Organized Interests
and American Democracy

Organized Interests and American Democracy

Kay Lehman Schlozman
John T. Tierney

Boston College

1817

HARPER & ROW, PUBLISHERS, New York
Cambridge, Philadelphia, San Francisco,
London, Mexico City, São Paulo, Singapore, Sydney

Sponsoring Editor: **Marianne J. Russell**
Project Editor: **Jo-Ann Goldfarb**
Cover Design: **20/20—Mark Berghash**
Text Art: **Reproduction Drawings Ltd.**
Production: **Willie Lane**
Compositor: **Donnelley/Rocappi Inc.**
Printer and Binder: **R. R. Donnelley & Sons Company**

Organized Interests and American Democracy

Library of Congress Cataloging in Publication Data

Schlozman, Kay Lehman, 1946-
    Organized interests and American democracy.

    Bibliography: p.
    Includes index.
    1. Pressure groups—United States.
I. Tierney, John T.,   1951-   .   II. Title.
JK1118.S38   1986   322.4′3′0973   85-5514
ISBN 0-06-045792-9

88   9 8 7 6 5 4 3

To Stanley and Susan,
who kept the pressure off

Contents

Preface   *ix*

1 Introduction   1

2 Interests in Politics   14

3 Interest Organizations in Politics   38

4 Who Is Represented?   58

5 Organizational Resources for Political Action   88

6 Interest Groups and Their Members   120

7 What Organized Interests Do: An Overview   148

8 Reaching Out to the Public   170

9 Influencing the Electoral Process   200

10 Financing Congressional Campaigns   221

11 Approaching Government Directly: Some General
Considerations   261

12   Lobbying Congress   289

13   Influencing the Executive Branch   322

14   Going to Court   358

15   Organized Interests and American Democracy   386

       Appendix A   The Washington Representatives Survey   411

       Appendix B   The Questionnaire   414

       Appendix C   The Catalogue of Organizations   428

       Appendix D   Additional Tables   430

       Index   434

Preface

Ours is an era of vigorous activity by organized interests in national politics. In the past two decades we have witnessed what seems to be a virtual explosion in demands by private organizations in Washington. While the media have made much of this development, political scientists have paid it less heed. In recent years scholars of politics have given admirable consideration to the electoral process as a linkage mechanism—tracking the changes in both citizen comportment and electoral institutions and outlining the implications of such changes for who is represented and how we are governed. At the same time, there has been far less attention devoted to analogous questions with respect to the private organizations that represent shared political interests in Washington. This book seeks to compensate for the relative neglect by academic analysts of organized interests in contemporary politics by probing what they are up to and what their activity means for public life in America.

This inattention to the place of organized interests in the current political scene is perhaps ironic, for interest groups once figured prominently in the scholarly understanding of the American political process, and some of the most provocative academic interpretations of American politics since the turn of the century place competition among organized private interests at the heart of the political process. Following the tradition laid out early in the century by Arthur Bentley, analysts of American politics during the 1950s—among them David Truman, Earl Latham, and Robert Dahl—characterized the political process not so much in terms of the static relations among institutions, as in terms of the dynamic relations among a plurality of contending groups.[1]

It is not simply that scholars recognized the centrality of interest groups to policymaking in America. They also drew conclusions about the meaning of a vigorous group process for democratic governance. Champions of group politics made a variety of arguments in its defense, contending that it enhances the mechanisms of representation, guaranteeing to ordinary citizens an effective voice in the halls of government; protects them from the coercive exercise of governmental power; precludes majority tyranny by accommodating the preferences of the most intensely concerned; ensures moderate policies and therefore political stability; and promotes political outcomes that approximate the public interest.[2]

No sooner had this perspective become dominant than it was questioned seriously. Part of the attack was empirical. On the basis of a systematic survey of lobbyists conducted during the late 1950s, Lester Milbrath concluded that interest groups did not have the determinative role in governing that had been attributed to them by the group theorists.[3] Similarly, on the basis of an in-depth study of organized activity on the issue of free trade, Bauer, Pool, and Dexter argued that the extent of interest group activity and influence had been overstated and that the world of lobbying was one in which overworked, harassed men rarely command resources equal to the task.[4]

Furthermore, such critics as E. E. Schattschneider, Mancur Olson, Grant McConnell, and Theodore Lowi regarded much more dubiously the implications of the process described by the advocates of interest group competition

[1]Arthur F. Bentley, *The Process of Government* (Chicago: University of Chicago Press, 1908); David B. Truman, *The Governmental Process* (New York: Knopf, 1951); Earl Latham, *The Group Basis of Politics,* (Ithaca, NY: Cornell University Press, 1952); and Robert A. Dahl, *A Preface to Democratic Theory* (Chicago: University of Chicago Press, 1956), and *Who Governs?* (New Haven: Yale University Press, 1961).

For contrasting evaluations of the contribution made by the group theorists and extensive bibliographical references, see Stanley Rothman, "Systematic Political Theory: Observations on the Group Approach," *American Political Science Review* 54 (1960): 15-33, and Robert T. Golembiewski, " 'The Group Basis of Politics': Notes on Analysis and Development," *American Political Science Review* 54 (1960): 962-971. For a more recent account, see G. David Garson, *Group Theories of Politics* (Beverly Hills, CA: Sage, 1978), Chapters 1-4.

[2]It is not our object here to engage in an exegesis of the contentions of earlier scholars who took seriously the role in the political process of organized private interests, and this brief enumeration of the thematic concerns of group theorists clearly does violence to the subtlety of the arguments made by the individual authors and to the differences among them. For example, Dahl's conception of the capacities of government to influence political outcomes clearly differs from Latham's; Truman places more emphasis upon the centrality of organized interests in influencing policy than does Dahl. There is no single work in which these themes are laid out systematically. However, it is this stereotype against which the critics of the group theorists of politics trained their ammunition.

[3]*The Washington Lobbyists* (Chicago: Rand McNally, 1959).

[4]Raymond A. Bauer, Ithiel de Sola Pool, and Lewis Anthony Dexter, *American Business and Public Policy* (Chicago: Aldine, 1963).

for the way we are governed.[5] Collectively, they made a number of points. They contended that, as interest groups usurp public authority, the boundaries between public and private spheres erode and that the resultant exercise of private power can be just as coercive—and much less accountable—than the exercise of public power. In addition, they pointed out, the pressure system is not universal: all interests are not equally well represented by organizations. In particular, two sorts of interests are less likely to receive sustained and vigorous representation: those of the disadvantaged—for example, welfare recipients, blacks, or the unemployed; and those of diffuse publics having no narrow stake in a controversy—for example, environmentalists, consumers, or taxpayers. Government policies, the critics argued, reflect this imbalance in the kinds of interests represented.[6]

At the same time, other analysts became concerned about a complementary theme. James Q. Wilson and Robert Salisbury considered the dilemmas confronted by those wishing to start a political organization—or keep one going—in light of the diverse motives of potential members, thus linking the problem of interest representation to the organizational maintenance needs of political associations.[7] Given the degree to which all these themes go to the heart of thinking about democracy, it is no wonder that a generation of academic observers of American politics took so seriously the role of interest groups.

In recent years political scientists have, by and large, either moved on altogether from concern with private organizations or focused upon the micro issue of the ways in which organizations attract and retain support from members.[8] The media, however, have not lost sight of these larger issues that once were so basic to the scholarly understanding of American politics, taking note

[5]E. E. Schattschneider, *The Semisovereign People* (New York: Holt, Rinehart and Winston, 1960); Mancur Olson, *The Logic of Collective Action* (Cambridge: Harvard University Press, 1965); Grant McConnell, *Private Power and American Democracy* (New York: Knopf, 1966); Theodore Lowi, *The End of Liberalism* (New York: Norton, 1969).

[6]Once again, this brief summary merges the arguments made by separate authors. Although compatible in substance, these authors differ both in approach and in the specific points they make.

[7]Peter B. Clark and James Q. Wilson, "Incentive Systems: A Theory of Organizations," *Administrative Science Quarterly* 6 (1961): 219–266; James Q. Wilson, *Political Organizations* (New York: Basic Books, 1973); Robert H. Salisbury, "An Exchange Theory of Interest Groups," *Midwest Journal of Political Science* 13 (1969): 1–32.

[8]There have been several thoughtful treatments of interest groups in recent years. See, for example, Jeffrey M. Berry, *Lobbying for the People* (Princeton: Princeton University Press, 1977); Terry M. Moe, *The Organization of Interests* (Chicago: The University of Chicago Press, 1980); Michael T. Hayes, *Lobbyists and Legislators* (New Brunswick, NJ: Rutgers University Press, 1981); John Chubb, *Interest Groups and the Bureaucracy* (Palo Alto, CA: Stanford University Press, 1983); and Andrew McFarland, *Common Cause* (Chatham, NJ: Chatham House, 1984).

Unfortunately, with a few exceptions, there has been a paucity of new systematic data collected since the 1950s. Jack L. Walker's recent work on interest groups is, however, based on systematic evidence. See "The Origins and Maintenance of Interest Groups in America," *American Political Science Review* 77 (1983): 390–406, and Thomas L. Gais, Mark A. Peterson, Jack L. Walker, "Interest Groups, Iron Triangles, and Representative Institutions in American National Government," *British Journal of Political Science* 14 (1984): 161–185.

of the recent proliferation of organized interest activity in Washington and speculating, in the best Progressive tradition, on the jeopardy in which it places democracy. Clearly, it is time to return to the themes that once animated academic inquiry into the character of public life in America and to integrate the insights of the recent work on the motives for organizational support into a measured assessment of both the role played by organized interests in the political process and the meaning of their activity for the way in which we are governed. By looking comprehensively and systematically at the world of organized interests in Washington—just what kinds of interests are represented, how the resources critical for political influence are distributed, how much activity there is and the forms it takes, when and where organizations get involved, when they are effective, how things have changed—this book seeks to overcome the relative disregard of this important political arena and thus to fill a 20-year gap.

In order to consider broadly the role of organized interests in national politics, we have compiled evidence from several sources. We have mined journalistic accounts and information collected by others such as the Federal Election Commission. In addition, we have assembled new data of our own: a set of interviews with 175 Washington representatives in organizations politically active at the national level; and tallies of the over 6,000 private organizations and nearly 3,000 political action committees active in Washington as of 1980.

The survey of Washington representatives is the primary source of evidence informing our analysis. Between October 1981 and May 1982, we conducted interviews with government affairs representatives in a sample of 175 organizations having offices in Washington. We devised a special sampling procedure such that active and well-funded organizations that build a large Washington operation—for example, General Electric, the American Bankers Association, or the American Medical Association—would have a greater probability of being selected than smaller, less active and affluent groups like the Moped Association of America, the Asphalt Roofing Manufacturers Association, or the American Association of Sex Educators and Counselors. (For a discussion of the many complex issues involved in designing such a sample and an elaboration of the procedure itself, see Appendix A.)

The sample we selected included 200 organizations—corporations, trade associations, unions, professional associations, civil rights groups, public interest groups, and so on. Of these we were able to contact and conduct interviews in 175 of them, including a broad range extending from the Liberty Lobby and the Child Welfare League to Common Cause, the National Association of Broadcasters, the National Education Association, and Standard Oil. Within each organization we sought to interview the individual having the broadest understanding of the organization and its involvement in politics. The interviews lasted roughly two hours each and covered a variety of subjects—among them the nature and extent of the organization's political activities, the techniques used to influence political outcomes, and the changes in Washington over the past decade or two that have had an impact on the way in which the organization approaches politics. (A copy of the questionnaire can be found in Appendix B.)

In order to get a sense of the range of organizations active in the capital, we also compiled two tallies. First, we enumerated and categorized the nearly 7,000 organizations listed in the *Washington Representatives—1981* directory as having a presence in Washington politics either by maintaining an office in the capital or by hiring counsel or consultants to represent them.[9] (The methods used are elaborated in Appendix C.) Using analogous methods we constructed a similar organizational census of the nearly 3,000 political action committees listed in the *PAC Directory* as having been registered with the Federal Elections Commission as of the end of 1980.[10]

As a complement to these efforts we wrote to over 200 additional organizations asking each to send us any published material that might help us understand the organization and its activities in Washington politics. While such materials cannot contribute in a systematic way to our understanding of organized interest politics, they supplement information from other sources about particular organizations active in Washington. Throughout our analysis, we have drawn extensively on these materials in illustrating general propositions.

Fortified with these varied kinds of information we have attempted to fill a wide canvas: to survey organized interest involvement in federal politics. To undertake such a comprehensive enterprise is surely to be guilty of hubris. This book encompasses many subjects—ranging from environmental groups to political action committees, from direct-mail fund raising to the nature of the public interest, from "capture" of executive agencies to the logic of collective action, from grass roots lobbying to organizational democracy—that could be, or have been, the subjects of whole books on their own. Clearly, by painting a panorama we are sacrificing the kind of detail and nuance that are possible when a single policy controversy or a single technique of influence or a single type of organization is the object of study.

However, there is a payoff as well as a cost to our strategy. By undertaking a systematic inquiry across the entire pressure scene we are able to pose questions that would be, quite simply, impossible to answer were we to concentrate on a smaller portion of the whole. The realm of organized interest politics is so vast—encompassing so many different kinds of organizations and so many different avenues of influence—that it is possible to locate an example to illustrate virtually any reasonable generalization one might put forward. Only by taking a more global view can we get a sense of the relative frequencies within this world of astonishing political diversity. Thus, although our approach forces us to forego particulars on occasion, it has the strength of permitting us to make comparisons across the entire realm of organized interests and to make reliable generalizations about that complex world.

[9] Arthur C. Close, ed., *Washington Representatives—1981* (Washington, DC: Columbia Books, 1981).
[10] Marvin Weinberger and David U. Greevy, compilers, *The PAC Directory* (Cambridge, MA: Ballinger, 1982).

ACKNOWLEDGMENTS

Because this research project was undertaken on a shoestring, it would never have been completed had we not benefited from generous assistance—much of it gratis—from many sources. We have a particular debt to the 175 Washington representatives who spoke with us. These are people for whom time is a precious resource. Their willingness to indulge us in interviews that were rarely brief and to elaborate on matters that bordered on the delicate was most impressive. Without their cooperation, this enterprise would surely have foundered.

We received capable and enthusiastic research assistance from a number of students. Maria Murray and Douglas Paxton performed superbly in assuming a share of the interviewing. Jerry Boren nursed the computer with rare perseverance and care. Taylor Bowlden, Maureen Casamayou, Daniel Felkel, Robert Gallagher, Elaine Korowski, Corinne Mellul, Lisa Reed, Diane Sullivan, and Robert Trombly cheerfully performed other general research tasks.

While the miracle of modern electronics relieved them of the burden of typing draft after draft, Jeanne Dotterweich and Yvette Forget assisted us in countless ways with unfailing efficiency and good humor. We shall miss them both.

Boston College provided services of many kinds. Data collection was supported by research funds made available to Boston College by the Mellon Foundation. The Boston College Computer Center supported both data analysis and word processing. In addition, the Fel-Pro, Inc., data processing department, under the supervision of John Barlow, punched the data. Boston College and Georgetown University made available summer research funds.

We appreciate the helpful editorial assistance we received from the staff of Harper & Row—particularly Marianne Russell and Jo-Ann Goldfarb. The manuscript benefited from the helpful comments of the reviewers who were asked by Harper & Row to examine an earlier draft: Dennis Ippolito, Albert Mavrinac, Bruce Robeck, Andrew Tuttle, and Betty Zisk.

We are grateful to our friends, colleagues, and teachers—Jeffrey Berry, Timothy Conlan, Robert Katzmann, David Manwaring, Grant McConnell, Francis Rourke, Robert Shapiro, and Susan Tierney—for helpful, critical readings of earlier drafts. We are especially indebted to James Q. Wilson and Sidney Verba. Not only does what we have learned from them inform these pages in fundamental ways, but each of them provided an insightful reading of an earlier version of the manuscript. To Sidney we owe special thanks for responding with enthusiasm to even our most half-baked thoughts and for continuing to give advisory opinions long after he should have withdrawn the intellectual welcome mat.

Our deepest gratitude is to Stanley and Susan who were far more patient than we had any right to expect. However, their extraordinary contributions went way beyond mere forbearance. Each of them provided invaluable logistical, intellectual, and emotional support. We appreciate their smarts, humor, and good cheer more than we can express. We are lucky to have them as the spice of our lives.

K. L. S.
J. T. T.

Organized Interests and American Democracy

1

Introduction

Recent decades have witnessed an expansion of astonishing proportions in the involvement of private organizations in Washington politics. From the Academy for Implants and Transplants to Zero Population Growth, interest organizations range from A to Z. From the American College of Nurse Midwives to the Casket Manufacturers Association of America, they embrace the human experience from cradle to grave. From Campbell Soup Co. to the Amalgamated Clothing and Textile Workers Union to the National Association of Home Builders, they attest to our efforts to provide for our most fundamental needs— food, clothing, and shelter. From the Cosmetic, Toiletry and Fragrance Association to the Recreation Vehicle Industry Association, they show our impulse to embellish the basics. And from the American Arts Alliance to the National Council of Churches, they indicate our loftier intellectual and spiritual aspirations.

Awesome in their sheer number and in the variety of their activities, such organizations exercise a profound, though not determinative, influence on the character of American politics. The object of this book is to investigate in the broadest terms the political dimensions of these private organizations: to enrich our understanding of the kinds of interests they represent in national politics; to probe the complex tasks that confront those who would nurture and sustain an organization having political goals; and to analyze the multiple techniques and complex strategies such organizations use to influence outcomes in Washington. In so doing, we shall be particularly interested in documenting

1

the many ways in which the realm of pressure politics has been altered over the past twenty years and to locate the sources of these developments in the changing legal, institutional, social, and cultural environment in which such politics are embedded.

THE MISCHIEFS OF FACTION

From the Founders through the muckrakers to reform-minded observers today, a steady refrain in American political commentary has been distrust of organized private power in politics. While the Progressives surely articulated this theme with unequaled verve and emphasis, it is James Madison's *The Federalist*, No. 10—the earliest, and to this day most elegant, expression of this concern—that serves as an inspiration to those who seek to understand the problem of organized conflict in American democracy.[1]

Madison's purpose in this celebrated essay is to demonstrate how the republican government proposed in the new constitution would ameliorate the "mischiefs of faction."[2] According to Madison, a faction is

> a number of citizens, whether amounting to a majority or a minority of the whole, who are united and actuated by some common impulse of passion, or of interest, adverse to the rights of other citizens or to the permanent and aggregate interests of the community.[3]

Madison proposes two alternatives for diminishing the jeopardy in which private rights and the public good are placed by factional strife. First, one could root out its causes in either of two ways. The spirit of faction would wither immediately if one were to quash the liberty that sustains it, but to do so would invoke a cure more pernicious than the malady:

> Liberty is to faction what air is to fire, an aliment without which it instantly expires. But it could not be less folly to abolish liberty, which is essential to political life, because it nourishes faction than it would be to wish the annihilation of air, which is essential to animal life, because it imparts to fire its destructive agency.[4]

The second expediency for erasing the causes of faction—making sure that everyone shares the same sentiments, obsessions, and interests—is, in Madison's view, simply infeasible. Conflict is inevitable, he says, not simply because of the imperfections in human reason, but because differences in matters of

---

[1] *The Federalist* (New York: New American Library, 1961), pp. 77–84.

[2] There are a number of provocative commentaries on *The Federalist*, No. 10, among them Robert A. Dahl, *A Preface to Democratic Theory* (Chicago: University of Chicago Press, 1956), Chapter 1; Martin Diamond, Winston Mills Fisk, and Herbert Garfinkel, *The Democratic Republic*, 2nd ed. (Chicago: Rand McNally, 1970), pp. 91–98; and Gary Wills, *Explaining America* (New York: Doubleday, 1981), Part IV. Diamond, Fisk, and Garfinkel interpret Madison as being less concerned about the dangers of multiple factions than do the other two authors.

[3] *The Federalist*, No. 10, p. 78.

[4] Ibid.

taste and morals and differences of interest are "sown in the nature of man." He argues, in particular, that "the most common and durable source of factions has been the various and unequal distribution of property."[5]

If, then, it is impossible to attempt to cure the mischiefs of faction by eliminating its causes, what are the prospects of ameliorating its effects? Madison takes up this question in the remainder of the essay. His first point is that if the faction is a minority faction, it threatens neither private rights nor the public welfare because the ordinary operations of republican government will permit the majority to prevail. What is of highest concern to Madison is a faction consisting of a majority, and he devotes considerable effort to demonstrating why in a republic—especially an extensive one encompassing many groups and interests—a factious majority will find it more difficult to coalesce and impose its will upon the nation.

The Federalist, No. 10, can hardly be used as an operational guide to understanding the problem of containing organized conflict in contemporary democracy. Madison's exposition as to why the republican government proposed under the Constitution would reduce the effects of factional strife—an exposition that was, of course, intended to be a polemic apology for that government rather than a philosophical inquiry—is less compelling than his diagnosis of the disease. In particular, we shall have occasion to question Madison's insouciance about minority factions with respect to Washington politics today. At many junctures we shall encounter situations in which intense and well-organized minorities enjoy political successes because they have the good fortune to be opposed by lukewarm majorities.[6] Still, Madison's observations about the inevitability in a free society of organized conflict among contending interests and the potential for mischief in such contention provide the inspiration for much of this inquiry into the world of contemporary interest politics in Washington.

ORGANIZED INTERESTS AND AMERICAN DEMOCRACY

Madison was only the first in a long line of observers of American politics to comment upon the crucial role played by organized interests. It is essential to republican government that citizens have mechanisms for transmitting information about their preferences to public officials. The election is only a very blunt instrument for the conveyance of such information. Winning candidates may be uncertain as to the wellsprings of their victories: approval of positions taken on particular issues (and, if so, which ones), personal magnetism, or generalized dissatisfaction with the performance of incumbents. Hence, they

---

[5]Ibid. pp. 78–79.

[6]In Madison's terms, however, we shall be unable to establish whether such a minority constitutes a faction, for Madison leaves much unspecified: What are the natural rights of individuals that demand protection from the government? How do we ascertain the public good? Hence, how do we know when a combination of citizens should be considered a faction?

may well find it difficult to interpret their mandates. The direct messages conveyed to political leaders by the vehicle of organized interest activity can be much more precise and, thus, can function as a critical supplement to elections in linking citizens to leaders. In short, once the political community grows beyond the manageable boundaries of the town meeting, some kind of private associational life becomes essential to democracy; in fact, it is difficult to imagine large-scale democracy without it.

Not only does organized interest activity, thus, go to the heart of governance in a democratic nation state, it also goes to the heart of what is most distinctive about democracy in America. Observers of public life in America have often remarked upon the strong undercurrent of voluntarism beneath it; that is, activities for which the state takes primary responsibility in other democratic polities—ranging from registration of voters to support of symphony orchestras—retain a strong voluntary component in the United States. This strand of voluntarism pertains to associational life as well.[7] Joint enterprises in seventeenth- and eighteenth-century Europe—whether educational, religious, commercial, or philanthropic—were undertaken under the sponsorship, protection, and, therefore, control of the sovereign. In the colonies, on the other hand, such associations developed without such a connection to the state and, thus, enjoyed neither the privileges nor the exclusive monopolies of their established counterparts across the Atlantic. This tradition of proliferation and voluntarism in associational activity has contributed to the distinctive character of contemporary American politics. In comparison to the democracies of modern Europe political organizations in America are distinguished not only by their autonomy from government and voluntary character but also by the vigor of their activity and the richness and variety of the interests they represent.

The relative importance of private organizations in American politics not only reflects but also reinforces these distinctively American tendencies. That political parties bear a rather smaller share of the burden of representation of collective citizen interests, with organized interests bearing a rather larger share, has consequences for the way we are governed. As opposed to electoral politics, interest politics is the arena of the organization of narrow publics having correspondingly narrow sets of concerns and issues. In addition, when votes are counted, numbers are determinative. In the domain of interest politics, however, the number of supporters is only one resource among many and carries less relative weight. Moreover, the realm of pressure politics is the one most hospitable to the translation of market resources into political activity. Given these special characteristics of interest representation via political organizations as opposed to parties, it is no wonder that the central role of organized interests in American politics has substantial implications for democratic governance.

[7]For an expanded discussion of the points made in this paragraph, see Oscar and Mary Handlin, *The Dimensions of Liberty* (Cambridge: Harvard University Press, Belknap Press, 1961), Chapter 5.

The past two decades have witnessed an expansion of significant proportions in the dimensions of organized interest activity in American national politics. This development, which has received substantial attention from the media, has generated relatively little comment from academic observers of American politics. In fact, it has been nearly twenty years since political scientists made a systematic study of the world of organized interests and the consequences of their activity for democratic governance.[8] In the interim there have been many innovations in American political and social life—ranging from modifications of congressional procedure to the emergence of various citizen movements, and from reforms of campaign finance to the introduction of new electronic technologies—that might be expected to have implications for the involvement of private organizations in national politics. Hence, the time is long overdue for a systematic and comprehensive consideration of organized interests in American democracy with a special focus on the nature and extent of the changes in the realm of interest politics.

This book seeks to address the need for a broad inquiry into the nature of organized interest activity and its place in the American political process. Implicit in such an enterprise are several ongoing questions that demand consideration.

How Do Organized Interests Go about Influencing Policy?   In order to investigate the broad outlines of organized interest involvement in American politics, certain building blocks are necessary. Because it has been some time since political scientists assembled such systematic information, it is important to examine in some detail the nuts-and-bolts aspects of how organized interests go about attempting to influence policy outcomes in Washington. In so doing, we shall attempt to use a wide-angle lens to get a picture of the range of such activity—how much there is and what kinds. To complement this broad perspective, we shall focus more narrowly on particular arenas in which organized interests are active—elections, Congress, the White House, the bureaucracy, and the courts—outlining their peculiar politics and describing the techniques of influence appropriate to each. We shall also probe the particular techniques used by organized interests, considering how they work, the resources they require, and the circumstances under which they are most effective. In short, a prerequisite for understanding the place of organized interests in Washington politics is, quite simply, a detailed understanding of what they do.

Who Is Respresented?   In order to comprehend the political role of organized interests, it is also necessary to have an understanding of the contours of interest representation—how many and what kinds of organizations are active on behalf of what kinds of interests in Washington and the kinds and level of

[8]For a brief summary of academic investigations of interest politics, see the Preface to this book.

resources at their command. Such an understanding will permit us to explore, from several perspectives, the implications of organized pressure politics for the representation of citizen interests. We shall investigate the degree to which organized interest politics broadens representation and the degree to which the pressure system is permeable—that is, whether the barriers to entry to competition in the marketplace of federal politics are so high as to impede the entry of newly hatched organizations. Furthermore, we shall probe whether the set of organizations active in Washington is exhaustive, representing all politically relevant interests, and whether it is unskewed, representing these myriad conflicting interests on nearly equal terms. With respect to these questions, it is important to understand whether certain kinds of interests are excluded or—by dint of lack of resources or scarcity of active organizations—underrepresented. Because they bear so directly on questions of equal protection of interests and one-person–one-vote, such considerations go to the center of the meaning of organized interest politics for democracy.

What Are the Pathways of Mutual Influence and Exchange?   It is customary to conceptualize interest organizations as the central link in a unidirectional process: groups of citizens delegate to such organizations the responsibility for representing their joint political interests; these organizations, in turn, take actions that influence the shape of public outcomes. In fact, however, the process is much more interactive, characterized by pathways of mutual influence and exchange. Individuals who share interests do not inevitably form organizations. There are many barriers to spontaneous organizational formation, and those who support collective political efforts may do so because some organizational inducement justifies the costs of their participation. Furthermore, it will become clear that definitions of common interest are often not simply given. On the contrary, Washington representatives—who are on the scene and thus in a good position to assess political realities—frequently take an active role in educating members as to what their best interests are.

     In addition, organized interests not only *affect* policy outcomes, they *are influenced* by the political system as well. In the course of our inquiry, we shall refer to various aspects of the political system—ranging from the Constitution to the internal structure of Congress to tax laws—having consequences for the extent of organized interest involvement and the forms it takes. Moreover, the unidirectional model errs in conceptualizing organized interests as battering rams hammering at policymakers. On the contrary, relationships between representatives of organized interests and public officials in both the legislative and executive branches are characterized by reciprocity and mutual exchange. Those in government can, of course, supply desired policy concessions to organized interests; however, organized interests command much that is valued by policymakers as well—not only information and political support but various services and, sometimes, future jobs. In short, then, the model that posits a one-way flow of influence from citizens through organized interests to the political system is too simplistic.

Do Organized Interests Influence Policy?　Although this study concentrates on detailing the activities of private organizations, rather than measuring their influence on policy, the age-old question of who governs on behalf of whom will never be far from our minds. We can approach this fundamental issue only obliquely. An inquiry concerned only with this question would involve sampling systematically from the universe of policy controversies and determining under what circumstances interest organizations are influential—or whether indeed they have any consequences at all. Our strategy, by contrast, was to sample systematically from the universe of organizations active in Washington because the evidence thus gathered would be germane to so many other themes we wished to explore. Although our mode of inquiry makes conclusions about the extent and nature of the impact on policy of organized pressure suggestive rather than definitive, we shall try, however, to make inferences about whether—and under what circumstances—organized interests affect government decisions.

According to the most extreme of the analysts of group politics during the 1950s, organized interests do not merely influence public policy, they determine it. In their view, policy outcomes are the vector sum of competing organized pressures. Except insofar as parts of the government pursue institutional self-interests and thus become merely additional contenders in the group struggle, government is reduced in this scheme to the role of umpire, ensuring that the contesting private groups play fairly:

> The legislature referees the group struggle, ratifies the victories of the successful coalitions, and records the terms of the surrenders, compromises, and conquests in the form of statutes. Every statute tends to represent compromise because the process of accommodating conflicts of group interest is one of deliberation and consent. The legislative vote on any issue tends to represent the composition of strength, i.e., the balance of power, among contending groups at the time of voting. What may be called public policy is the equilibrium reached in this struggle at any given moment, and it represents a balance which the contending factions of groups constantly strive to weight in their favor.[9]

Whatever the impact of organized interests on policy, the early group theorists surely erred in attributing to organized interests such a determinative role. It is fundamental to the nature of public power that the government is not simply a referee to private conflict, ratifying the victories of the strongest contenders in a pressure group free-for-all. If policy outcomes simply registered the relative strength of the organized pressures from various directions, there

[9]Earl L. Latham, *The Group Basis of Politics* (Ithaca, NY: Cornell University Press, 1952), pp. 35–37.

would be little reason to politicize issues by bringing in the government, for the result would be no different from that which obtained when the dispute was entirely private.

As is so often the case with academic interpretation, no sooner had the group theorists elaborated their viewpoint than they were beseiged by critics. Subsequent observers made a number of points to demonstrate that organized interests, far from being omnipotent, are in fact rather weak and that even though they may be able to affect the details of a policy proposal, their efforts rarely determine whether it succeeds or fails.[10]

Later on, we shall have occasion to scrutinize both the logic of this conclusion and the empirical assertions on which it rests. While it is surely the case that organized interests are rarely in a position to guarantee the enactment of policies they favor and not always in a position to block or stall the ones they do not, the passage or defeat of proposals may not be the most useful criterion for measuring organized influence. Affecting the details of policies is not merely a trivial form of influence. The world of pressure politics is a world of compromises and half-loaves. Often, when a policy outcome does not reflect the wishes of an organized interest, it is still substantially more congenial than it would have been had the organization not pressed its case.

Furthermore, although we do not have a systematic sampling of policy controversies from which to draw conclusions about the extent of pressure influence on policy, we shall adduce systematic data from various sources to demonstrate that some of the propositions central to the argument about the weakness of organized interests no longer hold. For example, contrary to what was described two decades ago, many contemporary organizations command adequate, even substantial, resources. If not in earlier years, now they are able both to undertake sophisticated efforts to mobilize general or specific publics and to engage extensively in various forms of electoral involvement, particularly in financing congressional campaigns. In addition, if organizations did not have the wherewithal to provide inducements to lawmakers in years past, they are now liberal in their use of an array of such perfectly legal inducements— among them PAC contributions, honoraria, and fact-finding trips.

Still, the activity of organized interests is only one of the numerous factors that shape what the government does. Others include the preferences of policymakers themselves, the residues of past policies, the limitations on what is technically or financially feasible, and the decisions of foreign powers. Not only are many factors beyond organized pressure responsible for forming policy, but the activities of organized interests do not even exhaust the supply of citizen inputs that influence government decisions. Citizens in American democracy have several vehicles for the expression of individual and collective

[10] Although they differ in approach and in particular arguments, both Lester Milbrath [*The Washington Lobbyists* (Chicago: Rand McNally, 1959), Chapter 17] and Raymond A. Bauer, Ithiel de Sola Pool, and Anthony Dexter [*American Business and Public Policy* (Chicago: Aldine, 1963), Chapters 21–24, 28] emphasize the weakness of pressure groups.

opinion. Public policies—especially major new policy initiatives—typically reflect citizen concerns as expressed in social movements, electoral results, and individual communications to policymakers in addition to inputs from organized interests. In short, organized interests are only one of many decisive factors in determining political outcomes.

What Are the Implications for How We Are Governed?   As we proceed, we shall attempt to be sensitive to the implications of contemporary pressure politics for the way we are governed. Group theorists of politics once argued that a political process in which interests are championed by vigorous private organizations has many benign consequences for civic life.[11] In particular, they contended that when a stratum of assiduous organizations pursuing narrow ends intermediates between ordinary citizens and political leaders, citizens are protected from manipulation and elites are protected from extremist demands for comprehensive change. Hence, political discourse is carried on in a more moderate voice.[12] Others pointed out that the political activists who lead and staff interest organizations are likely to be more committed to the procedural rules of democracy than are members of the mass public and concluded that when organizations are the primary vehicles for the expression of citizen demands, democracy is further protected.[13] More recently, this logic has come to be questioned. Many citizens' groups of both the left and the right—the legacy of the late sixties and early seventies—are intensely concerned about a single issue and express their demands with a stridency and incessancy that were once considered uncharacteristic of a citizen politics mediated by organizations. We shall consider the meaning for our politics of intensified activity by organized interests.

Even if it were to appear that our politics has been rendered more shrill by an escalated level of conflict among private organizations or that equal protection of interests is compromised by a politics of organized interests, it is not clear that anything can—or should—be done. At several junctures in our analysis we will be reminded of Madison's comments about "the mischiefs of faction" and his warning that to curtail the liberty that nourishes organized conflict would be a cure more destructive than the malady.

WHAT DO WE MEAN BY "ORGANIZED INTERESTS"?

By now it should be clear that we are covering the same terrain that is typically referred to as the politics of *interest groups* or *pressure groups*. Why do we adopt

[11] See the discussion of the group theorists in the Preface.
[12] This point is made by William Kornhauser in *The Politics of Mass Society* (New York: Free Press, 1959).
[13] Although he does not apply this principle to interest group activists in particular, Robert A. Dahl discusses the commitment to the democratic creed among members of the political stratum in *Who Governs?* (New Haven: Yale University Press, 1961), Chapter 28.

the clumsier and less familiar term *organized interests* instead? Except for occasional exceptions in the name of stylistic variety, we reserve the terms *interest groups* and *pressure groups* for membership associations.[14] Ordinarily, we use the term *organized interests* so as to include under our umbrella not only associations such as trade associations, unions, professional associations, and environmental groups that have individuals or organizations as members, but also politically active organizations such as universities, hospitals, public interest law firms, and, especially, corporations that have no members in the ordinary sense. Thus, our purview encompasses not only organizations like the United Mine Workers, the American Nurses Association, the American Farm Bureau Federation, the American Legion, the National Association for the Advancement of Colored People, the National Association of Realtors, and the Friends of the Earth, but also nonmembership organizations like Exxon, the Center for Law and Social Policy, and the University of California—all of which maintain offices in the capital.[15] Some of the issues we take up—for example, the rationality of decisions to join organizations or the problem of organizational democracy—apply to membership groups only. In such cases, the context makes clear that we are referring only to membership associations, and we revert to discussion of interest groups and pressure groups.

Ordinarily, then, the term *organized interests* is used here to denote the wide variety of organizations that seek joint ends through *political* action. Unlike, for example, a church group whose members work together to raise money for a new chapel, the organizations that concern us have collective goals that are politically relevant. However, the organizations with which we are concerned vary substantially in the degree to which political objectives are fundamental to their overall purposes. To a corporation like General Motors, politics

[14]Note that we do not use the term *lobbies* as a substitute for interest groups or pressure groups. Lobbying ordinarily denotes a particular kind of activity, direct contact between representatives of organized interests and policymakers. The organizations with which we are concerned use many techniques, of which lobbying is only one. Hence, when we discuss lobbying, we are giving the word a fairly precise meaning.

[15]We are eliminating from our range of concerns organizations that represent governments. In recent years, representatives of foreign and subnational governments have substantially increased their numbers and activity in Washington politics. Because they use many of the same techniques that are mobilized by private organizations, and because they are active and effective in Washington, we can address some of the same questions about their federal political involvement that we direct to the organizations that constitute our principal focus. However, studies of organized pressure in America ordinarily exclude them, and as discussed in Chapter 3, there are good theoretical reasons for so doing. As philosophers of the polity have known since the Greeks, there are important distinctions between public and private life. This is a book about *private* organizations in politics. Thus, in terms of representative functions of organizations in Washington politics, there is a difference between the governments of Kentucky, San Francisco, or Brazil and the private-sector organizations on which we concentrate.

There are also practical reasons for some of these decisions. Because foreign interests are prohibited by law from lobbying the federal government directly, they hire others—lawyer-lobbyists, public affairs consultants, and so on—to represent their interests. Since one of the principal sources of evidence on which we rely in this inquiry is a series of interviews with representatives of organizations that maintain their own government-relations offices in the capital, those who represent foreign interests as hired agents are beyond our reach.

is relatively tangential; the central goal is to manufacture autos and sell them at a profit. On the other hand, to citizens' groups like the Liberty Lobby and the League of Women Voters political objectives are more basic to the organizational purpose.

There are, of course, many social aggregates that are relevant for politics, and not all of them fall into our purview. Organized interests differ from social movements in the degree to which their activities are coordinated, although, of course, social movements often include an interest group component. Thus, the contemporary women's movement is a loosely structured aggregation that includes informal local groups and individual sympathizers, who may come together occasionally for joint activity, in addition to more formal associations like the National Organization for Women. Organized interests differ from social aggregates such as classes or ethnic groups not only in their degree of organization but also in the level of articulation of their political goals. Again, of course, such social collectivities may be represented by organizations that pursue their interests in politics. Finally, they differ from political parties in that they do not nominate candidates for office. Here again, there are affinities between the two categories of nongovernmental institutions. Organized interests, like parties, are involved in many aspects of the electoral process: registering voters, endorsing candidates, and donating manpower and money to campaigns. While the differences between, say, the National Association of Manufacturers and the Republican party as organizations are substantial indeed, minor parties—which in the American context rarely share in governing—are in many ways similar in scope of agenda and comprehensiveness of appeal to interest organizations.

Following common usage we refer to the involvement of organized interests in Washington as *interest politics* or *pressure politics*. The latter term may carry certain connotations that we do not intend. First, to some people the term *pressure politics* conjures up a process that is slightly disreputable. By using "pressure politics" and "interest politics" interchangeably, we mean to convey no such unsavory overtones. In addition, when we refer to pressure politics, we do not mean to equate organized interest politics with the application of pressure. Organized interests seek to influence political outcomes in many ways: by informing, by persuading, and by applying pressure. Of these, applying pressure is probably not even the most important.

One final bit of terminology bears clearing up. There are many terms used to refer to those who represent organized interests in federal politics—among them, *lobbyist, government-relations expert, public affairs consultant,* and *Washington representative*. The last term—one that has considerable currency these days, presumably because it conveys rather more professional distinction than *lobbyist*—is potentially confusing. It denotes not a member of the House of Representatives or any elected official, but, rather, any one of the many professional advocates who staff or are retained by organized private interests in the capital. Thus, in referring to *Washington representatives* we mean the government affairs professionals who work for private organizations and not the elected officials ordinarily associated with the term *representative* in discussions of republican governance.

ORGANIZED INTERESTS IN WASHINGTON: THE OUTLINE OF OUR INQUIRY

Let us preview briefly the principal topics of the chapters that follow. The main emphasis of Chapters 2 through 6 is on interest organizations themselves and their internal dynamics. Chapter 2 examines the nature of interests in politics and delineates the kinds of concerns—economic and noneconomic, private and public—that motivate organizations to pursue political action. Chapter 3 describes the various kinds of organizations—corporations, trade and other business associations, farmers' organizations, professional associations, unions, social welfare organizations, civil rights groups, citizens' and cause groups—that are active in Washington and sketches the ways in which they differ from one another in terms of their organizational structure, the nature of their membership (if any at all), and the number and content of their political objectives.

Chapter 4 investigates how many such organizations are active in Washington and how they are distributed among various organizational categories and explores changes over the past two decades in both the number and distribution of organizations active in Washington politics. Chapter 5 examines the various resources—money, members, contacts, reputation, and the like—that organizations mobilize to influence political outcomes, probing where such resources come from and how they are distributed among various kinds of organizations. Chapter 6 focuses, in particular, on membership groups and explores several aspects of the relationship between such organizations and their constituents: the motives that impel citizens to participate in joint efforts to pursue collective goods and the rationality of such participation; the problem of organizational democracy; and the multiple functions of the communications networks linking those in Washington to their constituents.

Chapters 7 through 14 focus on the efforts made by private organizations to influence political outcomes in Washington. Chapter 7 introduces this subject, provides an aerial overview of the range of organized interest activity—how much there is and what kinds—and discusses some of the difficulties in assessing whether organized interests have influence. Chapters 8 through 10 consider the ways in which organizations can affect politics indirectly, either by mobilizing the public or a narrower constituency to communicate with policymakers or by getting involved in electoral politics, paying special attention to the effects of new technologies that facilitate grass roots lobbying and to the growing role of private organizations in congressional campaign finance.

The remaining chapters delve into the ways in which organized interests approach government more directly. Chapter 11 discusses several aspects of the direct representation of interests, including the profession of lobbying and the patterns of conflict and cooperation that structure pressure politics. Chapters 12 through 14 examine the ways in which organized interests pursue their goals in each of the three branches of the federal government—Congress, the executive, and the courts—indicating some of the differences in the ways that organizations approach these institutions.

2

Interests in Politics

To study private organizations in American politics is to study the pursuit of interests: small aircraft owners seeking the relaxation of the regulations governing airport noise; bishops seeking federal tax credits for private and parochial school tuition; civil rights leaders seeking more vigorous implementation of the laws prohibiting racial discrimination in housing. After all, among the terms used for such organizations is *interest groups.* This chapter probes the nature of the interests that organizations hope to realize through political action.[1]

This chapter considers at some length the abstract, but very fundamental, issue of how we know what somebody else's political interests are, and we shall appraise the relative merits of two approaches to understanding of political interests. It also looks closely at the kinds of objectives that organizations pursue through political action, introducing some distinctions among categories of political interests: economic and noneconomic, public and private, and governmental and nongovernmental.

Although the notion of "interests" as the animus for political action is absolutely critical to the contemporary understanding of politics, both the term and the concept it signifies entered our political discourse only relatively re-

[1]When we refer in the course of this chapter—or in the course of this book as a whole—to an individual's or a group's "interests," we are referring to politically relevant interests and excluding the many senses in which someone can have interests (romantic, recreational, and so on) with respect to nonpolitical objects. There are, of course, clear affinities between the way in which a person might be interested in, or care about, political and nonpolitical matters; however, we are confining ourselves to political matters.

cently.[2] The concept of interests does not figure in the lexicon of premodern Western political thought. Classical and medieval political thinkers found the wellsprings of human motivation in two sources, reason and the passions. Among the central problems addressed by premodern political inquiry was how to restrain the passions—the lust for worldly gain, power, or success—that give rise to consequences so threatening to civil order. Reason being held sometimes ineffectual in taming passions, various thinkers proposed various antidotes to these vices—from moral education to religious orthodoxy to chivalrous pursuit of honor and glory.

The peculiarly modern linkage of reason to selfishness in the pursuit of interests has its source, as does much of modern Western political thought, in the writings of Machiavelli (1469–1527). By instructing the prince to mobilize rational will in the service of self-interest, Machiavelli began a profound transformation. He lauded the salutary effects of interested behavior, in which reason is harnessed in the orderly pursuit of selfish goals, contrasting this with the calamitous consequences that ensue from the rule of unbridled passions. From its roots in Machiavelli, the concept of interest emerged in Western political thought, wedding what had been considered since the ancients to be the principal sources of human motivation, reason and passion. In the process, each lost its most basic frailty: when yoked to reason, the passion of self-love was seen to be less degraded; when impressed in the service of selfish ends, reason was seen to be less impotent.[3]

As the concept of interest was adopted by thinkers of the seventeenth and eighteenth centuries—and acquired its present name—its meaning evolved, denoting first national interests in an era of conflict between states and later individual and group interests as internal political strife took precedence. By the eighteenth century, the term had assumed an even narrower meaning. Rather than signifying the reasoned pursuit of the range of human aspirations, interests became associated solely with the pursuit of economic advantage. At the same time, material acquisition, once labeled "avarice" and listed among the seven deadly sins, became so esteemed that Samuel Johnson was led to remark, "There are few ways in which a man can be more innocently employed than in making money."[4]

This conception of interested motivation in general, and of the primacy of economic gain among man's interests in particular, was an important political philosophical legacy to the Founders of the American republic—among them, of course, Madison. The government they designed and defended reflected this understanding of the role of self-interest in human activity and the responsibility of the government for providing an orderly context for individuals to pursue

[2]The discussion that follows is derived directly from Albert O. Hirschman's analysis in *The Passions and the Interests* (Princeton: Princeton University Press, 1977), Part I.

[3]Ibid., pp. 42–44.

[4]*Boswell's Life of Johnson,* Vol. I (New York: Oxford University Press, 1933), cited in Hirschman, *The Passions and the Interests,* p. 58.

their own ends. Thus, the concept of interest as it emerged in early modern political thought became an important part of the American political tradition.

WHAT IS AN INTEREST?

All of us are comfortable with statements regarding the best interests of children. No matter whether a child *prefers* cupcakes and Dr. Pepper to broccoli and milk, most of us would assert that it is in his *interests* to eat a nutritious diet. And, although a child might *want* to take a good swallow of household bleach, few would argue that it is in his *interests* to do so. But what about adults who, presumably, have acquired the faculties for making informed judgments for themselves? If a man wants to hang himself, are we acting in his best interests if we supply him with a rope?[5] If we take his own assessment of what is good for him—that is, if we consider his wishes to be his interests—then we should find him the nearest available rope. If, however, we were to make some independent determination of what is in his best interests, then we would probably hesitate before handing it over. This example illustrates the central dilemma of attempting to understand the interests of others.

While the concept of interest as a source of human motivation was bequeathed to us by the seventeenth- and eighteenth-century successors to Machiavelli, it was not until the late eighteenth and early nineteenth centuries that political philosophers focused on the problem of evaluating what is in somebody's best interests.[6] Two different approaches emerged. The first holds that each person is the best judge of his or her own interests. Therefore, to know somebody else's interests, it is sufficient simply to know his preferences. The interests-as-preferences concept is often called the *subjective* approach because the understanding of interests rests upon the individual's own concerns, desires, and wishes.

[5]This example is taken from W. J. Rees, "The Public Interest," *Proceedings of the Aristotelian Society,* Supplementary 38 (1964): 20. We pose this question to illustrate a dilemma. Rees, however, answers the query quite unambiguously.

[6]Among the recent scholarly discussions of the nature of political interests are the following: Arthur Bentley, *The Process of Government* (Chicago: University of Chicago Press, 1908), passim, especially pp. 208–214; John Plamenatz, "Interests," *Political Studies* 2 (1954): 1–8; S. I. Benn, "Interests in Politics," *Proceedings of the Aristotelian Society* 60 (1960): 123–140; Samuel Krislov, "What Is an Interest?" *Western Political Quarterly* 16 (1963): 830–843; B. M. Barry, "The Public Interest," *Proceedings of the Aristotelian Society,* Supplementary 38 (1964): 1–18; W. J. Rees, "The Public Interest," 19–38; David Truman, *The Governmental Process,* 2nd ed. (New York: Knopf, 1971), pp. 33–39 and passim; Isaac D. Balbus, "The Concept of Interest in Pluralist and Marxian Analysis," *Politics and Society* 1 (1971): 151–177; Hannah Fenichel Pitkin, *The Concept of Representation* (Berkeley: University of California Press, 1972), pp. 157–208 and passim; William E. Connolly, "On 'Interests' in Politics," *Politics and Society* 2 (1972): 459–477; J. David Greenstone, "Group Theories," in Fred I. Greenstein and Nelson Polsby, eds., *The Handbook of Political Science* (Reading, MA: Addison-Wesley, 1975), pp. 243–318; Nelson Polsby, *Community Power and Political Theory,* 2nd ed. (New Haven: Yale University Press, 1980), Chapter 12; and Andrew Reeve and Alan Ware, "Interests in Political Theory," *British Journal of Political Science* 13 (1983): 379–400.

The contrasting perspective, sometimes designated the *objective* approach, rests upon an outsider's evaluation of how an individual is affected by a given outcome rather than upon the wishes of the individual himself. Thus, according to this view, it is possible to impute interests to another on the basis of an informed assessment of what that person has at stake, irrespective of his or her own preferences. The logic behind this position is that there are many reasons why someone might lack adequate information to make accurate judgments about his or her interests. With respect to politics, for example, government policies may have effects of which those who stand to gain or lose are unaware. Nevertheless, those involved still have a stake in the outcome. Therefore, they have interests whether or not they have preferences.[7]

Interests as Preferences

In terms of intellectual utility, these two concepts are the obverse of each other. Each evades the problem the other confronts most fully. It is the virtue of the subjective approach that it accommodates most easily differences of taste. All of us do not want or care about the same things. A strategy allowing the individual to define his or her own interests thus permits the widest latitude for such differences in inclination. Furthermore, this approach avoids the arrogance and paternalism that inhere in assumptions that one can know what is best for others. In a sense, moreover, only this approach is compatible with the assumptions, so fundamental to democratic theory, about the capacities of the ordinary citizen to participate in government and to protect his own interests. To suggest that each of us is not the best judge of his own interest, then, is not merely condescending but potentially undemocratic.

There are, however, some serious difficulties with this approach. The equation between interests and preferences does not admit certain distinctions we commonly make about human motivations. With this formulation it is difficult, for example, to differentiate altruistic from self-interested behavior, for all behavior is by definition self-interested. Ordinarily, we distinguish between an industrialist who supports the relaxation of antipollution controls in the name of enhanced profits and another who, knowing full well that his profits might be higher if antipollution regulations were less stringent, nonetheless supports the stricter standards. It offends our common-sense understanding to

[7]A subjective definition of interests is usually associated with group theorists of politics and political scientists of a pluralist persuasion. Of the authors listed in footnote 6 as having given serious consideration to the problem of interests in politics, Bentley, Truman, and Polsby are among the proponents of this view, whereas Benn, Balbus, and Connolly are among those who incline to an objective view of how interests are ascertained.

Contrasting these two approaches to what constitutes an interest, Pitkin makes the point that when we talk about interests in the subjective sense—that is, in the sense of what we care about, are concerned about, or give our attention to—the converse of interested is uninterested or indifferent. When interests are construed in the objective sense—that is, in the sense of having a stake—the opposite of interested is disinterested or impartial. (See *The Concept of Representation,* p. 157.)

say that the behavior of the two industrialists is identical because each is defending his or her own self-interest, and that what differs is their interests.

Given this formulation, it is also a contradiction to assert that one can mistake his or her own interests. Because the evaluation of interests is complex, and because events frequently unfold in unexpected ways, we know that even the most careful attempts to assess self-interest often go awry. Doctors, for example, mounted a spirited campaign against national health insurance that successfully forestalled any major federal initiatives in this field for at least two decades. Only after the Democratic landslide that elected Lyndon Johnson to the presidency was the Medicare bill finally passed in 1965 over the opposition of physicians. The subsequent history of that policy has shown it to be an unanticipated financial windfall for the medical profession. Doctors have been among the principal beneficiaries of Medicare.[8] Had the doctors been privy at the outset to more complete information about the effects of the policies at issue, they might have defined their interests otherwise. They were, however, forced to make their initial determinations in the absence of such knowledge. If, in the light of the outcome, the doctors had reconsidered their stance toward Medicare, it probably would make more sense to argue that their original calculations were erroneous than to assert that their interests had changed.

These examples make clear that, in the absence of a Delphic oracle, even the most self-conscious estimate of self-interest might be mistaken.[9] An even more complicated intellectual problem occurs when those who are affected by a policy are unaware of it. Consider, for example, the unemployed. When jobless workers are asked to explain why they are out of work, they tend to discuss their situations in terms of various quite reasonable proximate causes: "Business was slow at the store," "Our plant lost a big order," or "A government contract was canceled." Not surprisingly, references to larger social forces as explanations of why they lost their jobs, or why they are having difficulty finding new ones, are much less frequent.[10] After all, it is easier to connect personal circumstances to the immediacies of one's personal orbit than to the workings of impersonal processes. Still, a trained economist might attribute these personal outcomes to the effects of macroeconomic policy as well as to the absence of back orders at a particular branch plant.

The question from our perspective is how we are to interpret the interests of these unemployed workers. Following the precepts of the interests-as-preferences approach, we might argue that the unemployed have no interests with respect to macroeconomic policy—because they have no opinions as to whether

---

[8] See Theodore R. Marmor, *The Politics of Medicare* (Chicago: Aldine, 1973), p. 123.

[9] Raymond A. Bauer, Ithiel de Sola Pool, and Lewis Anthony Dexter make some cogent observations on the subject of the difficulties inherent in making calculations of self-interest and give a fascinating, if dated, example in *American Business and Public Policy,* 2nd ed. (Chicago: Aldine, 1972), pp. 363–372, 472–475.

[10] Kay Lehman Schlozman and Sidney Verba, *Injury to Insult* (Cambridge: Harvard University Press, 1979) pp. 193–194.

interest rates should go up or down or whether the federal deficit is too great or too small. However, if they are, in fact, affected by such policies, it seems intuitively sensible to say that the unemployed have an interest in macroeconomic policy, even though they are unaware of those impacts and, hence, have no views on the subject.

Interests as Observable

The alternative perspective on the problem of how political interests are defined holds that an individual or group has interests in politics, apart from any expressed preferences; an informed, but unprejudiced, outsider can understand the interests of another by assessing what will most benefit him. This approach has the advantage that it fits well with at least one commonsense notion of interests. All of us—even the most dyed-in-the-wool partisans of the interests-as-preferences perspective—impute interests to others without first consulting them as to their opinions or observing their activity on behalf of a given policy. Thus, we say that retired people have an interest in higher Social Security payments, farmers have an interest in higher price supports, or students have an interest in low-interest federal loans. In making such assertions, we are alleging that the group in question is benefited by a given measure regardless of how group members themselves might feel about the subject or whether they have any feelings at all.

The notion that people have interests that are separate from their wishes and are, therefore, observable by an informed outsider obviates some of the difficulties discussed earlier. Because it becomes possible to know the interests of another, it becomes possible to distinguish altruistic from self-interested behavior and to differentiate conflicts of interest from conflicts of principle. Moreover, it becomes possible to assert that we have mistaken our interests, because we lack sufficient knowledge to make informed calculations, or because we are unaware of the ways in which social and political forces impinge on our lives.

Questioning the assumption that each of us is the best judge of his or her own interests also opens up lines of intellectual inquiry that are foreclosed prematurely when interests are equated with preferences. When preferences are no longer accepted as an axiomatic point of departure, then questions of where preferences come from, how they are shaped, and under what circumstances they change become legitimate. For example, during the 1950s women did not act collectively in politics; a decade later women's groups became an important political force. However, only if we adopt preferences as an object of inquiry rather than an axiomatic point of departure does it make sense to ask why there was no agitation for women's rights during the 1950s—a period when women faced widespread job discrimination. What social and cultural factors molded our perceptions of what was appropriate for women? What factors were responsible for the emergence of political activism on behalf of women's issues in the late 1960s? To what do we attribute the transformation in the way many women define what is in their best interests?

Clearly then, our definitions of what is best for us are rarely free, self-conscious choices made in the way that we assess the merits of the limited number of items on a restaurant menu—that is, made in the knowledge of all the available alternatives. Rather our preferences are influenced by a multitude of socially structured factors in our background and experience. The cues that we receive from family, school, church, and workplace, the messages that are promulgated through the media, the information that is disseminated (or withheld) by the government—all limit and shape in ways that have political effects what we consider to be in our best interests.

These considerations will concern us in several ways in the chapters that follow. Organizations that represent citizen interests are among the most important determinants of definitions of interest. Because they are on the scene day in and day out, persons who manage an organization's relations with the government have a knowledge of the potential effects of proposed policy changes that is denied to most organization members. As we shall see in Chapter 6, this first-hand intelligence allows these staffers to help members to know when their interests are threatened. This leads to a process of political education in which interests may be redefined. Hence, the political activity of an organization's government relations staff not only reflects but shapes the way that members understand their interests.[11]

In this process, interests are sometimes defined in ways that members find surprising, even uncongenial. An example of organizational intervention in the process of interest definition occurred recently. The American Medical Association suggested that doctors—whose fees had been rising at nearly twice the rate of inflation during the preceding year—should voluntarily freeze their fees for a year in order to obviate the need for congressional legislation that would place a mandatory freeze on Medicare fees.[12] Presumably, until so instructed by their professional association, very few doctors would have thought it to be in their best interests to forego an increase in income. Although there is no evidence in this case that the AMA leaders who made the suggestion were acting out of anything but a concern for the welfare of doctors, sometimes the organizational leaders and staff who actively promote particular definitions of member interests are animated by an agenda of their own concerns. Such instances raise thorny questions of organizational democracy, a problem taken up in Chapter 6.

A concern with the origins of political preferences and their relationship

---

[11] This understanding of the role of organizations in shaping member interests leads Philippe C. Schmitter to reject the ordinary term *interest representation* in favor of the clumsier *interest intermediation.* See "Modes of Interest Intermediation and Models of Societal Change in Western Europe," in Philippe C. Schmitter and Gerhard Lehmbruch, eds., *Trends toward Corporatist Intermediation* (Beverly Hills, CA: Sage, 1979), p. 93.

[12] *Newsweek,* March 5, 1984, p. 71.

to political activity is relevant in another way as well. Those who equate interests with preferences rarely take mass polls in order to determine who prefers what. Rather, they deduce the existence of shared preferences from political activity on behalf of a particular cause. This approach may become problematic when applied in reverse—that is, when lack of activity is understood as absence of joint interest.[13] Sometimes those whose life chances are likely to be seriously affected by a policy are not involved in trying to shape it. Such inactivity would not pose a puzzle to those who construe interests as preferences, for they would assume that it demonstrates that there is no joint desire to affect public outcomes. In making such an assumption, however, they would overlook not only the political and social forces that shape perceptions of interest but also the various impediments to political action by those who have joint interests. As we shall see in ensuing chapters, those who share common preferences are not always able to become active on behalf of those preferences. There are many barriers to organized political activity—including rational appraisals of the potential payoffs of collective action, lack of political resources, and intimidation by those in power—that dampen the participation of those with joint interests in politics. Once again, only when we loosen the connection between interests and preferences can we inquire into such matters.

Imputing Interests—Some Problems

If the adoption of this perspective makes possible certain kinds of intellectual analyses, it is not without its own problems. The notion that individuals have objective interests that can be ascertained by an informed observer seems to imply that the outsider himself is objective. Yet, it is surely the case that those who would presume to impute interests to others have their own values and may, in fact, not be fully informed.

The controversy over bilingual education for children whose first language is not English illustrates this point. In the early 1970s Congress mandated that such children should receive part of their education in their native tongues. The resulting programs have been steeped in controversy: antagonists assail them as costly and insist that in order to prepare children to cope most successfully in an English-speaking society, they need to concentrate on learning English; proponents argue that children learn most effectively when they master basic skills in their native languages before going on to learn a new one, and defend the role of bilingual education in sustaining cultural identity.

We could, in the name of ascertaining what is in the best interests of the children, turn to teachers as informed outside observers. Notwithstanding the claim of one teachers' union that "teachers want what children need," consult-

---

[13]On the problems with using political activity as an indicator of joint concern, see J. David Greenstone, "Group Theories," in *The Handbook of Political Science.* See also William A. Gamson, "Stable Unrepresentation in American Society," *American Behavioral Scientists* 12 (1968): 15–21.

ing educational experts would not be likely to provide a definitive answer. We would find that teachers' information is incomplete; there are serious gaps in educators' understanding of how students learn. Moreover, teachers are not objective. Inevitably, they have values of their own and, thus, appraise differentially the relative merits of cultural pluralism and economic success. They may even have something material at stake themselves if their own jobs are implicated in the outcome of the debate. Thus, we should be leery of the claims to greater information and objectivity of those who make judgments about the interests of others.

The example of the posture of the teachers with respect to bilingual education leads to the perhaps fatal shortcoming of the "objective" approach to interests—its failure to encompass differences of taste. As the proponents of this view recognize, there are many reasons why the members of a group might define their interests as they do. When a group does not act on behalf of its material self-interest, however, advocates of this approach may conclude prematurely that group members do not know their best interests and, then, search for the social roots of that lack of enlightenment.

However, when those to whom political interests might reasonably be imputed do not in fact pursue those interests, it may not reflect lack of awareness of their "true" interests. Sometimes the absence of political activism reflects what might be called a calculated quiescence, a conscious choice in the face of awareness of the potential costs involved in position taking. In the not too distant past, the potential civil rights activist in the Jim Crow South risked multiple reprisals, including physical violence; the Mormon woman with feminist inclinations risks estrangement from family and church if she becomes associated with feminist causes; and the union sympathizer in a nonunion shop risks losing his job if he makes overt gestures to organize the plant. In each case the absence of political action may reflect neither a failure to consider the effects of potentially beneficial policies nor a faulty appraisal of those effects; rather, the self-interested calculation must entail assessment of many factors, costs as well as benefits.

The preceding examples make clear that in any specific situation there are complicated trade-offs among many values we cherish—material enhancement, economic security, physical well-being, and psychic satisfaction, to name but a few. Thus, the process of defining what is in our best interests inevitably forces us to make choices among the many potential interests an outsider might be able to impute to us. There is no reason to expect that all individuals will have the same priorities when confronted with the need to choose among values. In our efforts to dig deeply into the sources of self-interest we must not forget the obvious: individuals differ in their inclinations, their values, and their tastes; and such differences of taste impel them to behave in ways that seem to certain outsider observers not to be in their best interests. After all, if a college student supports uncompromising foreign policies and believes that national security demands a well-trained army, who can say that he is acting contrary to his interests if he supports the draft and enlists in the armed forces, even if he is placing himself in potential physical jeopardy? Thus, when an individual does not pursue his narrowly defined interests in politics, it may, on the one hand, reflect a failure to assess those interests accurately—because interests are complex, because the information on which those assessments are based is always partial, and because the prevailing culture reinforces certain definitions of what is appropriate or natural. It may, on the other hand, simply show that individuals have different tastes, that one man's meat is another's endangered species.

As we analyze real cases of organized interests in action in the pages that follow, we shall attempt to be cognizant of the pitfalls of each of these perspectives. Like most political analysts, we shall in the name of brevity impute interests to a group—even in the absence of their expressed preferences—when government policies seem to have a clear impact on its members. In discussing any particular policy controversy, however, we shall attempt to be sensitive to what the individuals and groups involved—actual and potential—perceive to be in their best interests and take those perceptions seriously.

The difficult cases, of course, are those in which the content of expressed preferences or political action seems out of phase with the interests that might be attributed from an outsider's perspective. In such instances we shall attempt to understand what factors shape definitions of interest; what differences of taste or value induce individuals facing similar objective conditions to define their interests differently; and what information is available—or lacking—to facilitate the reasoned pursuit of perceived interests. We shall also be aware of the cues that are forthcoming from political organizations to their members, bearing in mind that the objectives of organization leaders and staff might differ from those of the rank and file. Finally, when the members of a group having a stake in the outcome of some policy controversy are inactive, we shall be motivated to probe further, seeking the roots of their quiescence in their own definitions of what is in their best interests, in rational calculations of the costs of position taking, and in the absence of resources for political action.

WHAT KINDS OF INTERESTS?

The discussion of the nature of interests in politics has said very little about their substance. Let us now consider the substance of the ends—economic and noneconomic, public and private—that organizations pursue in politics. Of course, organizations have nonpolitical objectives. They seek to further the interests of their members through activities outside the public arena; they seek to enhance themselves as organizations. While such goals will become relevant for our inquiry from time to time as we proceed, the focus in this section is on political objectives.

Economic and Noneconomic Interests

We pointed out earlier that as the term *interests* gained currency in early modern political discourse, its meaning narrowed, and it came to signify the interest in greater wealth. For many contemporary political analysts—not only Marxists but also those of a more conservative inclination—economic interests have a primacy among the goals sought through political action. Even though many important controversies—from pornography to women's suffrage to integration of schools—do not implicate pecuniary interests directly, economic conflict has been a leitmotif of American politics. And since the government is heavily involved in the economy—supervising macroeconomic performance, regulating industry, providing benefits for the needy, and acting as a major customer of the private sector—economic concerns are likely to be the sine qua non of political conflict in America.

Given the predominance of pocketbook interests in American politics, it is not surprising that the preponderance of organizations having a Washington presence unite those having joint economic interests at stake; more than three-quarters of the organizations that have their own Washington offices or hire Washington-based counsel or consultants to represent them bring together those who have in common their location in the economy.[14] When we begin to look more closely at interest group organizations in Chapter 3, particular attention will be paid to these business and occupational groups—corporations, trade associations, peak associations, professional associations, unions, and farm groups.

Although economic organizations are especially active in American politics, the pursuit of economic goals is not confined to groups organized around economic roles. Many groups that unite people on the basis of some other organizing principle have agendas laden with economic demands. The list of such groups is very long. Veterans, for example, receive an array of benefits from the federal government—disability pay, health and educational benefits, and preferential treatment in civil service hiring, to name a few—and veterans' groups like the American Legion and the Veterans of Foreign Wars are formidable advocates for the retention and enhancement of such material benefits. Similarly, senior citizens and civil rights groups have made vigorous efforts on behalf of the economic interests of their constituents. There are dozens of other examples of groups organized around some noneconomic principle—gender, ethnicity, and so on—that represent the shared economic interests of their members.

If economic conflict has been the dominant theme of politics in America (and virtually every other industrial democracy), then a consistent reprise has been conflict over nonmaterial interests and values. Since the early days of the republic, controversies over intangibles—political rights, liberty, security, beauty, cultural and moral values—have waxed and waned, engendering sentiments of an intensity and rancor not always present in the politics of economic competition.

Many of the noneconomic issues that have figured so prominently in the

---

[14]This figure is based on a tabulation of the organizations listed in Arthur C. Close, ed., *Washington Representatives–1981* (Washington, DC: Columbia Books, 1981). The mechanics of the enumeration are explained fully in Appendix C; the results of the tally are elaborated in Chapter 4.

politics of post-World War II America have antecedents in previous centuries. Issues involving race—currently embodied, for example, in the conflicts over forced busing to integrate schools and affirmative action programs in hiring—have a long and not terribly edifying history in our politics dating back at least as far as the Constitutional compromise that a Negro slave was to be counted as three-fifths of a person for the purposes of representation and taxation. The debate in 1984 surrounding the status of illegal aliens was one in a series of disputes over immigration stretching back over a century to the arrival of the first large groups of non-English-speaking and non-Protestant immigrants.

What sorts of values are at issue when citizens contend over nonpocket-book matters? Of course, the list of such intangibles is very long. However, two sources of recurring dissension deserve brief mention. Many of these conflicts involve the defense of the moral and cultural values that underlie a way of life. For example, according to one analysis of the temperance movement in the nineteenth century, what was at stake was not alcohol per se, but alcohol as the symbol of an entire way of life—a declining way of life that was rural, Yankee, Protestant, and dry and that was being laid seige by a complex of changes surrounding the emergence of an industrial order in the increasingly Catholic, immigrant, and wet cities.[15] An analogous argument could, it seems, be made about the quite vituperative contemporary debates surrounding pornography. Dirty books and movies come to symbolize the antithesis of a way of life that seems to many people to be under assault in the schools and in the media.

Sometimes what is at stake is power. It is axiomatic to our understanding of the political psychology of individuals that political men seek power, often for the other rewards on behalf of which it can be exercised, but sometimes for its own sake.[16] Yet we rarely apply this insight to groups. For disenfranchised groups, like blacks and women, the acquisition of group power has long figured importantly in the catalogue of group demands. For many decades it was a matter of establishing the fundamental political rights that citizens exercise in a democracy: the right to vote, to serve on a jury, to hold office, and so on. Now that these rights have been secured, the struggle to obtain equal political power focuses on different objectives, such as the attempt to place more blacks and women in public office.

Controversies involving values and ideas often pit one intangible against another. For example, in the political controversy over abortion, the principal antagonists appeal to differing moral principles: the opponents point to the right of the unborn to life; the advocates point to the right of a woman to choose freely whether to continue a pregnancy. There is also a continuing struggle between the claims of those who want to protect our First Amendment guarantees of free expression and the concerns of others who worry that the

---

[15] See Joseph R. Gusfield, *Symbolic Crusade* (Urbana: University of Illinois Press, 1963), especially Chapters 1, 6, and 7.

[16] For an animated journalistic account of the delights of exercising power, see Tom Wolfe, "The Ultimate Power: Seeing 'Em Jump," in Clay Felker, ed., *The Power Game* (New York: Simon and Schuster, 1969).

free flow of sensitive information in a democracy may jeopardize national security.

Many political conflicts, however, pit against one another combatants who have different kinds of interests at stake. Temperance enthusiasts, who were committed to moral values, met with vigorous opposition of brewers and distillers, who obviously had a material interest in the matter. Environmental issues often display a similar pattern of conflict. Supporters of environmental protection are animated by concern for beauty, the health of present and future generations, and the like; manufacturers and industrialists are understandably motivated by concern about their balance sheets. Many of the cases reviewed here conform to this pattern: antagonists on one side of a controversy having economic interests at stake; those on the other being concerned with intangibles.

Public and Private Interests

In addition to the fundamental distinction between economic and noneconomic interests, a second major distinction with respect to kinds of interests is between public and private interests. At least since Madison, observers of American politics and governance have raised concerns that the activities of organized interests are an impediment to the achievement of the common good. Furthermore, as shown in Chapter 4, broadly shared or "public" interests are underrepresented among organizations involved in Washington politics. For these reasons it seems appropriate to discuss the complex question of the nature of the public interest at some length and make clear what is meant when we refer to the *public interest*.

There is a long tradition within Western political thought of rumination upon the nature of the *public good* and the *commonweal,* terms that have now given way to the expression *public interest.* Public officials often appeal to the public interest in order to legitimate whatever policies they advocate. However, serious students of politics have achieved no consensus as to whether there even is such a thing as the public interest, much less what it is.[17] Contemporary

[17]The recent literature in political science on the concept of the public interest is quite voluminous. Among the works of the past few decades are the following: Frank J. Sorauf, "The Public Interest Reconsidered," *Journal of Politics* 19 (1957): 616-639; S. I. Benn, "Interests in Politics," *Proceedings of the Aristotelian Society* 60 (1960): 123-140; Glendon Schubert, *The Public Interest* (Glencoe, IL: Free Press, 1960); Carl J. Friedrich, ed., *NOMOS V: The Public Interest* (New York: Atherton Press, 1962); B. M. Barry, "The Public Interest," *Proceedings of the Aristotelian Society,* Supplementary 38 (1964): 1-18; W. J. Rees, "The Public Interest," *Proceedings of the Aristotelian Society,* Supplementary 38 (1964): 20; Richard Flathman, *The Public Interest,* (New York: Wiley, 1966); Virginia Held, *The Public Interest and Individual Interests* (New York: Basic Books, 1970); Theodore M. Benditt, "The Public Interest," *Philosophy and Public Affairs* 12 (1973): 291-311; Clarke E. Cochran, "Political Science and the 'Public Interest'," *Journal of Politics* 36 (1974): 327-355; Felix E. Oppenheim, "Self-Interest and Public Interest," *Political Theory* 3 (1975): 259-276; Barry M. Mitnick, "A Typology of Conceptions of the Public Interest," *Administration and Society* 8 (1976): 5-28; Candace Hetzner, "The Public Interest and Corporate Social Responsibility," paper presented at the Annual Meeting of the American Political Science Association, Washington, DC, September 1984.

analysts differ among themselves along several dimensions.[18] Some give the public interest a substantive meaning by introducing normative definitions of its content. But if such analysts agree that there is such a thing as the public interest and that we can discuss what it is, their descriptions of what *in fact* constitutes the common good are disparate to say the least. Sometimes the definitions are so general—for example, "the common good . . . is best conceived as the preservation and the improvement of the community itself"[19]—as to be of no guidance to the official who wishes to govern in the public interest. Sometimes, however, the definitions are quite specific—as, for example, the suggestion that the public interest is served by policies that promote racial tolerance, but not by those that induce racial bigotry.[20] Sometimes the focus is on the preservation of the community, as in the suggestion that policies that enhance national security are in the public interest. Sometimes the focus is on the development of the individual.[21] Thus, although many political analysts believe that the public interest does in fact exist, their elaborations of what it is are diverse indeed.

An alternative tack is taken by those who give to the term a procedural rather than a substantive meaning. Such thinkers conceive the public interest in terms of the process itself, rather than in terms of the outcome of those processes; that is, they posit that the public interest is realized when decisions are made and conflicts are resolved in accordance with certain prescribed methods. The specific procedures that are credited with the realization of the public interest are varied. Majoritarian democratic politics, the rule of law, the structure of legislative-executive relations, and the process of conflict and compromise among interest groups are all said to produce the public interest.[22] Finally, recent political scientists deny the usefulness of the concept for political analysis.[23] Basically, they subscribe to the precept that there is no public interest apart from the sum of the private utilities of individuals.[24]

[18]Therefore, exhaustive attempts to classify the various conceptions of the public interest invariably involve numerous categories based on the interrelationship of a large number of variables. See, for example, Mitnick, "A Typology of Conceptions."

[19]Cochran, "Political Science and the 'Public Interest'," p. 355.

[20]Edgar Bodenheimer, "Prolegomena to a Theory of the Public Interest," in Friedrich, ed., *NOMOS V,* p. 214.

[21]See, for example, Benn, "Interests in Politics," p. 139.

[22]Sorauf discusses procedural views of the public interest in "Public Interest Reconsidered," pp. 622–624, 629–633. See, also, Arthur Maass, *Congress and the Common Good* (New York: Basic Books, 1983), especially pp. 18–19.

[23]Among such analysts we would include Schubert in *The Public Interest.* Following the lead of Arthur Bentley in *The Process of Government,* group theorists of politics like David B. Truman see politics entirely in terms of the interests of individuals as represented by the groups of which they are members and, therefore, reject any notion of the public interest. Says Truman, "We do not need to account for a totally inclusive interest, because one does not exist" (*The Governmental Process,* p. 51).

[24]One way to avoid some of these difficulties is suggested by B. M. Barry in "The Public Interest," pp. 14–16. He distinguishes among the interests a person has in the various capacities in which he operates, indicating that a certain policy may be in his interests as a parent, as a businessman, as a house owner, or as a member of the public. On this basis, there are policies that will be to the benefit of all in their capacities as members of the public.

What Is a Public Interest Group?

> What exactly is meant when the media report that a lawsuit has been com-
> menced or a demonstration mounted by an organization described as a
> "public interest" lobby or a "public interest" group? Most such groups
> don't represent any broader interest than that of their own members—and
> most of them don't *have* all that many members . . . they grind a private
> ax—and claim that it really belongs to all of us.
>
> > Mobil Oil Advertisement, *Wall Street Journal,*
> > December 4, 1979, p. 2. © 1979 Mobil Corporation.
> > Reprinted with permission of Mobil Corporation.
>
> Any organized group of people constitutes a special interest—by definition
> . . . . Over the past decade there has come into existence something often
> referred to as "the public interest community." It consists of men and
> women with a common desire to emphasize certain values and certain per-
> spectives—e.g. a clean environment—that affect all of us alike, and to act
> on behalf of those values whenever and wherever they perceive the rest of
> us to be neglecting them. It does nothing to detract from anyone's efforts to
> suggest that even the noblest cause can at length become a vested inter-
> est, or that it may attract at least a few who are more interested in doing
> well than in doing good.
>
> > Citibank Advertisement, as appeared
> > in *The New York Times,*
> > February 22, 1978, p. A15.

Among the important developments of the 1960s was the emergence of a
number of groups representing broadly held interests—for example, consumer
groups, citizens' groups, environmental groups—that began to be called collectively "public interest" groups. In the aftermath of initial successes and favorable media coverage, an alternative view of this phenomenon took hold, such
that their antagonists routinely referred to "self-styled consumer advocate,
Ralph Nader" and "so-called public interest groups." If political scientists cannot arrive at a definition of the public interest, are the critics of the public
interest movement correct in arguing that there is no such thing as a public
interest group and that the interest represented by Ralph Nader is just as
special as that represented by Citibank or Mobil? It can be argued that there is
a difference between the kinds of interests being represented by, say, Common

---

Barry goes on to discuss the perplexing circumstance in which a person's interests in some
other capacity outweigh his interests as a member of the public. As a member of the public, a
student may have an interest in lower federal taxes; as a student, however, he may have a more
compelling interest in low-income student loans. As a member of the public, the businessman may
have an interest in environmental safety, but as an executive in a chemical company, he may have
an even greater stake in dumping toxic wastes. We should note both that this formulation makes
the implicit assumption of an objective view of interests and that Barry does not take into account
the circumstance, to be discussed later, in which a person has more than one interest in his capacity
as a member of the public.

Cause and the American Federation of Teachers. However, the matter is much more complicated than many public interest advocates would probably like.

A public interest group can be defined as one seeking a benefit, the achievement of which will not benefit selectively either the membership or the activists of the organization.[25] If the National Taxpayers Union is successful in promoting across-the-board tax cuts and reduced government spending, all taxpayers—not just NTU members or leaders—can enjoy the benefits. Thus, the National Taxpayers Union qualifies as a public interest group. Similarly, if the Consumers Union can realize its goal of inducing corporations to produce safer, more reliable consumer goods, everybody—not just the leaders and members of the Consumers Union—can benefit. It, too, qualifies as a public interest group.

Are All Public Interest Groups Liberal?   Sometimes, those who debunk public interest groups seem to assume that public interest groups are invariably liberal. This is hardly the case. Consider an organization like the Pacific Legal Foundation. The PLF is a public interest law firm that engages in litigation to defend, among other values, individual liberty, free enterprise, and economic development. In general, it opposes government regulation of the economy. Among its successful cases have been a challenge to the moratorium on the construction of nuclear facilities in California; a suit to compel the federal government to permit the use of DDT to control Tussock Moths in Washington; and the defeat of various governmental efforts to stop dams and water-delivery projects.[26] Such positions bring it into conflict with many better-known public interest groups.

In the process of defending economic liberty and development, the Pacific Legal Foundation has been accused of being a front for business rather than a public interest group. The PLF denies the charge vigorously and makes a fairly persuasive case to back up the assertion. The PLF claims to have 9,000 contributors, many of whom give small donations. According to their managing attorney, their contributors—like the contributors to their liberal antagonists—are drawn from the ranks of individuals, businesses, associations, and foundations. The PLF argues that it is no more captured by its benefactors than are the liberal public interest groups that rely upon individuals and foundations for support.[27]

The issue, however, bears further discussion. Consider the PLF's suit to

[25]This definition follows very closely that given by Jeffrey M. Berry in *Lobbying for the People* (Princeton: Princeton University Press, 1977), p. 7. Berry adds the stipulation that the achievement of the benefit not benefit the members or activists of the organization *materially*. We omit this criterion in order to classify as a public interest group an organization like the National Taxpayers Union.

[26]Information about the Pacific Legal Foundation is taken from "The New Wave of Public Interest Law," remarks made by their managing attorney, Raymond Momboisse, at a conference in January 1980, entitled *Public Interest Law: The Second Decade.*

[27]Ibid.

lift the moratorium on the construction of nuclear power plants in California. That suit sought a nonselective benefit for the people of California: a steady supply of low-cost electrical energy. However, some businessmen—for example, those involved in designing and building the plants and the reactors they house, and those involved in mining and processing nuclear fuel—surely stand to benefit selectively from the PLF's success. To the extent that the PLF lists among its contributors individuals, corporations, and trade associations standing to benefit selectively from its actions, its claim to status as a public interest group is vitiated. To the extent that its contributors are, quite simply, believers in free enterprise and economic growth who have no possibility of selective enrichment, then that claim is quite valid. In the absence of full disclosure of the names and affiliations of PLF contributors, we cannot judge definitively; however, there is no reason to cast doubt on the Pacific Legal Foundation's claim to be a public interest group.

Generally Available Benefits Versus Equally Available Benefits   A public interest group has been defined as one in which neither the membership nor the activists would benefit selectively from the achievement of group objectives. However, benefits that are *generally* available may not be *equally* available. As mentioned before, the National Taxpayers Union falls squarely under the public interest rubric. However, broad-based tax cuts rarely benefit all taxpayers equally. Leaving aside the problem that the effects of cuts in services that ensue from a reduced budget will affect citizens differentially, any specific tax cut will reduce the tax bills of those in some categories more than others. Similarly, if the government were to create a vast new wilderness area in, say, Wyoming, the resulting aesthetic pleasures would be available to all Americans. But surely city dwellers in Denver would find those pleasures more accessible than, for example, city dwellers in Miami.

A Single Public Interest?   Another complication is that in any particular political controversy there may be more than one public interest at stake.[28] Often, one of the competing interests will be intangible—safety, health, beauty—and the other material—reduced cost or increased economic growth. For example, there is no question that putting air bags into automobiles reduces the risk of injury to passengers in a collision; however, it also raises the cost to consumers. Thus, there are two generally available benefits at stake: on the one hand, safety, and on the other, reduced cost. Similarly, many people argue that there is a trade-off between pollution control and economic growth. As a barber in a Pennsylvania steel-producing town remarked, "When smoke is pouring, people get a haircut. When there isn't any smoke, people don't spend money."[29] Some-

[28] This point is made by Andrew S. McFarland in *Public Interest Lobbies* (Washington, DC: The American Enterprise Institute, 1976), pp. 37–40.
[29] Quoted by Charles O. Jones, *Dirty Air* (Pittsburgh: University of Pittsburgh Press, 1975), p. ix.

times, both broadly held benefits are intangible. For example, in the controversies surrounding the right of former CIA operatives to publish memoirs, the competing public interests are national security and the public's right to scrutinize what the government is doing.

Not only may there be diffuse public interests on both sides of a political controversy, there may be public and private interests on each side. Consider, for example, the conflict over offshore drilling for oil in the Atlantic on Georges Bank, one of the world's richest fishing areas. The competing public interests—environmental preservation and conservation of a natural supply of food, on the one hand, and exploitation of a potential source of abundant fossil fuel, on the other—are by now familiar. We should take note, in addition, of the private interests on each side of the dispute. The interest of the oil and gas companies in proceeding with the drilling is obvious. However, there is also the private interest of the commercial fishermen, who would probably oppose the drilling on the grounds of the danger of polluting the source of their livelihood.

Our observation that there are ordinarily several generally available benefits—or public interests—at issue in any given political conflict leads back to the question of differences of taste. When there are such competing public interests, then there are invariably differences of preferences with respect to them. The benefits of a wilderness preserve may be available to all who live near it. However, backpackers and bird-watchers are more likely to care about establishing such preserves and to take advantage of what they have to offer than are those whose recreational tastes lie in the direction of horse racing or chess.

Moreover, variations in individuals' preferences concerning alternative public interests are frequently socially structured. Consider, for example, Preservation Action, an organization that seeks government support (tax incentives, grants, and so on) to facilitate the preservation of buildings of historical significance. From its literature, Preservation Action seems unquestionably to be a public interest group; its supporters have no private benefit at stake. However, if Preservation Action is typical of other groups engaged in this enterprise, then its supporters are likely to be drawn disproportionately from the ranks of the upper-middle class and from those whose roots in America date back several generations. These are people whose economic security permits them to be more willing to forego the broadly shared benefits of economic growth when historical buildings give way to shopping malls, and whose family backgrounds give them strengthened ties with the more distant American past. Those with less economic security might be prepared to renounce aesthetic gratifications for jobs and commercial expansion.[30]

---

[30]Note that advocates of various diffuse interests agree that the trade-offs may not be as unambiguous as they are portrayed. Environmentalists assert, for example, that pollution control creates jobs (although different ones than might be destroyed). Preservation Action maintains that historic preservation often paves the way for economic revitalization and increased tourism, especially in downtown areas.

We have gone to some length to show that there is rarely just a single public interest at stake in any particular political conflict. That being the case, how do public interest groups presume to represent *the* public interest? Such a claim is clearly not legitimate. Thoughtful members of the public interest community do not claim to represent *the* public interest. Rather they attempt to take up the cudgel on behalf of what might otherwise be the unrepresented side of the question. For reasons that will be examined in some detail in Chapters 4 and 6, certain interests—the interests of those who dump chemicals into the water as opposed to the interests of those who drink it, the interests of those who raise beef as opposed to the interests of those who eat it, the interests of those who manufacture furniture as opposed to the interests of those who recline on it—are more likely to receive vigorous promotion in American politics. In general, public interest groups attempt to achieve some kind of balance by taking up the cause that has no organized voice and, thus, represent points of view that would not otherwise be articulated effectively.[31]

This, by the way, helps to explain why it sometimes appears as if all public interest groups are liberal. We mentioned that on any side of a political conflict there may be a mix of public and private interests at stake. Public interest groups favoring objectives like economic growth and lower costs to consumers will often find their goals to be coincident with those of private interests, especially business interests, that stand to benefit selectively from the outcome. This is less common for public interest groups favoring objectives like environmental preservation and consumer safety. When there are groups of the privately interested in the fray, the logic of trying to balance the civic discourse becomes less compelling. Hence, there is less necessity for public interest groups to take a position beside them or to speak loudly if they do. When the opposing position is not represented by privately interested groups, then public interest groups will be more likely to step in. Thus, public interest groups that oppose privately interested business groups are much more likely to achieve visibility than are public interest groups that support business.

Just in It for Themselves?   The upper-middle-class nature of the membership of organizations like Preservation Action and the Sierra Club has led critics to accuse such groups of being composed of elitists who have only their own interests at heart. By definition, of course, this accusation is unfair, since a public interest group has been defined as one in which neither members nor leaders benefit selectively from the realization of group goals. However, such critics are surely correct in locating the backbone of the current public interest movement in the middle and upper-middle classes. In this respect, contempo-

---

[31]On the question of how public interest groups construe their representative function, see McFarland, *Public Interest Lobbies,* pp. 8–12, 39; and David Vogel, "The Public-Interest Movement and the American Reform Tradition," *Political Science Quarterly* 95 (1980): 607–627.

rary public interest groups are very much in the tradition of historical movements for reform in America—abolitionism, temperance, and progressivism, to
list a few of the most obvious ones—that were rooted in the middle and upper-
middle classes. Furthermore, in their disproportionate recruitment of upper-
status citizens, public interest groups are similar to most other groups active in
Washington. When, in Chapter 4, we survey the Washington pressure community—that is, the whole set of organized interests involved in Washington politics—a pervasive upper-middle-class skewing becomes clear. Critics are also
accurate in arguing that members of public interest groups wish to see their
own preferences converted into public policy—preferences that are not necessarily universally shared. Indeed, those preferences might be opposed by a
majority of those from different social backgrounds or even by a majority of the
public at large.[32]

The question of whether those who act on behalf of broadly shared interests are "just in it for themselves" becomes even more compelling when it
comes to the leaders and staff of public interest groups. Once again, by definition, this clearly is not the case, at least in the narrow sense. However, the
accusation may apply to the career enhancement that can result from successes
in the public interest field. In fact, it seems that working for a public interest
group is hardly a short-cut to riches and fame—at least in the short run. Those
who work for public interest groups seem to labor for love not money: they
work long hours in surroundings that are not plush and do so at lower pay than
they could command in the private sector.[33] Moreover, they seem, almost universally, to care deeply about the causes to which they devote their efforts. This
emerged from the interviews we conducted with the 175 representatives in our
survey of organizations with Washington offices. When we posed an open-
ended question about what is most gratifying about the work they do, 70 percent of those affiliated with public interest groups, but only 30 percent of those

[32]For a discussion of this and related issues, see Jeffrey M. Berry, "Public Interest vs. Party
System," *Society,* May/June 1980, pp. 42–48.

[33]This generalization, based on both our observations and comments made in the course of
our Washington survey, is supported by various scholarly and journalistic accounts of life within
public interest groups that indicate that employees are overworked and underpaid. See, for example, Jeffrey M. Berry, "On the Origins of Public Interest Groups," *Journal of Politics* 10 (1978):
392–393, and Caroline E. Mayer, "Nader of the Lost Bark," *The Washington Post,* September 13,
1981, p. F3. With respect to the compensation of lawyers, in particular, see Burton A. Weisbrod,
"Nonprofit and Proprietary Sector Behavior: Wage Differentials Among Lawyers," *Journal of
Labor Economics* 1 (1983): 246–263.

An exception to the generalization that public interest groups overwork and underpay their
staff members is Common Cause. Andrew McFarland shows that at least through the late 1970s,
Common Cause staffers generally were paid the equivalent of the federal government salary for
their work—not as much, perhaps, as they would make in private firms, but more than their
counterparts in other public interest groups earned. Similarly, Common Cause staffers typically
worked 44 weeks, reflecting the preference of organizational founder John Gardner, who liked to
work nine-to-five and save his evening hours for reading. See McFarland, *Common Cause: Lobbying
in the Public Interest* (Chatham, NJ: Chatham House Publishers, 1984), p. 88.

associated with corporations and 32 percent of those employed by trade associations, mentioned something about the cause itself. It may be, however, that in the longer run, successes in the public interest sphere lead to lucrative offers in the private sector or government service. Unfortunately, there is no information available to assess whether this is a typical pattern or whether those who leave public interest groups earn even higher salaries than they would have had they gone directly to Houston, Wall Street, or the Environmental Protection Agency without having served such an apprenticeship.

Public Interest Groups: Concluding Remarks   Our discussion of public interest groups has focused on organizations like the National Tax Limitation Committee, the Friends of the Earth, and The Consumer Federation of America— organizations (both liberal and conservative) that seek broadly held interests that are shared by nearly everyone in the community. We have argued that, in terms of the kinds of interests they represent, public interest groups are different from private interest groups. In concluding, it seems appropriate to underline the implications of this line of reasoning.

First of all, since there are ordinarily broadly shared interests at stake on more than one side of any policy controversy, it should be clear that any claim to representing *the* public interest must be inherently suspect. In addition, in seeking generally available benefits, public interest groups may take positions that a majority of citizens deem not to be in the public interest. Moreover, public interest groups have no monopoly on the representation of broadly shared interests; on the contrary, the privately interested are often animated by a concern with diffuse public interests.[34] Finally, our discussion of the nature of the benefits sought by public interest groups implies no assessment of whether their programs are right-, or wrong-headed, their approach is flexible or stubborn, or their research is careful or slipshod. In short, the foregoing discussion is not intended to place public interest groups squarely on the side of the angels and to consign the privately interested to the company of Satan.

Organizations that act as advocates for broadly shared interests figure importantly in the understanding of pressure politics that informs later chapters. In order not to load the dice unfairly in their favor, from now on we shall not use the ordinary term *public interest groups* to refer to them. Rather, we

[34]When appeals to the public good are made by those who stand to benefit selectively from a particular policy outcome, it is often difficult to assess precisely the mix of sincerity and cynicism at work. Consider the posture of professors with respect to cuts in various forms of federal aid to universities. There are surely public benefits to be gained from having a well-educated citizenry and work force. However, when professors plead for a strong university system in the name of such general benefits, there is an ambiguity to their position. On one hand, they surely believe sincerely in the importance of higher education to the good of the nation; if they did not, they probably would not have become professors. On the other hand, their own livelihoods are at stake. Hence, it is not unreasonable to consider their seemingly public-spirited rhetoric as merely a cloak for the cynical advancement of their own private interests.

shall refer to these organizations as *citizens' groups,* in the hope that this term will carry fewer "white knight" overtones.[35]

A NOTE ON INTENSITY

Any discussion of the nature of political interests should include at least a passing reference to the problem of intensity. As should be quite obvious by now, all citizens have a multitude of politically relevant interests. Even the most involved cannot care with equal intensity about each of them. The problem for democratic theory is whether and how to make policy outcomes reflect the differences in intensity with which individuals hold their preferences.[36]

In general, individuals are more likely to be concerned about policies that affect them appreciably than about those whose effects, good or bad, are negligible. For example, auto workers are more likely to feel more strongly about the benefits of domestic-content legislation that specifies that imported automobiles must contain a certain proportion of American-made components than they do about the potentially inflationary consequences of the increases in the prices of foreign cars, consequences they would feel as consumers. Of course, there are exceptions. Certain moral issues—capital punishment, gun control, and abortion, to name a few—incite feelings of great intensity among partisans who have neither private nor material interests at stake. Still, citizens are ordinarily likely to care less deeply about what they have at stake as members of the public than about what they have at stake in other capacities. As we shall see more fully by the end of Chapter 4, what this means with regard to political controversies is that narrow private interests are more likely to receive spirited advocacy than broad public ones.[37]

The dilemma for democratic theory is to know how to weigh preferences that are held with differing intensity. On the one hand, serious students of American politics at least since Madison have been concerned with tyranny of the majority. Surely, the concern that a lukewarm majority will ride roughshod over the preferences of an impassioned minority is a real one. That is why constitutional guarantees of the procedural rights of minorities—the right to speak freely, assemble peaceably, and so on—are so crucial. But the substantive outcomes are important as well. The majority may respect the rights of the opposing minority with a delicacy bordering on perfection. If, however, when

[35]This language, should not, of course, be interpreted as implying that the members of organizations seeking more narrowly available benefits—unions, professional associations, and so on—are not also citizens.

[36]For an illuminating discussion of this issue, see Robert A. Dahl, *A Preface to Democratic Theory* (Chicago: University of Chicago Press, 1956).

[37]This point is made by E. E. Schattschneider in *The Semisovereign People* (New York: Holt, Rinehart and Winston, 1960), p. 35; James Q. Wilson in *Political Organization* (New York: Basic Books, 1973), pp. 332–337; and Mancur Olson, *The Logic of Collective Action* (Cambridge: Harvard University Press, 1965).

the shouting recedes, the majority simply votes down the opposition over and over again, then the Madisonians would be concerned. No matter how much the members of the smaller group care, they can never prevail.[38]

On the other hand, political thinkers of a more democratic temperament than Madison would likely be more concerned about the opposite problem: minorities' rule. That is, they would be likely to worry that zealous minorities would continually assert their will over that of the tepid majority and, therefore, that majority rule could never be realized. Furthermore, some observers argue that the American political process is uniquely hospitable to rule by groups representing narrow publics.[39] The history of governmental attempts to require registration of handguns illustrates this concern. For several decades, polls have shown that an overwhelming majority of the American public favors stricter firearms laws. For the past fifteen years, the American public has favored stricter federal handgun legislation by substantial margins. Largely as the result of the opposition of a few intensely committed groups—in particular, the National Rifle Association—no such measure has been passed.[40]

At a more practical level, it is difficult to ascertain how much an interested person or group cares about a particular issue. Some political observers take the amount of political activity on behalf of a certain position as an index of intensity of concern. This seems reasonable, as those who feel strongly about a particular matter would be more likely to get involved. This approach however, ignores the multiple barriers to joint political activity. Those with collective political concerns are not always active on behalf of those concerns. The next three chapters explore, among other things, the reasons why.

SUMMARY

This chapter has pursued a number of themes relevant to the interests that organizations seek through political action. We began by assessing two alternative perspectives on the problem of how we know what is in somebody else's best interests. The former holds that a person's interests are whatever he deems them to be—a point of view that makes ample allowances for differences of taste but falters in its insensitivity to the ways in which insufficient information can lead to mistakes in appraising self-interest. The latter holds that an informed, but impartial, outside observer can impute interests to another by

---

[38] Students of consociational democracies like Switzerland and the Netherlands point out that such democracies have altogether different arrangements for guaranteeing to the permanent minority a voice in government. See, for example, Arendt Lijphart, *The Politics of Accommodation* (Berkeley: University of California Press, 1968) and Kenneth McRae, ed., *Consociational Democracy* (Ottawa: McClelland and Stewart, 1974.)

[39] Among the authors who take this position are Schattschneider, *The Semisovereign People,* Chapter 2; Grant McConnell, *Private Power and American Democracy* (New York: Knopf, 1966); and Theodore J. Lowi, *The End of Liberalism,* 2nd ed., (New York: Norton, 1979).

[40] On public opinion and gun laws, see Robert Weissberg, *Public Opinion and Popular Government* (Englewood Cliffs, NJ: Prentice Hall, 1976), pp. 126–132.

evaluating what will benefit him most. This approach has the obverse virtues and flaws of the former. On the one hand, it allows for the possibility that people may assess their interests inaccurately, because they command incomplete information, or because their definitions of what is best for them are shaped by larger social and cultural forces of which they are not fully aware. On the other hand, this perspective is sometimes intolerant of differences in taste.

This chapter has also probed the substance of political interests, distinguishing first between economic and noneconomic interests. We made the point that material interests form the backbone of American political controversy and indicated not only that the large majority of groups active in American politics are organized around joint economic concerns, but also that groups organized along noneconomic lines often pursue economic objectives in politics. However, we went on to show that concern about a wide variety of intangible values has been a recurrent theme in the history of American political conflict and detailed some of those intangibles. We then proceeded to make the distinction between public and private interests, arguing that although political philosophers have achieved no consensus whatsoever as to the nature of the public interest, it is legitimate to consider as a public interest group any group seeking a benefit that, once achieved, would not benefit selectively either the members or the activists of the organization.

Finally, on a slightly different tack, we discussed the problem of differing intensities of preferences. Theorists of democracy have long noted the tension between the desire to preserve political equality and the desire to give special weight to the feelings of those who care most deeply. This issue will arise periodically in the pages that follow, especially when we consider the dilemma of how organizationally-based political inputs are to be weighed in a system that takes the one-man–one-vote principle of political equality as one of its central tenets.

3

Interest Organizations in Politics

So far, a great deal has been said about interests in politics, but relatively little about the many, many organizations that represent those interests. The organizations that represent collective interests in politics come in many sizes and shapes. Some have thousands of members, others have hundreds, and still others are merely letterhead organizations with no members at all. Some have individuals as members; others are composed of constituent organizations. Some are federal in structure, having national, state, and local units that operate with varying degrees of autonomy; most are unitary with no subsidiary components. Some have venerable histories; a few are self-consciously temporary, set up to do battle on a particular issue. Some are concerned about many issues; others concentrate on a single matter.

This chapter introduces the principal kinds of interest organizations and describes briefly what they do and what they look like. In particular, it examines how they vary in membership, organizational structure, and scope of political concerns. It aims to familiarize the reader with certain fundamental aspects of the categories of organizations that will be appearing most frequently throughout the remaining chapters.

Although this chapter is largely descriptive, later chapters examine aspects of internal organization having clear political consequences: variations in organizational resources (Chapter 5) and patterns of internal governance and communication (Chapter 6). This chapter says relatively little about the political implications of variations in organizational form. Political scientists do not know very much about how different kinds of interest organizations—membership as opposed to nonmembership, unitary as opposed to federal, and so on—vary in their political conduct. It may be that they have not hit upon the correct organizational variables that would explain diverse patterns of political involvement for different kinds of interest organizations. It is probably the case, however, that such organizational matters may have relatively limited political effects. One of the lessons of Chapter 7 is the remarkable similarity in the political strategies used by organizations that differ significantly in their organizational form. Differences in political approach among interest groups more likely are reflective of differences in the resources they command, the issues they tackle, and their tax status than of differences in organizational structure. Thus, the National Abortion Rights Action League (NARAL) and the American Medical Association (AMA) are both national voluntary associations having lots of members and state affiliates. Their approaches to politics are not dissimilar; however, in terms of the nature of its political activity, the AMA probably more closely resembles Exxon, which is a corporation and not a membership group at all, than it resembles NARAL. That resemblance, presumably, derives chiefly from the similarity in the scope of their resources and the nature of the political ends they pursue.

MEMBERSHIP ORGANIZATIONS

Although there are many politically active organizations in the organized interest world that have no members at all, when political scientists speak of interest groups, they are ordinarily referring to membership organizations of one type or another. Some national membership organizations have individual persons as members, others have organizations as members, and some have both.

Groups composed of individual members can be found virtually anywhere on the political landscape. Labor unions such as the National Association of Letter Carriers, professional societies such as the American Dental Association, civil rights and social welfare groups such as the National Association for the Advancement of Colored People and the American Civil Liberties Union, environmental and consumer groups such as the National Audubon Society and Consumers Union, ideological and cause groups such as Action on Smoking and Health and the Young Americans for Freedom—all are individual-membership organizations.

Many organizations have other organizations as members. Sometimes these organizations of organizations have as their members organizations that are themselves voluntary associations of individuals. Such organizations are often called federations. One such organization is the American Federation of Labor and Congress of Industrial Organizations (AFL-CIO), the peak labor organization composed of over one hundred operating unions having individuals as members.[1] Sometimes the constituent organizations are not membership groups at all. Many business associations fit into this pattern. Most trade associations and some peak business associations such as the National Association of Manufacturers and the Business Roundtable are composed of member corporations. They are organizations of organizations, but the components themselves are not membership organizations. While most membership organizations are composed either of individuals or organizations, many are hybrids, having *both* individuals and organizations as members. For example, the membership of the American Hospital Association includes 6,100 institutions (hospitals and related institutions like skilled-care nursing homes) and 25,000 individuals (hospital administrators and the like).[2]

In later chapters, readers will encounter time and again membership organizations from a few principal categories: peak business associations, trade associations, unions, professional associations, farm groups, citizens' groups, and civil rights and social welfare organizations. Let us examine these categories in turn, looking at the nature of their membership and the political issues with which they get involved.

Peak Business Associations

Among the more conspicuous pressure groups in Washington are the peak business associations—organizations that seek to advance the general interests of business and industry and to articulate the business perspective on broad policy issues. Perhaps the most prominent of these organizations are the Chamber of Commerce, the National Association of Manufacturers, the National Federation of Independent Business, and the Business Roundtable. Although they are very few in number, peak associations evince a remarkable diversity of organizational characteristics. On the one hand, the U.S. Chamber of Commerce—a traditional voice of American business—is a huge federation of state and local chambers of commerce, trade associations, individual companies and other commercial enterprises, and other business concerns, with a membership of 250,000, a budget of over $75 million, and a staff of over 400. On the other hand, the Business Roundtable has a membership restricted to the chief executive officers of roughly 200 of the nation's largest industrial, financial, and commercial institutions—firms like Shell Oil, GTE, Ford, IBM, and Caterpillar Tractor. Because much of the staff work for the Roundtable is done at the

[1] Federations differ in the way they structure membership in the national federation and affiliates. Workers become members of the AFL-CIO by virtue of their membership in one of the AFL-CIO's affiliated operating unions; thus, they do not join the AFL-CIO directly. The National Organization for Women (NOW) works differently. Membership in a state affiliate does not imply membership in the national NOW and vice versa; members join the state affiliates and the national separately and can join both.

[2] Unless otherwise indicated, all figures in this chapter on size of organizational membership, staff, and budgets are taken from Craig Colgate, Jr., ed., *National Trade and Professional Associations of the United States,* 18th ed. (Washington, DC: Columbia Books, 1983).

corporate headquarters of member companies, the Roundtable's staff for both its Washington and New York offices numbers only about 20 people.

The issues around which peak associations mobilize tend to be those that implicate the fortunes of business at large.[3] And when they get involved—as they do on matters like taxation and macroeconomic policy—they tend to be effective. During the Carter administration they scored a number of victories, defeating both the labor law reform bill and the consumer protection agency.

Trade Associations

The backbone of political activity on behalf of business has traditionally been the trade association. Indeed, trade associations are the most numerous of all organizations having Washington offices; there are nearly a thousand trade association offices in the capital. Like peak associations, trade associations are organizations of organizations. They unite companies in a single industry, companies that are ordinarily competitors in the marketplace but share mutual interests in politics. Trade associations vary enormously in size and political weight. On the one hand are Goliaths like the American Bankers Association with over 13,000 members and the National Association of Home Builders with nearly ten times that many, each having a budget well over $10 million; on the other are Lilliputians like the Bow Tie Manufacturers Association and the Post Card Manufacturers Association, each having fewer than ten member-companies and a budget under $10,000.

In their political activities, trade associations most frequently get involved in the kinds of regulatory issues in which government action affects an entire industry, thus placing marketplace antagonists in a position of mutual political interest. Two of the seemingly countless examples of trade association involvement in politics are the American Bankers Association's successful campaign to rescind a law that would have instituted tax withholding on interest and dividend income earned by individuals, and the American Iron and Steel Institute's longstanding effort to secure the enactment of legislation that would impose worldwide quotas on steel imports.

Trade associations not only represent the common political interests of their members but also provide them with various technical services of a non-political nature (as Chapter 6 indicates in greater detail). An important trade association function is to assist members—and the industry of which they are a part—in dealing with a wide assortment of mutual business problems. In so doing, a trade association may offer advice and assistance on accounting practices, advertising, product standardization, trade statistics, employee relations, and the like.

[3]See Andrew J. Glass, "NAM's New Look Is Toward Goal of Business Unity," *National Journal*, January 5, 1974, pp. 15–23; and Kim McQuaid, "The Roundtable: Getting Results in Washington," *Harvard Business Review*, May-June 1981, pp. 115–122.

Labor Unions

Labor unions are hardly the most numerous of Washington-based organizations, constituting little more than 100 of the thousands of organizations active in Washington. Yet they have a much larger membership than any other genre of political organization, over 20 million members, or roughly 24 percent of American workers.[4] Unions exhibit a federal organization that makes possible some degree of political division of labor. At the peak is the American Federation of Labor and Congress of Industrial Organizations (AFL-CIO), the grandparent union for many, though not all, of the operating unions. The AFL-CIO is very politically involved in a manner similar in form, though usually opposite in content, to peak business associations. That is, the AFL-CIO is active on issues of concern to the labor movement as a whole, such as repealing Section 14-b of the Taft-Hartley Act, which permits the states to bar union shops by enacting "right-to-work" laws. With respect to such issues, the AFL-CIO speaks for the labor movement as a whole (although some 20-odd percent of unionized workers, including those in such large and powerful unions as the Teamsters and the United Mine Workers, are not affiliated with it).

The AFL-CIO's political involvement is not limited to policies in which the labor movement has a direct stake. In addition to its "workers' ally" hat, the union often dons a "social justice" hat, acting as a spokesman for working people and the poor and taking liberal positions on a host of policy issues—for example, unemployment compensation, Social Security, and Medicare.

The operating unions—organizations such as the International Brotherhood of Electrical Workers and the United Steelworkers of America—ordinarily unite workers who share a joint occupation or are employed in the same or allied industries. (Of course, the operating unions may enroll workers from more than one occupation or industry. The American Federation of Teachers, for example, actively recruits nurses, government workers, and other white-collar personnel. In addition, a number of unions, especially large ones like the Teamsters, include workers from many occupations and a diverse group of industries.) Operating unions vary substantially in size of membership. Consider a few of the unions affiliated with the AFL-CIO: the Union of Journeyman Horseshoers has only about 400 members; the United Hatters, Cap and Millinery Workers has 10,000; the International Union of Bricklayers, 150,000; the United Brotherhood of Carpenters and Joiners, 750,000; and the American Federation of State, County and Municipal Employees, 1,200,000.

Compared with the AFL-CIO, operating unions get involved in political matters relevant to narrower categories of workers. For example, policy questions of ongoing concern to the International Ladies' Garment Workers Union include advocacy of amnesty for undocumented aliens and support for barriers

---

[4]U.S. Bureau of Labor Statistics figures for 1978 contained in U.S. Bureau of the Census, *Statistical Abstract of the United States: 1981,* 102nd ed. (Washington, DC: U.S. Government Printing Office, 1981), p. 411.

to the import of clothing manufactured abroad. Both of these issues might be expected to divide the labor movement as a whole. While the ILGWU's support for amnesty undoubtedly derives from a desire to organize and protect the large number of foreign workers in the garment industry, many unions might oppose amnesty for foreigners working illegally on the supposition that they are depriving American workers of jobs. With respect to trade barriers, a union like the International Longshoremen's Association might oppose any measure that would diminish commercial traffic between the United States and other nations.

The smallest components of the unions' federal structure are the locals. They have a crucial role in promoting the interests of their members in the workplace. However, with respect to national politics, they have a much more limited involvement than either the operating unions or the AFL-CIO.

Farm Groups

What is immediately apparent upon inspection of the constellation of farm groups is that the farm community is highly fragmented and divergent; there is no single agricultural interest. Farmers vary greatly with respect to the commodities they grow, the size of their farms, the mechanization of their operations, and their political predilections and activities. Vegetable growers, tobacco producers, feed grain and dairy farmers, cotton producers, and wheat farmers have relatively distinctive interests and problems, defined principally by their commodities. In addition to these natural cleavages in the farm community, conflicts and differences have emerged more clearly in recent years as agricultural production has become more specialized and as the technological revolution in farming has put greater economic pressure on farmers.

In view of this diversity within the farming community, it is not surprising that there are many different organizations representing farmers' interests. Several of the earliest interest organizations in the United States represent general farm interests. The oldest of these is the National Grange, founded in 1867. At one time the most politically aggressive advocate of farmers' interests, the Grange has been supplanted in that role by two other general farm organizations that have sharply divergent public stances. The largest of these is the American Farm Bureau Federation, with over three million farm families in its membership. Founded in 1919, the AFBF in recent decades has advanced free-market positions on American agricultural policy and has taken a decidedly conservative stance on many issues having little direct relevance to agriculture. Much smaller than the AFBF, but every bit its equal in political activism, is the National Farmers Union, with 300,000 farm families as members. Whereas the AFBF tends to be conservative in its policy preferences, the NFU is quite liberal, consistently advocating a larger role for government in agriculture, particularly in strengthening the family farm system and low-income farm groups. The differences in policy position between the AFBF and the NFU imply that, unlike the business community where the peak associations are ordinarily in agreement, members of the farming community have a choice between general organizations offering clear ideological alternatives.

The general farm organizations are not alone in representing the interests of farmers. Over the years many specialized commodity organizations have emerged to represent the interests of farmers producing particular commodities. These organizations—such as the American Soybean Association, the National Association of Wheat Growers, the National Cotton Council, and the National Milk Producers Association—unite farmers with businessmen such as seed producers and food processors, and reflect the growing specialization of American agriculture. Commodity organizations probably have greater success in shaping the details of farm commodity policies than do the general farm organizations. Their advantage in this regard is that they are able to focus on a narrower set of issues than can the general organizations and can work closely with members of the commodity subcommittees in Congress.[5]

Professional Associations

Several kinds of professional associations are active in Washington politics, all of them uniting individuals in the same or related occupations. Roughly two-thirds of them are organizations of people—scientists, librarians, dentists, social workers—whose shared occupation requires technical training and expertise. In addition, there are two subsidiary kinds of professional associations: organizations of professionals working in government, such as the National Association of Federal Veterinarians and the Association of Public Welfare Attorneys; and organizations of business executives and professionals working in business, such as the American Society for Personnel Administration and the Financial Executives Institute. Like unions, professional associations vary tremendously in size. Consider the following representative examples: the American Academy of Sports Physicians has only about 125 members; Clowns of America, 5,800; the American Institute of Architects, 38,000; the American Society of Mechanical Engineers, 100,000; and the American Nurses Association, 175,000.

Professional associations engage in both nonpolitical and political activities on behalf of their members. Like trade associations, professional associations assist their members by providing technical services and information. In order to inform members of technical developments in the field, they undertake a variety of activities; in particular, they publish journals and other materials and hold conferences and conventions.

Professional associations vary in terms of their political involvement. Professionals in fields that are heavily regulated by the government or are depen-

[5]On farm groups we have drawn on James E. Anderson et al., *Public Policy and Politics in America,* 2nd ed. (Monterey, CA: Brooks/Cole, 1984), pp. 347–355.

dent upon government grants or financing tend to be very active in politics; others are less so. What is more, while virtually every giant corporation or trade association is known as a political heavyweight, size alone does not predict activity for professional associations. Consider two of the oldest, largest, and most prestigious professional associations, the American Medical Association (AMA) and the American Bar Association (ABA). Both have in the neighborhood of 250,000 members and budgets running into the tens of millions of dollars. Yet, although no one would ever consider the ABA to be without political clout, the doctors field a much larger political operation than the lawyers, presumably because of the involvement of the government in regulating the delivery of medical care and paying for medical services for the poor and elderly.

Citizens' Groups, Advocacy Groups, and Cause Groups

The membership groups examined thus far have had a similar characteristic: each is organized around some economic interest or source of livelihood that its members have in common. But there are hundreds of voluntary membership organizations founded on common concerns of a noneconomic or nonoccupational nature. Among such associations are citizens' groups, advocacy groups, and cause groups.

As we saw in Chapter 2, citizens' groups differ from organizations like unions and trade associations in that they do not try to pursue selective benefits on behalf of their own members; rather, these organizations try to advance government policies and procedures that will benefit the public at large. Many of these—for example, the Friends of the Earth and the American Civil Liberties Union—are mass membership organizations of varying sizes, most of whose supporters make no more commitment than writing a $25 check. Others, like the Consumer Federation of America, are coalitions of a much smaller number of interested membership organizations.

Citizens' groups pursue a wide variety of goals in politics. Environmental groups like the Defenders of Wildlife and the Sierra Club press for policies that will result in clean air and water and the preservation of wilderness areas and wildlife. Taxpayers' groups like the National Tax-Limitation Committee and the National Taxpayers' Union promote reduced government spending and lower taxes. Some citizens' groups—for example, Common Cause—focus attention on the government itself. In order to render government both more open and more accountable, Common Cause supports adoption of a variety of measures designed, for example, to make information about the government more accessible to the public. In all these cases, what these citizen groups have in common is that they seek broadly held interests that are shared by nearly everyone in the community.

Other citizens' groups that we call *advocacy groups* seek selective benefits on behalf of groups of persons who are in some way incapacitated or are otherwise unable to represent their own interests. Organizations that promote the welfare of children—for example, the Children's Defense Fund and the Child Welfare League of America—fall into this category, as do organizations that press for the rights of prisoners, the retarded, and persons in nursing homes. In each case, those who run the organization or contribute to its maintenance enjoy no selective benefits for themselves if they realize their objectives, even though the public at large is not the direct beneficiary of their efforts.

Naturally, if organizational leaders or supporters of an advocacy group stand to benefit selectively from the policies being sought, then the organization would not properly be termed a citizens' or public interest group. An example is the National Association of the Deaf. Founded in 1880 to act on behalf of the deaf and those with impaired hearing, it includes among its members many persons who *do* have a selective interest at stake, including deaf adults, parents of deaf children, and professionals and students in the field of deafness.

Political scientists often refer to organizations they call *cause groups,* whose members care intensely about a single issue or small group of issues, ordinarily of a noneconomic character. The various organizations battling over abortion would be considered cause groups: on one side, advocating a ban on all abortions in order to protect the right to life of the unborn, are organizations such as the National Right to Life Committee; on the other, supporting access to abortion, are pro-choice organizations such as the National Abortion Rights Action League. Similarly, groups advocating various postures on foreign policy and defense issues would be considered cause groups. For example, the Committee on the Present Danger, which believes that a Soviet arms buildup threatens world peace and American security, and the American Committee on East-West Accord, which is interested in improving relations with the Soviets, are cause groups—as are the Arms Control Association and the Coalition for Peace through Strength, which take opposing positions on arms control issues.

From our perspective, however, cause groups are not a separate category of organization; rather, because neither their leaders nor their members would benefit selectively from the achievement of their goals, by our definition they are a kind—and not always a readily distinguishable kind—of citizens' group. In discussing the nature of the public interest, Chapter 2 made clear that in any policy controversy there is virtually always more than one public interest at stake. (Often the competing public interests take the form of the broadly shared interest in, say, consumer product safety or environmental preservation, on the one hand, and economic growth or lower prices, on the other.) As was pointed out, in addition, the positions taken by citizens' or so-called public interest groups often incite opposition from others who also have no selective interest at stake.

It is true that the issues around which cause groups cluster—gun control, teaching evolution in the schools, and the like—tend to incite passionate feelings within the public in a way that the fate of the coyote and the costs of funerals (issues that have been taken up, at one time or another, by some environmental or consumer group, respectively) do not. However, cause groups have no monopoly on either zeal or the ability to generate controversy. Environmental groups that oppose nuclear power generation in the name of public safety—for example, the Clamshell Alliance—display a tenacity that rivals that of the contending groups involved in the debate surrounding school prayer and incite considerable public antagonism. Thus, a group that one observer may regard as working for the public interest may be regarded by another observer as a bunch of zealots with a cause.

Civil Rights and Social Welfare Organizations

A final broad category of membership organizations includes civil rights and social welfare groups. Many of these are organizations that work to combat discrimination against members of a specific racial, ethnic, or gender group. For example, the National Urban League has labored for over 70 years to secure equal opportunities for blacks and other minorities. Other groups, such as the Women's Equity Action League and the National Organization for Women work to eliminate gender-based discrimination and to expand women's rights with respect to such matters as pensions, child care, health care, social security, and employment.

In addition, there is also a handful of groups organized to meet specific needs of the poor. For example, the National Rural Housing Coalition is a nonprofit membership organization that works to improve housing conditions and community facilities for people in small towns and rural areas. The now-defunct Full Employment Action Council lobbied for legislation to reduce unemployment and aid the unemployed. The activities of these and similar organizations are supplemented by church-related organizations such as the National Conference of Catholic Charities.

We shall see in Chapter 4 that civil rights and social welfare groups are very few in number; what is more, they have very few members considering the large size of their potential constituencies. With a limited number of exceptions, groups representing minorities and the poor are not large, mass-membership, voluntary associations. Membership groups representing the poor are almost invariably advocacy groups whose members and leaders are active on behalf of others whose poverty or minority status they do not share. Some are mass-membership organizations whose middle-class members are concerned about the poor. Others, as we shall see below, are coalitions either of local community organizations or of organizations such as labor unions and church groups originally formed for other purposes. The next three chapters will return periodically to the subject of organizations representing needy constituencies and discuss both the disadvantages under which they labor and the reasons why even large constituencies among the poor have difficulty fielding mass-membership organizations.

Coalitions

Earlier in the chapter we discussed membership groups—principally peak business and trade associations—whose members are organizations rather than individuals. While such organizations of organizations tend to be relatively permanent fixtures in the pressure group scene, sometimes organizations join together into coalitions that are less permanent, although perhaps more intense, marriages of convenience. Virtually all groups on the Washington scene—from business associations to labor unions to citizens' and social welfare groups—enter into coalitions of varying degrees of formality, homogeneity, and durability when it is deemed necessary or politically expedient for them to concert their activities in joint pursuit of shared goals.

Coalitions take on a variety of forms. They differ, first of all, in degree of formality. Some coalitions are quite formal in that they have a charter, an established dues structure, and the like. One such group was the Committee of Railroad Shippers, a group of automobile manufacturers and other rail users that lobbied on a rail deregulation bill in the late 1970s. That group even kept minutes of its meetings (apparently to guard against possible charges that it had violated antitrust laws). More typically, however, coalitions maintain highly informal organizational arrangements under which participating organizations are simply expected to contribute time, professional help, clerical services, and the like, according to their resources and their stake in the matter at issue. This informality has the dual advantage of minimizing power struggles and jurisdictional disputes.[6]

Coalitions also vary in how much the partners have in common. Some bring together a relatively homogeneous group of participants who share more than their stake in a particular policy decision. For example, the Clean Air Act Working Group consists of representatives of about 20 large corporations (most with interests in the automobile industry) trying to head off any tightening of the antipollution law. Others unite a wider array of organizations. For example, the National Coalition for Bankruptcy Reform was founded by an assortment of business organizations—automobile dealers, bank card companies, banks, collection agencies, credit unions, home furnishing and appliance dealers, and the like—concerned that existing bankruptcy laws made it too easy for people who could probably pay all or part of their debts to avoid doing so by declaring bankruptcy.

Finally, some coalitions bring together truly strange bedfellows—participants who seemingly have little in common and even less apparent inclination to join forces. For example, in 1979, Common Cause and Congress Watch (a subsidiary of Ralph Nader's Public Citizen) worked side by side with the American Conservative Union and the National Association of Manufacturers

[6]Many of the examples and substantive points in this section are drawn from Bill Keller, "Coalitions and Associations Transform Strategy, Methods of Lobbying in Washington," *National Journal*, January 23, 1982, pp. 119–123.

in support of a trucking deregulation bill. Such odd coalitions derive strength from their members' diversity; the unlikelihood of the alliance serves both to impress policymakers by the breadth of support and to diminish the scent of narrow self-interest that often surrounds lobbying campaigns.[7]

Finally, coalitions vary with respect to how long they persist as consciously coordinated groups. Some ad hoc coalitions are decidedly short-lived, dissolving once the issue of concern is resolved. Others—usually those concerned with problems that do not go away—become more institutionalized and persist as formal organizations for many years. An example is the Leadership Conference on Civil Rights, a coalition of about 150 national organizations that represent blacks, Hispanic and Asian Americans, labor, the aged, women, major religious groups, and minority businesses and professionals. First formed about 1950, the LCCR remains active today on matters affecting the rights of minorities, women, and the handicapped.

NONMEMBERSHIP ORGANIZATIONS

When we think about private organizations in politics, we tend to think of voluntary membership groups. However, nearly half the organizations having representation in Washington politics—such as corporations, public interest law firms, large hospitals and universities, radio and television stations, and think tanks—are not membership groups at all.[8] Interestingly, while these groups are, of course, very different from membership organizations in their internal dynamics, the evidence in Chapter 7 would indicate that they are not terribly distinctive in their political comportment. Let us look briefly at two main categories of nonmembership groups.

Corporations

Of nonmembership organizations, corporations are by far the most numerous. Among the most important changes in Washington politics in recent years have been the increasing political involvement of individual corporations and the increasing legitimacy accorded their activity. In terms of sheer numbers, the

[7]See James Q. Wilson, *Political Organizations* (New York: Basic Books, 1973), p. 317; and Lester W. Milbrath, *The Washington Lobbyists* (Chicago: Rand McNally, 1963), pp. 169–175.

[8]This figure and analogous figures cited in the next two paragraphs are based on a tabulation of the organizations listed in Arthur C. Close, ed., *Washington Representatives—1981* (Washington, DC: Columbia Books, 1981). The mechanics of that enumeration are explained fully in Appendix C; the results are elaborated in Chapter 4.

For corroborating evidence of the new prominence of nonmembership organizations in the Washington interest community, see Robert H. Salisbury, "Interest Representation: The Dominance of Institutions," *American Political Science Review* 78 (1984): 64–76; and Robert H. Salisbury, "Interest Groups: Toward a New Understanding," in Allan J. Cigler and Burdett A. Loomis, eds., *Interest Group Politics* (Washington, DC: CQ Press, 1983), pp. 354–367.

figures are quite arresting. Over three thousand corporations have some kind of Washington representation and well over five hundred—ranging from giants like Exxon and IBM to smaller companies like Western Airlines and Hershey Foods—have their own offices. Given how deeply the government's tentacles penetrate into the economy, it is not surprising that corporations find that they have business in Washington.

While corporations in general have become increasingly active in Washington politics over the past decade, there is great variation among corporations in their political involvement. Some, especially small ones, rely exclusively on their trade associations for representation; some, like Parker Pen and Firestone Tire and Rubber, hire Washington-based counsel or consultants; others, like Kraft Foods, have small offices in Washington; and still others, such as General Electric and General Motors, field large Washington offices with dozens of staff. What is more, an individual corporation's political involvement can vary over time depending on any number of factors, including what the government is doing, the availability of resources to devote to political activity, and the corporation's assessment of the ability of other organizations (such as trade associations) to represent its interests.

Public Interest Law Firms

So-called public interest law firms, such as the Center for Law and Social Policy, the Pacific Legal Foundation, the Media Access Project, and the National Prison Project, are a second type of nonmembership organization. A relatively new arrival on the Washington scene, public interest law firms began to emerge in noticeable numbers late in the 1960s and early in the 1970s.

By and large, their approach to representing the interests of the potentially unrepresented has been through the legal process; small staffs of attorneys, selecting test cases carefully, work diligently through the courts. Ordinarily, public interest law firms charge nothing for their services, depending instead upon a variety of other sources for their financial support—gifts from philanthropic foundations, government grants, court-awarded attorneys' fees, and individual contributions.[9]

Public interest law firms are siblings both to traditional citizens' groups like the Sierra Club and the Consumers Union and to traditional civil rights and civil liberties organizations like the National Association for the Advancement of Colored People and the American Civil Liberties Union. They are similar to these other organizations in their commitment to representing interests that might otherwise not find vigorous advocacy in the political process. They differ, however, in their internal structure: most public interest law firms do not have members. In addition, they differ in their emphasis on legal strat-

---

[9]See James W. Singer, "Liberal Public Interest Law Firms Face Budgetary, Ideological Challenges," *National Journal,* December 8, 1979, p. 2052.

egies for shaping policy, to the virtual exclusion of other techniques of influence.[10]

In more recent years, a new breed of conservative, business-oriented public interest law firm has sprung up to counterbalance the influence that the liberal public interest lawyers had gained over public policy. The newer groups—such as the Pacific Legal Foundation, discussed at length in Chapter 2—work principally to enhance economic growth and to reduce government regulation. These conservative public interest law firms began expanding in numbers and influence at the same time that the older, more liberal firms, already hard-pressed financially, started to have difficulties raising funds and avoiding cutbacks in their efforts.[11]

VARIATIONS IN GROUP AGENDAS

In addition to the presence or absence of a membership, another dimension on which organizations vary substantially is the size of their agendas. Some organizations are concerned with hundreds of issues at once; others pursue a single narrow objective. In examining the variation in the number of issues a group tackles, it is important to bear in mind that this is a continuum, not a set of discrete categories. There are no lines of demarcation that permit us to pigeonhole organizations neatly in terms of the number of their concerns.

Single-Issue Groups

Earlier in the chapter we discussed cause groups—organizations composed of individuals with a singular commitment to one or a few concerns, usually a social issue. The political strength of many single-issue groups is enhanced by the intensity of their members' commitment to their view of the issue. Issue-specific groups organized around social causes are probably the most conspicuous, but not the only, type of single-interest groups. Many organizations concern themselves with only a single issue. For example, an organization called U.S. Wheat Associates is the overseas market development arm of the wheat industry. Its exclusive purpose is to establish, expand, and maintain markets throughout the world for all classes of wheat grown in the United States. The implications of this kind of singularity of purpose for a nonideological organization are difficult to evaluate. No doubt there are organizational advantages to being able to concentrate attention and resources on a narrow range of con-

---

[10]There are exceptions to both of these generalizations. There are organizations—for example, the Food Research and Action Center, which is concerned with the food problems of the poor—that are structured as public interest law firms, but which have members in the manner of voluntary associations. In addition, some mass-membership organizations—for example, the ACLU—concentrate on legal strategies of political influence.

[11]See Singer, "Liberal Public Interest Law Firms Face Challenges," pp. 2052, 2055-2056; and Margot Hornblower, "Conservative Winds Reshape Public Interest Law," *The Washington Post,* January 14, 1980, p. A3.

cerns. Moreover, we would expect that while elected officials might discount the views of wheat exporters on, say, manpower policy or the arms race, they would probably listen attentively to wheat exporters who come to present their views on international wheat trade policies. In other words, organizations probably derive both internal strength and vitality as well as external political strength from having a narrow sphere of concern.

Multi-Issue Groups

Other organizations deal with a considerably broader set of issues. Although we might normally expect corporations to have relatively short lists of issues of political concern to them, this is certainly not the case with highly diversified conglomerates. Consider R. J. Reynolds Industries. Because its subsidiaries include R. J. Reynolds Tobacco (leader of the cigarette industry), Del Monte Corporation (a major food processor and marketer), Aminoil, USA (America's third largest petroleum exploration and production company), Sea-Land Service (the world's largest containerized cargo shipping company), Reynolds Industries must be concerned with policies in a number of areas, including tobacco, food and beverages, energy, and transportation.[12]

It is perhaps not surprising that a conglomerate whose subsidiaries are engaged in diverse industries would be involved in shaping policy in numerous fields. However, even organizations representing a single industry may have long agendas. Consider, for example, the Computer and Business Equipment Manufacturers Association (CBEMA), the trade association representing the manufacturers of data-processing and business equipment and allied products. Its roughly 40 member-companies engineer, manufacture, finance, sell, and provide support services for all types of office and business equipment, computer systems, and supporting equipment and supplies. Their products range from postage meters to photocopying machines to typewriter correction fluid. Given the range of the products manufactured by its members, it is perhaps not surprising that CBEMA concerns itself with a broad range of public policy issues: the availability, reliability, and quality of electric power sources; government procurement policies; the removal of barriers to the free flow of data between countries; strategic technology transfer policies; issues of personal privacy and data security in information processing; taxation; and telecommunications regulation.[13] What is more, in comparison with the number of issues tackled by giant diversified associations such as the American Retail Federation or the National Association of Home Builders, CBEMA's list is quite short.

[12]This information is drawn from *R. J. Reynolds Industries 1981 Annual Report,* R. J. Reynolds Industries, Inc., Winston-Salem, North Carolina.
[13]Computer and Business Equipment Manufacturers Association, "Challenges for the 80s," pp. 5–8.

Even further along the continuum are multi-issue groups—organizations with lengthy and diverse issue agendas. Perhaps the most obvious of such organizations are the peak business associations and labor unions. These are organizations that tend to be highly active on a wide variety of fronts simultaneously, monitoring and taking positions on issues ranging from pollution-control laws to Social Security and from tax incentives to housing subsidies. Still other multi-issue groups are the broad ideological organizations, such as the Americans for Democratic Action (ADA) and the Americans for Constitutional Action (ACA). Each of these organizations is continually alert to a wide variety of issues—economic and noneconomic, domestic and foreign—in part to aid them in assembling their evaluations of the ideological purity of members of Congress.[14] Finally, the list of multi-issue groups would also include an organization such as the Moral Majority. This is an organization linked to evangelical Protestantism that takes consistently conservative positions on a variety of social issues, ranging from school prayer to pornography and from television programming to capital punishment.

Does Size of Agenda Matter?

In recent years single-issue groups have been the target of a great deal of criticism. Therefore, it is worth considering briefly whether the size of a group's agenda has by itself an impact on its comportment in politics. The short answer is "not much." That is, there are no discernible and predictable differences between single-issue groups and multi-issue groups in terms of either their political strategies or their political effectiveness. One source of the criticism of single-issue groups has been concern about the increased emphasis by certain pressure groups on the tactic of targeting for defeat incumbent office holders who have taken "incorrect" positions on issues deemed especially important. While this approach to electoral competition may not lead to either elevated campaigning or enlightened government, single-issue groups are not alone in having adopted it. Organizations at all points on both the ideological and agenda-size continua—environmental groups as well as abortion opponents, the National Committee for an Effective Congress as well as the National Conservative Political Action Committee—have targeted their opponents.

Why do single-issue groups have such a bad name? Their antagonists have accused them of polarizing the public and argue that in their zeal to promote a single cause, these groups ignore other pressing concerns. To an extent, however, all this is largely a matter of whose ox is being gored. Everybody criticizes the single-issue groups with which he or she disagrees—especially the *successful* single-issue groups with which he or she disagrees. How-

[14]These evaluations will be discussed in Chapter 9.

ever, nobody likes the *multi-issue* groups with which he or she disagrees either.

What may, in fact, be at stake is not the singularity of the issue positions advocated but the singularity of purpose with which they are espoused. There is a long tradition in American politics of respect for willingness to compromise and intolerance for extreme positions. There are on the pressure scene today many groups who adopt positions with a single-mindedness bordering on intransigence. However, single-issue groups have no monopoly on shrillness and inflexibility. Organizations with many concerns as well as organizations with few, organizations on the left as well as organizations on the right, have adopted such postures toward politics.

THE INTERESTS OF GOVERNMENTS: A DIGRESSION

This is, of course, a book about private interests in politics. However, this chapter's brief survey of the principal categories of private organizations involved in Washington politics would be incomplete if it failed to mention a second set of organized pressures to which the federal government is subject: pressures from governments. Organized activity on behalf of other governments—foreign and subnational—as well as components of the federal executive branch has increased substantially in recent years. Because they have become so active and influential, and because in many ways they resemble private organizations in politics, the interests of other governments in Washington politics bear some attention.

Foreign Governments

Among the governments lobbying in Washington to advance their interests are foreign nations. The American national government adopts many different policies—defense, arms sales, foreign aid, immigration, import restrictions and other trade practices, and so on—that affect the economic development, political stability, and national security of other countries. As a consequence, most foreign nations now supplement the political efforts of their embassies with the services of lobbying agents in Washington. Although Congress has imposed registration requirements on lobbyists for foreign governments, very little stands in the way of foreign interests determined to promote their objectives with American national policymakers.[15] In addition to sending their own lobbying agents to Washington, foreign governments often hire American lobbyists to help them press their cases. There are roughly a thousand registered agents representing foreign interests in Washington.[16]

---

[15] Like most federal laws aimed at controlling the activities of lobbyists, the Foreign Agents Registration Act of 1938 (and later amendments to it) have only marginal impact on everyday lobbying operations in Washington.

[16] See Alan Dodds Frank, "The U.S. Side of the Street," *Forbes,* July 19, 1982, pp. 31–32.

The Federal Executive Branch

Among the most actively represented governmental interests are those of the White House and agencies of the executive branch of the federal government. Presidents since Dwight D. Eisenhower have maintained highly sophisticated congressional liaison operations in the White House to lobby Congress in support of presidential policy initiatives.[17] In addition, almost all cabinet-level departments (and many sub-agencies and bureaus as well) have congressional-relations divisions that lobby the legislative branch in much the same way that private interests do. An agency's lobbyists, usually called *legislative liaison officers,* work to maintain favorable relationships with Congress in an effort to make sure that cherished programs are not eliminated, that new proposals are given a fair chance, that necessary authorizations and appropriations are forthcoming, and that oversight hearings are not uncomfortably aggressive.[18]

The Intergovernmental Lobby

A relatively recent, and increasingly active, arrival on the Washington scene is the phalanx of representatives of other American governments—states, counties, cities, townships, and the like.[19] This *intergovernmental lobby* is so active in Washington because many of the domestic programs enacted by the federal government since the New Deal appropriate money that is to be spent by state and local governments, often in accordance with standards set by the federal government. Because the budgets and the policies of subnational governments are so heavily influenced by federal policy, these governments have seen the need to represent their interests in much the same way as private organizations present their opinions and policy preferences to the federal government.

The intergovernmental lobby includes such groups as the Council of State Governments, the National Governors Conference, the National Association of Counties, the National League of Cities, the U.S. Conference of Mayors, and the International City Management Association. All of these are organizations of public officials (elected or appointed) who exercise executive or legislative responsibilities in subnational governments. Such organizations are, in essence, the trade associations of the intergovernmental lobby. Just as the corporate members of trade associations may also maintain a capacity for independent political involvement, the municipal, county, and state members of such or-

[17]See the brief but illuminating discussion on executive liaison in Richard M. Pious, *The American Presidency* (New York: Basic Books, 1979), pp. 187–193.
[18]Congress long ago attempted to limit the practice of executive agencies lobbying Congress with appropriated funds, but the proscription is more often breached than observed. See Richard L. Engstrom and Thomas G. Walker, "Statutory Restraints on Administrative Lobbying—'Legal Fiction'," *Journal of Public Law* 19 (1970): 89–103.
[19]See Donald H. Haider, *When Governments Come to Washington* (New York: Free Press, 1974).

ganizations may participate in Washington politics on their own. Over two-thirds of the states and dozens of counties and cities, ranging from Houston to Hoboken, are listed in the *Washington Representatives* directory as having some kind of presence in the capitol.

A second component of the intergovernmental lobby is the growing array of organizations devoted to the concerns of the functional specialists—highway engineers, chief state school officers, county welfare directors, housing and re-development officials, and so on—in state and local governments and the agen-cies for which they work. These organizations enjoy considerable influence in Washington, not only because of the expertise of their members, but also be-cause they have strong support both from local politicians and from the func-tional specialists in the federal bureaucracy.[20] Again there are many organiza-tions representing the collective interests of such officials and their agencies:— for example, the National Association of County Park and Recreation Officials, the National Association of State Aviation Officials, the Council of State Plan-ning Agencies, and the National Association of County Aging Programs. Also, individual agencies are active in Washington on their own behalf. The Kansas City Board of Public Utilities and New York State Board of Education are only two of the many individual government agencies having representation in Washington.

Just as there are cleavages within other broad coalitions, the intergovern-mental lobby is often sharply divided along several dimensions of conflict.[21] Suppose, for example, the federal government proposed a new program to deal with the regional transportation problems of metropolitan areas. Within, for example, the National Governors Conference, Democrats might oppose Re-publicans, liberals might oppose conservatives, and Sunbelters might oppose Snowbelters. In addition, the mayors would probably want the money admin-istered by the cities, the governors by the states. Furthermore, highway officials would probably want to devote the money to roads, mass transit officials to subways and buses. Finally, if the actual grants were made, Phoenix might oppose Cleveland for its share of the booty. Even so, although its unity may be strained, the intergovernmental lobby is a formidable and growing presence in Washington.

Although the components of the intergovernmental lobby are not private voluntary associations, but are, instead, governments and associations of gov-ernment officials, they have so many affinities to private organizations that the boundary between these public sector organizations and the private ones ordi-narily subsumed under organized interest politics is often very fuzzy. Indeed, some organizations of government workers—the American Federation of State,

---

[20] For an illuminating discussion of the intergovernmental lobby and the influence of this "professional bureaucratic complex," see Samuel H. Beer, "The Adoption of General Revenue Sharing: A Case Study in Public Sector Politics," *Public Policy* 24 (1976): 127–195.

[21] See Timothy J. Conlan, "Congressional Response to the New Federalism: The Politics of Special Revenue Sharing and Its Implications for Public Policy," (Ph.D. dissertation, Harvard University, 1981), p. 453.

County, and Municipal Employees, the American Foreign Service Association, the Association of Former Members of Congress, to name a few—are considered private associations. These are organizations joined by individuals, not by governments. They are set up to represent the private interests of those individuals as government employees with respect to such issues as compensation and benefits.

Because the organizations in the intergovernmental lobby represent people in their capacity as citizens of various governmental jurisdictions (in much the same way that private organizations may represent them in their capacity as plumbers, Catholics, women, or gun-control advocates), many of the issues raised in succeeding chapters about private organizations in politics are equally relevant to the intergovernmental lobby. For example, with respect to techniques of influence, public sector organizations are virtually indistinguishable from private ones. To the extent that some states and localities do not maintain a separate presence in the capital, questions of equality of representation, discussed in Chapter 4, become germane. That is, the National Governors Association represents all citizens equally because each resides in a single state; however, what are the implications for political equality among citizens of the fact that Texas also maintains its own independent office in Washington, but Oklahoma does not? In short, the intergovernmental lobby is in many ways similar to the private associations in politics that constitute our central focus. These similarities, as well as the influence wielded by all these governmental actors in shaping policy, should be borne in mind in attempting to understand political outcomes in Washington.

SUMMARY

This chapter has examined the principal kinds of interest organizations encountered throughout the rest of the book and described briefly how they vary in terms of membership, organizational structure, and scope of political concerns. We have considered membership organizations representing the interests of business, labor, professionals, farmers, broad publics, issue activists, minorities, and the needy and introduced some of the principal categories of the nonmembership organizations that are so numerous in Washington these days. Finally, it is clear that the presence or absence of a membership is not the only dimension along which interest organizations vary: they also vary substantially in the size of their agendas, with some organizations focusing their attention on a single issue, and others attending to a much broader set of policy concerns.

In addition, it has been noted that private organizations are not alone in having representation in the Washington pressure community. A wide array of governments and officials have special Washington representation as well, including foreign governments, agencies of the American national government, state and local governments, and a host of elected and appointed officials at the subnational level.

4

Who Is Represented?

A little over a decade ago an analyst of interest activity in Washington made the following observation: "One answer to the question 'Who is in government relations?' might be 'Almost everybody'."[1] In one sense, this brief response is absolutely accurate. The organizational interests represented in Washington politics are staggering in number and variety. It is impossible to read a national newspaper or news magazine without encountering at least one example of an organization attempting to shape the policies of the federal government. One could populate an entire town with the over 8,000 people who, as Washington representatives, work on behalf of the interests of the more than 6,000 organizations that either employ them directly or retain them as counsel or consultants to influence government actions.[2] Ninety-seven of the 100 largest industrial corporations have some kind of representation in Washington politics; 81 of them have their own offices in the capital.[3]

Still, the matter bears further scrutiny. This chapter uses empirical evidence to delineate the contours of what we shall call the *Washington pressure community*—the set of organized interests active in Washington politics. Our investigation of the question of who is represented in Washington pressure

[1]Louis Anthony Dexter, *How Organizations Are Represented in Washington* (Indianapolis: Bobbs-Merrill, 1969), p. 17.
[2]Figures taken from Arthur C. Close, ed., *Washington Representatives,* 5th ed. (Washington, DC: Columbia Books, 1981).
[3]Figures calculated using the listing of the Fortune 500 contained in *The New York Times,* April 20, 1982, p. C16, and information contained in Close, ed., *Washington Representatives.*

politics focuses on two dimensions of organized interest politics: its *inclusiveness*—that is, the degree to which all individuals or all relevant interests are involved; and its *tilt*—that is, the degree to which certain kinds of individuals are especially likely to be active or certain kinds of interests especially likely to achieve representation.[4] In short, is almost everybody involved in Washington pressure politics? If all citizens are not involved as individuals in organized activity to influence what goes on in Washington, are then at least all politically relevant interests represented? If not, are certain kinds of interests more likely to be represented than others? As the evidence unfolds, it will become clear that the formulation that almost everybody is involved in government relations demands considerable qualification.

INDIVIDUALS AND ORGANIZATIONAL PARTICIPATION

At least since Tocqueville observed early nineteenth-century America, Americans have been known as joiners. By comparison with citizens of eleven other democracies for which data are available, Americans are relatively likely to be members of noneconomic voluntary associations. However, in many other nations the proportion of citizens in economic groups—in particular, trade unions, but also professional associations and the like—is substantially higher than in the United States. Overall, then, in terms of organizational membership, Americans fall in the upper-middle ranks of the list, behind the Scandinavians and ahead of the Italians, British, and West Germans.[5]

The results of a 1976 survey can be used to explore individual membership in political associations.[6] Respondents were asked several questions about their membership and activity in organizations.[7] Table 4.1 presents information

[4]E. E. Schattschneider originally raised these questions in *The Semisovereign People* (New York: Holt, Rinehart and Winston, 1960), Chapter 2. The conceptual framework of the present chapter relies heavily on Schattschneider.

[5]Based on data presented in Robert A. Dahl, *Dilemmas of Pluralist Democracy* (New Haven: Yale University Press, 1982), pp. 67–68. See also, Graham K. Wilson, *Interest Groups in the United States* (New York: Oxford University Press, 1981), pp. 132–144.

[6]These data come from the National Metropolitan Work Force Survey—a telephone survey, conducted in April of 1976, of 1370 working and unemployed members of the work force living in metropolitan areas. There is a paucity of recent survey data about organizational membership. While the best available, these data are not perfectly suited to our purposes because they exclude persons who live in rural areas and persons who are not in the work force (those who are in school, at home, unable to work, or retired). A national survey of the adult population would have been preferable. Furthermore, the respondents were not given an opportunity to specify the particular organizations with which they were affiliated. Thus, we do not even know whether these were organizations that presumed to influence politics, much less what joint political interests were organized or what issues were tackled. These data, available from the Inter-University Consortium for Political and Social Research at the University of Michigan, are analyzed in Kay Lehman Schlozman and Sidney Verba, *Injury to Insult: Unemployment, Class, and Political Response* (Cambridge: Harvard University Press, 1979).

[7]Specifically, respondents were asked whether they were union members and whether they were members of any group or organization aside from a labor union—"a fraternal or service organization, a veterans' group, a school service organization like the PTA, or business or professional organization."

Table 4.1   ORGANIZATIONAL MEMBERSHIP

	Members of an organization other than a union	Members of an organization or a union or both
Total[a]	40%	52%
Education		
Grade school	10	35
Some high school	22	44
High school graduate	27	44
Some college	38	49
College graduate	56	60
Graduate school	73	80
Occupation		
Professional/Technical	63	70
Manager/Administrator	48	51
Sales	34	39
Clerical	30	41
Crafts	35	64
Operative	23	48
Laborer	13	56
Service	33	40
Income		
Under $6,000	24	29
$6,000–10,999	27	42
$11,000–15,999	35	52
$16,000 and over	55	65

[a]Metropolitan American Work Force.
Source: 1976 Metropolitan Work Force Survey.

about organizational affiliation. The left-hand column shows the proportions of various groups indicating that they belong to an organization or group other than a union (for example, the Elks, the American Legion, the PTA, the American Medical Association, the Chamber of Commerce). The right-hand column gives the percentage indicating that they belong to such an organization or to a labor union or to both.

Table 4.1 makes clear that membership in organizations is neither inclusive nor balanced. Participation is not universal: only 40 percent of those interviewed are members of an organization other than a labor union, and only a bare majority, 52 percent, belong to either an organization or a union. Furthermore, organizational membership is not randomly distributed within the public. Rather, as with virtually all forms of political participation, upper-status individuals—those with high levels of education, prestigious jobs, and high incomes—are much more likely to be members of organizations than lower-status individuals. As shown in Table 4.1, only 10 percent of those who never went beyond grade school, as opposed to 73 percent of those with graduate training, are organization members. Similarly, 63 percent of those who work in professional and technical occupations but only 13 percent of those who work as laborers are members. Thus, individual membership in organizations is limited in scope; not everybody belongs. Furthermore, it has a tilt; it is skewed toward upper-status individuals.[8]

The right-hand column of Table 4.1, which shows the proportion in each group who are members of an organization or a union or both, demonstrates that union membership overcomes partially the socioeconomic skew in organizational membership. Figure 4.1, which repeats in graphic form the data for educational levels presented in Table 4.1, makes clear the degree to which union membership helps to narrow the gap in organizational membership between educational levels. The shaded portion of the bars indicates the percentage in each educational group who are members of organizations or groups other than unions. (Some of the organization members are, of course, members of unions as well.) The curve is quite steep. Only one-tenth of those in the lowest educational group belong to an organization, whereas nearly three-quarters of those at the highest educational level are members of an organization. The unshaded portion of each bar shows the increment added by those who are members of labor unions but not of any other organization. The overall curve is now less sharp; when union membership is added in, the gap between the lowest and the highest educational groups is reduced by nearly a third, from 63 percent to 45 percent. Organization membership retains a strong upper-status tilt even with union membership included; however, that tilt is not so acute.[9]

This socioeconomic skew exists for all forms of political activity—voting, campaigning, writing letters to public officials, and so on—not just for membership in organizations.[10] Membership in organizations, however, makes spe-

---

[8] Data from an older national survey, conducted in 1968, also confirm our findings. See Sidney Verba and Norman H. Nie, *Participation in America* (New York: Harper & Row, 1972), p. 181. In addition, analysis of an item from the 1976 Election Survey conducted by the Center for Political Studies at the University of Michigan produced identical results. Respondents were asked whether in the past two or three years they had "worked with others or joined an organization trying to do something about some national problem." The dual advantages of this question were that it was addressed to a national sample and that it asked about unambiguously political activity. However, since 92 percent of the respondents answered in the negative, we suspect that this question failed to tap long-term memberships in ongoing organizations like unions or professional associations.

[9] The reader might be puzzled by one aspect of the data presented in Figure 4.1. The increment contributed by union membership becomes progressively smaller as education increases. However, 7 percent of those with graduate training but only 4 percent of those with college degrees are members of unions but not of other organizations. This is probably due to the uneven distribution of union membership across occupations. Perhaps because of the unionization of nurses, teachers, musicians, and the like, professionals are actually the most heavily unionized white-collar workers.

[10] See, for example, Verba and Nie, *Participation in America,* Chapter 8, and Lester W. Milbrath and M. L. Goel, *Political Participation,* 2nd ed. (Chicago: Rand McNally, 1977), pp. 90–106. For explanations of why socioeconomic status is universally related to political participation, see Raymond E. Wolfinger and Steven J. Rosenstone, *Who Votes?* (New Haven: Yale University Press, 1980), Chapter 2; Gabriel A. Almond and Sidney Verba, *The Civic Culture* (Princeton: Princeton University Press, 1963), pp. 380–381; and M. Kent Jennings and Richard G. Niemi, *Generations and Politics* (Princeton: Princeton University Press, 1981), Chapter 8.

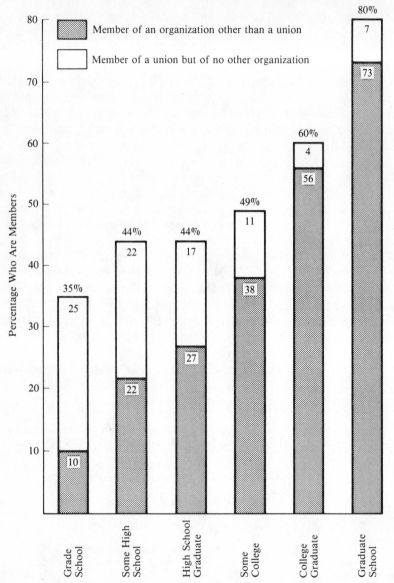

Figure 4.1 Organizational membership by education.
Source: 1976 Metropolitan Work Force Survey.

cial demands of a material nature that many other forms of political participation do not. These demands might pose a particular barrier to lower-status citizens. Consider the experience of the Massachusetts Welfare Rights Organization (MWRO), a now-defunct association of welfare recipients that was organized in the late 1960s. Unlike most organizations, the MWRO did not raise one barrier that clearly poses a special hurdle to the poor: it did not require its members to pay dues. Even so, the other costs of organizational activity proved prohibitive to a potential constituency whose financial resources were, by definition, severely limited. In order to attract members to meetings and rallies, the MWRO arranged for free transportation, free lunches, and free baby-sitting service.[11] For welfare recipients to provide these on their own would simply have entailed too much expense and bother. For those with greater resources, the costs of organizational membership and activity—from paying dues to paying a baby-sitter—represent much less of a drain.

THE CONTOURS OF THE WASHINGTON PRESSURE COMMUNITY

The evidence about individuals' memberships in groups gives us only indirect clues about the shape of collective representation in Washington. Surveys about membership in organizations necessarily miss an important component of the Washington pressure community. As we have seen in Chapter 3, many of the private organizations active in Washington today—in particular, corporations, but also public interest law firms and institutions like universities and hospitals—have no members in the ordinary sense of the word.[12] Other membership groups, most notably trade associations, unite member organizations that themselves have no individual members. Any understanding of the contours of interest representation in Washington must take account of such organizations in addition to membership groups. Moreover, in the abstract it is possible that even though individual participation in organizations is not universal, the set of interests represented is exhaustive because there are groups representing all possible political interests; that is, the interests and preferences of those who are not organizational members might achieve collective representation by dint of the efforts of others who are active. In order to consider these questions, it is necessary to look more directly at the set of organizations active in Washington politics.

Political Equality and Organizational Representation of Interests

The discussion of organizational membership for individuals focused on the level of inclusiveness and the degree of skew in organizational affiliations and made clear that organizational membership is marked more by inequality than by equality among citizens. When we move from consideration of individuals to consideration of sets of organizations, complex questions arise as to how to ascertain the degree of inclusiveness or skew. It thus becomes difficult to know what political equality would look like.

[11] Lawrence Neil Bailis, *Bread or Justice* (Lexington, MA: Lexington Books, 1974), p. 67.
[12] On this issue, see Robert Salisbury, "Interest Representation: The Dominance of Institutions," *American Political Science Review* 78 (1984): 64–76.

What is meant by political equality? When it comes to voting, the concept of equality of political inputs is relatively comprehensible—one-person–one-vote. Although the one-person–one-vote concept seems straightforward in the abstract, we need only recall the myriad political controversies having to do with the enfranchisement of disenfranchised groups, the nature of representative arrangements, and the construction of congressional district boundaries to understand the practical difficulties entailed in implementing even a relatively unambiguous formal political principle.

The meaning of political equality becomes somewhat more complicated when it is a matter, not of voting, but of direct expressions of preferences with respect to policy matters. Even then, however, we can propose a relatively straightforward, though abstract, formulation of political equality among individuals. The obvious utopian scheme for political equality would have all citizens equally active on all issues. This is, in essence, majoritarian democracy, a formula for the application of the principle of one-person–one-vote to the realm of nonelectoral political activity. To accommodate the principle of political equality to the existence of differing intensities of preferences, we can, again in the abstract, specify a circumstance in which all citizens are active on the policy questions about which they care—on as many or as few issues as are salient to them, devoting as much or as little activity to any particular issue as the intensity of their concern might dictate—so long as the total opportunity for input for any member of the political community is the same as for any other.

In light of these principles, how does one weigh political inputs that are organizationally based? Surely, equality among organizations is inconsistent with one-person–one-vote, for some organizations have many members while others have few, some organizations are well-off with respect to the skills and resources that enhance effectiveness in politics while others are impoverished, and some organizations are active on many issues while others have a short agenda of concerns. Hence, the volume of political input generated varies substantially across organizations, so that they (even organizations involved in a particular controversy) cannot be counted as equivalent units.

One way to reconcile the principle of equality among individuals with collective representation is to specify that "the resources of all organizations [be] effectively regulated so that they are proportional to the number of members."[13] Leaving aside both the myriad practical questions (for example, how actually to redistribute organizational resources, especially the nonmaterial ones such as skills) and the libertarian implications of such manipulations, it is clear that even as a formal solution to the problem of political equality, this scheme provides for a very different kind of equality than that which was posited for individuals. Because there is so much variation in the number of

---

[13]Dahl, *Dilemmas of Pluralist Democracy*, p. 84. Charles E. Lindblom discusses inequalities among organizational units in *Politics and Markets* (New York: Basic Books, 1977), p. 143. Jane J. Mansbridge also confronts some of these issues, though in a different context, in *Beyond Adversary Democracy* (New York: Basic Books, 1980), especially pp. 248–251.

issues on which individuals are active and the number of associations to which they belong, there will be significant inequalities among individuals in terms of their contributions to group-based political inputs.

It might be argued that multiple group memberships are simply a surrogate for intensity of preferences and that utopian schemes should admit the necessity of giving special weight to the views of those who care most. What the notion of regulating group resources in proportion to membership overlooks is that individuals vary in terms of the political resources—time, money, skills, contacts, and so on—that make it easier for some individuals to be joiners and more difficult for others. Not all inequalities in organizational membership reflect differences in intensity of preferences. Thus, in order to harmonize the concept of political equality for individuals with collective representation, we need then to specify abstract principles analogous to those posited earlier: each citizen's total share of the group-based input—whether as a member of one or several groups and whether on one or several issues—must be equal to every other citizen's.

Is the Washington Pressure Community Inclusive?

The first question to explore in assessing whether the Washington pressure community is inclusive is whether there are groups of persons who have mutual political interests but no organizational representation in Washington. History gives us good reason to suspect that any judgment on this matter may be flawed. Over the past three decades, a number of groups—among them, gay and handicapped people—have emerged and established an organized presence in Washington through new organizations such as the Gay Rights National Lobby and the Disability Rights Center. Just as gay and handicapped people were not politically organized thirty years ago and subsequently achieved a place in the Washington, there are presumably unorganized interests today whose joint political interests we are simply not perspicacious enough to identify and whose future emergence we are not prescient enough to anticipate. In the year 2000 we will probably look back at some group whose (at this point unanticipated) appearance on the political scene in the 1990s will seem very obvious in retrospect.

Even without such prescience, we can specify one group, homemakers, who would seem to have joint political interests but no organized representation in Washington. The vast majority of married women who are at home full time keeping house and raising children are dependent upon their husbands for financial support. Both state and federal laws contain many provisions relevant to homemakers' financial security should they be deprived of that support in the event of death or divorce.[14] Of course, there are a number of organizations representing the interests of women in Washington politics. Many of them—for

[14] Among them are laws governing the division of property in the case of a divorce and the procedures and penalties if the divorced husband fails to pay court-ordered alimony or child support; and laws specifying the rights of widows and divorcees to their former husbands' Social Security and pension benefits.

example, the National Military Wives Association, the National Beauty Cultur-ists League, and the National Association of Black Women Attorneys—are quite narrow in scope. Among such narrowly focused groups, however, there is not a single one devoted solely to the interests of homemakers.[15] Women at home probably do achieve some representation by some of the women's groups whose memberships and agendas are more inclusive—associations like the Na-tional Organization for Women (NOW)—but the peculiar set of concerns of homemakers is only one on a long list of policy objectives, and it probably ranks far from the top of the list of priorities of such organizations.

There are other groups as well that are not represented directly in Wash-ington politics. For example, there are no organizations specifically devoted to advocating the interests of many of the less advantaged beneficiaries of govern-ment programs—public housing tenants, food stamp recipients, and the like. In short, then, the Washington pressure community is not inclusive.

Is It Skewed?

If representation of interests in Washington politics is not universal, then it becomes important to investigate the potential skew in the interests that are represented—that is, to learn whether certain kinds of interests are more likely to be represented than others. Writing in the late 1950s, E. E. Schattschneider made two observations about the nature of organized interest representation in Washington: first, that it is limited in scope; and, second, that it is skewed in favor of groups representing the well-off, especially business, and against groups representing broad public interests and the disadvantaged.[16]

What are the contours of the Washington pressure community today? Table 4.2 presents the results of a tally of the nearly 7000 organizations listed in *Washington Representatives.*[17] The left-hand column shows the distribution for

[15]The most recent edition of the directory *Washington Representatives* (Close, ed., 7th ed., 1983) lists an organization called the Federation of Homemakers, whose existence would seem to contradict this generalization. However, according to the *Encyclopedia of Associations* [Denise S. Akey, ed., 17th ed. (Detroit: Gale Research Company, 1983), p. 1052], the Federation of Home-makers is a citizens' group concerned with educating consumers about the dangers of chemical additives in foods.

[16]*The Semisovereign People,* pp. 30–37.

[17]Appendix C describes the methods used in compiling this catalogue. The directory *Wash-ington Representatives* lists all the private organizations having an ongoing presence in the capital. For organizations having an office in Washington, the directory lists the address of the organization and names of important government affairs personnel; for those that do not maintain their own offices in Washington, the directory lists the names of their hired counsel or consultants. While this directory is surely the most nearly complete listing of private organizations with a sustained Wash-ington presence, we cannot be sure that it is an exhaustive inventory. Some organizations are probably missing. Furthermore, we are certain that, by using it as the basis of our discussion, we are neglecting the hundreds of local organizations that are occasionally active in Washington politics when their vital interests are in jeopardy. Such groups form an important component of the total pressure community.

In rechecking our figures prior to final publication of this book, we discovered a small number of errors (mostly rounding errors) in data that were previously published elsewhere. In case of discrepancies, the figures presented here are correct.

Table 4.2   THE WASHINGTON PRESSURE COMMUNITY

	Organizations having their own Washington offices	All organizations having Washington representation
Corporations	20.6%	45.7%
Trade and other business associations	30.6	17.9
Foreign commerce and corporations	.5	6.5
Professional associations[a]	14.8	6.9
Unions	3.3	1.7
Citizens' groups	8.7	4.1
Civil rights groups/Minority organizations	1.7	1.3
Social welfare and the poor	1.3	.6
New Entrants (elderly, women, handicapped)	2.5	1.1
Governmental units—U.S.	1.4	4.2
Other foreign	1.2	2.0
Other unknown[b]	13.4	8.2
	100.0%	100.2%
	(N = 2810)	(N = 6601)

[a]Includes, in addition to traditional professional associations, organizations of business executives, such as the Data Processing Management Association, and organizations of professionals working in government, such as the National Conference of Bankruptcy Judges.

[b]Includes, in addition to organizations we were unable to classify (292), nine small categories. Among them are farmers' organizations (46), veterans' groups (31), and religious groups (50). Of the nine categories, only educational organizations (124, or 1.9 percent) account for more than 1 percent of the total organizations classified. Otherwise, these categories account for less than 1 percent of the total each.

Sources: Based on information taken from Arthur C. Close, ed., *Washington Representatives—1981,* 5th ed. (Washington, DC: Columbia Books, 1981); and Denise S. Akey, ed., *The Encyclopedia of Associations,* 16th ed. (Detroit, MI: Gale Research Company, 1981).

the 2810 organizations (43 percent of the total) that have their own Washington offices. The right-hand column shows the distribution into categories of the 6601 organizations that achieve a presence in Washington politics either by maintaining an office in the capital to handle political matters or by hiring Washington-based counsel or consultants to assist them.

There is one obvious difference between the distributions in the two columns of figures that bears mention. Corporations constitute 45.7 percent of all organizations having a Washington presence but only 20.6 percent of those having Washington offices. This discrepancy reflects the fact that corporations are among the organizations relatively least likely to have their own Washington offices.[18] Ninety-seven percent of the social welfare organizations, 91 per-

[18]It is not surprising that corporations are less likely to open separate offices. Many organizations—among them very few corporations—choose to locate their national headquarters in the capital. Such organizations rarely have compelling reasons for choosing a particular locale over

cent each of the professional associations and citizens' groups, 83 percent of the unions, and 73 percent of the trade and other business associations, but only 19 percent of the corporations having Washington representation have their own Washington offices.[19]

This discrepancy should not blind us to the overall message of both columns of Table 4.2. Whether one considers all the organizations having a Washington presence or just those having their own Washington offices, it is clear that Schattschneider's observations two decades ago about the shape of the Washington pressure community are apt today. Taken as a whole, the pressure community is heavily weighted in favor of business organizations: 70 percent of all organizations having a Washington presence and 52 percent of those having their own offices represent business. The overrepresentation of business interests takes place at the expense of two other kinds of organizations: groups representing broad public interests and groups representing the less advantaged.[20]

Even making the perhaps dubious assumption that all unions, civil rights groups, minority organizations, social welfare groups, poor people's organizations, and groups organizing the elderly, the handicapped, and women represent political have-nots, less than 5 percent of all organizations having a Washington presence and less than 10 percent of those having their own offices there represent those having few political resources. Similar proportions obtain for the sum total of all the various kinds of organizations—consumer groups, environmental groups, civic groups, single-issue cause groups, foreign policy groups, and so on—that represent diffuse public interests; citizens' groups con-

---

Washington for their headquarters, and the propinquity to national politics makes the capital attractive. Corporations obviously consider many factors in addition to political convenience in choosing a site for their headquarters and cannot easily pull up stakes once settled. Many organizations with headquarters elsewhere also maintain offices in the capital. For several reasons, corporations are less likely to do so. First, although many corporations are very involved in politics, for many of them political activity is sporadic rather than constant. In addition, corporations are ordinarily members of trade associations having Washington offices and are thus represented on the scene even if they do not have their own offices. Moreover, corporations generally command the resources to be able to hire counsel or consultants to represent their interests if they do not have their own Washington offices.

[19]With respect to the other kinds of organizations on the list, foreign interests (enjoined by law from pressuring Congress directly) rarely open separate offices in Washington but, rather, hire counsel or consultants to represent them. Foreign nations, of course, maintain a direct presence through their embassies. As for other governments, in many cases *Washington Representatives* does not make clear whether U.S. governmental units have their own Washington offices because it tends not to list the address of the D.C. office, even when there is one. (This practice was changed in a subsequent edition of the directory.) Finally, only 55 percent of the civil rights groups have Washington offices. This reflects the fact that over 60 percent of the civil rights/minorities groups are not organizations like the National Association for the Advancement of Colored People or the Mexican-American Legal Defense and Educational Fund, most of which *do* have offices in the capital, but are Indian tribes, most of which hire counsel or consultants to represent them.

[20]In the remainder of this chapter we shall pay more attention to the tilt of the Washington pressure community against the less advantaged than to its bias against groups representing broad publics. This aspect will be elaborated in Chapter 6 when we consider the theories of Mancur Olson.

stitute only 4 percent of all organizations active in Washington politics and 9 percent of those having offices in the capital.

A Further Probe   The Washington pressure community, of course, includes groups organized around a vast array of dimensions—from occupation, race, age, and gender to hobbies. Consider that 51 percent of Americans are female and 49 percent are male; that 83 percent are white, 12 percent black, and 5 percent other races; and that 41 percent are under 25, 11 percent over 64, and the remainder in between.[21] Given the multiple axes of potential political conflict, it is difficult to know what a balanced pressure community would look like. We would not expect half the organizations in the pressure community to represent women and half to represent men, for the pressure community has to accommodate associations organized around many lines of political interest.

One way to understand the extent of the skewing is to consider the groups active on a single fault line of political cleavage. Figure 4.2 presents data on what is probably the single most important dimension of political conflict in American politics—economic roles. The left-hand bar presents data, based on the 1980 census, on the proportion of American adults in various economic roles. Most adults (59 percent) work in various occupations; others are unemployed and looking for work, in school, at home, unable to work, or retired. The right-hand bar, based on our catalogue of those organizations having offices in Washington, shows the distribution of groups organized around these roles.

We must caution that the correspondence between the economic roles in the left-hand bar and the economic groups in the right-hand one is far from perfect. Not all professionals, for example, are represented by professional associations. Some, such as elementary and high school teachers, are represented by unions. In addition, many of those included in the manager/administrator category—college deans, hospital administrators, and the like—are not employed by businesses and are represented, if at all, by professional associations. Furthermore, of the 92 educational organizations in the right-hand column, only one, the American Student Association, is an organization devoted to promoting the interests of students. In addition, none of the 39 women's organizations are expressly organized to act on behalf of the interests of homemakers. While these points lead us to treat the data in Figure 4.2 with circumspection, it should be noted that, in the absence of finer-grained categories, we are undoubtedly overstating the number of *people* in the business and professional categories and the number of *groups* representing homemakers and students. If anything, then, the set of economic interest groups is even more skewed than Figure 4.2 would indicate.

There is another dilemma underlying Figure 4.2. A plurality of the economic organizations in Washington are corporations and, thus, have no mem-

[21] Figures calculated from the U.S. Bureau of the Census, *Statistical Abstract of the United States,* 102nd ed. (Washington, DC: U.S. Government Printing Office, 1981), pp. 16, 25, 27.

Percentage of
U.S. Adults

Percentage of
Organizations

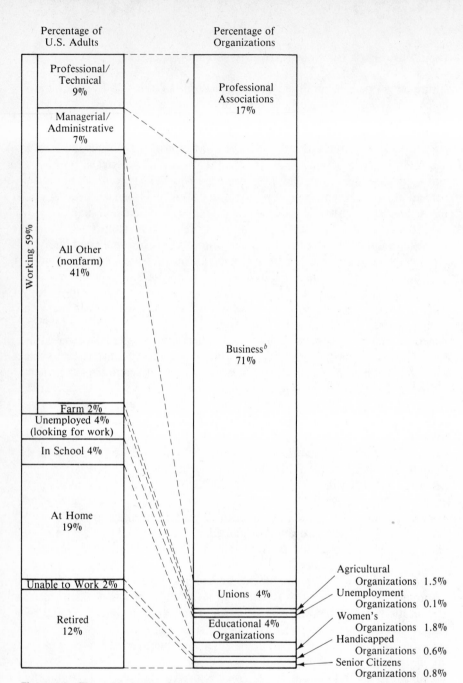

Figure 4.2   The public and the pressure community: Economic roles of adults and organizations.[a]

[a]Includes only organizations having Washington offices.

[b]Corporations, trade associations, other business associations, and associations of business professionals.

Sources: Information about the public based on U.S. Bureau of the Census, *Statistical Abstract of the United States,* 102nd ed. (Washington DC: U.S. Government Printing Office, 1981), pp. 379, 401–404. Information about organizations based on Arthur C. Close, ed., *Washington Representatives—1981,* 5th ed. (Washington, DC: Columbia Books); and Denise S. Akey, ed., *The Encyclopedia of Associations,* 16th ed. (Detroit, MI: Gale Research Company, 1981).

bers in the ordinary sense. When an organization has no members, whose interests can it be said to represent?[22] Presumably, the corporate constituency in politics extends to corporate managers, stockholders, employees, and consumers; and, presumably, in many instances the interests of these groups are compatible. However, if the number of conflicts between labor and management before the National Labor Relations Board or the number of class action suits undertaken against American Telephone and Telegraph are any indication, there are surely circumstances when what is good for General Motors is indeed not good for the country, or at least for those who build or buy GM automobiles. Some corporations consciously choose to place the interests of employees or customers before the short-term benefit of management or stockholders on the theory that such decisions make sound business sense. For example, a company might make marketplace decisions to cut profits rather than sustain a layoff in sluggish times or adulterate the quality of the product in inflationary periods. However, when there are conflicts within the corporate constituency, especially when those conflicts involve political matters, it is rarely the case that the interests of management take a backseat.

Bearing in mind all these qualifications, the broad outlines of the message contained in Figure 4.2 are quite clear. Considering the substantial portion of the pressure community consisting of groups organized about economic roles, the socioeconomic tilt of the Washington pressure system is unambiguous. The professionals and managers who might be considered to be "haves" constitute at most 16 percent of American adults; they are represented by 88 percent of the economic organizations.[23] Business organizations alone constitute 71 percent of the total. What is more, these data are for the distribution of organizations having their own offices in Washington. Had we used figures for all economic organizations involved in Washington politics—those that hire counsel or consultants as well as those that have their own offices—the data would have been even more skewed. Fully 93 percent of the economic organizations having a Washington presence represent business or professionals and 86 percent represent business alone.

The Multiple Representation of Business Interests

Recalling our earlier discussion, we might argue that it is not the number of groups representing a particular point of view so much as the equal representation of individuals that is critical for political equality. That is, workers might be just as well represented by a few large unions as business is by a much

---

[22] See the discussion of this issue and accompanying bibliography in Grant McConnell, *Private Power and American Democracy* (New York: Knopf, 1966), pp. 129–134.

[23] There is still another way in which these figures understate the number of business organizations in the pressure system. Since 1960, many smaller corporations with only trade association representation in Washington politics have been acquired by conglomerates with offices in Washington. The implication of this process is to increase the number of *companies* having direct representation in the capital without increasing the number of *offices* representing corporations.

higher number of smaller organizations if the total group-based political input were equal for all individuals represented. However, comparison with the structure of political representation of organized labor demonstrates that the structure of business representation is such that business interests are likely to enjoy multiple representation.

In terms of the level of aggregation of interest, the three kinds of business organizations in politics—firms, trade associations, and peak associations—are analogous to union locals, operating unions, and the AFL-CIO. At the peak, the representation of interests of business and labor is roughly equivalent. Several organizations—among them the Business Roundtable, the Chamber of Commerce, and the National Association of Manufacturers—represent the most general interests of business, while the AFL-CIO represents those of labor. At the most disaggregated level, however, the situation is entirely reversed. While individual firms frequently act on their own in politics, individual union locals rarely do so. Of course, there are many circumstances when firms compete with each other politically—for example, in defense procurement. When, as is often the case, an issue affects in similar ways the various companies in an industry, however, marketplace antagonists become political allies and the political activity of one firm represents others in the industry.

What is more, while each union local obviously belongs only to a single operating union, corporations, even small ones, belong to a number of trade associations. Large corporations, especially conglomerates, usually belong to dozens.[24] The following is a partial list of the more than 80 trade and other business associations to which General Electric belongs:

Aerospace Industries Association of America
Air Conditioning and Refrigeration Institute
American Mining Congress
American Public Transit Association
Association of Home Appliance Manufacturers
Atomic Industrial Forum
Business Roundtable
Chamber of Commerce
Edison Electric Institute
Electronics Industries Association
Health Industries Manufacturers Association
National Association of Broadcasters
National Association of Home Builders

---

[24]Social scientists have drawn from the union animus to "dual unionism" the conclusion that organizations jealously protect their turf from invasion by other organizations. However, this may not be the case with respect to trade and other business associations. Given the possibility of multiple memberships, business associations tend to proliferate and, on occasion, to represent very narrow interests. To illustrate, in addition to such a giant as the National Association of Home Builders, there are many groups having a much narrower focus—for example, the Door and Hardware Institute, the Foundation of the Wall and Ceiling Industry, the Log Homes Council, and the Resilient Floor Covering Institute. Such organizations often share members and are often allied.

> National Association of Manufacturers
> National Cable Television Association
> National Coal Association
> National Electrical Manufacturers Association
> Railway Progress Institute
> Society of the Plastics Industry
> Welding Institute

It would be folly to assume that these associations, and the more than 60 additional ones to which General Electric belongs, are always active on the same issues or are always allies when they are simultaneously active. The Atomic Industrial Forum and the National Coal Association, for example, presumably lock horns on the issue of nuclear power generation. Still, these many additional memberships must add considerably to the volume of a single corporation's political input.

Hence, in a particular political controversy, a unionized worker might be represented by his operating union and the AFL-CIO; a stockholder or manager in the same corporation might be represented by his own firm, by other firms in the industry, by one or more trade associations, and by one or more peak business associations. It is not, then, simply a matter of equal representation of individuals being provided by a multiplicity of smaller organizations as opposed to a few larger ones, for the proliferation of business organizations magnifies business input into politics.

The Tilt of the Pressure Community: A Qualification So far we have been arguing that the Washington pressure community is not inclusive and that it is skewed in favor of the well-off, especially business, and against broad publics and the less advantaged. However, the prominence in the politics of the past couple of decades of groups like the National Council of Senior Citizens and the National Organization for Women suggests a qualification to this formulation.

While the set of organized private interests arrayed along an economic dimension is clearly biased in favor of the well-off, quite the opposite is true when the sets of groups constellated around other axes of cleavage are examined. There are, for example, nearly 40 organizations on the Washington scene explicitly devoted to promoting the interests of women; there are none representing the interests of men. Analogously, while there are over a dozen senior citizens groups with offices in Washington, there are none representing the interests of the middle-aged. In addition, while organizations like the Italian American Forum, the Japanese American Citizens League, and the Ukrainian National Information Service promote the interests of Americans of foreign ancestry and defend their cultural distinctiveness, there is no Association of American WASPs to perform a similar function for the culturally dominant white Anglo-Saxon Protestants. There are organizations dedicated to promoting the interests of whites; however, unlike such civil rights groups as the National Association for the Advancement of Colored People and the National Urban League, groups like the Ku Klux Klan and the American Nazi Party operate almost entirely outside of ordinary pressure politics and lack political legitimacy.

It might be argued that members of the dominant age, gender, and racial group—middle-aged, white men—receive ample representation in the pressure community through their dominant role in the unions and business and professional associations that form the preponderance of organizations active in Washington. Still, it is important to note the fundamental difference between the distributions of groups organized along economic and noneconomic axes of cleavage. While the imbalance in the distribution of economic organizations is unmistakable, it is the have-nots among age, gender, and ethnic groups who command the preponderance of what organized political representation there is.

THE CHANGING PRESSURE COMMUNITY

If the contemporary Washington pressure community is tilted toward business—notwithstanding the presence in Washington of new groups like the National Center for a Barrier Free Environment, the Environmental Defense Fund, and the Lawyers Committee for Civil Rights under Law—what did it look like two decades ago when Schattschneider wrote? One of the most important changes in Washington politics over the past two decades has been the emergence of many new groups—ranging from Common Cause and Ralph Nader's Public Citizen to the National Urban Coalition and the Migrant Legal Action Project—representing broad publics and the less advantaged, precisely the kinds of interests that Schattschneider deemed not to be well organized.[25] As one prominent student of interest groups has observed: "Since the 1950s, a diffuse and uneven but nationwide process of political mobilization has been under way, bringing many new elements of the population into closer contact

[25]This development has received considerable attention from both journalists and scholars. See, for example, "The Swarming Lobbyists," *Time,* August 7, 1978, pp. 14–22; "Single Issue Politics," *Newsweek,* November 6, 1978, pp. 48–60; and John Herbers, "Grass Roots Groups Go National," *New York Times Magazine,* September 4, 1983, p. 22 ff. Among the academic observers who have noted this trend are Andrew McFarland, *Public Interest Lobbies* (Washington, DC: American Enterprise Institute, 1976); Jeffrey M. Berry, *Lobbying for the People* (Princeton: Princeton University Press, 1977); David Vogel, "The Public-Interest Movement and the American Reform Tradition," *Political Science Quarterly* 95 (1980–1981): 607–627; Jack L. Walker, "The Origins and Maintenance of Interest Groups in America," *American Political Science Review* 77 (1983): 394–396; Jack L. Walker, "The Mobilization of Political Interests," paper delivered at the Annual Meeting of the American Political Science Association, Chicago, September 1983, pp. 15–18; and Andrew S. McFarland, *Common Cause: Lobbying in the Public Interest* (Chatham, N.J.: Chatham House, 1984). Michael T. Hayes ["Interest Groups: Pluralism or Mass Society?" in Allan J. Cigler and Burdett A. Loomis, eds., *Interest Group Politics* (Washington, DC: CQ Press, 1983), pp. 110–125] notes the rise of citizens' groups but draws different conclusions about the implications of the trend.

with the nation's political process."[26] Another has noted "a renaissance in citizen activism."[27] With the mobilization of new interests over the past two decades, the nature of the Washington pressure community has undoubtedly been altered. There is good reason to suppose that it is less exclusive and less skewed than in the past.

The Explosion in Organized Activity

Systematic data confirm the popular impression that many new citizens', civil rights, and social welfare organizations have emerged since 1960. We were able to locate the dates of founding of 80 percent of the nearly 3000 organizations listed in the *Washington Representatives—1981* directory as having their own offices in the capital. Figure 4.3 shows the distribution of these dates for various categories of organizations. The overall finding in Figure 4.3 is the large number of new groups on the scene. Fully 40 percent of the organizations having offices in Washington have been founded since 1960 and 25 percent since 1970. Equally striking is the distribution for the various categories. Seventy-six percent of the citizens' groups, 56 percent of the civil rights groups, and 79 percent of the social welfare and poor people's organizations but only 38 percent of the trade associations and 14 percent of the corporations were founded since 1960. In addition, 57 percent of the citizens' groups and 51 percent of the social welfare and poor people's organizations but only 23 percent of the trade and other business associations and 6 percent of the corporations were founded since 1970.[28] These figures confirm the observation that there has been an explosion in the number of groups representing the interests of broad publics and the disadvantaged.

Clearly, then, the pressure community has expanded in scope, but how has the entry of all these new groups altered its skew? Unfortunately, *Washington Representatives,* which is the nearest equivalent to an exhaustive directory of the organizations active in national politics, has been published only since 1977. However, the Index to the *Congressional Quarterly Almanac* for 1960 permits an approximate construction of the distribution of politically active organizations at the time Schattschneider wrote. The results of that inquiry are presented in Table 4.3.[29] In comparing the pressure community of 1960 with

[26] Jack Walker, quoted in Dom Bonafede, "Interest Groups Pressing for Earlier, More Active Role in the Electoral Process," *National Journal,* May 14, 1983, pp. 1005–1006.

[27] Harry C. Boyte, *The Backyard Revolution* (Philadelphia: Temple University Press, 1980), p. 3.

[28] These figures are similar to those presented by Walker in "The Origins and Maintenance of Interest Groups," p. 394.

[29] The Index to the *Congressional Quarterly Almanac* is not meant to be an exhaustive guide to all private organizations active in Washington analogous to the *Washington Representatives* directory. Rather, the Index includes all the private associations mentioned in the *Almanac* either in the articles on policy matters or in the listings of associations registered with Congress under the Provisions of the Federal Regulation of Lobbying Act of 1946. We categorized and enumerated the 523 organizations contained in the 1960 Index in the same manner that we treated the organiza-

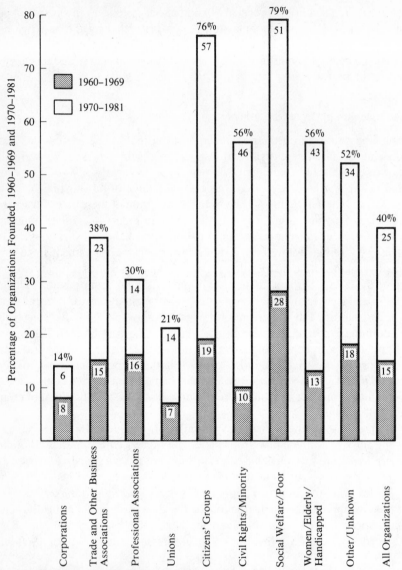

Figure 4.3 Dates of founding of organizations having Washington offices. Percentage of organizations founded, 1960–1969 and 1970–1981.

Sources: Calculated from information contained in Denise S. Akey, ed., *Encyclopedia of Associations,* 17th ed. (Detroit, MI: Gale Research Company, 1983), and the various volumes published by Moody's Investors Service (New York: Moody's Investors Service, 1982).

tions contained in *Washington Representatives.* Because the *CQ Almanac* Index cannot be used to locate foreign interests and subnational U.S. governments active in Washington, we have eliminated these categories from the figures for 1980.

Table 4.3   THE CHANGING WASHINGTON PRESSURE COMMUNITY

	1960	1980	
	Organizations listed in CQ	Organizations having their own Washington offices	All organizations having Washington representation
Corporations	16%	21%	52%
Trade and other business associations	41	32	20
Professional associations	5	15	8
Unions	11	3	2
Citizens' groups	9	9	5
Civil rights/Social welfare/Poor	2	3	2
Women/Elderly/Handicapped	2	3	1
Other/Unknown	15	14	9
	101%	100%	99%
	(N = 523)	(N = 2721)	(N = 5769)

Sources: Based on information from *Congressional Quarterly Almanac—1960* (Washington, DC: Congressional Quarterly, 1960); Arthur C. Close, ed., *Washington Representatives—1981,* 5th ed. (Washington, DC: Columbia Books, 1981); and Denise S. Akey, ed., *The Encyclopedia of Associations,* 16th ed. (Detroit, MI: Gale Research Company, 1981).

the set of organizations having their own offices in the capital two decades later, it is clear that there is less change than political scientists might have expected. Although the balance between corporations and trade associations has changed, the total business presence (corporations and trade and other business associations taken together) has diminished relatively little, from 57 percent to 53 percent of all organizations. The most substantial alteration is the increase in the proportion of professional associations and the corresponding decrease in the proportion of unions.

However, because the *CQ Almanac* Index clearly includes not only organizations that represent themselves but also those that hire professional lobbyists to handle their government relations, it is probably more appropriate to compare the figures for 1960 with the figures for all organizations having a Washington presence in 1980 (shown in the right-hand column of Table 4.3). This comparison leads to a somewhat different conclusion. In spite of all the newborn organizations representing the interests of diffuse publics, minorities, poor people, the elderly and other disadvantaged groups, business actually is a more dominating presence in Washington now than it was two decades ago. Considering all organizations having representation in Washington, the proportion representing the interests of business rose from 57 percent to 72 percent since 1960. The proportion of citizens' groups decreased from 9 percent to 5 percent of all organizations, and the proportion representing labor plummeted from 11 percent to 2 percent.[30]

Movement In and Out of the Pressure Community

How can the data about the birth of new groups representing the previously underrepresented be reconciled with evidence indicating the increasing over-representation of business? The discussion so far may have lent a misleading aura of immutability to the set of organizations active in national politics. In fact, the pressure community is quite fluid. Changes in its composition from one time to another represent not only the entry into politics of fledgling organizations but also the mobilization for politics of previously apolitical organizations and the exit of both organizations that leave politics either temporarily or permanently, while continuing to function as organizations, and of organizations that go out of business altogether. Quite simply, organizations vary in terms of the constancy of their political activity. Some, especially those having offices in Washington, are on the scene year in and year out. Others participate more sporadically, becoming galvanized for politics only on those occasions when a specific issue impinges upon their vital interests. Some groups are intentionally temporary, formed to deal with a particular policy matter.

The data in Table 4.4 allow us to get a better feel for the movement of organizations in and out of the pressure community. Using various sources, we were able to amass information about the subsequent histories of three-fourths of the organizations listed in the Index to *Congressional Quarterly Almanac* of 1960. As shown in Table 4.4, there is a remarkable amount of continuity. Sixty percent of all the organizations listed in 1960—or 79 percent of those for which we could find information—were on the scene two decades later (having been listed in *Washington Representatives—1981*). We could establish that another 9 percent—or 12 percent of those we could trace—were still active as organizations but were not involved in Washington politics (not having been included in *Washington Representatives*). We could confirm that an additional 7 percent—or 9 percent of those we could locate—had become inactive as organizations or gone out of business entirely. Some of these defunct organizations—for example, the National Committee to Liberalize the Tariff Laws on Art and the Committee for the Return of Confiscated German and Japanese Property—

[30]It is possible that the *CQ Almanac* Index is not only incomplete but unrepresentative. In order to ascertain whether the 523 organizations listed in 1960 were a representative sample of the organizations active in Washington at that time, we attempted to compare the distribution of organizations in the 1981 *CQ Almanac* Index with that gleaned from the tally of organizations listed in *Washington Representatives*. Unfortunately, the *CQ Almanac* Index has changed its format since 1960. The 1981 Index lists only 70 organizations. Given the expansion in the number of organizations active in Washington politics, this is clearly a much less comprehensive catalogue than in the earlier volume. Hence, it seems that the 1981 Index cannot be used to detect whatever bias may be present in the 1961 Index.

Table 4.4   STATUS IN 1980 OF ORGANIZATIONS ACTIVE IN WASHINGTON POLITICS IN 1960

	Organizational status					
	Still active in politics	Still active, not in politics	Inactive/ Out of business	No information		
Corporations	63%	8	0	29	= 100%	(N = 84)
Trade and other business associations	61%	6	10	24	= 101%	(N = 216)
Professional associations	79%	7	0	14	= 100%	(N = 28)
Unions	77%	7	4	12	= 100%	(N = 56)
Citizens' groups	33%	13	27	27	= 100%	(N = 46)
Civil rights/Social welfare/Poor	50%	12	0	38	= 100%	(N = 8)
Women/Elderly/ Handicapped	78%	11	0	11	= 100%	(N = 9)
Other/Unknown	46%	18	3	33	= 100%	(N = 76)
All organizations	60%	9	7	24	= 100%	(N = 523)

Sources: Compiled from information contained in the following: Denise S. Akey, ed., *The Encyclopedia of Associations,* 17th ed. (Detroit, MI: Gale Research Company, 1983); Arthur C. Close, ed., *Washington Representatives—1981,* 5th ed. (Washington, DC: Columbia Books, 1981); Craig Colgate, Jr., ed., *National Trade and Professional Associations of the United States,* 18th ed. (Washington, DC: Columbia Books, 1983); *Congressional Quarterly Almanac—1960* (Washington, DC: Congressional Quarterly, 1960); *Directory of Corporate Affiliations—1983* (Skokie, IL: National Register Publishing Company, 1983); Baldwin H. Ward, ed., *Ward's Directory of 55,000 Largest Corporations* (Petaluma, CA: Baldwin H. Ward Publications, 1981).

have names that suggest organizations purposely founded to deal with a specific issue. Thus, it is not surprising that they passed from the scene along with the issues on which they were intended to do battle. Others, such as the Clothespin Manufacturers of America and the Mobile Homes Dealers National Association, sound more like the kind of traditional organizations that we expect to persist from year to year. The received social science wisdom about the adaptive capacities of organizations to the contrary, it is clear that some organizations do go out of business.

Citizens' groups are an exception to the general pattern that emerges from Table 4.4. Only 33 percent of the citizens' groups listed in 1960 were still active in politics two decades later. Fully 27 percent (a substantially higher figure than for any other type of organization) were not around at all. Considering only those organizations for which we have information, 80 percent or more of the corporations, trade and other business associations, professional associations, unions, organizations of women, the elderly, and the handicapped, and civil rights and social welfare organizations—but only 45 percent of the citizens' groups—that were active in Washington in 1960 were listed twenty years later.

It is worth mentioning, as well, that the turnover in citizens' groups has been accompanied by some alteration in the distribution of kinds of groups. There has been a decline in the relative number of civic groups (e.g., League of Women Voters) and foreign policy groups (e.g., Committee for Collective Security) and an increase in the relative proportion of environmental groups (e.g., Friends of the Earth) and consumer groups (e.g., Public Citizen). Although some of the specific issues have changed—from loyalty oaths and temperance to handguns and abortion—the relative weight of single-issue groups has remained unchanged. In light of the difficulties of obtaining information about small (and, in some cases, now defunct) organizations and the lack of precise boundaries among categories, the following figures should be interpreted cautiously; they do, however, suggest these shifts in emphasis among citizens' groups:

	1960	1980
Consumer groups	4%	10%
Civic groups	22	13
Environmental groups	11	23
Foreign policy groups	33	22
Single-issue groups	13	15
Other citizens' groups	17	17
	100%	100%
	(N = 46)	(N = 269)

The greater weight of consumer and environmental groups among citizens' groups has led some observers to speculate that the unusual turnover that has characterized citizens' groups in the past may not carry over into the future.

This investigation of the fate of the organizations mentioned by the *Congressional Quarterly* has demonstrated something about the relative propensities of organizations to continue to be involved in politics, to become politically deactivated, or to go out of existence completely. Unfortunately, however, it is impossible to trace an additional process that affects the overall contours of the pressure community: the mobilization into national politics of existing, but previously apolitical, organizations. Many observers have remarked upon the importance of this process in recent years, especially with respect to business.[31]

[31] The recent political activation of business organizations has been discussed in many places. See, for example, Philip Shabecoff, "Big Business on the Offensive," *New York Times Magazine,* December 9, 1979, pp. 134–146; Richard E. Cohen, "The Business Lobby Discovers That in Unity There Is Strength," *National Journal,* June 28, 1980, pp. 1050–1055; David Vogel, "The Power of Business in America: A Re-appraisal," *British Journal of Political Science* 13 (1983): 19–43; and Graham Wilson, "The Changing Role of Business in the U.S.A.," paper presented at the Annual Meeting of the American Political Science Association, Chicago, September 1983.

It is this process of mobilization of previously politically inactive organizations that accounts for the discrepancy between the results reported here and Walker's finding that "citizen groups make up a much larger part of the total than ever before." ("On the Origins and Maintenance of Interest Groups," p. 395.)

Because the listing in the Index to the *CQ Almanac* cannot be considered as comprehensive as that in the *Washington Representatives* directories published since 1977, it cannot be used as a baseline for tracing the growth of the pressure system. It would be inaccurate to conclude either that all existing organizations not listed by *CQ Almanac* were uninvolved in politics as of 1960 or that the pressure system has expanded from far fewer than 600 organizations to well over 6000.

One bit of evidence from our Washington representatives survey provides indirect confirmation of the significance of the political activation of organizations previously outside politics. We asked the respondents in our sample when their organizations had first established offices in the national capital. Sixty-one percent of the organizations in our survey have opened a Washington office (often a national headquarters) since 1960, and 38 percent since 1970. Furthermore, 36 percent of the organizations in our sample—including 42 percent of the corporations and 55 percent of the professional associations—are organizations that existed as of 1960 but have established offices in Washington since then, presumably indicating the increased salience of national politics both to organizations originally established for other purposes and to organizations long active in politics whose political interests had become so compelling that they established a permanent beachhead in Washington. These figures, of course, do not capture the large number of organizations—a group including, as we have seen, a disproportionately large share of corporations—that have decided to hire government affairs professionals to represent their interests but do not have their own offices in the capital. Thus, it is clear that the process of organizational politicization has been an important one in recent years, particularly for corporations and professional associations. Unfortunately, however, we cannot track it with precision.

The Changing Pressure Community: Summing Up   It is now possible to draw together the various lines of argument and indicate how the net result of all these processes of change could be a pressure community whose contours have been altered relatively little. To summarize, a very large share of the civil rights and social welfare organizations and of the groups representing women, the elderly, and the handicapped are young, having been established since 1960. However, there are still so few of them compared with other kinds of organizations that, even though their numbers have grown substantially, they do not form a more significant component in the pressure community.

Many new citizens' groups have also been born over this period. As in the case of the organizations just mentioned, there are still too few of them to figure significantly in the pressure community. What is more, the citizens' organizations that were part of the pressure system as of 1960 seem to have been characterized by unusually high rates of attrition, which has had the effect of reducing their overall representation in Washington.

The pattern for unions is quite different. Union representation has remained remarkably stable over the last two decades. The number of unions has not grown significantly. Furthermore, a large proportion of the unions active in 1980 were on the scene in 1960. This stability, in a period during which many new organizations have appeared and many old ones have been politically mobilized, yields a situation in which the union share of organized interest representation has diminished substantially. A similar, though less exaggerated, pattern is characteristic of trade associations as well. The birthrate for trade associations has been somewhat lower than for other kinds of organizations. In addition, because so many trade associations were already active in politics in 1960, the process of political activation has been less pronounced than for corporations. The net result is that trade associations, while still a crucial component of the pressure community have lost their former unambiguous predominance. At one time, trade associations were deemed the backbone of the pressure community. It would be an overstatement to make such a claim today.

The pattern for corporations—and, to a lesser extent, professional associations—is different again. The birthrate for these organizations, especially corporations, is relatively low. However, the massive mobilization of organizations formerly outside Washington politics more than compensates for the low rate of entry of newborn organizations. Thus, in spite of their low birthrates, both professional associations and corporations have increased their share of the pressure community. Corporations alone account for 52 percent of the organizations that either maintain offices in the capital or hire counsel or consultants to represent their interests. This massive influx of corporations has meant that in spite of the relative eclipse of trade associations, the overall business share of the organized representation in Washington has been enhanced.

In short, then, we have traced various processes of change, the effect of which has been to leave the structure of the pressure community more or less unaltered. It should be noted, however, that these trends have been sequential as well as simultaneous. The explosion in citizens' group activity occurred in the earlier part of the two-decade period reviewed. The countermobilization of business began only in the mid- to late 1970s in response to the victories that had been scored by citizens' groups in the years immediately preceding. Therefore, it is possible that had we been able to enumerate the organizations active in Washington in 1975, the pro-business bias would have been somewhat less acute.

GROUP REPRESENTATION AND POLICY CONTROVERSIES

One of the principal empirical findings of this chapter has been that in spite of the emergence of new organizations like the Consumer Federation of America and the Solar Lobby, groups representing broadly shared interests constitute only a very small part of the pressure community. This is surely a finding having significance for the nature of political competition and the outcomes of public controversies. Fortunately, there is a theory that explores systematically the implications for policy conflict of this imbalance in representation: James Q. Wilson has elaborated in detail the consequences for policy controversies of the fact that interests shared by narrow publics are more likely to be given representation in political conflicts than are the interests of diffuse publics.[32]

Fundamental to Wilson's analysis is his understanding that the structure of conflict and the nature of the political process surrounding a particular policy issue will be determined by the degree to which the costs being imposed and the benefits being conferred are widely distributed or narrowly concentrated; and that the politics of a particular policy will vary depending on whether a new policy is being adopted or an existing one is being implemented or altered. To illustrate: a policy proposal that would lead to an increase in the income tax rate, to general price increases, or to a higher crime rate would be considered to have *distributed costs;* one producing cleaner air or higher social security benefits, on the other hand, would be said to have *distributed benefits;* a policy imposing a costly regulation on a particular industry (say a requirement that funeral directors make detailed listings of prices) would entail narrowly *concentrated costs;* and subsidies paid to particular industries or occupations, such as tobacco farmers, or licenses granted by the government for the operation of facilities, such as television or radio stations, confer *concentrated benefits.* Wilson presents four categories of policy controversies, each displaying one of the different possible configurations of costs and benefits and each characterized by a unique pattern of political conflict.

Majoritarian Politics: Distributed Benefits and Distributed Costs   Some policies—for example, social security, Medicare, or national defense—confer benefits on large numbers of persons at a cost that all or most of society must pay. Wilson argues that although interest groups—in particular, peak business and labor associations—are not entirely absent from debate over such issues, organized interest conflict ordinarily plays a subsidiary role when these issues are resolved. In their initial stages, "majoritarian" issues often involve highly ideological conflict that engages the two political parties, with Democrats lining up behind extending benefits and Republicans opposing any wider government role. Deadlock over such issues is sometimes broken when the public registers its aggregate opinion in a decisive presidential election. At the behest of the president, a new (or a beefed-up) congressional majority may vote significant new policies that confer distributed benefits.

---

[32]Wilson has presented this analytical scheme in varying forms and with varying degrees of elaboration in the following: *Political Organizations* (New York: Basic Books, 1973), Chapter 15; "The Politics of Regulation," in James W. McKie, ed., *Social Responsibility and the Business Predicament* (Washington, DC: Brookings Institution, 1974), pp. 135–168; "The Politics of Regulation," in James Q. Wilson, ed., *The Politics of Regulation* (New York: Basic Books, 1980); *American Government: Institutions and Policies,* 2nd ed. (Lexington, MA.: Heath, 1983), especially Chapter 14. We have used many of Wilson's examples in our brief outline of his scheme.

Interest Group Politics: Concentrated Benefits and Concentrated Costs   Sometimes policies confer benefits on one narrowly concentrated, identifiable group and impose costs on another narrowly concentrated, identifiable group. For example, when Congress approves subsidies to sugar beet farmers, it creates benefits for some farmers but imposes higher production costs on candy and soft-drink manufacturers. Under such circumstances, the process is likely to be dominated by organized interest activity because each side has a strong incentive to try to affect the outcome through the exercise of its political influence. The general public, however, is likely to remain relatively uninformed or indifferent about such issues.

Client Politics: Concentrated Benefits and Distributed Costs   When the benefits of a policy or program are concentrated but the costs are to be borne by everybody—or at least by a substantial portion of society—the political activity surrounding the issue is likely to be unbalanced. Organizations representing the beneficiaries will be vigorous in their support of the proposal, but since the costs are distributed at a low per capita rate over a large number of people (through price increases or generally higher taxes), the public has little incentive to organize in opposition. Examples of such policies are veterans' benefits and agricultural subsidies. Such policies tend to produce symbiotic relationships between the government officials who authorize and administer these programs and the beneficiaries or "clients," who work hard to maintain and expand their benefits. To the extent that these programs encounter any organized opposition at all, it is likely to come from consumer and taxpayer groups.

Entrepreneurial Politics: Distributed Benefits and Concentrated Costs   In some cases a policy will confer general (though perhaps barely noticeable) benefits on society as a whole or some large part of it at a cost to be borne by some small, identifiable segment of society. For example, automobile safety or antipollution regulations—and most other consumer protection laws, for that matter—are intended to improve the health and well-being of the public at large; however, such regulations may impose initially heavy costs on manufacturers. In some respects it is astonishing that policies of this kind ever get enacted. The beneficiaries, members of the public at large, are unlikely to mobilize in support of the policy. Those who would have to bear the costs, however, have a powerful incentive to mobilize in opposition. Moreover, the structure and procedures of the American political system tend to favor groups opposed to the adoption of a measure by giving them multiple opportunities to block, delay, or modify it.

In spite of these formidable obstacles, many policies of this type have been enacted over the past two decades, often because of the activity of a *policy entrepreneur*—someone in or out of government who, through adroit use of the media, can mobilize public support by appealing to widely shared values such as a concern about health, safety, or environmental preservation and by making opponents seem self-serving and careless of the public interest. While organized activity on such issues is often confined to groups representing the interests of the narrow publics that would have to bear the costs, in recent years policy entrepreneurs have frequently gotten support from organizations, such as the Consumers Union or Friends of the Earth, representing the interests of the broad publics that would benefit from the proposed policy. Sometimes the work of these policy entrepreneurs is facilitated by a scandal or a crisis. The thalidomide disaster in 1961 spurred passage of drug amendments the following year; costly oil spills off the coast of Santa Barbara, California, helped those pushing for passage of the Water Quality Improvement Act of 1970.

Unfortunately, as Wilson acknowledges, policy controversies cannot always be fitted neatly into this scheme. Wilson gives no criteria, numerical or otherwise, for determining before the fact whether the costs and benefits in a given political controversy are concentrated or distributed. Rather than considering distributed and concentrated costs or benefits as dichotomous categories, it seems more appropriate to think of them as anchor points on a continuum along which many intermediate cases might be arrayed. In addition, the distribution of costs and benefits is only one of a variety of factors that determine whether a particular interest will have organized representation in a policy controversy. As we shall demonstrate in the next two chapters, other factors that may make a difference include the adequacy of organizational resources, the presence of skillful and committed leadership, the ability to provide selective benefits, and the size of the organization's attentive constituency. Nevertheless, Wilson's scheme has great utility because of its capacity to explain how and why group activity is likely to configure around a given policy controversy. Moreover, it contains a lesson critical for understanding the role of organized interests in political conflict, namely, most political controversies do not involve a head-on collision between two well-organized and deeply committed organizations. On many issues only one side receives vigorous organized interest advocacy; representation of the opposing point of view comes, if at all, from other political actors rather than from interest organizations. On some issues, furthermore, organized interest activity is subsidiary to the role played by the parties, Congress, and the president.

SOME CAVEATS

Let us be clear as to what is *not* implied by the foregoing analysis of the contours of the Washington pressure community. First of all, inequalities in representation are not necessarily translated into proportional inequalities in influence. Contrary to the claims of the most ardent of the group theorists, organized interest politics is only one part of the sum total political conflict in Washington; government is no mere punching bag registering the relative strength of the blows from organizations to which it is subjected. At various times and under various circumstances, governmental institutions—the courts, Congress, the presidency, some agencies within the executive branch—have championed the interests of the less advantaged and broad publics, interests that are not well represented within the Washington pressure community. In addition, other kinds of citizen politics—both electoral and social movement politics—act as an engine for the representation of some of the interests that are less well served through pressure politics.

Moreover, in spite of the unambiguous tilt of the pressure community, it does not exclude broad publics and the disadvantaged altogether. A number of narrow but nonaffluent publics—for example, the elderly, the handicapped, and blacks—are represented in Washington by effective organizations that have helped to secure policy victories on their behalf. Similarly, the extensive environmental and consumer legislation of the late 1960s and early 1970s resulted, at least in part, from the presence and activity of new citizens' groups in Washington.

Furthermore, even when a group has no direct representation in Washington, it sometimes achieves secondary representation through the efforts of others working on their own behalf. For example, primary and secondary school students enjoy only minimal organizational representation in Washington; however, their interests are sometimes lent secondary advancement by teachers pursuing their own ends. Similarly, the interests of those needing public housing achieve some representation through the self-interested activities of the building industry. In short, a by-product of organized interest activity by the kinds of interests that are predominant in pressure politics may be the benefit of those less well represented. It is crucial to point out, however, that such secondary advocacy is not inevitable. Furthermore, secondary advocates, when they are available at all, make imperfect substitutes for direct participation in politics. While the unemployed—a group having little or no continuing, direct representation in Washington politics—are aided by the organized efforts of labor unions, mayors, and social service administrators, these surrogate advocates have their own sets of concerns that do not necessarily coincide fully with those of the unemployed. Hence, while the unemployed would surely be worse off if no one were active on their behalf, they would probably be better off if they also made their case themselves.[33]

A final point is that simply because business interests are well represented in Washington does not necessarily mean that business always speaks with one voice. On many issues, business organizations are in conflict. For example, defense procurement pits firms against one another as they vie for government contracts. Similarly, licensing of television stations by the Federal Communications Commission produces competition between companies. Sometimes industries are political antagonists. For example, banks and savings and loan associations frequently conflict over government regulation of the services each is permitted to provide. In other circumstances a single industry may be involved in a political controversy that is ignored by the business community at large.

[33] See Schlozman and Verba, *Injury to Insult,* Epilogue.

When the Federal Trade Commission threatened to regulate the advertising on children's television programs, the manufacturers of breakfast cereals were galvanized into action, but the manufacturers of, for example, automobiles and cigarettes had nothing to do with the conflict. In short, to assert the overrepresentation of business interests is not to presume the unanimity of business interests.

SUMMARY

This chapter has demonstrated that a lot of activity and many groups do not necessarily imply either universal representation of interests or equal representation of individuals. There are serious problems for democratic theory in reconciling the underlying principle of political equality (or one-person–one-vote) with representation of collective interests by organizations. Given the problems of unknown levels of skills and resources, variations in numbers of group members and size of agenda, the multiple dimensions of political conflict, the possibility of structured duplications of political representation, and the importance in Washington politics of organizations having no members in the ordinary sense, there is simply no way to specify in the abstract what an unbiased pressure community would look like.

Systematic empirical investigation, however, makes clear that the Washington pressure community is both narrow in scope and skewed. With respect to inclusiveness, not all potential interests are represented by organizations. In terms of skew, organization members are drawn disproportionately from the ranks of upper-status individuals—those with high levels of income, education, and occupational prestige. As for the kinds of interests represented, the number of organizations in the Washington pressure community is tilted heavily in favor of the advantaged, especially business, at the expense of the representation of broad publics and the disadvantaged. Surprisingly, in spite of the appearance of new groups representing the previously underrepresented, the imbalance of the pressure community seems to have become more pronounced in recent years. Thus, Schattschneider's observation that "the flaw in the [organized interest] heaven is that the heavenly chorus sings with an upper-class accent" continues to be accurate.[34] Although it is impossible to ascertain what an unbiased pressure community would look like, it is clear that, whatever the contours of that utopia, it would not resemble what we have.

[34]Schattschneider, *The Semisovereign People,* p. 35.

5

Organizational Resources for Political Action

Without sufficient resources interest groups cannot expect even to survive as organizations, much less to have an effect on political outcomes. This chapter discusses the resources—money, supporters, information, and so on—that a group can mobilize in order to maintain itself over time and to influence public policy. The discussion has two principal parts. First, we shall describe some of these resources, examining what makes them useful and what importance attaches to them. Second, we shall explain the role of political resources in enhancing or diminishing inequalities in collective political representation, focusing on both the minimum level of resources needed for a group to become active in Washington politics and the distribution of resources among various kinds of organizations.

This chapter is not meant to be a general statement on the nature of the resources useful in politics. Various political resources tend to be differentially useful to different political actors depending on the circumstances. Consequently, some political resources that carry substantial weight in certain political contexts—for example, a big city mayor's control of patronage jobs—are of much more limited utility in pressure politics.[1] As a matter of fact, different kinds of organizations need and value different levels and kinds of resources.

---

[1]There are, of course, exceptions. While jobs do not figure importantly in the array of resources that organized interests wield in Washington, it has been argued that policymakers in the executive branch are often induced to be less vigorous in their regulatory efforts because they do not want to foreclose opportunities for private sector employment after leaving government service.

The large membership that is the source of some organizations' strength would be an albatross to others; the budget that is ample for one organization would be scanty for another. Thus, the discussion that follows focuses not only on the range of political resources mobilized by interest groups but on their differential utility to various kinds of organizations.

MONEY AS AN ORGANIZATIONAL RESOURCE

The primary political resource that organizations command is, of course, money. What makes money important in politics is its convertibility—the fact that it can easily be transformed into other valued political resources. In short, money buys things. However, it should be made clear at the outset that while money is a crucial political asset, it is far from the only one; and organizations that are not well-heeled can often compensate for their lack of financial wherewithal with other resources—an appealing cause, a large membership, or a particularly skillful and dedicated staff.

One of the legacies of nineteenth-century lobbyists like Samuel Ward—who regaled politicians at nightly banquets of ham boiled in champagne and paid off the gambling losses of debt-ridden legislators—is the stereotype of the fat-cat lobbyist living opulently and spending lavishly.[2] It was not until the mid-1950s that political scientists, armed with the tools of systematic political inquiry, looked more carefully at the world of lobbying. What they found was that pressure groups fell "far short of the omnipotent, well-oiled machines that are portrayed in the political literature."[3] On the contrary, the groups studied "suffered from shortages of money, skilled personnel, information and time." Instead of lobbyists with bottomless purses inhabiting posh quarters, researchers found "only harassed men with tight budgets" operating out of "surprisingly modest" offices. In short, according to these researchers, "the image of lobbyists wallowing in ill-gotten and ill-spent lucre is one of the great myths of our time."

These observations were very influential in subsequent political analysis and became the basis of a counterorthodoxy. Although the stereotype of the well-heeled lobbyist has undoubtedly persisted in the popular mind, the reigning image in political science for the past two decades has been of the harassed Washington representative in slightly shabby quarters, always stretching a tight budget in order to make do.[4] This revised image is once more in need of

---

[2] Karl Schriftgiesser, *The Lobbyists* (Boston: Little, Brown, 1951), p. 14.

[3] This quote and all the others in this paragraph are from Raymond A. Bauer, Ithiel de Sola Pool, and Lewis Anthony Dexter, *American Business and Public Policy* (Chicago: Aldine, 1963). The five quotes may be found on pages 349, 341, 345, 343, and 341, respectively.

[4] As is not infrequently the case, when one stereotype is superseded, the opposing one is reified. The argument made in Bauer, Pool, and Dexter is more complex, more ambiguous, and in a sense more confusing than subsequent discussions based upon it would indicate. While their analysis did become the basis for the alternative image of the down-at-the-heels lobbyist, such characterizations overlook subtleties of their argument and exaggerate their conclusions.

reassessment. Although, as we shall see, groups vary widely in terms of the dollar resources they command, the notion that most lobbying organizations are financially hard-pressed simply does not accord with today's realities. Of course, there are still offices in Washington like the Environmental Policy Center's—with its peeling walls and splintering floors. Professional staffers, who handle most of their own typing and paperwork, jockey for workspace in cramped quarters amidst the clatter of typewriters and telephones. Much more common, however, are offices like du Pont's—roomy, thickly carpeted, handsomely furnished, and well-staffed with clerical help—or the Washington quarters of the United Auto Workers, located in an elegantly appointed nineteenth-century townhouse in a posh downtown neighborhood.

Of course, it should be made clear that, because our Washington sample was designed deliberately to select large and active organizations, we were presumably exposed to disproportionately few of the organizations that are hand-to-mouth operations. However, as Appendix A indicates, we oversampled precisely those kinds of organizations that are likely to feel short of resources (as is demonstrated later in the chapter). Without generalizing unnecessarily, we know first-hand that the portrait of the impoverished pressure group is far from universally applicable.

WHERE DOES THE MONEY COME FROM?

Groups organized for political action raise their money in a variety of ways. Corporations are in the enviable position of being able to finance their lobbying operations out of their own general revenues. Thus, when Ford Motor Co. decides that it wants to establish a formidable political presence in Washington, it merely needs to allocate in its budget whatever amount it chooses to spend for that purpose.

The financial problems of creating and maintaining a political presence in Washington are considerably more complicated for noncorporate interest groups. Most groups raise money from many sources—not just one source. When we talked with the Washington representatives in our sample, we inquired about the sources of financial support for their organizations. We showed respondents affiliated with organizations other than corporations a card listing eight possible funding sources and asked them to indicate the ones that account for 10 percent or more of their revenues. Table 5.1 lists these funding sources and shows for each the percentage of organizations that derive at least 10 percent of their total revenue from that particular source.

As these data indicate, virtually all noncorporate interest groups rely on dues contributed by individual and/or organizational members. Of course, they vary widely in the percentage of their annual revenues accounted for by membership dues. For example, the annual budget of the National Association of Manufacturers is almost entirely based on revenues from member dues.[5] By

---

[5]Karen DeW. Lewis, "NAM Turns Pragmatic in Opposing Federal Restraints on Industry," *National Journal,* June 1, 1972, p. 940.

Table 5.1   SOURCES OF INTEREST GROUP REVENUE

Source	Percentage of organizations receiving at least one-tenth of total revenue from each source			
	Trade associations	Unions	Citizens' groups	All organizations
Individual dues	60%	83%	60%	65%
Member organization dues	43	22	22	27
Individual gifts and donations	0	6	70	27
Foundation grants	0	0	30	15
Corporate gifts	0	0	22	13
Staff-generated revenue	43	6	56	41
Income from investments and endowments	27	11	13	18
Grants from the federal government	3	0	9	13
	(N = 30)	(N = 18)	(N = 23)	(N = 106)

Source: Washington Representatives Survey.

contrast, the annual dues of the almost 17,000 active members of the American Society of Hospital Pharmacists account for only 19 percent of that organization's annual budget.[6]

As the data in Table 5.1 indicate, some organizations—most of them citizens' groups—also rely heavily on monetary gifts and donations from individuals or corporations and on grants from foundations. The Sierra Club is a good example of an organization that receives such funds. For example, in 1982 the Sierra Club received over $5,725,000 in dues from its roughly 318,500 members. But in addition the Sierra Club received nearly $3.5 million in gifts from over 45,000 donors. Nearly 80 percent of those donations came in amounts of less than $50. Among the 460 donors whose gifts were in excess of $500 were corporations such as Burlington Northern Railroad, Exxon, Penn Central, and Time, Inc., as well as over 25 foundations.[7]

The ability of an organization to attract gifts and donations is enormously affected by the particular status it has been accorded under provisions of the Internal Revenue Code. For example, Section 501(c)(3) of the code exempts certain organizations from having to pay taxes and also allows individuals donating money to such organizations to deduct the amount of their donation from their taxable income. Among the groups eligible for this tax status are various not-for-profit organizations, such as religious groups, charities, literary and scientific organizations and groups committed to the prevention of

[6]"Proceedings of the 32nd Annual Session of the ASHP House of Delegates," *American Journal of Hospital Pharmacy,* August 1981, pp. 1193–1194.
[7]"Associates of the Sierra Club," *Sierra,* November–December 1982, p. 1377.

cruelty to children or animals. Naturally, this tax status has important political and organizational consequences. A group with 501(c)(3) status is more likely to get big contributions from donors who are seeking a tax deduction. Such a group is also permitted to receive grants from private foundations. Although 501(c)(3) status may thus constitute a vital financial resource, it also imposes some limitations on the activities of groups that have it. They are restricted in the amount of their activity that can be devoted to lobbying Congress, but are permitted to advocate positions before administrative agencies and to provide Congress with information on legislative proposals.[8]

Staff-generated revenues are another important source of organizational income. As shown in Table 5.1, citizens' groups and trade associations are especially likely to rely on such revenues for a significant portion of their budgets. (Professional societies also tend to draw substantial revenues from this source.) In all these cases, an important organizational function is the dissemination of various kinds of information to members about developments in the industry, profession, or policy area of mutual concern. The magazines, pamphlets, reports, informational booklets, and the like that are sold to members and the public enhance the organization's budget. Similarly, the conferences, meetings, seminars, and training sessions frequently held by trade associations and professional societies generate revenue.

A source of revenue for a few groups is income from financial investments and endowments. Organizations having extra resources beyond those needed for ongoing organizational activities are in a position to invest the surplus and, thus, enjoy added income. The American Medical Association, for example, brought in almost $4 million in 1978 from investment income alone.[9]

A final source of revenue for a few groups sprinkled among the various organizational types is the federal government.[10] The government rarely contributes money to the operating budget of an organization for its discretionary use; rather, federal money comes with strings attached. Usually, it must be used for the performance of specified functions, such as operating federally approved programs, collecting and evaluating data, or assisting the group's members in complying with federal law. For example, in 1981 the American Public Transit Association derived about 18 percent of its budget from federal money, most of it for research contracts to apply new technology to buses and rail-transit systems. And although the American Council on Education typi-

---

[8]Lest it seem as if organizations qualifying for 501(c)(3) status enjoy an enormous advantage, it should be recalled that corporations can deduct both trade association dues and lobbying expenses from their taxable income. For more on the political consequences of 501(c)(3) status—and on the *government's* occasional political manipulation of it—see Jeffrey Berry, *Lobbying for the People* (Princeton: Princeton University Press, 1977), pp. 45–55.

[9]"American Medical Association Financial Statements," *Journal of the American Medical Association* 24 (May 18, 1979): 2153.

[10]Jack L. Walker discusses federal government support for interest groups, and relates it to the emergence of many new organizations in "The Origins and Maintenance of Interest Groups in America," *American Political Science Review* 77 (1983): 390–406.

cally derives 30 to 40 percent of its annual operating income from federal sources, the use of those federal dollars is carefully restricted: most of it comes from the Defense Department for evaluating military courses for academic credit and from the State Department for the international exchange program the ACE operates for university professors.[11]

Interestingly, the small number of organizations receiving federal funds are scattered among various kinds of organizations.[12] For example, while only a small portion of the trade associations in our sample (3 percent) rely on federal funds for more than 10 percent of their budgets, some businesses and trade groups derive huge portions of their budgets from federal funds. In 1981, for example, the National Alliance of Business received $10.8 million of its $12.5 million budget from the federal government, and federal funds accounted for $760,000 of a $2.6 million budget for the National Savings and Loan League. Among civil rights and social action organizations, federal money accounts for a large portion of the budgets of the National Urban Coalition ($2.5 million of a roughly $5 million budget in 1981) and of the National Urban League ($18.2 million of $25.2 million in 1980), but less than 10 percent of the budget of the National Association for the Advancement of Colored People (NAACP). And whereas the Children's Defense Fund derives none of its budget from federal funds, the Planned Parenthood Federation of America gets half of its budget from federal sources.[13] In short, even organizations of similar type or with similar missions differ in the extent to which they rely on federal funding sources.

Direct-Mail Fund Raising

Many national membership organizations such as cause groups, ideological organizations, and consumer and environmental groups raise money by sending letters to hundreds of thousands of individuals deemed likely to be supportive of their work and likely to make a contribution to help finance it. This kind of direct-mail fund-raising effort has become particularly prominent in recent years both with the growth of political consulting firms that specialize in this kind of work and with the increased accessibility of high-speed computers that facilitate the maintenance of specialized mailing lists containing millions of names and addresses.

Typically, the first step for a group eager to raise money through a direct-mail campaign is to hire consultants and rent mailing lists. Consultants are

[11] Rochelle L. Stanfield, " 'Defunding the Left' May Remain Just Another Fond Dream of Conservatives," *National Journal*, August 1, 1981, pp. 1375–1377.

[12] We should note that the groups that rely most heavily on federal funds—organizations representing state and local governments—are not included in our sample. It is not uncommon for such organizations as the U.S. Conference of Mayors and the National Governors' Association to derive over half of their operating income from federal funds. See Stanfield, " 'Defunding the Left' May Remain Just Another Fond Dream of Conservatives," p. 1376.

[13] Ibid.

necessary because direct-mail fund raising is a business of slim profit margins and is best left to people who have the specialized expertise and equipment necessary to put out an effective mailing.[14] Perhaps the most important function the consultants perform is helping to select a fertile list or set of lists likely to generate the maximum response. The best lists ordinarily come from the membership rosters of other, similar interest groups; from the list of donors to particular political campaigns; and from the lists of subscribers to magazines having similar ideological leanings.

Although some organizations have been able to sustain themselves through direct-mail fund raising, the practice is far from a sure bet. The upfront costs of prospecting for new members and new contributors are enormous; both hiring consultants and renting mailing lists are expensive. Consequently, it can be several years before direct-mail appeals become profitable to a group, and some organizations never recover from having invested large amounts of seed money in what turn out to be unfruitful ventures. For example, later in the chapter we shall see that a fledgling organization, the Center for Strategic Petroleum Understanding and Research (SPUR), spent thousands of dollars on direct-mail consultants and test mailings before it became clear that the organization's cause was not one to induce potential donors to open up their wallets.

Mailing for Dollars: An Experiment In order to trace the paths connecting organizations that share mailing lists, we decided to run a small experiment. We enrolled Daniel Aaron Schlozman—who, at the tender age of four months, had not yet had the good fortune to receive any political junk mail—in a number of different organizations that use direct-mail solicitation. We used slightly different versions of his name—Daniel A., D. Aaron, Dan, and so on— in enrolling him in four conservative organizations (the National Right to Life Committee, the National Rifle Association, the Conservative Caucus, and the National Right to Work Committee) and four liberal ones (the Sierra Club, Common Cause, National Abortion Rights Action League, and Handgun Control). In spite of a cover letter giving clear directions to enroll young Mr. Schlozman as a member and including the required fee, the last two organizations never seem to have recorded his membership. Hence, the paragraphs that follow describe the avalanche of mail generated by six of the original eight organizations.

Our experiment confirmed the common wisdom about direct-mail fund raising. Danny received a torrent of mail. Over the next eighteen months his six memberships were responsible for 248 pieces of mail—some 18 pounds worth! In addition to 135 requests for money, this mail included newsletters, magazines, petitions to sign, and preprinted postcards to dispatch to lawmakers in Washington. Although the conservative organizations have a reputation for

---

[14]On direct-mail consulting firms, see Larry Sabato, *The Rise of Political Consultants* (New York: Basic Books, 1981).

using direct-mail techniques with particular sophistication, as the following figures make clear, the liberal and conservative organizations stuffed the mail-box with nearly equal vigor:

	Pieces of mail sent by organization
Sierra Club	35
Common Cause	32
Conservative Caucus	36
National Right to Life	35
National Rifle Association	33
National Right to Work Committee	14
	185

In addition to the 185 pieces of mail from the six organizations of which he was a member, Danny received a total of 63 pieces of mail from 32 other organizations that rented or bought mailing lists including his name. Three of the six organizations—the Conservative Caucus, the Sierra Club, and Common Cause—were responsible for all but two of these pieces. Table 5.2 lists the organizations that rented or purchased lists originally owned by one of these three organizations. As one would expect, there is a great deal of ideological compatibility among the organizations using each of the listings.

The contents of this direct-mail bonanza were also of interest. Most of the envelopes were carefully designed to reduce the likelihood that they would simply be tossed into the wastebasket unopened. The letters themselves were typically long, emotion-laden appeals intended to make the recipient afraid or angry by describing some person or group actively working against the interests of the soliciting group and, presumably, against the recipient himself. (We should also note that when Danny failed to renew his memberships, he received personal phone calls from most of the organizations urging him to renew.)

INFORMATION, EXPERTISE, AND SKILLS

Money may be the preeminent political resource, but it is surely not the only one. In a technological age, several types of political, technical, and organizational skills are critical for effective political action. An organized interest must, first of all, be on top of the political situation. This involves, at the outset, an understanding of government as it exists on paper: which institutions and governmental organizations have authority or responsibility with respect to particular policy areas; what laws and regulations are presently in place; and so on. It encompasses, moreover, an understanding of the relevant political realities: which individuals and groups are lined up in support of and in opposition to various proposals; which of them are powerful; and how much they care.

Table 5.2   WHO SHARES MAILING LISTS?

National Conservative Caucus membership produced mail from:
 Americans Against Union Control of Government
 American Association of Retired People
 Association of Concerned Taxpayers
 Committee for the Survival of a Free Congress
 Congressional Club Foundation [Jesse Helms]
 Conservatives against Liberal Legislation
 Leadership Action
 National Tax Limitation Committee
 Ray Shamie for U.S. Senate
 Senator Orrin Hatch Election Committee
 Taxpayers Education Lobby
 Young Americans for Freedom

Sierra Club membership produced mail from:
 Barney Frank for Congress
 Campaign to Save the Massachusetts Bottle Bill
 Committee for the Future of America [Walter Mondale]
 Committee to Re-elect Senator Kennedy
 Defenders of Wildlife
 Environmental Defense Fund
 Greenpeace, USA
 National Audubon Society
 Nature Conservancy
 Solar Lobby

Common Cause membership produced mail from:
 Campaign to Save the Massachusetts Bottle Bill
 Cousteau Society
 League of Women Voters
 Linus Pauling Institute of Science and Medicine
 National Association for the Advancement of Colored People
 National Organization for Women
 National Women's Health Network
 Public Citizen
 Simon Wisenthal Center
 Union of Concerned Scientists

For example, if lobbyists for the American Hospital Association want to influence congressional action on Medicare reimbursement policy, they must understand (among many other things) how the House Ways and Means Committee operates and how its members are likely to align themselves on the issue; what is the policy stance of the Health Care Financing Administration (the executive agency responsible for Medicare administration); how the nation's Blue Cross plans (and other Medicare fiscal intermediaries) feel about a change in reimbursement policy; what is the political strategy of the Federation of American Hospitals (the hospital association which represents for-profit institutions); and what position (if any) the American Medical Association has staked out on the issue and whether it will jump into the fray.

Equally important is technical expertise: the technical training and information needed to comprehend the substance of a particular policy area or problem, including the logic and dimensions of the problem itself, its multiple causes and effects, and the probable ramifications of various proposed solutions. To return to the example used above, if lobbyists for the American Hospital Association wish to have a meaningful role in shaping federal policies to contain rising hospital costs, they must be thoroughly conversant with the intricacies of medical economics, the likely consequences of specific cost-control proposals, and the relative merits of state regulation as well as the incentives that govern the behavior of health professionals in hospitals. Not only does such information make it easier for an organized interest to define its goals and ascertain the consequences of various policy proposals, but it is also an important resource in approaching public officials. In order to design sound programs, policymakers need technical information from organizations. The organization that is armed with accurate, detailed, and pertinent information will find officials more responsive, especially if that information has been framed so as to place it in the most politically congenial light.

Of course, it is not sufficient for an organized interest to command information and expertise; it is vital to be politically skilled as well. Any catalogue of such skills would be seemingly endless. It would include an ability to frame issues in such a way as to attract allies and divide opponents, a sense of timing, a facility in marshaling facts and presenting arguments, and a nose for assessing the strengths and vulnerabilities of one's antagonists.

Personnel

There are two ways for an organization to acquire these various kinds of skills and knowledge: one is to hire as staff members persons who possess them; the other is to retain them from the outside. The offices of the political organizations in Washington vary widely in the size and sophistication of their staffs. Two of the larger Washington operations are the U.S. Chamber of Commerce and the American Association of Retired Persons, both of which have full-time Washington staffs of over 400 persons. Most Washington offices of organized interests are more modestly staffed, however. The Washington operation of Bethlehem Steel has a staff of about 30. The American Trial Lawyers Association has a Washington staff of two—a director and an assistant, who does everything from gathering statistics and information to typing reports and letters. Furthermore, some organizations rely heavily on unpaid volunteers to help run their operations; others rely exclusively on a paid staff of persons experienced in government relations work.

Hiring people with talent, skill, and experience is expensive. Some organizations are in a much better financial position than others to pay attractive salaries. As shown by the following 1983 and 1984 figures, these salaries range widely:[15]

President, Chamber of Commerce of the U.S.	$275,000
Executive Vice-President, American Medical Association	$216,723
President, American Petroleum Institute	$199,166
President, International Brotherhood of Teamsters	$173,056
President, Air Line Pilots Association	$163,701
President, National Association of Broadcasters	$127,000
President, AFL-CIO	$110,000
President, National Education Association	$ 61,423
President, National Organization for Women	$ 49,000
President, Common Cause	$ 48,539

These figures confirm our discussion in Chapter 2 about the relative financial sacrifices made by many of those who work for citizens' groups, social welfare and civil rights organizations, and the like. In order to attract talented professionals, such organizations must rely on a commitment to the cause as an incentive, since the financial incentives they are able to offer are, by Washington's standards, relatively weak.

Hired Professionals   The other way that organizations can acquire the skills and expertise needed to function effectively in Washington politics is to hire outsiders to assist them. There are several kinds of outside professionals, having different kinds of professional experience, whose skills can be purchased.[16] There is no single form of organizational base for these "hired guns." Some work out of law firms; others out of public relations firms of varying sizes; and still others hang out their own shingles as political consultants or public affairs representatives. In terms of the array of services they provide, these various kinds of government relations firms range widely from those specializing in a single type of assistance (such as expertise in direct-mail fund raising) to those having a complete repertory of public affairs capabilities.

[15] Figures for Teamsters Union and AFL-CIO are taken from "Teamsters' President Earned Nearly $500,000 for 4 Posts," *New York Times,* June 20, 1984, p. A20. All others are from Robert D. Hershey, Jr., "Some Lobbyists and Their Salaries," *New York Times,* November 8, 1983, p. A24. Copyright © 1983/1984 by the New York Times Company. Reprinted by permission.

[16] Political scientists have paid relatively little systematic attention to these kinds of government affairs professionals. Thus, we are unable to draw conclusions as to whether it makes a difference for the political process if the interests of organizations are represented by such outside specialists rather than organization government affairs staff.

On Washington lawyers see Mark Green, *The Other Government: The Unseen Power of Washington Lawyers* (New York: Grossman, 1975), and Albert R. Hunt, "The Power Brokers," *Wall Street Journal,* March 23, 1982, pp. 1, 23. For an excellent analysis of the Washington public relations world a quarter century ago, see Stanley Kelley, Jr., *Professional Public Relations and Political Power* (Baltimore: Johns Hopkins University Press, 1956). For a contemporary journalistic account, see Michael Gordon, "The Image Makers in Washington—PR Firms Have a Natural Home," *National Journal,* May 31, 1980, p. 884.

Lawyers are among the most numerous and important of these outside professionals. Whether they work for one of the long-established Washington firms like Covington and Burling, for one of the increasing numbers of out-of-town firms that have set up offices in the capital in recent years, or for one of the "full-service lobbying firms" that concentrate virtually exclusively on government relations work, lawyer-lobbyists do little of the kind of legal work that is ordinarily associated with the practice of law. A lawyer-lobbyist is more likely to draft a bill than a will and more likely to spend time in a Senate committee hearing room than in a courtroom. Lawyer-lobbyists are called upon to perform a variety of tasks for their clients. Among the most important is reconnaissance, the monitoring of government activity for any developments that might bear on the client's interests. Also fundamental are the many activities—drafting bills and regulations, composing statements and testimony, assembling research and technical data, gaining access to key policymakers, talking with government officials, planning political strategy, and so on—that are associated with direct attempts to influence government. They may also be involved in setting up and running a political action committee for the client.

The functions that public relations agencies perform for their clients are not altogether different from those of the lawyer-lobbyists. With the obvious exceptions of strictly legal work (courtroom litigation, representation before administrative law judges, and the like), the big public relations firms provide a full range of lobbying services. In addition to the usual stock of lobbying activities, public relations firms offer their clients a much wider array of services—for example, orchestrating grass roots political efforts, conducting opinion surveys, handling press relations, arranging social events and receptions, and putting together advertising campaigns.

The activities of these hired guns, then, are substantially similar to those of the salaried staff members of organizations. In view of this similarity, we might be led to inquire why organizations hire them. In the case of organizations without their own Washington offices, the answer is clear: these professionals serve as a surrogate Washington office, performing the functions a Washington office would perform. It is, however, less obvious why an organization that already has an office in the capital (often a large, professionally staffed one) retains outside government affairs assistance. Although our interviews with Washington lobbyists produced no systematic data on this question, they did furnish us with some insight.

There are, of course, many different reasons for employing an outside professional in government relations. Sometimes clients turn to knowledgeable outside lobbyists in order to supplement their own substantive expertise about the matter at hand. Moreover, since lobbying always involves the accumulation and expenditure of political capital, an organization may retain outsiders if it has already gone to the well too many times with a key policymaker and is not in a position to ask for another private meeting or another favor. A "hired gun" brings to the task his own supply of capital to be spent.

It seems that the primary reason that organizations need the services of outsiders, however, is to gain *access* to those members of Congress or executive branch officials to whom the client does not have easy entree. Even organizations that have their own well-known and well-connected lobbyists seldom have close relations with all the public officials who may have a decision-making role on a particular issue. Thus, to make contact with officials who otherwise might not be reached, they turn to an outside lobbyist who can either arrange for the desired meeting or personally present the organization's case. The many former government officials—representatives, senators, and cabinet officers as well as lesser bureaucrats and staffers—who become government relations professionals are particularly likely to have extensive contacts and, thus, to be able to offer their clients access to key policymakers. The celebrity status of these former government officials—and other well-known superlobbyists—can be helpful in making a case both to policymakers and, more importantly, their staff.

Organizations vary in the degree to which they have the need and the budgetary wherewithal to hire various kinds of specialists and professionals. To explore the matter more fully, we asked the respondents in our survey whether their organizations have on their staffs, or hire from the outside, various kinds of experts. The results of that inquiry are presented in Table 5.3. Virtually all the organizations hire legal expertise: three-quarters include lawyers on the organization staff; four-fifths (many of which also have staff lawyers) hire outside attorneys. Over three-quarters have access to public relations consultants, more frequently from within the staff than from the outside.

Table 5.3 also makes clear that citizens' groups are less likely than other kinds of organizations to retain public relations experts. As discussed in Chapter 7, citizens' groups are particularly likely to pursue political strategies involving direct appeals to the public. In view of their reliance on such strategies, their relative neglect of this particular sort of expertise for hire is perhaps surprising. As shall be demonstrated later in the chapter, citizens' groups feel strapped financially. Their relative lack of reliance on public relations consultants thus may reflect the absence of resources rather than the absence of need for such expertise. Finally, about one-third of the groups hire pollsters and direct-mail fund-raising specialists. Not surprisingly, it is the citizens' groups that are most likely to employ the latter kind of expert.

MEMBERSHIP

An important resource for some political organizations is membership. While an attentive and supportive constituency can be a crucial asset, membership has some special characteristics as a political resource: with respect to money in politics, the more the better; with respect to members, the situation is more complicated. Unlike a small budget, a small membership may be preferable to a large one under certain circumstances.

Table 5.3 EMPLOYMENT OF EXPERTS

	Corporations	Trade associations	Unions	Citizens' groups	All organizations
Percentage of organizations having on staff:					
Lawyers	85%	79%	74%	67%	75%
Public relations consultants	72	61	63	46	64
Pollsters	11	3	16	8	12
Specialists in direct-mail fund raising	7	7	47	44	23
Percentage of organizations hiring from the outside:					
Lawyers	87	79	94	76	80
Public relations consultants	34	54	56	33	41
Pollsters	21	30	50	33	30
Specialists in direct-mail fund raising	7	4	28	73	22
Percentage of organizations having access to (either on staff or from outside):					
Lawyers	96	100	95	88	94
Public relations consultants	78	79	74	67	76
Pollsters	31	30	47	38	36
Specialists in direct-mail fund raising	14	7	58	78	33

Source: Washington Representatives Survey.

Membership Size Contradictory expectations might be posited with respect to the value of a large membership as a political resource. On the one hand, a large membership can be an important organizational resource in several ways. First, large numbers of people can pool their time, energy, information, money, and contacts and thereby transform meager individual resources into significant collective ones. In addition, a large membership confers greater legitimacy on the demands an organization makes of public officials. Not surprisingly, the president and members of Congress are more likely to listen seriously to an organization that represents 100,000 persons than to one that represents 100 persons. Furthermore, if a group's members are distributed across many congressional districts, it will be able to make legitimate demands on a broad range of public officials and, therefore, increase its influence.

On the other hand, a small membership can be a useful resource. Economist Mancur Olson holds that because of what is called the "free rider problem," rational individuals will join large groups only under certain specified conditions.[17] According to this logic, problems of organizational maintenance are considerably greater for large rather than small groups. Since Olson's theory is discussed at length in Chapter 6, there is no reason to elaborate here. For the moment, let it suffice to assert that Mancur Olson's formal theory leads to the conclusion that a large constituency is an organizational burden.

A few groups do deliberately limit membership in the expectation that exclusivity begets prestige. The Business Roundtable, for example, zealously limits its membership to some 200 chief executive officers of the nation's largest commercial enterprises. The selectivity of this membership roster no doubt adds to the organization's aura (or at least the Roundtable thinks it does). An unusual organization that draws distinction, if not great strength, from its purposely limited size is the Boone and Crockett Club. Started in 1887 by Theodore Roosevelt, the Boone and Crockett Club is the nation's oldest society devoted to wildlife conservation. As one of its brochures indicates, regular voting membership in the club is limited under its bylaws to "one hundred big game hunters of the highest ethical caliber . . . [each of whom] is required to have taken in 'fair chase' at least one adult male individual of each of three of the various species of North American big game animals."[18]

Cohesion   It is certainly preferable for an organization to have a united, cohesive membership rather than a factious membership beset by quarrels and squabbles. A cohesive membership frees an organization from having to devote time and other resources to the resolution of disputes. Moreover, having a cohesive membership places an organization in a strengthened position in the eyes of governmental policymakers. That is, cohesion provides an organization with a legitimacy that is lacking when an organization's members are conspicuously at odds with one another over public policy issues.

Density   One final characteristic of an organization's membership that affects its usefulness as a political resource is its density—that is, the proportion of its potential constituency that is mobilized. It is clear that enhanced density confers political legitimacy and thus increases political effectiveness. Policymakers are more likely to be persuaded by a group that represents a substantial portion

---

[17]Mancur Olson, Jr., *The Logic of Collective Action* (Cambridge: Harvard University Press, 1965).

[18]"The Boone and Crockett Club: What It Is and What It Stands For," undated brochure, p. 1.

of its potential membership than by one that mobilizes a smaller share of its possible supporters. For example, the National Organization for Women is a large group by Washington standards, having over 150,000 members; however, its political effectiveness is hampered by the fact that its membership constitutes such a small share of American women.

REPUTATION

An organization's reputation for credibility and trustworthiness and for power is among its most important resources. A reputation for being credible and trustworthy is especially critical for those organizations whose representatives have direct contact with government officials. Insofar as an organization ordinarily buttresses its case with facts, and insofar as public officials rely upon such information in formulating policy, it is vital to an organization that policymakers regard its recommendations and supporting evidence as being credible and worthy of trust. It is certainly a commonplace among Washington lobbyists that few things will damage a group's cause so much as a reputation for playing fast and loose with the facts. Furthermore, other political actors inside and outside government must know that the organization plays by the rules of the game—that it does not engage in illegal activities, that it keeps its commitments, and that it is honest and forthright in its dealings with others.

A different kind of politically useful reputation is a reputation for being powerful. Confronted with a reputedly powerful opponent, government officials or activists in other private organizations may reason that it is folly to waste their own resources for little or no gain. Hence, they may choose to refrain from doing battle at all or, at least, decide to shape their own positions to give the least offense to the allegedly formidable antagonist. What makes a reputation for power so valuable, then, is that an organization enjoying it can influence political outcomes without expending resources. In short, an organization thought to be powerful can often enjoy the benefits of power without having to exercise it.[19]

WHICH RESOURCES ARE VALUED?

This chapter has elaborated at some length the kinds of resources that an interest group involved in political activity might find helpful in influencing policy outcomes, but very little has been said about their relative importance. The data from our Washington representatives survey can help in investigating which ones of the many possible political resources are deemed particularly important by Washington representatives of organized interests. Keeping in mind the degree to which different political resources are of differential impor-

[19]Matthew A. Crenson discusses this logic and applies it to the issue of air pollution in *The Un-Politics of Air Pollution* (Baltimore: Johns Hopkins Press, 1971).

tance to different political actors in different political settings, we compiled a list of eight resources that we expected to be generally relevant for private organizations in politics. These eight are:

A large membership
A large budget
Control over technical information and expertise
Well-known and respected leaders
A reputation for being credible and trustworthy
A wide circle of contacts
Strategically placed allies
An appealing cause

We asked our respondents to look at the list and tell us, first, which two of the eight are most important to their particular organizations and, next, which two are least important to their organizations. The results of that inquiry are given in Table 5.4. A reputation for being credible and trustworthy is unambiguously in first place. Eighty-one percent of those interviewed chose a reputation for credibility as one of the two most important resources to their organizations. In last place, equally unambiguously, is a large budget. A paltry 3 percent of our respondents rated it as one of the two most important, and 56 percent considered one of the two least important. The other six resources are clustered together surprisingly closely in the collective estimation of our respondents.

Table 5.5 permits further investigation of the relative value placed on various resources by the four kinds of private groups for which we have suffi-

Table 5.4 RELATIVE IMPORTANCE OF ORGANIZATIONAL RESOURCES

	Percentage of respondents citing resource as:			
	Most important	No mention	Least important	
A reputation for being credible and trustworthy	81%	18	1	= 100%
A wide circle of contacts	24%	67	9	= 100%
Well-known and respected leaders	21%	67	12	= 100%
Control over technical information and expertise	25%	58	17	= 100%
An appealing cause	14%	70	16	= 100%
Strategically placed allies	11%	69	20	= 100%
A large membership	21%	37	42	= 100%
A large budget	3%	40	56	= 99%

Source: Washington Representatives Survey.

Table 5.5 IMPORTANCE OF ORGANIZATIONAL RESOURCES BY ORGANIZATION TYPE

Net evaluations of resources (percent "most important" minus percent "least important")

	Reputation	Contacts	Leaders	Expertise	Cause	Allies	Membership	Budget
All Organizations	80%	15%	9%	8%	1%	−10%	−20%	−54%
Corporations	88	31	6	20	−6	2	−62	−57
Trade associations	80	17	3	−9	−3	0	−23	−37
Unions	63	10	5	−22	12	−22	32	−53
Citizens' groups	68	0	12	12	20	−32	16	−68

Source: Washington Representatives Survey.

cient numbers in our sample to make possible more intense analysis. Table 5.5 presents figures on the importance of the various resources to corporations, trade associations, unions, and citizens' groups.[20] Each number on the table represents the difference between the percentage of respondents indicating that a particular resource is most important to their organizations and the percentage indicating that it is least important. Consider, for example, the fifth column, summarizing the evaluations of the relative importance of an appealing cause as a political resource. Twenty-four percent of those associated with citizens' groups indicated that an appealing cause is one of their two most important resources; 4 percent indicated that it is one of their least important. The net figure, then, is 20. Only 6 percent of the corporate representatives, on the other hand, considered an appealing cause to be one of their most important resources, while 12 percent considered it to be among the least important. The net figure for corporations, then, is -6.

What is most striking about the figures in Table 5.5 is the similarity among the various kinds of organizations. With a single, understandable exception, there seems to be a rough congruence among the various categories of organizations with respect to the emphasis they give to different kinds of political resources. All of them value credibility and denigrate money. The sole exception is the assessment of the importance of a large membership. Corporations (which are of course not even membership groups) and, to a lesser extent, trade associations (which traditionally have relatively few members) deem it of little importance; on the other hand, unions and citizens' groups (which traditionally claim to represent the great mass of ordinary citizens) value a large membership relatively highly. In short, then, organization representatives in Washington echo Shakespeare's famous lines in *Othello.* Note that it is, of course, the villainous Iago who intones piously:

Who steals my purse steals trash; 'tis something, nothing;
'Twas mine, 'tis his, and has been slave to thousands
But he that filches from me my good name
Robs me of that which not enriches him,
And makes me poor indeed.

Othello, Act III, Scene iii

[20]Given the very small number of civil rights and social welfare organizations among Washington-based interest groups, it is not surprising that our sample contained only eight such organizations. Still, especially in view of some of the themes that will be pursued later in the chapter, it is unfortunate that there are too few cases of representatives of the poor and racial minorities to permit further analysis.

POLITICAL RESOURCES AND THE SHAPE
OF THE PRESSURE COMMUNITY

The discussion in Chapter 4 of the contours of the Washington pressure community left out one piece of the puzzle. We argued there that in terms of the private organizations on the Washington scene, some potential political groups are simply not represented at all; others, most notably the disadvantaged and diffuse publics, are clearly underrepresented, while the well-off, especially businesses, are overrepresented. However, such a distribution is not necessarily incompatible with the egalitarian principle of one-person–one-vote as long as the total group-based input for any citizen is equal to that for any other and as long as the distribution of political resources among organizations reflects the same principle of equality among individuals. Chapter 4 demonstrated both how unlikely it is that individuals would actually enjoy equality of political input and how the structure of the representation of business interests renders it peculiarly likely that they would achieve multiple representation. Now we are in a position to sketch in the puzzle's missing piece—the role of political resources in enhancing or diminishing these inequalities in collective political representation.

Fielding a Shoestring Washington Operation

One way to understand more fully the limited scope of the Washington pressure community is to draw an analogy between the representation of collective interests in Washington and the pursuit of pecuniary gain in a capitalist economy. In both cases a pivotal question concerns the height of the barriers to entry into the market.[21] If the threshold level of resources needed for effective participation is too high, then those with few resources will be frozen out of the competition and the scope of the pressure system will be narrowed. Consequently, it is important to know the minimum start-up costs for a group of collectively interested individuals wishing to become active in Washington politics and to ascertain whether those costs are prohibitive to groups attempting to enter the political marketplace.

It is probably impossible to specify a precise dollar figure for the minimum needed by a group wishing to establish an ongoing presence in Washington politics. However, we can take an initial cut at understanding the level of resources needed by such a group by taking a closer look at the National Low Income Housing Coalition, the organization of the 175 in our survey sample that manages on the lowest budget.[22] Admittedly, our sample was deliberately

---

[21] Robert A. Dahl discusses the concept of a threshold level of resources needed for entry into politics in *Who Governs?* (New Haven: Yale University Press, 1961), p. 238.

[22] Information about the Low Income Housing Coalition culled from Rochelle L. Stanfield, "Beleaguered Lobbyists for the Poor—Taking Allies Where They Can Find Them," *National Journal,* September 20, 1980, pp. 1556–1560, and by the same writer, "Cushing Dolbeare Champions

designed to tap organizations that are large and active; therefore, the lowest-budget organization in our sample is, presumably, far from the most impecunious in the capital.

Still, the National Low Income Housing Coalition, a bipartisan advocacy organization concerned about low-income housing issues, gives every indication of being a shoestring operation. With the aid of a computer to manage the finances and keep track of the list of over 1500 supporting local and national groups, and second-hand duplicating and collating machines, Cushing Dolbeare, the founder and president, and Kate Crawford operate the Coalition out of an office in a converted garage adjacent to Dolbeare's house on Capitol Hill. Because their secretary left when they could no longer pay her salary, they do all their own office work. In their circular for May 28, 1981—a mimeographed document that makes the average college syllabus look like an invitation to the White House—they apologize for the ten-week lapse since their previous communication and explain that they do not have the cash to indulge in any but the most urgent communications. In short, then, if the National Low Income Housing Coalition is in any way typical, surprisingly little is needed in the way of financial resources to establish an effective presence in Washington. It would seem that, given sufficient enthusiasm and perseverance, virtually any group could locate an empty garage, wheedle some cast-off office equipment, and—presto!—be in business as an interest group.

Unfortunately, the matter is not concluded so easily. Most nascent groups do not have a Cushing Dolbeare at the helm—willing to devote 60 hours a week, essentially without pay, to a cause about which she cares deeply. It is not simply her persistence but, according to others in Washington, her persuasiveness and her knowledge (the fruit of over thirty years in the housing field) that render Dolbeare so effective. Thus, Dolbeare brings—more or less as a volunteer—the kinds of skills and expertise as a lobbyist that ordinarily can be purchased only at a very high price. What is more, Dolbeare lives in Washington, which means that she can press her case without having to pay large sums for long-distance phone calls, airplane trips, or high-priced Washington-based counsel or consultants. Clearly, then, propinquity to national political life is another money-saving resource. Finally, for all the spartan surroundings and skeletal staffing, the Coalition's budget for 1981 was roughly $61,000. While such a figure represents mere pocket change to an organization like the American Petroleum Institute with its annual budget of nearly $50 million, $61,000 is a very substantial sum to, say, an emerging welfare rights or migrant workers' organization.[23]

Low-Income Assistance," *The Washington Post,* March 6, 1982, pp. E15–16, as well as various Coalition pamphlets and newsletters and our interview with Dolbeare.

[23] API budget figure cited in "Recession Creams the Lobbyists," *Business Week,* December 13, 1982, p. 25. Budget figure for the National Low Income Housing Coalition supplied by Cushing Dolbeare. In a telephone interview January 14, 1983, Dolbeare indicated that increased member-

It is unrealistic to conclude from Cushing Dolbeare's example that $61,000, an empty garage, a creaky mimeograph machine, and two very able and selfless individuals constitute the minimum for entry into the national political marketplace. Even if this brief case study cannot be used to affix a price tag on collective participation in Washington politics, it does illustrate something about the degree to which the political system is permeable. Most important, there are many resources—ranging from enthusiasm, skills and experience to an appealing program and proximity to Washington politics—that can help compensate for the absence of cash. Cushing Dolbeare manages on such limited finances because she mobilizes such intangible resources so effectively as a substitute.

Starting a Washington Operation: Organization as a Resource   One resource that can offset lack of money is organization itself. It requires far fewer material resources for an established, but apolitical, organization to enter politics than for a nascent group of individuals to form an organization for the purpose of coordinating joint political activity. An organization that already has a functioning office, a dues-paying membership, an up-to-date mailing list, and an experienced staff—in short, an apparatus readily diverted to political tasks—can get into the business of political influence far more cheaply than a group of individuals starting from scratch. A number of organizations in our sample were able to maintain quite comfortable Washington offices on budgets little higher than Dolbeare's. The reason is that the organizational maintenance tasks that consume so much time and money for Dolbeare and Crawford—communicating with members, maintaining a mailing list, keeping the books, and so on—are handled elsewhere, at the organizations' headquarters. Thus, for an ongoing organization the marginal costs of mobilizing for politics are relatively low.

For a newly emergent organization, however, the start-up costs are considerably higher. Consider, for example, the brief history of the Center for the Study of Petroleum Understanding and Research (SPUR).[24] In 1980 Ira Nerkin, then a young lawyer with the Consumer Protection Division of the Federal Trade Commission, was concerned that the inadequacy of the American strategic petroleum reserve rendered the United States vulnerable to another disruption in the international petroleum supply—just as it had during the Arab oil

---

ship contributions had raised their 1982 budget well beyond its 1981 level, permitting Dolbeare and Lawson to cut back on the outside consulting they had been doing to support the organization and, wondrously, to contemplate moving the Coalition out of Dolbeare's garage and into an honest-to-goodness office. [Rochelle L. Stanfield ("Dolbeare Champions Assistance," p. E16) quoted a 1982 budget figure of $142,000 for the Coalition; Dolbeare indicated that she did not know the source of that figure and placed the 1982 budget at nearer to $113,000.]

[24]Information about SPUR taken from personal interviews with SPUR's founder and from "Here's a Man Who Believes in a Strategic Oil Reserve," *Energy Daily*, April 24, 1981 and *Inside D.O.E.,* May 15, 1981.

boycott of the winter of 1973–74. Nerkin, no stranger either to Washington politics or to public interest efforts, decided to found a citizens' group to press for an increase in the amount of petroleum stockpiled for strategic purposes. Having raised sufficient seed money from private sources, he established an office on Capitol Hill, hired a small staff, and retained expert talent to advise him on the use of direct-mail techniques. However, when his efforts generated too little support to sustain his young organization, he was forced to close up shop before SPUR's first birthday.

The example of Nerkin's efforts to do something about a strategic oil reserve is clearly an instructive one. What is not clear, however, is how general is the phenomenon we have described. When an organization like SPUR disappears, it leaves barely a trace. Therefore, it is impossible to ascertain how many organizational efforts end up in failure for lack of sufficient financial resources. Even more to the point, it is impossible to judge how many embryonic groups lacking Nerkin's experience and his access to seed money never even get to the point of forming an organization. Because we cannot locate such nascent but unsuccessful organizations, we cannot measure the degree to which inadequate resources inhibit group formation. Still, the fate of SPUR makes clear that the barriers to entry to political competition are sufficiently high as to render the pressure community exclusive. In other words, the scope of the pressure community is narrowed by the high threshold of resources necessary for involvement in Washington politics.

The Distribution of Political Resources

We are, of course, interested in skew as well as in inclusiveness. That is, we are interested in knowing not only which groups are frozen out of the pressure community by virtue of their lack of resources but also how the distribution of resources among political associations articulates with the inequalities of representation discussed in Chapter 4.

Comparing Resources   At least with respect to tangible resources like budget and staff, it should be a relatively straightforward task to make comparisons among organizations. After all, political scientists are constantly making comparisons to the effect that "Representative Green is more powerful—more politically savvy, more persuasive, or whatever—than Representative Gray," comparisons that can be neither quantified nor verified. Even if comparisons of skill and experience are risky, people and dollars at least can be counted. Therefore, it should be possible to map with considerable accuracy the distribution of such tangible resources among organizations. Alas, although we went to no little trouble to ask the respondents in our Washington representatives survey about the size of their organizations' budgets and staff, we learned that it is very difficult to make comparisons among organizations with respect to resources because the dimensions of the tasks to be accomplished with those resources vary so substantially.[25]

Most importantly, in several respects the volume of the political undertaking varies tremendously from organization to organization. This is, in part, a function of the wide dispersion among organizations in the length of their political agendas. As discussed in Chapter 3, organized interests range from single-issue groups like abortion opponents, on one hand, to multi-issue organizations like the peak business and labor associations, on the other.

Clearly, a group that fights many battles spreads its resources more thinly than one that engages in less frequent political conflict. This places consumer and, to a slightly lesser extent, environmental groups at a comparative disadvantage. With the exception of a handful of organizations like the Citizens Communications Center, the Aviation Consumer Action Project, the National Association of Railroad Passengers, and the National Association of Insured Persons, all of which represent consumers of specific products or services, most consumer groups—for example, Consumers Union or Public Citizen—are all-purpose; that is, they represent the interests of those who use a stunning array of products and services—ranging from microwave ovens to pharmaceuticals to breakfast cereals to smoke detectors. Such a consumer organization, therefore, must develop a research capability and expertise across an intimidatingly broad range and must be prepared to fight skirmishes on multiple fronts. On the other hand, the industries with which the consumer groups are often at odds can ordinarily concentrate their resources. They need the resources and substantive expertise only to defend their own products and can stand on the sidelines when a Ralph Nader takes on another industry.[26] Thus, what seems like a hefty organizational budget for an organization like Public Citizen pales in comparison to the sum total of the budgets of its many industrial antagonists.[27]

[25] From the figures given by the respondents in our Washington representatives survey, it is clear that our general queries about budget and staffing prompted some respondents (especially those for whom the Washington office serves as national headquarters) to give us the total figures for all the activities, political and nonpolitical, of the organization; some to give us the figures for the operating budget and staffing of the Washington office; and some to give us the figures for the organizations' government affairs operation. Therefore, apart from the substantive difficulties discussed below in comparing tangible resources across organizations, there is a methodological difficulty with the imprecision of our questions about budget and staffing that render the data collected of very limited utility. Given the variations in organizational structure among the groups in our sample, it is doubtful that even more precisely worded items would have elicited data appropriate for making meaningful comparisons among organizations with respect to budget and staffing.

[26] The requirement that a consumer group develop expertise on such a staggering number of issues may help explain why consumer groups, particularly subsidiaries of the Nader conglomerate, are frequently accused of supplying slipshod research or faulty information. It would be impossible for Nader's organization to develop the kind of thorough understanding of baby cribs, funeral homes, wood-burning stoves, and pork sausages that the relevant industries command. Thus, it may be that because consumer groups must represent such diverse consumer interests, they are forced not only to stretch their resources thinly but also to risk superficiality in their policy presentations.

[27] It should be noted that in spite of their inclusive agendas, some consumer organizations— for example, the Consumer Federation of America—have quite small budgets.

The size of the political task varies not only with the length of the political agenda but also with the nature of the resources available elsewhere in the organization. When, for example, a corporation needs complex technical information to buttress its political case, its Washington office can get in touch with the appropriate department at corporate headquarters. Because there is extensive research capacity available elsewhere in the organization, the Washington office of a corporation ordinarily needs to do little research.

Quite the contrary is true for an organization like Common Cause, a nonpartisan citizens' group concerned with overseeing the operation of the federal government. Perhaps the single most important activity of the headquarters of Common Cause in Washington is research, to assemble the kind of data about how the government works that the ordinary citizen cannot easily provide for himself. Common Cause is often cited as having one of the highest budgets among those attempting to influence the federal government. However, while the budget of Common Cause has to cover an extensive research operation, the government affairs divisions of many organizations, especially corporations, have no major research responsibilities at all. Thus, it is difficult to compare the budget of the Washington office of Common Cause with that of RCA.

An analogous point can be made with respect to the organizational maintenance activities of various groups. The organizations in our sample diverge markedly in the degree to which they must devote precious time and money to the task of keeping on business. Once again, corporations and, to a somewhat lesser extent, trade associations are in a privileged position. While those in a corporation's Washington office do have to justify their activities to their higher-ups, raising money just to keep the Washington office open is not a significant activity. For many of the organizations in our sample—especially civil rights, social welfare, and citizens' groups—raising money is an activity of such major importance that it sometimes interferes with the pursuit of central organizational goals.

Furthermore, while the Washington offices of corporations ordinarily devote time to keeping corporate headquarters informed, this is usually a much less burdensome (or at least less costly) job than communicating with a large and far-flung membership. Such organizational maintenance chores can swallow enormous amounts of resources for a membership group, especially one without a clearly defined and well-heeled constituency. For all these reasons then—differences in the size of the political agendas of various organizations, in the resources available to the government affairs operation from elsewhere in the organization, and in the degree to which resources must be devoted to organizational maintenance—it is impossible to make comparisons among organizations with respect to their budgetary or staff resources.[28]

[28] Although comparisons of the budgets of various kinds of organizations are probably inappropriate, it is possible to compare the budgets of the Washington offices of various corporations with one another. A superficial examination of the figures supplied to us by the corporations

Which Organizations Feel Needy?

Although we deem it unwise to use the raw data on budgets and staffing to arrive at an approximation of the distribution of resources among organizations, some tentative generalizations can be made on the basis of our respondents' subjective perceptions of resource needs. Earlier in the chapter (Tables 5.4 and 5.5) we discussed our respondents' replies to a series of questions about the relative importance of various organizational resources. We followed up these questions by asking our respondents to look at the list again and indicate, if they could enhance their organizations' stock of resources, which *two* of those on the list they would choose to increase. Ironically, the very resources that were earlier deemed least important—a large budget and strategically placed allies—are the most frequently desired. Thirty-four percent of the Washington representatives indicated they would like to enhance their organization's budget, and 33 percent said they would like more strategically placed allies. Only 20 percent indicated they would like to increase their stock of the resource that was overwhelmingly cited as being most important: a reputation for credibility.

Once again, it is not the raw frequencies, but rather the pattern of responses among organizations, that is instructive. Consider Table 5.6, which presents the distribution of preferences for increased resources for corporations, trade associations, unions, and citizens' groups. While the different kinds of organizations are in substantial agreement with respect to the resources they deemed important—they placed credibility first and budget last—the pattern of their preferences for increased resources is quite complex. When it comes to contacts, expertise, leaders, and allies, the various kinds of organizations are in rough agreement in terms of their desire for more resources. There is somewhat more divergence with respect to credibility and, to a lesser extent, cause. Corporations and, then, trade associations are especially likely to indicate that they would like to enhance their reputation for being credible and the appeal of their cause.

There is the greatest dispersion in the preferences of the various kinds of organizations when it comes to desiring a larger membership or budget. In this case, it is the unions and citizens' groups that feel deprived. In light of the

---

in our sample indicates that there is surprisingly little relationship between the volume of a corporation's business with the government and the size of its Washington office. Sometimes, two corporations in the same industry—therefore, facing analogous regulatory problems or attempting to sell the same goods and services to the government—have government affairs operations on a substantially different scale from each other. Sometimes corporations for which the government looms large as a policeman or a customer have relatively small offices and vice versa. Our speculative interpretation is that the levels of budget and staffing of a corporation's Washington office are as dependent upon the political and entrepreneurial skills of the vice-president for governmental affairs who runs it as upon the level of its interactions with the government. Because the budget of a Washington office is so insignificant an entry on a corporate balance sheet, a Washington representative who is politically effective can easily justify expanding his government affairs operation.

Table 5.6 PREFERENCES FOR INCREASED RESOURCES BY ORGANIZATION TYPE

	Reputation	Contacts	Leaders	Expertise	Cause	Allies	Membership	Budget
				Percentage desiring more of resource				
All organizations	20%	26%	10%	15%	11%	33%	26%	34%
Corporations	35	30	13	17	26	44	0	9
Trade associations	24	21	9	15	12	33	27	33
Unions	0	21	16	5	0	26	47	58
Citizens' groups	8	17	4	12	4	33	46	58

Source: Washington Representatives Survey.

discussion earlier in the chapter, it is not surprising that the different kinds of organizations vary so widely in terms of their desire for more members. What are most striking, however, are the figures for increased budget. While a mere 9 percent of the corporations express a need for more money, 58 percent of both the unions and the citizens' groups indicate a desire to increase their budgets. Thus, in spite of their protestations that a large budget is not an important resource to their organizations, unions and citizens' groups are substantially more likely to feel a financial pinch.

This conclusion about the perceived need for more material resources is supported by other comments made by our respondents in the course of our interviews. Among the open-ended questions was one that asked respondents to think about some recent policy controversy in which their organizations had been ineffective and to discuss the reasons why. This query elicited an array of responses ranging from the modal one (22 percent), "Public opinion was against us," to "We ran into opposition from key policymakers" to "Our timing was off" to the 4 percent who told us "We never lose." The second most common response, expressed by 19 percent of the respondents, was to the effect that the organization lacked the funds or resources to carry on the fight effectively. Again it is the pattern of the responses that is instructive. As shown in Table 5.7, only 2 percent of those affiliated with corporations, 16 percent with trade associations, and 29 percent with unions—as opposed to 68 percent of those affiliated with citizens' groups—indicated in response to the open-ended

Table 5.7   PERCEIVED RESOURCE NEEDS BY ORGANIZATION TYPE

	Corporations	Trade associations	Unions	Citizens' groups
Would like to enhance budgetary resources	9%	33%	58%	58%
Insufficient resources cited as source of ineffectiveness in recent policy controversy	2%	16%	29%	68%
Insufficient resources cited as biggest source of frustration	5%	11%	0%	47%
Perceived organizational strength compared with opponents:				
Stronger than opponents	22%	41%	29%	12%
About as strong	33	41	7	35
Weaker than opponents	44	18	64	53
	99%	100%	100%	100%
	(N = 52)	(N = 35)	(N = 20)	(N = 25)

Source: Washington Representatives Survey.

question that the absence of material resources had impeded political effectiveness.

There is a similar pattern in the responses to an open-ended question about the greatest sources of frustration in being a Washington representative. Again the query evoked a broad range of reactions. Some complained that the government, especially Congress, is too slow and unresponsive; others spoke of headaches in trying to educate corporate headquarters or a recalcitrant membership; still others had gripes of a more personal nature about the problems of living and working in Washington. Fourteen percent of our respondents indicated that the lack of resources is the greatest source of frustration. Again, as shown in Table 5.7, the distribution of responses among various kinds of organizations is striking. Five percent of the corporate representatives, 11 percent of the trade association representatives, none of the union representatives, and 47 percent of the citizens' group representatives complained about the absence of resources.

Table 5.7 reports the responses to a question that bears attention here. We asked our respondents to compare the strength of their organization with that of its antagonists. Overall, the respondents tended to feel somewhat weak: 25 percent indicated that their organizations are stronger than their antagonists and 40 percent that their organizations are weaker. An examination of the various kinds of organizations reveals a slightly different pattern from that which emerged over and over on the questions about resources. As shown in Table 5.7, the trade associations feel relatively the strongest, with corporations, trade unions, and citizens' groups following in that order. We do not want to exaggerate the importance of this particular finding. Subjective perceptions of organizational strength presumably are shaped by many factors in addition to the availability of sufficient resources. In this particular case, the weakness perceived by the unions and the citizens' groups probably reflects, at least in part, the presence in the White House of an administration that was quite hostile to them. Still, it is interesting that, in terms of subjective perceptions, feelings of both poverty and weakness tend most commonly to be typical of unions and citizens' groups.

The Tilt of the Pressure Community—Some Further Thoughts

These data tend to reinforce our earlier conclusions about the nature of the tilt of the pressure community. As shown in Chapter 4, in terms of the sheer number of organizations sustaining a presence in Washington, there are relatively few organizations representing either the interests of the disadvantaged or the interests of broad publics. It is possible, however, that a few large groups might theoretically provide the same collective input as many small ones if the group-based input represented individuals equally and if the distribution of resources across organizations reflected the principle of one-person–one-vote. At least with respect to subjective perceptions of the adequacy of material resources, however, the pressure community is doubly skewed. The distribution of resources reinforces the advantage that accrues to the well-off, especially business, in terms of both the number of organizations and the way in which the structure of representation virtually guarantees duplication of representation.

Our analysis has been weakened by our inability to analyze systematically the data for social welfare and civil rights groups; there are simply too few of them in the sample to derive meaningful figures. However, a close reading of the interviews with the few such groups included in the sample would indicate that whatever resource problems the unions and citizens' groups face, the representatives of the poor and racial minorities face even more acutely. Thus, in spite of the growth over the past two decades in the number of organizations designed to represent the disadvantaged and broad publics, the heavenly chorus continues to sing with an upper-class accent. If the strong sense imparted by citizens' groups and, to a lesser extent, unions, that they are needy is a reflection of reality, then the distribution of resources exacerbates the problem of skew in the pressure community.

Analysis of the tilt in the pressure community can be pushed one step further by considering, not the way that resources are distributed among organizations of various types, but the way in which resources are distributed among organizations of various ideologies. We asked our respondents whether they would describe their organization as liberal, middle-of-the-road, or conservative. Most of them found this a manageable question, although for some reason a particularly large number of corporate representatives either refused to answer or could not accommodate themselves to one of the three categories.[29] (Note that these are the respondents' own views of the ideological leanings of their organizations. Based on what we knew of their positions on political issues, we did not always consider their self-labels accurate. Naturally, however, we did not substitute our own judgment for theirs.)

Table 5.8 presents data about subjective perceptions of resource poverty from the perspective of organizational ideology. The message of Table 5.8 is unambiguous. The distribution of resources, at least as perceived subjectively, places conservative organizations at an advantage. Let us look briefly at the separate items. When asked which resources they would choose to increase, 55 percent of those affiliated with liberal organizations, but only 24 percent of those affiliated with conservative ones, indicated that their organizations could use a larger budget. With respect to the open-ended questions, 40 percent of those attached to liberal organizations, but only 12 percent of those attached to

---

[29]Because a large number of corporations did not answer this question, and because—as discussed in Appendix A—our sample overrepresents unions, citizens' groups, and civil rights and social welfare organizations, we would expect the overall distribution of ideologies among groups active in Washington to be skewed in a more conservative direction than the raw figures reported at the bottom of Table 5.8. However, this is no barrier to our making comparisons between the liberal and conservative organizations taken separately.

Table 5.8　PERCEIVED RESOURCE NEEDS BY ORGANIZATIONAL IDEOLOGY

	Liberal	Middle-of-the-road	Conservative
Would like to enhance budgetary resources	55%	18%	24%
Insufficient resources cited as source of ineffectiveness in recent policy controversy	40%	5%	12%
Insufficient resources cited as biggest source of frustration	24%	11%	3%
Perceived organizational strength compared with opponents:			
Stronger than opponents	13%	23%	48%
About as strong	20	46	30
Weaker than opponents	67	32	22
	100%	101%	100%
	(N = 47)	(N = 48)	(N = 44)

Source: Washington Representatives Survey.

conservative ones, attributed policy ineffectiveness to lack of resources; 24 percent of the representatives of liberal organizations, as opposed to a mere 3 percent of the representatives of conservative ones, said that insufficient resources constitute a major source of frustration. Overall, then, 80 percent of those affiliated with liberal organizations, as opposed to only 34 percent of those affiliated with conservative ones, expressed a need for greater resources at some point in the interview.

When it comes to feelings of relative organizational strength, the figures are analogous. Two-thirds of those representing liberal organizations, but less than a quarter of those representing conservative organizations, feel weaker than their opponents; on the other hand, nearly half of those representing conservative organizations, but barely over one-tenth of those representing liberal ones, feel stronger than their principal antagonists. Again the data on perceptions of organizational strength undoubtedly reflect the presence of Reagan in the White House. However, they are obviously consistent with the other evidence about the ideological tilt introduced by the distribution of resources within the pressure community. Thus, the pressure community is skewed in yet another way—in favor of conservative points of view.

SUMMARY

This chapter has described the many resources that organized interests can mobilize in attempting to influence political outcomes—not only money but also information, expertise and skills, membership, and reputation. Furthermore, we have investigated the way in which the distribution of financial resources affects the inclusiveness and skew of the pressure community. It seems that the pressure community is somewhat impermeable; some groups (there is no way to measure how many) lack sufficient resources even to establish an effective presence in Washington politics. The existing distribution of financial resources, however, not only narrows the scope of the pressure community but also contributes to its tilt. At least in terms of perceived relative deprivation, the very business interests that were found in Chapter 4 to be advantaged in terms of the numbers of organizations active in Washington are also advantaged in terms of access to financial resources. Obviously, however, organizations that are less well-endowed financially often command other resources—an appealing cause, political skill, enthusiasm, support, and reputation—that compensate for their small budgets.

6

Interest Groups and Their Members

The discussion so far has treated organized interests as if they were congeries of like-minded individuals that develop spontaneously and pursue common goals under the aegis of a similarly interested leadership and staff. Unfortunately, this formulation is too simple. It contains a number of implicit assumptions that demand further scrutiny. We already have reason to question whether organizations inevitably spring forth when they are needed. Further, one well-known theory posits that, unless certain conditions obtain, a rational individual may have no incentive to join an organization whose goals he shares. What is more, the members of an organization may not be of one mind on all the policy matters that fall under its purview; their differences in age, race, taste, or whatever have implications for the definition and pursuit of the joint interests around which the group is organized. In addition, there may be no automatic congruence between the interests of organizational leaders and staff and those of members; leaders and staff may favor the interests of one internal faction over another or may even have interests of their own that conflict with those of the rank and file taken as a whole.

This chapter probes several issues bearing on the internal dynamics of organizational operations and considers the interests and motivations of various people involved in organizations: those who found them, those who staff them, and those who join them. In particular, we investigate the questions of where organizations come from and why people join them. Then, we consider the ways in which organizational leaders and staff represent, or fail to represent, the interests of ordinary members and the reciprocal ability of ordinary members to render leaders and staff accountable for what they do. Finally, we discuss the patterns of communication between leaders and staff, on the one hand, and rank and file, on the other, indicating the multiple purposes that can be served by such communication. In so doing, we encounter several major theories about behavior in organizations, including Mancur Olson's logic of collective action and Robert Michels's iron law of oligarchy.

Since this is a book about organized interests in politics, it might seem beside the point to spend a great deal of time poking at the insides of organizations. However, matters germane to the relations between organizations and their members are central to our overall study because they bear so fundamentally on the issue of which interests are represented—and which most effectively—in politics. Since we assume that interests having an organizational advocate are more likely to receive vigorous representation in the political process, then the issues of whether organizations emerge automatically and how the interests of rank and file are represented by leaders and staff are relevant to understanding who is represented in politics. The debates surrounding these matters are complicated. In contending with these questions, we may seem to stray from our basic concern with the political role of interest groups. Yet, issues surrounding the relationship between organizations and their constituencies are pivotal for one of the most fundamental matters in the study of pressure groups in politics: the representation of interests.

WHERE ORGANIZATIONS COME FROM

Political scientists during the 1950s seemed to assume that interest groups would emerge more or less automatically in response to environmental changes that rendered necessary the representation of new interests in politics. In discussing the proliferation of organizations, David B. Truman alludes to two kinds of disturbances that might stimulate the growth of new organizations.[1] First are changes, ordinarily of an economic or technological character, that have an impact upon the division of labor in society. As society becomes ever more complex, processes of social and economic differentiation, coupled with technological advances, give birth to new interests that naturally seek organizational embodiment and articulation. Consequently, there are many organizations currently active in Washington whose presence would have been unimaginable in an earlier era. For example, the National Cable Television Association, the National Computer Graphics Association, the American Academy of Physicians Assistants, and the U.S. Hang Gliding Association are all relatively young associations representing interests that have emerged re-

[1] *The Government Process,* (New York: Knopf, 1951), Chapters 3–4. Truman's approach is discussed in Robert H. Salisbury, "An Exchange Theory of Interest Groups," *Midwest Journal of Political Science* 13 (1969): 1–31, and Jeffrey M. Berry "On the Origins of Public Interest Groups: A Test of Two Theories," *Polity* 10 (1978): 379–397.

cently as the result of the growth of new technologies, new industries, new professions, or new ways of producing goods and services.

A second kind of disturbance occurs when some kind of disruptive factor—a war, a recession, a technological innovation, or even a newly organized group—upsets the equilibrium among social groups and makes it advantageous for some group to organize in order to restore a more satisfactory equilibrium.[2] For example, when student loan programs fared badly in the first round of Reagan budget cutting, students organized for political battle in order to avoid a similar fate in subsequent Reagan budgets.

David Truman's suggestions about the origins of interest groups are more or less implicit in his discussion. Therefore, it would be unfair to raise his insights to the level of theory and to demand of them the kind of rigor one expects of theoretical propositions. Still, there are two problems with the environmental disturbance theory. First, one environmental disturbance it overlooks is the role of government itself in creating or sustaining various interests.[3] For example, the American Farm Bureau Federation, the largest of the general farm organizations in the United States, emerged not from the spontaneous organizational impulse of American farmers but as a result of a 1914 law that established the Agricultural Extension Service (AES) to furnish farmers with advice on improving crop production. Many of the local agents of the AES formed local organizations, or "farm bureaus," to help them establish good relations with the farmers in their areas. By 1915 local bureaus began forming state federations, and in 1919 the national organization was founded.[4] Government also stimulates the formation of new organizations or the growth of existing ones by funding, underwriting, or otherwise supporting their activity. Even so redoubtably antigovernment an organization as the U.S. Chamber of Commerce was established at the behest of the federal government.[5] In addition, many of the organizations in the so-called intergovernmental lobby were sponsored, in effect, by the federal government through its sizable grants. Over the

[2]Because the factor producing disequilibrium can be another group, Truman concludes that organizations will be formed in waves. Finding itself challenged by a new association, a potential group will organize defensively to contend with its recently hatched rival. Thus, associations beget associations. Scholars have discerned waves of organizational coalescence during the nineteenth and early twentieth centuries, but find a steady, unabated increase in the number of organizations since World War I. See, for example, James Q. Wilson, *Political Organizations* (New York: Basic Books, 1973), pp. 198–211, and Jack Walker, "The Origins and Maintenance of Interest Groups in America," *American Political Science Review* 77 (1983): 390–406. Our own data confirm the steady increase in the number of associations since the Progressive era.

[3]On the issue of government encouragement of group formation, see Robert H. Salisbury, "Are Interest Groups Morbific Forces?" paper presented to the Conference Group on the Political Economy of Advanced Industrial Societies, August 1980; and Jack L. Walker, "The Mobilization of Political Interests," paper presented at the Annual Meeting of the American Political Science Association, Chicago, September 1983.

[4]On the origins of the Farm Bureau, see O. H. Kile, *The Farm Bureau Through Three Decades* (Baltimore: Waverly Press, 1949), and Grant McConnell, *The Decline of Agrarian Democracy* (Berkeley: University of California Press, 1953).

[5]Sar A. Levitan and Martha R. Cooper, *Business Lobbies* (Baltimore: Johns Hopkins University Press, 1984), p. 18.

past two decades, government funds seem to have become an increasingly important resource for newly emergent organizations, especially those in the nonprofit sector.[6]

Another problem with Truman's environmental disturbance argument is that it assumes that interest organizations emerge more or less automatically when changes in the environment render them necessary and does not treat the failure of potential interests to become organized as a problem meriting extended analysis. But, of course, political organizations do not emerge automatically even when government policy encourages them or circumstances seem to require them. Someone has to exercise leadership to get them started.

The Logic of Collective Action

Whether David Truman or his intellectual successors ever, in fact, explicitly stated that potential interests are inevitably represented by organizations when threatening changes occur is a matter of some academic dispute.[7] Nevertheless, it is quite clear that political scientists of the 1950s and early 1960s tended to emphasize the degree to which the pressure community is permeable and the likelihood that pressure on one side of an issue would beget opposing counterpressures.[8] The first to dissent explicitly from this position was E. E. Schattschneider. As we saw in Chapter 4, Schattschneider observed that the representation of latent interests is not at all automatic. In fact, he argued, what is most striking about the pressure system is that it is small: "The range of organized, identifiable, known groups is amazingly narrow; there is nothing remotely universal about it."[9] Furthermore, there are two kinds of interests in particular that are likely to remain unorganized, the interests of the disadvantaged and broad publics.

While Schattschneider observed intuitively that the emergence of organized interests is by no means inevitable, Mancur Olson drew much the same conclusion half a decade later on the basis of a much more rigorous logic. An economist, Olson had the insight to see the relevance of economic theory for various kinds of noneconomic, collective, goal-directed activities, including one particular kind of such activity: lobbying. Thus, he took what economists had long known about the behavior of firms and applied it, with quite startling results, to the behavior of individuals deciding whether to join interest groups.[10]

---

[6] Walker, "The Origins and Maintenance of Interest Groups."

[7] See, for example, Robert A. Dahl, *Dilemmas of Pluralist Democracy* (New Haven: Yale University Press, 1982), Appendix A.

[8] For example, Lester Milbrath asserts that "an important factor attenuating the impact of lobbying on governmental decisions is the fact that nearly every vigorous push in one direction stimulates an opponent or coalition of opponents to push in the opposite direction." *The Washington Lobbyists* (Chicago: Rand McNally, 1963), p. 345.

[9] *The Semisovereign People* (New York: Holt, Rinehart and Winston, 1960), p. 30.

[10] *The Logic of Collective Action* (Cambridge: Harvard University Press, 1965).

To understand Olson's theory it is necessary to understand the concept of a collective good.[11] A collective good is any benefit that if available to one member of the community cannot reasonably be denied to any other, regardless of whether he or she bore any of the cost of providing it. National defense and clean air, for example, are both collective goods. Clearly, if the government provides for adequate security from foreign intrusion or ensures that the atmosphere is healthy, such benefits will be available to all in the community: those who did not vote for the incumbents in office, as well as those who did; those who are delinquent in their taxes, as well as those who paid on time; and so on.

We ordinarily think of collective goods in terms of government benefits that are universally available. However, it is clear that interest groups can use political action to seek benefits that are collective with respect to the members of some smaller group of citizens—benefits that would be available regardless of whether the members of the narrower public are organization members or not. Thus, for example, if the National Education Association is successful in persuading Congress to funnel more federal dollars to localities to subsidize the training of teachers or to increase their salaries, all teachers can benefit from the windfall, NEA members and nonmembers alike. Similarly, if the Pharmaceutical Manufacturers Association succeeds in making it easier for new drugs to be approved by the government and marketed, all drug companies, not just PMA members, can enjoy that improvement in their business climate.

Olson uses an economic logic to reach the conclusion that "rational, self-interested individuals will not act to achieve their common or group interests."[12] He begins by describing what constitutes rational behavior in an economic situation that has relevance for various kinds of collective action.[13] Consider a perfectly competitive industry, say, growing wheat, in which prices are falling to the point where it is no longer profitable to produce. Presumably it would be in the best interests of all the farmers if each farmer were to cut back production somewhat so that the price of wheat would rise, therefore increasing his own profits and those of the whole industry as well. However, the rational individual farmer would not, in fact, decrease his production. Calculating that his own contribution to a joint effort to cut production would be too small to make an appreciable difference, he would have an incentive to become a free rider. That is, he would figure that by cutting his production voluntarily he would only hurt himself without changing market conditions sufficiently to affect the price of wheat. If everybody else withholds part of his crop, the single individual who does not—the free rider—will be able to fetch a very high price. Therefore, if every rational wheat farmer pursues his individual interest, no one

[11]What Olson calls a collective good is ordinarily called a "public good" in the literature on public finance. We will use the former term in order to avoid confusion with an alternative meaning of "public good." In *The Federalist,* Madison uses "public good" to refer to what we might now call the "public interest."

[12]*The Logic of Collective Action,* p. 2.

[13]Ibid., p. 9.

curtails production and the collective effort—which is clearly in the best interests of all farmers—fails.

Olson points out that political interest groups confront precisely the same dilemma as wheat farmers. Consider any of the myriad government policies that benefit some subgroup within the public. Commercial fishermen presumably have a joint interest in the 200-mile offshore fishing limit, which protects them from foreign competition in American waters, and handicapped people in wheelchairs presumably have a shared interest in the installation of ramps to make public buildings accessible. Yet, no individual fisherman has an interest in supporting the National Federation of Fishermen, and no individual handicapped person has an interest in supporting the American Coalition of Citizens with Disabilities. Because the benefits being sought are collective benefits to the group as a whole—that is, because once provided they cannot reasonably be withheld from anyone who qualifies—the rational individual has an incentive to become a free rider. Thus, it is not rational for a single individual to contribute his time or money to an organization *whose goal he shares* if he cannot appreciably enhance the organization's ability to attain that goal. Because his efforts will be too small to make a significant contribution to the joint endeavor, the rational individual will allow others to assume the organizational burden and wait to reap the collective benefits. What this means, of course, is that rational individuals will not work together to further their common interests and that the emergence of organizations to act as advocates for shared interests is by no means automatic.

Why Are There Any Interest Groups at All?

One need not be a devotee of the directory of *Washington Representatives* to know that, contrary to the foregoing logic, there are thousands of interest groups active in Washington politics. Why? Mancur Olson makes clear that if certain specified conditions obtain, we can expect organized pressure group activity. For one thing, if the group can coerce individuals to support collective efforts, then the free-rider problem can be overcome. The state, of course, can compel us to do our share in providing collective goods. If we do not pay taxes, we risk going to jail. Under ordinary circumstances, however, voluntary interest groups cannot force potential members to participate. Therefore, we will have to look elsewhere for the explanation of the existence of organized political groups.

If the group is small, the rational individual has an incentive to support a joint effort to supply a collective good.[14] When the group is small enough, the

---

[14]Ibid., pp. 22–65. Olson's argument about the relationship between group size and group behavior is far more complex than the fragment presented here. Olson goes into some detail about the multiple disadvantages suffered by large groups. Not only are members of large groups likely to have no incentive to contribute to the provision of collective goods, but large groups are harder to

individual can calculate that his contribution to the joint effort will in fact have some impact on the group's ability to secure the desired collective benefit. Thus, it is not irrational for the individual to participate. This is an insight with important implications for the shape of the Washington pressure community. Olson's argument means not only that organizations representing small groups are much more likely to be formed than organizations representing large ones, but also that organizations representing the interests of large publics will be a relative rarity in interest politics. Thus, the pressure community will overrepresent the interests of narrow publics at the expense of broad ones. Furthermore, contrary to what intuition might tell us, a large constituency, far from being a political resource, may in fact be a political liability, for small groups face a much lower organizational hurdle.

There is another circumstance under which even large groups may be formed. If the organization can supply its members with selective benefits—that is, with benefits available to organization members only—then rational individuals are given an incentive not to become free riders.[15] Most organizations do provide their members with some benefits that are denied to nonmembers. Among the most important is information. Virtually all membership organizations have newsletters or magazines of varying degrees of frequency and interest that are sent to members. In addition, many organizations—in particu-

---

organize. The costs of coordination and organization increase with size, thus rendering it even more unlikely that a large group will be able to organize in order to provide itself with a collective good. (See pp. 46–48.)

Olson also delves into the effects of group composition. If the group contains members of quite different sizes, or if the group contains a few members who are particularly interested in the collective good, then the prospects of supplying that benefit are enhanced, for there are individual members who have an incentive to bear a substantial part, or all, of the cost of providing the collective good. (See pp. 35–36.)

Olson's conclusions on the effects of size are quite controversial even among those who are congenial to his general approach. See, for example, Norman Frolich, Joe A. Oppenheimer, and Oran R. Young, *Political Leadership and Collective Goods* (Princeton, NJ: Princeton University Press, 1971), Chapters, 1–2, Appendix 1; John Chamberlin, "Provision of Collective Goods as a Function of Group Size," *American Political Science Review* 68 (1974): 707–716; and Russell Hardin, *Collective Action* (Baltimore: Johns Hopkins University Press for Resources for the Future, 1982), Chapter 3.

[15]Ordinarily, the selective benefits provided by organizations to their members are economic in character, while the collective benefits are political (policies favorable to all members of a certain category whether or not they are organization members). There are exceptions, however. Organizations not infrequently provide collective benefits that are economic. For example, the Brick Institute of America has various programs designed to give an economic boost to the brick industry. For example, the BIA touts the advantages of building with brick by advertising on behalf of the industry in *Architectural Record* and magazines servicing the home building and home mortgage finance industries. In addition, it provides assistance to schools in developing vocational programs in bricklaying, as described in *Brick and Clay Record* (October 1978). These programs promote the brick industry as a whole and therefore provide *economic* benefits to companies that are not BIA members as well as to those that are.

Conversely, under rare circumstances, government policies can provide selective rather than collective benefits. For example, sections of the Wagner Act that provide for unions to act as collective bargaining agents for workers constitute a government policy that allows unions to supply selective benefits for members.

lar, trade and professional associations—make available to members various kinds of highly useful technical information. For example, the Food Marketing Institute, the trade association of the grocery industry, publishes information about consumer attitudes—which grocery items they think are outrageously priced, what factors they consider in choosing a place to shop, what they do to economize on food, and so on—that can help owners of groceries and super-markets make their stores more attractive to consumers. Organization members have an opportunity to gain valuable information—as well as to make contacts, see friends, and have a good time—at conventions, conferences, and trade shows sponsored by the organization. SNAXPO '82, the annual convention of the Potato Chip/Snack Food Association held at Caesar's Palace in Las Vegas, featured, for the enlightenment of participating snacksters, a speech by former Secretary of State Henry Kissinger as well as workshops on various aspects of the production and marketing of snack foods.

Most organizations provide, in addition to technical information, other selective benefits tailored to the nature of the particular industry, occupation, or profession represented. Unions provide a variety of job-related benefits—among them, collective bargaining with management, grievance procedures, and often pension fund management—that are critical to the job security and economic well-being of members. In a closed shop the selective benefit is, in effect, the job itself, for nonunion members are barred from employment in closed shops. (A worker in a closed shop, thus, has little choice about union membership. Given these circumstances, it is ambiguous whether it is more appropriate to describe a union with a closed-shop agreement as an organiza-tion that overcomes the free-rider problem by providing a very highly valued selective benefit—a job—or as an organization that has the ability to coerce membership.) Many other organizations provide appropriate selective benefits to members, even if these benefits may not be so highly valued as those offered by unions. Of course, the content of such benefits varies from organization to organization, depending upon the needs of the members. For example, both to reassure consumers and, presumably, to stave off regulation by the government, the Recreation Vehicle Industry Association certifies that the mobile homes, travel trailers, and campers produced by member companies comply with strict safety standards. The RVIA's seal of compliance is affixed to each vehicle for the consumer to see.

In addition, many organizations make available selective benefits that are less obviously tailored to the purposes of the organization and the special needs of its members and are therefore more clearly related to issues of organizational maintenance and survival. Interestingly, such benefits—reduced-cost travel op-portunities, insurance policies, disability and pension plans—tend to be quite similar across organizations, regardless of whether the members happen to be farmers or professors.

Mancur Olson's logic of collective action bears lengthy consideration be-cause his argument is complicated and because it has serious implications for the representation of joint interests in politics. Olson makes clear both that organizational representation of common interests is by no means automatic and that citizens' groups will be at a special disadvantage with respect to the free-rider problem. Not only do such organizations appeal to large constituencies (and thus have the additional difficulties that Olson argues accompany increased size), but also they are not in a position to provide highly valued selective goods to their members. Some citizens' group do, of course, supply selective benefits. Most send magazines or newsletters to members, some of them lushly designed; the American Automobile Association provides members with maps to aid in planning motor trips and towing assistance when they are stranded; the Audubon Society admits members to its sanctuaries for free; and the Sierra Club offers discounts on its books and publications. Under ordinary circumstances, however, the selective benefits that citizens' groups are able to provide hardly seem to justify the cost of membership. Still, there are many groups representing broad publics that are active and effective in Washington politics. Their existence is in one sense an implicit refutation of Olson. But when viewed from another perspective—that is, when we consider that most consumer and environmental groups enroll only a minuscule proportion of all who share their goals—Olson's view is confirmed.

Scholars interested in Olson's argument have subjected it to extensive comment and criticism and have tried to test how well it holds up empirically.[16] Most of the inquiries have focused not on citizens' organizations or ideological groups but on economic groups, for which the pull of selective economic incentives is presumably quite strong. The evidence, in fact, is somewhat mixed but indicates that while economic motives are usually of primary importance to group members, political goals figure significantly as well.[17] That is, organization members are motivated by the lure of economic benefits that are available on a "members only" basis; however, they seem to be animated by a sense of responsibility for assuming a fair share of the burden of supplying collective political benefits as well.

Motivations for Group Membership

In short, the empirical evidence seems to confirm James Q. Wilson's observation that "people join associations for many different reasons—some for status,

---

[16]A helpful essay summarizing the various lines of criticism of Olson's theory and an extensive bibliography are contained in Brian Barry and Russell Hardin, eds., *Rational Man and Irrational Society?* (Beverly Hills, CA: Sage, 1982), pp. 19–37, 391–400. Terry M. Moe summarizes empirical evaluations of Olson's argument and provides some additional data in *The Organization of Interests* (Chicago: University of Chicago Press, 1980), Chapters 7–8, and "Toward a Broader View of Interest Groups," *Journal of Politics* 43 (1981): 531–543.

[17]On the evidence from experiments designed to assess the propensity of individuals to assume a share of the costs of providing collective goods, see Gerald Marwell and Ruth E. Ames, "Experiments in the Provision of Public Goods, I," *American Journal of Sociology* 84 (1979): 1335–1360, and "Experiments in the Provision of Public Goods, II," *American Journal of Sociology* 85 (1980): 926–937.

some for money, some for power, some from a sense of guilt, some because they have been asked by a friend to whom they do not wish to say no."[18] Wilson elaborates this common-sense observation with a taxonomy of the various kinds of incentives—which he calls material, solidary, and purposive—that organizations can offer to induce membership support.[19] Material incentives are the kinds of tangible benefits—money, discounts, or goods and services—for which one would ordinarily have to pay on the open market. These are the kinds of benefits that Olson stresses.

Unlike material incentives, solidary ones are intangible. The many kinds of emotional satisfactions that derive from dealing with others are all solidary incentives for organizational support. The pleasures of friendship and companionship, the self-esteem and prestige attached to being respected by others, the thrills and ego-trips concomitant to rubbing elbows with the powerful and emerging victorious from the political fray—all these are emotional gratifications that can accompany organization membership and support. Although solidary benefits, especially friendship and companionship, seem particularly important in small groups, even large groups can make them available to members. For example, those attending the Potato Chip/Snack Food Association's SNAXPO '82 were regaled by strolling minstrels—Italian, Mexican, and German—at the gala cocktail buffet and entertained by Les Brown's Band of Renown at the annual banquet. For all the importance of the information shared at SNAXPO, it is surely the case that the participants also had a good time together.

A final incentive, what Wilson calls a purposive incentive, is the belief in the goals of the organization and the sense of satisfaction that derives from contributing to a cause in which one believes. With respect to purposive incentives, it is not the selfishness or unselfishness of the goals of the organization but, rather, the motivation of the individual joining that is crucial. Thus, purposive incentives animate not only those who support organizations with altruistic purposes—for example, charities and advocacy groups—but also those who support private interest groups, not out of a desire to take advantage of the selective benefits available to members, but out of a sense of responsibility for assuming a fair share of the collective burden in furthering the cause.

On the basis of this brief survey, several generalizations emerge about the various kinds of material and psychological benefits that organizations offer their members to induce them to join and give support. For one thing, most organizations attempt not to rely on a single kind of incentive but, rather, to develop an array of incentives. For example, while unions are able to offer valued material benefits (job security, collective bargaining agreements, and so on), one look at a union magazine makes clear the importance of intangible inducements for generating membership support. The pages are filled with newsy items about the activities of local unions and their members, kudos to

[18]*Political Organizations* p. 26.
[19]Ibid., Chapter 3.

activists and officers; and exhortations about the importance of union spirit. In addition, within a single organization different individuals may value different kinds of benefits. Finally, while the primary motive for organizational membership seems to be, as Olson predicted, rational economic self-interest, intangible gratifications are important as well.[20]

The Rationality Threshold   If the costs of organizational involvement are low enough, the rationality mechanism identified by Olson does not seem to be triggered; that is, there seems to be a threshold level for costs, below which members do not bother to make rational calculations of economic self-interest. The point at which it becomes worthwhile to make such calculations clearly varies with the resources of the group member. When organization membership entails high opportunity costs—that is, when it involves sacrificing something else of value—then we can expect the kind of behavior that Olson predicted. When it does not—and for the well-heeled it often does not—then we can expect potential members not to require selective benefits as an inducement to join.[21]

This is a point with important implications for our understanding of the contours of the Washington pressure community. For the poor the costs are never negligible. Thus, organizations representing the poor cannot count on that cushion of support that rests below the point at which rationality calculations become salient and, therefore, they face special difficulties in getting and keeping going. Consider the organizational maintenance problems confronted by the organizers of the Massachusettes Welfare Rights Organization. Committed to organizing welfare recipients, a constituency with little experience in and few resources for political participation, these activists adopted a strategy that allowed them to generate support for collective goods—increased welfare rights and benefits from the government—by supplying members with selective ones. Having no resources to provide selective benefits on their own, the orga-

[20]Olson does refer on occasion to noneconomic incentives (see, for example, pp. 60–65, 159–165). He argues that psychological benefits are analogous to selective economic benefits—that is, available to association members only. However, to treat psychological rewards as simply additional selective benefits for members is to reduce the theory to a tautology. That is, any organization that is a going operation must, by definition, be supplying its members with selective benefits. If no economic ones can be located, then it is assumed that psychological ones are taking their place. Although this formulation makes Olson's theory impossible to disconfirm, it still points to an important truth about political organizations—that they must provide their members with some kinds of benefits if they are to be able to induce membership support. For a discussion of this issue, and the degree to which it is damaging to Olson's argument, see Brian Barry, *Socialists, Economists and Democracy* (Chicago: University of Chicago Press, 1978), p. 33.

[21]David March, "On Joining Interest Groups," *British Journal of Political Science* 6 (1976): 257–271.

This point is also made with respect to municipal membership in various associations of cities by William P. Browne, "Benefits and Membership: A Reappraisal of Interest Group Activity," *Western Political Quarterly* 29 (1976): 269. Barry also discusses this point in *Socialists, Economists and Democracy*, pp. 34–35.

Andrew McFarland points out that the citizens' lobby Common Cause has a membership of preponderantly upper-middle-class persons for whom the opportunity costs are less than they would be for median-income persons. See McFarland, *Common Cause: Lobbying in the Public Interest* (Chatham, NJ: Chatham House, 1984), p. 58.

nizers generated support for their group by helping members obtain government benefits for which they were already eligible. This was a sound strategy for attracting members but was of little use in inducing welfare recipients to support the organization in a sustained fashion. Once members had acquired whatever government benefits were available (the selective benefits), they tended not to participate in the organization's efforts to exact collective benefits from the government.[22] The costs of group participation on behalf of policy goals—baby-sitters, bus fares, and so on—were simply prohibitive to the poor, who could not afford to expend their scarce resources for the potential achievement of less immediate collective goals. All this helps us understand why not only the interests of diffuse publics but also the interests of the poor are underrepresented in politics. For those with few resources the costs of organizational membership are rarely low enough to justify efforts to seek collective benefits.

Organizations and Entrepreneurs

While Olson's work is useful in indicating what groups must do if they wish to keep going, it is of less help in understanding how associations come into being.[23] In explaining how associations come to be organized before they are in a position to maintain themselves by distributing selective benefits, some scholars point to the efforts of organizational entrepreneurs.[24] The role of the entrepreneur vis-à-vis a political association is analogous to that of the founder of a business enterprise. However, where the business entrepreneur is assumed to be motivated by a desire to maximize profits, the organizational entrepreneur may be prompted by any of a wide range of desires. He may aspire to further a cause in which he believes, to enhance his career, or to associate with the powerful. Whatever his motives, he must be enthusiastic and persevering enough to undertake what is not an easy task, supplying sufficient benefits of one kind or another to persuade potential members to assume the costs of organizational involvement. The previous chapter cited the case of Ira Nerkin, a young lawyer who started an organization to press for increases in the nation's strategic petroleum reserve. This is a matter about which Nerkin cared intensely and which he was willing to pursue at considerable personal cost. In spite of Nerkin's best efforts, his nascent organization foundered, in part because he was unable to find that elusive mix of incentives that would elicit paid membership support from enough members.

[22] Lawrence Neil Bailis, *Bread or Justice* (Lexington, MA: Lexington Books, 1974), Chapters 3–4.

[23] This point is made both by Wilson in *Political Organizations,* p. 22, and by Barry and Hardin, *Rational Man and Irrational Society?,* pp. 28–29.

[24] A number of authors discuss the role of entrepreneurs in acting as organizational midwives, among them, Salisbury, "An Exchange Theory of Interest Groups," pp. 11–15; Frolich et al., *Political Leadership and Collective Goods;* Wilson, *Political Organizations,* Chapter 10; Berry, "On the Origins of Public Interest Groups," pp. 388–393; and Walker, "The Mobilization of Political Interests." On the entrepreneurial role of John Gardner in starting Common Cause in 1970, see McFarland, *Common Cause,* especially pp. 196–198.

A focus on the entrepreneur helps solve another puzzle with respect to Olson's theory. Olson talks about lobbying—that is, organization efforts to seek collective policy benefits from the government—as a "by-product," an incidental activity undertaken by an organization that is set up for another purpose, namely to provide selective benefits for its members.[25] If, however, lobbying is merely a by-product, and if members only join organizations in order to take advantage of the selective benefits they provide, then one might well inquire why interest groups bother to lobby at all—since it is the selective benefits that are their raison d'être.[26] Once again, the role of the entrepreneur is central. More than the ordinary member, the entrepreneur is likely to care about promoting the policy goals of the organization—whether because he is committed to them or because he likes political battle or because he is advancing his own career. Thus, if—as Olson tells us—ordinary members are relatively indifferent to the efforts of an association to supply collective goods, we must look to the entrepreneur to take the lead in seeking policy benefits.

This raises a much larger issue, one that students of organizations have pondered for more than half a century. Lurking in the preceding discussion is the notion that organizational leaders may have very different interests and preferences from ordinary rank-and-file members. Thus, the internal politics of organizations raise the fundamental questions of representation and accountability that theorists of republican democracy have so long pondered.

THE PROBLEM OF ORGANIZATIONAL DEMOCRACY

Citizens in democratic political communities have long relied on representative arrangements to overcome the inefficient and cumbersome aspects of direct democracy. Analogously, when people come together to achieve collective ends in private associations, control is almost inevitably delegated to a small group of leaders. In the process the issues of representation and citizen control that figure so critically in theories of the democratic state become relevant to the internal politics of private organizations. Should leaders act as the trustees of the interests of organization members, or should the leaders serve as instructed delegates, mirroring the preferences of the rank and file?[27] Just as these questions take on an added dimension in government when officials or agencies

[25] Olson, *The Logic of Collective Action,* pp. 132–135.

[26] If, as a number of authors suggest, organization members are buying selective benefits with their dues and the efforts to secure collective benefits are financed out of the surplus or profit that remains to the entrepreneur after he has paid for the selective benefits (see for example, Salisbury, "An Exchange Theory of Interest Groups," p. 27), then why is there not more marketplace competition in the provision of such benefits? Why do not other organizations, unburdened by aspirations to influence public policy and therefore relieved of the necessity to finance a political operation, not emerge to provide the selective benefits at a lower cost?

[27] For a discussion of this dilemma in representation, see Hanna Pitkin, *The Concept of Representation* (Berkeley: University of California Press, 1967).

have their own interests at stake, the fact that organization leaders may have interests different from those of the members is also problematic.

The work of Robert Michels, an Italian-Swiss sociologist whose seminal analysis of democracy in large organizations appeared in 1915, leads us to expect that the internal politics of voluntary associations will tend to be decidedly nondemocratic.[28] According to Michels, delegation of power in organizations introduces a separation between the leaders and the led—what he calls the "iron law of oligarchy." This separation gradually widens as the leaders develop skills, gain the knowledge and experience necessary to manage a large and complex organization, and begin to identify their own interests with the survival of the organization. The knowledge and political skills of the leaders, as well as their control over the organization's financial resources and internal communications channels, allow them to consolidate their positions of power. Having grown accustomed to the exercise of power and its perquisites (fancy offices, good salaries, the solidary satisfactions of holding a position of leadership, the opportunity to rub elbows with government officials, etc.), the organization leaders become preoccupied with perpetuating their rule and neglect organizational goals.

According to Michels, the leaders also develop a feeling of superiority to the members in the process. The leaders come to identify psychologically with the organization itself and tend to see their interests as being the organization's interests. Any challenge to their personal rule is interpreted as a challenge to the organization itself, and the challengers are branded as rebels. All of this is made worse, Michels argues, because in contrast to the leaders, most of the organizational rank and file are generally indifferent to what goes on in the organization. Ordinary members are likely to have a poor understanding of politics (inside and outside the organization) and willingly relinquish their political rights to the leaders. Since the apathy of the rank and file is matched by the leaders' greed for power, the result is control of the organization by an unresponsive oligarchy whose members use the organization to serve their own ends. Literature on organizations subsequent to the work of Michels has qualified and supplemented his ideas about the anti-democratic bias in modern organizations. Today, Michels's views seem to be generally regarded by other writers as overly deterministic and too broadly generalized.[29]

[28]Robert Michels, *Political Parties,* trans. Eden and Cedar Paul (New York: Free Press, 1958), especially Part VI, Chapter 2.

[29]For some prominent modern criticisms of Michels, see Alvin Gouldner, "Metaphysical Pathos and the Theory of Democracy," in Amitai Etzioni, ed., *Complex Organizations: A Sociological Reader,* (New York: Holt, Rinehart and Winston, 1961), pp. 78–82, and Maurice Duverger, *Political Parties* (New York: Wiley, 1963), especially p. 135.

Recent sociological analysis of social movements such as the Black Power movement, new-Pentecostal religious movements, and some branches of the environmental movement presents a model that stands, not surprisingly, in sharp contrast to that of Michels. Describing the structure of such movements as "segmentary, polycephalous, and reticulate," Luther P. Gerlach finds them composed of a range of diverse groups with no central command or decision-making structure. See

Does Organizational Democracy Matter?

Although social scientists have devoted a great deal of attention to the issues raised by Michels, there is an alternative perspective on these matters. The argument can be made that the emphasis on democratic arrangements within organizations is misguided. According to this point of view, adherence to the procedural niceties of democratic governance merely hampers the effective pursuit of external organizational objectives. In order to deal effectively with political rivals and governmental officials, organization members should not waste precious resources on internal squabbles, but should conserve them for the real battles with external antagonists.[30] The League of Women Voters, for example, is one organization that may be less effective because it is procedurally democratic. At every stage there is consultation between League officers and members on matters ranging from the selection of issues for action to the definition of appropriate League posture. Thus, the League can be sure that the positions it adopts reflect members' preferences. However, these procedures are not very efficient. When issues arise unexpectedly, the League cannot act quickly. By the time the League has deliberated, dissected, debated, and decided, the time for action may have passed. Futhermore, displays of internal disagreement may simply dilute the organization's leverage in the larger political environment; it is useful to present a united front. From this perspective, associational democracy may squander the resources or diminish the cohesion an organization needs to accomplish its external goals and prevail over its political opponents.

It is certainly possible to posit circumstance for which this argument seems compelling. For example, the absence of a meaningful role for rank-and-file members in choosing leaders or setting policy may not be a problem if an organization's members are homogeneous in their interests, like-minded with respect to organizational goals, and unanimous in their satisfaction with organizational leadership. If there are no differences of opinion or interest among members, then democratic procedures may only introduce disabling conflicts and unnecessary inefficiencies.

Similarly, the absence of procedural democracy is presumably of little consequence when organization members are limited in their commitment to the organization, apathetic with respect to its activities, and free to leave it if they are dissatisfied. Another way of putting it is in terms of Albert Hirschman's formulation: the opportunity of members to exercise their "voice" option (by "attempting to change, rather than escape from, an objectionable state of affairs" in the organization) may be less important when they also have the option of "exiting."[31] For example, environmental group members whose involvement consists solely of writing $20 checks each year for membership dues

---

"Movements of Revolutionary Change: Some Structural Characteristics," in Jo Freeman, ed., *Social Movements of the Sixties and Seventies* (New York: Longman, 1983), pp. 133–147.

[30] Wilson, *Political Organizations,* pp. 236–237.

[31] Albert O. Hirschman, *Exit, Voice and Loyalty: Responses to Decline in Firms, Organizations, and States* (Cambridge: Harvard University Press, 1970).

presumably care little whether they have an effective voice in the selection of the organization's leaders or issue agenda. On the whole, they are likely to be happy to let the organization be run by a small oligarchy of persons who have a consuming interest in its work. If dissatisfied, they can simply let their membership lapse the next time there is a request for renewal in the mailbox. The American Civil Liberties Union (ACLU), a civil liberties organization with many Jewish members, learned this lesson in the late 1970s. Over strong objections from many members, ACLU leaders decided to defend the right of the American Nazi Party to hold a march in Skokie, Illinois, a suburb of Chicago that is home to several thousand survivors of Nazi concentration camps. In the aftermath of that decision, nearly 30,000 ACLU members withdrew, taking with them some $500,000 in annual financial support.[32] The option of exiting or leaving the organization is likely to be especially attractive to disgruntled members if there is an alternative organization, offering similar benefits, available to represent their interests. Thus, the importance of providing members with a voice in the organization's direction diminishes if members can express their discontent by leaving the organization and taking their support elsewhere.[33]

In some organizations, alternative institutionalized mechanisms—different from the arrangements associated with citizen control in a democratic nation-state—facilitate the articulation of the interests of various subgroups in the organization. The American Hospital Association (AHA), for instance, explicitly recognizes that America's hospitals and hospital professionals are diverse and specialized. For example, the needs of a small, rural hospital differ from those of a large, inner-city hospital; the problems of nursing care institutions and psychiatric hospitals differ still more. To accommodate all these diverse constituencies (and to provide for the expression of their special interests), the AHA maintains formal organizational subunits to provide special technical assistance as well as specialized representation on national issues.[34] Consequently, when there are systematic differences among the AHA's members, internal mechanisms already exist for the effective expression of particularized interests. Under such circumstances, the absence of formal arrangements for internal democracy may not be of significance to rank and file. In short, then, there are various circumstances under which the interests of organization members are not jeopardized by the absence of internal democracy.

When Democracy Does Matter

But the need for internal democracy in voluntary associations must not be dismissed too lightly, for just as there are circumstances in which it may be

---

[32]"Why the ACLU Defends Nazis," *U.S. News and World Report,* April 3, 1978, p. 49. The decline in support for the ACLU was temporary, however; within a year the ACLU recovered many of its estranged members.

[33]On the other hand, as Hirschman points out, "the *effectiveness* of the voice mechanism may be strengthened by the possibility of exit." *Exit, Voice and Loyalty,* p. 83.

[34]"Hospital Is Our Middle Name," undated brochure printed by the American Hospital Association.

relatively unimportant, there are others in which the need for it is equally clear. If there are no serious differences of opinion or interest within an organization's rank and file, then democratic arrangements are unnecessary and possibly counterproductive. However, few organizations are characterized by such unanimity; rather, members are likely to be divided by differences in age, taste, race, region, sex, and so on.[35] For example, in a labor union there may be systematic differences among older and younger workers. Older workers, anticipating retirement and future health problems, often want a larger pension and medical benefit package and greater deference to seniority; younger workers, facing the immediate expenses of raising a family and meeting the mortgage payments, often prefer higher wages to increased benefits. Age is only one of many possible cleavages dividing the interests of group members. For example, an organization of handicapped persons may be internally divided on the basis of specific disabilities. The visually handicapped will want a larger share of the limited public funds available to aid the handicapped devoted to educational programs for the blind; the physically handicapped will want more money used to construct ramps and elevators in inaccessible facilities. In addition, wheelchair riders need ramps cut into street curbings so that they can traverse urban intersections; blind people need curbs to guide their canes.[36]

The kind of arrangement mentioned earlier—in which the American Hospital Association provides institutionalized mechanisms for the articulation of the interests of various subgroups in the organization—is quite rare. When no such substructures are present in an organization, internally democratic decision-making arrangements may be important for dealing with structured, systematic differences among members. If there are no mechanisms built into a group's organizational structure to give form to the expression of divergent member interests, some persons within the group may be consistently denied representation of their interests. The guarantees of procedural democracy are also significant when organizational membership is not entirely voluntary, or when leaving the organization is not really an option—that is, when the benefits of membership are unavailable elsewhere or are very highly valued, or when the penalties for nonmembership are simply too severe.

Finally, when there are differences of opinion or interest among members, adherence to norms of procedural democracy can lend legitimacy to an organization's efforts to influence policy. Organization leaders who can demonstrate that they speak not merely for themselves but for their members can presumably make more effective arguments before policymakers.

[35] In *Private Power and American Democracy* (New York: Random House, Vintage Books, 1966, Chapter 5), Grant McConnell makes this point and discusses the importance of associational democracy more generally.

[36] See Steven V. Roberts, "Handicapped Are Feeling New Strength in Congress," *New York Times,* May 13, 1979, p. 8E, and Neal R. Peirce, "The Great Wheelchair Flap," *Washington Post,* December 28, 1978, p. A23.

The Special Case of Trade Unions   Scholars concerned about the problem of organizational democracy have paid special attention to trade unions. This is understandable because unions evince many of the characteristics associated with a situation in which internal democracy might matter. For example, union members are unlikely to be unanimous in their interests and opinions; as we have seen, there are likely to be structured conflicts among union members. Moreover, unions customarily cloak themselves in all sorts of rhetoric indicating a commitment to democratic norms.

On the other hand, the organizational characteristics of trade unions also suggest that they are organizations particularly vulnerable to oligarchical tendencies.[37] After all, for most workers, expressing their dissatisfaction by leaving the union is not a realistic option because the costs of exiting are simply too great. Union members typically derive highly valued exclusive benefits from their membership (including the very right to work in a union shop). In addition, given the animus to what is called "dual unionism," workers usually have no alternative organizations to which they can turn to receive similar benefits. And because union leaders therefore have little reason to fear a mass exodus of unhappy members, they may feel less constrained than leaders in other organizations to defer to members' wishes.

Furthermore, Michels cautions that when the elected officers of an organization receive very different (or much more valuable) rewards than the members, they have a strong motive to hold on to their offices and the attendant prerogatives and perquisites. Unlike the officers of, for example, the American Medical Association or the American Institute of Architects, union leaders do, in fact, typically enjoy substantially greater incomes than the workers who make up the rank–and–file membership. In addition, most union leaders undoubtedly derive psychological satisfaction from their positions as officeholders or from the opportunity to associate with public officials. In other words, the gap in status between that of the typical union leader and the typical member is likely to be relatively great; according to Michels, officers would therefore be likely to cling especially tenaciously to the perquisites of their positions.

Although all these circumstances seem to impel union governance toward oligarchy, genuine organizational democracy is not uncommon in American trade unions. Even allowing for the possibility that much of the apparent democracy is mere gesture—a symbolic obeisance to the procedural niceties of democracy in a society that values democracy—unions are more democratic than the iron law of oligarchy would predict. For example, almost all unions use referenda to provide for rank-and-file input on such matters as new programs, officers' salaries, strike actions, and approval of collective bargaining

---

[37]Seymour Martin Lipset, *Political Man* (Garden City, NY: Doubleday, Anchor Books, 1963), pp. 388–389. Also see Nicos P. Mouzelis, *Organization and Bureaucracy* (Chicago: Aldine, 1971), pp. 65–66.

agreements. (These referenda are not merely symbolic; not infrequently, union memberships veto negotiated settlements.) Moreover, virtually every union constitution provides for a periodic convention of delegates selected by the various locals in the organization. Important matters such as amendments to the union constitution, dues increases, major new programs, collective bargaining goals, and public policy objectives to be pursued at state and national levels are debated and resolved at these conventions. In many unions the convention delegates also elect the leadership.[38]

In some unions, rank-and-file members elect their leaders by direct vote. For example, both the United Mine Workers and the United Steel Workers have systems for the direct election of major officers; in both unions, these elections in recent years have been more than mere symbolic exercises. For instance, in 1982 rank-and-file members of the United Mine Workers—a union long known for bitter, even violent, internal conflicts—chose an insurgent candidate for the union presidency over the powerful incumbent.[39]

In a few unions there are not only direct elections in which officers are chosen but also ongoing factions or internal political parties to organize the expression of internal conflict and make it easier for rank-and-file members to make informed choices. For almost sixty years the International Typographers Union has maintained a competitive party system in which organized factions regularly contest national union elections and occasionally transfer control of the union.[40] Another major union that has maintained a competitive party system throughout the greater part of its history is the American Federation of Teachers, an AFL-CIO affiliate founded in 1916 and composed primarily of public school teachers. Since 1935, AFT elections have involved formally organized opposition groups that compete for control of the union. Usually there have been two major political parties, called caucuses, inside the AFT, although in periods of internal political realignment there have been as many as three. These opposing groups perform the functions commonly attributed to political parties. They adopt different policy positions and thereby offer the union's rank and file identifiable choices; they hold primaries to select candidates for union office; they draft and adopt platforms; they conduct campaigns to enroll membership and elect candidates; and they frequently vote as blocks in AFT conventions.[41] In short, these examples suggest, at the least, that or-

[38] Derek C. Bok and John T. Dunlop, *Labor and the American Community* (New York: Simon & Schuster, Touchstone Books, 1970), pp. 70–77.

[39] The insurgent's campaign was aided by a $200,000 war chest raised entirely from union members and by the fact that earlier UMW reforms guaranteed him the right to express his views in the union's newspaper. See William Serrin, "Democracy by Unions," *New York Times,* November 15, 1982, p. A17; "Generals of Shrinking Armies," *Time,* November 22, 1982, p. 87; and "Coal Miners Vote for a New Generation," *Business Week,* November 22, 1982, p. 31.

[40] On the ITU, see the classic study by Seymour Martin Lipset, Martin Trow, and James Coleman, *Union Democracy: The Inside Politics of the International Typographical Union* (New York: Free Press, 1956).

[41] See Gerald Morris, "Teachers and Union Democracy" (Ph.D. dissertation, Harvard University, 1976).

ganizational democracy is alive in American trade unions—both industrial unions such as the UMW and white-collar unions such as the AFT.

Organizational Democracy: Some Data

Anxious to examine associational democracy more systematically, we asked the representatives of membership organizations in our survey a set of questions focusing on their organizations' electoral arrangements for choosing officers. We probed, in particular, to learn whether elections were contested and, if so, whether competing candidates represented stable parties or factions that continue from one election to the next. Our emphasis upon partylike competition reflects the understanding, widely shared among analysts of elections, that vigorously contested elections in which candidates are associated with ongoing, identifiable parties or factions are distinctive in several ways: voter turnout tends to be higher; candidates are more likely to take distinguishable positions on the issues; voters are more likely to cast ballots on the basis of some understanding of the choices being offered; and voters are given a chance to make retrospective evaluations of the performance of the current administration regardless of whether the incumbents are running.[42]

Table 6.1 presents the results of our inquiry. The findings are mixed, supporting neither an "iron law of oligarchy" nor an opposing "iron law of democracy." It is clear that the *forms* of electoral democracy are preserved

Table 6.1   ELECTORAL COMPETITION IN MEMBERSHIP ORGANIZATIONS

	Trade associations	Unions	Citizens' groups	All membership groups
Officers chosen in elections	85%	100%	73%	86%
Elections are ordinarily contested	31	68	54	46
Parties or factions in contested elections:				
1. As proportion of such organizations having contested elections	50	64	43	53
2. As proportion of all such organizations choosing officers in elections	14	37	27	23
3. As proportion of all such organizations	12	37	20	20
	(N=34)	(N=19)	(N=15)	(N=102)

Source: Washington Representatives Survey.

[42]For the seminal statement of this point of view, see V. O. Key, Jr., *Southern Politics* (New York: Random House, Vintage Books, 1949), Chapter 14.

almost universally. Note that 86 percent of all the membership groups choose their officers in elections, even though in only 46 percent of these organizations are there ordinarily opposing candidates in the elections. Furthermore, in only 53 percent of the organizations having contested elections—or only 20 percent of all the membership groups—do the candidates represent parties or factions.

Moreover, our interviews indicate that when there are parties or factions, they vary substantially both in their durability and in the degree to which they act, from election to election, as stable objects of loyalty to individual members. In addition, the axes of cleavage about which such persistent rivalries emerge are diverse indeed. Sometimes, as in one white-collar union, the competition is between the ins and the outs, the incumbents and the challengers. In such a case, the electoral issues focus on the relative ability and effectiveness of alternative leaders rather than on matters of policy. Sometimes the division is ideological. For example, according to the executive director of the American Political Science Association, electoral competition inside the association has largely been an ideological matter, with the opposition coming from the political left. The issue at stake is whether the APSA should become more politicized as an organization, staking out positions on a wide variety of public problems. Sometimes, subgroups within an organization have conflicting interests. The director of governmental affairs of the Railway Labor Executives Association, an organization composed of chief executive officers of railway labor unions described "stable, consistent interest factions" pitting nonoperators, who care for tracks and equipment, against operators, who run trains. Sometimes, what is at stake is personalities, not policy issues. In addition, our respondents described factions rooted in competition between large and small firms, members in different regions, and so on.

The figures in Table 6.1 for the various categories of organizations are also interesting. It is, in fact, the labor unions that are most likely to choose their officers in contested elections in which the candidates represent parties or factions. Since unions provide benefits that are highly valued and since disgruntled union members are unlikely to have an alternative organization to join if they decide to exit, this is perhaps not surprising. Interestingly, citizens' groups are least likely to choose their officers in elections. This fact is consistent with an accusation that is sometimes leveled at citizens' groups—that they are staff organizations that are internally undemocratic.[43] However, in contrast to union members, members of citizens' groups ordinarily can quit without serious loss if they are unhappy. What is more, members of citizens' groups seem to be the least intensely involved organization members: only 22 percent of the citizens' group representatives—as opposed to 38 percent of the union representatives and 66 percent of the trade association representatives—describe their members as quite involved. Thus the stakes are not high for members of citizens'

---

[43]Michael T. Hayes makes such an argument in "Interest Groups: Pluralism or Mass Society?" in Allan J. Cigler and Burdett A. Loomis, eds., *Interest Group Politics* (Washington DC: CQ Press, 1983), pp. 110–125.

groups. Under such circumstances, democratic guarantees may lose their urgency. On the other hand, members of citizens' groups may not have enough information about what is going on in the organization to be able to exercise the option of quitting in an informed way.

The logic is somewhat different for trade associations. Association representatives report that their members are involved, and 85 percent of the trade associations elect officers in elections. However, only 31 percent of these elections are contested, and even fewer are characterized by ongoing factional competition. The absence of electoral democracy in trade associations probably reflects the number of options open to the dissatisfied trade association member. As shown in Chapter 4, trade associations tend to proliferate, and individual firms tend to belong to a number of them. The processed food industry, for example, is represented in politics not simply by such large organizations as the National Food Processors Association and the American Frozen Food Institute, but also by a host of more specialized ones such as the National Pretzel Bakers Institute, the Association for Dressings and Sauces, and the Pickle Packers International. Given the number and specialization of such organizations, there is likely to be an institutionalized mechanism for the expression of subgroup preferences when there is structured conflict within a large industry. What is more, the benefits provided by trade associations are often available elsewhere. Companies can often purchase them on the open market (or as nonmembers from the trade association at a higher price) or provide them for themselves. Of course, many corporations do not rely exclusively on the political efforts of their trade associations but, rather, maintain their own offices in the capital. In short, under these circumstances as well, democratic guarantees lose their urgency.

THE PROBLEM OF BUREAUCRATIC RESPONSIVENESS

It may be, however, that such electoral arrangements are meaningless if organizational officers who are elected in regular, free, and competitive elections are, in fact, mere figureheads in a staff-run operation. An appointed staff, of course, is beyond the reach of electoral accountability. These staff members, on the scene year after year while elected officers come and go, are indeed powerful, and their presence raises the problem of making sure that the paid staff who make up an organization's relatively permanent bureaucracy is responsive to members' wishes.[44] The concern is that as an organization becomes more and more established, it will acquire a larger and more specialized staff (typically not drawn from the ranks of the organization's members). These persons who have control of the organization's administrative apparatus will progressively become concerned primarily with protecting the organization and their own security within it. Consequently, the elites will become risk-averse, pursuing

[44]On this matter, see the concerns of Michels, *Political Parties,* pp. 382, 386, 405–406.

more conservative external goals and generally taking more cautious political action than the rank and file would prefer.

The paid staff ordinarily has considerable power in running organizations, but it is not clear that staff members are inevitably cautious. There are many examples of contemporary organizations whose elites regularly adopt more militant or more progressive positions than those favored by the membership. For example, the staff of the National Council of Churches has frequently adopted more politicized, more progressive stands on issues of civil rights and social welfare policy than local churches would. The AFL-CIO is another organization whose large, bureaucratized staff is commonly regarded as being more liberal than most of the organization's members.[45] And the decision, referred to earlier, by the leadership and staff of the American Civil Liberties Union to defend the right of Nazis to march could hardly be described as cautious or self-protective.

There are two ways of explaining cases in which organizations adopt positions on public policy issues that are different from members' preferences.[46] First, such deviations may occur in organizations where the national leadership does not have to worry much about trying to keep the rank and file member happy because maintenance of the membership is the responsibility of local or constituent units of the organization (the local church, the local union, or the local chapter). Second, group organization may sometimes disregard members' preferences in order to maintain the goodwill and commitment of another important constituency, the organization's staff. This is especially likely in organizations that pay their professional staff members low salaries relative to what they could earn in other settings. To retain the services of these staff members, group leaders may have to compensate them with the nonmonetary incentive of purposive satisfaction and allow them a hand in choosing the goals of the organization and in other tasks that will give them the sense that they are accomplishing things and fulfilling an important purpose.

Typically, however, an organization's leaders—elected or appointed officials and their staffs—are less likely to defy members' wishes than to defer to them. For the very reasons outlined earlier, in many organizations the administrative elites spend large amounts of time and resources trying to determine members' preferences and are likely to be deferential to—not defiant of—members' wishes. The leaders defer to the members in order to maintain the organization—that is, to ensure that it will be able to obtain the essential resources (money, personnel, goodwill, political support, and so on) necessary for it not merely to survive but to prosper. Since in most voluntary associations an important source of such resources is the membership, the administrative elites do not go out of their way to alienate the members.

---

[45] This point is made by a number of authors. See, for example, J. David Greenstone, *Labor in American Politics* (New York: Random House, Vintage Books, 1969), p. 343; Bok and Dunlop, *Labor and the American Community,* p. 460; and Wilson, *Political Organizations,* pp. 226–227.

[46] Wilson, *Political Organizations,* pp. 226–227.

COMMUNICATING WITH MEMBERS

In discussing the problem of organizational democracy—and the relationship between the interests and preferences of members and those of leadership and staff—we have focused on questions of democratic representation and, thus, assumed implicitly an upward flow of communications from members to leaders and staff. Important as this upward flow may be with respect to theoretical questions of representation and accountability, we should not neglect the opposite side of the exchange, the flow of information downward from leaders and staff to rank and file. Our interviews with the Washington representatives contacted in our survey make clear that they consider this process important.

As shown in Table 6.2, 72 percent of the Washington representatives indicated that they spend a great deal of time on such communications. In addition, only 7 percent said that they devote little or no time to communicating with members or corporate headquarters. This pattern is more or less uniform across the various categories of organizations. Although unions and citizens' groups are somewhat less likely than corporations and trade associations to dedicate a great deal of time to keeping members informed, the overall similarities among kinds of organizations overshadow the differences. When we

Table 6.2 INTERNAL COMMUNICATIONS WITHIN ORGANIZATIONS

How much time and resources of Washington office are devoted to internal communications with members/corporate headquarters?

	Corporations	Trade associations	Unions	Citizens' groups	All organizations
A great deal	79%	77%	63%	57%	72%
Some	15	19	32	38	20
Little	6	3	5	5	6
Almost none	0	0	0	0	1
	100%	99%	100%	100%	99%

In general, which is more important component—communications with government officials or communications with own members/corporate headquarters?

	Corporations	Trade associations	Unions	Citizens' groups	All organizations
Government officials	46%	34%	41%	50%	39%
Equally important	39	47	29	30	42
Own members/ Corporate headquarters	15	19	29	20	18
	100%	100%	99%	100%	99%
	(N=46)	(N=32)	(N=17)	(N=20)	(N=153)

Source: Washington Representatives Study.

asked which, in general, is a more important component of the organization's work—communications with government officials or communications with members (or corporate headquarters)—a surprising 42 percent of those responding indicated that the two kinds of communications are equally important. Of course, they consider communications with government to be crucial; still, in no category did a majority of the respondents indicate that communications with government take precedence.

Early Warning System

These communications are used to achieve several different, sometimes simultaneous, purposes. First, the communications serve as a kind of early warning system—that is, a means of keeping members from being surprised or being taken unaware by political or governmental developments.[47] An organization's members rely on their leaders and staff to monitor what is happening in government—the introduction of new legislation in Congress, the scheduling of new rule-making proceedings at an executive agency, and the like—that may have an impact on the members' interests. The communication of this accumulated political intelligence typically occurs through a regular medium, such as an organizational magazine or newspaper. Many organizations also publish regular reports or newsletters that perform this function. For example, every three months the American Bankers Association (ABA) publishes for the private use of ABA members a "Government Relations Status Report," an exceptionally detailed document that runs more than a hundred pages. The report furnishes members with useful information on recently enacted legislation, on issues pending in Congress and before regulatory agencies, and on the implications of recent court cases. For each specific item (such as changes in estate and gift taxes or bankruptcy laws) the report provides a concise background briefing on the subject, an indication of how government action would affect bankers, a statement of the ABA's position on the matter, a notice about its current status, and the name and phone number of an ABA staff member in Washington who can be contacted for further information. Clearly, those receiving such sophisticated information are in a superior position to act in defense of their interests.

Educating Members

Downward communications also serve to educate members about the political process itself by explaining, for example, the structure and operation of institu-

[47] See Milbrath, *The Washington Lobbyists*, pp. 202–206, and Lewis Anthony Dexter, *How Organizations Are Represented in Washington* (Indianapolis: Bobbs-Merrill, 1969), pp. 102–111. Organizations also see the process in these terms, as evidenced by an article in a Chase Manhattan Bank publication that referred to the bank's Washington lobbying operation as "an early warning system for Chase." [Carl G. Mueller, "The Chase-Washington Dialogue," *Chase Directions* (Summer 1980), p. 3.]

tions, the mechanics of grass roots organizing, the subtleties of political strategy, and the importance of careful timing. Organizations typically tailor their communications to their particular constituencies in order to make matters of politics and government understandable. For example, the American Society of Mechanical Engineers uses sophisticated flowcharts to explain governmental processes to its members. A common element in the educational efforts of large organizations is providing members with "how to" booklets describing in detail such matters as how to communicate effectively with legislators about pending legislation. The standard version of such advice includes these kinds of tips:

- Keep your letters brief and to the point.
- Identify your subject clearly, providing the name and number of the legislation about which you are writing.
- State your reason for writing. Your own personal experience is your best supporting evidence.
- Don't be argumentative and don't engage in name-calling.
- Never threaten political repudiation if the member of Congress disagrees with you.
- Avoid standard phrases that give the appearance of form letters.

Organizations often furnish their members with a sample text to help them in drafting their own letters to legislators.

Communications from leaders and staff to members permit an organization's Washington officials to help members (or corporate headquarters) to understand what they can reasonably expect, both from government and from the organization itself, and to interpret governmental actions that are likely to affect the members. Thus, leaders and staff perform an additional educational and interpretive function: assisting members in understanding the complexities of Washington politics that render necessary accommodation and compromise in the face of competing demands made by public officials and other private interests.[48] By helping them appreciate the positions of government and the nature of the other interests that the government must take into account, interest groups thus function as intermediaries, helping constituents to adapt, accommodate, and adjust.

"Farming" Members

Of course, organizational communications can be used for purposes other than informing members on the substance of issues and educating them about the processes of government and politics. Leaders and staff also use internal communications to "farm," or cultivate the members' support for favored policy positions and programs. It is commonplace for the leaders and staff in Wash-

---

[48] Lewis Anthony Dexter argues that this interpretive function is a crucial one. *How Organizations Are Represented in Washington,* pp. 103–104.

ington to spend lots of time and resources trying to persuade members (or corporate headquarters) that some matters are more worthy of attention than others and some courses of action are more appropriate. This often requires leaders and staff to generate a flood of information in support of their case and to make personal appearances at local membership meetings to solidify support and justify their positions.[49]

It is probably even more common for the Washington leaders and staff of an organization to use its information network as a way to claim credit for developments that members (or headquarters) are likely to regard as beneficial or favorable to their interests. For example, virtually every major union has a regular magazine or newspaper that serves as a report to the members on what the leaders have done for them lately. *The Postal Record,* the monthly magazine of the National Association of Letter Carriers, is filled not only with the latest information on members' benefits but also with pictures and prose designed to demonstrate how tirelessly the union's president is working on the members' behalf. The unions are hardly alone in this regard. For example, the four-page March 1982 issue of the National Association of Home Builders' *Government Affairs Monitor* contains four photographs, all of them featuring the association's president talking with various public officials, including President Reagan. This display of eager effort on behalf of members is typical of the way in which organizations use the instruments of communication to let members know how valuable and active the leadership is.[50]

How are we to understand the function an organization's Washington office serves in communicating with members—as a means of intelligence gathering and dissemination, a means of Machiavellian manipulation, or a means of interpretive intermediation? It can, of course, be all three simultaneously in varying proportions. Effective communications—even the same communications—emanating from the same office can operate on many levels at once.

SUMMARY

This chapter has explored a variety of issues bearing on the internal dynamics of organizational operations and has probed the diverse interests and motivations of various people in organizations—those who establish them, those who maintain them, and those who join them. In particular, it examined some of the sources of organizational formation and the assortment of incentives that lead people to become members. In addition, the chapter investigated some of the problems that obtain when members of an organization are not of one mind on policy matters or when the interests of organizational members are not congru-

---

[49]On the concept of "farming" the constituency, see Milbrath, *The Washington Lobbyists,* p. 205, and Browne, "Benefits and Membership," pp. 261–263.

[50]It is not easy to say, in the abstract, whether this behavior confirms Michels's notions that members are manipulated by oligarchic leaders or whether much of it is simply a reflection of inflated egos.

ent with those of the leaders and staff. The internal operations of organizations are complex and dynamic. Organizational maintenance requires that a delicate balance of incentives, including a host of intangible gratifications, be supplied not only to members but to staff and officers as well. Moreover, this balancing act presumably makes the various elements in an organization more accommodating to one another's interests and preferences than the "iron law of oligarchy" would suggest.

Most of the balance of this book examines the activities of organized interests as entities operating in the larger political process—trying to shape public opinion and the outcome of elections, and pressing their interests before Congress, the executive branch, and the courts. In the main, we shall be referring to organizations as if they were monolithic, rational actors pursuing their goals. But the lessons of this chapter are that no matter how single-minded they may seem, they face critical internal tasks related to the generation of support and the resolution of internal conflict.

7

What Organized
Interests Do:
An Overview

The discussion so far about the nature of interest representation and the internal structure and politics of organizations has important implications for the way in which organized interests get involved in politics; however, most of the material up to this point has been essentially preliminary to our primary concern with the role of organized interests in the policymaking process. Here these matters will be considered more directly. Later chapters investigate the various efforts of organized interests to affect political outcomes indirectly by influencing public opinion and election results, and directly by lobbying Congress and the executive branch and by going to court. This chapter lays the groundwork for what is to come by treating several topics: the multiple techniques that organized interests use to influence what the federal government does; various factors that can affect the courses of political action that organized interests choose; and the relationships among representation, access, and influence by organized interests.

In order to understand how organized interests approach the enterprise of influencing political outcomes, it is necessary to know just what they do. Leaving more detailed examination for later chapters, let us begin with an overview of the many techniques that organizations use in their efforts to shape government policy: what they are; the extent to which different kinds of organizations use them; and the degree to which their use has changed over the past couple of decades.

TECHNIQUES OF INFLUENCE

In an effort to piece together a comprehensive picture of exactly what techniques groups use in their efforts to influence, either directly or indirectly, what goes on in government, we devised a list of 27 such techniques. The list includes both direct and indirect forms of influence: that is, activities in which the organization itself makes the case, as when testimony is given at an agency hearing, as well as those in which the organization attempts to influence policy outcomes either by mobilizing the public or its constituency or by affecting electoral results. The list embraces traditional forms of articulating positions, such as contacting officials directly, as well as nontraditional modes of expressing views, such as engaging in demonstrations or protests. It incorporates methods mobilizing various kinds of political resources—money, information, constituency size and cohesion, and appeal of the organizational cause. And, of course, the list includes techniques appropriate to each of the traditional institutional arenas—legislative, executive, and judicial.

We presented our respondents with this list and asked them to indicate, with respect to each one, whether or not the group uses it. Table 7.1 shows the results of that inquiry, listing in descending order the proportion of groups using each of the 27 methods. At the top of the scale, virtually all our respondents, 99 percent of them, testify at hearings; 98 percent contact officials directly; and 95 percent talk shop with officials in informal settings. At the bottom, only 20 percent engage in protests and demonstrations. Surely, the nature of our sample affects the results shown in Table 7.1. Given our deliberate attempt to sample active organizations, it is not surprising that Table 7.1 shows a great deal of activity. Still, what is striking about these figures is just *how much* organizations do. Seventeen of these techniques are used by at least three-quarters of the groups, and 21 are used by at least half. Figures not contained in Table 7.1 indicate that the median number of techniques used by an organization is 19, and the modal number of techniques is 21.

To probe further, it makes sense to ask whether different kinds of groups are specialists in different kinds of activities. Table D.1 (in Appendix D) gives the figures for the four kinds of organizations—corporations, trade associations, unions, and citizens' groups—that are sufficiently numerous in our sample to permit further investigation. What is striking is the overall similarity among the four categories of organizations with respect to the various techniques they employ. Among the most heavily used activities (those on the top half of the list, employed by at least 80 percent of all organizations), in only two cases do fewer than 70 percent of the organizations in a specific category use it. (Only 67 percent of the corporations report that they talk with people from the press and the media, and only 58 percent of the citizens' groups indicate that they mobilize influential constituents to contact legislators.)

Further down the list some differences do appear. Citizens' groups seem

Table 7.1   PERCENTAGE OF ORGANIZATIONS USING EACH OF TECHNIQUES
            OF EXERCISING INFLUENCE

1. Testifying at hearings	99%
2. Contacting government officials directly to present your point of view	98
3. Engaging in informal contacts with officials—at conventions, over lunch, and so on	95
4. Presenting research results or technical information	92
5. Sending letters to members of your organization to inform them about your activities	92
6. Entering into coalitions with other organizations	90
7. Attempting to shape the implementation of policies	89
8. Talking with people from the press and the media	86
9. Consulting with government officials to plan legislative strategy	85
10. Helping to draft legislation	85
11. Inspiring letter writing or telegram campaigns	84
12. Shaping the government's agenda by raising new issues and calling attention to previously ignored problems	84
13. Mounting grass roots lobbying efforts	80
14. Having influential constituents contact their congressional representative's office	80
15. Helping draft regulations, rules, or guidelines	78
16. Serving on advisory commissions and boards	76
17. Alerting congressional representatives to the effects of a bill on their districts	75
18. Filing suit or otherwise engaging in litigation	72
19. Making financial contributions to electoral campaigns	58
20. Doing favors for officials who need assistance	56
21. Attempting to influence appointments to public office	53
22. Publicizing candidates' voting records	44
23. Engaging in direct-mail fund raising for your organization	44
24. Running advertisements in the media about your position on issues	31
25. Contributing work or personnel to electoral campaigns	24
26. Making public endorsements of candidates for office	22
27. Engaging in protests or demonstrations	20

Source: Washington Representatives Survey.

substantially less likely than the other kinds of groups to make financial contributions to candidates (presumably because many of these groups have tax-exempt status, which restricts their political activity). In addition, there are several techniques that seem to be employed more frequently by certain groups. Unions and citizens' groups seem to be much more likely to publicize candidates' voting records and, not surprisingly, to engage in direct-mail fund raising. Furthermore, there are several techniques—donating manpower to campaigns, endorsing candidates, and engaging in protests—that are virtually exclusive to the unions. Still, with respect to techniques used, it is the similarities rather than the differences across types of groups that are striking.

We asked our respondents, in addition, to scan the entire list of 27 activities and choose those three that consume the largest share of the group's time and resources. As shown in Table 7.2, which lists for each of the techniques the

Table 7.2   PERCENTAGE OF ORGANIZATIONS FOR WHOM TECHNIQUE CONSUMES TIME AND RESOURCES

1. Contacting government officials directly to present your point of view	36%
2. Testifying at hearings	27
3. Presenting research results or technical information	27
4. Mounting grass roots lobbying efforts	26
5. Shaping the government's agenda by raising new issues and calling attention to previously ignored problems	20
6. Entering into coalitions with other organizations	20
7. Consulting with government officials to plan legislative strategy	19
8. Attempting to shape the implementation of policies	17
9. Alerting congressional representatives to the effects of a bill on their districts	14
10. Sending letters to members of your organization to inform them about your activities	12
11. Helping to draft legislation	12
12. Engaging in informal contacts with officials—at conventions, over lunch, and so on.	10
13. Talking with people from the press and the media	10
14. Inspiring letter writing or telegram campaigns	10
15. Making financial contributions to electoral campaigns	8
16. Helping draft regulations, rules, or guidelines	7
17. Having influential constituents contact their congressional representatives' office	6
18. Engaging in direct-mail fund raising for your organization	5
19. Serving on advisory commissions and boards	4
20. Filing suit or otherwise engaging in litigation	4
21. Running advertisements in the media about your positions on issues	3
22. Publicizing candidates' voting records	2
23. Contributing work or personnel to electoral campaigns	2
24. Doing favors for officials who need assistance	2
25. Engaging in protests or demonstrations	1
26. Attempting to influence appointments to public office	0
27. Making public endorsements of candidates for office	0

Source: Washington Representatives Survey.

percentage of respondents indicating that it consumes time and resources, there is quite a bit of dispersion in the responses, and no single technique is chosen by a majority of the respondents. There is, however, a rough correspondence between those techniques that are employed by the largest share of organizations and those that are most frequently cited as consuming time and resources. Contacting officials directly and testifying at hearings are used virtually universally; they also consume time and resources for the plurality of organizations. On the other hand, engaging in informal contacts with officials and sending letters to organization members to keep them informed are also employed by nearly all groups; however, they are much less frequently mentioned as consuming time and resources.

While there was rough congruence among the various kinds of organizations in terms of the kinds of techniques they use, there is more disparity with respect to the kinds of techniques they cite as consuming time and resources.[1] (See Table D.2 in Appendix D for the evidence on which this paragraph is based.) Corporations are substantially less likely than trade associations, unions, or citizens' groups to indicate that testifying at hearings or shaping the government's agenda consume time or resources. Corporations and citizens' groups are much more likely than unions or trade associations to indicate that presenting research results is a time- or resource-consuming activity. Citizens' groups mention more frequently than other kinds of organizations that talking to the press and the media consumes time and resources. Once again, however, it is the unions that evince an unusual pattern of responses. They are less likely than the other kinds of groups to mention contacting officials directly, entering into coalitions, consulting with government officials to plan legislative strategy, or shaping implementation as activities that consume resources, and they are much more likely to mention making financial contributions.

MORE ACTIVITY?

The common wisdom among journalists and politicians is that there has been an explosion in organized interest activity in recent years. *Time* has called this "an era of the strenuous clique and the vociferous claque" in which "factions of all sizes and configurations, alike only in self-service and single-mindedness,

---

[1] Thomas L. Gais and Jack L. Walker, ("Pathways to Influence in American Politics: Factors Affecting the Choice of Tactics by Interest Groups" paper presented at the Annual Meeting of the Midwest Political Science Association, Chicago, April 1983), seem to reach similar conclusions in a sophisticated analysis of the results of a mail survey. However, because their measures are highly aggregated and because their level of analysis is quite abstract, it is hard to make explicit comparisons. In addition, differences between the two samples are surely responsible in part for any discrepancies. We include unions and corporations, while Gais and Walker do not. In addition, all our organizations have their own Washington offices. Therefore, it is not surprising that we find a greater prevalence of what they call "insider strategies."

tend to dominate virtually every salient issue."[2] According to *Newsweek*, it is an age of "Me-first factionalism" in which "every conceivable issue seems to have competing pressure groups—from gun control and import quotas to abortion and nuclear power."[3] Those in Congress experience it firsthand. According to Senator Gary Hart of Colorado:

> I hate to get on the plane for Denver. For three hours the lobbyists just line up in the aisle to get a word with me. Most of them are special pleaders for business, and they generally have two messages. The first is that there is too much government, too much taxation and spending—and that they want something specific from the federal government.[4]

These sentiments are echoed by Senator Daniel Patrick Moynihan of New York, who complained that the lobbyists "come at you in relays. It's like the human wave approach to legislation. They never stop."[5]

It is important to subject the accounts of journalists and politicians to the light of systematic data, for there is always the possibility that the expansion in group activity is merely illusory. It may be that the most successful lobbying has traditionally been that which is least overt, the regularized interactions between organization representatives and government officials that proceed largely unnoticed by the public. Perhaps what has happened is that a few groups—Common Cause would be a good example—have arrived on the scene making a lot of noise. Disclaiming or lacking the access enjoyed by insiders of the old school, such groups deliberately bring their message to the public, often as dramatically as possible, by fine-tuned direct-mail campaigns and the skillful use of other new technologies. The noise is amplified when these groups receive the media coverage that their publicity-engendering tactics are designed to attract. Thus it may take relatively little innovation to give the appearance of a burst of new activity.

There is strong evidence that the expansion in group activity perceived by public officials and journalistic observers is real, not spurious. Chapter 4 showed that there are many new groups on the Washington scene. Fully 40 percent of the organizations having offices in the capital were born since 1960; in addition, over 60 percent of them opened their Washington offices since then.

Furthermore, in terms of what the groups are doing, there is additional confirmation for the journalistic perception of an expansion in group activity in recent years. Among the first questions we asked our respondents was an open-ended one inquiring about the changes over the past decade in the way their

---

[2]"The Menace of Fanatic Factions," *Time,* October 23, 1978, p. 73.
[3]"Single Issue Politics," *Newsweek,* November 6, 1978, p. 48.
[4]Ibid.
[5]Quoted in David Shribman, "Lobbyists Proliferate—So Do Headaches," *New York Times,* July 25, 1982, p. E5.

groups went about trying to influence what goes on in Washington. The question, not surprisingly, netted dozens of answers going off in many directions. However, the single most frequent reply—articulated by 32 percent of the respondents—was some variation on the simple theme "We are more active than we used to be."[6] The government affairs representative for a national teachers' organization discussed this change in terms of the increasing politicization of its membership:

> It's a much more sophisticated approach now. We have a lot of political activists in our locals—people we can count on to work in campaigns. There is a major change or difference in our membership and their attitude. In 1968, we didn't even come out in support of Humphrey because, at that time, people didn't think that a national teachers' association had a role in politics. Now it's the rare local that doesn't think that everything is tied to politics.

The representative for a major peak association of businesses discussed his organization's escalating political involvement in different terms:

> There are more people in the act and more issues to deal with. For example, in the 93rd Congress, we had 40 issues; in the 94th, 71 issues; in the 95th, 101 issues; in the 96th, 132 issues. Hopefully, that's tapering off now.

We immediately followed up this open-ended question with a closed-ended one asking about changes in the group's level of activity over the past decade. A remarkable 88 percent of the respondents indicated that their groups had become more active in recent years; 9 percent said that their activity level was largely unchanged; and a mere 3 percent said that their activity had diminished.[7]

We can probe this issue further by returning to our list of 27 methods of political influence. Each time a respondent indicated that his group utilized a given technique, we inquired whether its use of that method had increased, decreased, or remained the same in recent years. Table 7.3 shows, once again in descending order, the proportion of groups reporting increased use of a particular technique in recent years. Again there is a range: 68 percent of the groups in our sample are having more contact with people from the press and the media, while only 9 percent are engaging more frequently in protests and

---

[6]This figure underrepresents the number of references to this theme because it does not include the many additional respondents who amplified this theme by citing some specific change, such as the growth of government activity, that has had the effect of increasing their involvement in politics.

[7]We are unsure of the effect of our sampling technique on these figures. It is difficult to know whether, in systematically sampling organizations with *high* levels of Washington activity, we also sampled organizations with *increasing* levels of Washington activity. We do not know whether the *National Journal* is systematically less likely to report on an active organization whose activity is, nonetheless, not growing.

Table 7.3   **PERCENTAGE OF ORGANIZATIONS USING EACH OF TECHNIQUES MORE THAN IN PAST**

1. Talking with people from the press and media	68%
2. Entering into coalitions with other organizations	68
3. Contacting government officials directly to present your point of view	67
4. Testifying at hearings	66
5. Sending letters to members of your organization to inform them about your activities	65
6. Presenting research results or technical information	63
7. Mounting grass roots lobbying efforts	59
8. Inspiring letter writing or telegram campaigns	58
9. Engaging in informal contacts with officials—at conventions, over lunch, and so on	57
10. Attempting to shape the implementation of policies	56
11. Helping to draft legislation	54
12. Shaping the government's agenda by raising new issues	54
13. Consulting with government officials to plan legislative strategy	54
14. Having influential constituents contact their congressional representative's office	52
15. Making financial contributions to electoral campaigns	49
16. Alerting congressional representatives to the effects of a bill on their districts	45
17. Helping to draft regulations, rules, or guidelines	44
18. Filing suit or otherwise engaging in litigation	38
19. Serving on advisory commissions and boards	32
20. Engaging in direct-mail fund raising for your organization	31
21. Attempting to influence appointments to public office	23
22. Doing favors for officials who need assistance	21
23. Running advertisements in the media about your position on issues	19
24. Publicizing candidates' voting records	19
25. Contributing work or personnel to electoral campaigns	18
26. Making public endorsements of candidates for office	14
27. Engaging in protests or demonstrations	9

Source: Washington Representatives Survey.

demonstrations. What is noteworthy, however, is how much increase there has been. In 14 of the 27 cases, at least half the respondents reported they were using a technique more in recent years. Viewed from another perspective, the median group reported increased utilization of 13, or just under half, of these methods.

The other side of this coin is perhaps even more striking. Our data on the proportion of groups reporting *decreased* use of a particular technique in recent years reveal a very narrow range; for each of the 27 techniques, the proportion of groups reporting a decrease in use was 5 percent or fewer. (The average across all 27 techniques was a decreased use by only 2 percent of the groups.)

A Transformation in Techniques of Influence?

It is possible that there has been not only an expansion in group activity but also a transformation of its character. Two of the principal changes in our larger political environment—the revolution in assorted electronic technologies and a reinforcement of the nexus between the congressional representative and his or her district—may well be giving rise not simply to more activity but also to entirely new kinds of activity or at least to enhanced salience of some forms of activity at the expense of others.

We might reasonably expect recent developments in mass communications and data-processing technologies to add new weapons to an organization's arsenal, facilitating its use of indirect forms of lobbying in order to influence the decisions of government officials. The electronic and print media make it easier than ever to reach not only the public at large but also special publics with messages specially designed to maximize their popular appeal. Given the sophistication and effectiveness of these communications technologies, we might expect to find organizations relying increasingly on such methods as direct-mail fund raising, efforts to generate letters and telegrams to public officials, and advertising campaigns in the media to explain positions on issues.

Similarly, it seems sensible to predict that the approaches taken by organized interests would be altered by the strengthening of the ties between the congressional representative and his or her district. Academic observers of Congress point to a cluster of phenomena to demonstrate that in recent times the modern legislator is not so much an instructed delegate as a parochial advocate, attentive both to the expressed preferences and the particularistic needs of constituents.[8] Given this enhanced sensitivity to what the folks back home are telling legislators, we would expect organized interests to place special emphasis upon certain strategies and methods: for example, framing appeals to legislators in terms of the specific effects of a proposed measure upon their own districts; bringing influential constituents from the district to Wash-

---

[8]On this theme see, for example, Morris Fiorina, *Congress—Keystone of the Washington Establishment* (New Haven: Yale University Press, 1977); John A. Ferejohn, *Pork Barrel Politics* (Stanford: Stanford University Press, 1974); David Mayhew, *Congress: The Electoral Connection* (New Haven: Yale University Press, 1974); Richard Fenno, *Home Style* (Boston: Little, Brown, 1978); and Steven V. Roberts, "Congressmen and Their Districts: Free Agents in Fear of the Future," in Dennis Hale, ed., *The United States Congress: Proceedings of the Thomas P. O'Neill, Jr., Symposium on the U.S. Congress* (Chestnut Hill, MA: Boston College, 1982), pp. 65–83.

ington in order to present a case to their own representative rather than relying on the persuasiveness of their permanent Washington lobbyists; and generating communications from constituents. Here our expectations of the effects of changes in the nature of congressional representation reinforce our expectations of the effects of new technologies. Both point in the direction of increased salience of indirect lobbying techniques in which groups mobilize citizens at the grass roots to communicate with policymakers.

However, considering the evidence in Table 7.3 from the perspective of these hunches, our expectation that the advent of computers or the importance of advocacy representation would transform organized interest activity is not borne out.[9] Table 7.3 does not indicate selective increases among the clusters of techniques that are either electronically relevant or constituency-based. Certainly, at the top of the list is one method of influence for which we would anticipate huge increases in an electronic age—talking with people from the press and media. However, two others that might also be related to new communications technologies—engaging in direct-mail fund raising and running ads in the media—are near the bottom. Techniques specified as particularly relevant to an era of close links between legislators and constituents seem anchored in the upper-middle ranges of the list, far from the bottom but not at the top. In short, there is no selective increase in either electronically related or constituency-based modes of interest group activity. Use of these forms of interest representation has, of course, skyrocketed, but so too has the use of the time-honored direct methods of contact and consultation. Thus, the massive increase in pressure activity is built upon expanded use of various kinds of weapons in the organizational arsenal.

CHOOSING A COURSE OF POLITICAL ACTION

The discussion so far has made clear that most organizations have many arrows in their quivers, many techniques that they can use in approaching the task of political influence. In the face of so many options, how do they choose which ones to use? As a preliminary to the detailed examination in later chapters of organized activity in various arenas, let us consider some of the factors that shape the particular strategies and tactics an organization adopts in pursuit of its political objectives.

Deciding to Act at All

The first decision faced by those who design political strategy for an organization is whether to act at all. Sometimes, of course, external events dictate that

---

[9]This theme is treated at greater length in Kay Lehman Schlozman and John T. Tierney, "More of the Same: Washington Pressure Activity in a Decade of Change," *Journal of Politics* 45 (1983): 351–377.

there is essentially no alternative but to get involved. In particular, actions taken by other political actors—especially government officials—provide the impetus for political activity.[10] For example, when the staff of the Federal Trade Commission decided to recommend rules requiring that used car dealers inform potential buyers of the known defects of cars offered for sale, automobile dealers had little choice but to get involved if they wished to protect their interests. Hence, the National Automobile Dealers Association swung into action to block the adoption of such a rule. Less frequently, organizational maintenance considerations provide the impetus for an organization to become active. For example, citizens' groups, especially those that use direct-mail to raise funds, sometimes latch onto highly visible and emotional issues in order to sustain membership involvement.[11]

While the decision to become politically active is sometimes determined by exogenous forces, organizations frequently take the initiative themselves. It is by no means inevitable that issues of concern to an organization will become objects of public policy concern unless the organization itself puts them on the government's policy agenda. Thus organized interests not only react to political developments and the actions of others, but they also take advantage of opportunities to place issues on the policy agenda.[12] For example, in the early 1970s two groups representing the handicapped, the National Association for Retarded Children and the Council for Exceptional Children, were instrumental in drawing attention to the educational needs of handicapped youngsters. Without the efforts of these groups to raise the issue and press the government to do something about it, the Education for All Handicapped Children Act—which secured for handicapped children the right to free and appropriate educational programs, whenever possible in settings with nonhandicapped children—would never have been passed.[13] Groups concerned with civil rights, the environment, and consumer protection also are well known for their successful efforts to shape the government's agenda.

In addition to blocking initiatives to which they object and trying to draw attention to new concerns, many organized interests also have to work to keep alive an issue that might pass off the government's agenda but for sustained

[10]On the way in which the political involvement of organized interests frequently reflects efforts to block changes in public policy initiated by other actors, see John W. Kingdon, *Agendas, Alternatives, and Public Policies* (Boston: Little, Brown, 1984), pp. 52–54.

[11]See R. Kenneth Godwin, "Lobbying Choices of Citizen Action Groups" paper presented at the Annual Meeting of the Midwest Political Science Association, Chicago, April 1984, p. 15.

[12]Because questions of the permeability of the American political system both to new groups and to new issues have been part of the multifaceted critique of pluralist analysis, the process of political agenda setting is often considered to be the virtually exclusive preserve of organized interests. As shown in Table 7.1, interests do devote time and resources to identifying problems and bringing them to the attention of government. However, organized interests are only one factor among many (and probably not the most important one) having a role in determining the contours of the policy agenda.

[13]On the history of this bill, see Erwin L. Levine and Elizabeth Wexler, *PL94–142: An Act of Congress* (New York: Macmillan, 1981).

efforts to retain it. An example is the continuing effort by the United Auto Workers to press for adoption of national health insurance long after other supporters had given it up as a dead issue.[14]

A variety of factors place important boundaries on the nature of the substantive demands organized interests can make and on the kinds of issues they can raise. Most fundamentally, the Constitution limits the kind of goals organized interests may pursue. For example, a church group proposing that Congress make weekly attendance at religious services mandatory for all Americans would get nowhere because such a bill would be clear violation of the First Amendment. American political culture places another boundary on what organizations demand; that is, the shared definitions and expectations that Americans have of government and its proper role shape the structure of the policy agenda. For example, commitments both to capitalism and to limited government are central strands in the American political culture. These commitments imply that an organization suggesting broad-scale public ownership of economic enterprises (railroads, airlines, utilities, and so on)—a pattern typical of many industrial democracies—would probably make little headway.[15]

Finally, past policies often circumscribe the kinds of proposals or options that organizations can offer for reasonable consideration by policymakers. For example, the formulation of transportation policies is shaped by the federal government's historical commitment to policies favorable to the growth and economic stabilization of the automobile industry. Any proposal by a citizens' group favoring much heavier federal commitment to mass transportation would have to conform to the legacies of past decisions: the existence of a vast network of interstate highways; an automobile industry employing, directly or indirectly, millions of workers; and so on. Not only would the realities of the current transportation infrastructure place technical limits on what policymakers can do, but the proponents of mass transportation would face organized political pressures generated by all those having a stake in previous policies. In short, then, there are some demands that are simply impractical for an organization to make.

Deciding What to Do

Once the initial decision to engage in political action has been made, an organization must choose its particular strategies and tactics. The constitutional prin-

[14]Kingdon points out that while some of this promotion is attributable to union ideology, the UAW also has a self-interested motive in pushing national health insurance, which would remove the issue of expensive health benefits from collective bargaining—a step that would be "particularly advantageous to a union such as the UAW since its health insurance benefits are impressively complete and thus unusually expensive." *Agendas, Alternatives, and Public Policies,* p. 51.

[15]On this point, see Anthony King, "Ideas, Institutions, and the Policies of Governments," *British Journal of Political Science* 3 (1973): 291–313, 409–423.

ciples of federalism and separation of powers divide sovereignty among the national, state, and local governments, and among the legislative, executive, and judicial branches. These constitutional arrangements multiply the number of institutions involved in policymaking and therefore increase the number of points of access open to an organized interest intent on influencing the course of policy decisions. This implies that there are a number of arenas in which a particular controversy might be played out. Hence, in the American context, strategic considerations may be more complicated than in political systems in which decision-making authority is less widely dispersed.[16]

If it has any choice in the matter, an organization is likely to try to locate a controversy in the institutional setting most likely to produce favorable results. This was the strategy pursued in the 1940s and 1950s by civil rights groups seeking equal rights for blacks. Recognizing the futility of attempting to deal with all-white Southern legislatures and the difficulties of approaching a Congress whose powerful members were drawn disproportionately from the ranks of Southerners, civil rights leaders concentrated on the federal courts and waged a patient, protracted legal struggle. A typical pattern illustrating organizational attempts to move a policy conflict into the arena most likely to yield a congenial outcome involves a trade association, certain of losing in its efforts to persuade a hostile regulatory agency to drop a potentially burdensome rule, taking its case to Congress, where it may have enjoyed victories in the past, where it may have many friends, or where its political resources may be brought to bear with more favorable effect.

Sometimes, of course, an organized interest has no choice as to the institutional arena in which a policy contest will be waged. A corporation may be sued by a group of its employees who charge it with violating federal antidiscrimination laws. If the corporation is to fight on this issue, it must do so in court, perhaps by questioning the constitutionality of affirmative action programs. Similarly, if a congressional subcommittee has started hearings with the intention of legislating a change in the minimum wage, labor and business organizations will fight at least the initial rounds on Capitol Hill.

Choosing Tactics   Once the arena is set (either because it has been forced on or chosen by the attentive interests), it narrows, at least for the moment, the range of political activities that an organized interest will find suitable. For example, as shown in later chapters, an organization going to court will necessarily behave differently than if it were lobbying Congress or trying to persuade the president's aides. Still, within any particular institutional arena, choices remain as to how to achieve political objectives.

An organization's decisions on such matters are shaped by a variety of

---

[16]On the way in which groups in Britain focus on the national administrative departments or ministries, where most of the important decisions are made, and on the case of the British Medical Association in particular, see Harry Eckstein, *Pressure Group Politics* (Stanford: Stanford University Press, 1960), especially Chapter 3.

factors—among them, what is legal. Of course, tactics such as bribery, black-mail, and fraud are illegal. In addition, as will become clear in later chapters, there are many other legal restrictions on the activities of organized interests. Such measures regulate, for example, the political activities of organizations having 501(c)(3) tax status; the size of contributions to legislative campaigns; and the circumstances under which lobbyists may approach executive officials about matters at issue in an administrative hearing or an adjudicatory proceeding. Chapter 11 considers briefly the extent of illegal activity among organized interests. To summarize the argument there, while it is impossible to assess with certainty the effectiveness of such legal restrictions, the common wisdom among political scientists is that there are so many legal avenues of influence that very few organizations resort to illegal methods.

Perhaps the most important factor affecting an organization's strategic choice of lobbying techniques is its resources. Chapter 5 made clear the many ways in which resources shape the opportunities and activities of organized interests. Most obviously, an organization with plenty of money enjoys options that less wealthy organizations lack. It can hire well-known lobbyists, mount expensive public relations campaigns, mobilize members at the grass roots, and the like. The size and geographic distribution of an organization's membership may also dictate its choice of lobbying techniques; if there are many members spread throughout most congressional districts, and if the organization has the means to mobilize them, a campaign of grass roots pressure may be an option.

The nature of the cause also has an impact on the choice of political techniques. Whereas a corporation fighting to ward off potential new limits on the rate at which it dumps pollutants into a river will work hard to minimize the visibility of the issue, an environmental group working for cleaner water will try to attract public attention to the issue. However, the same environmental group that goes to the public for support when it is dealing with such a highly emotional issue as toxic wastes will rely on behind-the-scenes lobbying of government officials when the issue is more technical in nature, such as the best available technology for manufacturing and handling PCB.[17]

Finally, an organization's choice with respect to tactics will be affected by what has worked in the past. Previous success not only generates the conclusion that a given technique is effective but also yields useful political experience in the employment of that technique. Hence, an organization that has enjoyed great success in Congress by joining in lobbying coalitions with other organizations is likely to consider such an option favorably in the future. Interestingly, an organization that enjoys the capacity for a particular kind of action may be pushed by the "law of the instrument" to pursue it. For example, because a group has a mailing list and the computer capabilities for grass roots mobilization, it may feel that it must use these facilities to justify its earlier investment.[18]

---

[17]Godwin, "Lobbying Choices of Citizen Action Groups," pp. 5–6.
[18]Ibid., p. 6.

Similarly, some large organizations have separate, well-differentiated subunits handling different operations. In such cases, the organization's choice of lobbying technique may result from the pushing and tugging that goes on among the unit responsible for mass mailings and member alerts, the unit in charge of research and information, and the unit involved with direct lobbying.[19]

REPRESENTATION, ACCESS, AND INFLUENCE

So far we have focused upon the question of how organizations go about trying to influence political outcomes in Washington. We have not, however, shed any light on a more fundamental issue: whether or not they are successful. Clearly, organizational input is not equivalent to political influence. Political outcomes are decided by a multiplicity of factors, only one of which is organized interest activity, and political scientists of an earlier era erred in attributing to organized interests a virtually exclusive role in policy determination.[20] We will not be able to answer definitively the question of whether activity by organized interests yields political influence. However, the issue is so critical to any inquiry into the place of organized interests in American politics that it bears discussion.

The evidence on which we are relying was not designed for the purpose of measuring political influence. In conducting our survey of Washington representatives, we sampled from the universe of Washington-based private organizations and asked our respondents about the government affairs activities of their organizations. The data thus gathered told us much that is important about the Washington pressure scene—what kinds of techniques are used to influence politics, what resources are important, what works and what fails, how things have changed, who talks to whom, and so on. However, the data are not appropriate for measuring the relative decisiveness of various political forces in making policy. Tackling the question of organized interest influence necessitates, not a sample of organizations, but a sample of policy controversies. If a random selection of cases could somehow be generated, then careful scrutiny of the details might yield generalizations about the extent of the political impact of organized interests.[21]

We do not have such a sample of cases. While we chose organizations

[19] Ibid., p. 11.

[20] See the discussion of the group theorists' perspective on the determination of policy in Chapter 1.

[21] Had we such a sample, our assessment of organized interest influence would have to allow for the fact that organized interests can have an impact on the course of political events even when there is no apparent controversy and no decisions get made. For analysis of this complicated issue, see Peter Bachrach and Morton S. Baratz, "Two Faces of Power," *American Political Science Review* 56 (1962): 947–952, and "Decisions and Nondecisions," *American Political Science Review* 57 (1963): 641–651. They elaborated on the process they call "nondecision-making" in *Power and Poverty* (New York: Oxford University Press, 1970).

To see how an organized interest can keep an issue off the policy agenda merely by virtue of its formidable reputation for power, see Matthew A. Crenson, *The Un-Politics of Air Pollution* (Baltimore: Johns Hopkins Press, 1971).

randomly in conducting our survey, there is good reason to suspect that the *cases* presented here are, in fact, a biased selection. In the chapters that follow, we examine many cases that demonstrate clear victories for organized interests—for example, the Calorie Control Council's successful attempt to prevent the Food and Drug Administration from banning the use of saccharin; the obstruction by the used car dealers of a regulation that would have required them to list the known defects on the autos they sell; the establishment of a separate Department of Education at the behest of the National Education Association; the promulgation of strict standards of access by handicapped members of the Architectural and Transportation Barriers Compliance Board; and the Food Research and Action Center's successful class action suit on behalf of those who had been deprived of food stamp benefits through administrative error. In so doing, we overlook many examples of stunning defeats for organized interests: the failure of the food industry to achieve an overhaul of the nation's food safety laws; of the American Medical Association to get an antitrust exemption from the Federal Trade Commission; of the American Petroleum Institute to obtain accelerated decontrol of natural gas; of the National Coalition to Ban Handguns to win passage of gun control legislation; and of labor unions to secure labor law reform.[22]

For good reason, the cases used here for illustrative purposes are skewed in the direction of demonstrating the successes of organized interests; in searching for examples of the use of a particular technique of political influence we were naturally drawn to those cases that would show the *effective* use of that technique, since cases in which the efforts of organized interests were half-hearted or bumbling are surely less useful for explaining how organized interests go about achieving their goals. Hence, the cases we use, taken together, surely overstate the proportion of unambiguous victories enjoyed by organized interests. Thus, we would not want to use our case material as the basis for generalizations about the level of influence of organized interests.

Thinking About the Influence of Organized Interests

What is more, it is inappropriate to infer the degree of policy influence enjoyed by an organization that has been active on a particular controversy simply from the outcome. Because political outcomes are decided by a multiplicity of factors, only one of which is organized interest activity, it is important to examine the entire course of the controversy in detail. Such scrutiny might show, for example, that a decision favorable to an organization resulted, not from its own efforts, but from unsolicited intervention of a friendly legislator, or that an apparent defeat masks effective political action that forestalled an even more substantial rout. Hence, the appropriate way to consider the influence of orga-

[22]The first three of these cases are discussed in Paul Taylor, "Lobbyists Lose the Game, Not the Guccis," *Washington Post,* July 31, 1983, p. A1.

nized interests in politics is to ask not "Who won?" but "Would the final outcome of the controversy have been less congenial to the organized interests in question had they not been politically active?"

To illustate, consider the announcement early in the Reagan administration of a plan to curtail enforcement of a package of nursing home reform regulations promulgated late in the Carter administration. Clearly, this constituted a defeat for an organization like the National Citizens Committee for Nursing Home Reform. However, scrutiny of the life history of this controversy demonstrates that the Reagan administration had originally planned to scuttle the regulations entirely. When the National Citizens Committee stirred up a huge public outcry, the administration backed down and, instead of canceling the regulations, decided only to limit their implementation.[23] In this case, then, the National Citizens Committee for Nursing Home Reform sustained a defeat, but it was not without influence. Had the committee not gotten involved at all, the defeat would have been even more damaging. Once again, in considering the question of the impact of organized interests, what is critical to assess is not who was the victor and who the vanquished but, rather, whether attempts at influence had an effect on the outcome. Moreover, it is critical to bear in mind that the activity of organized interests is only one among many factors shaping the outcome.

Access and Influence

As will become clear in the pages that follow, a steady refrain by lobbyists is that they are only seeking access, not influence. In light of the importance that lobbyists themselves attach to the distinction, it seems appropriate to probe further. Upon examination it appears that the boundary between access and influence is less clearly defined than it is sometimes assumed to be.

In order to understand the relationship between access and influence, consider the circumstance in which the government hears nothing at all from one of the contesting parties in a particular policy controversy. The question of government intervention on behalf of the textile workers who are subject to byssinosis, an occupation-related disease, commonly known as brown lung, provides an example. Government regulations designed to protect textile workers should, of course, be based on technical information about the extent and the seriousness of the problem. Exhibit 7.1 contains information culled from pamphlets published by two organizations with reason both to have access to relevant evidence and to have an intense concern about the issue—the American Textile Manufacturers Institute, whose member companies bear the cost of

[23]For the progression of events, see Robert Pear, "Reagan Officials Seek to Ease Rules on Nursing Homes," *New York Times,* December 20, 1981, pp. 1, 26; Robert Pear, "Schweiker Declares Nursing Home Rules Will Not Be Relaxed," *New York Times,* March 21, 1982, pp. 1, 34; Robert Pear, "Schweiker Seeking to Loosen Nursing Home Rules," *New York Times,* May 25, 1982, p. A21; and Robert Pear, "Nursing Homes Offer Strong Arguments for Re-Regulation," *New York Times,* October 23, 1983, p. E5.

any regulations, and the Amalgamated Clothing and Textile Workers, whose members are exposed to the disease. Exhibit 7.1(a) presents the gist of the industry's case; Exhibit 7.1(b), the union's.

It is apparent that the industry and the union differ on virtually every relevant aspect of the controversy: how many textile workers are exposed to byssinosis; whether all textile workers afflicted with chronic lung diseases have byssinosis; how effective job reassignment programs have been; and whether the industry has been concerned about the welfare of employees and responsive to the problem. Thus, it is possible to impart quite varied impressions of the "truth" about this policy matter. Clearly, policymakers having access to information from only one of the two parties would be likely to design different sets of regulations aimed at ameliorating brown lung.

Together with arguments made earlier to the effect that there is nothing automatic about the representation of all possible political points of view, this example suggests that access and influence are not fully separable. Reasonable arguments can ordinarily be made on more than one side of a political issue. A policymaker who hears from only one side—or who hears much more from one side than the other—is likely to be persuaded by the arguments and information to which he or she is exposed. Hence, if access is unequal, it would not be surprising if it were to have consequences for influence.

The Importance of Representation by an Organization

Implicit in our discussion is not only the notion that it matters for policy outcomes whether the government hears from all sides in a political conflict, but also the notion that jointly interested individuals who are represented by an ongoing organization are more likely to be effective than those who communicate with government on their own or who are represented by nascent organizations. The interested individual is more likely to be politically influential if he acts in concert with others. It is not simply the jointness of the activity that matters, not simply the fact that lawmakers are more likely to be persuaded if it becomes clear that the opinion being expressed is widely shared. Rather, organization is itself a resource. Those who share a point of view on some policy matter but have no organization to act as the vehicle for the expression of their common interests are likely to find themselves at a distinct disadvantage.

As the previous chapter indicated, one of the important functions of an organization's Washington representative is to monitor government policy, identifying measures under consideration that may have an impact on the organization's members so that they are not confronted with any surprising and disastrous *faits accomplis*. Individuals acting on their own or contemplating starting an organization lack this kind of ongoing intelligence. In addition, established organizations have many resources—access, contacts, skills, and reputation, to name a few—that give them a head start over organizations just

Exhibit 7.1(a)   THE BYSSINOSIS CONTROVERSY: THE INDUSTRY'S CASE

- At hearings held in 1977 on the cotton dust standard the American Textile Manufacturers Institute submitted data involving medical examinations and histories of 37,000 employees. Results of the study indicated that less than 1 percent exhibited both subjective (employee says he has a problem) and objective (tests indicate a breathing problem) symptoms of byssinosis.

- The number of incidences of byssinosis is grossly exaggerated. A more realistic figure is 2,330.

- In its chronic irreversible stage, byssinosis is indistinguishable from other chronic lung diseases such as bronchitis and asthma. Bear in mind that 20 percent of the total U.S. adult population suffers some form of chronic lung diseases, no matter where they work or live. To complicate the matter even further, these lung problems are often the result of a combination of such factors as heredity, old infections, atmospheric pollution, socioeconomic conditions, and personal habits. In the case of cotton textile workers it would be misleading, and in the vast majority of cases medically and morally incorrect, to blame disability on dust exposure alone.

- Industry's concern for employee health has prompted the establishment of medical screening programs throughout the textile industry. Data and techniques obtained from medical research are being used by the industry to scientifically detect potential employee health problems.

- Textile companies have implemented job reassignment programs that are designed to reassign employees who have been diagnosed as cotton dust reactors.

- The textile industry has attempted to provide the best health-oriented working environment for its employees. Textile companies have spent millions of dollars on dust control technology and equipment.

- No one has greater concern for the health and welfare of textile workers than does the industry itself. The textile industry has repeatedly stated its support for workers' compensation benefits under state laws for employees who have been diagnosed by competent pulmonary specialists as having disabling byssinosis.

- As early as 1973, the textile industry demonstrated its concern for the cotton dust problem by introducing a Work Practices Standard for Raw Cotton Dust. This voluntary effort by industry was designed to provide guidelines that would provide medical surveillance and reduce work exposure to cotton dust, minimizing the risk of those employees exposed.

Source: All items are direct quotations selected from pamphlets supplied to us by the American Textile Manufacturers Institute: "Some facts about 'PRESUMPTIVE DIAGNOSIS' of occupational diseases—a threat to the entire workers' compensation concept;" "SOME FACTS about the cotton textile industry and the cotton dust problem from the people most directly involved;" and "Facts about cotton dust, byssinosis, and the textile industry."

Exhibit 7.1(b)   THE BYSSINOSIS CONTROVERSY: THE UNION'S CASE

- At least 150,000 of the 800,000 textile workers in the United States suffer from some degree of brown lung. Thirty-five thousand are totally disabled.

- In the early stages, Brown Lung victims suffer from shortness of breath, tightness of chest and cough upon return to work on Mondays. Later, these symptoms extend to other work days, and finally they become more severe, and continuous, resulting in total and permanent disability.

- Doctors in [textile mill] towns have frequently entered into an unspoken conspiracy with textile management. Instead of telling mill workers that they have byssinosis, doctors refer to their condition as bronchitis, asthma or emphysema. They neglect to tell workers that these are the lung conditions which result from byssinosis.

- Even though a great number of workers did poorly on their lung tests, only 3 of the 1,400 workers employed [at West Point-Pepperell, Inc.] were offered transfers [to less dusty jobs] by the company. And these were never told anything about any disease called brown lung or byssinosis by any company doctor or nurse.

- Of the 35,000 cases of disabled brown lung victims, only some 400 have received compensation. . . . The plain fact is that the state system of Workers' Compensation is rigged against the victims of industrial disease. They have the heavy burden of proving not only that they are totally disabled, but that their disability comes from conditions they were exposed to on the job.

- The textile industry has a big stake in suppressing the facts about brown lung. If the victims were able to collect the Workers' Compensation they are entitled to, it would cost the industry hundreds of millions of dollars in increased insurance premiums. It would cost additional hundreds of millions to clean up the mills in order to prevent future cases of brown lung.

- The Public Health Service decided, over strong industry pressure, to re-evaluate the situation. The employers tried to suppress the investigation. A doctor commissioned by the Public Health Service to conduct research among cotton mill workers was denied access to the mills as a result of a boycott organized by the Georgia Textile Manufacturers Association. He had to do his research with cotton mill workers at the United States Federal Prison in Atlanta.

Source: All items are direct quotations selected from pamphlets supplied to us by the Amalgamated Clothing and Textile Workers Union: "The Right to Breathe: Where did it go and how did I lose it?" and "Fact Sheet: The OSHA Cotton Dust Standard."

getting off the ground. Besides, the members of an emergent group in the process of getting organized will find the start-up costs substantial: electing officers, raising money, recruiting members, and the like, all swallow time and resources that the already organized can devote to the business of political influence.

An example from the early years of the Reagan administration can serve to underline the proposition that organization is itself a political resource, placing the members of an ongoing group at an advantage over those who promote their joint political preferences either by acting as individuals in parallel or by forming a new organization around their commonly held interests. Let us consider three groups of citizens who are the beneficiaries of federal largesse: veterans, college students, and welfare recipients. All three are large, geographically dispersed groups. In terms of sheer numbers, all three figure significantly in the constituency of virtually every member of Congress, and all three derive benefits from the federal government that impinge seriously on day-to-day life.

With respect to organizational resources, however, these three groups are not similar at all. Veterans are represented by a number of well-known and active organizations in Washington including the Veterans of Foreign Wars and the American Legion. College students also have a Washington-based organization to represent their interests, but the American Student Association is no match for the veterans' organizations in terms of any of the resources that contribute to effectiveness in politics. Students do, however, have an organizational infrastructure on individual campuses—not only student governments but student newspapers as well—that can potentially be mobilized for political action. Furthermore, that they are ghettoized in dormitories and student cafeterias helps overcome some of the barriers to communication that hamper efforts to organize the unorganized. Welfare recipients, however, have none of these actual or potential organizational resources: no association already on the Washington scene and no network of local organizations that could be readily converted into a political battalion.

The determinants of the treatment of various groups in the first two Reagan budgets were undoubtedly very complex. It is surely foolish to ascribe budgetary outcomes to a single factor. Furthermore, others lobbied on behalf of these programs. In each case the professionals who provide the specified services—medical personnel, college teachers and administrators, social workers and so on—and the government agencies that implement the programs acted as advocates for program beneficiaries. Still, it is interesting to note that in a period of wholesale amputation of benefits programs, the veterans fared well in both of the first two Reagan budgets; students, having been taken unaware the first time around, girded for action in 1982 and yielded no substantial ground in the second Reagan budget; welfare recipients sustained serious losses in both heats. Whatever the specific explanations for these results, it is probably not irrelevant that the organizational resources of the three groups were so much at variance.

SUMMARY

This chapter sets the stage for those that follow. First, we presented an aerial snapshot of the involvement of organized interests in the policy process. What is especially striking is simply how much organized interests do. Moreover, although there is a certain amount of specialization, and although various kinds of groups differ in the activities they indicate consume the most time and resources, there is a remarkable congruence among different kinds of organizations with respect to their political activities. In addition, not only is there a lot of interest group activity, but there is more interest group activity. This is a function, as shown in Chapter 4, of the large number of newly arrived organizations—both newborn and previously apolitical—that have established a presence in the capital. Furthermore, as our interviews demonstrate, all groups, even previously active ones, are doing more. The effect is therefore multiplicative; with more organizations each doing more, the product is an explosion in the amount of organized interest activity in Washington.

We also considered some of the factors that shape an organization's decision whether or not to get involved in a particular political matter. Sometimes there is no choice. Sometimes, however, organized interests take initiatives without any external impetus, acting instead to try to shape the policy agenda. In their agenda-setting activities, organized interests are limited in the nature of the substantive demands they can make or issues they can raise by a wide variety of factors, ranging from provisions of the U.S. Constitution to the limitations imposed by past policies.

Once in the fray, an organization may have extensive strategic and tactical choices. Although the institutional arena in which a political conflict will be waged is sometimes settled in advance by the actions of others, when an organization has a choice, it will try to locate a political conflict in that setting most likely to produce favorable results. Once strategic matters have been settled, an organized interest still must choose among assorted political tactics. Its choice of tactics will be shaped, once again, by numerous considerations, ranging from what is legal to the nature and amount of its resources.

The final portion of the chapter treated several abstract considerations with respect to the fundamental question of whether organizations have influence. It is clear that political activity can by no means be equated with political influence. What is more, the appropriate standard for judging an organization's influence is not its apparent victory or defeat but the degree to which the outcome reflects its activity. In addition, we demonstrated that access and influence cannot be divorced as completely as they are in the parlance of some lobbyists. Finally, it is clear that those whose interests are represented by ongoing organizations are at an advantage over those who try to protect their interests either without benefit of organization or through nascent organizations.

8

Reaching Out to the Public

Most of the activities of organized interests in Washington are conducted in relative obscurity—out of the glare of public attention, if not expressly behind closed doors. Consequently, unless the media highlight them, ordinary citizens will not be aware of the efforts made by organized interests to influence public outcomes. Sometimes, however, an organization deliberately raises its profile and appeals to the public. This chapter considers the many forms of indirect lobbying through which organizations try to influence government action by enlisting the sympathies or support of the public.

By reaching out to the public, an organization can serve one or both of two purposes. Public appeals can be used to persuade—that is, to convince an audience either to be generally favorable to an organization and its perspectives or to adopt the organization's position on a particular policy issue. Public appeals can also be used to mobilize—that is, to activate the audience to do something, usually to communicate their like-minded opinions to policymakers. Furthermore, public appeals can be directed to various kinds of targets. On one hand, they may be aimed at the public at large. On the other, they may be intended for one of two sorts of narrower publics: either for a circumscribed group (ordinarily actual or potential supporters of the organization) likely to be especially concerned about the issues in question; or for opinion leaders, those elites strategically positioned to influence the attitudes of others. Although distinguishing among the various purposes and targets of public appeals is useful in analyzing particular cases, it should be borne in mind that actual communications may attempt to accomplish multiple ends, or appeal to more than one audience, simultaneously.

This chapter takes as its principal focus the various techniques that organizations use in approaching the public. As will become clear, strategies of political influence based on public communications are nothing new, and there is ample historical precedent for many of the techniques used today. However, in an electronic age, political public relations has become a highly professionalized and complex business, applying to the dissemination of positions on public issues the same techniques and skills that are used to market hair spray and barbecue sauce. Indeed, many of the firms most prominent in the marketing of consumer goods have added political work to their public relations repertoires. In order to show how organizations go about influencing the public, this chapter examines many of the techniques available to them. In addition to seeing how various techniques work, we shall be sensitive to whether they work at all. After all, in all government relations efforts there is a danger not simply that attempts at influence may fail to have their intended effect, but that they may actually backfire by mobilizing the opposition. This danger is particularly great when the scope of a conflict is broadened by appeals to the public. Thus, we shall be certain to include consideration of cases in which an attempt to reach out to the public was counterproductive.

Any discussion of the techniques of public persuasion and mobilization must entail concern with organizational resources. Many of these techniques— for example, sending out mass mailings or advertising on television—are very costly and are therefore beyond reach of organizations with slender budgets. Others—for example, holding press conferences or mounting demonstrations— are considerably less expensive and are used more heavily by organizations commanding scant financial resources.

There is, however, another side to the question of resources. When an organization tries to appeal to the public, it helps not only to have money but also to have an appealing message. As we saw in Chapter 5, many organizations that are financially needy support causes that generate natural public sympathy. In approaching the public, such organizations may be forced to eschew some of the more expensive techniques of public communication, such as advertising, in which there is control over the content of the message. However, because they hold policy positions that have intrinsic public appeal, they can get by without the purchase of advertising because the media's routine, free coverage of their points of view is generally sympathetic and favorable. Conversely, organizations having more money but less obviously appealing policy goals will do what they can to avoid ceding to unfriendly media control of what the public learns about them. Thus they are likely to utilize costly techniques affording maximum control over content so as to be able to package their positions in the most appealing way. Similarly, organizations concerned that they do not get a fair shake from the media will avoid free, but potentially unflattering, media coverage. Furthermore, when it comes to indirect lobbying, numbers are also an important resource. For many organizations, a large constituency helps compensate for a lack of financial resources.

SHAPING PUBLIC OPINION AND POLITICAL CLIMATES

Since it is with the citizenry that ultimate sovereignty rests in a democracy, it is not surprising that organized interests make considerable efforts both to attract public attention to their activities and concerns and to cultivate a favorable impression of themselves and their positions. And as we shall note several times in this chapter, lobbying the public effectively is such a sophisticated enterprise that organizations often hire public relations experts to do the job.

Advertising

One of the most conspicuous ways in which groups try to shape public opinion and the general political climate is by conducting large-scale advertising campaigns designed, not to promote a product or service, but to make a statement about the organization itself, its work, and its views. Anyone who reads magazines or watches television is barraged by what is generally known as "idea" or "institutional" advertising. As prominent as it might seem, however, only a minority of organizations use it. Table 8.1 presents data about the multiple ways in which organizations approach the public. Running advertisements in the media does not rank particularly high on the list of techniques of influence. Only 31 percent of our organizations do it, making it twenty-fourth out of twenty-seven, and only 3 percent indicate that it consumes great amounts of time and resources, making it twenty-first on the list. Unions are somewhat more likely to use this technique than are other kinds of organizations. A bare majority, 55 percent, of the unions run ads in the media; however, none deem it an especially important activity.

In the course of this chapter, it will become obvious that various technological innovations—the advent of television, the development of high-speed data processing, the invention of laser printers—make it easier for groups to communicate with the public. However, there is considerable historical precedent for attempts to influence American political life by rousing public opinion. In particular, advertising campaigns are not a new weapon in the arsenal of organized interests. In fact, organizations have used them for many years. One of the first "modern" uses of such advertising was by the American Telephone and Telegraph Company, which in June of 1908 launched a magazine advertising campaign intended in part to improve customer cooperation but designed primarily to defuse public uneasiness about the telephone monopoly.[1] In the

---

[1]A copy of the first in the series of AT&T ads can be found in Anthony Galli, "Corporate Advertising: More than Just a Nice Warm Feeling All Over," *Public Relations Journal,* November 1971, p. 22.

Table 8.1 USE OF TECHNIQUES OF PUBLIC PERSUASION AND MOBILIZATION

Percentage of groups using technique

	Corporations	Trade associations	Unions	Citizens' groups	All organizations	Rank[a]
Talking with people from the press and media	67%	89%	95%	96%	86%	8
Inspiring letter-writing or telegram campaigns	83	89	100	83	84	11.5
Mounting grass roots lobbying efforts	81	80	100	71	80	13.5
Having influential constituents contact their congressional representative's office	77	94	85	58	80	13.5
Running ads in the media about your position on issues	31	31	55	33	31	24
Engaging in protests and demonstrations	0	3	90	25	20	27

Percentage for whom technique consumes time and resources

	Corporations	Trade associations	Unions	Citizens' groups	All organizations	Rank[a]
Talking with people from the press and media	4%	9%	0%	26%	10%	13.5
Inspiring letter-writing or telegram campaigns	2	12	20	9	10	13.5
Mounting grass roots lobbying efforts	22	18	53	44	26	4
Having influential constituents contact their congressional representative's office	0	12	13	4	6	17
Running ads in the media about your position on issues	4	0	0	0	3	21
Engaging in protests and demonstrations	0	0	7	0	1	25

[a]Overall rank on list of 27 techniques.
Source: Washington Representatives Survey.

late 1940s and early 1950s, as part of its campaign against the enactment of national health insurance, the American Medical Association spent tens of millions of dollars on radio, magazine, and newspaper advertisements attacking "socialized medicine." The AMA spent an additional large sum in fees to Whitaker and Baxter, the public relations firm that orchestrated the AMA's broadside attack on President Truman's health insurance proposal.[2]

Although the use of advertising by organized interests is not the innovation of an age of media prominence, its use now is in several ways broader than in the past. It is not simply that there is more organizational advertising than before—more groups sponsoring more ads. In addition, it seems that it is now possible to convey a broader set of messages through advertisements. Observers of organized pressure once emphasized that organizations would undertake public relations campaigns only very cautiously, both because they are very expensive and because they can backfire.[3] That is, there was a perceived danger that a costly campaign would succeed only in mobilizing the opposition without winning new converts. The inference was that advertising was an option only if the organization's cause was a potentially appealing one. Today, however, it is common for messages of seemingly more limited appeal to be dressed up and taken out in public.

Consider the advertising campaigns undertaken in recent years by the tobacco companies and by their trade association, the Tobacco Institute. Traditionally, tobacco interests have operated effectively but quietly in Washington, relying on friendly legislators from tobacco states for cooperation.[4] Such a low-profile approach would seem consistent with a product having a long-standing reputation for association with serious health problems. More recently, however, tobacco interests have taken their case to the public in a series of skillfully phrased ads. The ads, run in various news magazines, convey several messages, among them: the tobacco industry generates jobs and tax revenues, thus rendering the multimillion dollar tobacco price support program a virtual bargain to taxpayers; like nonsmokers, smokers have rights, upon which zealous nonsmokers should not trample unreasonably; and the public should be skeptical of the scientific evidence that smoking causes diseases.[5] What is noteworthy about these advertising campaigns is not simply the indubitable skill with which they are produced but the ability of their sponsors to package in an engaging way controversial messages of potentially limited appeal.

[2] See Stanley Kelley, Jr., *Professional Public Relations and Political Power* (Baltimore: Johns Hopkins Press, 1956), pp. 83–87.

[3] See, for example, V. O. Key, *Public Opinion and American Democracy* (New York: Knopf, 1961), pp. 514–518, and L. Harmon Zeigler and G. Wayne Peak, *Interest Groups in American Society,* 2nd ed. (Englewood Cliffs, NJ: Prentice-Hall, 1972), pp. 115–119.

[4] On the tobacco lobby in politics, see A. Lee Fritschler, *Smoking and Politics,* 3rd ed. (Englewood Cliffs, NJ: Prentice-Hall, 1983).

[5] See ads in *Newsweek,* November 20, 1978, pp. 32–33, and *Parade Magazine,* February 19, 1984, p. 9. Also see, on the latest campaign of the R. J. Reynolds Tobacco Company, Philip M. Boffey, "Health Groups Assail Cigarette Ads," *New York Times,* February 17, 1984, p. A17.

Advertising professionals distinguish between two major forms of idea advertising.[6] One form, used most heavily by large corporations or business associations, is known as "image" advertising. Its purpose is to project an artfully contrived general impression of the sponsoring organization—either to establish an image where none existed before or to improve an organizational image tarnished by events or by negative public attitudes. The other is called "advocacy" advertising and is used by all kinds of organizations to elucidate controversial public issues in ways that cast the interests and positions of the sponsoring organization in the most (and, often, those of opponents in the least) positive light. Although we shall discuss these two kinds of institutional advertising separately, in practice the differences between them are often quite blurry. An organization may use the same ad both to project a certain image of itself and to advocate a particular policy position.

Image Ads Image advertising typically focuses on the characteristics of the sponsoring organization's "personality"—its policies, functions, objectives, ideals, and standards. Most image advertising is intended, therefore, to *educate* the audience about the organization, its activities, and concerns. Frequently, image ads aim to create goodwill toward the sponsoring organization by trying to demonstrate what a "good citizen" the organization is. This is a common tactic in industries that are the object of some public distrust. For example, in order to "help defend, spread understanding of, and preserve the health of one of the critical industries in the nation," the Chemical Manufacturers Association in the early 1980s launched a campaign aimed at "opinion leaders" and "influentials" by placing ads in such publications as *Time, The Smithsonian,* and *The Washington Post.* The ads involved a series of portraits of persons employed by chemical manufacturing companies whose jobs involve protecting the safety and health of the workers and of the public—safety engineers, industrial hygienists, toxicologists, epidemiologists, occupational physicians, and nurses. The point, of course, was to demonstrate the seriousness of the industry's efforts to anticipate and control potential health hazards from chemicals.[7]

Other industries rely on image advertising as well. For example, the timber industry has had to combat public concerns about the ecological impact of its timber cutting and logging practices. The Weyerhaeuser Company ("the tree-growing company") has long sponsored advertising designed to portray the firm as a friend of wildlife. As early as 1952, Weyerhaeuser hired a big advertising agency in the Pacific Northwest to help inaugurate an advertising program featuring the paintings of some of America's top wildlife artists. As the environmental and ecological movements acquired urgency in the late

[6]See S. Prakash Sethi, *Advocacy Advertising and Large Corporations* (Lexington, MA: Lexington Books, 1977).

[7]"The Trouble with CMA's Ad Campaign," *Chemical Week,* September 23, 1981, pp. 14–16. For examples of the ads, see *New York Times,* September 30, 1981, p. A31, and *Time,* November 16, 1981, p. 3.

1960s and early 1970s, Weyerhaeuser took its advertising campaign to television, with commercial air time on NCAA football, ABC's Wide World of Sports, and NFL Monday Night Football.[8]

Advocacy Ads   Whereas image ads are meant to make their sponsoring organization look good—socially responsible, beneficent, concerned with the public interest—advocacy ads convey specific messages about the sponsoring organization's public policy postures.[9]

A variety of organizations run advocacy advertisements. Among the most prominent are the newspaper ads sponsored by Mobil Oil. Mobil's public affairs department in New York has over a hundred employees and an annual budget of well over $20 million. Its most regular outlet is the prestigious op-ed page of *The New York Times*. Mobil has run ads in the lower right-hand corner of the *Times* op-ed page every Thursday morning since 1972—so regularly, in fact, that in advertising jargon, the "Mobil Oil position" denotes that particular corner of the page opposite a newspaper's editorial page. While some of Mobil's messages are image ads designed to celebrate the good works of the corporation, many have been advocacy ads touting the benefits of economic growth and the need for more oil exploration.[10] Similarly, the American Federation of Teachers, the AFL-CIO affiliated teacher's union, runs an advocacy ad each Sunday in *The New York Times* elucidating the viewpoint of the union's president on various issues related to education.

Their regular appearance renders the advocacy ads of Mobil and the AFT especially conspicuous. However, such regular campaigns are exceptional. Organizations are more likely to utilize advocacy when a particular issue of pressing concern arises. For example, in the first year of the Reagan administration, the American Federation of State, County, and Municipal Employees (AFSCME), the nation's largest union of public employees, mounted an ambitious ad campaign in the print media arguing that the Administration's tax cuts and budget cuts were harder on middle-class working people than on wealthy persons. AFSCME also spent $400,000 on a series of one-minute television spots—aired on 37 stations in 13 major cities—critical of cuts in Social Security benefits that Reagan had proposed in May 1981.[11]

What Difference Does Institutional Advertising Make?   Do these public relations efforts in fact change any minds? Drawing upon the literature of mass communications, political scientists have generally held that these ads are more

[8]Richard Londgren, "Weyerhaeuser Company: Exploring Conservation Concepts," *Public Relations Journal*, November 1974, pp. 34–36.

[9]Sethi, *Advocacy Advertising and Large Corporations*, p. 4, and Chapter 1.

[10]See Michael Gerrard, "This Man Was Made Possible by a Grant from Mobil Oil," *Esquire*, January 1978, p. 143.

[11]See "Union Plans TV Ads Against Pension Cuts," *New York Times*, September 15, 1981, p. D29.

effective in increasing the salience of convictions than in changing them; that is, they serve to channel and strengthen latent opinions and to provide information to support preexisting attitudes.[12] This classical view of the impact of political advertising is based on the results of early voting studies, conducted in the pretelevision era of the 1940s. More recently this view has been modified by the results of studies of the effects of political advertisements in electoral campaigns and of mass-communications campaigns designed to promote socially desirable behavior (reducing litter, preventing forest fires, and so on).[13] Unfortunately, there do not seem to be any empirical tests of the impact on attitudes of institutional advertising.

One indirect test emerges from a study of spending in referendum campaigns conducted in four states between June 1976 and November 1980.[14] According to the study, the high-spending side prevailed in 40 out of 50 ballot issues. For 32 of these issues, public opinion data were available to indicate changes in public mood as the referendum campaign progressed. In 12 cases there was little or no such change. Interestingly enough, in 17 of the remaining 20 cases public opinion moved in the direction of the position advocated by the high-spending side. (In all but two of these cases, the movement was sufficient that the high-spending side was able to prevail.) In only three of the 32 cases did high spending seem to backfire; that is, in only three cases did the public move over the course of the campaign away from the position supported by the high-spending side. Of course, the study relates spending to vote outcomes. We do not know what the money was spent on, whether those who changed their minds were those exposed to sponsored communications, and what other influences were at work. Still, these results suggest that we should not dismiss prematurely the conclusion that institutional advertisements have some effect on public attitudes.

Regardless of whether this kind of advertising accomplishes the narrow objectives of its sponsors, it has other potential consequences. Questions have been raised about what it is doing to the quality of our political discourse. These ads are sometimes misleading. While outright misstatements of fact are presumably quite rare, these ads often use statistics in ways that are, at the least, self-serving. Moreover, institutional advertisements are frequently quite shrill and provocative, using an emotion-laden pitch to play on the public's fears, frustrations, and anger. The inflammatory rhetoric may be accompanied by gut-wrenching photographs—such as pictures of aborted fetuses or of hunters clubbing baby seals. Although such ads may be successful in advancing

[12]See Zeigler and Peak, *Interest Groups in American Society,* pp. 114–115.

[13]For a review of the literature on advertising in electoral campaigns, see Herbert Asher, *Presidential Elections and American Politics,* 3rd ed. (Homewood, IL: Dorsey Press, 1984), pp. 221–233. On campaigns designed to promote socially desirable behavior, see Ronald E. Rice and William J. Paisley, eds., *Public Communications Campaigns* (Beverly Hills, CA: Sage, 1981).

[14]Betty H. Zisk, "Winning State Referenda: Money vs. Peoplepower," paper presented at the Annual Meeting of the American Political Science Association, Chicago, September 1983.

cherished positions and casting opponents' views in the worst possible light, they do not always contribute to reasoned discussion of serious public matters. Of course, this is one of numerous circumstances with respect to organized pressure when our reactions are governed by the substance as well as the form of the communication. People tend to be more offended by strident messages when they disagree with them, more tolerant when they agree. However, organizations at all points on the political spectrum make emotional appeals. Neither liberals nor conservatives have a monopoly on sensationalism in their advertisements.

INDIRECT USES OF THE MEDIA

So far we have been examining the ways in which organizations use the media directly by paying to have specific messages conveyed. Equally important, however, are the several ways in which organizations use the media indirectly, by inducing the media to cover organizational activities and spread word of their purposes. Using the media indirectly rather than directly involves clear trade-offs for an organization. When an organization sponsors advertisements, it has complete control over the content and a measure of control over the timing and placement of the public communication. This control is lost when the organization relies on the media to run their own stories about organizational activities and goals. When the media produce their own material, the result may not show the organization at its best. Important facts may be overlooked or bungled; the relative emphasis may differ from what the organization would like; or the organization may, quite simply, be cast in a negative light. There are, however, compensating benefits. Helping the media to spread the word on its own is, of course, much cheaper than paying for expensive ads or programming. Furthermore, on the principle that having someone else tell your story is more effective than telling it yourself, the message gains credibility when articulated by another source.[15]

Cultivating the Media

In order that media coverage may be as favorable as possible, most organizations make efforts to shape the ways in which the media report their activities and take steps to ingratiate themselves with reporters. As shown in Table 8.1,

---

[15]On this point see Zeigler and Peak, *Interest Groups in American Society,* pp. 118–120. This principle also explains why organizations sometimes make considerable efforts to obscure the sources of public messages (usually by creating dummy committees to act as fronts). V. O. Key notes that such "concealment seems to occur most frequently among business groups, although the general principle probably is that any group that feels itself to be in the doghouse will tend to hide behind false fronts when it propagandizes the public." *Public Opinion and American Democracy,* p. 517.

Washington representatives in the overwhelming majority of the organizations in our sample—including almost all of the trade associations, unions, and citizens' groups and two-thirds of the corporations—spend time talking with people from the press and the media. This seems, however, to be an important enterprise only to those associated with citizens' groups, 26 percent of whom selected it as an especially time- or resource-consuming activity (making it fifth on their list of 27 techniques of influence). It is perhaps not surprising that citizens' groups place particular emphasis upon their dealings with the media, for such groups rely on public support to survive. Moreover, many of them lack the resources to pay for all the publicity they feel they need.

Business organizations, on the other hand, approach the media quite differently. They are more likely to command the slack resources needed to buy sufficient media time to present their side of the story. In addition, they perceive an antibusiness bias in the news media—an unwillingness to treat the business viewpoint objectively or to give the business community equal access for the presentation of its views.[16] Feeling that they do not get a fair shake in news coverage or in editorials, business organizations often prefer to make their own case to the public so that they can control the contents of the message.

In dealing with the media, part of the task is simply to cultivate the goodwill of the journalists who might cover the organization. Most Washington correspondents for major newspapers (and increasingly these days, for television networks as well) are assigned to regular "beats"—that is, they cover developments relating to specified institutions, agencies, or policy areas. Just as elected politicians and appointed officials develop mutually dependent relationships with these reporters, so do Washington lobbyists. The reporters depend on lobbyists (as well as on government officials) for information about current and future developments in their areas of concern. The lobbyists are able to furnish reporters with background information, authoritative responses, quotable quotes, and occasional "scoops." The reporters can be reciprocally useful to the lobbyists. From reporters, lobbyists may glean information or insights into their opponents' strategies. More important, reporters have significant, though not determinative, control over what is broadcast or published about an organization. Therefore, shrewd lobbyists are selective about the information

[16]See Sethi, *Advocacy Advertising and Large Corporations,* Chapter 3, and Bernard Rubin, *Big Business and the Mass Media* (Lexington, MA: Lexington Books, 1977). Additional confirmation of this perception emerges from our interviews. We asked our respondents which two of eight political forces listed on a card they considered to be their principal competitors in influencing members of Congress. Corporate respondents (39 percent) were the most likely to cite the media as a principal competitor. Interestingly, respondents from citizens' groups—23 percent of whom chose the media from the list—were next in terms of their likelihood to cite the media as a principal competitor. (Only 18 percent of the union representatives and 13 percent of the trade association representatives gave this response.)

Our concern here, however, is not to evaluate or confirm the business community's perception that the media do not treat it fairly but, rather, to show the consequences of that perception for political activity.

they release—and about the reporters to whom they release it—and attempt to stay in the good graces of appropriate reporters.[17]

Organizations with local chapters or affiliates often encourage local officers to nurture similar relationships with representatives from the local media. For example, the National Association of Letter Carriers in 1980 distributed to all its branches a booklet entitled "Public Relations," which included instructions on, among other things, how to make contacts with local reporters and editors. After advising local officers how to compile a "press list" of media contacts and how to conduct themselves during an initial appointment, the brochure instructs:

> After your first meeting, stay in contact with at least the major media on a regular basis. . . . Follow these hints for a good relationship: Try to discover each reporter's attitudes—particularly on labor issues—and how they affect his or her reaction to your message. Always deal only in facts—never opinions, guesses or assumptions. Exaggerating the truth can damage your credibility. Say nothing "off the record." It's the reporter's job to report what is said, both formally and informally.[18]

Attracting Media Attention

Organizations are ordinarily not content simply to establish good relationships with the media; they also attempt to attract media attention. One way to do so is to provide them with actual copy. Some organizations get their views before the public by retaining the services of a so-called media distribution service that works at getting its clients' views placed in small newspapers and with small radio and television stations. Such a service learns what message the client wants to convey and then produces a package of editorials and light feature articles designed to create a climate of sympathetic public opinion toward the client and its goals. The distribution service promises its clients that the pieces will be run verbatim in hundreds of news outlets.[19] As a follow-up, the organization that has retained the distribution service can send out reprints of articles thus inspired to policymakers and other salient publics. In this way it can further disseminate its point of view while obscuring its original source.[20]

A similar technique has been used by some organizations to reach a television audience. For example, when the Food and Drug Administration

---

[17]Obviously, not all relationships between reporters and lobbyists are friendly. Some lobbyists are quite cynical about the treatment their organizations are likely to receive by reporters and therefore seek to minimize the release of information to the media. The head lobbyist for one of the large airlines insisted that in dealing with reporters, "the trick is to keep them from knowing what you're up to."

[18]National Association of Letter Carriers, *Public Relations* (Washington, DC: Research and Education Department, 1980), pp. 9, 12, 13.

[19]Bill Keller, "Special-Interest Lobbyists Cultivate the 'Grassroots' to Influence Capitol Hill," *Congressional Quarterly Weekly Report,* September 12, 1981, p. 1741.

[20]David L. Paletz and Robert M. Entman, eds., *Media Power Politics* (New York: Free Press, 1981), p. 135.

ruled that a certain pharmaceutical company's product was the only safe one in a particular category of drugs, the company hired a public relations firm to make the most of it. The PR people prepared a videotape in the form of a news report on the FDA ruling showing the name of their client's product as being "the only safe one in the circumstances." The tape was distributed to several hundred stations and included a script in case a local television station wanted to furnish its own narration. More than half the television stations to which the videotape was sent used it as a news item.[21]

Interestingly, while some of the technology is new, such media-manipulation strategies are not without historical precedent. In the 1920s organizations would distribute what was called "boilerplate," a plate containing a story of general interest that could be placed directly on a printing press without further typesetting. Using such plates permitted a harried editor to generate copy with almost no extra work. According to a contemporary analyst, "the insidious part of the procedure is in the fact that this propaganda is disguised as a legitimate news item, the source of the data and the name of the interested party not being mentioned. The unsuspecting reader does not realize that the stuff before him, news in outward seeming, is in reality distributed by an interested organization."[22] Just as the "boilerplate" of yore was viewed as having insidious aspects, media distribution services today are criticized for masquerading propaganda as news.

There are, of course, other ways to attract media coverage, and organizations often manufacture opportunities to obtain attention from the media. Sometimes organizations stage dramatic public gestures, called "media events," in order to attract coverage. For example, in recent years Greenpeace, the activist environmental organization, has regularly won widespread media attention through such risky confrontational tactics as trying to disrupt the work of Russian whaling fleets, Norwegian and Canadian seal hunters, and British nuclear transport ships.

Organizations also hold press conferences in order to get their messages out. The release of a new study report, policy statement, or position paper provides an appropriate occasion for a press conference. For example, early in 1983, the Children's Defense Fund (CDF) held a press conference to highlight its release of a study report on the effects of Reagan administration budget cuts in health services for poor mothers and their children. The organization received good media coverage on the issue, in part because of the respect commanded in Washington by CDF's executive director, Marian Wright Edelman.[23] As a means of utilizing the media to disseminate a point of view, press

[21] Michael R. Gordon, "The Image Makers in Washington—PR Firms Have Found a Natural Home," *National Journal,* May 31, 1980, p. 888.

[22] Pendleton Herring, *Group Representation before Congress* (Baltimore: Johns Hopkins University Press, 1929), p. 70.

[23] See "Group Says Budget Cuts Hurt Health of the Poor," *Boston Globe,* January 12, 1983, p. 6.

conferences have obvious advantages. They entail few financial costs, a paramount consideration to organizations with strained financial resources. In addition, they permit the organization to retain some control over the content of the communication. However, it is possible to "cry wolf" by holding press conferences too frequently; overuse can dilute their impact.

Protests and Demonstrations

For groups that lack either the means or the organizational temperament to use the more conventional ways of gaining public attention, protests and demonstrations are an alternative tactic. As shown in Table 8.1, few of the organizations in our Washington sample use this tactic; as a matter of fact, it ranks last on the list of 27 techniques of influence. It is not surprising that only 20 percent of the organizations surveyed engage in protests and demonstrations. Such tactics have long been the ultimate recourse—and sometimes the only technique available—to the relatively powerless.[24] No matter how substantial the variations in the resources they command, all the organizations in our sample are well beyond what has been called the "threshold of civic group participation."[25] All of them have the wherewithal to maintain an office in Washington, and all of them have achieved legitimacy as actors in national politics.[26] Thus, for all the differences in their resources, they all are able to use conventional techniques of political influence and have at least some status as insiders.

Table 8.1 also makes clear that use of this technique is quite uneven across the various kinds of organizations. In general, organizations with roots in social movements—for example, civil rights and women's groups—are the most likely to use such tactics. In particular, where a social protest wing coexists with an organizational one, the continued use of direct action tactics is likely. Hence, nine out of ten unions engage in protests and demonstrations, as do one-fourth of the citizens' groups. The business community eschews demonstrations almost completely; none of the corporations surveyed engage in protests (they are more likely to be targets thereof), and only one trade association reported doing so. It is hardly surprising that business organizations do not use protest tactics. They do not need to do so. Their substantial resources enable them to engage extensively in more traditional modes of public persuasion and direct lobbying. In addition, they enjoy considerable access to relevant policymakers. Moreover, such tactics are simply inconsistent with the dignified image business wishes to project.

[24]The theme of protest as the tactic of the powerless is explored in Michael Lipsky, *Protest in City Politics* (Chicago: Rand McNally, 1970), especially Chapters 1, 6, and 7.

[25]Ibid., p. 167.

[26]At this point it is useful to recall the special characteristics of our sample. As described in Appendix A, we sought to sample organizations that are particularly active in Washington. Hence, all the organizations sampled not only maintain offices in the capital but also have achieved sufficient weight and presence to have been mentioned (many of them numerous times) in the *National Journal.*

That unions use protest extensively is also not too surprising. Mass demonstrations have long been a tactic used by organized workers to express their collective will. Strikes against employers are a standard part of labor's repertoire of bargaining strategies. Unions engage in mass actions not only for economic purposes but for political ones as well. Furthermore, although unions command substantial resources, engaging occasionally in protests can serve as a useful supplement to more conventional tactics by invoking important symbols: the deep roots of the labor movement in a tradition of direct action; the size of union membership; and the identification of the labor movement with all who are deprived.

For those that use them, mass demonstrations can be strategically and organizationally useful in several ways: as a tool for attracting public attention; as a means of attracting new members, motivating existing ones, and increasing their sense of solidarity; and as a source of both political leverage and credibility for a group.[27] Moreover, a well-orchestrated demonstration generates publicity. Consider some of the scenes: 50,000 antiabortion activists staging a March for Life on the steps of the U.S. Capitol; a Solidarity Day demonstration with 250,000 labor union members gathering around the Washington Monument and then marching to the Capitol to protest President Reagan's budget cuts and tax policies; 1,000 physically handicapped children and adults—some hobbling on crutches, others rolling their wheelchairs—marching down Pennsylvania Avenue to protest reductions in social services for the disabled.[28] The media heed such events.

By mobilizing and solidifying rank-and-file members, demonstrations can also serve organizational maintenance needs. This was, in fact, one of the articulated reasons for the AFL-CIO's sponsorship of the Solidarity Day demonstrations in 1981. Inspired partly by the bravado of the workers' union in Poland, but also by a growing perception that organized labor had lost clout in American politics, AFL-CIO president Lane Kirkland believed that a massive turnout of workers from all over the country would energize affiliated unions and also serve notice of the vitality of the labor movement.[29]

Finally, protests may be effective as a source of political leverage for a

[27]See James Q. Wilson, *Political Organizations* (New York: Basic Books, 1973), pp. 282, 283. The multiple functions of protest tactics imply that they are being directed at several targets: potential group members, the media, other groups, and government officials. A number of authors have remarked upon the competing claims of these various publics and the difficulties involved in attempting to appeal to them simultaneously. On this issue, see Lipsky, *Protest in City Politics.*

[28]For a news account of the 1980 March for Life, see Leslie Bennetts, "Thousands March in Capital, Seeking Abortion Ban," *New York Times,* January 23, 1980, p. A12. On the Solidarity Day demonstration, see Eric Pianin and Warren Brown, "250,000 March to Protest Reagan's Policies," *Washington Post,* September 20, 1981, p. A1. On the demonstration by the handicapped see Sandra R. Gregg, "Physically Handicapped Protest Cuts in Services," *Washington Post,* September 10, 1981, p. C5.

[29]See David S. Broder, "AFL-CIO Leader Riding a Big Bet," *Washington Post,* September 20, 1981, p. A1.

group. If demonstrations are large enough, elected officials may feel that they cannot afford to ignore the policy preferences of sponsoring organizations. Also, when a group stages a sit-in or sets up a picket line or behaves disruptively, it may succeed in making life sufficiently unpleasant for those inside that they will make concessions simply to restore order.[30] One study of the Massachusetts Welfare Rights Organization, found that when welfare mothers held mass demonstrations at the office of a welfare administrator, they were often able to secure special-needs grants in exchange for a promise to put an end to the commotion and the noisy confrontations.[31] We should note that these kind of disruptive tactics, when they are used at all, are typically invoked by the most resource-poor organizations. None of the organizations in our survey mentioned disruptive activities. If they use them at all, they use them sparingly.

Earlier in the chapter we referred to the possibility that if they alienate the previously inattentive or mobilize opponents, attempts to carry a message to the public may be not merely ineffective but actually counterproductive. This is a particular danger with protests. On some occasions, demonstrations and protests backfire. For example, in 1979 the American Agriculture Movement organized a "tractorcade" into Washington to demand higher farm prices. Over 2,000 farmers steered their tractors into the city for a month of aggressive demonstrations and threatening confrontations with public officials. The demonstrations were well designed to attract a steady stream of media coverage: tractors and other rigs tying up traffic on metropolitan Washington highways during rush hours and parked on the lawn between the Washington Monument and the Capitol; and unruly farmers throwing a goat over the White House fence. This is the stuff of which sure spots on the network news are made, but rather than inducing public sympathy, the media attention generated popular wrath. Public indignation was exacerbated when the federal government had to spend $3.6 million to repair damage the farmers had done throughout the city. Moreover, government officials also reacted testily to the farmers' threatening tactics, as evidenced by statements by congressional leaders to the effect that the farmers had "got out of hand" and "hurt the cause of farmers."[32]

MOBILIZING PRESSURE: GRASS ROOTS LOBBYING

The discussion so far has focused on the techniques that organizations use in their efforts to shape broad public opinion and manipulate the general political climate. However, when politicians regard the public's preferences, what often matters to them is not an amorphous perception of the views of the general public but, rather, the understanding that there is a narrower group of citizens who care intensely about a policy matter and are likely to act on their views.

[30]This point is made by Wilson, *Political Organizations,* p. 282.
[31]See Lawrence N. Bailis, *Bread or Justice* (Lexington, MA: Lexington Books, 1974), pp. 47–54.
[32]Steven V. Roberts, "Mass Protest Has Simply Gone Out of Style: 'Tractorcade' Demonstrators Go Home, Leaving Mostly Anger Behind," *New York Times,* March 18, 1979, p. E7.

Therefore, an organization's ability to convince policymakers that an attentive public is concerned about an issue and ready to hold them accountable for their decisions may be critical in determining policy outcomes. Recognizing this, interest organizations expend considerable effort preaching to the converted—that is, communicating with those who agree with the organization's point of view in order to generate expressions of opinion to public officials. Hence, in many of their public relations efforts, organizations are attempting not to persuade but to mobilize.

Government affairs experts in Washington today use a variety of techniques—loosely gathered under the rubric "grass roots lobbying"—to raise the profile of an issue on the policy agenda and to demonstrate to policymakers that there are interested constituents attending to what they do. Grass roots lobbying can refer to any of several activities, including: (1) arranging for legislators at home in their districts to meet with representatives of the organization so that the lawmakers can be "educated" as to its position and the strength of its views; (2) bringing influential constituents to Washington to meet directly with public officials about an issue; (3) organizing networks of grass roots activists who can be relied on to contact policymakers in response to an organizational "action alert"; and (4) finding ways to produce huge floods of letters, telegrams, or phone calls to government offices advocating a particular stance on a given issue. In short, grass roots lobbying is essentially any means by which a group generates public pressure on those in government.

Not surprisingly, grass roots campaigns are most frequently aimed at Congress; because electoral cycles render legislators periodically accountable to their constituencies, they are a natural target for the expression of citizen opinion. All the examples in this chapter are taken from the realm of legislative politics. However, as we shall see in Chapter 13, those in the executive branch—in the White House and the agencies—have constituencies as well. Hence, it should be borne in mind that grass roots efforts are sometimes directed at the executive branch, especially when regulations are being considered. In addition, since our principal concern here is with organized efforts to bring *indirect* pressure to bear on policymakers, we shall put off until later chapters an examination of those forms of grass roots pressure that involve direct contacts—either in the congressional district or in Washington—between elected officials and group members.

It is evident from the data in Table 8.1 that the use of these techniques is widespread. A substantial majority of our respondents—80 percent—indicated that their organizations mount grass roots lobbying efforts. Not only do most organizations engage in grass roots lobbying, but it is clearly an important activity to them. Twenty-six percent of our respondents (including 53 percent of those affiliated with unions and 44 percent of those affiliated with citizens' groups) indicated that mounting grass roots lobbying efforts consumes organizational time and resources—making it fourth on the list of 27 activities. It seems logical that these two kinds of organizations would place emphasis upon grass roots lobbying. Unions are large organizations. Grass roots lobbying allows them to make the most of their greater numbers and to demonstrate to policymakers the extent of support for a particular policy position. Many citizens' groups have 501(c)(3) tax status, which limits their ability to lobby Congress directly. Therefore, they find it useful to rely upon indirect forms of influence in approaching public officials. In addition, a substantial majority of organizations in all categories use two specific forms of grass roots lobbying: inspiring letter-writing or telegram campaigns and having influential constituents contact their congressman's office. (With respect to generating communications from influential constituents, there are some variations across the different kinds of organizations. Trade associations are especially likely to use this technique, and citizens' groups are relatively unlikely to do so.)

Inspiring "Spontaneous" Grass Roots Pressure

Organizations of all types have developed elaborate systems for producing a flow of "spontaneous" communications from concerned citizens to their legislators. When Congress was considering increasing milk price supports in 1980, legislators heard from thousands of worried managers of fast-food restaurants: the industry's trade association had put out an issue alert. After the introduction in Congress in 1981 of various bills that would alter the jurisdictions of federal courts, legislators heard from thousands of concerned citizens opposed to any move that might weaken the independence of the federal courts: Common Cause had put out an issue alert. When a House committee in 1982 was deliberating on a bill to deregulate the American Telephone and Telegraph Company, legislators heard protests from thousands of telephone company managers and employees: not only had AT&T put out an issue alert, but so had the Communications Workers of America, 90 percent of whose members are AT&T employees. In each of these cases, some of the letters that reached congressional offices may have sprung unsolicited from conscientious citizens, but it is safe to assume that most of the communications had resulted from the efforts of a national organization.

An organization cannot expect to mount a successful campaign of grass roots pressure unless it has established reliable procedures and communications systems for alerting its own natural constituency of the need for pressure. Most organizations these days have well-developed systems for the coordination of their grass roots lobbying programs. Consider, for example, the FMC Corporation, one of the world's largest producers of machinery and chemicals for industry and agriculture. In 1982 it operated 137 manufacturing facilities and mines in 29 states and abroad. FMC maintains a nationwide network of managers designated as Legislative Action Program (LAP) Representatives. These FMC managers are expected to remain abreast of current issues of concern to the company; this is a task facilitated by assorted notices that emanate regularly from FMC's government affairs staff in Washington—the FMC

Washington Report, the *Issue Advisory,* and *Action Requests.* The key function of these LAP representatives is to contact their legislators on issues deemed important by the corporation's Washington staff. The LAP representative receives an *Action Request* from Washington, and depending on how much time is available, the manager may be asked to write a letter, send a mailgram, or make a telephone call in support of the approved corporate position on an issue. Less frequently, the Washington office may also ask its LAP representatives to organize a letter-writing campaign within their own facilities or help in some other way to generate support for the corporate position among community leaders and the local media.[33]

Grass Roots as High-Tech: The Chamber of Commerce   The U.S. Chamber of Commerce has added a particularly sophisticated electronic dimension to its grass roots capability.[34] In addition to maintaining the conventional communications channels such as action alerts, newsletters, and the like, the Chamber has linked its Washington headquarters to its local affiliates by means of its own private, closed-circuit television network—the American Business Network, or Biznet for short. Started in 1982, Biznet represents both great costs and great potential for the Chamber. The organization spent $6 million for the new television studio and satellite dish now in place at the Chamber's Washington headquarters. Moreover, the annual cost of producing and sending programming over Biznet is estimated to range from $1.5 to $3 million a year. These costs are recovered by fees charged to hundreds of subscribers throughout the country—mostly corporations, local chambers of commerce, and trade associations willing to pay $15,000 to $20,000 for a satellite receiving dish plus an additional $5,000 in annual subscription fees.[35]

Although the Chamber's Biznet system is still too new to judge whether its effectiveness justifies its costs, it is clear that the potential power of Biznet lies in its ability to stimulate, almost immediately, an outpouring of concerted pressure to influence legislation while there is still time to do something about it. If Biznet operates as the Chamber hopes, it may well give the business community a competitive edge in the stimulation of grass roots pressure, for the costs of this technology place it beyond the embrace of most citizens', civil rights, or social welfare groups. However, only rarely does an organization need

---

[33]FMC, "Legislative Action Program Notebook." If an FMC manager disagrees personally with the corporate position on an issue, he is not required to support it but must notify the Washington office so that the government affairs staff can ask another manager in that congressional district to contact the legislator.

[34]For a general account of the Chamber's grass roots program, see Burdett A. Loomis, "A New Era: Groups and the Grass Roots," in Allan J. Cigler and Burdett A. Loomis, eds., *Interest Group Politics* (Washington, DC: CQ Press, 1983), pp. 169–190. See also William H. Miller, "Business Gets Its Lobbying Act Together," *Industry Week,* December 5, 1977, p. 72.

[35]Bill Keller, "Chamber Lobbying Will Take to the Air," *Congressional Quarterly Weekly Report,* November 14, 1981, p. 2235; and Robert K. Massie, "How the Chamber Lobbies: Giving America the Business," *The Nation,* May 8, 1982, pp. 550–551.

to generate grass roots pressure on such short notice. On most important issues, Congress moves slowly and deliberately, so those affected have time to antici- pate the need for a grass roots campaign and to lay the groundwork for it. Furthermore, the stimulation of pressure from community notables such as prominent business leaders is only one form of grass roots lobbying. As we shall see in what follows, another technique for bringing pressure to bear on legislators is to attempt to mobilize the mass public.

Inspiring High-Volume Pressure

When a resourceful organization wants to be sure of winning legislators' atten- tion to an issue, one of its best options is to try to create the semblance of a popular movement in support of the organization's cause. (As we shall see, sometimes groups manage this task so well that they actually do create a popu- lar movement, not merely the semblance of one.) To achieve this objective, organizations sometimes use provocative advertisements or direct-mail appeals to inspire deluges of cards, letters, telegrams, and phone calls to Capitol Hill.

The Saccharin Case   An example of particularly effective use of advocacy advertising to mobilize the general public to communicate with policymakers was the campaign undertaken by the Calorie Control Council in opposition to a proposed ban on the use of saccharin. After reviewing the final results of a study by the Canadian government showing that laboratory rats fed high dos- ages of saccharin suffered an alarming incidence of cancer, the Food and Drug Administration proposed the ban in March of 1977. The proposed ban threat- ened food and drug products important to many different groups of persons, including dieters, drug manufacturers, diabetics, and heart patients. As the saccharin controversy unfolded, associations representing all these interests be- came active in trying to influence government policy on the subject. But the leading role in opposition to the ban was assumed early and vigorously by the organizational representative of the interests of diet food and soft drink pro- ducers, the Calorie Control Council (CCC).

Determined to fight the FDA's proposed ban, the CCC, with the help of some of the nation's largest advertising and public relations firms, launched a huge advertising campaign. Six days after news of the proposed saccharin ban was out, double-page advertisements sponsored by the CCC appeared in news- papers all over the United States, at a cost the Council admitted to be in the "high six-figure range."[36]

The two-page ad (with a banner headline, "Why the Proposed FDA Ban on Saccharin Is Leaving a Bad Taste in a Lot of People's Mouths") ridiculed

---

[36]Linda Demkovich, "Saccharin's Dead, Dieters Are Blue, What is Congress Going To Do?" *National Journal,* June 4, 1977, pp. 18–19.

the FDA and the scientific tests that led to the proposed ban. The text read, in part:

> For over 80 years people have been using saccharin. It has been used in an incredible variety of foods and drinks. It is consumed by millions of people all over the world every day.
>
> In all this time, there has never been a case of anyone having a significant adverse effect from consuming saccharin.
>
> And yet, the FDA is now proposing a ban on saccharin!
>
> Why?
>
> Well, you see, in Canada they conducted some research on rats, feeding them giant quantities of saccharin and then feeding the same high dosages to the offspring from infancy until their demise. The result was that some second generation rats in this experiment developed bladder tumors.
>
> So how does all this relate to humans? Not well at all. We know the dosages of saccharin fed the rats in the Canadian study were more than the amount a human would receive from drinking 1,250 twelve-ounce diet beverages a day over a lifetime! That's 117 gallons of liquid, or over 4,000 packets of saccharin a day for a lifetime! . . .
>
> If you find this action [the FDA's proposed ban] ridiculous, you're not alone. It's just another example of the arbitrary nature of BIG GOVERNMENT. It's left a bad taste in the mouths of millions of people all over America. Fortunately, we can all conduct our own experiments in this matter. It's called an experiment in democracy. And it works like this—WRITE OR CALL YOUR CONGRESSMAN TODAY AND LET HIM KNOW HOW YOU FEEL ABOUT A BAN ON SACCHARIN.[37]

The second page of the ad then listed the names and addresses of relevant policymakers and urged readers of the ad to "make this experiment in democracy really work. Your action now could make all the difference."

The CCC's ad was a stroke of political genius. First, the ad effectively ridiculed the Canadian laboratory tests, and made the test procedures and results appear absurd in the eyes of lay persons.[38] (Indeed, the reference to an equivalent human saccharin ingestion of 1,250 sodas a day stuck in readers' minds, and throughout the balance of the saccharin controversy that reference became a stock part of opponents' arguments.) Second, the ad invoked the symbol of Big Government arbitrarily meddling in the everyday personal decisions of consumers. In addition, because the ad was sponsored by the CCC rather than by, say, Pepsico, it seemed less self-serving to readers. Finally, the ad appealed to consumers' loyalties to products they not only enjoyed but presumed to have health benefits.

[37] *Washington Post,* March 13, 1977, pp. 18–19.

[38] In fact, the tests were conducted by trained experimental toxicologists according to procedures commonly used in the profession.

The best indicator of the ad's genius is that it achieved its intended effect. In following weeks, mail from irate citizens poured into congressional offices and into the offices of HEW and the FDA. Joseph Califano, the HEW Secretary, reported that his department was getting "more [mail] than HEW has ever gotten on any other issue," virtually all of it opposed to the ban.[39] Members of Congress also reported being deluged.[40] Not surprisingly, Congress eventually passed—and President Carter signed—legislation postponing the ban. The soft drink industry's effectiveness at arousing popular passions has given it a formidable reputation in Washington, and subsequent FDA attempts to deal with saccharin have failed. While we cannot infer that the CCC's efforts alone determined the outcome of this controversy, surely the amount of mail stimulated by the ads was an important factor.

The volume of the response in the saccharin case is even more impressive when compared with another recent example of successful grass roots lobbying: the torrent of mail that arrived on Capitol Hill urging repeal of a provision in the 1982 tax bill that would have required commercial banks and savings and loan associations to withhold 10 percent of the interest and dividends paid to depositors. The main objective of the provision had been to capture income that taxpayers failed to report. To the bankers, however, the provision meant administrative headaches. In order to exert pressure on behalf of the repeal of this provision, the American Bankers Association and the U.S. League of Savings Institutions—with the assistance of one of the nation's leading advertising firms—undertook a multimillion dollar, multifaceted public relations campaign.[41]

One of the linchpins of this effort was the generation of volumes of mail from bank customers. Senate offices reported receiving from 150,000 to 300,000 letters, mailgrams, and postcards apiece on this issue. In contrast to the CCC, which stimulated an outpouring of mail solely through the medium of newspaper ads, the bankers were able to rely on an established network, the millions of customers with whom they are in touch regularly by mail. This provided a ready-made communications channel. By including an appeal for action with the monthly statement, the bankers were able to reach a large number of interested citizens directly in a way that the CCC could not. In short, the saccharin case makes clear both the devotion of diet soda drinkers to their product and the extraordinary achievement of the CCC in generating mail from the public at large.

[39] Quoted in *Washington Post,* March 29, 1977, p. A6.
[40] *Congressional Quarterly Weekly Report,* March 26, 1977, p. 539.
[41] On the banking lobby's fight to repeal the withholding provision, see Bill Keller, "Lowest Common Denominator Lobbying: Why the Banks Fought Withholding," *The Washington Monthly,* May 1983, pp. 32–39. See, also, Paul Gardner and Ronn Kirkwood, "The Ability to Say 'No': An Analysis of Executive and Legislative Behavior in the Interest Withholding and Social Security Reform Debates," paper delivered at the Annual Meeting of the Midwest Political Science Association, Chicago, April 1984.

Direct Mail

Although timely and provocative advertising campaigns can be remarkably effective in mobilizing the mass public, most groups seeking to stimulate constituent pressure cannot expect a broad base of popular support. Therefore, they are eager to focus their efforts on identifiable, special segments of the public that are likely to be sympathetic and supportive. To reach these special publics, many groups—especially citizens' groups—have turned to the use of direct-mail campaigns. Direct mail is used in politics for several purposes— raising funds, persuading recipients of the rightness of a cause, and mobilizing them to contact lawmakers about it. However, as shown by the brief discussion in Chapter 5 of the use of direct mail as a fund-raising tool, direct-mail campaigns tend to be quite expensive. Therefore, organizations that send out letters urging recipients to make their views known to legislators are also inclined to try to recover some of their costs at the same time. In short, the various functions of direct mail are often so closely intertwined that they are difficult to separate in practice.

Direct-mail campaigns vary greatly in their cost and in their levels of sophistication, but all such campaigns consist of the same basic components: (1) assembling a mailing list; (2) preparing the letter's "packaging"; and (3) developing the right "pitch" in the text of the letter so that the recipient is persuaded to take action. Whether a group is mailing to 500 persons or to 500,000, it goes through each of these steps.

The Mailing List   Perhaps the most important part of the direct-mail process is assembly of the mailing list. Since the purpose of a mailing is to urge supportive action from the recipients, a group wants to send its letters only to persons most likely to respond to its appeal. Of course, organizations that have members enjoy an advantage here: they have a natural constituency of persons they can call on for active support. However, organizations that have no members or that wish to appeal beyond their membership base to a broader public have the option of renting or purchasing lists. Finding useful lists is easier than it used to be because distribution of mailing lists has become a big business, with assorted firms in most major cities brokering lists among eager political organizations.[42] Furthermore, high-speed data processing makes it possible to use the lists selectively. When, for example, Rep. Barney Frank of Massachusetts used the Sierra Club list as the basis for a fund-raising letter during his 1982 campaign for reelection, he presumably sorted by zip code, selecting only the Sierra Club members in his district.

Designing the "Package"   Putting together a list is only the beginning of the process. The second step involves designing the "package"—the mailing enve-

[42]See Deborah Baldwin, "Ideology By Mail," *The New Republic,* July 7–14, 1979, p. 20.

lope, the letter itself, and any enclosures—to attract the recipients' attention
and to induce them to open it and read it through to the end. First of all, of
course, the sponsoring organization wants to reduce the chances that its letter
will go straight from the recipient's mailbox into the wastebasket. Therefore, in
order to increase the chances of a letter being read, direct mailers employ
various techniques to make it seem less like "junk mail." For example, in 1982
a coalition of telecommunications firms was pressing for legislation that would
effect the breakup of the American Telephone and Telegraph Co. As one part
of its effort, the coalition of AT&T competitors sent out a mailing of some
70,000 pieces that included a controversial gimmick. Each envelope was
stamped with an imitation of the Bell System logo along with the attention-
grabbing warning: "Notice of Telephone Rate Increase Enclosed." With an
envelope well-designed to ensure that recipients would not lightly toss it away,
the letter's contents warned that unless the recipient helped lobby for the
breakup of AT&T, telephone rates would double.[43]

Similarly, since direct-mail experts have discovered that an envelope with
a licked stamp looks more like a personalized letter and is, therefore, more
likely to be opened and read, many organizations avoid metered mail; some
even see to it that the stamps are affixed at a slightly cockeyed angle to
strengthen the impression that the letter emanated from a human.[44] Likewise,
many organizations use high-speed letter-quality printers to address their envelopes so as to avoid the preprinted address labels that stigmatize a direct-mail
letter.

Preparing the "Pitch"   The key to making direct-mail an effective stimulant of
grass roots action is appealing to the recipient's emotions. The letter's text, or
"copy," has to carry the full burden of informing, agitating, and prompting. As
a consequence, direct-mail appeals for grass roots help usually cast issues (as
well as political enemies) in the starkest, most overblown terms, playing on the
recipients' fears, angers, and political prejudices. For example, in the early
1980s the handgun lobby mounted an unusually bitter attack on the Department of the Treasury's Bureau of Alcohol, Tobacco and Firearms (ATF) in an
effort to eliminate the bureau or, at least, to reduce the enforcement powers it
received under the Gun Control Act of 1968. Hard pressed to cite legitimate
matters warranting its members' alarm, the Gun Owners of America seized on
the ATF's offering of "honorary Junior Special Agent" cards to children who
tour the agency's Washington Museum—a practice much like the airlines giving a set of plastic pilot's wings to children taking their first flight. The Gun
Owners of America warned in a mass mailing:

43 Bill Keller, "Computers and Laser Printers Have Recast the Injunction: 'Write Your
Congressman,' " *Congressional Quarterly Weekly Report,* September 11, 1982, p. 2247.
44 Larry Sabato, *The Rise of Political Consultants* (New York: Basic Books, 1981), p. 240.

MOBILIZING PRESSURE: GRASS ROOTS LOBBYING

> Your gun rights won't be worth a red cent if Federal agents recruit your neighbor's children to spy on you. The ATF recently offered to make our American youngsters "Junior Special Agents."
>
> Sounds harmless enough, doesn't it? But what will these Junior Special Agents be doing? There's no doubt in my mind that ATF is encouraging them to spy on their parents and neighbors. Tomorrow while you're at work these kids could be sneaking around your property. You can expect them to be peeking in the windows of your house or car trying to find out more about your hunting rifle or gun collection.
>
> Then, for an impressionable youngster, the most important part of all—sending a SECRET report to the Government. That is when you can expect the senior ATF agents to take over from the kids. And that is when you start becoming the "hunted instead of the hunter."
>
> All because an unsuspecting youngster has been duped into joining an organization that looks suspiciously like the "Hitler Youth." Is it any wonder that the ATF has been called "an American Gestapo"?[45]

In addition to arousing the emotions, a typical letter from an interest group tries to convey a sense of urgency. Thus, in a letter promoting People for the American Way—a liberal organization founded in 1981 to oppose the conservative religious organization, the Moral Majority—television producer Norman Lear wrote: "If I live to be a thousand . . . I may never write a letter more important to me than this one." Some variation on the "this is the most important letter you'll receive this year" line crops up frequently because direct-mail experts have found it effective.[46]

These communications also try to make it easier for an inexperienced citizen to write a letter by including pertinent background information, summaries of points that might be made in letters, and names and addresses of relevant policymakers. Sometimes a preprinted and addressed card is enclosed so that those who lack the time or inclination to compose their own letters can register their views.

Proxy Lobbying

One problem with using advertisements and direct mail to prod supporters into communicating with policymakers is timing: a grass roots campaign may generate letters or telegrams too early or too late to help. Some interest groups have tried to solve this timing problem by using a technique known as *proxy lobbying*—collecting proxies from supporters and dispatching communications

---

[45]Cited in Patricia Rachal and John T. Tierney, "Traffic in Cant," *New York Times,* September 8, 1981, p. A23. Copyright ©1981 by The New York Times Company. Reprinted by permission.
[46]Sabato, *Rise of Political Consultants,* p. 242.

in their names when it is deemed expedient. The National Education Association (NEA), for example, uses proxy lobbying. With its highly regarded lobbying machine of 1.7 million members, the NEA does a remarkably effective job of getting teachers to send letters and telegrams and make phone calls. However, during the summer when teachers are on vacation, the organization has a harder time of it. Consequently, the NEA has secured permission from 100,000 teachers to sign their names to telegrams on issues ranging from tuition tax credits to Social Security. The telegrams pour into Congress whenever the NEA needs them, whether or not the teachers "sending" them know it.[47]

Of course, an organization runs risks when it mails letters under the names of persons whose names appear on some acquired list. During deliberations on the 1982 tax bill, Maine's U.S. senators began receiving numerous telegrams from grocers back home opposing a proposed increase in the cigarette tax. When Senator William S. Cohen wrote back to them, some of the constituents complained that they had never written to him. And several of Cohen's letters were returned to his office marked that the constituent was long dead. It turns out that the telegrams had been sent by the Tobacco Institute, using a list supplied by the Maine Retail Grocers Association. When the association decided to oppose the cigarette tax, it sent its 350 members a letter saying their names would be used unless they objected. Only two did, and the other 348 names were turned over to the Tobacco Institute.[48]

Is "Contrived" Pressure Really Pressure?

The discussion so far has focused on various means by which organizations—often at tremendous financial cost—orchestrate grass roots pressure on policymakers. We have seen how such campaigns can be successful in flooding government mailboxes and have considered numerous cases in which a favorable policy outcome ensued. However, we cannot conclude that the grass roots lobbying effort was responsible for the ultimate resolution of the controversy. After all, the conventional wisdom has generally held that communications inspired by organizations usually betray their origins and that elected officials ignore or discount constituent communications bearing the scent of having been orchestrated. According to one set of observers, "While legislators give their mail serious consideration, generally they are not receptive to letters whose actual origin may have been with a constituent but whose wording bears close resemblance to thousands of others. . . . Considered singly, the letter-writing campaign is probably the least effective and most relied-on lobbying technique."[49]

---

[47]Keller, "Computers and Laser Printers," p. 2247.
[48]Ibid.
[49]Zeigler and Peak, *Interest Groups in American Society,* p. 153. This view is generally derived from Lewis A. Dexter, "What Congressmen Hear: The Mail," *Public Opinion Quarterly* 20 (1956): 16–57.

We asked the respondents in our survey of Washington representatives about this problem with letter-writing campaigns. Because of the rich responses they provided, it is difficult to give statistical summaries of their replies. What seems clear, however, is that many groups, acting on the conventional wisdom, bend over backward to camouflage the fact that the pressure has been orchestrated by an office in Washington. Over two-thirds of the organizations that inspire grass roots pressure make some attempt to see that the letters or contacts seem spontaneous and sincere. For example, many organizations find it best not to provide their members with mail-in postcards or prewritten texts; instead, they furnish members with a summary of salient points and instruct them to compose their own letters, perhaps even to write in longhand. As the vice-president of Washington operations for a large membership organization told us: "We try to avoid form letters. We send them the information and ask them to tailor it to themselves and make it personal." In an interesting twist, the Washington bureau director of a leading civil rights group indicated that the more illegible and ungrammatical the letters generated by her organization, the greater the likelihood they would be taken seriously.

One technical innovation relieves grass roots letter writers of any need to be creative. The "package" sent out to the grass roots includes not only the conventional statement laying out the issue and the organization's position, but also a fully prepared, thoughtful letter that the constituent is to sign and send to his congressman or senator. This is no mere form letter; it is printed on colored paper and imprinted, in letterhead style, with the constituent's name and address to make it resemble personal stationery. Moreover, to reduce still further the chances that congressional offices will spot these as form letters, the sponsoring organization prepares return letters using many different paper sizes and colors, type styles, and text wordings. (To benefit those who find signing and posting the letter too much trouble, the cover appeal sometimes extends an option: "Because time is short, you might choose to call us toll free . . . and authorize us to send, at no cost to you, a public service message on your behalf to your Congressman.")[50]

Although many organizations go to great lengths in attempting to disguise the extent to which constituents' communications have been concerted, some lobbyists feel such efforts are unnecessary. Certain developments in congressional politics over the past decade would seem to enhance the potency of a grass roots lobbying campaign that generates a large *number* of communications, even if they are obviously stimulated. As discussed in Chapter 7, scholars indicate that in recent times lawmakers in Congress increasingly act as parochial advocates, attentive both to the expressed preferences and the particularistic needs of constituents.[51] Legislators, especially newcomers, feel electorally vulnerable. Their activities evince an increasing concern for the feelings and

---

[50] Keller, "Computers and Laser Printers," pp. 2246, 2240.
[51] For references to the literature, see footnote 8 in Chapter 7.

special needs of constituents. They pay more attention to individual casework; they dicker with complex formulas to guarantee the most generous package of federal goodies to the district; and they listen for any tremors that would indicate shifts in constituency opinion.

Reflecting this climate, many of the lobbyists we interviewed indicated that if the communications arrive in sufficient *quantity* in congressional offices, they will be heeded no matter how orchestrated they seem. As one prominent lobbyist (and son of a former congressman) told us:

> Members [of Congress] have to care about this mail, even if it's mail that is almost identically worded. Labor unions do this sort of thing a lot. The congressman has to care that *somebody* out there in his district has enough power to get hundreds of people to sit down and write a postcard or a letter—because if the guy can get them to do *that,* he might be able to influence them in other ways. So, a member has no choice but to pay attention. It's suicide if he doesn't.

Talking with a reporter, Richard Conlan, staff director of the House Democratic Study Group, echoed these comments:

> The conventional wisdom you'll hear is that a few thoughtful letters have more impact than 100 names on a petition. That's generally true. But a lot of these new members are like cats on a hot tin roof and they start dancing all over. They can't take any pressure at all—including contrived pressure.[52]

Further confirmation of this view emerges from the results of a 1981 survey of Capitol Hill staff aides. The results of that study show that "orchestrated mail from constituents" ranks eleventh overall on a list of 96 types of communications that may influence the decisions of members of Congress. (The types of communications listed in the study included constituent letters, editorials in major daily newspapers, telephone calls from friends, visits from lobbyists, and television documentaries.)[53] It would seem, in short, that although members of Congress may not be fooled by contrived constituency pressure, they do not feel free to ignore it.

Grass Roots Lobbying: Something New?

Because grass roots lobbying campaigns rely so heavily on data processing and other electronic innovations, it is easy to lose sight of the fact that grass roots lobbying is not the invention of our era. This, too, is an ancient weapon in the

---

[52]Quoted in Keller, "Lobbyists Cultivate 'Grass Roots,' " p. 1740.
[53]See "Orchestrated Mail Does Influence Staff—Who Says So? Staff.," *The Congressional Staff Journal,* November/December 1981, p. 7.

pressure group arsenal. At the start of the century, without so much as a microchip to aid it, the Anti-Saloon League had a mailing list of over half a million people.[54] However, we know from observers at the time that the Anti-Saloon League was not unique. As described in the 1920s, the techniques of grass roots lobbying were remarkably similar to those of today.[55] Moreover, membership organizations of the time were not alone in using these techniques; there is evidence that corporations have long made it their business to mobilize their employees to act on behalf of preferred political positions with a heavy-handedness that would probably not be accepted today.[56]

Indeed, even the extraordinary sensitivity of contemporary politicians to mass-generated communications—which we attributed, at least in part, to recent changes in congressional politics—is not an entirely new development. Writing in1928, one observer contradicted the frequent assertions by legislators that orchestrated mail has no effect on their votes: "In a close congressional district, or one in which a close primary contest is in prospect, as few as six letters from voters with whom the Member [of Congress] is acquainted have been known to change his vote."[57] In short, while grass roots efforts may be facilitated by electronic innovations, neither attempts to mobilize the public nor legislative sensitivity to orchestrated communications are unique to our era.

SUMMARY

This chapter has examined the many ways in which organized interests try to influence political outcomes by persuading or mobilizing either the public at large or special, narrower publics of interested citizens or opinion leaders. We have probed the assorted techniques that groups use to draw attention to an issue and to shape public opinion—advertisements, "canned" editorials and news items, media events, press conferences, and protests and demonstrations. We have also explored many of the techniques used to mobilize citizens to communicate with public officials. We saw, for example, that many organizations maintain intricate communications systems to alert their members of the need to contact policymakers, and that advertisements and direct-mail appeals can be used to stimulate communications from broader publics. In addition, we assessed the impact of contrived pressure on legislators' deliberations.

Several themes run through this discussion of organized attempts to mold

[54]Peter Odegard, *Pressure Politics: The Story of the Anti-Saloon League* (New York: Columbia University Press, 1928), p. 76.

[55]See Pendleton Herring's description in *Group Representation before Congress*, p. 70.

[56]See May 2, 1913 letter to the employees of the Great Western Sugar Company, in Peter Odegard, *Current History* 31 (1930): 695–696, quoted in Helen M. Muller, ed., *Lobbying in Congress* (New York: Wilson, 1931), p. 82.

[57]Richard Boeckel, *Regulation of Congressional Lobbies* (Washington, DC: Editorial Research Reports, 1928), p. 18.

public opinion and action. The first is that all organizations are not equally advantaged in the use of these indirect lobbying techniques. Although technological advances have made things like the maintenance of computerized mailing lists economically feasible even for relatively impecunious groups, the effective use of most of the techniques described in this chapter is expensive, thus placing better-financed groups at a distinct advantage. We saw in Chapter 5 (Table 5.2) that citizens' groups were the least likely to report having access to public relations experts. This chapter, however, has made clear that citizens' groups rely heavily on political strategies involving public persuasion and mobilization. This suggests that their relative lack of use of public relations expertise reflects a scarcity of resources rather than an absence of need. However, it is also apparent that an appealing message can compensate for slender finances when reaching out to the public. Organizations whose causes generate natural sympathy can take advantage of free media coverage and need not rely solely on the expensive techniques that permit maximum control over content.

Second, contrary to the impression one gets from assorted journalistic and academic analyses of contemporary pressure politics, the techniques currently used to cultivate public opinion and encourage popular reactions are nothing new. Changing technologies have made some of these techniques easier, faster, or less costly to use (undoubtedly helping to account for the increases in their use), but as our historical references indicate, virtually all of the techniques examined in this chapter have long been used in one form or another.

Finally, extensive use of these techniques may be debasing the quality of our public discourse. The public relations professionals who formulate the campaigns that take an organization's political case to the public use techniques developed in the marketing of consumer products. Classical notions of democracy do not envision that public discussion should consist of the selling of political ideas like the selling of so many cakes of soap. Furthermore, many of the communications might be deemed irresponsible because they use inflammatory rhetoric to appeal to public fears, prejudices, and ignorance, or because they misrepresent to the public the nature of the facts or the source of the message or to policymakers the spontaneity of the response. Thus, critics argue not only that the clarity of our collective political vision and the quality of our political discourse are sullied but also that campaigns of public mobilization subject already skittish legislators to irreconcilable cross-pressures and therefore undermine the ability of elected representatives to deliberate thoughtfully and exercise statesmanlike judgment.

These considerations bring us squarely back to Madison's concerns in *The Federalist,* No. 10. If it is true that organized attempts to reach out to the public debase political discourse, then such attempts can be numbered among the "mischiefs of faction." However, it is important to recall Madison's warnings about the folly of curtailing the liberties that sustain such mischiefs. Any attempt to circumscribe such public appeals would be a fundamental violation of the rights we enjoy as citizens. Indeed, as Madison reminds us, it would be a cure worse than the disease. Hence, public officials—especially those in Congress—bear a special burden. Since contrived pressure is likely to be an inevitability, they must assume the responsibility for achieving some kind of balance as representatives—that is, to remain responsive to citizen concerns while not capitulating to orchestrated expressions of opinion.

9

Influencing
the Electoral
Process

There is a second route by which organized interests seek indirect political influence, the electoral process. Because they command resources of great utility to candidates—votes, manpower, and money—they are in a position to have an impact both upon electoral outcomes and upon the comportment of winners once they take office. This chapter focuses upon the various electoral activities of organized interests that depend upon the first two of these resources: votes and manpower. The next chapter, which treats political action committees, concentrates on the last of this trio of electoral resources: money.

ORGANIZED INTERESTS AND POLITICAL PARTIES

The involvement of organized interests in the electoral process brings them into contact with the other set of major private institutions linking citizens to policymakers in American democracy: political parties. It has been traditional to differentiate political parties from interest groups along several dimensions: to point out, for example, that parties address a wide range of issues while organized interests have a more limited agenda of policy concerns; that parties encompass a broad spectrum of identifiers having divergent preferences while organized interests unite smaller numbers of people who share certain specialized concerns; and that parties are characterized by greater longevity than organized interests.[1]

[1] See, for example, Robert J. Huckshorn, *Political Parties in America*, 2nd ed. (Belmont, CA: Brooks/Cole, 1984), pp. 288–289.

As tendencies, these distinctions undoubtedly hold. However, the world of organized interests is so diverse as to contain dozens of contradictory examples. For instance, as discussed in Chapter 3, many political organizations—ranging from the Americans for Democratic Action to the Moral Majority—address multiple issues. In addition, the roughly 15 million members of AFL-CIO affiliates (a number that surpasses the vote for any minor-party candidate in American history) include persons of diverse background, interest, and opinion. In addition, many organizations active in Washington are long-lived; the American Medical Association actually predates the Republican party.

In fact, in an age of weak political parties and an increasing role for organized interests in electoral politics, what is noteworthy is the extent of overlap between political parties and organized interests in terms of their activities, objectives, and functions. Both sets of institutions participate in nominating candidates, working for their election, and financing their campaigns; both try to influence appointments to government office; both have policy goals they seek to realize; and so on. Still, the two sets of institutions are not utterly indistinguishable. One observer characterized their differing emphases as follows: "[M]ost students of government see a pressure group as 'issue or policy oriented' and a political party as 'election or personality oriented.' A party is seen as primarily motivated toward capturing and operating the government; the interest group's motivation is to shape public policy."[2]

Party and Organized Interest Strength

The common wisdom among political scientists is that party and organized interest strength are inversely proportional: where parties are strong, organized interests are weak and vice versa.[3] Our own era is one of interest group strength and party weakness. Among the important trends noted by observers of American politics of the past two decades has been the progressive enfeeblement of our parties.[4]

---

[2]Hugh Bone, "Political Parties and Pressure Group Politics," *Annals of the American Academy of Political and Social Science* 319 (September 1958): 74.

[3]This point is made by E. E. Schattschneider in "Pressure Groups versus Political Parties," *Annals of the American Academy of Political and Social Science* 259 (September 1948): 18–19. A contemporary statement of this theme can be found in Jeffrey M. Berry, *The Interest Group Society* (Boston: Little, Brown, 1984), Chapter 3.

[4]The theme of party weakness is elaborated in many places, among them, Walter Dean Burnham, *Critical Elections and the Mainsprings of American Politics* (New York: Norton, 1970), Chapter 5; Norman H. Nie, Sidney Verba, and John Petrocik, *The Changing American Voter* (Cambridge: Harvard University Press, 1976), Chapter 4; Everett Carll Ladd, Jr., with Charles D. Hadley, *Transformations of the American Party System,* 2nd ed. (New York: Norton, 1978), Chapter 7; and Austin Ranney, "The Political Parties: Reform and Decline," in Anthony King, ed., *The New American Political System* (Washington, DC: American Enterprise Institute, 1978), Chapter 6. More recently, observers have noted a countertrend, a revitalization of party organization at the national level. See, for example, David Adamany, "Political Parties in the 1980s," in Michael Malbin, ed., *Money and Politics in the United States* (Chatham, NJ: Chatham House Publishers, 1984), Chapter 3.

This decline in party strength has several facets. At the level of the ordinary citizen, there has been an erosion of party loyalties, increased split-ticket voting, and a tendency for partisans to defect in casting ballots. At the level of the parties as institutions, reforms (especially in the Democratic party) have deprived party leaders of important prerogatives and responsibilities, and direct primaries, civil service systems, and political action committees have encroached on many traditional party functions. Furthermore, new compaign technologies—polling, direct-mail fund raising, and television spots—have spawned a new genre of campaign specialists, whose expertise is not party-based. It has also been argued that the rise of citizens' groups, which offer to ordinary citizens an alternative route for the expression of their views, has contributed to the atrophy of the parties.[5]

Evidence from state legislatures confirms the inverse relationship between party and organized interest strength: nine of the ten states categorized as having weak pressure groups have strong parties; only one of the 22 states categorized as having strong pressure groups has strong parties.[6] Unfortunately, there is no evidence from national politics to supplement these state-level data. It would be useful to trace the vicissitudes in the fortunes of organized interests with reference to changing party strength—to learn, for example, whether a period of party resurgence like the 1930s was one of waning organized interest influence.

The Ties between Parties and Organized Interests

In many democracies there are strong and continuing ties between the national political parties and the organized interests that share their programmatic goals. In particular, trade unions are likely to be allied with labor or social democratic parties. Although organized interests play a substantial role in supporting candidates and financing campaigns in the United States, their links to parties as institutions are weaker than elsewhere.[7] We asked the Washington representatives in our survey about the partisan inclinations of their organizations. A majority (59 percent) indicated that their organizations are closer to one of the two parties. Of course, the direction of such partisan leanings varies with the kind of organization. Business organizations, not surprisingly, favor

---

[5] See Jeffrey M. Berry, "Public Interest vs. Party System," *Society*, May/June, 1980, pp. 42–48.

[6] Sarah McCally Morehouse, *State Politics, Parties, and Policy* (New York: Holt, Rinehart and Winston, 1981, pp. 107–118). Morehouse measures party strength by averaging the governors' vote percentages in gubernatorial primaries. She classifies pressure group strength on the basis of a reading of the state literature. See also, L. Harmon Zeigler and Michael Baer, *Lobbying: Interaction and Influence in State Legislatures* (Belmont, CA: Wadsworth, 1969), pp. 23–37, 144–151.

[7] Morehouse argues that the European model holds for states having strong, programmatic parties; that is, in states where the parties compete with each other on the basis of distinctive policy positions, organized interests tend to affiliate with their natural allies. *State Politics, Parties, and Policy*, pp. 115–116.

the Republicans: 60 percent of the trade associations lean toward the Republicans and only 7 percent lean toward the Democrats; among corporations, the most avowedly nonpartisan of the organizations in the sample, 37 percent are closer to the Republicans, 5 percent to the Democrats. Labor, on the other hand, is overwhelmingly pro-Democratic: 95 percent of the unions lean toward the Democrats, none toward the Republicans. Citizens' groups also incline toward the Democrats: 57 percent of those sampled feel closer to the Democrats, 14 percent to the Republicans.[8]

In spite of their frequent partisan leanings, evidence emerges at various points in the interview that organized interests do not consider the national parties critical factors in their attempts at policy influence. For example, we asked our respondents to indicate which two of eight political forces (excluding other interest groups) listed on a card they considered their principal competitors in influencing members of Congress. Most frequently mentioned was the White House, chosen by 38 percent as their major rival. Six of the remaining seven choices are clustered close behind: in descending order, congressional staff (28 percent), other members of Congress (26 percent), members' constituencies (25 percent), and executive branch agencies, public opinion, and the media (24 percent each). Only the political parties were not deemed serious opponents; a mere 6 percent selected the parties from the list as a principal source of competition.

We also posed a series of questions to learn who talks to whom in Washington.[9] For example, we asked our respondents how likely they were to consult and cooperate with various political actors when planning political strategy on policy matters. The replies range substantially. Only 4 percent of the respondents indicated that they are not too likely to consult with congressional committee staff, and 6 percent that they are not too likely to consult with friends in other organizations. Party leaders in Congress lag considerably farther behind: 34 percent of the respondents said that they are not too likely to consult and cooperate with party leaders in Congress, making them sixth on a list of ten. Furthermore, the political parties seem to be largely excluded from such policy

[8]We surmise that these figures may overstate the Democratic leanings of the citizens' groups in Washington. As indicated in Appendix A, our weighted sample drawn from the index to the *National Journal* overrepresents citizens' groups. We attribute this overrepresentation to the journalistic ethic of giving full coverage to both sides of a story even when the size of the contending forces is quite uneven. We suspect, on this basis, that we have oversampled not simply citizens' groups but liberal citizens' groups as well. Conservative groups that defend broadly held interests in economic growth or reduced prices and taxes are often allied with organizations that have private interests in avoiding government regulation, exploiting natural resources, and the like. Journalistic coverage of political controversies often focuses on the antagonism between liberal environmental or consumer groups, on the one hand, and such private interests, on the other, and leaves their conservative public interest allies in the background. On this basis, we suspect that the same bias that accounts for the overrepresentation of citizens' groups in the sample caused an overrepresentation of *liberal* citizens' groups as well. Thus, these figures may overrepresent the affinities between the Democratic party and the public interest community.

[9]The items discussed in this paragraph and the one that follows will be analyzed in greater detail in Chapter 11.

networks. Fully 84 percent of the respondents indicated that they are not too likely to plan political strategy with party leaders at the national committees.

Similar findings emerge from a question about the relative importance of 13 different channels of information for finding out about what the government is doing. Again, congressional committee staff are the vital link; only 1 percent of our respondents indicated that they are not too important as a source of information. As before, the replies then range considerably. Once again, however, party leaders in Congress were far from the top of the list: 41 percent of the respondents deemed them not too important, placing them well down the list. Finally, in distant last place are the political parties: 80 percent of the respondents indicated that party leaders at the national committees are not too important as a source of information.[10]

Party conventions, especially presidential nominating conventions, do, however, bring organized interests into periodic contact with parties. As will be discussed later in the chapter, a few organizations (usually ones with large constituencies) seek to place members as delegates at party conventions. Larger numbers of organizations attempt to influence the content of party platforms. Such activities imply direct communication with the national parties. In summary, then, it seems that what day-to-day contact exists between organized interests and the political parties is ordinarily mediated through congressional party organizations. Except at the time of party conventions, the policy networks of organized interests more or less exclude the national parties.

Organized Interests and Election Results: The 1980 Election

The foregoing seems to imply that parties and organized interests operate in relative isolation from one another and to support the notion that while administrations might come and go with the vagaries of electoral outcomes, the Washington pressure community marches on unperturbed. However, the reality is more complicated. Our interviews with Washington representatives make clear that electoral outcomes can have a significant impact on the fortunes of organized interests even though the links between parties and organized interests are indeed weak. It matters to organized interests who holds office. While Washington representatives have to learn to deal with public officials regardless of their party or ideology, their task is made much easier when policymakers are like-minded. Because our interviews were conducted between November 1981 and May 1982, we were able to probe the effects of the 1980 election, an election that brought with it change of partisan control of both the White House and the Senate and that ushered in the most significant departure in public policy at least since the 1960s, if not since the New Deal of the 1930s.

---

[10]Unfortunately, these lists did not include reference to various subsidiary party organizations such as the Democratic Study Group and the Republican Congressional Campaign Committee with whom organized interests might also have contact.

An overwhelming 91 percent of our respondents—ranging from 86 percent of those affiliated with corporations to 100 percent of those attached to citizens' groups—indicated that the 1980 election had made a difference to their organizations.

The responses to an open-ended probe as to *how* things had changed under Reagan fell into three broad categories. A few respondents remarked that the change of administrations had brought to Washington a new set of incumbents who had to be cultivated and educated. Implicit in such comments was the assumption that it was simply the change of personnel, rather than the particular partisan or ideological character of the Reagan administration, that implied extra effort during the inevitable period of transition. In addition, however, many of the respondents pointed out that their access to policymakers had changed. For some, such as the government affairs operation of the American Petroleum Institute, the change in administration facilitated access. For others, such as a lobbyist for a social welfare organization focusing on housing: "[I]t turns life upside down. It means we no longer have the information sources; we don't have the personal contacts. We must start all over again. There are a lot of people who are unwilling to speak up even if they are in favor of your policy stands because you are a potential enemy." Finally, many talked about the substantive content of policy. According to the executive director of a consumer organization focusing on broadcasting: "The changes have threatened to wipe us out. The administration challenges every policy and issue that we stand for. Our work has become that much more important." To the Chamber of Commerce, on the other hand, the policy changes were welcome:

> For years this organization has advocated less government, less government spending and lower taxes. Usually this fell on deaf ears. Finally, now the Administration advocates what we've always believed. They've been of great assistance. The fact that the Senate is controlled by the same party is also helpful . . . We have government leaders who think the same way we think. It's a delightful relationship that we have with the White House—from the President on down.

Of course, the Reagan administration has affected different kinds of organizations differently. Of those organizations indicating that Republican control of the White House and Senate had an impact on their fortunes (beyond that expected when there is simply a new set of incumbents with whom to get acquainted), 93 percent of the unions and 76 percent of the citizens' groups—but only 19 percent of the trade associations and 9 percent of the corporations—indicated that life had been harder since the change. Analogously, in response to a query about any alteration in their organizations' level of influence with the new administration, those affiliated with 77 percent of the unions and 59 percent of the citizens' groups—but only 6 percent of the trade associations and 4 percent of the corporations—said that their influence had decreased.[11] The figures for organizations professing different ideologies are equally striking. Ninety percent of the liberal organizations—as opposed to 29 percent of the middle-of-the-road and 7 percent of the conservative organizations—indicated that life had been harder since the change of administration. Similarly, 67 percent of the liberal organizations—but only 14 percent of the middle-of-the-road and 2 percent of the conservative ones—said that their influence had decreased.

In short, the relationship between the parties and the Washington pressure community is complex. On one hand, in spite of the fact that a majority of the organizations in our Washington representatives survey have partisan leanings, most of the dealings they have with party leaders take place either in the congressional context or at presidential nominating conventions. They have very little to do with the national party organizations on a day-to-day basis. On the other hand, whatever the level of interaction with the parties, the Washington pressure community is not insulated from the effects of electoral outcomes. Because elections bring to office new sets of incumbents—especially when, as is periodically the case, they constitute an approximation of a national decision on major questions of policy—electoral results can have a significant effect on the prospects of organized interests. The 1980 election, a notable one in many respects, had an impact on virtually all of the organizations included in our sample. Thus, even though the institutional links between the parties and the Washington pressure community are quite weak, organized interests are not unaffected by the electoral verdicts that turn administrations in and out of office. Rather, under certain circumstances, national choices rendered in elections have substantial consequences for organized interests as well.

ORGANIZED INTERESTS IN ELECTORAL POLITICS

That organized interests devote so much energy to activities associated with the electoral process implies, of course, a recognition of how much elections affect them. Organizations that get involved in electoral politics may be pursuing either or both of two goals. One objective in electoral activity is to influence the outcome of electoral contests and, by affecting who wins or loses, thereby to elect more sympathetic public officials. The implicit assumption is that candidates who are like-minded on the broad or narrow set of issues with which the

[11]It is interesting that a number of organizations reported a contradictory impact with respect to membership support. Several respondents from civil rights and citizens' groups indicated that although access to policymakers had become more difficult and administration policies were antagonistic to their goals, their memberships had grown in the wake of the 1980 election as liberals awoke to the jeopardy in which pet causes had been placed. At least one trade association representative made the opposite point with respect to membership. According to an executive at the Independent Petroleum Association, "It's ironic. It's given our membership the impression that government is in friendly hands which makes them more complacent. So now we have to work harder to motivate them."

organization is concerned would, if left to their own devices once in office, promote the causes dear to the organization; therefore, what is needed is quite simply to make sure that such candidates are victorious. The goal of electing ideologically congenial candidates and defeating hostile ones dictates that the organization locate races in which there is a genuine choice on salient issues and support the ideologically compatible candidate with endorsements and campaign assistance. This strategy dictates that contributions of money and manpower be directed to candidates who need assistance and who seem to have a reasonable chance of winning. In particular, assistance is targeted to marginal races; not only are scarce resources not to be squandered on certain losers, no matter how ideologically virtuous, but they are not to be dissipated on sure winners of similar purity.

A second aim in electoral activity is to influence, not electoral results, but the behavior of eventual office holders and, thereby, government policy. That is, the purpose is either to demonstrate enough political muscle or to create a sufficient sense of indebtedness on the part of the eventual winner that, once in office, he or she will be responsive to the organization's political needs. In pursuing this aim, organizations not only give support—endorsements and campaign and financial assistance—to particular candidates, they sometimes work through the parties, attending party conventions and influencing party platforms. This objective generates a different set of strategic criteria. The ideological conformity of the candidate and the marginality of the race recede in importance. The only ideological test applied is that the candidate be receptive to persuasion and not downright antagonistic in policy orientation. Organizations seeking to affect the behavior of officeholders are particularly likely to pursue two strategies in selecting candidates to assist: to help incumbents who are on key committees (especially powerful ones with positions of institutional leadership in policy areas of concern); and to concentrate on races in geographically critical districts, such as where an association has many members or a corporation has a branch plant. As before, organizations seeking to influence the behavior of elected officials avoid sure losers. However, since the goal is to ensure that officeholders feel compelled to be responsive, organizations active in electoral politics frequently aid certain winners, even candidates running without opposition.

Presumably, different kinds of organizations are differentially likely to pursue one or the other of these strategies in electoral politics, depending upon the size, geographical dispersion, and intensity of commitment of the membership; the number and nature of the organization's policy concerns; the extent and nature of its resources; and so on. However, these strategies are not mutually exclusive alternatives. While some organizations probably pursue one to the exclusion of the other, it is quite possible to combine them in various ways—for example, by pursuing different strategies in different races; by emphasizing one strategy at one time and the other during a later electoral cycle; or by varying the strategy according to what kind of assistance is at stake. Still, while particular organizations presumably hybridize, it is useful to understand the twin objectives of electoral involvement.

Interest Groups at Party Conventions

Most electoral activity by organized interests entails supporting particular candidates. Periodically, however, they make the parties the target of their participation in the electoral process, usually in conjunction with party conventions. Probably reflecting the differences in the kinds of organizations that lean toward each of the parties, such party-based attempts at influence are relatively more conspicuous in the Democratic than the Republican Party. Certain kinds of organizations—in particular, those representing large blocs of potential voters and those commanding limited financial resources—are especially likely to press their claims upon the parties. Thus, unions, ideological groups, and organizations representing women and racial and ethnic minorities (most of which feel closer to the Democrats) are relatively more likely to make the parties a target of their activity and, especially, to attempt to make party platforms reflect their particular concerns. The kinds of organizations that have traditionally felt more at home with the Republicans—in particular, business and conservative professional associations—incorporate involvement in electoral politics, especially campaign giving, into their overall political strategies; however, they are less likely to make particular claims upon the parties.

When the parties gather—at least every four years to nominate a presidential candidate, sometimes more frequently—there are always many organization members in attendance. Ordinarily, these delegates do not attend the convention in their capacity as organization members. However, a few groups make efforts to assemble blocs of delegates—often with their own whip systems—who will function as representatives of the organization. At the 1984 Democratic convention, several organizations contributed substantially to the number of delegates pledged to Walter Mondale. Of 2067 delegates who arrived in San Francisco pledged to Mondale, 573 were members of unions affiliated with the AFL-CIO; 220 were members of the National Education Association; and 280 were members of the National Organization for Women.[12] Presumably, this particular form of electoral participation is confined to a few organizations that have large constituencies. Still, with the decline in the number of public officials at nominating conventions, the number of delegates who are organizational representatives or issue activists has increased correspondingly.[13] Thus, nominating conventions, especially those of the Democratic

[12]Walter V. Robinson, "The Common Roots of Mondale Delegates," *Boston Globe,* July 9, 1984, p. 7.
[13]Michael J. Malbin, "Conventions, Platforms and Issue Activists," in Austin Ranney, ed., *The American Elections of 1980* (Washington, DC: American Enterprise Institute, 1981), pp. 134–135.

party, include large numbers of delegates who carry with them a policy agenda for the party.

Influencing Party Platforms   An organization that sends a large bloc of delegates to a party convention is in a position to demonstrate to candidates and party leaders that it is a force with which they must contend. In addition, an organization with a bloc of delegates is in a position to place members on the platform committee and to influence the outcome of platform disputes if they are taken to the floor. However, many groups—not just those with blocs of delegates—try to ensure that the platform reflects their concerns and interests. In 1976, for example, the subcommittees of the Republican platform committee heard from representatives of no fewer than 164 groups, ranging from the National Association of Independent Colleges and Universities to the Citizens for Highway Safety.[14] Some of the groups expressing their views—for example, the American Federation of Teachers and the National Association of Social Workers—are not known to be closely associated with the Republicans. Given the heterogeneity of the Democratic voting coalition, it is not surprising that a host of groups seek to have their concerns incorporated into the Democratic platform. In 1984, the list of groups seeking favorable platform planks included unions, environmental groups, gay rights advocates, peace activists, blacks, senior citizens, Hispanics, and Asian-Americans.[15] A few groups mount an all-out effort to influence the platform. In 1980, abortion opponents focused on the Republican platform, antinuclear and gay activists on the Democratic platform. These groups launched carefully coordinated campaigns: attending candidate forums, participating in the delegate selection process, placing them on appropriate platform subcommittees, attending regional platform committee meetings, and lobbying other platform committee members.[16] It is interesting to note that it was an ideological group that focused its efforts upon the Republican platform, rather than an organization drawn from the set of business associations that function as the Republicans' natural constituency.

INFLUENCING ELECTORAL OUTCOMES

In an era of candidate-, rather than party-based, campaign organizations, the electoral involvement of organized interests takes the form, by and large, not of activity at party conventions, but of assistance to particular candidates. Organized interests use several techniques to help favored candidates win election. Table 9.1 repeats information already presented in Chapter 7 regarding the use of various techniques to influence elections. We asked our respondents about

[14]Huckshorn, *Political Parties in America,* pp. 305–307.
[15]Timothy Clark, "Democrats in Search of a Platform All Can Stand on," *National Journal Campaign Monthly,* June 1984, pp. 1, 10.
[16]Malbin, "Conventions, Platforms, and Issue Activists," pp. 100–110, 121–126.

four different techniques of influence relevant to the electoral process: publicizing candidates' voting records, making public endorsements of candidates for office, contributing work or personnel to electoral campaigns, and making financial contributions. Table 9.1 makes clear that this kind of activity—unlike, for example, testifying at hearings or lobbying directly—is far from universal. Of the organizations in the sample, 44 percent publicize voting records, 22 percent endorse candidates, 24 percent donate manpower, and 58 percent give money to campaigns.

What is more, unlike most of the activities in which organized interests engage, there are systematic differences among different kinds of organizations with respect to various campaign activities. Corporations and trade associations confine their electoral participation, by and large, to making financial contributions, an activity in which they engage quite heavily. Unions, on the other hand, are quite involved, participating almost universally in all four activities. Three-fourths of the citizens' groups publicize candidates' voting records. Otherwise, their electoral activity is relatively limited—reflecting, presumably, the constraints on campaign activity imposed on many of them by 501(c)(3) tax status. Leaving for the next chapter the complex and controversial subject of financial contributions to campaigns, let us investigate in somewhat more detail the other techniques used by organized interests to evaluate and support candidates for public office.

Evaluating Candidates: Scorecards

In order to cue their own members or the general public as to which candidates are worthy of support, organizations evaluate candidates for office in several different ways. Many organizations put together scorecards—summaries of selected roll call votes in Congress designed to show the level of support by each incumbent for measures of importance to the group. A typical scorecard displays each incumbent's votes on from a half dozen to two dozen measures and provides in addition a summary score (usually between 0 and 100). Because the measures used in the tally may involve complicated parliamentary maneuvering, it is not always clear what an aye vote signifies. Therefore, in listing the roll calls used in the tally, the preferred organizational position is always made explicit. These scorecards are ordinarily mailed to group members as a pamphlet or published in the organization's magazine or newsletter. The following excerpts from the 1982 Voting Record of the National Council of Senior Citizens (NCSC) are typical. The roll calls are summarized in the following manner:

> 4. H.R. 4560—Labor-HHS Education Appropriations, Fiscal 1982—A vote on an amendment by Rep. Thomas Bliley (R-VA) to bar enforcement of a provision in the budget reconciliation bill (P.L. 97–35) that prohibited Medicare and Medicaid reimbursement for drugs for which the Food and Drug

Table 9.1 USE OF TECHNIQUES OF ELECTORAL INFLUENCE

	Corporations	Trade associations	Unions	Citizens' groups	All organizations	Rank[a]
Making financial contributions to electoral campaigns	86%	66%	90%	29%	58%	19
Publishing candidates' voting records	28%	37%	90%	75%	44%	22.5
Contributing work or personnel to electoral campaigns	14%	23%	70%	33%	24%	25
Making public endorsements of candidates for office	8%	9%	95%	29%	22%	26

[a]Overall rank on list of 27 techniques of influence.
Source: Washington Representatives Survey.

Administration had not completed an evaluation of effectiveness. Adopted 271–148 on October 6. A "No" vote is an NCSC vote.[17]

Obviously, such a description makes sense only to reasonably sophisticated persons. The summaries for the incumbents along with the 1981 and cumulative scores are presented as follows:

	Issue number											
Iowa	1	2	3	4	5	6	7	8	9	10		
1. Leach (R)	W	W	W	W	R	R	W	R	W	W	30	33
2. Tauke (R)	W	W	W	W	W	R	W	R	W	R	30	24
3. Evans (R)	W	W	W	W	R	W	W	R	W	W	20	20
4. Smith (D)	W	R	W	R	R	R	R	R	R	R	80	82
5. Harkin (D)	R	R	R	R	R	–	R	R	R	R	100	88
6. Bedell (D)	W	R	R	R	R	–	–	R	W	–	71	72

(R = Voted Right; W = Voted Wrong; – = Absent)[18]

Some organizations seek through their scorecards to summarize the legislator's overall position on a general set of issues. For example, the Americans for Democratic Action (ADA) seeks to measure overall liberalism, the Americans for Constitutional Action (ACA) and American Conservative Union (ACU) overall conservatism; the Committee on Political Education (COPE) of the AFL-CIO attempts to rate members in terms of support for workers both union and nonunion, the Chamber of Commerce in terms of support for business; and the League of Conservation Voters (LCV) seeks to evaluate responsiveness on environmental issues.[19] Candidates sometimes publicize these scores in order to enhance their own image or embarrass an opponent. Although there is no systematic evidence on the use of group scores as a campaign tool, the common wisdom is that a low LCV score can be damaging and, depending on the district, a high ADA score can be a death warrant if exploited by an opponent.[20]

While these organizations seek to summarize the posture of a candidate with respect to a broad class of issues, many more organizations construct scorecards based on a narrower set of concerns. The scorecard compiled by the Veterans of Foreign Wars (VFW), a veterans' organization with 1.5 million members, is typical. The scorecard is based on roll call votes on 14 measures—

[17]"Voting Record—97th Congress, First Session, 1981," *Senior Citizens News,* February 1982, p. S–2.

[18]*Ibid.*

[19]For a discussion of what these groups claim they are rating, as well as a general discussion of legislative scorecards, see Bill Keller, "Interest Groups Rate Members of Congress," *Congressional Quarterly Weekly Report,* July 3, 1982, pp. 1607–1613.

[20]The ADA maintains that it is visibility on issues of particular concern to the constituency, rather than a high ADA score, that is responsible for getting liberals into electoral trouble. See Linda L. Fowler, "How Interest Groups Select Issues for Rating Voting Records of Members of the U.S. Congress," *Legislative Studies Quarterly* 7 (1982): 403.

7 each having to do with veterans' benefits and defense preparedness.[21] Such a scorecard is supposed to help members in deciding which candidates to support. It is easy to understand why such an organization would compile a scorecard; with a large membership distributed over every legislative district, VFW members are in a position to have an impact at the polls. The memberships of a number of other groups—for example, unionized workers, teachers, and gun owners—are also sufficiently large and geographically dispersed to possess potential electoral clout. However, much smaller organizations—for example, the Independent Petroleum Association of America, a trade association with 7,500 members—have also adopted the practice of rating legislators. Such an organization cannot expect to exercise great influence at the polls. However, its scorecard can provide useful information to member companies that make financial contributions through political action committees as they select candidates to receive funds.

For the National Federation of Independent Business (NFIB), a 620,000 member association of small businesses, the scorecard of legislative roll calls is part of an overall political strategy.[22] Just before an important measure is to be called up for a floor vote, the NFIB sends each legislator a personal letter outlining the organization's position on the matter and a follow-up postcard specifying the measure as a "key small business vote" that will probably be a component in the annual rating. The NFIB publishes the results of its tally with as much publicity as possible. Legislators who receive a passing grade of 70 are named "Guardians of Small Business" and awarded the small-business equivalent of an Oscar, a pewter minuteman statuette. The NFIB explicitly links the scorecard to campaign contributions by endorsing all "Guardians" and contributing to the campaigns of those who face stiff electoral competition. In addition, the NFIB sends a donation to challengers running against incumbents who have failed by receiving a summary score lower than 40. Thus, the NFIB's annual rating becomes part of its lobbying strategy as well. Because they have been warned what might be included in the annual rating, legislators have the information needed to boost their scores and thus qualify for both campaign contributions and the favorable publicity that an NFIB endorsement generates locally.[23]

Critics of legislative scorecards raise a number of objections to the technique.[24] It is often argued that ratings distort a legislator's whole record both

[21]Cooper T. Holt, *Voting Record—95th Congress-96th Congress* (Washington, DC: VFW Political Action Committee, 1981).

[22]On the NFIB's rating system and its place in the organization's overall political strategy, see Bill Keller, "Small Business Lobby Plays Trick or Treat," *Congressional Quarterly Weekly Report,* March 21, 1981, p. 509.

[23]The practice of altering roll call behavior in the hope of gaining a more favorable rating from some interest group may not be confined to legislators courting the NFIB. See "When Lobbyists Grade the Lawmakers," *U.S. News and World Report,* April 14, 1980, p. 53.

[24]For a summary of the arguments made about scorecards, see Bill Keller, "Congressional Rating Game Is Hard to Win," *Congressional Quarterly Weekly Report,* March 21, 1981, pp. 507–516.

because they focus on only a few votes and because it may not be clear of what the selected votes are an index. One study of interest group ratings points out that on one occasion the same nay vote was interpreted as an indicator of liberalism by the ADA and conservatism by the ACA, and that on another bill the ACA rated a nay vote as a correct conservative position, while another conservative organization, the ACU, deemed it an incorrect one.[25] Another argument is that because groups often change their rating technique from year to year, the meaning of the rating is not stable over time—even when the organization maintains that it is measuring the same dimension each year.

Still another argument is that by focusing on roll call votes only, the scorecards fail to take into account a legislator's behavior during the period when a bill is actually shaped—before it comes to a final vote on the floor. It is, for example, a well-known practice for an opponent of a measure to make valiant efforts to cripple it while it is being considered in committee or to add weakening amendments while it is being debated on the floor and then ultimately to vote for the weakened measure on the final roll call so as to be able to go on record as being a supporter. Still another objection is that the scorecards make no allowances for the reasons for a legislator's vote. If an organization decides that an aye vote is a correct one on a particular bill, it will not differentiate the legislator who voted against it because it was too weak from the one who voted against the bill because it was too strong. In short, then, the critics charge that scorecards are inaccurate and easily subject to misinterpretation and exploitation. In recognition of such criticisms, some organizations preface their scorecards with explanatory statements describing the limitations of the information contained therein, but most do not bother with such consumer warnings.

Endorsements

A somewhat less common way in which interest groups evaluate candidates for office is by making explicit endorsements. As we saw in Table 9.1, this technique is almost exclusively in the province of the unions, most of which make endorsements. For example, just before the 1982 California and Oregon primaries the International Longshoremen's and Warehousemen's Union devoted a full page in its newspaper to its endorsements, designating choices in 60 races and 16 ballot propositions.[26] In this case, while the party of the endorsed candidate is noted, and the three candidates who are union members are flagged, there is no further discussion of the reasons for the choices. Like scorecards, endorsements are ordinarily intended to provide members of a large organization with information useful in making vote choices. However, a few organizations—especially, but not exclusively, citizens' groups—make endorsements with the aim of instructing a more general audience. In addition, endorsements

---

[25] Cited in Fowler, "How Groups Select Issues," pp. 401, 411.
[26] *The Dispatcher,* May 7, 1982, p. 10.

can be used by even small groups to give cues to members as to which candidates are worthy of financial and campaign support. Finally, a few bellwether organizations—most notably the Business-Industry Political Action Committee—pinpoint worthy candidates in competitive races in order to convey information to other organizations as to where to channel their campaign funds and assistance.

There is no systematic evidence regarding the effect of endorsements upon vote choices. Anecdotal evidence suggests that organizations have a great deal of difficulty delivering large blocs of voters. Organization members rarely vote in unison and are reluctant to be shepherded in casting ballots. In 1980, for example, Carter was the beneficiary of a large number of union endorsements. (A few unions—including the nation's largest, the Teamsters—did support Reagan.) However, only 50 percent of voters from union households cast ballots for Carter.[27]

Endorsements may have an impact on balloting not only by an organization's constituents but by members of the public as well. In 1984 Walter Mondale received early endorsements from many organizations including the AFL-CIO, the National Organization for Women, and the National Education Association. His subsequent actions—for example, his selection of Geraldine Ferraro as a running mate—were widely interpreted as evidence that he had become a captive of "the interests." Whether this reputation cost him more votes than he gained by his responsiveness to various groups representing larger constituencies is, as of this writing, impossible to judge.

A recent Gallup Poll suggests that union endorsements may, in fact, backfire.[28] While a plurality of those polled, 41 percent, indicated that a union endorsement would have no effect on their behavior at the polls, the remainder indicated by a ratio of nearly two to one that a union endorsement would actually make them less likely (35 percent) rather than more likely (18 percent) to vote for a candidate. Not surprisingly, the figures for members of union households are more or less reversed: 32 percent indicated that they would be more likely and 18 percent that they would be less likely to choose a candidate endorsed by a union; 47 percent said that a union endorsement would make no difference to them. While these figures might seem to indicate that a union endorsement will undermine a candidate's performance at the polls, it is unwise to overinterpret them. The query presumes that voters in fact know which candidates have been endorsed by unions. Since it seems likely that union members would be much more likely to know of such endorsements (which are ordinarily announced in the union press), it may well be that they do not have the boomerang effect suggested by the Gallup Poll results.

As our earlier discussion of the endorsements gathered by Mondale implied, organizations can also use endorsements to gain leverage with candi-

---

[27] Figure cited in William Schneider, "The November 4 Vote for President," in Ranney, ed., *The American Elections of 1980,* p. 254.

[28] "Poll Says Labor Endorsement May Have Negative Influence," *New York Times,* June 12, 1983, p. A32.

dates. The National Organization for Women (NOW) endorsed front-runner Mondale even before the 1984 presidential primaries. This early endorsement was made, not only to instruct NOW members how to vote in the upcoming primaries, but also to achieve two goals—access to the Mondale campaign and the inclusion of a woman on the Democratic ticket.[29] (Whether or not the result of NOW's endorsement, both objectives were realized.)

Targeting

The underside of endorsing candidates is targeting them: constructing a hit list of candidates, usually incumbents with low group ratings, to be defeated. In the recent past, the practice of targeting candidates was first used by an environmental group, Environmental Action, in the early 1970s.[30] Environmental Action selected 12 powerful incumbent legislators, all of whom had poor records on environmental issues, and dubbed them the "Dirty Dozen." The Dirty Dozen became the targets of a clever advertising campaign, and an impressive number of them were ultimately defeated: of the 52 incumbents who were listed over the course of five elections, 24 were defeated in the year they were members of the Dirty Dozen.

More recently the tactic of targeting has been adopted by a number of conservative organizations that use direct-mail techniques to raise staggering amounts of money (commonly in relatively small sums) from large numbers of people. Of such organizations probably the best known is the National Conservative Political Action Committee (NCPAC).[31] Beginning late in the summer of 1979, NCPAC initiated a bitter media attack against several liberal Senate incumbents. The barrage of NCPAC-sponsored advertisements focused on issues like government spending, national defense, and abortion. The campaign had an impressive incessancy: one NCPAC ad attacking Senator Church ran 150 times a day for five weeks throughout Idaho. NCPAC ads soon gained a reputation for having only a casual regard for the truth. One ad aimed at Senator Tom Eagleton (D-Missouri) maintained that he had voted to give "$75 million in aid to a revolutionary government in Nicaragua," when in fact Eagleton had voted against the measure.[32] Another claimed that Birch Bayh (D-Indiana) had voted in favor of a $1.4 billion cut in the defense budget. Bayh had been absent for the vote.[33] NCPAC's reputation for disrespect for the canons of honesty was reinforced when the *Washington Post* (August 10, 1980)

[29] For an account of the NOW endorsement, see Jane Perlez, "Women, Power, and Politics," *New York Times Magazine,* June 24, 1984, pp. 23–24, 26.

[30] On Environmental Action's targeting of the Dirty Dozen, see Bill Keller, "The Trail of the Dirty Dozen," *Congressional Quarterly Weekly Report,* March 21, 1981, p. 510.

[31] Information about NCPAC taken from Brad Bannon, "NCPAC's Role in the 1980 Senate Elections," *Campaigns and Elections,* Spring 1982, pp. 43–46.

[32] Cited in Mark Shields, "Running with NCPAC," *Washington Post,* April 17, 1981, p. A13.

[33] Cited in Bannon, "NCPAC's Role in the Senate Elections," p. 44.

quoted NCPAC national chairman Terry Dolan as having said: "A group like ours could lie through its teeth and the candidate it helps stays clean."[34]

Assessments of NCPAC's success in 1980 vary. That four of the six Senate incumbents targeted by NCPAC were, in fact, defeated—leading to Republican control of the Senate for the first time since the early 1950s—has prompted many observers to attribute real influence to NCPAC's efforts. Others argue that these vulnerable Democrats would have lost in the Reagan tide anyway or that they were defeated *in spite of* NCPAC efforts, which, in fact, generated sympathy for the victims of its mudslinging campaigns. Candidates targeted by NCPAC fared rather better in 1982. For the 1982 election, NCPAC raised an astonishing $9,990,931. Of this, NCPAC spent only 34 percent or $3,440,381 on candidates.[35] This record of expenditures reflects the high cost of raising money through the mail, even when an organization has an operating mailing list.

Although we have described a targeting campaign as essentially a negative endorsement, there is clearly much more at stake than a hostile evaluation of a candidate. Organizations that compile scorecards or make endorsements need not devote extensive resources to backing up their assessments. Organizations that target candidates bolster their appraisals of candidates' defects with tremendous amounts of cash. Thus, as a technique of electoral influence, targeting entails contribution as well as evaluation. This brings us to to the central set of activities of interest groups in the electoral process—assisting candidates with contributions of services, personnel, and money. The remainder of this chapter treats the first two. Chapter 10 takes up the last.

Providing Campaign Assistance

Organizations can assist candidates in various ways in their campaigns. A few organizations, especially ideological PACs, provide services of a technical nature. The National Committee for an Effective Congress, for example, assists candidates with campaign organization, media relations, polling, and so on.[36] Another service, highly valued by candidates, is help with fund raising. A Washington representative might sponsor a fund raiser for a candidate, make phone calls to encourage friends in other organizations to attend a fund-raising event, or provide the group's membership list if it would be a promising source of contributors. The most common kind of nonfinancial campaign aid is to provide workers. Many organizations—especially unions, but also, to a lesser

---

[34]This remark has been widely quoted. See, for example, Bannon, "NCPAC's Role in the Senate Elections," p. 44.

[35]Figures taken from Adam Clymer, "PAC Gifts to Candidates Rose 45% in Latest Cycle," *New York Times,* April 29, 1983, p. A16.

[36]On the services provided by ideological PACs, see Margaret Ann Latus, "Assessing Ideological PACs: From Outrage to Understanding," in Malbin, ed., *Money and Politics in the United States,* pp. 159–161.

extent, citizens' groups—mobilize members to volunteer to help with various election-related tasks. Of necessity, such efforts must have a strong local component. Therefore, only an organization with a local infrastructure and a fairly substantial membership can engage in such activities.

A number of groups organize their members to conduct nonpartisan registration and get-out-the-vote drives. This is the only kind of electoral activity that citizens' groups enjoying tax-exempt [IRS–501 (c)(3)] status are permitted by law to undertake.[37] Even then, 501(c)(3) organizations are allowed to conduct such drives only under restricted circumstances.[38] Unions and corporations, prohibited by federal law from making direct contributions to campaigns, are free, however, to pay for nonpartisan electoral activities out of their treasuries. Because they have sufficient numbers of members to constitute a manpower resource and because their members are less likely to be politically active than members of management, it is, in fact, unions that are particularly likely to engage in nonpartisan voter education campaigns.

Although organized interests are undoubtedly animated by norms of civic virtue when they undertake nonpartisan registration and get-out-the-vote drives, they are usually impelled as well by an underlying desire to mobilize voters sympathetic to their policy goals. Such concerns are implicit in the instructions given to organizers of such activities in the "Organizer's Manual" of the Fair Budget Action Campaign (FBAC)—a coalition of over 80 civil rights, religious, consumer and poor people's organizations, unions, and so on, concerned about the impact of cuts in funding for social programs under the Reagan budgets.[39] Given the FBAC's desire to register low-income people (according to the manual, three of four of whom do not vote), the instructions suggest food stamp distribution centers and unemployment offices as sites for registration activities. Large numbers of low-income people congregate in such places. Because they have to kill time while waiting in line, they would have time both to fill out the necessary registration forms and to listen to a canned spiel (also included in the manual) explaining the effects of the Reagan budgets on their lives and exhorting them to register and vote. The instructions also include suggestions for how to follow up registrants and make sure that they get to the polls. In counseling organizers to undertake voter education drives, the FBAC is presumably concerned not only with bringing into politics previously disenfranchised citizens out of deference to the norms of democracy but also with bolstering the ranks of the like-minded.

Organizations that are not tax-exempt are not restricted to nonpartisan electoral activities. Most organizations that mobilize their members to participate in electoral politics, therefore, supplement efforts to boost registration and

[37] For a discussion of 501(c)(3) status and its implications for political activity, see Chapter 5.

[38] For a discussion of the legal restrictions placed upon even nonpartisan electoral activities by 501(c)(3) status, see Fair Budget Action Campaign, "An Organizer's Manual," 2nd ed. (Washington, DC: Fair Budget Action Campaign, 1982).

[39] Ibid.

turnout with support for favored candidates. What is more, if appropriately structured by an organization with a vigorous local component, such activities can be a part of an integrated grass roots program of lobbying, letter writing, and fund raising.

While it is unions that are most likely to marshal their membership to help in campaigns, the National Association of Home Builders (NAHB)—the 125,000-member trade association of the housing industry—has what is, at least on paper, the most impressive grass roots electoral strategy. A 250-page manual, "Blueprint for Victory: Homebuilder's Political Offensive," outlines all aspects of the NAHB's "G. I. [Get Involved] Program" with staggering completeness and attention to detail. "Blueprint for Victory" is concerned entirely with techniques of grass roots, especially electoral, influence; substantive policy issues are mentioned not at all. Among the subjects covered are how to survey NAHB members, their families, employees, and suppliers in order to generate a master list of those whose livelihoods depend upon home building; how to make sure that they are registered and able to get to the polls; how to conduct a house-to-house or telephone canvass on behalf of favored candidates in order to identify sympathetic voters; how to assess where campaign assistance is most needed; and how to organize a "Victory Caravan" to transport volunteers to more distant precincts to help in crucial, but understaffed campaigns.

"Blueprint for Victory" deals with these subjects with an astonishing meticulousness. Among the details included are how to calculate how many phones are needed for a phone bank to make a given number of calls, where to place campaign literature to maximize the likelihood that it will be read by temporarily absent home owners when they return, and reminders to give a party at the end of each day of campaigning to show appreciation to volunteers. Lest anything be left to the imagination, the manual includes both sample conversations with voters and prototypes of all materials that might be needed—sign-up sheets, handwritten "Sorry we missed you" notes to leave when no one is home, and even patterns for how to divide up a neighborhood when canvassing in teams. While it is difficult to translate such a master plan into actual volunteers, and while there are no systematic assessments of the impact on electoral campaigns of group-based volunteers, it would seem that these efforts must be helpful to the candidacies they are intended to promote.

SUMMARY

This chapter has indicated just how complicated the relationship between the Washington pressure community and the national political parties is. Although a majority of the organized interests in our Washington sample have partisan leanings, there is very little day-to-day contact between organized interests and the national parties except for that which surrounds periodic party conventions. What contact exists involves party leaders in Congress rather than the national party organizations. Still, the kinds of macrolevel policy choices made by electoral majorities are fraught with potential consequences for organized interests. The 1980 election, which in many ways has been interpreted as such a majority decision, had an impact—differential across various kinds of groups—on virtually every organization in our sample.

That there is limited cooperation between party and interest organizations does not prevent organized interests from participating in the electoral process. This chapter has discussed both organized interest activity at party conventions as well as several of the techniques that organized interests, especially unions, use to influence electoral outcomes: scorecards, endorsements, targeting, and providing assistance to campaigns. The technique of electoral influence that is used by the most organizations and that consumes the most resources, however, is the funneling of financial contributions to campaigns. It is to this controversial activity that we now turn.

10

Financing Congressional Campaigns

Since long before Marcus A. Hanna amassed a Republican campaign chest of over $3.5 million by assessing corporations and banks for a predetermined campaign gift in order to finance William McKinley's 1896 presidential race, organized private interests have sought indirect influence on political outcomes by donating large sums to electoral campaigns. Perhaps no aspect of organized interest participation in American political life generates such intense controversy as the role that group-based money plays in filling the coffers of candidates for office. This chapter continues the project begun in the last—to understand how organized interests go about trying to influence electoral results—by focusing on the activities of political action committees (PACs), the organizations that funnel organized interest money into campaigns.

THE PAC EXPLOSION

PACs are nonparty committees, set up in accordance with federal law, to collect money and disburse it to candidates for office. Most PACs are established as the campaign giving arm of another organization—a corporation, a union, a professional association, or the like. Contributions from the PAC are ordinarily construed as still another instrument through which the parent organization can realize its political goals. However, some PACs—for example, the National Committee for an Effective Congress (which supports liberals), the National Pro-Life Political Action Committee (which supports opponents of abortion), and the Hawaiian Golfers for Good Government (which supports goodness knows whom)—are what the Federal Election Commission (FEC) calls "non-connected." Such PACs are not affiliated with another organization but, rather, are founded solely to make collective efforts on behalf of candidates they deem deserving.

Most PACs have names that leave little doubt as to the identity of the organization that is its sponsor or the issues that are of central concern. Thus, FEC lists include, for example, American Medical PAC (AMPAC), sponsored by the American Medical Association; General Dynamics Voluntary Political Contribution Plan, sponsored by General Dynamics Corporation; the United Steelworkers of America Political Action Fund, supported by the United Steel-workers; and Voters for Choice, a nonconnected PAC that supports pro-abortion candidates. Sometimes, the names border on the cute: Six PAC is the name of the political action committee of the National Association of Beer Wholesal-ers; Snack-PAC of the Potato Chip/Snack Food Association; CALF is the acronym of the National Cattlemen's Association's Cattlemen's Action Legislative Fund. A few PACs have civic-minded monikers: the Brotherhood of Railway and Airline Clerks calls its PAC the Responsible Citizens Political League, and International Paper Co. calls its PAC the Voluntary Contributors for Better Government. Such designations not only bespeak civic virtue, they make it more difficult for the attentive public to identify the ultimate source of the funds.

Whether or not the emergence of PACs is, as some have maintained, the most significant development in American politics of the past decade, there is no question that, by any measure, the increase in PAC activity has been of stunning proportions. Between the end of 1974 and the end of 1982, the number of PACs registered with the FEC jumped more than sixfold from 608 to 3371.[1] In dollar terms, contributions to federal campaigns skyrocketed over the same period from $12.5 million to $83.1 million.[2] Even adjusting for the effects of inflation, that expansion is remarkable; expressed in terms of 1974 dollars, PACs donated $42.7 million to federal candidates in 1982, an increase of nearly three-and-a half times over the eight-year period.[3] While overall campaign spending has soared as well, the increase in PAC contributions has outstripped the increase in campaign expenditures. In 1972 PAC contributions accounted for 13.7 percent of the spending in House and Senate races; by 1982 the analogous figure was 24.2 percent.[4] In short, then, any set of relevant figures demonstrates unambiguously an enhanced role for organization-based giving in congressional elections.

[1] Figures taken from Federal Election Commission press releases of January 17, 1982 and April 29, 1983.

[2] Figures taken from Congressional Quarterly, *Dollar Politics,* 3rd ed. (Washington, DC: Congressional Quarterly, 1982), p. 18, and the FEC press release of April 29, 1983.

[3] Figure for 1982 calculated by applying a deflator based on the annual Consumer Price Index to the figure given above.

[4] Figure for 1972 given in Congressional Quarterly, *Dollar Politics,* p. 45. Figure for 1982 calculated from data contained in the FEC press release of April 29, 1983.

ORGANIZED CAMPAIGN GIVING AND THE LAW

Hanna's now infamous 1896 fund-raising effort on behalf of McKinley elicited one in a series of periodic outbursts of reformist fervor that have characterized electoral history in America. This particular wave of enthusiasm resulted in the passage of the nation's first campaign finance law, the Tillman Act of 1907, which outlawed campaign contributions from corporations. This measure, like subsequent regulatory legislation, was sufficiently dense with loopholes to be honored mostly in the breach.[5] After decades of virtually meaningless regulation, the reformist impulse intensified during the 1960s. Since the early 1970s Congress has enacted several pieces of legislation that, as implemented by the Federal Election Commission and interpreted by the courts, have had an enormous impact on giving by organizations.[6]

The first of these measures was the Federal Election Campaign Act (FECA) of 1971. Its impact on organized giving was relatively limited. However, among other things the FECA of 1971 did require candidates to report the sources of their receipts on the theory that disclosure would minimize corruption by making clear to whom candidates were beholden. If the quid pro quo of campaign donations from organized interests has traditionally been policy favors, then the scrutiny to which disclosure subjected officeholders would presumably deter them from making overt trades.

The disclosures surrounding Watergate made apparent that, as a prelude to the 1972 election, Nixon's Committee to Re-Elect the President (CREEP) had collected colossal sums, much of it in cash and much of it before the April 7, 1972 cutoff date, after which the new disclosure provisions would go into effect. In response to renewed pressure for reform, Congress legislated once again. The FECA of 1974, technically a series of amendments to the 1971 law, was the most sweeping campaign reform act in American history. Its many provisions included public financing of presidential elections, the creation of the FEC, and streamlined requirements for disclosure. Most relevant for organized giving was the provision that limited political committees to $5,000 per candidate per election (with primaries, runoff primaries, and general elections each considered as separate elections) but placed no aggregate ceiling on what a PAC could disburse.[7]

[5]There are numerous helpful summaries of federal campaign laws regulating PACs. See, for example, Herbert E. Alexander and Brian A. Haggerty, *The Federal Election Campaign Act* (Los Angeles: Citizens' Research Foundation, 1981), Chapters 1–4, and Congressional Quarterly, *Dollar Politics*, pp. 3–27, 41–46.

[6]The following discussion focuses only on those provisions of the regulations that pertain to giving by organizations and omits reference to many other provisions—for example, those governing federal funding of presidential elections or giving by individuals—that are of critical importance for campaign finance in America.

[7]The provisions of the 1974 amendments are not ironclad. For a discussion of some of the loopholes and ambiguities, see Alexander and Haggerty, *The Federal Election Campaign Act,* pp. 52–54; Elizabeth Drew, "Politics and Money—Part I," *The New Yorker,* December 6, 1982, pp. 60–64; Brooks Jackson, "Loopholes Allow Flood of Campaign Giving by Business, Fat Cats," *Wall Street Journal,* July 5, 1984, pp. 1, 16; and John Holcomb, "Contribution Strategies of Business PACs," paper delivered at the Annual Meeting of the American Political Science Association, Washington, September 1984.

The 1974 amendments contained, in addition, another section bearing significant implications for organized giving. Since many unions hold government manpower contracts, organized labor—then the leader in group-based campaign contributions—was concerned that the 1971 law continued a ban on campaign giving by government contractors. Therefore, labor lobbyists made sure that the 1974 amendments specified clearly that government contractors could establish and administer PACs.

The Sun Oil Decision

This provision had important consequences that did not become apparent until somewhat later. In the immediate wake of the Watergate revelations of massive corporate giving to CREEP, corporations were understandably somewhat reluctant to avail themselves of the opportunity to establish PACs. Then, in 1975, the Sun Oil Co. asked the FEC for an advisory opinion as to whether a company could use corporate funds to set up and administer a PAC and to solicit voluntary contributions from its employees and stockholders. (Corporate funds could not, of course, be given directly to candidates.) Sun Oil also sought to use a payroll deduction (or checkoff) plan as a mode of collection. In a controversial 4–2 decision that, not surprisingly, outraged labor, the FEC approved Sun Oil's requests with the stipulation that solicitation practices must be set in such a way that employee contributions would be genuinely voluntary.[8] Thus, the FEC gave a green light to corporations to use funds from the company treasury to set up political action committees. Since the Sun Oil decision, the number of corporate PACs has multiplied several fold, and as we shall see, corporate PAC dollars have surpassed giving by other kinds or organizations.

The Supreme Court Decides

Soon after the passage of the 1974 amendments to the FECA, a diverse group of libertarians of both the right and the left went to court to challenge various provisions of the act that, they argued, represented an unconstitutional infringement on First Amendment rights of freedom of expression. This suit raised a question that underlies almost all attempts to regulate collective efforts to influence politics, especially attempts to regulate campaign giving, the trade-off between political equality and free speech. Unregulated giving may open the door to differential impact on electoral outcomes and differential responsiveness to big givers; thus, it may compromise the norm of one-person–one-vote. Attempts to restrict giving, however, may jeopardize the liberty, so essential to democracy, to influence what the government does. While the Supreme Court's decision in *Buckley* v. *Valeo* (1976) did not resolve this dilemma in an unambig-

[8]Later in the chapter we shall return to the issue of the degree to which such contributions are genuinely voluntary.

uous way, the collective pronouncements of the justices show far more deference to the free speech guarantees of the First Amendment than to the equal
protection clause of the Fourteenth.[9]

The Court did, in fact, uphold the limitations on individual and group
giving to candidates' campaigns. However, the decision overturned many other
provisions of the law, including the limitations on independent spending on
behalf of candidates. The Court reasoned that if these expenditures are indeed
made in a genuinely independent fashion (that is, without the candidate's
knowledge or supervision), they constitute a form of protected free speech and,
therefore, cannot be subject to limitations. This has had important ramifications for groups like the National Conservative Political Action Committee
(NCPAC) that make most of their expenditures independently; they are, in
effect, exempt from the spending limitations written into the FECA.

Certain aspects of the decision in *Buckley* v. *Valeo* forced Congress to act
again in 1976. Labor unions used the opportunity created by renewed discussion of campaign finance to attempt to ameliorate the effects of the Sun Oil
decision. They were successful in having incorporated into the 1976 amendments to the FECA a provision that limited corporate PACs to soliciting stockholders, executives, and managerial personnel and their families only and
union PACs to soliciting union members and their families only. (Twice yearly
corporate and union PACs are permitted to solicit all employees by mail so
long as the contributions are anonymous. An independent third party is to be
in charge of keeping the books and forwarding donations to candidates.) In
addition, the amendments contained a provision requiring anyone making an
independent expenditure of over $100 on behalf of a candidate to swear that
the expenditure was truly independent. The amendments also contained further
limitations on giving. No individual may give more than $5,000 to a single
PAC, and no PAC may give more than $20,000 to a national committee of a
political party.

Aside from the FEC regulations that implement the legislation of the
1970s, as of this writing there has been no major legislation affecting organized
campaign giving since the amendments of 1976. There is, however, continuing
agitation for reform. Two of the more frequent suggestions are public financing
of congressional elections in a manner analogous to the public funding of
presidential contests and a limit on the aggregate amount a candidate can
accept from PACs.

It is interesting that there has been something of a reversal in the partisan
support for such major reforms.[10] In the early 1970s many Republicans, perhaps fearing the well-established giving power of labor, supported measures

[9]On this point, see the discussion and attendant references in David Adamany, "Money,
Politics, and Democracy: A Review Essay," *American Political Science Review* 71 (1977): 301.
[10]On the changing politics of electoral reform, see Stuart Rothenberg, *Campaign Regulation
and Public Policy: PACs, Ideology, and the FEC* (Washington, DC: The Free Congress Research
and Education Foundation, 1981), p. 33.

that would have limited the electoral finance capabilities of unions and corporations. It was Democrats who, at the behest of labor, made sure that the campaign finance reforms did not preclude a role for significant giving by private organizations. More recently, the support for limiting the role of PACs has come from Democrats. Republicans, who—like their Democrat counterparts—seem not to have anticipated the explosion of giving by corporate PACs, tend to oppose any major overhaul.

MANAGING A PAC

Because PACs raise so dramatically questions of organizational democracy and leadership accountability to the preferences of supporters, it is important to know something about how they manage their internal affairs. In order to understand how they go about soliciting contributions, making decisions, gathering information to inform those decisions, and responding to the preferences of donors, we took the opportunity of the interviews we conducted with Washington representatives to ask about PAC activity. Of the 175 organizations in our sample, 101 have PACs. These 101, however, are in one fundamental respect not representative of the universe of PACs. By definition, all the PACs in our sample fall into that minority that have access to a Washington office. There is evidence that PACs having a Washington connection are distinctive in their behavior: they tend to pursue pragmatic, insider strategies and to be particulary concerned about maintaining access to legislative policymakers.[11]

Furthermore, PACs having access to an office in the capital tend to be substantially larger. Of the 200 PACs that gave the largest aggregate sums in the 1979–1980 electoral cycle, 81 percent either maintain their own offices in Washington or are affiliated with organizations that have offices in the capital. (Of the remainder, just under half are represented in Washington politics by counsel or consultants.)[12] These 200 large PACs, by the way, accounted for over two-thirds of the total given by the over 2,000 PACs that made contributions in the 1979–1980 electoral cycle. In short, if PAC activity is construed in terms of the total number of dollars contributed rather than in terms of the total number of PACs, the PACs in our sample are not unrepresentative.

Considering the seemingly narrow range of PACs in our sample, it is interesting that what emerged from our interviews is that there are several patterns—rather than a single pattern—of PAC management, involving varying loci of authority and varying degrees of involvement by donors and Wash-

[11] See Theodore J. Eismeier and Philip H. Pollock III, "Political Action Committees: Varieties of Organization and Strategy," in Michael Malbin, ed., *Money and Politics in the United States* (Chatham, NJ: Chatham House, 1984), p. 126; and Larry J. Sabato, *PAC Power* (New York: Norton, 1984), p. 42.

[12] Based on information assembled from *The PAC Directory*, compiled by Marvin Weinberger and David U. Greevy (Cambridge, MA: Ballinger Publishing Company, 1982); and Arthur Close, ed., *Washington Representatives—1981*, 5th ed. (Washington, DC: Columbia Books, 1981).

ington staff. In many PACs a formal committee makes the important decisions. The description offered by a lobbyist for a Fortune 100 industrial is typical:

> The PAC Executive Committee makes the decisions. The president of it is usually a president of one of our operating companies. The vice president is usually the head of the Washington office. The secretary is usually someone well-placed in the corporate law department. The treasurer is usually someone in the financial department. Other members represent the different operating companies on an equal basis.
>
> The frequency of our meetings varies. We have no set schedule of meetings. We are not active in non-election years. If you are going to plan a solicitation of your employees, it must be timely. Therefore, we are more active in election years.

Some, like the associate director of a major trade association in the finance industry, describe a much more informal process centered within the Washington office: "The PAC committee consists entirely of the lobbyists and myself. . . . We meet weekly or whenever necessary." The president of another trade association was quite straightforward in describing an informal, but centralized, process: "I am responsible for making the decisions, but we don't divulge this to our members." A third pattern involves formal consultation with members. The director of government relations at the National Education Association describes the process as it works in her union:

> Local committees interview each candidate. For every candidate who had an interview, we provide all the information we can assemble: voting records, records of our meetings with them, and any other intelligence we can muster. The committees make recommendations to their state boards; the state board either confirms the recommendation or sends it back. The recommendations then come to the national NEA-PAC. It's a *very* structured process.

As shown in Table 10.1, reliance upon a formal committee is the modal pattern. Corporations, in particular, use formal committees to structure PAC management. Although trade associations, like corporations, use the formal committee mechanism, they are the kind of organization most likely to rely on informal processes. Unions favor no single organizational principle and are the kind of organization most likely to report formal processes of consultation with members or member organizations.[13] Table 10.1 also makes clear the extent of participation of the Washington offices of these organizations. Only 4 percent

---

[13]Whether this consultation with union members is mere form is another question. Larry Sabato (*PAC Power,* p. 36) and Michael Malbin ("Looking Back at the Future of Campaign Finance Reform," in Malbin, ed., *Money and Politics in the United States,* pp. 258–259) both argue that union leaders have particular autonomy from members in making decisions about contributions.

Table 10.1 RUNNING A PAC

How is PAC decision making managed?

	Corporate PACs	Trade association PACs	Union PACs	All PACs
1. By a formal committee	87%	50%	21%	63%
2. By an informal process	8	45	36	22
3. By consulting with members or donors	5	5	43	15
	100%	100%	100%	100%

From where is the PAC managed?

	Corporate PACs	Trade association PACs	Union PACs	All PACs
1. From the organization's Washington office	15%	65%	46%	37%
2. From elsewhere, with input from the Washington office	82	35	36	59
3. From elsewhere, without input from the Washington office	3	0	18	4
	100%	100%	100%	100%
	(N = 43)	(N = 23)	(N = 18)	(N = 101)

Source: Washington Representatives Survey.

of the organizations having PACs—all of them PACs that consult formally with members—report no input at all from the Washington office. Otherwise, the nature of the input varies with the pattern of decision making. In 88 percent of the PACs that are run by committees, the decisional locus is outside Washington, but there is input from the Washington office. On the other hand, 90 percent of the PACs that are run informally are managed directly out of the Washington office.

Gathering Information

In making decisions about whom to support, PAC managers use information from a variety of sources. The comments of the legislative liaison for the National Association of Letter Carriers show a typical approach:

> We monitor hearings, request calendars for hearings and monitor them. We keep in contact with staff and members on committees that we are concerned with. We also read the *Congressional Record*. People also call us. We seldom miss anything because we cover all the sources. We also contact friends in other organizations. We help each other out.

In some organizations, the introductory phase of the intelligence gathering is carried out locally. For example, according to the vice-president of legislative and political affairs for a peak business association:

> We have six regional offices and each has its own political affairs manager. The initial research is done by people in these offices. They determine candidate vulnerability and demographics. They are in constant contact with us, and then they send reports to the Public Affairs Department.

More systematically, of the respondents in PAC-affiliated organizations, 52 percent indicated that the preferences of others in the organization constitute an important source of information, and 60 percent said that they consult published sources.[14] Fifty-nine percent indicated that, because they are on the scene on a long-term basis, their own knowledge about candidates is critical. As a lobbyist for one of the nation's largest banks remarked: "We work with these people every day. We know who is doing what to whom." Thirty-three percent mentioned friends in the district or other organizations. Not surprisingly, only 10 percent of the respondents in PAC-affiliated organizations mentioned party sources. The Realtors Political Action Committee (RPAC), well-known both for the overall magnitude of its giving and for the effectiveness of its operations, uses an unusual technique to assess candidates, the "congressional candidates questionnaire." The 1982 version of the questionnaire was long (seven pages) and tricky. RPAC's political director recalled with glee receiving phone calls from desperate candidates hungry for clues as to how best to answer questions on such complex matters as the economics of inflation so as to ingratiate themselves with the Realtors. RPAC dispensed many campaign donations but no questionnaire assistance.[15]

Soliciting Contributions

With respect to solicitation practices, our knowledge is somewhat sketchy.[16] Unions tend to solicit at the local level with local union officials contacting union members either individually or jointly at a meeting. Many unions, like their corporate counterparts, are moving toward using payroll deduction, or checkoff, plans. Corporations vary in the techniques they use to solicit PAC

---

[14]For reasons we do not understand, there are substantial differences among various kinds of PACs with respect to their use of published sources: 85 percent of the union PAC respondents, but only 25 percent of the trade association PAC respondents, mentioned referring to printed materials in gathering information about candidates.

[15]See James M. Perry, "How Realtors PAC Rewards Office Seekers Helpful to the Industry," *Wall Street Journal,* August 2, 1982, p. 1+.

[16]See Congressional Quarterly, *Dollar Politics,* p. 44; Edward Handler and John R. Mulkern, *Business in Politics,* (Lexington, MA: Lexington Books, 1982), Chapter 3, and Edwin M. Epstein, "The Emergence of Political Action Committees," in Herbert E. Alexander, ed., *Political Finance* (Beverly Hills, CA: Sage, 1979), pp. 181–182.

contributions. Some, like the unions, approach executives directly either as individuals or as a group. Some use the mails. Often, there is a suggested contribution, usually ranging up to 1 percent of the executive's annual salary. Corporations also vary in terms of how deeply into the ranks of management they dip. Some collect only from a small number of top executives; others from the ranks of management more generally.

Most corporations do not solicit stockholders or nonexecutives. Mobil Oil, one of the companies that does ask stockholders to contribute, has applied the checkoff principle to dividends. The company sent letters to all 160,000 of its individual shareholders requesting that they agree to an automatic deduction from dividend checks to benefit Mobil PAC.[17] Ideological PACs, of course, rely on the kinds of direct-mail techniques described in Chapters 5 and 8 to raise money.

One frequently heard allegation is that contributions to PACs are not genuinely voluntary. The charge that solicitation is coercive is leveled at corporations in particular, presumably because corporations have the widest array of sanctions to apply to those who fail to take part in the joint effort. There is journalistic evidence to support this accusation. According to one such report, during their annual salary review, executives at a company having one of the nation's largest corporate PACs are told that they are getting a special bonus and then are requested to make a donation to the PAC. The implication, of course, is that the bonus is to be applied to the contribution.[18] Scholarly analysts tend to indicate that the coercion implied by journalistic anecdotes is not general.[19] Corporate PACs have, according to a survey conducted by the National Association of Business PACs, a median participation rate of only about 20 percent.[20] This figure would indicate that if there is attempted coercion, it is not very effective. What is more, many corporate PAC managers go out of their way to make sure that giving is anonymous by discouraging personal solicita-

---

[17]Monica Langley, "Mobil Asks Holders to Finance Its PAC Via Their Dividends," *Wall Street Journal,* June 19, 1984, p. 22.

[18]Morton Mintz, "Corporation Politics," *Washington Post,* May 18, 1980, p. 1. See also, Nicholas Goldberg, "Showdown in the Boardroom," *Washington Monthly,* December 1983, pp. 14–19, and Douglas N. Dickson, "CORPPACS: The Business of Political Action Committees," *Across the Board,* November 1981, p. 21.

[19]See, for example, Handler and Mulkern, *Business in Politics,* pp. 49–56; Frank J. Sorauf, "Accountability in Political Action Committees: Who's in Charge?", paper delivered at the Annual Meeting of the American Political Science Association, Denver, September 1982, pp. 14–15; and Ann B. Matasar, "Corporate Responsibility Gone Awry?: The Corporate Political Action Committee," paper delivered at the Annual Meeting of the American Political Science Association, New York, September 1981.

Interestingly, both the FEC and the courts have reached the same conclusion. In 1979 the International Association of Machinists sued ten large corporations having active PACs, charging that they were engaging in "inherently coercive" practices in their methods of solicitation. The Machinists lost their case before the FEC and subsequently lost in court as well. See Herbert Alexander, *The Case for PACs* (Washington, DC: Public Affairs Council, 1983), pp. 24–25.

[20]Figure cited in Sorauf, "Accountability in Political Action Committees," p. 15.

tion and using independent third parties as intermediaries in carrying out transactions.[21]

CAMPAIGN GIVING STRATEGIES

Perhaps the most important question is what PACs expect to achieve with their donations. In Chapter 9 we delineated two common strategies in aiding candidates. In one the objective is to influence the outcome of electoral contests and, by affecting who wins or loses, thereby to elect a more sympathetic set of public officials; in the other, the aim is to influence, not electoral results, but the behavior of eventual officeholders and, thereby, government policy. We also pointed out that various kinds of organizations are not equally likely to pursue one or the other of these strategies in electoral involvement and that it is possible to combine them in various ways.

Who Gets PAC Money?

As an initial cut at understanding how PACs proceed in giving, let us consider what kinds of candidates benefit from their largesse. In our analysis we focus on races for House of Representatives in 1980. We choose congressional races because the campaign reforms of the 1970s mandating public financing of presidential elections have moved the focus of organized giving at the federal level to the legislative branch. We concentrate on the House rather than the Senate because the greater number of races makes it less likely that our findings will be distorted by a few aberrant cases. We use 1980 as the most recent election for which data were available at the time we did our analysis.

Figure 10.1, which gives the average 1980 PAC receipts for various categories of candidates running for the House of Representatives, makes clear several attributes that seem to predict PAC receipts.[22] First, as shown in Figure 10.1(a), incumbents and to a somewhat lesser extent open seat contenders (that is, candidates running in districts in which there is no incumbent) collect far more from PACs than challengers (that is, candidates running against incumbents). In 1980 the average House candidate received $44,200 from PACs. However, the average incumbent received $62,500 and the average challenger only $20,500. What is more, winners collected nearly three times more than losers. Interestingly, even candidates running without opposition collect sub-

[21] Handler and Mulkern (*Business in Politics,* p. 50) point out that, ironically, a corporation's best efforts at maintaining the anonymity of PAC donors are undermined by federal laws governing disclosure. A PAC must turn over to the FEC—which in turn publishes the information—the names of all those who give more than $100 or who earmark their contributions.

[22] Calculated from data compiled by the authors from *FEC Reports on Financial Activity—1979–1980: Final Report U.S. House and Senate Races,* January 1982, and Michael Barone and Grant Ujifusa, *The Almanac of American Politics—1982* (Washington, DC: Barone and Company, 1981).

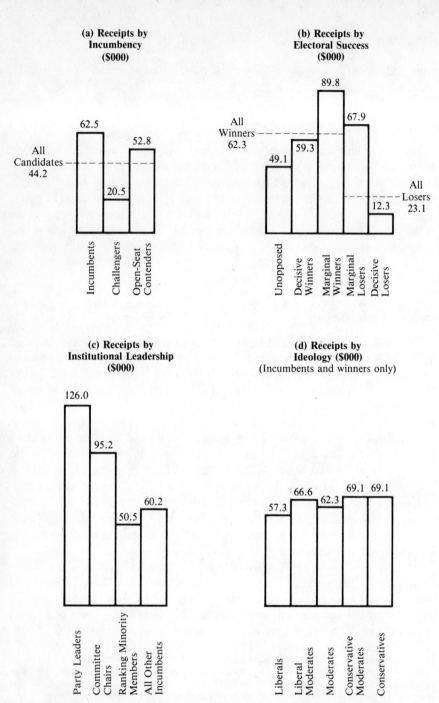

Figure 10.1 Who gets the PAC money? (Average PAC receipts of 1980 House candidates in thousands of dollars.)

Source: Calculated from data compiled by the authors from *FEC Reports on Financial Activity—1979–1980: Final Report of U.S. House and Senate Races* (January 1982), and Michael Barone and Grant Ujifusa, *The Almanac of American Politics—1982* (Washington, DC: Barone and Company, 1981).

stantial sums from PACs. The figures in Figure 10.1(b) indicate that marginal races (races in which the winner garners no more than 55 percent of the two-party vote) attract more money than ones in which the outcome is more decisive. In tandem with the finding that winners collect more than losers, this means that among winners the smaller the share of votes received, the higher the PAC receipts; among losers average PAC receipts diminish as share of votes diminishes.

In addition, as shown in Figure 10.1(c), PAC contributions seem to flow to those who occupy positions of power within the House. Party leaders and committee chairs raised significant amounts from PACs—$126,000 and $95,200, respectively. We should note that ranking minority members, the senior Republicans on each of the House committees, actually collected less from PACs than the average incumbent. Finally, as indicated in Figure 10.1(d) liberals received somewhat, but not substantially, less than conservatives from PACs.[23] With respect to party, Figure 10.2 shows that in the aggregate Democrats received a bit more from PACs in 1980 than Republicans did. In fact, however, it is only Democratic incumbents who outcollected their Republican counterparts. Republican challengers and open-seat contestants actually received substantially more from PACs than Democrats of analogous incumbency status.

Giving by Union and Corporate PACs

Let us probe the question of what kinds of candidates are favored by PAC donations by considering contributions by labor and corporate PACs.[24] Given the affinities between business and the Republicans on the one hand, and labor and the Democrats, on the other, it seems appropriate always to distinguish the partisanship of the candidate. Indeed, in 1980 labor PACs gave an average of $20,200 to Democratic candidates and $1,000 to Republican candidates. Corporate PACs, on the other hand, donated an average of $18,200 to Republicans and $10,700 to Democrats.

[23]Candidates were categorized in terms of ideology in the following manner. For each an ideology score was calculated by taking the average of the candidate's ADA score and 100 minus his ACA score. Then candidates were grouped in quintiles on the basis of the result. We used 1980 ADA and ACA scores (culled from the *Almanac*) for all incumbents and 1981 scores (supplied to us by the two organizations) for all nonincumbent winners. Such information is, of course, not available for nonincumbent losers. This fact should be borne in mind in interpreting the data in Figure 10.1(d).

[24]We would have liked to have been able to investigate, as well, patterns of giving among other kinds of organizations—in particular, trade associations and single-issue groups. Unfortunately, the way in which the FEC presents data renders this impossible. The FEC divides PACs into seven categories that may have great utility for other purposes but are of little analytical use from our perspective. Each of the categories mixes organizations that in political terms are very different from one another: for example, the "trade-member-health" category combines trade associations, professional associations, and a miscellany of membership groups; the "corporations-without-stock" category includes the National Women's Political Caucus Campaign Support Committee and Handgun Control, Inc., as well as many savings and loan associations; the "noncon-

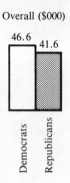

Overall ($000)

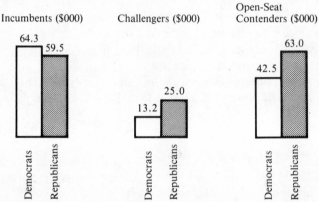

Figure 10.2   PAC receipts by party and incumbency. (Average PAC receipts of 1980 House candidates in thousands of dollars.)

Source: Calculated from data compiled from the authors from *FEC Reports on Financial Activity— 1979–1980: Final Report of U.S. House and Senate Races* (January 1982), and Michael Barone and Grant Ujifusa, *The Almanac of American Politics—1982* (Washington, DC: Barone and Company, 1981).

The data presented in Figure 10.3 confirm that giving by union and corporation PACs falls into already familiar patterns. Both give more to incumbents than to challengers, more to winners than to losers, and more to incumbents having positions of institutional leadership within the House than to other incumbents. However, there is an interesting difference between labor

nected" category includes, in addition to various ideological and cause PACs, the Footwear Distributors PAC, the Futures Industry Good Government PAC, and the Kentucky Gasoline Dealers Association PAC. Not only do the FEC categories group together PACs that we would consider very different from one another, they place in separate categories PACs that we might consider similar. For example, the National Rifle Association Political Victory Fund is classified under trade-member-health, and the Citizens Committee for the Right to Keep and Bear Arms under nonconnected. Analogously, the League of Conservation Voters is placed in trade-member-health, and the California League of Conservation Voters in nonconnected. Thus, for most purposes we are forced to ignore the FEC's classification of PACs. As indicated in footnote 40, even the corporate category is problematic.

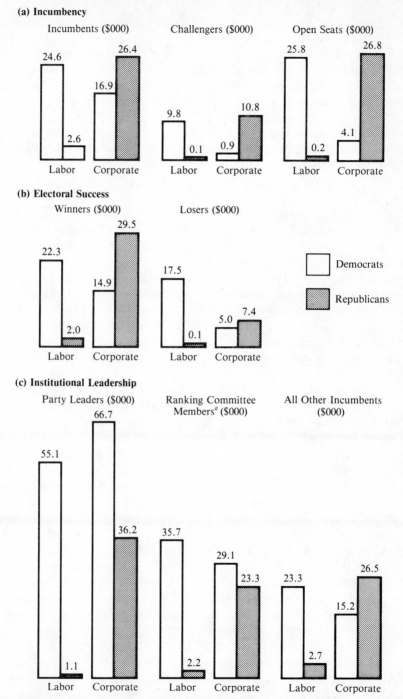

(a) Incumbency

Incumbents ($000)   Challengers ($000)   Open Seats ($000)

Incumbents: Labor — 24.6 / 2.6; Corporate — 16.9 / 26.4

Challengers: Labor — 9.8 / 0.1; Corporate — 0.9 / 10.8

Open Seats: Labor — 25.8 / 0.2; Corporate — 4.1 / 26.8

(b) Electoral Success

Winners ($000)   Losers ($000)

Winners: Labor — 22.3 / 2.0; Corporate — 14.9 / 29.5

Losers: Labor — 17.5 / 0.1; Corporate — 5.0 / 7.4

Democrats
Republicans

(c) Institutional Leadership

Party Leaders ($000)   Ranking Committee Members[a] ($000)   All Other Incumbents ($000)

Party Leaders: Labor — 55.1 / 1.1; Corporate — 66.7 / 36.2

Ranking Committee Members: Labor — 35.7 / 2.2; Corporate — 29.1 / 23.3

All Other Incumbents: Labor — 23.3 / 2.7; Corporate — 15.2 / 26.5

Figure 10.3 Receipts from labor and corporate PACs, by party. (Average receipts of 1980 House candidates in thousands of dollars.)

[a]Democrats—Committee chairs; Republicans—Ranking minority members.

Source: Calculated from data compiled by authors from *FEC Reports on Financial Activity—1979–1980: Final Report of U.S. House and Senate Races* (January 1982), and Michael Barone and Grant Ujifusa, *The Almanac of American Politics—1982* (Washington, DC: Barone and Company, 1981).

and corporate PACs. Corporations are, quite simply, less partisan than unions in PAC giving. While labor PACs donated less than 5 percent of their aggregate contributions to Republicans in 1980, corporate PACs gave nearly 40 percent of theirs to Democrats. However, only certain Democrats benefited from this bipartisan corporate generosity. As shown in Figure 10.3(a), while labor union PACs donated only very small sums to the coffers of incumbent Republicans, corporate PACs contributed substantial amounts to incumbent Democrats. With respect to challengers and open-seat contenders, however, unions gave virtually nothing to Republicans and corporations gave little more to Democrats.

This relatively bipartisan spirit on the part of corporate PACs shows up in Figure 10.3(b) as well. Although both kinds of PACs prefer winners to losers, corporate PACs devote an especially large share of their contributions to winners. While 65 percent of labor PAC contributions went to winners, just under 80 percent of corporate PAC donations in 1980 went to winners. (In interpreting these figures it is helpful to remember that because a number of candidates ran unopposed, 53 percent of the candidates were winners.) In short, Figure 10.3(b) shows that labor gave very little to Republicans regardless of their eventual electoral performance, but gave quite liberally to Democrats who went down in ultimate defeat. Corporations, on the other hand, gave very little to losers of either party, but gave fairly generously to Democratic winners.

The same pattern continues in Figure 10.3(c). Both labor and corporate PACs contribute more to party leaders and ranking committee members than to ordinary incumbents. Once again, however, unions gave almost exclusively to Democrats. However, not only were corporations generous to Democratic leaders and committee chairs, they gave more to these powerful Democrats than to their Republican counterparts. Presumably, the willingness on the part of corporate PACs to fund Democratic incumbents and leaders would diminish dramatically if the Democrats lost control of the House and, therefore, of the power that accrues to the majority party. Still, corporations at this point devote a substantial share of their PAC resources to powerful Democrats.

These figures lead us to an understanding of PAC giving by union and corporate PACs—but especially corporate PACs—as motivated by a desire to ingratiate powerful legislators; hence, the disproportionate gifts to incumbents, winners, and leaders and the corporate PACs' willingness to fund Democrats in these categories. However, the data in Figure 10.4 suggest that it would be premature to conclude that what animates campaign giving by these two kinds of PACs is a cynical desire to buy responsiveness from powerful officeholders, whoever they might be. Figure 10.4 shows the average 1980 PAC gifts from union and corporate PACs to candidates of varying ideologies. Clearly, in funding incumbents and winners (ideological data being unavailable for nonincumbent losers), ideology is of critical importance to both labor and corporate PACs. The measure is one of overall liberalism or conservatism, not of candidate responsiveness on a narrow set of issues of concern to particular compa-

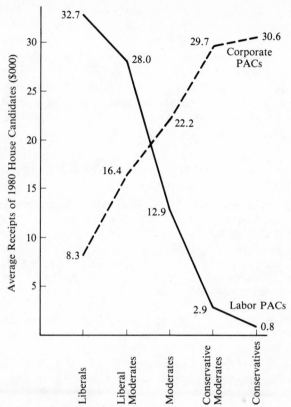

Figure 10.4   Receipts from corporate and labor PACs, by ideology, for winners and incumbents only. (Average receipts of 1980 House candidates, in thousands of dollars.)

Source: Calculated from data compiled by the authors from *FEC Reports on Financial Activity—1979–1980: Final Report of U.S. House and Senate Races* (January 1982), and Michael Barone and Grant Ujifusa, *The Almanac of American Politics—1982* (Washington, DC: Barone and Company, 1981).

nies or unions. The relationship between campaign giving and candidate ideology is a robust one for both labor and corporate PACs: for the former, contributions fall with increasing conservatism; for the latter, contributions rise with increasing conservatism. Thus, it is clear that for neither labor nor corporate PACs is it simply a matter of money seeking power. Both kinds of PACs obviously also seek out like-minded candidates who can be trusted to be supportive, even if left to their own devices.[25]

[25] A detailed study by J. David Gopoian of PAC giving by corporations in the defense, oil, and auto industries and unions confirms that both general ideology and positions on particular issues are related to PAC giving. "What Makes PACs Tick? An Analysis of the Allocation Patterns of Economic Interest Groups," *American Journal of Political Science* 28 (1984): 259–281.

Understanding Giving—The PACs' Point of View

This survey of the kinds of candidates that are likely to benefit from PAC generosity gives important clues as to what PACs are up to. We can get another perspective by considering what those who run PACs *say* they are up to. Many PACs have formulated brief statements summarizing the criteria to be used in giving. A few that we have seen are collections of civic-minded platitudes; most, however, are quite straightforward. The listing composed by the steering committee of the PAC of a large insurance company is typical:

> The Committee has established the following criteria to select candidates to whom contributions may be made:
>
> 1. The candidate's general philosophical outlook on matters of importance to private enterprise, as revealed in Chamber of Commerce of the United States (COCUSA) and Americans for Constitutional Action (ACA) ratings.
> 2. With respect to incumbents, the individual's committee and/or Congressional leadership assignment (with substantial weight given to individuals on committees likely to be considering legislation of major concern to [the company]).
> 3. Again with respect to incumbents, the individual's previous stand on issues of importance to [the company], independent of the criterion in paragraph (1).
> 4. With respect to non-incumbents, the general attitude and voting record of the incumbent and the challenger's chances for victory and need for financial support.
> 5. Any constituent relationship which [the company or its subsidiaries] might have with a particular candidate.

We asked our Washington representatives whose organizations had PACs an open-ended question about the criteria used by the PAC in making contributions. Then, we showed them a list of possible criteria and asked them to choose the two that are most important in selecting candidates to receive PAC donations. In their replies to the open-ended question, the respondents referred to ten possible factors, eight of which we had anticipated and included on the list. Table 10.2, which summarizes the results of these inquiries, indicates that the criteria spelled out so explicitly by the insurance company quoted above are common ones. As shown in the right-hand column, a majority of the respondents mentioned as considerations the candidate's position on a few issues of special concern to the organization, general ideology, and committee assignments. Fewer mentioned the location of the candidate's district, the closeness of the race, and the candidate's position as a committee chairman, as well as helping "friends." Fewer than one in five indicated that they take into account the likelihood that the candidate will win, the size of the candidate's war chest relative to his opponent's, and the candidate's party. The figures in the left-

Table 10.2   WHY PACs CONTRIBUTE

	Percentage of respondents	
	Citing criterion as especially important[a]	Mentioning criterion[b]
The candidate's position on a few issues of special concern to your organization	59%	74%
The candidate's general ideology	50	57
The candidate's committee assignments	46	57
The locations of the candidate's district	22	34
How close the race is	15	31
The candidate's position as a party leader or committee chairman	15	27
"We help our friends"[c]	—	20
The likelihood that the candidate will win[c]	—	15
The size of the candidate's war chest relative to his opponent's	1	8
The candidate's party	1	3

[a]Selected from list of eight as one of two most important.
[b]Either mentioned in discussion or selected from list.
[c]Not included on list of eight.
Source: Washington Representatives Survey.

hand column indicating which criteria were cited as especially important are, of course, lower in magnitude; they are, however, in the same rank-order.

Table 10.3 presents these data for the three kinds of PACs for which we have sufficient cases to warrant inclusion. Overall, corporate, trade association, and union PACs tend to emphasize similar criteria in selecting candidates to receive campaign funds. However, there are a number of discrepancies that deserve mention. Although corporations deem the candidate's position on a few particularly salient issues an important consideration, they are rather less likely to mention that criterion than are trade association or labor PACs. They are, however, especially likely to single out the geographical location of the candidate's district, presumably reflecting a desire to be on good terms with legislators representing areas in which they have branch plants or subsidiaries. They are, also, more likely than trade associations or unions to mention the candidate's chances of winning. Trade associations are distinctive in the degree to which they seem to ignore general ideology and emphasize a favorable posture on a few important matters and committee assignments. Unions seem relatively insensitive to the candidate's committee assignments and rather more concerned about the closeness of the race.[26]

[26]These findings are consistent with Gopoian's. See his results for further elaboration of, for example, the particular industries in which different criteria are likely to be especially important. Eismeier and Pollock ("Political Action Committees Varieties of Organization and Strategy," pp,

Table 10.3   CRITERIA USED BY DIFFERENT KINDS OF PACs

Percentage mentioning or selecting as important from list

	Corporate PACs	Trade association PACs	Union PACs
The candidate's position on a few issues of special concern to your organization	65%	83%	89%
The candidate's general ideology	67	30	61
The candidate's committee assignments	67	70	44
The location of the candidate's district	60	17	22
How close the race is	26	17	50
The candidate's position as a party leader or committee chairman	28	35	22
"We help our friends"	14	22	22
The likelihood that the candidate will win	23	4	0
The size of the candidate's war chest relative to his opponents	7	9	11
The candidate's party	2	0	11
	(N = 43)	(N = 23)	(N = 18)

Source: Washington Representatives Survey.

In view of the importance to PACs of both a candidate's positions on salient political issues and his general ideological posture, we were interested to know how they behaved if they misjudged a candidate's predilections or if the candidate changed his views. Hence, we asked our respondents whether they had ever had to withdraw support from a candidate whom they had supported in a previous election. Forty-four percent—40 percent of those from corporate PACs, 33 percent of those from trade association PACs, and 73 percent of those from union PACs—replied that they had.

In their supplementary comments the respondents made clear that such withdrawal does not necessarily imply punishment. A number of ideological PACs made the point that their objective is to elect like-minded legislators, not to get anything from them once they are in office. As incumbents, these new legislators are in a position to raise ample funds in subsequent elections. Thus ideological PACs are relatively unlikely to support the same candidates from one election to the next. A spokesman for the Young Americans for Freedom, a conservative youth organization, made this point: "We get them into Con-

136–137) and Holcomb ("Contribution Strategies of Business PACs," pp. 8–14) suggest that PACs in industries subject to industry-specific regulation are relatively likely to pursue pragmatic strategies.

gress and then move on to new people unless the incumbent has been unusually helpful or is having a tough time in his reelection bid." A number of respondents echoed this last point. They indicated that a candidate who faces a tough challenge in one election may not need help in the succeeding one. Therefore, if they do not fund a previously supported candidate, it need not reflect any abandonment by the PAC. Labor PACs, more sensitive than their business counterparts to the marginality of the race, made this point frequently. Therefore, their relative propensity to withdraw support from candidates who had received contributions in the past probably reflects their desire to direct contributions to candidates who need the money as well as their well-known desire to reward friends and punish enemies. Sometimes, however, withdrawal of support from a candidate represents punishment for failure to deliver. As one trade association executive put it: "It depends on their voting record. If you gave to them and then they end up screwing you, you're not going to support them again."

Split Giving

We asked our respondents whether they ever have occasion to give to more than one candidate in a race for a single office, a practice called "split giving."[27] Split giving has a bad name among those involved with PACs. Because the split giver is guaranteed to have backed a winner, the practice has an aroma of the cynical purchase of influence. This kind of disapproval was expressed by many of our respondents. According to one corporate director of federal affairs, split giving is not only bad ethics, it is bad politics: "That practice is a real mistake. You don't win friendships by it; you just win enmity. A guy will call you up and instead of thanking you for the $1,000 you gave him, he'll get on your back for giving his opponent $1,000 as well."

Although our respondents disapprove of contributing to more than one candidate in a race, many of them do it—at least on occasion. Fifty-three percent of the PACs in our sample—58 percent of the corporate, 57 percent of the trade association, and 43 percent of the union PACs—have engaged in split giving.[28] It is clear from our respondents' explanatory remarks that they use this technique, not because they want to guarantee the indebtedness of the victor in races where the outcome is in doubt, but because under certain unusual conditions they find themselves cross-pressured. Under certain circumstances, a general election might pit against one another two old friends of the PAC: if redistricting forces two incumbents into a single race; if a friendly senator is challenged by a representative who is also an ally; if a congenial representative is challenged by a friend out of the state legislature.

[27] For a helpful discussion of split giving that reaches conclusions similar to those presented here, see Handler and Mulkern, *Business in Politics*, pp. 84–89.

[28] In responding that they have at some point given to more than one candidate in a contest, 6 percent of the PACs—including 5 percent of the trade association and 12 percent of the labor PACs—qualified their answers to indicate that while they have engaged in split giving on occasion, they do so only rarely or under extraordinary circumstances.

Sometimes the dual contributions represent differing preferences or perceptions within various parts of the organization. Corporate subsidiaries might find their political interests antagonistic and, therefore, might wish to back opposing candidates in the same race. In a typical pattern, the organization's Washington office wishes to back one candidate (often an incumbent on a key committee), while the folks in the district wish to support his opponent (often an ideologically more congenial challenger). In this last, not altogether rare circumstance, the Washington office itself may have divided loyalties and end up supporting both a powerful, strategically placed incumbent and his ideologically preferable challenger.

Split giving, however, does not always reflect unusual circumstances that put the organization in a cross-pressured position. Some of our PACs admitted quite freely to wanting a seat on the victory wagon. According to a Washington representative for one of the nation's largest airlines: "We call it covering our bets. We do it in a close race—to make sure we're on the right side of the winner." Another major airline achieved the same effect with a post-election gift: "We supported an incumbent who lost. Then we got in with the new guy after he won. We got on the bandwagon and welcomed him to Washington with a contribution." Only a minority of PACs contribute in this way; those that do, use this kind of split giving relatively infrequently. Still, by their own admission, some PACs use split giving to ensure that they are on the right side of the winner, whoever he or she may be.

BRIBERY OR EXTORTION?

At least some of the evidence considered so far would lead to cynicism about the aims of PACs: the amount of PAC money collected by incumbents running without opposition; the tendency of PAC money to gravitate toward winners and incumbents in positions of power; the threat implicit within some PACs' practice of withdrawing support from those who do not deliver; and the custom of some PACs of contributing to both candidates in a race so as to be sure of being in the good graces of the winner. However, the decision making of PAC managers is only half the story. The discussion so far has examined only one side of what is in fact an exchange. Our respondents made clear that it is not as if the congressional candidates were reluctant virgins helpless before the onslaught of ardent PACs. It is apparent that the candidates are just as eager to receive the booty as the PACs are to give it. It seems that PACs are quite simply besieged with requests for money from candidates. One small trade association PAC reported receiving more than 500 requests for donations— over 20 pounds worth—in a three-month period.[29] A Washington representative for a large corporation told us that his PAC received its first request for a campaign donation for the 1982 election the Friday after the 1980 election.

[29]Reported in Albert R. Hunt, "An Inside Look at Politicians Hustling PACs," *Wall Street Journal*, October 1, 1982, p. 33.

Ordinarily the requests for donations come in the form of invitations to fund raisers. Sometimes fund raisers feature some kind of gimmick to spark interest.[30] It may be a celebrity. While Elizabeth Taylor was married to Senator John Warner (R-Virginia), she was a fixture on the Republican fund-raiser circuit. It may be entertainment: for his annual fund raiser, Rep. Andy Ireland (D-Florida) books a block of tickets at the circus and arranges for the performers to give a private show in an adjacent tent. It may be a regional theme, such as a Texas barbecue or a New England clambake. More commonly, however, the fund raiser is a Washington cocktail party. The candidate stands at the doorway as the lobbyists, who have usually paid in the neighborhood of $250 to attend, file in.[31] The lobbyists introduce themselves, not by name but—lest anyone be confused as to the purpose of the ritual—by organizational affiliation. So what the candidate hears is a litany of "Hello, I'm with RCA" . . . or the National Automobile Dealers Association or Lockheed or the Consumer Bankers Association or the Edison Electric Institute or the Federation of American Hospitals. And if the candidate is someone like Orrin Hatch (R-Utah), the chairman of the Senate Labor and Human Resources Committee who collected over $900,000 from PACs during his 1982 campaign for reelection, he will greet guests not with a "How are you?" or a "Thank you for coming," but with "We won't forget you."[32] Sometimes a fund raiser will be sponsored, not by the candidate him or herself, but by a friendly organization or a Washington super lobbyist.[33] This kind of assistance, of course, leaves a grateful policymaker in its wake.

Saying No to Candidates

In view of the shamelessness with which candidates dun PACs for money, we were anxious to know whether PAC managers feel pressure from candidates to provide financial support. Therefore, we asked our respondents whose organizations have PACs a closed-ended question about how often they feel free to refuse candidate requests. We followed that question with open-ended ones about what the consequences might be if they were to refuse and whether their interests would be damaged if they did not support a candidate who asked for it. The replies, summarized in Table 10.4, tell a mixed story. On one hand, as shown in Table 10.4(a), our respondents do not feel constrained by requests from candidates: 78 percent feel free to refuse most of the time and only 2

[30] For these and additional examples, see Congressional Quarterly, *Dollar Politics,* pp. 62–63.

[31] The following description of fund-raiser etiquette is taken from Lynn Rosellini, "Fund-Raisers Feature Wall-to-Wall Lobbyists," *New York Times,* April 12, 1982, p. A20. All the organizations named are listed by Rosellini as having had a representative in attendance at the fund raiser described in the article.

[32] Hatch's comportment at a fund raiser that netted $500,000 is described in Lois Romano, "The Catch for Hatch," *Washington Post,* October 1, 1981, p. C1. Figure for Hatch's PAC receipts supplied by the FEC.

[33] On this practice, see Drew "Politics and Money—Part I," pp. 106–112.

percent rarely feel free to refuse. In relative terms, those representing trade associations feel themselves to be in the position of least flexibility: 57 percent of them feel free to refuse most of the time, and 43 percent feel free to refuse only some of the time.

Although our respondents seem to have no compunctions about rejecting candidates' pleas for money, the figures in Table 10.4(b) indicate that they are divided in their judgments about the possible repercussions of refusing: 47 percent of the respondents indicated that there would be no damage to their interests were they to say no to a candidate; 12 percent indicated that it would be unlikely; and 41 percent felt there might be some consequences. Our respondents' supplementary remarks can help us understand what is behind this

Table 10.4   DO CANDIDATES APPLY PRESSURE?

(a) How often do you feel free to refuse these requests—most of the time, some of the time, or rarely?

	Corporate PACs	Trade association PACs	Union PACs	All PACs
Most of the time	90%	57%	80%	78%
Some of the time	5	43	20	19
Rarely	5	0	0	2
	100%	100%	100%	99%

(b) What might be the consequences for your organization if you were to refuse such a request? (Probe) Do you ever feel that your interests would be damaged if you don't provide support for a candidate who asks for it?

	Corporate PACs	Trade association PACs	Union PACs	All PACs
No consequences in case of refusal	40%	50%	38%	47%
Unlikely to be damaging consequences	16	15	8	12
Might be damaging consequences	45	35	54	41
	101%	100%	100%	100%

Source: Washington Representatives Survey.

seeming lack of consensus. Part of the resolution to the contradictory replies undoubtedly has to do with psychological differences among our respondents; some simply are more likely to perceive pressure and are less capable of withstanding heat than others. As one corporate lobbyist put it, "Any time anybody who can do a favor for you asks you for money, you can read pressure into it. But that's a mind set. It's probably not fair to impute pressure."

Those who felt that refusing a candidate's request would have no deleterious effects made several different points. One lone idealist from a large organization of business professionals expressed the view that there would be no bad consequences: "Legislators, hopefully, have a much broader view of the overall picture than to be guided in their actions by that kind of thing." The respondent from Business-Industry Political Action Committee (BIPAC) predicted no consequences for an entirely different reason. A few of the organizations in our sample—among them BIPAC—concentrate solely on electing sympathetic legislators. Thus, there are no reciprocal requests once a candidate takes office: "We are not knocking on anyone's door after the election. It's a luxurious position. We are immune to what others see as retribution. There is no way to apply it to us."

A number of those who fear no consequences from saying no to candidates never really put the system to the test. Quite simply, they would not *want* to refuse a friend. For example, according to a spokesman for a large conglomerate: "Normally, these calls come from people with whom we already have a good working relationship. We're friends. We try to help each other. We don't want to jeopardize that." A lobbyist for the National Association of Letter Carriers explicitly articulated this risk-averse strategy: "We haven't been stupid enough to offend our friends in high places." In fact, even the most cavalier of our respondents does not necessarily take chances. He described with glee fielding calls from arrogant legislators:

> These congressmen just keep getting bolder and bolder. If they don't meet our criteria, we don't give the money. I just love to get a Member on the phone. He'll call and ask for a contribution and I'll just run down the list of votes he's opposed us on. I'll say, "You didn't vote for us on Synfuels; you didn't vote for us on natural gas. . . . How do you expect us to give you money?!" Then they'll start stuttering and stammering, "Well, I . . . uh, I, well . . ." It's great. I love it. These guys think they're gods and they deserve a contribution if they can pronounce their own names.

In short, this corporate vice-president feels perfectly free to risk offending those who do not support his company anyway. His answer does not make clear whether he would feel equally free to reject a request from, say, an old friend who was running unopposed and, therefore, would not need the money.

Many of those who expressed a sense of greater constraint indicated that the implication of failing to support a candidate would be, not to create an overt opponent, but to enjoy diminished access to policymakers. One corporate lobbyist drew that lesson from a recent experience:

> At a fund-raiser breakfast the other morning a prominent southern senator said in a drawl, "My door is always open, but to you here today, the door will be open a little wider." You can't use money to change opinions, but you can use money to get in the door.

Another echoed this sentiment and indicated that members of Congress know who has contributed to their campaigns: "Some congressmen keep records of who has given to them and who hasn't. I've had that happen—a guy keeps a list in his drawer and decides whom he will see on the basis of whose names are on the list." A Washington representative with a prominent association of professionals also predicted that there might be repercussions, but elaborated by indicating that his organization, like many of those quoted earlier, takes no chances:

> Most members of Congress and their staff try not to make it a threatening request. But there's no question that if you're not on the list of contributors, you can expect a phone call asking, "What's the problem? Why didn't you support me?" Most of them don't have to threaten. We know who can help us and who can hurt us.

When such a call comes, according to one corporate lobbyist, the heat is on: "Are you kidding me? Of course you feel pressure. If a member of Congress calls you on the phone, you feel the pressure."

Saying No to PACs

By concentrating on legislators' ever bolder and more frequent requests for donations, the discussion so far has probably given the inaccurate impression that all in Congress are members of this hungry pack. In fact, a growing number of candidates are refusing to accept money from PACs.[34] This is a sufficiently recent phenomenon that it is impossible to gauge its dimensions and potential—that is, to know how many candidates are renouncing PAC contributions and how their numbers are changing. Furthermore, it is difficult to assess whether the decision not to accept PAC donations is animated by distaste for PACs or by desire to avoid being criticized as a captive of interested campaign donors or both. Still, it will be interesting to see whether this nascent trend gathers momentum.

[34]On this phenomenon, see Chris Black, "Once Seen as a Boon, PAC Money Now Avoided," *Boston Globe,* May 6, 1984, p. 1, and Laurence Collins, " 'PACs Vobiscum, Not with Me,' Political Candidates Proclaim," *Boston Sunday Globe,* July 22, 1984, p. A20.

POLITICAL EQUALITY AND PAC GIVING

In line with our ongoing concern with understanding who is being represented in organized interest politics, it seems sensible to raise with respect to PAC giving some of the same questions that we asked about group representation in Chapter 4—that is, to know where the PAC money comes from and the degree to which PAC giving exacerbates or ameliorates other political inequalities. Defenders of PACs make two arguments with respect to representation: that PACs broaden participation in politics by bringing in as donors ordinary citizens who might otherwise not be politically involved; and that they guarantee representation to all politically relevant groups. The comments of Representative Bill Frenzel (R-Minnesota) express this point of view: "[PACs] increase participation in the political system. . . . Every group in the world has now got a PAC, and it seems to me that tends to take a little sting out of saying certain people or certain forces are controlling the government."[35]

Systematic data confirm that PACs do mobilize as donors citizens who would probably not make campaign contributions through party or candidate organizations. In Chapter 4 we pointed out that people with prestigious occupations and high levels of income and education are especially likely to be active in politics. This socioeconomic skewing is especially pronounced when it comes to campaign giving. PAC donors are considerably more likely to enjoy high levels of income and education than are members of the electorate who do not contribute to campaigns.[36] However, comparing those who contribute only to PACs with those who donate to campaigns through party or candidate organizations in addition to—or instead of—PACs, we find that the PAC donors are less skewed sociologically than are other kinds of givers. They are more likely to be under 35 and less likely to have incomes in the upper range than are other kinds of contributors. These socioeconomic contours presumably reflect the success of union PACs in mobilizing their members to contribute. Forty-two percent of the PAC donors—as opposed to only 19 percent of the contributors to either parties or candidates—are from union households.

Data about the characteristics of donors tell only a part of the story of the overall shape of PAC giving, however. The comparisons between PAC donors and nongivers and between PAC donors and party and candidate contributors treated each individual as a unit. When it comes to campaign contributions, however, not all individuals are equal; some people wish to—and are able to—give far more than others.[37] Indeed, a 1981 BIPAC survey showed that the

[35]Quoted in Alexander and Haggerty, *The Federal Election Campaign Act,* pp. 70–71.

[36]The evidence on which this discussion is based is presented in Ruth S. Jones and Warren E. Miller, "Financing Campaigns: Modes of Individual Contribution," paper delivered at the Annual Meeting of the Midwest Political Association, Chicago, April 1983, pp. 30–36.

[37]Not surprisingly, studies have shown that while education is the most potent resource for becoming a political activist, money is the most valuable resource for becoming a big giver. See,

average corporate donor gave $160 to the company PAC. The Steelworkers checkoff plan allows union members to donate either two cents per workday or five dollars per year to the PAC.[38] The data from the 101 organizations in our sample that had affiliated PACs confirm these discrepancies: on average, the corporate PACs collected 12 percent of their total receipts in amounts over $500; trade association PACs 11 percent of their total in amounts over $500; and union PACs 0.3 percent of their total in amounts over $500. Thus, since equal rates of participation need not imply equal yield in dollars, any reasonable discussion of the slant in compaign giving must quickly depart from notions of one-person–one-dollar.

Table 10.5 presents the results of a tally (analogous to the catalogue of organizations having a Washington presence that we presented in Chapter 4) of the nearly 3,000 PACs listed in *The PAC Directory* as having been registered with the FEC between the beginning of 1977 and the end of 1980.[39] In terms of numbers of PACs, what is interesting about the distribution in the left-hand column is how similar it is to the distribution of organizations having Washington representation shown in Table 4.2. The preeminence of business organizations among PACs is striking: 61.6 percent of all PACs represent corporations or trade and other business associations. The remainder of the distribution is also similar to the distribution of interest organizations, although labor union and agricultural PACs represent a rather larger share—and civil rights, poor people's, and social welfare groups and organizations representing women, the elderly and the handicapped an even more minuscule share—of PACs than they did of interest organizations.

In terms of contributions, the pattern is slightly, but not substantially, different. The share derived from business is once again large: 59 percent of all PAC donations in the 1979–1980 electoral cycle originated from corporations or trade and other business associations. In this case, however, the portion attributable to corporations is slightly smaller and that attributable to business associations correspondingly higher. With regard to contributions, the labor share of the distribution, 21 percent, is considerably higher than its share of the distribution of PACs, indicating that the average individual union PAC is a

---

Larry L. Berg, Larry L. Eastland, and Sherry Bebitch Jeffe, "Characteristics of Large Campaign Contributors," *Social Science Quarterly* 62 (1981): 412, and Edmond Constantini and Joel King, "Checkbook Democrats and Their Copartisans," *American Politics Quarterly* 10 (1982): 74.

[38] Both figures cited in Congressional Quarterly, *Dollar Politics*, p. 44.

[39] As indicated in footnote 21, the seven categories used by the FEC to classify PACs have limited utility from our perspective. Therefore, we undertook to take a census of our own. In categorizing PACs we used the same classificatory criteria (elaborated in Appendix C) employed in creating our tally of interest groups having a presence in Washington politics.

The PAC Directory (compiled by Marvin Weinberger and David U. Greevy), lists 2,968 PACs registered as of the end of 1980; in its press release of January 17, 1982, the FEC gives the total number of PACs as of December 31, 1980 as 2,551. This discrepancy may reflect the fact that the *Directory* includes PACs that registered with the FEC during 1977 and 1978 but did not file subsequent reports. As Larry Sabato points out (*PAC Power*, p. 8) many of these are "paper PACs" that contribute little or nothing.

Table 10.5 DISTRIBUTION OF PACs BY ORGANIZATIONAL TYPE AND SHARE OF PAC GIVING

	Share of all PACs	Share of all PAC giving[a]
Corporations	44.7%	37.4%
Trade and other business associations	16.9	21.5
Professional associations	5.7	7.2
Agricultural associations	1.9	2.9
Unions	12.8	21.3
Citizens'/Ideological groups	4.2	5.2
Civil rights/Minority organizations	0.2	—
Social welfare and the poor	0.3	—
Women/Elderly/Handicapped	0.6	0.6
Other/Unknown	12.9	3.8
	99.9%	99.9%
	(N = 2968)	(N = $55 million)

[a]Donations to House and Senate candidates 1979–1980.

Sources: Based on information contained in *The PAC Directory,* compiled by Marvin Weinberger and David U. Greevy (Cambridge, MA: Ballinger, 1982), Section II, Part B, and *FEC Reports on Financial Activity— 1979–1980: Final Report U.S. House and Senate Races,* January 1982.

comparatively large giver. Except for the fact that PACs in the "other/un-known" category, account for a much smaller portion of the actual donations, the distributions in the two columns are otherwise remarkably similar.

Even though the early 1980s saw the birth of PACs like Senior PAC and the League of United Latin American Citizens, FEC figures make clear that the business share of PAC activity has grown over the past ten years. In 1974 corporate PACs represented 15 percent of the total number of PACs and accounted for 20 percent of the total PAC contributions to congressional candidates; by the end of 1982 corporate PACs represented 44 percent of the total number of PACs and donated 33 percent of the total contributions.[40] The figures for labor PACs tell the same story in reverse. In 1974 labor PACs represented 33 percent of the total number of PACs and gave 50 percent of all PAC donations; by the end of 1982 labor PACs represented only 11 percent of

[40]Our figures for corporate contributions do not jibe perfectly with those supplied by the FEC. This reflects, once again, the problems from our perspective of the way in which the FEC classifies PACs. The FEC's corporate PAC category includes some PACs—for example, the Young Americans for Freedom PAC—whose parent organizations are legally chartered as corporations. Such PACs, however, are not what we ordinarily think of as corporate PACs. Furthermore, the FEC has a separate category, containing a diverse set of PACs, for corporations without stock. We considered many of these PACs—for instance, those organized to solicit the officers of savings and loans associations—to be corporate PACs. All told, we find more corporate PACs than are contained in the corresponding FEC category.

all PACs and contributed only 24 percent of the total PAC donations.[41] Furthermore, labor contributions have become of diminished importance to the Democratic party: in 1974 labor PAC contributions represented 69 percent of all PAC contributions to Democratic candidates for the House; by 1980 that figure had been reduced to 43 percent.[42]

The meaning of these figures is subject to some dispute. The argument has been made that the increase in corporate PAC giving is more apparent than real. According to this perspective, what has happened in the aftermath of the reforms of the 1970s is that donations from corporate executives that used to be disguised as individual contributions and given under the table in "double envelopes" are now given openly and legitimately by company PACs. Thus, what we have is in a sense old wine in new bottles.[43] If this line of argument is correct—that is, if increasing contributions by corporate PACs represent only the rechanneling of funds previously given less openly—then it contradicts another contention made by the friends of PACs, that they mobilize for political participation individuals who would not otherwise be active.

There is also disagreement about how to interpret the overall distribution of giving among various kinds of PACs. One line of argument holds that the figures underestimate the aggregate contribution of labor because they do not include what unions are able to spend directly from their own treasuries on nonpartisan activities such as registration drives.[44] An opposing viewpoint holds that the figures in fact obscure the extent of business contributions because so much of the giving that is funneled directly through party and candidate committees is derived from business sources.[45] Studies of campaign giving show that a substantial proportion of big donors to both parties are recruited from the ranks of business.[46] This point was underlined by the oil industry lobbyist who was quoted to the effect that only one-third of the donations originating in the independent oil industry arrive via PACs.[47]

Table 10.5 contains several other lessons in addition to the relative balance between business and labor activity. First, there is virtually no representation among PACs of the poor and racial minorities. In the words of Senator

[41]Calculated from figures given in FEC press releases of January 17, 1982 and April 29, 1983. Unfortunately, we cannot use FEC data to calculate analogous figures for trade association and citizens' PACs.

[42]Figures given by Gary C. Jacobson in "Money in the 1980 Congressional Elections," paper delivered at the Annual Meeting of the Midwest Political Science Association, Milwaukee, April 1982, Table 5.

[43]See Michael J. Malbin, "Neither a Mountain nor a Molehill," *Regulation,* May/June 1979, pp. 41–43.

[44]See Michael J. Malbin, "Labor, Business and Money—A Post-Election Analysis," *National Journal,* March 19, 1977, p. 412.

[45]See David Jessup, "Can Political Influence Be Democratized?" in Michael J. Malbin, ed., *Parties, Interest Groups, and Campaign Finance Laws* (Washington, DC: American Enterprise Institute, 1980), pp. 26–31.

[46]Constantini and King, "Checkbook Democrats and Their Copartisans," p. 74.

[47]Drew, "Politics and Money—Part I," p. 63.

Robert Dole (R-Kansas), "There aren't any Poor PACs or Food Stamp PACs or Nutrition PACs or Medicare PACs."[48] There are, in fact, a small number of PACs registered with the FEC that fall into this category; however, they gave no money at all in the course of the 1979–1980 electoral cycle. Other groups commanding relatively few political resources—women, the elderly, and the handicapped—also are significantly underrepresented in PAC giving. Most of the small amount of money given by PACs representing such groups came from PACs representing women. PACs representing the handicapped contributed nothing at all.

In a further parallel to the contours of the Washington pressure community as a whole, the interests of diffuse publics are also very unevenly represented in PAC activity: 4.6 percent of all PACs, contributing 5.2 percent of the 1979–1980 total, fall into this category. It is worth looking more closely at the composition of the diverse group of 128 citizens' PACs. Fully 50 percent of these PACs, donating 43 percent of the 1979–1980 citizens' PAC money, represent single-issue or cause groups—pro- and antiabortion, pro- and antigun control, and so on. Another 30 percent, accounting for 52 percent of the 1979–1980 citizens' PAC donations, are general ideological PACs—such as the Committee for the Survival of a Free Congress or the Fund for a Democratic Majority—whose purpose is to elect candidates to Congress of either a conservative or a liberal coloration. Very few of these groups represent the kind of environmental or consumer interests by which business organizations feel so besieged. Of the nearly 3000 PACs, there are only 17 concerned with environmental preservation and energy conservation and only one representing the interests of consumers. The environmental and energy PACs contributed a total of only $45,454, representing 1.5 percent of the citizens' PAC donations and .08 percent of all contributions in 1979–1980. The lone consumer PAC contributed nothing at all.

Of the 110 ideological, foreign policy, and cause PACs, we were able to classify all but two as either liberal or conservative.[49] Of these PACs, 84 percent are conservative and only 16 percent are liberal. In terms of their contributions, the figures are skewed, though somewhat less so: 68 percent of the 1979–1980 total came from conservative groups, 32 percent from liberal ones. (If the environmental and energy PACs are included and considered to be liberal, the figures change very little: 67 percent of the money originated with conservative PACs, 33 percent from liberal ones.) Because they include only direct contributions to candidates and omit independent expenditures, these figures actually overestimate the representation of liberal points of view in ideological PAC

---

[48] Quoted in "Money Talks, Congress Listens," *Boston Globe,* December 12, 1982, p. A24.
[49] In virtually all cases where we did not recognize the PAC, we could discern from its name the nature of its ideological leanings. We considered pro-abortion, pro-gun control, and peace PACs to be liberal; anti-abortion, anti-gun control, and pro-national security PACs to be conservative. The two PACs that we did not classify are Californians for Bilingual Education and Committee for Humane Legislation.

giving. In partisan terms, approximately 85 percent of all independent expenditures in 1982 were made on behalf of Republican candidates or against Democrats; the National Conservative Political Action Committee (NCPAC) alone accounted for 60 percent of the independent expenditures in that year.[50]

Our discussion of the contours of PAC giving can be given two quite different interpretations. On the one hand, when compared to a pre-Watergate system of free-for-all giving by individuals, PAC-based congressional campaign finance indeed democratizes giving. The set of citizen donors mobilized by PACs (and PACs only) is much less skewed in socioeconomic terms than the group of individuals who give to campaigns through party or candidate organizations in addition to—or instead of—through PACs. On the other hand, PAC contributors are, like any set of political activists, skewed sociologically. What is more, because not all PAC donors can afford to give equally, PAC money is in the aggregate far less balanced in its sources than is the group of individuals who give to PACs: business is well represented, and the disadvantaged, especially the poor and minorities, are hardly represented at all in PAC giving. In addition, the interests of certain diffuse publics, especially environmentalists and consumers, figure only marginally in PAC giving.

PACS AND POLICY INFLUENCE

Among the most serious issues debated by the defenders and detractors of PACs is whether the quid pro quo of the campaign contribution is a policy favor and, therefore, whether a system of campaign finance relying heavily on PAC giving to incumbents undermines the integrity of the policy process.[51] Naturally, PAC contributions do not affect voting on all issues, or even on all the issues in which PACs have an interest. Students of Congress make the point that legislators are subject to multiple pressures when they vote—most importantly, the claims of party, constituency, and individual conscience.[52] Therefore, it is reasonable to expect PAC influence to diminish on visible issues that engage intense partisan conflict, constituency preferences, or personal commitments on the part of the legislator himself. Conversely, the possibility of PAC influence would probably be enhanced to the degree that an issue of low visibility generates no strong partisan conflict, constituency opinion, or feelings on the part of the legislator.

---

[50]Figures given in Frank Sorauf, *What Price PACs?* (New York: The Twentieth Century Fund, 1984), p. 54. Note that we are making the not always accurate assumption that Republican candidates are more conservative than Democrats.

[51]This is an issue that divides observers sharply. For one view, see Drew, "Politics and Money—Part I." For the opposite, see Robert J. Samuelson, "The Campaign Reform Failure," *The New Republic,* September 5, 1983, pp. 28–36, and Alexander, "The Case for PACs." For a position between these two, see Sorauf, *What Price PACs?,* pp. 59–61, 89–92.

[52]See, for example, Warren E. Miller and Donald E. Stokes, "Constituency Influence in Congress," *American Political Science Review* 57 (1963): 45–56; Aage R. Clausen, *How Congress-*

It is quite easy to assemble a litany of quotations from legislators of both parties confirming the diagnosis of the associate director of legislative affairs at Common Cause who told us that "there is a lot of 'institutional bribery' in the way we finance campaigns." For example, according to one House Republican, "PACs not only buy incumbents, but affect legislation."[53] It is, of course, equally possible to compile a list of affirmations by PAC managers and legislators to the effect that "the idea that there is a quid pro quo is balderdash" and that, furthermore, when a legislator votes for a measure supported by a donor-PAC, we might mistakenly attribute his vote to PAC influence when, in fact, he was only voting as he would have anyway.[54]

Several of the PAC managers in our sample argue that PAC contributions buy access, not floor votes. As one of the corporate PAC managers put it, "You can't use money to change opinions, but you can use money to get in the door." Legislators often echo this point. Tony Coelho (D-California), chair of the Democratic Congressional Campaign Committee, replied when asked what donors could expect for their cash: "Access. Access. That's the name of the game. They meet with the leadership and chairmen of the committees. We don't sell legislation; we sell the opportunity to be heard."[55]

Can a Mere $5,000 Make a Difference?

Defenders of PACs argue that contributions from individual PACs are too small to buy influence. PACs are limited to giving $5,000 per candidate ($10,000 if there is a primary and $15,000 if there is a runoff primary as well). In fact, average contributions are substantially below this upper limit: among PACs registered as having contributed at least $5,000 in 1979–1980, the average contribution to a Senate candidate was $1,243; the average to a House candidate $702.[56] Therefore, according to this logic, the contribution of any single PAC rarely represents a substantial share of a candidate's total receipts, and it

men Decide: A Policy Focus (New York: St. Martin's Press, 1973); and John W. Kingdon, *Congressmen's Voting Decisions* (New York: Harper & Row, 1973).

[53] Quoted in Mark Green, "Political PAC-Man," *The New Republic,* December 13, 1982, p. 18; see also, ibid., the quotations from Reps. Glickman (p. 19), Jacobs (pp. 21–22), and Leach (p. 19). In addition, see quotations from Rep. Downey in "Speaking Out," *People against PACs* (Washington, DC: Common Cause, 1983), p. 13; and from Reps. Panetta (p. 67) and Shannon (p. 101) in Drew, "Politics and Money—Part I."

Occasionally a legislator makes a damaging admission like the following: "Asked whether he was uncomfortable about accepting a personal payment from [a company interested in a tax bill] within weeks after playing a prominent [legislative] role . . . [one] Senator said, 'God no, I figured they might owe it to me.'" "Top PAC Man," *Wall Street Journal,* April 24, 1984, p. 15.

[54] Quoted in Walter Isaacson, "Running with the PACs," *Time,* October 25, 1982, p. 24; see also quotations from Rep. Klinger in Congressional Quarterly, *Dollar Politics,* p. 82; and from Budde (p. 18) and McCarthy (p. 19) in Green, "Political PAC Man."

[55] Quoted in Drew, "Politics and Money—Part I," pp. 93–95. See also Culver's statement to the same effect (p. 129).

[56] Figures taken from Eismeier and Pollock, "Political Action Committees: Varieties of Organization and Strategy," p. 132.

can hardly have a significant effect on a legislator's behavior in office.[57] This argument, however, misconstrues both the structure of the representation of interests by organizations and the structure of political opposition on many issues.

A single PAC donation is often not the only one representing a particular interest. As discussed in Chapter 4, the representation of an industry by both its trade association and individual companies implies that the interests of a particular industry are likely to be represented by multiple organizations. This logic applies to PAC contributions as well. Consider, for example, the chemical industry, one not ordinarily cited for free-spending habits in campaign dona- tions. The components of the industry—its trade associations and individual corporations—are not included on lists of big campaign contributors. As a matter of fact, the largest contributor from the chemical industry was only the forty-fifth largest contributor in 1980 and only one other was on the list of the top 50 contributors. Together, however, the 120 corporations included on the *PAC Directory* listing of chemical industry companies contributing over $5,000 donated a total of over $4.4 million to candidates for Congress in 1979–1980.[58] Similarly, in the same electoral cycle, oil and gas interests donated over $6 million.[59] Thus, it is clear that—in industries having a sufficient number of companies large enough to field their own PACs—the total to a particular candidate can be many times the limit for a single PAC, a sum of sufficient size that the recipient might feel constrained not to offend the contributing indus- try. Because the individual PACs that are part of the industry may not rival the well-known mega-PACs (such as the PACs of the United Auto Workers, the American Medical Association, and the National Association of Realtors), which are traditionally among the biggest total givers, the industry's status as a major PAC giver and the size of its aggregate contributions may go unnoticed.[60]

[57]This argument has been made in a number of different places. See, for example, the comments of Rep. Timothy E. Wirth in "Views Differ on PAC Money's Role," *Congressional Quarterly Weekly Report,* March 12, 1983, p. 504; and Michael J. Malbin, "Of Mountains and Molehills: PACs, Campaigns, and Public Policy," in Malbin, ed., *Parties, Interest Groups, and Campaign Finance Laws,* pp. 157–177.

[58]Figure calculated from information contained in Weinberger and Greevy, compilers, *The PAC Directory.*

[59]Figures for spending by the oil and gas industry taken from Brooks Jackson, "Oil and Gas Interests Pumped $4.3 Million into Political Coffers," *Wall Street Journal,* September 27, 1982, p. 14. (The figure given in the title of the article refers to contributions as of the end of July, 1982 for the 1982 election. Since a large portion of all contributions is given in the final weeks before the election, Jackson predicted that 1982 spending by oil and gas interests would surpass that in 1980.)

[60]The implication of this logic is that "Top 10" lists enumerating the largest PACs can be very misleading. In industries in which there are a large number of relatively small and geographi- cally dispersed companies, virtually all the PAC contributions are funneled through trade associ- ations. The companies themselves are too small to field individual PACs. Thus, the PACs of the realtors and the home builders associations are famous for their aggregate size. However, individual real estate brokers and individual contractors (with the exception of a few large builders) do not have their own PACs, in contrast with the situation in the chemical or petroleum industries. Thus, lists of the largest PACs misrepresent the overall distribution of PAC giving.

Furthermore, donations on one side of an issue are not necessarily met by equal and opposite donations on the other. We have already seen that—contrary to the optimistic assessment that "every group in the world has now got a PAC"—the proliferation of PACs has not yielded full mobilization of all interests, much less equal representation of all interests. Thus, when a contribution buys access to present what is sincerely believed to be a legitimate case—and there is no opposing donation—then even relatively small sums can have a potential impact. On issues of low visibility, when not all parties to a controversy are represented among campaign donors, a lawmaker can allow himself the luxury of being guided by the wishes of even small campaign contributors without giving offense to anyone else. Consistent with our contention in Chapter 7 that the distinction between access and influence is sometimes overdrawn, we need assign no venality to legislators to assert that even small contributions might influence behavior. Legislators who hear a convincing argument on one side of a controversy, and are not exposed to the equally compelling case that might be made in opposition, need not be motivated by a desire to guarantee future contributions if they act in accordance with the wishes of a donor. They have, however, been influenced by the inequality of access that results from a system of campaign financing that relies in such large part upon PAC donations to incumbents.

Do PAC Donations Matter?: Systematic Assessments

Another observation made by those who maintain that PAC money does not affect policy is that it is impossible to assess the effects of PAC contributions because we do not know whether or not legislators whose votes reflect the preferences of PAC donors might, in fact, be behaving as they would have anyway. The PAC managers in our sample make a point of rewarding friends. Presumably, the beneficiaries of such generosity would be supportive in any circumstance. These contributions to friends might be erroneously interpreted as having bought votes when those votes were forthcoming anyway.

Political scientists who analyze roll call voting in Congress use sophisticated statistical techniques to overcome this objection. While such techniques do not permit the conclusion that a *specific* lawmaker was—or was not—influenced by PAC contributions in voting on a certain issue, they do permit inferences about whether *in the aggregate* acceptance of PAC donations increased significantly the chances that a legislator would vote in accordance with the PACs' wishes.

At this point, however, the systematic evidence is still incomplete. There are now several studies, of varying quality, that attempt to assess whether PAC giving by a specific organization influences roll call votes on a particular issue. The results are mixed. A few of these studies have found no relationship between PAC spending and roll call voting. Most have uncovered statistically significant relationships of varying strength (ranging from weak to robust) between PAC receipts and roll call votes, controlling for other relevant factors such as party, constituency characteristics, and ideology.[61] Some of these studies are flawed methodologically, and there is considerable dispute among the authors as to both which statistical tools are most appropriately applied and whether the particular issues selected are ones on which PAC influence should have been expected. It is clear that further studies are needed to acquire a fuller understanding of the circumstances under which PAC contributions are likely to have an influence on roll call votes and the relative strength of that influence.

In order to assess the legislative effect of PAC donations, it is necessary to have not only additional statistical studies of roll call votes but also detailed inquiries into legislative maneuvering. The discussion in Chapter 9 of legislative scorecards made clear that roll call voting is only one of an array of legislative behaviors. Frequently, a legislator's behavior with respect to less visible activities (planning legislative strategy, shaping the details of bills, introducing amendments, and so on) is at odds with the direction of his or her vote on the floor. A really thorough evaluation of the impact of PACs would have to encompass these less visible activities as well in order to determine how PAC recipients are behaving behind the scenes.

Until more studies are conducted it seems prudent to reserve final judgment. The evidence reviewed here gives cause for concern, though not hysteria, that PAC contributions intrude into the making of policy. The systematic evidence currently available gives no reason to conclude that the Congress is "the best that money can buy." It does not, however, justify dismissing the possibility that under certain circumstances PAC contributions can have a significant effect on the comportment of lawmakers in Congress.

SUMMARY: THE CONTROVERSY OVER PACS

Since PACs are among the most controversial recent developments in the conduct of American politics, it seems appropriate to review some of the evidence presented here and consider how it impinges on the arguments for and against PACs. The debate is carried on in terms of some of the values most fundamental to American democracy—liberty, equality, accountability, the quality

---

[61]Henry W. Chappell, Jr., "Campaign Contributions and Voting on the Cargo Preference Bill: A Comparison of Simultaneous Models," *Public Choice* 36 (1981): 301–312; Dickinson McGaw and Richard McCleary, "The Corporate-Labor PAC Struggle: A Vector ARIMA Time Series Analysis," paper delivered at the Annual Meeting of the American Political Science Association, Denver, September 1982; W. P. Welch, "Campaign Contributions and Legislative Voting: Milk Money and Dairy Price Supports," *Western Political Quarterly* 35 (1982): 478–495; John P. Frendreis and Richard W. Waterman, "PAC Contributions and Legislative Behavior: Senate Voting on Trucking Deregulation," paper delivered at the Annual Meeting of the Midwest Political Science Association, Chicago, April 1983; Kirk F. Brown, "Campaign Contributions and Congressional Voting," paper delivered at the Annual Meeting of the American Political Science Association, Chicago, September 1983; and Diana Yiannakis, "PAC Contributions and House Voting on Conflictual and Consensual Issues," paper delivered at the Annual Meeting of the American Political Science Association, Chicago, September 1983.

of the electoral process, and the integrity of the legislative process. In part, the disagreements rest on how the evidence is interpreted: it is possible, for example, to construe in quite different ways the meaning for political equality of a system of campaign finance relying heavily on PAC contributions. However, there are clear trade-offs among these competing values. Any assessment of PACs thus also rests on the relative priority assigned to them.

One point made repeatedly in defense of PACs is that to curtail organized giving is to place unconscionable limits on the first-amendment rights of citizens to act collectively to influence government. The Supreme Court's decision in *Buckley* v. *Valeo* echoes this concern with freedom of expression. PAC opponents rarely explicitly deny the importance of free speech. Rather, if they deal with the issue at all, they point to the existence of multiple alternative routes for the expression of joint opinion and assert that they are sufficient guarantors of liberty.

The implications for political equality are somewhat more complicated. Those who defend PACs contend that they encourage participation and thus broaden the citizen base of the political system. Indeed, PACs do mobilize ordinary citizens to become contributors. Furthermore, a campaign finance system that relies in part upon PACs is less biased in favor of the well-off than a system of free-for-all giving by individuals would be. In addition, restrictions on PAC giving would introduce another kind of political inequality: wealthy candidates, who are not limited in what they can spend on their own behalf, would have an even greater advantage and politics would become even more "a rich man's game." However, not all interests are represented equally in PAC donations. The interests of business achieve ample representation; the interests of the disadvantaged and certain broad publics far less. In terms of political equality, a system of congressional campaign finance that drew upon the public treasury would surely be less skewed.

Speaking to somewhat different sets of issues, PAC supporters and opponents reach opposite conclusions about the effects of PAC contributions on accountability. Defenders of PACs argue that, since the current system of campaign finance includes provisions for disclosure, it is possible for the public to know the sources of a candidate's funds and to evaluate his performance in office in light of that knowledge. It is easier to determine the possible policy agenda behind a contribution from a PAC than a contribution from an individual. Since many of those who now give through PACs would continue to contribute individually if PAC donations were restricted, voters are in a much better position at present to ascertain who is beholden to whom for what and, thus, better able to hold lawmakers accountable.

With respect to the consequences for accountability, a second argument in defense of PACs hinges on the role played by PAC contributions in rendering congressional elections competitive. According to this logic, only if incumbents can be defeated can they be held accountable for their performance in office. It has been established that, all other things being equal, the more a challenger spends, the better his or her chances of beating the incumbent. Spending by incumbents, which seems to be largely a defensive response in the face of a strong challenger, does not similarly enhance his or her share of the vote.[62] Therefore, even though incumbents receive a disproportionate share of the contributions from PACs, if challengers are cut off from the supply of PAC money, they will be unable to amass sufficient cash ever to unseat incumbents. In this way, the availability of PAC money enhances accountability by increasing the ability of challengers to defeat incumbents. This reasoning explains the negative reaction among PAC defenders to the proposal for public financing of congressional campaigns, which they dub the "incumbents protection act" because it would presumably deny to challengers sufficient funds to mount a winning campaign.

Those less friendly to PACs wonder aloud why congressional incumbents, who receive much the larger share of PAC money and who are generally prone to take care of themselves, would oppose a measure that would purportedly guarantee them reelection. They argue that if legislation establishing federal financing of congressional election placed sufficient funds in the hands of challengers, it would enhance the ability of candidates to challenge incumbents successfully and thus make it easier to hold legislators accountable.[63]

Opponents of the current system also make the argument that PAC giving nationalizes the raising of campaign money, attenuating an important link between the legislator and his district, thus making it more difficult for voters to hold lawmakers accountable. Because the legislator is not beholden to his constituents for contributions, he can ignore their wishes more freely. Two points need to be made about this line of reasoning. First, what is alleged to be taking place is a somewhat special kind of nationalizing process. PAC giving may move the center of financial gravity from the districts to Washington. However, unlike the many nationalizing processes that have characterized American politics since the founding, this would not have the effect of counterbalancing particularistic tendencies. Rather it would substitute fragmentation along functional lines for fragmentation along geographical lines. Thus the effect would not necessarily be to stimulate legislators to take a broader, more national view. Rather the consequence might be to induce them to replace one kind of parochialism for another: seeing issues from the narrow perspective of truckers, rather than the narrow perspective of Manhattanites, or from the limited point of view of chiropractors, rather than from the limited point of view of Californians.

[62]On the question of how additional spending alters the electoral prospects of challengers and incumbents, see Gary C. Jacobson, "Public Funds for Congressional Candidates: Who Would Benefit?" in Herbert E. Alexander, ed., *Political Finance* (Beverly Hills, CA: Sage, 1979), pp. 99–128, and Gary C. Jacobson, *Money in Congressional Elections* (New Haven: Yale University Press, 1980).

[63]On the difficulty of assessing the effects of public financing of congressional elections, see Jacobson, "Public Funds for Congressional Campaigns," pp. 109–124.

Secondly, the argument that PAC giving weakens the links between legislator and district and therefore undermines accountability is made without benefit of empirical support. Since it contradicts the findings of scholars of the contemporary legislative process—who make a strong case that the bonds between congressmen and constituents have been, if anything, reinforced in recent years—it cannot be considered compelling without supportive evidence.[64]

There is similar disagreement as to the meaning of PAC activity for the quality of the electoral process. The experience with PAC-based independent expenditures has not been elevating. Some of the PACs that make independent expenditures have shown little regard for the niceties of the truth, producing campaigns that are at once dirty and polarizing. Many—though not all—friends of PACs join PAC antagonists in this view.[65] However, those who defend PACs conclude that the experience with independent expenditures renders direct PAC contributions to candidates all the more necessary. Since the *Buckley* decision endowed independent expenditures with protected status, none of the proposed reforms, including federal financing of congressional campaigns, would curtail them. In fact, reforms aimed at limiting the role of organization-based contributions would leave the field open for these kinds of expenditures.

PAC defenders make another point about the effects of PAC-based contributions on the quality of the electoral process. Although the media commonly rue skyrocketing campaign costs in an era of jet travel and television, most thoughtful observers agree that the sums spent on campaigns are not in themselves exorbitant and that it is important that a sufficient supply of campaign capital be forthcoming from somewhere.[66] The activities that permit campaigns to act as vehicles for the mobilization and education of voters are expensive; restrictions on PAC contributions as a source of campaign dollars would jeopardize these activities and thus the voter participation and discussion of issues that they foster.

A final concern is the impact of PAC contributions on the integrity of the legislative process. PAC opponents argue that in the current system of campaign finance, PAC donations constitute a form of what our respondent from Common Cause called "institutional bribery." As indicated earlier in the chapter, some of the assertions forwarded to deny this point of view do not withstand scrutiny, and the systematic evidence that can be used to evaluate this

[64]Variations on the theme of the modern legislator's attentiveness to the district can be found in David Mayhew, *Congress: The Electoral Connection* (New Haven: Yale University Press, 1974); Morris Fiorina, *Congress—Keystone of the Washington Establishment* (New Haven: Yale University Press, 1977); and Richard F. Fenno, *Home Style: House Members in Their Districts* (Boston: Little, Brown, 1978).

[65]See, for example, Malbin, "Of Mountains and Molehills," p. 181. For a contrasting view, see Rothenberg, "Campaign Regulation and Public Policy," pp. 42–44.

[66]A strong case is made that "most campaigns have too little, not too much money" in *An Analysis of the Impact of the Federal Election Campaign Act, 1972–78: Report to the Committee on House Administration of the U.S. House of Representatives* (Cambridge, MA: Institute of Politics, John F. Kennedy School of Government, Harvard University, 1979), p. 1.

point is incomplete. There is, however, sufficient information to indicate that easy dismissals of this concern are not warranted.

In short, any set of campaign finance regulations—or any set of political arrangements, for that matter—involves complicated trade-offs among cherished values: the right of the individual to influence public life, on one hand, and political equality and the integrity of the political process, on the other. However, as with controversies over so many procedural matters in politics, some of the concerns of those who argue so heatedly about the effects of PAC contributions on contemporary civic life are substantive, not procedural. That is, some who argue so persuasively in favor of retaining a role for PACs in campaign finance are politicians who themselves, or whose ideological or partisan colleagues, fare well when PACs divide up the booty. Some who advocate change are positioned less well to take advantage of PAC largesse without serious compromise of principle. It is, as we have pointed out with respect to a number of other procedural issues, a matter of whose ox is being gored.

11

Approaching Government Directly: Some General Considerations

In an era of heavy governmental involvement in virtually every aspect of American life, direct interchanges between government officials and Washington representatives occur in many arenas and take many forms. It is no longer simply a matter, if it ever was, of lobbyists confining their activities to button-holing legislators in the anterooms of Congress during the afternoon and bailing them out of their gambling debts at night. The three chapters that follow this one look closely at the ways in which organized interests attempt to influence policy in each of the three branches of the federal government: Congress, the executive, and the courts. However, before proceeding to an analysis of the involvement of private organizations in each of these separate policymaking arenas, we take up several discrete topics that are more generally relevant to the business of approaching government directly. Let us begin by considering the profession of being a Washington representative for an organized interest.

PROFESSIONALISM IN WASHINGTON REPRESENTATION

Lobbyists generally perceive that their profession is held in low esteem by Americans. One lobbyist epitomized the situation in the opening pages of his memoires:

> My mother has never introduced me to her friends as "My son, the Lobby-ist."

My son, the Washington Representative, maybe. Or the Legislative Consultant. Or the Government Relations Counsel. But never as the Lobbyist.

I can't say I blame her. Being a lobbyist has long been synonymous in the minds of many Americans with being a glorified pimp.[1]

Roland Oulette of the American League of Lobbyists, the organization that serves as the professional association of Washington representatives, takes this problem more seriously. He is concerned that lobbying as a profession does not enjoy a positive image within the public, and his organization undertakes many activities designed to improve the reputation enjoyed by government affairs specialists. He half-seriously suggests that what the profession needs is for there someday to be a television series featuring a lobbyist in a more favorable light—perhaps something like a Perry Mason of the government relations set— doing battle against all odds to preserve industry tax breaks, increase government subsidies for agricultural commodities, or prevent cuts in educational programs for handicapped children. According to Oulette, one of the inhibitions to public acknowledgment of the professional nature of lobbying is that there are no specific educational requirements for entry.[2]

This comment, echoed by lobbyist Charls Walker in his keynote speech to the League's 1981 conference, elicited the following tongue-in-cheek suggestion as to what the appropriate academic preparation might look like:

Let's imagine what a B.L.T. (bachelor of lobbying technique) curriculum might look like:

- *Arm Twisting 101:* Fundamentals of purveying information about your client's annual revenues, campaign contributions, and computer mailing lists. Euphemisms, code words and double-talk throughout history.
- *Introduction to Legal Semantics:* Points of distinction between "fit" and "not unfit," "ethical" and "not illegal." Implications of "receiving" versus "accepting" large sums of cash.
- *Senior Thesis:* Write a press release explaining why federal subsidies, price guarantees and government-granted monopolies are essential to the preservation of free enterprise.[3]

The absence of respect accorded to government relations as a profession is perhaps ironic, for a number of the respondents in our Washington survey remarked that the whole enterprise of Washington representation has become both more sophisticated and more professional over the past decade. They indicated over and over that it is no longer sufficient just to know the right

---

[1]Charles B. Lipsen and Stephan Lesher, *Vested Interest* (Garden City, NY: Doubleday, 1977), pp. 2–3.
[2]Interview, July 16, 1982.
[3]Gregg Easterbrook, "They Don't Get No Respect," *Common Cause,* December 1981, p. 23.

people. Now they must also marshal complicated and well-reasoned arguments. As the vice-president of government affairs for an international airline told us:

> The lobbying process has become more complex and requires more so-phistication. The old boy network has broken down. Now a lobbyist has to be much more articulate about the issues.

Furthermore, lobbyists buttress their arguments with complex technical information and research findings. Such data not only aid the government in making sound policy but help to present a group's case in a favorable light. A senior lobbyist for a large chemical company summed up the situation:

> Insofar as much of the legislation we deal with is technical, we're doing a lot more providing of research results and technical information. We often think of ourselves as educators. Up until ten or twelve years ago, the issues were not so technical and complex. As the issues increased in technicality, no one congressman could be expected to know all the technical information about the issues. As a result, there is a greater reliance on staff by congressmen and, in turn, the staffs rely on special interest groups for information.

Providing technical information clearly ranks high among the activities in which Washington representatives engage: 92 percent of our respondents indicated that they present research results and technical information to policy-makers; 63 percent said that they are doing it more in recent years.

The claim on the part of Washington representatives that their work has taken on a new level of sophistication and professionalism seems to be a common refrain with plenty of historical precedent. Describing certain congressional reforms that had the effect of opening the legislative process to public scrutiny, one author, writing in 1928, remarked that there had been "a revolution in lobbying methods . . . [that] has given to the title 'legislative agent' something of a professional standing," and that many lobbyists of the day saw a "welcome recognition by Congress of the new dignity of their calling and of the importance of the part they now play in the making of legislative decisions."[4]

The Underside of Lobbying

To the vice-president for governmental affairs at a large corporation, the new sophistication and complexity of lobbying are linked to a decline in the amount

---

[4] *Regulation of Congressional Lobbying* (Washington, DC: Editorial Research Reports, 1928), pp. 2–3. A similar celebration of the professionalism of the "new lobbyist" is contained in Richard W. Gable, "Interest Groups as Policy Shapers," *Annals of the American Academy of Political and Social Science* 319 (September 1958): 90.

of sleazy activity that we associate with lobbying in the age of the robber barons:

> To a large extent, the three B's—booze, bribes, and broads—have disappeared. Not altogether, you understand. But today, a good lobbyist must have the ability to draw up factual information—a lot of it—in a short period of time for people on the Hill who want it. . . . Nowadays, taking somebody to a football game or a goose hunt just doesn't quite make it.

It is interesting that our respondents, ordinarily quite forthcoming, did not respond to our inquiries about the seamy side of lobbying with their usual loquacity. In general, they feel that government affairs work as practiced today involves very little explicitly illegal activity. When asked about the Abscam scandals, in which members of Congress accepted bribes from FBI agents posing as lobbyists, only 3 percent of our respondents indicated that this sort of thing goes on all the time; 63 percent said that it happens only infrequently. In relative terms, those associated with corporations are somewhat more likely to regard it as a rare form of activity, while those associated with citizens' groups are least likely to think it is rare. (There was quite a bit of missing data on this question because many respondents simply refused to answer, saying that in their experience they had never been exposed to any such activity.)

Our respondents' uncharacteristic reticence limits our ability to draw conclusions about the extent of unsavory activity. However, there is nothing in the 175 interviews conducted for our Washington representatives survey (or in the half-dozen additional interviews we conducted with various policymakers and lobbyists to probe this particular question more deeply) to contradict the common wisdom among political scientists that there are so many legitimate avenues of influence in Washington politics that bribery is unnecessary.[5] A number of the people to whom we spoke indicated that any illegal dealings that might have transpired in days of yore surely had disappeared in post-Watergate Washington. While such comments would indicate that Washington pressure politics are cleaner than they once were, there is a striking similarity between what was being described as the reigning ethic for the post-Watergate 1980s and what Walter Lippman saw 50 years earlier:

> Bribery which consists of direct payment by private interests to officials is not very common in American politics today. But there are many subtle kinds of bribery which are very common. There is the bribe of campaign contributions. There is the bribe of free and favorable publicity. There is the bribe of reelection and promotion. There are all the bribes of little privileges

[5]For a presentation of this point of view, see Henry A. Turner, "How Pressure Groups Operate," *Annals of the American Academy of Political and Social Science* 319 (September 1958), p. 67, and Lester Milbrath, *The Washington Lobbyists* (Chicago: Rand McNally, 1963), pp. 274–282.

and special favors. There are the bribes of inside knowledge, the profitable tips on the stock market, real estate developments, public contracts, future fees, jobs for relatives, business for the partner of the officeholder. There are social bribes, election to clubs, invitations to dinner, visits to and from the elite, a good start for little Cuthbert and little Violet. There are bribes of vanity, to be flattered and made a fuss over. There are in short all the inducements, tragic and comic alike, for which men who put a low price on themselves sell their souls.[6]

Our interviews made clear that government affairs professionals still use these subtle forms of payment in their dealings with policymakers. Fifty-six percent of our respondents reported that they do favors for officials who need assistance; however, only 21 percent indicated that they have increased their use of this tactic in recent years, and only 2 percent deemed it an activity that consumes a great deal of time or resources. (Although, as we shall see in Chapter 13, organized interests have various resources at their disposal that can be used to induce cooperation from executive agencies, the kind of favors discussed here are directed, by and large, at members of Congress and their staffs and, occasionally, at presidential candidates.)

Our respondents do perform favors, and our interviews and the popular press contain abundant examples of the kinds of services rendered. Perhaps the most common kind of favor is the provision of information about technical matters to legislative staff. This activity is so obviously related to policy and to ordinary processes of interest advocacy that it might not even be considered a favor at all. In addition, some of the assistance provided to members of Congress, such as services extended to needy constituents, would probably not offend even the most tender-minded reformer. For example, a drug company executive described a situation in which, in response to a congressional request, he helped arrange for FDA approval of an experimental drug to help a young constituent afflicted with a rare disease. Other favors involve making life easier for policymakers. A lobbyist for a major health insurance company told us that his company programmed its computer to identify claims submitted by congressional lawmakers and other public officials so that they could be treated with kid gloves.

Many of the favors done on behalf of legislators involve helping them either to get reelected or to stay in touch with constituents. We have already discussed at length the most common of these favors, the PAC donation, as well as such related services as sponsoring fund raisers. Furthermore, because members of associations have concerns—and often an occupation—in common, their mailing lists are in demand by legislators wishing to send a message to a specially targeted population. Using such lists, a legislator can write a

---

[6]Quoted in Helen M. Muller, ed., *Lobbying in Congress* (New York: H. W. Wilson Company, 1931), p. 82.

personal letter to all the beneficiaries—doctors, teachers, home builders, whomever—of a particular piece of special interest legislation indicating his support of the measure.[7]

The kinds of favors that border most closely on bribery are those that involve payments of cash or the provision of goods and services for which policymakers would ordinarily have to expend personal funds. According to the manager for government relations of a large professional association:

> There's not too much of the illegal stuff but a lot of things that border on it: hunting lodges and fishing trips and golf vacations to Florida; big dinners. What's the real difference between a $10,000 cash payment to a senator and paying for a $10,000 dinner party to which the senator is free to invite his favored constituents and friends?

Such favors vary widely and are usually done on an ad hoc basis. One corporate lobbyist admitted that he now regrets having lent the company limousine to a congressman for his daughter's wedding. We could multiply such presumably unusual examples.

However, there are certain regularized channels for the funneling of cash or its equivalent to legislators. One is the honorarium. It is common practice for organizations to ask lawmakers to address conventions or meetings. The speech usually lasts less than a half hour; it is often a canned spiel and it rarely has been written by the legislator himself. Since the organization ordinarily picks up the tab for the speaker's expenses, and since association meetings and conventions are frequently held in attractive resorts, the lawmaker may get a free minivacation as part of the deal. Although there is a limit to how much a legislator can be paid for a single appearance—currently $2,000—there is no limit on the number of times he can address the same organization within the same year. Legislators are limited by law to a total of $20,940 annually in honoraria. (These rules are subject to frequent revision and may have been changed since this writing.) In 1982 members of the House and Senate earned over $4.5 million in such fees, twice what they had earned the year before. While some lawmakers donate their speaking earnings to charity, over 90 percent is kept by legislators for their own personal use.[8] Interestingly enough, Congress has seen fit to outlaw such speaking fees for policymakers in the executive branch, presumably to avoid potential conflicts of interest. As in so many other cases, however, Congress has exempted itself from the strictures it places on others.

[7]See William Haydon, "Confessions of a High-Tech Politico," *Washington Monthly,* May 1980, pp. 43–48.

[8]Figures taken from Brooks Jackson and Edward F. Pound, "Fees for Congressmen from Interest Groups Doubled in Past Year," *Wall Street Journal,* July 28, 1983, pp. 1, 14. On the rules governing honoraria, see Martin Tolchin, "Moonlighting Senators Race for Year-End Income," *New York Times,* December 13, 1983, p. B10. See also Mark Green and Michael Waldman, "Dishonoraria," *New York Times,* January 7, 1983, p. A25.

Policymakers—and their families—can get free vacations courtesy of organized interests in another way as well. It is legal for private organizations to pay for travel expenses (transportation, meals, and lodging) incurred on "fact-finding" trips so long as there is a "direct relationship to official duties." Although executive branch personnel also take advantage of opportunities to take fact-finding excursions and attend conventions and conferences in appealing spots, the rules governing congressional behavior are, once again, considerably more relaxed than those Congress has applied to the executive branch.[9] Whereas most executive branch personnel are barred by ex parte rules from discussing pending cases with interested parties, legislators have left themselves and their staffs untouched by restrictions on the places or the manner in which they are permitted to have contacts with those who have business before them. And although the ethics committee in each house of Congress will give advisory opinions to legislators who inquire about appropriate standards of conduct, interpretation of these standards rests with legislators themselves.

It is clear that at least some legislators take advantage of the freedoms they enjoy. For example, the chairman of the House Ways and Means Committee, the committee which handles tax matters, is in a position to influence the fortunes of virtually every organized interest on the Washington scene. Thus, contact with any of them can be legitimately construed as related to public business. The current chair of Ways and Means, Representative Dan Rostenkowski (D-Illinois), has not been shy about accepting hospitality. Over the six-month period beginning in November 1981, Rostenkowski was out of Washington for at least 45 days, in posh watering holes from Hawaii to Florida, as the guest of organizations ranging from the Outdoor Advertisers Association of America to the Distilled Spirits Council of the United States.[10]

These kinds of practices—the acceptance of honoraria and expense-paid travel—raise precisely the kinds of questions discussed so extensively in the previous chapter on PAC contributions. Persons involved in such practices tend to emphasize the educational function of interchanges in informal settings. They argue, furthermore, that policymakers are not swayed by such largesse and that what is being purchased is not influence but access. However, as indicated in Chapter 7, the line between access and influence is at best vague, since the former is often so crucial to achieving the latter. Critics worry that the various inducements constitute a form of legal and regularized bribery and argue that many organizations, particularly those representing the poor and others with few political resources, cannot afford them.

In summary, it is surely the case that now that congressional policymak-

---

[9]On the extension of association and corporate hospitality to policymakers in the Department of Defense, see Gordon Adams, *The Iron Triangle* (New York: Council on Economic Priorities, 1981), pp. 175–180.

[10]All information in this paragraph is taken from Ted Gup, "Golfing No Handicap for Rostenkowski," *Washington Post,* June 6, 1982, pp. A1–2, and Ted Gup, "Life in the Tax Lane: Staff Gets Trips, Too," *Washington Post,* June 7, 1982, pp. A1–2.

ing is more specialized and complex than in previous eras, there seems to be greater demand for lobbying that is professional and informed on the substance of the issues. However, a more professional demeanor in presenting arguments and technical information does not preclude the use of the kind of techniques that leave reformers queasy. Although the three B's have clearly not disappeared, their use does not seem to have accelerated as quickly as the employment of other techniques of influence. There does seem, however, to have been a clear increase in some of the completely legal inducements—PAC contributions, honoraria, fact-finding trips—that organizations can use to gain a sympathetic hearing from legislators or their deputies. Our original formulation thus requires slight modification. The received wisdom of earlier decades still holds today—that is, that bribery is a rarity in Washington pressure politics because there are so many legitimate channels for interest advocacy. However, some of the many legal channels for the expression of collective interests involve increasing amounts of cash being directed to legislators for their electoral and personal use.

LINKS WITHIN THE SYSTEM

Also relevant to the general issue of how organized interests approach the federal government are the links among the various institutions and actors on the Washington scene. We shall examine this subject from a variety of perspectives, considering in sequence the recruitment of former policymakers by private political organizations, the various institutional targets of pressure activity, the networks of communication linking Washington representatives with those in government, and finally the patterns of conflict and cooperation among organized interests.

The Revolving Door

One of the better-known linkages in Washington politics is the well-known interchange of personnel between the federal government and the private sector, a pattern of movement so regularized that it has been dubbed "the revolving door." Any election that brings a flock of new elected and appointed officials to Washington creates an equally large troop of former policymakers whose experience and contacts in government are marketable to the myriad private organizations that are involved in Washington politics. The movement is not confined to the former legislators and cabinet officials whose fancy offers are often chronicled in the press in the aftermath of an election. Like their bosses, staffers and lesser officials find the skills and knowledge acquired while in the government to be in demand in the private sector. The path through the revolving door is so well-trod that periodically a corporate ad like the following will turn up in the *Wall Street Journal* making the whole business explicit:

Table 11.1 THE REVOLVING DOOR

Percentage of organizations in which a professional on staff of Washington office has previously worked in the federal government[a]

	Corporations	Trade associations	Unions	Citizens' groups	All organizations
Federal government	90%	97%	65%	82%	86%
Executive branch	60	63	31	55	52
White House	8	15	6	10	9
Congress	46	63	31	30	46

[a] Figures probably underestimate number of organizations with staff who have worked in these institutions; (see footnote 12).

Source: Washington Representatives Survey.

"VICE PRESIDENT GOVERNMENT SYSTEMS—We are searching for a senior executive . . . DOD experience particularly helpful."[11]

One of the employment destinations of former government officials is lobbying. They may be employed directly by organized interests: former Senator Gaylord Nelson (D-Wisconsin) became the chairman of the Wilderness Society; Ron Ziegler, Nixon's press secretary, the president of the National Association of Truck Stop Operators. Others, like former Representative Wilbur Mills (D-Arkansas) and former Senator Jacob Javits (R-New York) join Washington law firms where they take on government relations tasks for clients. Still others—for example, Charls Walker, who was undersecretary in the Treasury Department under Nixon, and Anne Wexler, who was assistant to the president for public liaison in the Carter White House—hang out shingles as lobbyists for hire. Whichever particular professional designation a former policymaker adopts, he or she puts valuable skills and experience at the disposal of the organizations represented. Of critical importance is expertise—both technical knowledge of a particular substantive public policy area and political knowledge of government processes. Of equal significance is access—a wide network of contacts and personal acquaintance with key policymakers.

Table 11.1 shows that almost all of the organizations in our sample hire staff through the revolving door. In 86 percent of our organizations—ranging from 97 percent of the trade associations to 65 percent of the unions—a professional on the Washington staff has worked for the federal government. The pattern of former employment is particularly interesting. In view of the size of the federal bureaucracy and the attention that political scientists have paid to interchanges of personnel between agencies of the executive branch and the

[11] *Wall Street Journal,* November 22, 1983, p. 24.

private interests they regulate, it is not surprising that the largest number of organizations, at least 52 percent, employ former executive branch personnel.[12] In light of how relatively few people work in the White House, it is also not surprising that only 9 percent of our organizations have former White House employees on staff.

What is interesting is that nearly as many organizations, at least 46 percent, have staff with experience in Congress as have staff with executive branch experience. Political scientists have raised many questions about the effects on policymaking of the circulation of personnel between the executive branch and the private sector. There appears to be good reason to raise the same kinds of questions with respect to the revolving door between Capitol Hill and private interests. For our organizations at least, the phenomenon is of almost equal dimensions. It is interesting to note, in addition, that all kinds of organizations hire government relations specialists through the revolving door. That business organizations have former government employees on their staffs has been documented in the media. Less attention has been paid to the fact that citizens' groups and, to a lesser extent, unions engage in the practice as well.

Our figures for the numbers of organizations that hire former federal employees to do government affairs work are only a small part of a larger story. Former government employees are retained by private organizations, not simply to staff their Washington offices, but in many other capacities in which their substantive knowledge and political skills and contacts would prove useful. Defense contractors are notorious for the number of former Defense Department officials they recruit. One study of eight of the largest defense contractors found that they had hired 1,455 former military and 186 former civilian employees during the 1970s.[13] The practice is hardly confined to the defense industry, however. Former government lawyers from virtually any agency can find opportunities to represent clients from regulated industries. Other kinds of professionals in government—for example, scientists from the Food and Drug Administration—also find their expertise in various policy matters and their knowledge of how the government works to be useful to private employers. Our

---

[12]On the exchange of personnel between executive agencies and the private sector, and the meaning of that exchange for governance, see the discussion and attendant bibliographical references in Paul J. Quirk, *Industry Influence in Federal Regulatory Agencies* (Princeton: Princeton University Press, 1981), pp. 143–174, 187–191. We will return to this subject in greater depth in Chapter 13.

Because of a peculiarity in the way we constructed our questionnaire, the figures in the lower part of Table 11.1 probably underestimate interest group employment of former policymakers in the separate institutions. We asked our respondents if they had ever worked for the federal government and, if so, what they had done. If not, we asked if anyone else in the organization had ever worked for the federal government and, if so, what they had done. In the cases in which the respondent had been a government employee, say, in the executive branch, we would not pick up his coworker who had been a congressional staffer. Therefore, the actual figures are probably higher than those reported in Table 11.1

[13]Figures given in Adams, *The Iron Triangle,* p. 84.

figures are only part of the story in another way as well, since people move through the revolving door in both directions. Government agencies often re- cruit specialists from regulated sectors of the economy. Not surprisingly, these people bring to government service valuable expertise. They also bring with them perspectives gained from private sector experience that complicate the making of policy, especially regulatory policy. This issue, on which political scientists have pondered at length, will be taken up in Chapter 13.

There are laws that regulate the traffic of personnel from government to the private sector.[14] As amended by the 1978 Ethics in Government Act, these statutes prohibit former employees of the executive branch from ever represent- ing a client before an agency on a matter in which he or she "had substantially and personally participated while at the agency." Furthermore, former officials are not allowed to represent clients personally (although they can act as advi- sors) before their former agencies on matters that had once fallen within the orbit of their "official responsibility." High-level officials are barred from hav- ing any contact with their former agencies for a year after leaving. How well these measures deal with potential conflicts of interest in the executive branch is a matter of some dispute. Some reformers argue that they do not go far enough. Other observers reply that these laws discourage able people from serving in government and are thus counterproductive.

What is interesting, however, is that these restrictions do not apply to former legislators and their staff. We have seen that a substantial number of former congressional staffers find employment as lobbyists or public affairs specialists. Given the explosion in the size of legislative staffs during the 1970s, this trend has probably gained momentum in recent years. This would, presum- ably, raise precisely the same questions of bias and conflict of interest that are taken so seriously when it comes to the executive branch. Nevertheless, Con- gress has not seen fit to apply to itself the same standards it imposes on others.

Institutional Targets of Pressure Activity

The focus in the next three chapters will be upon the efforts made by organized interests to shape policy outcomes in each of the branches of the federal gov- ernment. We also wanted to get a sense of their relative centrality to the activity of organized interests. Therefore, we asked our respondents to evaluate the importance of various institutions—Congress, the White House, executive agencies, and the courts—as objects of Washington activity, recognizing, of course, that the focus of an organization's activity might well change from issue to issue or even over the life span of a single issue. The replies are summarized

[14]These regulations are summarized in Adams, *The Iron Triangle*, pp. 81–82; and Stuart Taylor, Jr., "Those Job-Hopping Carter People," *New York Times*, May 10, 1981, Section 3, pp. 1, 15.

in Table 11.2. Congress is clearly the premier institutional target: 89 percent of our respondents rated Congress as a very important focus of activity, and only 2 percent deemed it not very important. The courts are equally clearly of secondary importance: only 22 percent ranked the courts as a very important focus of activity for their organizations, and 51 percent considered the courts not too important. As shown in Table 11.2(b), these relationships are uniform across the various categories of organizations; all of them placed Congress well in front as the most important institutional focus and the courts in distant last place.

When it comes to the White House and, to a lesser extent, the executive branch agencies, however, there are some discrepancies among the four kinds of organizations. Corporations and trade associations were more likely to see the White House as an important target than were unions and citizens' groups; trade associations were, by far, the most likely and citizens' groups the least likely to deem executive agencies an important focus of activity. The differential focus on the executive agencies may reflect, in part, differences in the nature of the business that different kinds of organizations transact with the government. It may also reflect the structure of the executive branch. Some interests—for example, labor unions and agricultural organizations—have corresponding advocacy agencies in the executive branch with which they deal on a continuing basis; others do not. In addition, it seems that the relative emphasis placed by business organizations on contact with the executive, especially

Table 11.2 INSTITUTIONAL TARGETS OF ORGANIZATION ACTIVITY

(a) Recognizing that the focus of your activity may change from issue to issue or even over the life span of a single issue, in general, how important is [each institution] as a focus of your organization's activity—very important, somewhat important, or not too important?

	Very important	Somewhat important	Not too important		
Congress	89%	8	2	=	99%
White House	55%	32	12	=	99%
Executive agencies	65%	28	6	=	99%
Courts	22%	27	51	=	100%

(b) Percent responding "very important"

	Corporations	Trade associations	Unions	Citizens' groups
Congress	94%	91%	95%	92%
White House	67	59	37	40
Executive agencies	68	82	58	40
Courts	18	21	28	28

Source: Washington Representatives Survey.

the White House, reflects the particular character of the incumbents at the time the interviews were conducted. Chapter 9 examined the differential impact on the fortunes of various kinds of organizations of the arrival in Washington of the Reagan administration. Perhaps unions and citizens' groups were devoting less attention to the White House because they were not getting a receptive hearing there.

This suspicion gains some credence from the evidence presented in Table 11.3, which shows our respondents' evaluations of the changing importance of the various institutional targets. Again, Congress is most likely and the courts least likely to have been deemed increasingly important as a focus of activity. Once again, various kinds of organizations differ in their assessment of the White House. As shown in Table 11.3(b), corporations and trade associations are more likely than unions and citizens' groups to have reported growing importance of the White House as a point of contact. Figures not given in the table tell the same story: 25 percent each of the unions and citizens' groups, as opposed to 4 percent of the corporations and 3 percent of the trade associations, indicated that the White House has become less important as a focus of activity. Another bit of data also suggests that the Reagan White House is differentially receptive to various kinds of interests. We asked our respondents which two on a list of eight political institutions and actors they considered their principal competition in influencing the decisions of Congress. Eighty-two percent of the respondents from the unions and 50 percent of those from citizens' groups, as opposed to 36 percent of those from trade associations and 10

Table 11.3 CHANGING IMPORTANCE OF TARGETS OF ORGANIZATION ACTIVITY

(a) Over the past decade has [this institution] become more important, less important, or stayed about the same as a focus of your organization's activity?

	More important	About the same	Less important	
Congress	58%	39	3	= 100%
White House	49%	40	12	= 101%
Executive agencies	49%	43	8	= 100%
Courts	31%	62	7	= 100%

(b) Percent responding "more important"

	Corporations	Trade associations	Unions	Citizens' groups
Congress	60%	54%	62%	59%
White House	61	53	38	35
Executive agencies	50	54	44	45
Courts	23	50	33	24

Source: Washington Representatives Survey.

percent of those from corporations, chose the White House as a principal competitor.

Networks of Information and Consultation

Responses to two additional sets of items provide further confirmation that Congress is central to the activities of organized interests and that various categories of organizations are differentially likely to have dealings with the executive branch. We asked our respondents about the importance of 13 different channels of information in keeping themselves posted about what is going on in government. As shown in Table 11.4, congressional committee staff are clearly the most important source of information about what the government is up to: 86 percent of the respondents—in roughly equivalent proportions across all kinds of organizations—indicated that they are a very important source of information, and only 1 percent deemed them not too important. In addition,

Table 11.4   INFORMATION NETWORKS

To keep yourself posted as to what the government is up to, how important is each of the following possible channels of information?

	Very important	Somewhat important	Not too important	
1. Congressional committee staff members	86%	13	1	= 100%
2. Friends in other private organizations	67%	26	8	= 101%
3. Congressional members' personal staff	66%	26	8	= 100%
4. Members of Congress	61%	23	16	= 100%
5. Newspapers like the *Post* and the *Times*	50%	37	13	= 100%
6. *The Federal Register* or other government publications	49%	30	21	= 100%
7. The trade press	45%	33	22	= 100%
8. Mid-level bureaucrats	38%	39	24	= 101%
9. Party leaders in Congress	35%	24	41	= 100%
10. White House staff	30%	30	40	= 100%
11. Journalists	29%	39	31	= 99%
12. Cabinet officers or their deputies	27%	28	45	= 100%
13. Party leaders at the national committees	10%	9	80	= 99%

Source: Washington Representatives Survey.

three of the four sources of information cited by a majority of respondents as being very important are congressional.

A question about networks of consultation and cooperation in the planning of political strategy on policy matters elicited similar results. As shown in Table 11.5, congressional committee staff once again head the list: 85 percent of the respondents—across various categories of organizations—indicated that they almost certainly would plan strategy with them; only 4 percent reported that they would not be too likely to do so. Furthermore, a majority of respondents indicated that they would almost certainly consult and cooperate with four of the ten sets of political actors on the list; three of these were congressional.

In both cases there is evidence of greater involvement with the executive branch on the part of business organizations, as opposed to unions and citizens' groups. Thirty-six percent of the corporate and 47 percent of the trade association respondents, as opposed to 16 percent of the union and 13 percent of the citizens' group respondents, indicated that White House staff are an important source of information. Similarly, 26 percent of the corporate and 41 percent of the trade association respondents, as opposed to 16 percent of the union and 14 percent of the citizens' group respondents, indicated that they

Table 11.5 NETWORKS OF POLICY CONSULTATION AND COOPERATION

When you plan your political strategy on policy matters, how likely are you to consult and cooperate with the following political actors?

	Almost certainly	Somewhat likely	Not too likely	
1. Congressional committee staff members	85%	12	4	= 101%
2. Members of Congress	79%	12	9	= 100%
3. Friends in other private organizations	65%	28	6	= 99%
4. Congressional members' personal staff	60%	30	10	= 100%
5. Influential grass roots contacts	55%	23	22	= 100%
6. Party leaders in Congress	39%	27	34	= 100%
7. Mid-level bureaucrats	28%	28	44	= 100%
8. White House staff	27%	31	42	= 100%
9. Cabinet officers or their deputies	26%	35	39	= 100%
10. Party leaders at the national committees	8%	8	84	= 100%

Source: Washington Representatives Survey.

almost certainly would consult and cooperate on policy matters with White House staff. Interestingly, these relationships hold, with slightly greater strength, for mid-level bureaucrats and cabinet officers. (Complete data on which these generalizations are based can be found in Table D.3 of Appendix D.) As before, these patterns are presumably evidence of the differential receptivity to various kinds of organizations of the executive branch under Reagan. Citizens' groups might not be expected to have strong links with the bureaucracy because they do not have a single agency with which they do business on an ongoing basis. Unions do, however, have a clientele agency, the Department of Labor, with which they might be expected to have close ties. The absence of links between unions and the executive branch at the time the interviews were conducted thus seems especially noteworthy.

Subgovernments

We have seen that contacts between organized interest representatives and government policymakers entail mutual exchanges of information and consultation and cooperation on policy matters rather than simple one-way communications. This observation leads us to consider the kind of stable relations between public and private actors that are sometimes called "subgovernment politics." Subgovernments are relatively narrow, circumscribed, and autonomous sets of actors that operate virtually without interference to make routine policy in a given substantive policy area.[15] Subgovernments tend to be characterized by a low degree of turnover and relative impermeability to new members. The members of a subgovernment tend to know one another; their relationships tend to be long-term and stable. One particularly rigid form of subgovernment that is frequently discussed is the "iron triangle," which is a subgovernment consisting of an agency or bureau within the executive branch, a committee or subcommittee within Congress, and an organized interest united by their concern with a given policy matter. Iron triangles have been said to govern in many policy areas—for example, defense procurement, veterans' benefits, and agricultural subsidies.

Recently it has been argued that an increasingly open politics of highly technical issues is characterized less by subgovernments (especially iron triangles) than by "issue networks."[16] Issue networks are webs of policy activists

[15]The subgovernment phenomenon was originally described in Douglas Cater, *Power in Washington* (New York: Random House, 1964), and J. Leiper Freeman, *The Political Process* (New York: Random House, 1965). Randall B. Ripley and Grace A. Franklin use the concept in their analysis of federal policymaking, *Congress, the Bureaucracy, and Public Policy* (Homewood, IL: Dorsey Press, 1976). In addition, numerous authors have applied the concept to policymaking in a single substantive policy area. See, for example, Adams, *The Iron Triangle,* pp. 24–26; and A. Lee Fritschler, *Smoking and Politics,* 3rd ed. (Englewood Cliffs, NJ: Prentice-Hall, 1983), pp. 6–8.

[16]See Hugh Heclo, "Issue Networks and the Executive Establishment," in Anthony King, ed., *The New American Political System* (Washington, DC: American Enterprise Institute, 1978), pp. 87–124. Thomas L. Gais, Mark A. Peterson, and Jack L. Walker also conclude that iron

both within and without the government who are linked by their common commitment and expertise with respect to a particular issue area. They differ from subgovernments in being more porous and less clearly delineated: membership in issue networks is not frozen but, rather, shifts over time; the boundaries of issue networks are indistinct. Issue networks mobilize not only individuals with common political and technical skills and concerns, but institutions and organizations as well. Issue networks are larger than subgovernments, and membership in issue networks is based as much on shared policy expertise as on mutual political interest.

Although our data permit us to establish the existence of links between private organizations and public officials for the purpose of exchanging information and planning strategy, they do not permit us to map particular subgovernments or issue networks. Our data have two limitations from this perspective. First, we talked on a systematic basis only to representatives of organized interests and not to policymakers in the legislative or executive branches. Furthermore, while our sample has admirable breadth, it does not run deep. We talked to organizational representatives in a wide array of policy domains, ranging from transportation to education to finance to civil rights. In any particular policy area we have too few respondents to draw definitive conclusions.

We do, however, have some evidence that supports the notion of the more extensive, less clearly defined issue network rather than the ossified subgovernment. Our respondents' accounts of their legislative activities make clear that congressional policy is no longer made by circumscribed groups of powerful lawmakers. As will be shown in the next chapter, the changes that political scientists have observed in Congress over the past decade have had consequences for organized interests. The proliferation of subcommittees, the diminished importance of seniority, the increase in congressional staff, the greater number of policy entrepreneurs, and the rapid turnover in membership all imply that interest representatives must interact with a much larger number of legislators and staff than before. It is no longer sufficient simply to have close connections with a few powerful committee chairmen. Now lobbyists must cultivate contacts with a number of subcommittees and with a plurality of lawmakers attached to each one. All of this has the effect of broadening the relevant policy network in Congress. Similarly, with the establishment of a more vigorous presence on the part of citizens' organizations in Washington politics—especially among consumer and environmental groups—it is more difficult to confine policymaking to narrowly circumscribed sets of actors.

Our respondents' comments about relations with various components of the executive branch provide indirect evidence to suggest that the links are

---

triangles no longer govern policymaking—if they ever did. ["Interest Groups, Iron Triangles, and Representative Institutions in American National Government," *British Journal of Political Science* 14 (1984): 161–185.] Their findings parallel those presented here.

more fluid and less rigid than implied by the concept of subgovernment. At several junctures in the last several chapters, we have pointed out that the arrival in Washington of the Reagan administration had consequences for the fortunes of various kinds of organized interests and, in particular, seems to have affected their relationships with the executive branch. Presumably, subgovernments—especially, iron triangles—should be impermeable to the vagaries of electoral results. That unions (which have their own sponsoring agency, the Department of Labor) and citizens' groups have such weak connections to the executive branch leads us to conclude that policy networks are not immutable.

Our interviews with Washington representatives do make clear, however, that there is structure to their interactions with policymakers and that even though they must cultivate an expanded set of public officials, they still deal with a relatively limited set of government actors. Our respondents were, for example, quite reluctant to comment about the Washington scene in general. When we asked, for instance, a series of open-ended questions about which organizations active in Washington were gaining or losing power, our respondents tended to prefer to discuss only their own policy realm, indicating that there are narrower policy spheres in which these groups operate and sets of policy actors with whom they deal on an ongoing basis. In short, then, although our data do not make it possible to specify membership in particular issue networks, they do suggest the appropriateness of the image of the more extensive, less sharply delineated issue network.

Coalitions

The discussion so far has focused on the links between organized interests and various parts of the government. However, among the most important links in Washington interest politics are those that connect organized interests with one another. Chapter 3 introduced the notion of coalitions among organizations and some of the many forms they take. It was pointed out that coalitions vary in the degree to which they are structured formally by having scheduled meetings, an established dues structure, and so on; in the degree to which they are heterogeneous, bringing together partners who have little in common save their concern about a single issue; and in the degree to which they are long-lived, persisting beyond the resolution of a single controversy.

Our respondents confirm what newspaper accounts of policy disputes frequently indicate—that coalition-building is a crucial part of any organization's strategy of influence. As earlier chapters made clear, there is quite a bit of evidence to this effect. Chapter 7 indicated that 90 percent of the organizations in our sample enter into coalitions with other organizations. In response to an item about communications links through which political actors in various institutional settings plan joint strategy, 65 percent of our respondents reported that they would almost certainly consult and cooperate with friends in other organizations when planning strategy on policy matters. (Only 6 percent indicated that they would not be too likely to do so.) As such, friends in other organizations rank third on a list of 10 political actors. As a source of information about what the government is doing, friends in other private organizations rank even higher. Sixty-seven percent of our respondents said that they consider friends in other organizations very important as a channel of information, making it second on a list of 13 possible information sources. (Only 8 percent indicated that friends in other organizations are not too important as a source of information.)

What is more, coalitions among private organizations seem to be not simply an important, but an increasingly important, component of Washington politics. Sixty-seven percent of our respondents indicated that their organizations had increased their commitment to coalitional activity over the past decade. In terms of increasing use by Washington organizations, entering into coalitions ranks second on the list of 27 techniques of influence. The executive vice-president of a well-known environmental group told us:

> We build our strategy around coalitions. These coalitions are sometimes very informal, without a letterhead; sometimes they're formal.
>
> We try to go beyond the environmental community for coalitions when we're working on an issue. We try to look for the economic interests in an issue and try to build alliances with them. We've learned that the merits of environmental arguments alone aren't sufficient to carry the day. So we try to frame our concerns in line with one of the economic interests involved. Consequently, sometimes the unions are with us; sometimes they're against us. We've had coalitions with farmers, ranchers, Indians, and so on. When we were fighting off-shore oil drilling, for example, to put together a coalition with the commercial fishermen—a group whose obvious economic interest was threatened by the possibility of offshore drilling.

Patterns of Conflict and Cooperation: Lowi's Arenas of Power   The discussion so far has focused on the importance of coalitions, not on their substance. Useful for understanding who coalesces or conflicts with whom is Theodore J. Lowi's concept of arenas of power. Lowi's theory posits that patterns of conflict and cooperation among organized interests vary systematically with the nature of the policy at issue. He defines three different kinds of domestic policies, each having a characteristic configuration of organized interest activity—distributive, regulatory, and redistributive.[17] Let us describe briefly what is meant by each of these.

---

[17]Lowi lays out these categories in "American Business, Public Policy, Case-Studies, and Political Theory," *World Politics* 16 (1964): 677–715. He elaborates them (and adds a fourth category with which we will not deal here) in "Four Systems of Policy, Politics, and Choice," *Public Administration Review* 32 (1972): 298–310. We should note that his scheme is multidimensional. Each of the arenas is characterized not simply by a unique pattern of interest group interaction, but by a singular configuration of governmental actors, kind of power structure, and mode of bargain-

Distributive politics is, in essence, the politics of federal subsidy. Defense contracts, research grants to universities, special tax provisions, and federal aid for airport, road, or harbor construction are all examples of distributive policies. These policies are characterized by the way in which the benefits at stake can be disaggregated and granted to or withheld from individual supplicants in a manner reminiscent of the awarding of patronage jobs by a big-city machine. A billion-dollar program can be cut into a large number of nickel-and-dime items, thus widening access to the largesse contained in the distributive pork barrel. The politics of distributive issues tends to be nonconflictual because any party that feels deprived can simply be cut in for a share of the booty and the policy further disaggregated. In terms of organized interest activity, distributive politics tends to involve interests that are similarly disaggregated. In general, the individuals, firms, or localities seeking subsidies, grants, tax loopholes, or contracts are the principal actors. The characteristic bargaining style of the distributive arena tends to be the mutual back-scratching of logrolling as coalitions are formed between parties having nothing in common except their willingness to indulge another's desire to capitalize on governmental generosity in order that they may be similarly indulged in return. Policy is thus not made in a comprehensive way but, rather, emerges as the result of the accretion of many individual decisions.[18]

Regulatory policies involve government attempts to control potentially harmful private activities: deceptive advertising, the sale of unsafe products, monopolistic business practices, coercive union organizing techniques, the pollution of streams and rivers, and so on. Because regulatory policies involve the enunciation of general principles, they cannot be infinitely disaggregated like distributive policies. In addition, while the costs of the items in the distributive pork barrel are borne by the taxpaying public and may therefore be seen as being borne by no one at all, the objects of regulatory policies are only too aware that they are bearing costs. Because the burden of such rules ordinarily

---

ing. In this context, we will concentrate, not surprisingly, on Lowi's predictions about the nature of interest group interactions in each of the three arenas. (We should also note that there are affinities between Lowi's categories and those developed by James Q. Wilson. See Chapter 4 for an elaboration of Wilson's method of classifying policies.)

One study that uses Lowi's categories extensively to understand policymaking at the federal level is Ripley and Franklin, *Congress, the Bureaucracy, and Public Policy.* David Vogler also uses Lowi's scheme to investigate the nature of interest group influence in Congress in *The Politics of Congress,* 4th ed. (Boston: Allyn & Bacon, 1983), pp. 249–282.

[18] Implicit in Lowi's concept of distributive politics is the notion that there is unlikely to be countervailing pressure looking out for the taxpayer's interest in keeping down overall levels of spending. This may no longer be true, however. Since 1964, when Lowi first published his scheme, we have entered an era in which the ability of the American economy to sustain consistent growth—and the wisdom of steadily increasing government expenditures—have been called into serious question. Furthermore, changes in the budgetary process imply that the federal budget as a whole is subjected to greater scrutiny than before. It will be interesting to see whether distributive politics will be transformed in an age of scarcity, taxpayer revolts, and budget reconciliation acts. Ripley and Franklin (*Congress, the Bureaucracy, and Public Policy,* Chapter 4) point out that subgovernment dominance is especially likely to occur in the distributive arena.

falls on an entire industry, the groups involved in disputes over regulatory matters are typically trade associations, groups of firms that, although they ordinarily compete with one another in the marketplace (or for a defense contract), have common political interests.

While the coalitions formed on distributive matters are characteristically stable marriages of noninterference, the coalitions formed in the regulatory arena are typically temporary unions of organizations sharing a joint interest with respect to a particular measure. It is in regulatory politics that we find shifting coalitions among strange bedfellows, the kind of alliances of convenience to which a lobbyist for the National Association of Manufacturers was referring when he said: "On the Hill today, there are no permanent friends and no permanent enemies. There are only permanent interests."[19] Sometimes coalitions on regulatory matters bring together groups that are ordinarily antagonists. For example, Ralph Nader and the American Conservative Union found themselves on the same side on the issue of trucking deregulation. Sometimes these issues split old friends, as on the question of what to do about acid rain. Two solutions are proposed—requiring coal-burning utilities to install expensive scrubbers to reduce sulfur dioxide emissions or requiring them to burn costly low-sulfur coal. The coal industry, united on many political matters, is divided. In the East, where the coal is high-sulfur, the industry favors the former solution; in the West, where the coal is low-sulfur, the industry favors the latter.[20] Sometimes the members of coalitions in the regulatory arena are groups that ordinarily have little to do with one another. For example, the television networks joined forces with the cereal manufacturers over the regulation of TV advertising aimed at children. Such interests are ordinarily neither allies nor antagonists. Thus, the characteristic relations among groups are highly pluralistic in the regulatory arena; temporary coalitions form on the basis of mutual interest and dissolve when the matter at issue has been resolved.

In contrast to the unstable coalitions typical of the politics of regulation are the predictable, almost frozen coalitions that emerge when redistributive issues are at stake. Redistributive policies—the graduated income tax, welfare, public housing programs, manpower programs, and so on—reallocate benefits and burdens across broad aggregates of citizens. Such policies involve, as much as any in American politics, the interests of social classes or the "money-providing" as opposed to the "service-demanding" sectors of society.[21] Conflicts over redistribution tend to be highly visible and to engage liberals and conservatives in ideological and often partisan conflict. In terms of organized interest activity, redistributive issues tend to activate peak associations: on the liberal

---

[19]Quoted in Walter Guzzardi, Jr., "Business Is Learning How to Win in Washington," *Fortune,* March 27, 1978, p. 54.

[20]See "Acid Rain Dissolves the Lobbies," *Fortune,* August 22, 1983, pp. 85, 88.

[21]Lowi uses these terms—originally Wallace Sayre's—in "American Business, Public Policy, Case-Studies, and Political Theory," p. 711.

side, the AFL-CIO, the peak labor association; on the conservative side, the National Association of Manufacturers, a peak business association.

The coalitions that do battle on redistributive issues show a striking propensity to emerge over and over in similar form. Thus, one study of the politics of the Full Employment and Balanced Growth Act of 1978 (the Humphrey-Hawkins bill) found that the alignment of political forces on this largely symbolic measure to provide work for the unemployed was, by and large, the same as that which had prevailed 30 years before when Congress had passed the Full Employment Act of 1946.[22] What is more, although any particular redistributive measure may mobilize narrow interests having a special stake—doctors on Medicare, home builders on housing, and teachers on federal aid to education—the coalitions built around redistributive matters in quite different substantive policy areas have a remarkable resemblance to one another.

Thus Lowi identifies characteristic patterns of conflict over public issues, not within substantive policy areas such as health, education, or energy resource development, but within his three arenas of power. Politics in each arena has its own special configuration of institutional relationships, style of bargaining, and—most important for our purpose—structure of organized interest involvement. Coalitions crystallize differently in each of the three arenas. On distributive issues stable partnerships are formed in which there is mutual cooperation without joint interest; on regulatory issues, unstable alliances emerge, temporarily uniting interests having a common position on a single issue; and on redistributive issues, stable coalitions that persist from issue to issue join partners sharing an overall liberal or conservative political posture. In addition, organizations of differing levels of aggregation tend to focus on different arenas. Individual firms or localities tend to be involved in distributive politics, trade associations in regulatory politics, and peak associations in redistributive politics.[23]

Lowi's general scheme has been criticized on several grounds.[24] One charge that is sometimes leveled is that policymaking in actual political controversies often takes on attributes associated with the politics of more than one arena. Hence it is sometimes difficult to place a specific policy in one of the three categories. A well-known study of the passage of the Medicare bill in 1965 argues that the conflict assumed a shape typical of redistributive issues.[25] Yet, an analysis of the role of organized interests in congressional policymaking places exactly the same political controversy in the regulatory arena.[26] A second

[22] See Kay Lehman Schlozman and Sidney Verba, *Injury to Insult: Unemployment, Class and Political Response* (Cambridge: Harvard University Press, 1979), pp. 338–341.

[23] Lowi, "American Business, Public Policy, Case-Studies, and Political Theory," p. 709.

[24] See, in particular, the discussion and bibliographical references in Michael T. Hayes, "The Semi-Sovereign Pressure Groups: A Critique of Current Theory and an Alternative Typology," *Journal of Politics* 40 (1978): 138–139.

[25] Theodore R. Marmor, *The Politics of Medicare* (Chicago: Aldine, 1973), pp. 108–111.

[26] Vogler, *The Politics of Congress*, p. 272.

criticism is that Lowi's scheme accommodates economic issues far more easily than it does cultural issues such as abortion, crime control, or gay rights.

An additional point made about Lowi's arenas of power is that the political patterns typical of an ongoing policy may well differ from those evinced when the policy was first adopted.[27] An emerging issue may generate substantial conflict, particularly if a significant expansion of governmental powers is entailed. Once a policy is in place, it ordinarily loses its controversial character and politics of a more routine sort take over.[28] Important new initiatives in, say, manpower development may be accompanied by political conflict characteristic of redistributive issues, with long-established coalitions of liberals and conservatives battling each other and involvement of peak associations. When such policies come up for renewal, however, the bargaining may take on a more distributive character—as spokespersons for various categories of jobless workers (for example, the young or the handicapped) and officials of private and public agencies that administer the programs compete for specific benefits.[29]

Changing Patterns of Conflict and Cooperation   Our interviews with Washington representatives suggested to us some ways in which patterns of interaction among organized interests may have changed over the two decades since Lowi originally described his three arenas of power. We asked our respondents whether there are any organizations that they would consider their allies on most issues and any they would consider their opponents on most issues. Their replies attest to the existence of both stability and instability in the alliances among private groups. On the one hand, only 4 percent of those answering could not name a single group they considered an ally or an antagonist, indicating the presence of ongoing structures of competition and cooperation among organized interests. On the other, 33 percent said something to the effect of "it all depends on the issue" or "our coalitions shift" or named the *same* group as both an ally and an opponent, indicating the coexistence of pluralistic patterns of temporary, issue-specific alliance and opposition.

Because our respondents named hundreds of specific organizations in response to these questions, we have aggregated their replies in Table 11.6. We considered the "business" category to encompass corporations, trade associations, and peak business associations as well as general references to "business." We included under the "labor" designation all references to specific

[27]This point is made, in particular, by James Q. Wilson, *Political Organizations* (New York: Basic Books, 1973), pp. 330–331. Ripley and Franklin weave this qualification to Lowi into their application of his scheme to federal policymaking (*Congress, the Bureaucracy, and Public Policy,* Chapters 4–6).

[28]For a discussion of the politics of policy "rationalization" as opposed to the politics of policy "breakthrough," see Lawrence D. Brown, *New Policies, New Politics: Government's Response to Government's Growth* (Washington, DC: The Brookings Institution, 1983).

[29]On the politics of the renewal of the Comprehensive Employment and Training Act, see Schlozman and Verba, *Injury to Insult,* pp. 337–338.

Table 11.6   PATTERNS OF COMPETITION AND COOPERATION AMONG ORGANIZED INTERESTS

	Among business organizations	Among labor organizations	Among citizens'/ consumer/ environmental organizations
Corporations indicating they have:			
Allies only	66%	2%	0%
Both allies and antagonists	23	11	6
Antagonists only	0	19	53
Neither allies nor antagonists	11	68	40
	100%	100%	99%
Trade Associations indicating they have:			
Allies only	56%	12%	0%
Both allies and antagonists	26	3	0
Antagonists only	12	21	38
Neither allies nor antagonists	6	65	62
	100%	101%	100%
Unions indicating they have:			
Allies only	0%	79%	26%
Both allies and antagonists	16	5	0
Antagonists only	53	0	0
Neither allies nor antagonists	32	16	74
	101%	100%	100%
Citizens' Groups indicating they have:			
Allies only	0%	12%	68%
Both allies and antagonists	4	0	0
Antagonists only	64	4	12
Neither allies nor antagonists	32	84	20
	100%	100%	100%

Source: Washington Representatives Survey.

unions or to "labor" in general. We gathered under the rubric of "citizens'/ consumer/environmental" all references to specific groups or to these categories in general. If a respondent named one organization within a given community as an ally and another organization within the same community as an opponent, we considered the respondent to have both friends and enemies within that particular community—even though the same particular organization was not named simultaneously as an ally and an opponent. For example, a defense contractor might have named a corporate competitor in defense procurement as an antagonist and a trade association in the industry as an ally. In such a case we categorized the corporation as having both allies and antagonists within the business community, even though the allies and antagonists are different organizations.

Not surprisingly, organizations tend to have ongoing friendships with other organizations in their own communities. Eighty-nine percent of the corporations, and 82 percent of the trade associations cited allies within the business community. (Of these, 23 percent of the corporations, and 26 percent of the trade associations also have opponents within the business community.) Eighty-four percent of the unions reported alliances with other unions. (Of these, 5 percent indicated that other unions are also antagonists.) Sixty-eight percent of the citizens' groups indicated bonds with other citizens', consumer, or environmental groups. Furthermore, very few of our respondents reported antagonists drawn from their own communities. None of the corporations and 12 percent of the trade associations said that they have consistent opponents and no consistent allies within the business community; none of the unions and 12 percent of the citizens' groups listed antagonists but no friends within their respective communities.

Table 11.6 also indicates a not terribly surprising antagonism between business and labor. Thirty percent of the corporations and 24 percent of the trade associations mentioned antagonists drawn from the ranks of labor. Unions seem even more hostile to business: 69 percent of the unions listed opponents from the business community. Interestingly, Table 11.6 attests to the existence of at least some links between business and labor: 13 percent of the corporations, 15 percent of the trade associations, and 16 percent of the unions reported that they have allies within the opposite community. In view of the fact that the mainspring of politics in most industrial polities is the conflict between business and labor, even these tenuous links might seem surprising. We surmise that, in an age of scarcity, business and labor have some common as well as many opposing interests. For example, workers and management have joined forces in seeking government aid for ailing heavy industries (for example, on the Chrysler loan) and in seeking relief from foreign competition. Where business failure threatens large numbers of union jobs, labor and management have coincident interests.

Table 11.6 contains the somewhat unexpected finding that the antagonism between business and labor that is so fundamental to the politics of industrial democracies is overshadowed by the enmity between the business community and the axis of interests grouped under "citizens'/consumer/environmental." Business organizations are much more likely to mention such groups as consistent opponents than to mention unions: 59 percent of the corporations and 38 percent of the trade associations listed such groups as antagonists. Correspondingly, 68 percent of the citizens' groups reported opponents drawn from the ranks of business. Furthermore, the subtheme of cooperation amidst conflict that underlay the business-labor conflict is barely perceptible when it comes to citizens' organizations. None of the business or citizens' organizations in our sample mentioned allies but no opponents within the opposite community, and only 6 percent of the corporations and 4 percent of the citizens' groups listed both allies and opponents within the opposite set of groups.

Consistent with these results are the replies to another question. We asked our respondents how the rise of consumer and environmental groups had affected their ability to operate effectively in Washington. Only 2 percent of the respondents from corporations and 3 percent of the respondents from trade associations—as opposed to 69 percent of those from unions and 82 percent of those from citizens' groups—indicated that the rise of such groups had made it easier to operate effectively. On the other hand, 70 percent of the corporate and 66 percent of the trade association respondents—but none of the union and only 14 percent of the citizens' group respondents—said that this trend had made it harder to operate effectively.

All this may be evidence of a second set of stable antagonisms in Washington politics. Lowi pointed out that redistributive issues call forth time and again a set of frozen liberal and conservative coalitions. Our data would suggest that consumer and environmental issues elicit a consistent, though more fluid, set of coalitions pitting a segment of the business community against advocates of the broadly shared interests in consumer protection and environmental preservation. Such issues do not engage the attention of the business community as a whole in the way that redistributive issues do. What is more, on any particular issue, consumer and environmental groups may find allies within the business community. For example, environmentalists have joined forces with commercial fishermen on off-shore drilling; consumer groups have allied with insurance companies on the issue of installing passive restraints in automobiles. Still, although the precise content of the coalitions will vary from issue to issue, there seems to have emerged a consistent antagonism between business and citizens' groups. One explanation for the emergence of this hostility focuses upon the changing nature of government regulation in the early 1970s. Regulatory innovations during that period, especially in the fields of occupational health and safety and environmental preservation, were not—like previous attempts to regulate freight rates or drug safety—industry-specific. On the contrary, they affected business as a whole rather than particular industries. This had the effect of lending to new regulatory efforts a redistributive character.[30]

The responses to these questions also shed light on an issue raised in Chapter 4—the question of whether the political interests of business are uniform. Clearly, the business community does not always act in unison. Relatively few political controversies mobilize the business community as a whole. However, lack of uniformity of interest within the business community does not necessarily imply conflict among business interests. In our Washington representatives survey, only a minority of those associated with business—23 percent of those affiliated with corporations and 38 percent of those affiliated

---

[30]David Vogel makes this point in "The Power of Business in America: A Re-appraisal," *British Journal of Political Science* 13 (1983): 36.

with trade or other business associations—could identify *any* consistent opponents within the business community, and most who could named allies within the business community as well. Thus, clashes between business interests do not seem to be the norm. A more common pattern entails involvement of a portion of the business community—perhaps in conflict with consumer or environmental groups—and the indifference of the remainder.

There is another change in the patterns of conflict and cooperation among organized interests that bears brief mention. Lowi indicates that the principal private actors in the regulatory arena are trade associations because regulations ordinarily affect the fate of entire industries. While the structure of conflict has not changed since Lowi wrote, the nature of interest representation seems to have been altered. As indicated in Chapter 4, the past two decades have witnessed a massive migration of corporate public affairs offices to Washington. These days, not only trade associations but also individual corporations—often acting in concert with both their marketplace competitors and their trade associations—are active with respect to regulatory issues. Evidence of the involvement of individual corporations on regulatory issues emerged spontaneously in the course of the interviews as Washington representatives with corporations discussed issues on which they had been active in the recent past. In addition, 66 percent of them mentioned trade associations in their industries as consistent allies, and none listed them as consistent antagonists or both allies and antagonists. Thus, although regulatory issues continue to engage the interests of industries as a whole, individual corporations—now equipped with an enhanced capacity for political activity—get involved as well.

SUMMARY

This chapter has covered several discrete topics relevant to the ways in which organized interests approach the federal government directly. It began with a discussion of professionalism in Washington representation and the ancillary subjects of bribery and the kinds of favors and rewards that organized interests can provide to public officials. Although the increased specialization and complexity of policymaking in the modern era push lobbyists to make their case with substantive arguments and relevant information, there seems also to have been a simultaneous increase in some of the kinds of inducements—such as honoraria and cushy fact-finding trips—that organized interests can use to gain a more sympathetic hearing from policymakers, especially those on Capitol Hill.

Another prominent linkage between organized interests and government officials is the "revolving door" through which personnel pass on their way from jobs in government to employment in private organizations or vice versa. Most of the organizations in our survey hire staff through the revolving door and draw them in almost equal proportions from the executive branch and from Congress. However, when it comes to lobbying activity, Congress is clearly the central focus of most organizations. Naturally, organized interests are differentially likely to have principal dealings with different governmental institutions, but it is to congressional policymakers that the bulk of organizations look in an effort to keep themselves informed about what the government is up to, and it is congressional actors (committee staff members, in particular) with whom organized interests are most likely to consult and cooperate in planning political strategy on policy matters. While organizations in all categories are in agreement in the centrality of position they assign to Congress, different kinds of organizations attribute differential importance to the White House. Various bits of evidence indicate that the Reagan White House is more receptive to business organizations than to unions or citizens' groups.

Finally, we investigated the relationships among private organizations that are said to obtain in three arenas of power. Our data indicate that for the most part, organizations tend to have ongoing friendships with other organizations in their own segment of the Washington interest community and are unlikely to have antagonists within those ranks. In addition, the traditional enmity between business and labor that is said to be characteristic of politics in industrial democracies has been (perhaps only temporarily) overshadowed by antagonism between the business community and the axis of interests represented by citizens' groups, especially consumer and environmental organizations. Another important change in the nature of interest representation in Washington is the importance of corporate political activity as a supplement to trade association activity on issues having industrywide consequences.

12

Lobbying Congress

This chapter and the two that follow examine the various direct ways in which organized interests attempt to influence policymaking in each branch of the federal government: Congress, the executive branch, and the courts. Our concerns in these chapters are several: to understand the techniques organized interests use in each of these institutional settings; to examine how changes in institutional structure or procedure affect group activity; and to explore whether—or under what conditions—organized interests are influential in each branch of government. In addition, this particular chapter includes a brief appendix devoted to examining what Congress has done over the years to regulate lobbying activity.

CONGRESS AND ORGANIZED INTERESTS

In addition to mobilizing "indirect" grass roots pressure on legislators and helping them win elections—activities examined in the last three chapters— organized interests carry their case directly to the legislature. The direct approach of legislative lobbying involves organizational representatives in diverse tasks that put them in the thick of the legislative process. Lobbyists representing organized interests are a seemingly ubiquitous force on Capitol Hill, forging mutually beneficial relationships with legislators and their staffs, and finding ways to make the structure and operation of Congress work for them.

As in many other aspects of the political behavior of organized interests, the interactions between lobbyist and legislator are reciprocal or mutually beneficial: each participant has resources of various kinds—information, strategically placed allies, political support, and the like—that the other needs.[1] This mutuality of need binds legislators and lobbyists and draws representatives of organized interests into virtually every detail of both congressional politics and the legislative process.

Much of the direct lobbying by organized interests—just like the indirect forms—is designed to mobilize as well as to persuade; that is, many of the contacts between legislators and lobbyists involve, not attempts to convince opponents of the logic of a particular point of view, but attempts to collaborate with allies so as to maximize joint effectiveness. Thus, in reviewing the various kinds of contacts that the representatives of organized interests have with policymakers in Congress, it is well to remember that organized interests find it useful to conspire as well as to convert.

There are, of course, many ways that an organized interest may try to influence the course of legislative policymaking. We asked the respondents in our survey about eight different techniques of influence relevant to the legislative process: testifying at hearings, meeting with legislators to advocate a position, engaging in informal contacts with officials, presenting research results or technical information, helping to plan legislative strategy, helping to draft legislation, alerting members of Congress to the effects of a bill on their districts, and doing favors. Table 12.1 highlights information from Chapter 7 about the use of these various techniques. The data make clear that some of these activities are nearly universal among organized interests, and all of them (even the performance of favors) are used by a majority. In light of the evidence from the previous chapter that the vast majority of our respondents consider Congress the primary institutional target for their Washington activities, the emphasis they place on approaching Congress directly is easy to understand.

LOBBYING CONGRESS DIRECTLY

For an organized interest bent on influencing the course of congressional policymaking, there is no substitute for direct contact with individual congressmen and legislative aides. Just about all the Washington representatives interviewed in our survey, 98 percent, reported that their organizations use this technique, and clearly it is an important one: 36 percent of our respondents indicated that contacting officials directly consumes time and resources, more than any other technique. (These direct contacts between lobbyists and legislators have long been a source of concern to political reformers and have been regulated—

---

[1]On this theme see Raymond A. Bauer, Ithiel de Sola Pool, and Lewis Anthony Dexter, *American Business and Public Policy,* 2nd ed. (Chicago: Aldine, 1972), especially Chapter 24; L. Harmon Zeigler and Michael A. Baer, *Lobbying: Interaction and Influence in American State Legislatures* (Belmont, CA: Wadsworth, 1969), pp. 8–13; and Michael T. Hayes, *Lobbyists and Legislators* (New Brunswick, NJ: Rutgers University Press, 1981).

Table 12.1 USE OF TECHNIQUES OF INFLUENCE IN CONGRESS

	Corporations	Trade associations	Unions	Citizens' groups	All organizations	Rank[a]
Testifying at hearings	98%	100%	100%	100%	99%	1
Contacting officials directly	100%	97%	100%	100%	98%	2
Engaging in informal contacts—at conventions, over lunch, etc.	98%	97%	95%	96%	95%	3
Presenting research results or technical information	94%	89%	90%	92%	92%	4
Consulting with officials to plan legislative strategy	90%	89%	85%	83%	85%	9.5
Helping to draft legislation	86%	94%	85%	74%	85%	9.5
Having influential constituents contact their congressional representatives	77%	94%	85%	58%	80%	13.5
Alerting members of Congress to the effects of a bill on their districts	92%	74%	85%	58%	75%	17
Doing favors for officials who need assistance	62%	56%	68%	54%	56%	20

[a]Rank on list of 27 techniques of influence.
Source: Washington Representatives Survey.

although not effectively—by law. For a brief examination of what Congress has done to control the interactions among legislators and lobbyists, see the appendix to this chapter.)

In a private meeting in a legislator's office, organized interests can present their arguments away from the scrutiny of the media and beyond the manipulative reach of political competitors. Furthermore, this kind of direct contact affords lobbyists the opportunity to cultivate personal relationships with policymakers. As lobbyist and legislator get to know one another, mutual confidence, trust, and understanding grow. For the lobbyist, these bonds mean that getting access will be less of a problem: it is no longer "the lobbyist from XYZ Corporation" who wants a word with the congressman or top staff aide, but "Jim." For the policymakers, these direct interactions mean access to various kinds of information, assistance, and services that lobbying organizations can furnish.

Once forged, these relationships make it easier for lobbyists and legislators to meet briefly and speak frankly with one another without having to engage in the preliminaries and the posturings that necessarily characterize their early meetings. Whereas it is difficult for a lobbyist unknown to a legislator to command the latter's attention during a brisk walk between congressional office buildings, Jim from XYZ does not have to introduce himself, explain his organizational affiliation, and so on. He can spend the three-minute walk communicating a message, not identifying himself. These advantages of familiarity can be considerable for a lobbyist who needs to deliver information quickly right before a hearing or a vote. For this reason, diligent lobbyists routinely call on legislators' offices just to keep in touch, even if there is no measure pending that is of particular concern. Such visits are useful for cultivating access at those times when it is needed on short notice. These routine calls also serve another purpose for lobbyists, allowing them to demonstrate to others in the organization that they are working industriously to promote their interests. Furthermore, lobbyists hired from outside the organization (as opposed to salaried organizational employees) can bill for the time they spend keeping in touch with legislators and their staffs.

Although lobbyists ordinarily cultivate such congenial relationships as widely as possible, they are likely to be especially concerned with being on good terms with lawmakers who sit on the committees and subcommittees with which they have ongoing dealings. In particular, lobbyists attempt to nurture cordial relations with the chairs and ranking minority members of such committees. Furthermore, in selecting targets for legislative lobbying, representatives of organized interests ordinarily waste little effort attempting to convert diehard opponents. Rather, they concentrate on persuading those sitting on the fence and planning legislative strategy with allies.

Over the years organized interests have used many tactics for cultivating the access they need to make their pitch. In recent times lobbyists have learned to take advantage of legislators' increased electoral insecurity and their sensitivity to the expressed preferences and particularistic needs of their constituents.[2] Organized interests find that among the most productive ways to command a legislator's attention is through his constituents. Chapter 8 showed how Washington-based organized interests build pressure for their causes by inspiring floods of letters and telegrams from constituents to congressional offices. This use of constituents in the lobbying process also has a more direct form that one Washington insider facetiously called "the Utah plant manager theory of lobbying."[3] Simply put, the theory is that a senator from Utah may not make time to meet with a Washington lobbyist for a large conglomerate, but if the company sends in the manager of a branch plant located in the state, the senator can hardly refuse to see him.

The extensive application of the "Utah plant manager" approach is testimony to its reputed utility in getting access to legislators: 80 percent of all the organizations in our survey reported that they have influential constituents contact their congressional representative's office. Citizens' groups—only 58 percent of which reported having influential constituents contact their lawmakers—are relatively least likely to use this technique. This may reflect the very nature of the interests represented by such groups. Because they represent broadly shared public interests and because their members do not stand to benefit selectively from policy victories, there is no real analogue to the Utah branch plant manager, and membership in citizens' groups is rarely concentrated in a few intensely interested constituencies. The tendency of citizens' groups not to rely on this technique may also be a reflection of their relatively skimpy financial resources; for a citizens' group, the opportunity cost of bringing the Utah chapter president to Washington may simply be higher than it is for other kinds of organizations.

That trade associations use this technique most heavily (94 percent report doing so) confirms our impression that trade associations and peak business associations have particularly finely tuned systems for getting influential members to lobby their legislators. The Business Roundtable—a peak business association with a membership consisting of the chief executive officers of almost 200 of the nation's largest industrial, financial, and commercial institutions— was explicitly founded on the premise that the member of Congress who cannot find time in his schedule to meet privately with an unknown lobbyist from the business community will *make* time when the head of General Motors requests an appointment. Perhaps the most sophisticated program for applying pressure from influential constituents is that of the U.S. Chamber of Commerce, which

---

[2] Among the academic observers who have documented legislators' increased electoral insecurity and sensitivity to constituents' needs are David Mayhew, *Congress: The Electoral Connection* (New Haven, CT: Yale University Press, 1974); Morris Fiorina, *Congress—Keystone of the Washington Establishment* (New Haven; Yale University Press, 1974); and Richard F. Fenno, *Home Style: House Members in their Districts* (Boston: Little, Brown, 1978).

[3] Quoted in Bill Keller, "Special-Interest Lobbyists Cultivate the 'Grass Roots' to Influence Capitol Hill," *Congressional Quarterly Weekly Report,* September 12, 1981, p. 1741.

maintains a network of Key Resource Personnel (KRPs) in towns throughout the United States. A KRP is an individual member of the national Chamber (through his company or local chamber) who has direct access to a representative or senator. The access these KRPs enjoy derives, not from their institutional status as plant managers or state chapter presidents (although they may be these, too), but from their personal status as friends, relatives, or major campaign contributors of the lawmaker. The Chamber uses these relationships to gain access to legislators and win a friendly hearing for business's viewpoint.[4]

Capitol Hill is not the only setting for the interchanges between lobbyists and legislators. Some of the contact between lawmakers and interest representatives occurs naturally as these people conduct their lives in Washington; they see each other at meetings, at receptions and parties, and in the neighborhoods they cohabit. More to the point, however, are the myriad opportunities arranged by organized interests for their representatives to meet more informally with legislators.

"Social" Lobbying   The dean of nineteenth-century lobbyists, Samuel Ward, once held that "the way to a man's 'aye' is through his stomach."[5] Although the arts of influence have changed considerably from the days when lobbyists routinely plied congressmen with wine, women, and song, contemporary organized interests almost all engage in "social" lobbying, nurturing relationships with government officials by providing them with relaxation and entertainment: cocktail parties, three-martini lunches, lavish dinners, tickets to the theater or to sporting events, deep-sea fishing expeditions, and the like. A lobbyist who provides such pleasures has a chance to cultivate a legislator's friendship and trust. The idea is to provide a relaxed setting in which legislators and representatives of the interests can get to know one another better and discuss matters of mutual concern. Most such meetings are quite low key and involve no direct lobbying by interest representatives; if they need to ask for a legislative favor, they make the request at some other time.[6]

It is difficult to assess the extent to which this kind of social lobbying implicitly puts a lawmaker under obligation to his hosts. The interpretation given by lobbyists themselves is that what is being purchased is not influence but access. But as earlier chapters have indicated, such a distinction is difficult

---

[4]For examples of the KRP network in operation, see Mark Green and Andrew Buchsbaum, "How the Chamber's Computers Con the Congress," *Washington Monthly* 12 (May 1980): 49–50.

[5]Quoted in Karl Schriftgiesser, *The Lobbyists* (Boston: Little, Brown, 1951), p. 14.

[6]For example, at their regular "Capitol Hill Breakfasts," officers and lobbyists for the American Institute of Certified Public Accountants (AICPA) make it a point not to present legislators with a list of the profession's grievances or requests for special assistance. Although direct advocacy is avoided at breakfast itself, it occurs throughout the rest of the day as group representatives fan out in small groups for additional meetings with legislators in the Senate and House office buildings. For a description of the AICPA's "Congressional Breakfast Program," see Thomas G. Bisky, "Capitol Hill Breakfasts," *Journal of Accountancy,* August 1981, pp. 50–52.

to sustain in practice. In any political dispute there is rarely only one side to the story. The examination in Chapter 7 of the byssinosis controversy showed that a policymaker who listens to two sides of a story would be likely to have a different impression of the dimensions of a problem and the wisdom of proposed remedies from that of a policymaker who hears one side only. A legislator who hears from one interested party is not necessarily acting on feelings of indebtedness for hospitality rendered if he is persuaded by the obviously sincere and seemingly reasonable arguments being offered by his onetime hosts, for he has not been exposed to the equally sincere and reasonable positions taken by the opposition. Hence, while it is important to distinguish access from influence in the abstract, access probably begets influence in practice. Correlatively, unequal access presumably begets unequal influence.

Not all organizations have the wherewithal to engage in the more elegant forms of social lobbying. For example, in 1981, just before the House Appropriations Committee held its markup sessions on the Defense Department budget, the vice-president for government affairs at Hughes Helicopters Inc.—the prime contractor on a controversial attack helicopter that had run substantially over the original cost estimates—learned that two committee members wanted to go elk hunting. He arranged for the two to take a three-day hunting trip in Montana and found a speaking engagement for one of them in order to pay the costs of the trip.[7] Presumably, the lobbyists for a smaller, less affluent organization like the Coalition for a New Foreign and Military Policy—a group committed to reducing federal military spending in favor of spending on "human needs"—would be hard-pressed to make such arrangements.

Testifying at Hearings

In addition to the many informal avenues of access to legislators, lobbyists for most organized interests avail themselves of a more formal mode: testifying at congressional hearings. Indeed, this is the most widely used of the 27 techniques of influence. What is more, the Washington representatives with whom we spoke deemed it an important activity: 27 percent mentioned testifying at hearings as one of the three activities on the list of 27 that consume the most time and resources. (Only contacting officials directly was chosen more frequently.)

It is not surprising that testifying is such a widely used technique. After all, the practice of holding committee hearings is associated historically with

---

[7]See Walter Pincus, "Helicopter Maintenance on the Hill," *Washington Post,* March 14, 1982, pp. A1–2. To appreciate more fully the David-and-Goliath character of this case and others like it, one need only consider how Hughes's resources in this lobbying effort were supplemented by those of some other corporate giants that are major subcontractors on the Apache helicopter program—General Electric, Martin-Marietta, Litton, Rockwell International, and Teledyne Ryan Aeronautical.

the right of citizens to petition government, either in support of or in opposition to a proposed action.[8] And at least one scholar has argued that the development of the public hearing in the United States "was a consequence of the
proliferation of interest groups and of the challenge to established interests that
their claims constituted."[9] But the exceptionally widespread use of formal testimony as a lobbying technique by contemporary organized interests has far
less to do with its historical origin than its extraordinary usefulness.

Foremost, of course, is that hearings are an opportunity for interest
groups to present carefully reasoned arguments and technical information
bearing on the issue at hand. Witnesses at hearings often supplement their
testimony with the submission to the committee of stacks of documents to
substantiate the organization's position further. Interests also get involved in
congressional hearings in order to shape the legislative record in ways that may
work to their advantage at later stages of the policymaking process, when
executive agencies or the federal courts are scrutinizing the record to gain a
better understanding of congressional intent. Testifying at hearings may also
provide organizations with access to key legislators whom they may not have
been able to contact in more private and direct ways. Finally, the presentation
of testimony before congressional committees may be a way for an organization's leaders or Washington representatives to persuade members (or corporate headquarters) that they are actively pursuing the organization's political
interests.

In addition, congressional hearings sometimes offer organized interests a
propaganda forum that is virtually unparalleled in Washington. On occasion,
the subject of a hearing invites such widespread attention that participating
interests can count on having network television correspondents and reporters
from the major print media among their audience. In light of the potential
benefits of an effective appearance at such a hearing, organizations sometimes
go to great lengths to make their testimony outstanding. They hire public relations consultants to help them rehearse their statements before the hearing;
they try to make sure that on the day of their testimony the hearing room is
filled with their members or allies; they prearrange for friendly committee
members to ask leading questions designed to permit them to make their best
case; and they hire political consultants to help them "clean up" their remarks
before the hearing transcripts are printed.[10]

Just as organized interests use congressional hearings to their best advantage, the appearance of interest representatives at hearings is often orchestrated
to advance the interests of committee members or staff. Legislators and their
aides may use organized interests to develop a hearing record that will be useful
for the subcommittee or committee in justifying its decisions to other policy

[8]William J. Keefe and Morris S. Ogul, *The American Legislative Process,* 5th ed. (Englewood
Cliffs, NJ: Prentice-Hall, 1981), pp. 205.

[9]David B. Truman, *The Governmental Process* (New York: Knopf, 1953), p. 373.

[10]See Bill Keller, "Special-Interest Lobbyists Cultivate the 'Grass Roots,' " p. 1742.

actors in Congress or in other branches.[11] Legislators and their aides may also manipulate the hearing machinery so as to make their preordained decision on a bill appear to be a legislative judgment reached by rational, objective deliberation. They may do this in many ways: by inviting the most cogent and convincing witnesses to testify on behalf of the measure; by trying to minimize the number of strong opposition witnesses; by giving "friendly" witnesses free rein to make their strongest case but bearing down on "unfriendly" witnesses with embarrassing or confining questions; by arranging for the hearing to end at a favorable time; and so on.[12]

Providing Information

The discussion so far has examined some of the forms that lobbyist-legislator contacts take, but has revealed relatively little about the substance of those contacts. Let us now consider the kinds of information and services that lobbyists furnish to legislators in order to understand both why lawmakers give lobbyists so much of their time and how lobbyists exercise influence over the legislative process.

Legislators' greatest need is for information. Members of Congress are confronted with a staggering number of complex issues about which they are expected to make informed judgments. In the face of these complexities, members of Congress need all the help they can get in trying to determine the consequences of their assorted legislative decisions—who will be affected, in what ways, to what extent, and with what reaction.[13]

The kind of detailed, up-to-the-minute information that legislators need is often difficult to obtain and expensive to collect. Nevertheless, organized interests find it useful to try to produce such information when congressional policy issues touch their areas of concern. Nearly all organized interests with Washington offices do this. Over 90 percent of those contacted in our survey indicated that their organizations present research results and technical information. Moreover, as Chapter 7 indicated, this activity is an important one: 27

[11]On this point, see Kenneth J. Meier and J. R. Van Lohuizen, "Interest Groups in the Appropriations Process: *The Wasted Profession* Revisited," *Social Science Quarterly* 59 (1978), p. 494.

[12]See Julius Cohen, "Hearing on a Bill: Legislative Folklore?" *Minnesota Law Review* 37 (1952): 38–39. Cohen also indentifies other manipulative tactics used by legislators and aides to further their policy goals: writing the committee report in such a way as to bring out the best features of the testimony favoring the bill and the most unfavorable features of the opposition's testimony; ignoring facts or evidence which do not support their preconceived notions or preferences; and "killing the bill with kindness"—that is, giving it such a lengthy hearing that neither house of Congress has time to consider the measure prior to adjournment.

[13]Richard A. Smith argues that it is virtually impossible for members of Congress to engage in such an exercise because their time is limited and the calculations are so complex. Consequently, legislators construct "interpretations" of the consequences of their decisions—simple models of the ways in which their decisions affect their constituents and ultimately affect their own personal goals. See "Advocacy, Interpretation, and Influence in the U.S. Congress," *American Political Science Review* 78 (1984): 44–63.

percent of our respondents selected it from the list of 27 activities as one that consumes time and resources, putting it in second place along with testifying at hearings.

Technical Information   Input from organizations is likely to be especially important on issues involving highly complex economic or technical problems. Consider, for example, the policy area of nuclear power, which is affected by complicated, risky, and uncertain scientific and technological processes. Policy decisions relating to the timing and direction of nuclear energy development depend on technical information concerning the health and safety effects of the nuclear fuel cycle, the reliability and cost of different technologies, and the availability of various alternative energy resources. Because scientists and antinuclear groups also provide information, the Atomic Industrial Forum (AIF) lacks a complete information monopoly. However, the AIF's input is important. Politicians have to rely on the industry not only to provide them with answers to technical questions but also to inform them of the assumptions embedded in those answers and their implications for policy choices. It is with respect to this last set of questions that the provision of information begins to merge with advocacy.

The discussion about political resources in Chapter 5 indicated that the most highly valued is a reputation for credibility. In line with this, the respondents in our survey stressed that the information they present must be accurate and reliable because they would lose legislators' confidence if they were found to be misrepresenting the facts. Many of them dwelled on the untoward consequences of presenting bad advice or distorted information. If it were detected or if it led to the embarrassment of those who relied on it, the organization responsible for it could lose badly needed contacts and channels of communication. Thus, in presenting information to Congress, organizations avoid outright misrepresentation but attempt to place the facts in a favorable light.

For their part, legislators and their staff aides understand that the information provided by organized interests is tendentious—that, especially when information is supplied to buttress a particular point of view, the process of gathering and presenting information entails selection and, thus, inevitably introduces bias. In a recent study exploring how Congress deals with highly technical issues, one legislative staff aide is quoted as saying:

Everybody has a vested interest, and it's reflected in what they're telling you. But I honestly find it easier to deal with information when you know there's a vested interest, because you can interpret that information according to the bias, which is easier in some cases than testing the accuracy of the data itself.[14]

[14]Susan E. Fallows, "Technical Staffing for Congress: The Myth of Expertise" (Ph.D. dissertation, Cornell University, 1980), p. 103.

Another congressional staffer echoed this concern:

> If we don't know about an issue or a technology, we talk to everyone we
> can about it. We talk to the lobbyists. The industry and environmental
> groups are always anxious to see you. . . . We know we're getting biased
> information from everybody. But in just about every case we can pretty well
> figure out what the direction of that bias is and what effect it's likely to have
> on the data. We look for areas of agreement and assume that stuff is valid.
> On the things where disagreement exists, you keep going to other sources
> to try to finally elucidate the common ground and the area of dispute. Then
> in that area, we have to use our judgment.[15]

In their emphasis upon the importance of hearing from all points of view, these
remarks highlight once again concerns about equality of representation. Chapter 4 demonstrated that not all interests are equally likely to receive vigorous
advocacy; in particular, the interests of broad publics and those having few
political resources are at a disadvantage. In addition, several earlier chapters
have shown that organizations in a position to offer inducements such as honoraria or campaign contributions enjoy increased access to policymakers. What
this means is that policymakers will not always have information from multiple
sources to sift and evaluate. In such cases, legislators who are sensitive to the
potential bias in the information provided by an interested party have no countervailing information against which to measure it.[16]

Political Intelligence   Organized interests also trade political intelligence with
policymakers in Congress. A member of Congress intent on winning passage of
a favored piece of legislation will exchange information with an allied interest
about the alignment of political support and opposition to the measure, the
likely tactics of opponents, and so on. Perhaps the most valuable political
intelligence an organization can provide to a legislator is information about
how his or her home district would be affected by the enactment of a bill. It is
not always easy for a legislator's staff to derive this kind of information from
the kinds of aggregate data that are so often employed in debates on national
policy issues. But the organized interests that are often the sources of the
aggregate data are in a position (and have an incentive) to furnish information
about a bill's effects on particular states or localities. As noted above, one of
the ways organizations deliver this information to lawmakers is by bringing
local notables to Capitol Hill to emphasize the effects of proposed legislation at
home.

[15]Ibid., pp. 103–104.
[16]It is also true, however, that these processes are highly interactive. Legislators and their
staff aides seek out information from the organized interests. It is not just a matter of organized
interests providing biased information.

On this basis it is not surprising that the figures in Table 12.1 show that high percentages of the corporations and unions in our survey reported "alerting members of Congress to the effects of a bill on their districts" as a technique of influence. Most corporations and unions regularly monitor legislative proposals that would have discernible effects on their local operations or memberships, and it is easy for them to put these consequences in terms that are "politically meaningful" to a member of Congress. Lockheed can demonstrate to a legislator the effects on his or her district if Congress fails to appropriate money for an aerospace system manufactured there; the National Association of Letter Carriers can tell a legislator how many mailcarriers in his district would lose their jobs if Congress mandated an end to Saturday mail deliveries. Conversely, the kinds of widely shared collective ends pursued by most citizens' groups do not always lend themselves easily to disaggregation, so it makes sense that substantially fewer citizens' groups (58 percent) report the use of this kind of political intelligence as a lobbying technique.

Providing Services, Assistance, and Support

In addition to furnishing members of Congress with information, organized interests also provide them with a wide assortment of valued services, assistance, and support. As earlier chapters have shown, some of this comes in the form of honoraria, PAC contributions, and the like. Organized interests also provide legislators with assistance and services of a more policy-relevant character. In doing so, interests are not mere suppliants, earnestly imploring legislators to decide in their favor; they provide members of Congress and their staffs with valued information and assistance that can work to the mutual advantage of both parties. And much as they may complain of being besieged by swarms of lobbyists, legislators also benefit substantially from interest groups' efforts on their behalf.

The American legislative process is a labyrinth, perplexing even to those who have negotiated its pathways for years. Although members of Congress have no shortage of help in performing basic legislative chores, the assistance they get from organized interests can be especially helpful. As shown in Table 12.1, 85 percent of those interviewed in our survey—across all kinds of organizations—reported that they help to draft legislation, and an equal proportion reported that they help in planning legislative strategy.

Representatives of organized interests typically have a thorough understanding of existing laws and programs and can provide useful aid in fashioning a bill that has an appropriate fit with existing statutes and governmental activities. Moreover, because lobbyists are so thoroughly a part of the "issue networks" that underpin most policy areas, they are in a position to advise their congressional allies on the best legislative strategy for coalescing needed majorities and neutralizing opponents. Organized interests can offer crucial strategic advice on such matters as the timing of an amendment or the substance of a substitute bill, the need to compromise on a contested provision, and the best procedural defense against the stratagems of opponents. For example, an organization opposed to a bill may see that it has substantial support in a standing committee and strong support in both houses of Congress, but still kill the measure by working successfully with allies on the Rules Committee to see that the bill is not allowed to reach the floor for a vote.

In addition to helping members of Congress usher a bill through complex legislative processes, organized interests also furnish them with various kinds of assistance that otherwise ease their work as elected officials. Chapter 10 explored what is surely the most conspicuous form of such assistance offered by organized interests: help in financing electoral campaigns. Not only do organizations give to legislative campaigns through their PACs, but they may also give additional assistance by holding a fund raiser. In addition, there are many other kinds of assistance that are less well known but important nevertheless.

For example, interest groups write a lot of the speeches that members of Congress give and a lot of the articles that appear under legislators' by-lines. Although the sizable personal staffs with which contemporary lawmakers are endowed furnish their bosses with much of the verbiage that is politicians' stock-in-trade, friendly organizations are also a frequent provider of this kind of service. A professional society or union that invites a member of Congress to give the keynote speech at its convention may receive an affirmative answer only if it agrees to furnish a prepared text. A legislator who supports a particular trade association's position on impending legislation may authorize the trade group to write a magazine article or newspaper op-ed piece to be submitted in his name. Both parties to such an arrangement benefit. The organization that may otherwise have trouble getting its position before the public has it conspicuously advocated by a member of Congress; for his part, the legislator gets the publicity benefits of having his name in print and wins both credit with the group's immediate constituents and credibility with a wider audience of sympathetic supporters.

LOBBYING ACTIVITY IN A CHANGED CONGRESS

As a legislative body, Congress has traditionally been characterized by a fragmentation of power that has provided avenues of access for organized interests. Over the past decade students of Congress have documented a number of changes on Capitol Hill that have had the effect of dispersing power in Congress even more. Among these changes are the proliferation of subcommittees, the diminished importance of seniority, the increase in the numbers and professionalism of congressional staff, the greater number of policy entrepreneurs, the requirements for open meetings, and the rapid turnover in congressional membership. These changes have had consequences for the organized interests that approach Congress, multiplying the number of actors in Congress to whom an organized interest might usefully seek access and increasing the number of points in the lawmaking process at which interests may try to exert influence.

These changes have thus led to an across-the-board increase in the volume of legislative lobbying. They have left organized interests bent on influencing officials with little choice but to escalate the range and volume of their activities. However, while all kinds of organizations reported increasing their Washington political activity in response to these changes in Congress, the changes seem to have had a differential impact on the ability of various kinds of groups to achieve their political goals. As the following discussion makes clear, citizens' groups view these changes as being much more benign than do other kinds of organizations.

In view of the many changes in governmental procedure and structure over the past decade, we wanted to understand their impact on organized interests and therefore asked the Washington representatives in our survey about them. Early in our interviews we asked our respondents whether there had been changes over the past decade in the way their organization goes about trying to influence what goes on in Washington. We were surprised neither that the answers to this open-ended question went off in a variety of directions nor that the most common reply was something to the effect that "we are more active these days." However, we were somewhat surprised when the largest number of our respondents attributed their increased activity to recent changes in congressional organization and procedure.[17] Because the political patterns are intricate, these changes—and their consequences—bear closer scrutiny.

Multiplication of Subcommittees   In the aftermath of procedural reforms in Congress—especially the House—that diminished the powers of committee chairmen and multiplied the number of subcommittees, it is no longer possible for an organized interest to make its case effectively by contacting only a few powerful legislators.[18] This complaint surfaced repeatedly in our interviews. For example, the director of a large federation in the food industry lamented: "It used to be that if you had connections with a few powerful chairmen in Congress, you were all set. Now it is important to have contact with a wide number of members." The vice-president for governmental affairs of one of the

[17] In response to this open-ended inquiry, a few of our respondents (5 percent) linked their increased activity to the escalated efforts of their opponents. Fourteen percent of those replying to our open-ended question mentioned that their organizations had become more politically involved in response to the fact that the government has grown so much and become so much more intrusive. Twice as many (28 percent) connected their increased activity to the changes in Congress. For a discussion of these findings, see Kay Lehman Schlozman and John T. Tierney, "More of the Same: Washington Pressure Group Activity in a Decade of Change," *Journal of Politics* 45 (1983): 351–377.

[18] On this point, our findings support the argument of Roger Davidson, "Subcommittee Government—New Channels for Policymaking," in Thomas E. Mann and Norman J. Ornstein, eds., *The New Congress* (Washington, DC: American Enterprise Institute, 1981), p. 130.

big oil companies expressed a similar sentiment regarding the consequences of this fragmentation of power: "With the dramatic changes in Congress, we have had to broaden our operation. We must make a lot more contacts with people on the Hill. We have to touch more bases; knowing the committee chairman is not enough."

Not only must organized interests now cultivate a broader range of individual contacts than they did before, but they must also respond to the expanded information demands from the growing number of subcommittees. The changes in the field of nuclear energy have been particularly striking. Prior to 1976, one committee—the Joint Committee on Atomic Energy—had jurisdiction over nuclear matters. Since that panel was abolished in 1976, the number of congressional committees with jurisdiction over energy matters has soared. Today, legislative, budget, or oversight jurisdiction over nuclear power is shared by 28 committees (and 53 subcommittees) of the House and Senate. In the 96th Congress (1979–1980), hearings on nuclear energy issues were held before 39 committees and subcommittees, and nuclear industry representatives were keeping track of more than 150 bills dealing with some aspect of nuclear power.[19]

Lobbying activity has increased not only because there are more subcommittees whose jurisdictions touch each organization's interests, but also because single committees and subcommittees no longer exercise the control over legislation they once did. With the growing tendency to refer bills to multiple committees, and with the general relaxation of the norms inhibiting floor challenges to committees, threats to a group's legislative interests may come from anywhere in the chamber and at many more points over a bill's progress through the legislative labyrinth.[20]

The Role of Staff The expansion and professionalization of congressional staff have also led to more work for organized interests. Like the fragmentation of power among legislators, the proliferation of staff has changed the operating environment of congressional lobbyists. As a veteran lobbyist for the American Medical Association put it:

> When I came to Washington, congressmen had staffs of four; senators, fifteen. Today, congressmen have at least fifteen aides and senators, eighty. That's one of the big changes in lobbying. Today, you have to fight your way through a crowd of ambitious aides to get to the person you need.[21]

[19]The nuclear power example is somewhat unusual because the policy area had originally been governed by only one committee. However, the fragmented jurisdictional authority described here is common in other policy areas as well.

[20]See Davidson, "Subcommittee Government," pp. 120–128.

[21]AMA lobbyist James Foristel, quoted in Dennis L. Breo, "I've Been in on the Whole Show," *American Medical News,* June 22, 1979, p. 6.

The increased size and importance of congressional staff mean that organized interests have many more people with whom they need to establish contacts. The reason for this is twofold. First, it is true that staff members can provide valued access to the legislators, so the cultivation of good working relationships with them is obviously desirable for an organized interest. Second, staff members (in part because there are more of them, in part because their bosses are more likely than before to have an independent power base) are increasingly seen as a policymaking force in their own right.[22]

The modern tendency for staff members to have entrepreneurial instincts poses both problems and opportunities for outside interests. On one hand, a friendly entrepreneurial staff member can serve as a sponsor for an organization eager to see a cherished policy proposal find a place on the government's agenda.[23] On the other hand, the presence of entrepreneurial staff multiples the sources of potential opposition and thus forces organizations to touch even more bases on Capitol Hill. Commenting on the size and professionalism of congressional staff, an executive in one of the peak business associations complained:

> It has increased the number of things that have to be done—the number of people we have to contact. The problem is that these people [staff] constitute an unseen, unelected government. Some of the committee staff members are more important than the legislators themselves. There are people up there [on the Hill] just taking action on their own. They're in a position to change dramatically the presumed intent of a law as they write up committee reports.

Echoing these sentiments, the director of government relations for one of the major automobile manufacturers remarked:

> Each staff member tends to be ambitious and energetic. They tie into issues and become advocates. I think the general increase in legislative activity in recent years is partly due to the increase in legislative staff.

In other words, the increasing number of prima donnas among legislators and their staffs means more work for organized interests.

Sunshine Laws   Sunshine laws have opened up once-secret meetings to public scrutiny. These reforms have also created new opportunities for organized interests to have access to legislative processes and have thereby escalated their work load. Particularly significant are the rules adopted by both chambers liberalizing access to conference committee and markup sessions. According to the legislative counsel for one of the major hospital associations:

[22]See Michael J. Malbin, *Unelected Representatives: Congressional Staff and the Future of Representative Government* (New York: Basic Books, 1980).

[23]Ibid., p. 27.

It's great for the lobbyists, but the members of Congress hate it. There in the back of the hearing room are all these lobbyists watching a markup session and giving a thumbs up or a thumbs down to specific wordings or provisions. It's a fishbowl for them.

Markups of tax bills are especially likely to attract hordes of business lobbyists eager to protect their clients' profits from unfavorable changes in the tax laws. Hundreds of lobbyists pack into the hearing rooms (and the corridors outside) on the chance that they might be able to affect the wording of a crucial provision; a subtle nuance or a quick word with a staff member or legislator may make all the difference. Some legislators regard the process with an eye for its comic features, joking that they could look at the size of the audience and tell how big a loophole they were trying to close; if not many people showed up, they need not bother. Others view it less warmly. Looking out at the hundreds of business lobbyists clogging a Senate Finance Committee hearing room during its markup of a tax bill in 1982, Senator Daniel Patrick Moynihan, (D-New York) said to a reporter: "When the Administration proposed to abolish the only piece of social legislation that passed during the Carter administration, the Child Welfare and Adoption Assistance Act of 1980, there may have been a dozen people here. Look who's here today. It's squalid."[24]

Turnover in Membership   Another development in congressional politics that has meant more work—and, therefore, increased activity—for many organized interests is the accelerated turnover in congressional membership. Throughout the twentieth century, the tenure of legislators in the House and Senate increased.[25] This trend reversed during the 1970s as more and more lawmakers voluntarily left Congress before retirement age.[26] In 1971, the ratio of newcomers (two terms or fewer) to veterans (ten terms or more) was 1.2 to 1. By 1981, that ratio had risen to more than 3 to 1, and a majority of those in both House and Senate had served six years or fewer.

A number of our respondents commented that the absence of institutional memory that follows from such a rapid turnover has forced them to intensify their educational efforts as they patiently inform programmatically

[24]Quoted in David Shribman, "Lobbying Aides Wait, of Course, in a Lobby," *New York Times,* July 2, 1982, p. D4. For more on the throngs of business lobbyists who pack into the markup sessions on tax bills, see this article and also Lynn Rosellini, "Tax Lobbyists Learning How to Lose," *New York Times,* August 13, 1982, p. D6.

[25]Samuel P. Huntington, "Congressional Responses to the Twentieth Century," in David B. Truman, ed., *The Congress and America's Future* (Englewood Cliffs, NJ: Prentice-Hall, 1965), pp. 8–9.

[26]This point is made by Norman J. Ornstein, in "The House and the Senate in a New Congress," in Mann and Ornstein, eds., *The New Congress,* pp. 373–374. Figures in this paragraph are taken from this source.

ignorant legislators and staff members about the purposes, operation, and benefits of cherished programs. The director of a feisty social welfare action group described the Sisyphean task this way:

> One problem is that half the Congress has served fewer than six years. Much of the case made for food programs in the late 1960s was made to people who are no longer on the Hill. Current members of Congress only see the success of those earlier efforts; they look around now and, finding less malnutrition, don't see there's *still* a problem. Consequently our lobbying task is being willing to tell the same story time after time to one legislator after another—making them see that hunger and malnutrition are reduced now *because* those programs [food stamps, school lunches, etc.] are in place and that we can't afford to eliminate them. You have to have stamina to tell the story over and over—to persuade people who don't understand.

Thus, in yet another way, the impact of changes on Capitol Hill is to demand that a conscientious organization augment its efforts.

Coalitional Teamwork in Congressional Lobbying   Few, if any, organizations have sufficient resources to cover this balkanized, individualistic Congress with their own lobbying corps. This is one of the reasons for the recent rise in coalitional activity noted in Chapters 3 and 11. By joining together with other organizations that have similar goals and complementary contacts and resources, an organized interest has a better chance of winning a legislative objective that would elude it if it were to act on its own. A well-known union lobbyist pointed to coalition building as the key innovation over the past decade in the way her organization tries to influence what happens in Congress:

> We've discovered that it's easier to lobby for issues you're concerned about if you have others to help you do the job. There is no discipline in Congress any more. Congressional voting blocs really have to be put together ad hoc on every issue. With 535 members of Congress it would be almost impossible for any one organization to cover the whole Congress.
>   In coalitions, the various organizations divide up and see those members of Congress with whom they have the most rapport or clout, whether because of sizeable constituencies in the district, past political support, or whatever. It works.

Since the organization and structure of Congress no longer permit even the most resourceful of organized interests to press a policy issue singlehandedly, acting jointly thus permits organizations to pool resources and take advantage of the special strengths and contacts of each member organization. Joining coalitions not only helps member organizations to cover all the necessary bases in Congress, but it enhances their chances of legislative success in another way as well. Since the organizations involved in coalitions work hard to iron out any differences they might have so as to present Congress with a united front, they reduce the level of conflict that legislators see and thus make it more likely that Congress will act favorably on these "predigested policies."[27]

Old-fashioned Lobbying: Why the Increase?   The evidence about the impact of changes in Congress upon the activities of organized interests helps solve an earlier puzzle. In Chapter 7, in the course of the discussion of the increase in the use of various techniques of influence, the hypothesis was raised that there would be selective escalation in the use of certain of them—those facilitated by electronic technologies and those capitalizing upon the close relationship between legislator and district. Clearly, there has been increased use of such methods of influence. However, there has also been enhanced use of old-fashioned methods of direct lobbying.

The foregoing analysis of the implications for organized interests of the changes in Congress helps explain why. These changes, taken collectively, spell both more opportunities for influence and more work for representatives of organized interests: more policymakers with whom one must consult and to whom one must present a case; more freshmen and issue amateurs requiring education; more meetings to attend; more hearings at which to testify and present technical information; and more campaigns demanding contributions. These developments imply an increase in virtually all the techniques relevant to legislative influence. In particular, however, they imply an increase in the use of those techniques associated with old-fashioned lobbying. Thus, it is clear why the employment of these traditional methods has risen as quickly as the use of the clusters of electronically related or constituency-based methods.

Organizational Effectiveness in a Changed Congress

In light of the magnitude of these changes, it is important to explore further their impact on the functioning of organized interests in Washington. We asked our respondents about several of these changes specifically, inquiring whether a particular change had made it harder or easier for their organizations to operate effectively in Washington or whether it had made relatively little difference. Their answers are summarized in Table 12.2. This series of questions tapped a different dimension from the earlier open-ended one. Whereas our respondents had earlier mentioned changes in Congress as having affected the overall volume of their activity, here they discussed the changes as having affected their

---

[27]This point is made by Douglas W. Costain and Anne N. Costain, "Interest Groups as Policy Aggregators in the Legislative Process," *Polity* 14 (1981): 249–272. The term "predigested policies" is the Costains' (p. 271).

**Table 12.2   THE IMPACT OF CHANGES IN CONGRESS ON ORGANIZATIONAL
ABILITY TO OPERATE EFFECTIVELY**

**(a) How has change affected organization's ability to operate effectively—made it
easier, harder or made relatively little difference?**

	Easier	Little difference	Harder	
Growth in congressional staff	21%	31	48	= 100%
Increasing number of subcommittees in Congress	12%	31	57	= 100%
Decreased power of appropriations subcommittees in the changed budgetary process	15%	38	47	= 100%
Sunshine laws	36%	53	12	= 101%
Increasing ability of Congress to generate its own information through service agencies like CBO	42%	43	15	= 100%

(b) Net effect of changes for different kinds of organizations[a]

	Corporations	Trade associations	Unions	Citizens' groups	All organizations
Only easier	6%	9%	6%	33%	14%
Easier on balance	8	6	12	24	15
No change	22	16	25	19	21
Harder on balance	24	34	31	10	25
Only harder	39	34	25	14	26
	99%	99%	99%	100%	101%

[a]The figure for the net effect was calculated by subtracting the number of changes that were deemed to make it harder from the number deemed to make it easier.
Source: Washington Representatives Survey.

ability to realize their policy goals.[28] As shown in Table 12.2(a), some of these changes—the growth in number of congressional staff, the increasing number of subcommittees in Congress, and the decreased power of appropriations sub-committees in the changed budgetary process—were seen as reducing organizational effectiveness. Others—such as sunshine laws and the increasing ability of Congress to generate its own information through service agencies like the Congressional Budget Office—were seen as enhancing organizational effectiveness.

[28]We have two reasons for drawing the inference that this question tapped a different dimension from the earlier open-ended one. First, as we have seen, our respondents indicated that both the increasing number of subcommittees and sunshine laws augment the lobbying workload. However, when asked how these changes affect the ability of their organizations to operate effec-

What is especially striking is how these reforms have affected the ability of various kinds of organizations to realize their policy goals. The dispersion of responses is particularly large with respect to the growth of congressional staff. On balance, the growth of staff was said to make life harder: 71 percent of the corporate, 58 percent of the trade association, and 62 percent of the union respondents took this position. However, only 10 percent of the respondents from citizens' groups indicated that the increase in staff makes it harder to operate effectively, and 48 percent actually reported that it makes things easier. This point is echoed by the responses to an item that asked respondents to indicate which two of eight political forces (excluding other organized interests) listed on a card they considered their principal competitors in influencing members of Congress. Forty-six percent of the corporations and 39 percent of the trade associations—but only 6 percent of the unions and none of the citizens' groups—cited congressional staff members as principal competitors. Presumably, these results indicate the entrepreneurial instincts of congressional staff.

While their increasing number has meant more work for organizations across the board, congressional staff seem to be especially responsive to the substantive policy concerns of the citizens' groups.[29] The growth in congressional staff is the only change for which respondents from the various kinds of organizations did not agree as to its impact on the ability to operate effectively. However, with one minor exception (50 percent of the union respondents, as opposed to 48 percent of those from citizens' groups, indicated that sunshine laws make things easier), the respondents from citizens' groups consistently reported most favorably about the impact of these changes upon their ability to operate effectively.

Table 12.2(b) makes clear the degree to which these changes have operated to the advantage of citizens' groups. This measure is constructed by subtracting the number of changes that the respondent considered to make life harder from the number deemed to make life easier. (Those who considered none of the changes to make things harder and those who deemed none of them to make life easier were placed in the appropriate extreme categories.) Fifty-seven percent of the citizens' group respondents—as opposed to only 14 per-

---

tively, respondents across all categories of organizations agreed that the increase in the number of subcommittees makes life harder, while sunshine laws make life easier. In addition, if our respondents had been principally concerned about the dimensions of the work load in answering this question, then the organizations with the least financial resources (and therefore the least capacity to expand their political activity substantially) would presumably have been most likely to say that these changes make life harder. Instead, as we shall soon see, it is the citizens' groups whose Washington representatives were most likely to see these changes as making it easier for their organizations to operate effectively.

[29]The ambivalence with which corporate respondents view congressional staff is especially noteworthy. In response to items about communications links, they—like their counterparts in other kinds of organizations—reported that they consider congressional staff an important source of information and that they are likely to consult with congressional staff in planning strategy on policy matters. However, they were especially likely to indicate that the increase in the number of congressional staff is a hindrance.

cent of the corporate, 15 percent of the trade association, and 18 percent of the union respondents—received scores indicating that the net effect of these changes is to make it easier to operate effectively. Similarly, only 24 percent of the citizens' group respondents—as opposed to 63 percent of the corporate, 68 percent of the trade association, and 56 percent of the union respondents— received scores indicating that the net effect of these changes is to make it harder to operate effectively. Hence, while various changes in congressional structure and procedure seem to have enhanced the work load of all kinds of organizations, they seem to have been of particular assistance to citizens' groups in their efforts to influence congressional outcomes.

DOES LOBBYING MAKE A DIFFERENCE?

The most important question, of course, is whether all the effort that organized interests expend in attempting to influence Congress in fact makes any difference. As the discussion in Chapter One indicated, at one time political scientists attributed to interest groups premier power in determining policy outcomes in Congress.[30] However, the image of a political process dominated by organized interests was soon replaced by one of a political process in which organized interests play a limited role.[31] According to the new model, interest activity is hardly the mainspring of congressional policymaking. For several reasons, organized interests rarely determine policy outcomes on important issues; the best that they can hope to do is to influence the details of policies.[32]

This latter conclusion hinges upon several assertions about the nature of organized interests, the nature of political conflict in Washington, and the nature of congressional representation. Among these contentions are that organized interests in Washington are too resource-poor to be effective;[33] that they have too few tools for rewarding or punishing members of Congress to exercise political leverage;[34] that the impact of organized efforts at influence is vitiated by the fact that pressure on one side of an issue is inevitably met with opposing pressure;[35] that lobbyists tend to approach only those lawmakers who already agree with them and thus that they function not as "agents of direct persuasion" but as "service bureaus" for supportive legislators;[36] and that legislators

[30] See the discussion and attendant references in Chapter 1.

[31] See Bauer, Pool, and Dexter, *American Business and Public Policy,* especially Parts IV–VI, and Lester W. Milbrath, *The Washington Lobbyists* (Chicago: Rand McNally, 1963), especially Chapter 17.

[32] Ibid., pp. 343, 354.

[33] Bauer, Pool, and Dexter, *American Business and Public Policy,* pp. 324, 341–349.

[34] Milbrath, *The Washington Lobbyists,* pp. 342–343; Andrew Scott and Margaret A. Hunt, *Congress and Lobbies: Image and Reality* (Chapel Hill, NC: University of North Carolina Press, 1966), pp. 84–94; and Zeigler and Baer, *Lobbying: Interaction and Influence in American State Legislatures,* pp. 202–203.

[35] Milbrath, *The Washington Lobbyists,* p. 345.

[36] Bauer, Pool, and Dexter, *American Business and Public Policy,* pp. 350–352.

are essentially free from pressure because they only pay attention to what they want to hear.[37] Although this multifaceted argument contains important insights, it requires substantial revision—both because it underestimates the significance of certain kinds of influence and because it is based on data that are now obsolete.

Consider the underlying contention that organized interests are rarely responsible for broad new policy initiatives—their role being confined to influencing the technical details of measures the passage or failure of which they are powerless to determine. It is surely the case that major policy departures—such as railroad regulation at the end of the nineteenth century, welfare measures during the New Deal, civil rights legislation during the 1960s—are rarely, if ever, the product only of organized interests' efforts. On the contrary, such policy innovations ordinarily reflect the intrusion into legislative politics of any of several factors—popular movements, electoral verdicts, or presidential intervention. However, policymaking of this level of novelty and visibility is hardly typical. In politics of a more routine sort, especially the renewal of ongoing policies, organized interests can play a much more substantial role.

Furthermore, the ability to have an impact on the details of a policy is not in the least a trivial form of influence. On the contrary, one of the axioms of policy analysis is that to know what a piece of legislation actually does, it is important to look beyond its broad purposes to the particulars; it is the details that specify such critical matters as when the measure is to take effect, whom it covers, how much is to be spent, and who has what authority to implement it.[38] How such particulars are defined determines whether a measure will be a mere symbolic gesture or a potentially effective policy. Thus, even if the impact of organized interests were confined to influencing details—and later it will be shown that it is not—such influence should not be dismissed as negligible.

Moreover, the components of this argument rest on empirical assertions that no longer hold. Chapter 5 showed that most organized interests in Washington could not be characterized as resource-starved. If it was ever true that lobbyists were overworked and underpaid, hard-pressed to stretch the available resources to do the job, it is for the most part no longer so. Of course, resources are very unevenly distributed in the world of Washington lobbying, and some

---

[37] Ibid., pp. 414–424. See also Lewis A. Dexter, "The Representative and His District," in Theodore J. Lowi, ed., *Legislative Politics U.S.A.,* 2nd ed. (Boston: Little, Brown, 1965), pp. 89–90. In summarizing this argument, we have drawn on the helpful synthesis in Costain and Costain, "Interest Groups as Policy Aggregators," p. 250.

[38] For a compelling example of the degree to which the details of a measure, rather than its ostensible purposes, define what it is really all about, see A. Lee Fritschler, *Smoking and Politics,* 3rd ed. (Englewood Cliffs, NJ: Prentice-Hall, 1983), pp. 113–114. According to Fritschler, the Cigarette Labeling and Advertising Act of 1965—billed as a public health measure—actually contained significant concessions to the tobacco industry and was construed by a some as a boon to tobacco interests. Tobacco-state legislators voted for it, and most of the opposing votes came from liberal Democrats.

organizations are forced to manage on relatively little. Still, the 1960s view of the lobbyist as pauper is no longer valid.

In addition, organized interests now command various means of reward and punishment. The most obvious of these are campaign contributions. As Chapter 10 demonstrated, organized interests are now heavily involved in the financing of increasingly expensive congressional campaigns. In 1980 the average House incumbent running for reelection collected $62,500—or 38 percent of total receipts—from PACs; the average Senate incumbent collected $309,000—or 26 percent of total receipts—from PACs. While campaign donations are the most obvious of the inducements that organized interests can offer to legislators, there are many others as well—among them, lecture fees, fact-finding vacations and so on. Exactly what kind of leverage such benefits confer on pressure organizations is a complex issue that the standard interpretation—that they enhance access, not influence—oversimplifies. However, the old argument that there are no rewards to mete out simply no longer holds.

The argument that any particular interest can exercise only limited influence because organized pressure on one side of an issue elicits opposing pressure on the other conveys an important insight about the policy process: when it comes to influence in Congress, other interests are among the most serious competitors that organized interests face. When a group faces organized opposition, it rarely emerges from a policy controversy with an unqualified victory. However, as earlier chapters have shown, this sort of balanced competition is not inevitable. Chapters 4 and 6 presented the theories of E. E. Schattschneider and Mancur Olson, which would predict that not all latent interests can be expected to organize in opposition to established groups. Chapters 4 and 11 presented the theories of James Q. Wilson and Theodore J. Lowi, whose works on the patterns of group conflict suggest that most policy controversies do not involve head-on conflicts between organized interests.[39]

Several statistical studies also support the notion that organized interests are not always active on both sides of an issue. One analysis of the participation by blocs of organized interests in congressional hearings over a sixteen-year period found 55 percent of the hearings examined to be noncompetitive.[40] Another study of how congressmen decide how to vote on legislation found

[39] For an illuminating discussion of the "configuration of demand" among interest groups for public policies, also see Hayes, *Lobbyists and Legislators*. Hayes shows that there are great variations among policy proposals with respect to the patterns of interest group demands. Sometimes group pressures cancel each other out, leaving congressmen relatively free; sometimes group pressures are all one-sided and "overwhelming." (Hayes, p. 4.) Furthermore, Jack L. Walker reports that only 59 percent of the respondents in his 1980 survey of interest groups reported that they had an organized opponent. See "The Mobilization of Political Interests," paper delivered at the Annual Meeting of the American Political Science Association, September 1983, p. 42.

[40] Robert L. Ross, "Relations Among National Interest Groups," *Journal of Politics* 32 (1970): 106–108. In a study of legislative lobbying in Iowa, Charles W. Wiggins and William P. Browne found that in 77 percent of the cases in which there was organized interest testimony on one side of a bill, there was no countervailing organized interest testimony on the other side. "Interest Groups and Public Policy within a State Legislative Setting," *Polity* 14 (1982): 548–558.

organized interests active on both sides of an issue in only 12 percent of the cases examined.[41] Thus, while competition among organizations provides an important check on the influence of interests under certain circumstances, it does not inevitably do so.

Another component of the interests-are-weak argument is that lobbyists interact only with friendly lawmakers for whom they act as "service bureaus." This chapter has made clear that lobbyists continue to furnish members of Congress with all sorts of services. However, it is not at all clear that they only approach legislators who already share their views. In fact, the whole logic of the increasingly prevalent coalitions among organized interests is that taken together their members will have a very large number of friends. Thus, by concentrating on friends only, a coalition will be able to cast a very wide collective net, using joint contacts to approach virtually all members of Congress. In short, although organizations still may not make direct approaches to legislators with whom they lack good relations, they will find some other means of making the case—either through another organized interest, through a known intimate of the legislator, through another member of Congress, or by mobilizing pressure from within the legislator's constituency. Furthermore, working with allies in order to maximize effectiveness can be an important pathway to influence. Converting opponents is only one way to have an impact on policy outcomes; collaborating on strategy so as to make the most of a situation is another.

The argument that legislators are free of pressure because they only hear what they want to hear is difficult to evaluate. It is surely the case that some legislators selectively perceive all communications as supportive.[42] Also, there is evidence that individual legislators vary in their susceptibility to pressure; some have thinner skins than others.[43] However, the balance of systematic evidence seems to suggest that legislators overestimate the degree to which their records are subject to district scrutiny and underestimate the latitude of action afforded them by their constituents.[44] Contemporary analysts of Congress have observed that—in spite of high rates of incumbent retention in the House, though not the Senate—lawmakers feel electorally vulnerable and are sensitive to the expressed preferences and particularistic needs of those in the district.[45] Through their increasingly sophisticated campaigns to mobilize constituents for political action, organized interests prey upon legislators' sense of electoral vulnerability.

Members of Congress themselves provide evidence that they do indeed

[41] John W. Kingdon, *Congressmen's Voting Decisions* (New York: Harper & Row, 1973), p. 142.

[42] Dexter, "The Representative and His District," p. 181.

[43] Ibid.

[44] Donald E. Stokes and Warren E. Miller, "Party Government and the Saliency of Congress," in Angus Campbell et al., eds., *Elections and the Political Order* (New York: Wiley, 1967), pp. 194–211.

[45] See Mayhew, *Congress: The Electoral Connection,* and Fiorina, *Congress—Keystone of the Washington Establishment.*

feel pressure from organized interests. It is now commonplace to read of legislators who quit Congress, listing among their reasons for retirement the relent-
less pressure brought to bear by the special interests; it is also commonplace to
read of legislators' complaints about pernicious effects of PAC involvement in
elections or about the ferocity of the pressure they feel from constituents mobilized by organized interests.[46] For example, among the more outspoken critics
of interests' pressures in Congress is Representative Michael L. Synar (D-Okla-
homa), who has complained that special interests have become a powerful,
intimidating force in the halls of the Capitol—in his words, a "petrifying
force."[47]

When Are Organized Interests Most Likely to Prevail in Congress?

This discussion leads us to question the common wisdom among political scientists that organized pressure is a minor factor in congressional policymaking
and suggests some circumstances under which the activity of organized interests is especially likely to be effective. First, the extent of lobbying impact is
likely to vary with the nature of the issue. Interest organizations' influence is
likely to be less substantial on highly visible issues that engage public passions
or media coverage and on issues in which there are strong competing ideological, partisan, or constituency pressures. Conversely, organized interests are
more likely to be able to affect legislative outcomes on issues that are shielded
from public or media scrutiny and that do not articulate with deeply felt convictions, lines of party cleavage, or particularistic constituency needs.

In addition, lobbying success is likely to vary with the nature of the
demand. It is an old chestnut in American politics that organized interests in a
defensive posture—that is, organized interests that are resisting some proposed
change—are at an advantage over their opponents who seek to alter the status
quo.[48] The complexities of the congressional policy process are such that any

---

[46]See "Why Lawmakers Are Quitting in Droves," in *U.S. News and World Report,* October
11, 1982, pp. 51–52. See also the comments of Rep. Barber Conable (R-New York) in Steven V.
Roberts, "Moving to Limit the Impact of PACs," *New York Times,* August 16, 1983, p. A20.

[47]Quoted in David Shribman, "An Angry Young Congressman Criticizes Special Interest
Groups," *New York Times,* January 11, 1981, p. 24.

[48]This observation can be found over and over again in the literature on interest groups. See,
for example, David B. Truman, *The Governmental Process* (New York: Alfred A. Knopf, 1951), pp.
391–392, and Lewis A. Dexter, *How Organizations Are Represented in Washington* (Indianapolis,
IN: Bobbs-Merrill, 1969), p. 62. It is given empirical verification in Wiggins and Browne, "Interest
Groups and Public Policy within a State Legislative Setting," pp. 551–552.

Milbrath (*The Washington Lobbyists,* pp. 349–350) challenges this common wisdom. He
shows that there is no relationship between whether an organization in its broad policy is trying to
"change or preserve the *status quo* in society" and its lobbyist's evaluation of whether the organization is successful. This finding, however, is somewhat problematic. Milbrath does not explain what
criteria he used to categorize organizations as "defensive" or "offensive"; he does not present the
actual data but, rather, only reports the conclusion. Furthermore, it is not clear that respondents'

congressional policy measure must clear multiple hurdles, thus providing organized interests with many opportunities to delay or kill it. Furthermore, internal rules such as the Senate provision for unlimited debate contribute to the overall congressional bias in favor of the legislative status quo.[49] Hence, an organization that seeks to have a measure defeated is at a strategic advantage over one that seeks to have a measure passed. Moreover, organizations whose demands are narrow are more likely to achieve success than those whose demands are more encompassing. In particular, organizations can ordinarily have greater influence on single, discrete amendments to bills than on entire pieces of legislation. Amendments are generally specific and technical (thus increasing the influence of the information provided by the group); this makes them both narrower in impact and harder to understand (thus decreasing the breadth of attention they are likely to attract).[50]

The probability of success for an organized interest also depends upon the structure of conflict in a particular controversy. Organized pressure on Congress is less likely to bear results if it is met—as it often is—by opposing pressure. However, as mentioned above, on many issues, especially those in which either the costs or the benefits of a policy (but not both) are widely distributed, there is no such contest between organized interests. When there is vigorous activity by a private organization on one side of an issue, and no countervailing activity on the other, lobbying is likely to have an impact on policymaking in Congress.

However, the countervailing activity need not come from another organization in order to check organized influence. Interests that have no organizational embodiment often find champions among policymakers. It is clear that policy entrepreneurs—whether animated by a desire to feather their own nests or by a concern about a public problem—often take up the cudgel on behalf of the interests of the resource-poor or broad publics and prove formidable antagonists to organized interests. In addition, an organized interest that has a close relationship with an agency within the executive branch often has a very valuable partner in approaching Congress. If the organization deals only with a single agency, and if that agency has no other competing groups within its constituency, that partnership is especially likely to be effective. Naturally, it is important for an interest organization to have allies in Congress as well. Good relationships with key legislators or committee staff members can be enor-

---

appraisals of their organizations' success measure actual policy impact. In addition, in an era of concern over budget deficits, it is not clear that all organizations that oppose the status quo in society necessarily oppose the policy status quo. Consider the Food Research and Action Center, an organization concerned with the food problems of the poor. FRAC is an organization that would legitimately be considered to oppose the social status quo. However, FRAC has been fighting proposed cuts in food stamp benefits. As such its legislative posture has been defensive.

[49]See Lewis A. Froman, *The Congressional Process* (Boston: Little, Brown, 1967), pp. 188–193.

[50]On this point, see Randall B. Ripley, *Congress: Process and Policy,* 3rd ed. (New York: Norton, 1983), p. 301.

mously helpful: if, for example, an organization can line up support among key actors on the legislative committees and on the Rules Committee, its chances of success may be enhanced substantially.

Many kinds of interests have acquired additional political advantage in recent years by institutionalizing networks of strategic allies in Congress in the form of congressional caucuses. Often with the encouragement and assistance of the relevant organized interests, members of Congress have organized themselves into scores of groups geared to advance certain kinds of interests—racial, ethnic, regional, occupational, and issue. There are caucuses for the interests of women, blacks, Hispanics and the Irish; caucuses for solar energy, the arts, and jewelry manufacturers; caucuses for residents of the Sunbelt and for New Englanders; and caucuses for civil servants and for senior citizens. There is a Steel Caucus, a Mushroom Caucus, a Textile Caucus, a Veterans' Caucus, a Shipyard Coalition, and so on.

To a certain extent, there is nothing out of the ordinary here. Congress has always had informal cliques, clubs, alliances, organized voting blocs, and caususes.[51] But what distinguishes today's caucuses from earlier ones is their number (there were only 4 in the early 1960s, but more than 70 by 1982), their diversity, and most of all their institutionalized character. Many of them have paid staff members, office space, dues-paying members, formal bylaws, and elected officers. For the interests so represented, these caucuses function as the legislative equivalent of a clientele agency in the executive branch, a governmental counterpart that can serve as an in-house lobbying operation and that facilitates access, the dissemination of information, and the design of legislative strategy.[52]

The effectiveness of organized interests in approaching Congress also varies with their resources. Of course, as Chapter 5 demonstrated, various resources are differentially useful under different conditions. And, of course, money is only one of the resources that organized interests can mobilize in the name of political influence—although it is an important one. In dealing with Congress, other resources—for example, an appealing cause, a skillful staff, or a widely dispersed and attentive membership—can often compensate for an absence of cash. However, the total package of resources that an organization brings to the political fray in Congress has a significant bearing on the outcome.

In short, then, the degree to which organized interests wield influence in Congress is a complex question. Our assessment of the evidence with respect to the contemporary legislative process suggests that it is too simplistic just to

---

[51]See, for example, James Sterling Young, *The Washington Community, 1800–1828* (New York: Columbia University Press, 1966), and Ross K. Baker, *Friend and Foe in the U.S. Senate* (New York: Free Press, 1980).

[52]See Susan Webb Hammond, Arthur G. Stevens, Jr., and Daniel P. Mulhollan, "Congressional Caucuses: Legislators as Lobbyists," in Allan J. Cigler and Burdett A. Loomis, eds., *Interest Group Politics* (Washington, DC: CQ Press, 1983), pp. 275–297.

dismiss lobbying influence as negligible. The influence of organized interests seems to be highly variable. Depending on the configuration of a large number of factors—among them the nature of the issue, the nature of the demand, the structure of political competition, and the distribution of resources—the effects of organized pressure on Congress can range from insignificant to determinative.

SUMMARY

This chapter has examined the many different ways in which organized interests lobby members of Congress directly in pursuit of their ends. These direct contacts among lobbyists and legislators occur in many different settings and take many different forms, including the provision of information, favors, services, and political support that organized interests use in their efforts to win allies inside the legislature.

There are many ways in which recent changes in the structural and political complexion of Congress have affected the lobbying activities of organized interests. These changes generally have required a lot more work from organizations serious about advancing their goals in Congress. They have more hearings and committee meetings to attend, more persons whose consent and support they must seek. In addition to forcing interest organizations to redouble their efforts, the fragmentation and decentralization of power in Congress have strengthened the role of organized interests in the legislative process. It is now easier for outside forces to influence what occurs in Congress, and there is ample reason to believe that the lobbying efforts of these organizations make a difference.

In the next chapter we shall see that the executive branch of government is also highly permeable, affording organized interests multiple avenues for participation in the policymaking process. Organizations' lobbying activities may be less conspicuous in the executive arena than in the legislative, but they are no less pervasive.

APPENDIX: Regulating Lobbying

Prompted by disclosures of venality and corruption or by concern over the sheer volume of organized interest activity, Congress has intermittently investigated lobbying and lobbyists and has considered ways to regulate lobbying activity. In considering measures to regulate lobbying, Congress has always had to balance its desire to protect itself from corrupting influences against the constitutional protections of the First Amendment, which requires that "Congress shall make no law . . . abridging the . . . rights of the people . . . to petition the Government for a redress of grievances." Furthermore, legislators have shown a marked reluctance to deny themselves perquisites they enjoy. Hence, for the most part, the efforts of reformers over the years have done little to restrict the activities of lobbyists.

As early as 1852, the House of Representatives sought to protect itself from the supplications of lobbyists who posed as journalists by prohibiting hired lobbying agents from plying their trade from the newsmen's seats in the House chambers.[53] The early decades of this century were marked by repeated congressional investigations of lobbying abuses. For example, after a decade of congressional concern about the pressure tactics used by private utilities, Congress mounted an intensive investigation of the lobbying methods of utility companies.[54] As a result of the investigation, Congress inserted a provision in the Public Utilities Holding Company Act of 1935 requiring the registration of lobbyists representing holding companies before Congress, the Federal Power Commission, or the Securities Exchange Commission. Lobbyists for shipping and commercial maritime interests were placed under a similar enjoiner by the Merchant Marine Act of 1936. And two years later, the Foreign Agents Registration Act of 1938 (which has been amended frequently since its passage) required that anyone in the United States representing a foreign government or principal register with the Justice Department.

All these piecemeal efforts at lobby registration set the stage for a more general law enacted in 1946. The Joint Committee on the Organization of Congress, set up to consider various issues pertaining to the organization and operation of Congress, included lobbying activities among its areas of focus. On the basis of the committee's recommendations, Congress in 1946 passed the Legislative Reorganization Act, which included the first general lobby registration laws.

FEDERAL REGULATION OF LOBBYING ACT

The 1946 act regulating lobbying prompted little debate at the time of its passage, perhaps because it in no way directly restricts the activities of lobbyists but merely imposes registration and disclosure requirements. Specifically, the act requires any person hired for the *principal purpose* of influencing legislation to register with the Secretary of the Senate and the Clerk of the House, and to file certain quarterly financial reports, disclosing the amount of money received and spent for lobbying. Of course, any measure designed to protect Congress from corrupting influences had to defer to constitutionally protected rights of free speech, association, and petition. Insisting that "professionally

---

[53]See Hope Eastman, *Lobbying: A Constitutionally Protected Right* (Washington, DC: American Enterprise Institute for Public Policy Research, 1977), p. 5.

[54]In response to intensive lobbying by the utilities, a special investigative panel set up by the Senate charged that the utilities had financed thousands of phony telegrams to Congress, in which the names of the "senders" had been picked at random from telephone books. The scheme was revealed by a 19-year-old Western Union Messenger. See Schriftgiesser, *The Lobbyists,* p. 71.

inspired efforts to put pressure upon Congress cannot be conducive to well considered legislation," the congressional architects of the law eschewed direct restrictions in favor of identification, disclosure, and publicity:

> The availability of information regarding organized groups and full knowledge of their expenditures for influencing legislation, their membership and the source of contributions to them of large amounts of money, would prove helpful to Congress in evaluating their representations without impairing the rights of any individual or group freely to express its opinion to the Congress.[55]

Surely congressional sensitivity over constitutional rights was not the only reason for this less restrictive approach to the regulation of lobbying. Among the other reasons was the belief that one of the principal problems of lobbying was that lobbyists often were not straightforward about whom they were representing. There was also a fear that sharper restrictions would handicap legitimate lobbying activity but still not affect the more serious forms of venality, corruption, and abuse. In addition, some members of Congress were undoubtedly eager not to close off avenues to possible lobbying careers they might wish to pursue upon leaving office. Finally, lobbyists themselves were opposed to more severe restrictions and made their views known.[56]

Whatever the explanations for its substantive content, the 1946 lobbying law is generally considered ineffective and limp. For example, it is restricted in its scope. It applies only to lobbyists' efforts to influence Congress, not to their lobbying of the executive branch; only to contacts between lobbyists and legislators, not to contacts between lobbyists and congressional staff; and only to efforts to influence, not to efforts to inform. Furthermore, in deference to the First Amendment, the law imposes virtually no restrictions. Instead, it merely asks for a modicum of information: who is being hired for the purpose of influencing legislation, who is putting up the money, and in what amounts. As one observer noted within a few years of its passage:

> The lobbyist for the National Association of Rabbit Fur Raisers is still at liberty to corner [a congressman] in the corridors of Capitol Hill and urge him to vote a heavy tariff on South African skunk, to ply him with Manhattans at the Carlton cocktail room, to furnish him with statistics for a slashing speech that will be heard by six conferees but will roll with onomatopoeia through the pages of the *Congressional Record*. All the lobbyist has to do is admit his profession, name his employers, define the terms of his employment, and submit his expense account.[57]

[55] U.S. Congress, House, *Organization of the Congress,* H. Rept. 1675, 79th Cong., 2d sess., 1946, p. 26. Excerpt cited in Davidson and Oleszek, *Congress and Its Members,* p. 364.
[56] See Schriftgiesser, *The Lobbyists,* Chapters 6, 8.
[57] Ibid, p. 78.

In addition, the act is ambiguous. The language of the law is exceedingly vague and fails to make explicit to what activities it applies. While the law specifically exempts testimony before congressional committees, it does not define exactly what activities are covered.[58] In light of this ambiguity it is not surprising that some of those who do not register argue that their activities consist only of attempts to inform legislators, not to influence them. What is more, the law failed to provide an effective mechanism for enforcement of its own provisions. No agency was charged with monitoring compliance, and Congress has never specifically authorized money for its enforcement. Although the Clerk of the House and the Secretary of the Senate receive the registrations and reports, these officials are not empowered to investigate the reports or to compel anyone to register.

Furthermore, although the Supreme Court upheld the constitutionality of the law in 1954, the decision in *United States* v. *Harriss* (347 U.S. 612) narrowed its coverage and opened several major loopholes, effectively exempting many organizations and individuals from the registration and reporting requirements. The court held that individuals and organizations using their *own* money only to finance their legislative lobbying activities do not fall under the purview of the law. (However, if they also solicit, collect, or receive money for that purpose, they are not exempt.) The court also held that registration requirements apply only to persons and groups whose "principal purpose" is to influence legislation. These interpretations have given many representatives of organized interests double grounds on which to avoid registering.[59]

Also, the original bill defined lobbying as any attempt "to influence, directly or indirectly, the passage or defeat of any legislation by the Congress of the U.S."[60] However, the *Harriss* decision held that the Act applies only to direct contacts, thus exempting from the law's requirements individuals or organizations that confine their activities to the generation of grass roots pressure on Congress.

Given the ambiguities in the law and the narrowness of the Supreme Court's ruling, it is no surprise that the financial disclosure statements filed by lobbying organizations vary enormously. Some heavily active organizations report only minimal expenditures on their lobbying activities, typically arguing that most of their spending is for public information purposes, research, and the like. Other organizations make more of a good-faith effort to file accurate

[58]This exemption was further expanded in 1950 by a federal court holding that the exemption also extended to persons who assisted in the preparation of congressional testimony [*United States* v. *Slaughter* (89 F. Supp. 205)]. This exemption seriously reduced the applicability of the 1946 act since—as this chapter has shown—testifying before congressional committees is one of the leading activities of lobbyists.

[59]See Davidson and Oleszek, *Congress and its Members,* p. 364. See, also, Daniel P. Mulhollan, "An Overview of Lobbying by Organizations," in U.S. Congress, Senate, *Senators: Offices, Ethics, and Pressures,* Commission on the Operation of the Senate, 94th Cong., 2d sess., 1977, pp. 157–192.

[60]Federal Regulation of Lobbying Act of 1946, sec. 307.

reports on their lobbying expenditures. The result is that they often end up with reputations as "big lobby spenders," when in fact they merely are filing more complete reports than other groups that may be spending just as much or more on lobbying.[61] Furthermore, the Justice Department, which has power to prosecute violators, has adopted a policy of investigating lobbyists only when it receives complaints. It has initiated only five prosecutions (some involving several individuals) from 1946 to 1979.[62]

EFFORTS TO REVISE THE 1946 LAW

Widespread dissatisfaction with the 1946 act has prompted many efforts to revise the law, but Congress has been repeatedly unsuccessful at enacting a meaningful substitute. A number of proposals to regulate lobbying have won support of congressional subcommittees or full committees but have failed to win enactment. The 94th Congress, which marked the apogee of government openness, came closest to enacting a tough lobbying law. Nearly all sides agreed that the 1946 law should be revised (if only because it is so widely ignored), but when new legislation began to make its way through Congress, it was opposed by virtually every major lobbying group in Washington, with the exception of Common Cause. A formidable coalition made up of unlikely allies fought the measure. Among the groups opposed to the bill were the AFL-CIO, Ralph Nader's Congress Watch, the National Association of Manufacturers, the Sierra Club, the Chamber of Commerce of the United States, the American Civil Liberties Union, the League of Women Voters, and the U.S. Catholic Conference. The members of the coalition succeeded in frustrating the congressional sponsors of the bill by blocking formation of a conference committee to resolve conflicts between bills passed by the House and the Senate. The bill died when Congress adjourned in 1976. At the urging of Common Cause, House and Senate committees took up the battle once more in 1979. Once again the legislation failed to move in the face of strong opposition from lobbyists for all sorts of interests. Since then, similar bills have also failed to survive the opposition.

[61] Congressional Quarterly, *The Washington Lobby,* 3d ed., (Washington, DC: Congressional Quarterly, 1979), p. 20. This volume, from which we have drawn for this appendix, has an excellent summary of the federal laws and regulations governing lobbying activity. See pp. 19–24.
[62] Ibid., p. 23.

13

Influencing
the Executive
Branch

Congress is by no means the only branch of government toward which organized interests direct their efforts to influence policy. As the presidency and the bureaucracy have expanded in size, scope, and power, they, too, have become essential targets for organized interest activity. In fact, the executive branch is in many cases a more important part of the national policymaking process than Congress is. The executive branch initiates policy proposals and administers the policies that have won congressional enactment. Unless an organization is effective at cultivating support for its interests among the appropriate executive branch officials, even its most stunning victories on Capitol Hill may go for naught.

This chapter examines the influence of organized interests on the executive branch, focusing first on the strategies and mechanisms organizations use in an attempt to influence the White House. Although the president is less accessible than other government officials, there are still multiple avenues for group influence on presidential decision making. The discussion will then turn to the administrative and regulatory agencies with several aims: to explore the various ways in which organized interests seek to cultivate support inside the bureaucracy; to consider the various theories of agency "capture" propounded by political scientists to explain the relationships between agencies and their constituencies; and to assess the impact on organized interest politics of various changes in executive branch procedures.

Many of the principles developed in the previous chapter's discussion of congressional lobbying also pertain to the executive branch. As with legislative lobbying, access to appropriate policymakers is critical for lobbying success. In this case, however, access—at least to the president and sometimes to his aides—may be considerably more limited than access to congressional policymakers. Another principle that continues to be relevant is that the relationships between lobbyists and policymakers are reciprocal: lobbying is not a one-way street. However, the content of the exchanges differs because the needs of policymakers in the White House and the agencies differ from those of policymakers in Congress.

Some of the kinds of inducements that help create access to legislators and facilitate dialogue with them—PAC contributions, honoraria, fact-finding trips, and so on—are of diminished importance in the executive branch. As Chapter 11 indicated, executive branch policymakers are enjoined from accepting some of the hospitality that their counterparts in Congress are permitted to accept. In addition, there is relatively little in the way of hospitality (dinners at fancy restaurants, tickets to football games, etc.) that organized interests can offer to the president. Organized interests may, of course, seek to meet the electoral needs of presidential candidates. However, with federal financing of presidential elections, PAC donations play a smaller role in presidential than congressional elections.

What the president often needs most from organized interests is not electoral support but support for policy initiatives. The White House spends considerable resources cultivating organized interests in order to line them up behind policies that the president would like to see enacted. What policymakers in agencies often need most is support in dealing with Congress. Because Congress is the source of both authorization and appropriation, executive agencies are often vulnerable to Congress. Organized interests can function as invaluable allies to agencies in their dealings with the legislature.

ORGANIZED INTERESTS AND THE WHITE HOUSE

Recent history has witnessed a veritable revolution in the nature of presidential power and the organization of the presidential office. Throughout the twentieth century, especially since the New Deal, the president has become the principal source of policy leadership in American national government. Presidential policy initiatives dominate the legislative agenda; presidential preferences determine bureaucratic priorities; and presidential rhetoric shapes public opinion. And as the government has grown, the number of presidential appointments has mushroomed. At the same time, not surprisingly, the presidential office has grown spectacularly and the president is surrounded by hundreds of aides who give him advice, plan his schedule, and manage his relations with Congress, the media, organized interests, and the like. What is more, the various agencies of the Executive Office of the President—the Office of Management and Budget, the National Security Council, and the Council of Economic Advisers—provide the president with expertise and policy planning in critical areas.[1]

These developments have had an effect on organized interest activity that is in some ways analogous to the impact of the changes in Congress discussed in Chapter 12. As the presidency increasingly has become the focal point in national policymaking, organized interests have recognized the significance of the White House as a target. (As indicated in Chapter 11, only 12 percent of those interviewed in our Washington representatives survey regarded the White House as "not too important" as a focus of organizational activity.) Organized interests understand that the president has the ability to affect their political fortunes in many ways—through his power of appointment, by the timing or urgency of his legislative initiatives, and by withholding or conferring his support for their efforts. Therefore, they naturally try to influence presidential decisions on matters germane to their interests. In addition, the proliferation of presidential staff has fragmented what has sometimes been construed as a monolithic office and thus multiplied the points of access for organized interests. Hence, it is not surprising that White House lobbying has increased substantially since the New Deal.

The President's Needs

According to one perspective in political science, the White House is the part of the federal government most responsive to the national interest broadly defined and least permeable to the importunes of narrow interests. This view holds that the president is more likely than Congress to stand in defiance of narrow private interests since the heterogeneity of his constituency not only instills in him a responsiveness to the public at large but makes it politically sensible for him to be attentive to broader interests.[2] However, just as organized interests have come to acknowledge the centrality of the presidency in contemporary American government, modern presidents have come to recognize their dependence on organized interests.[3]

Part of this dependence is electoral. As mentioned in Chapter 10, organized interests have a long history of (sometimes illegal) participation in presidential campaign finance. With the passage in 1974 of amendments to the

[1]See Thomas Cronin, *The State of the Presidency,* 2nd ed. (Boston: Little, Brown, 1980), and Stephen Hess, *Organizing the Presidency* (Washington, DC: The Brookings Institution, 1976).
[2]See, for example, Grant McConnell, *Private Power and American Democracy* (New York: Knopf, 1966), pp. 351–352; Grant McConnell, *The Modern Presidency* (New York: St. Martin's Press, 1976), p. 42; and Theodore J. Lowi, *The End of Liberalism,* 2nd ed. (New York: Norton, 1979), p. 302.
[3]See Benjamin I. Page and Mark P. Petracca, *The American Presidency* (New York: McGraw-Hill, 1983), Chapter 7; Joseph Pika, "The President and Interest Groups," in Edward N. Kearney, ed., *Dimensions of the Modern Presidency* (St. Louis, MO: Forum Press, 1981), Chapter 3; and Martha Joynt Kumar and Michael Baruch Grossman, "The Presidency and Interest Groups," in Michael Nelson, ed., *The Presidency and the Political System* (Washington, DC: CQ Press, 1984), pp. 282–312.

Federal Election Campaign Act of 1971, which provided for federal funding of presidential campaigns, that financial role has receded substantially. Organizations, of course, do continue to play a part in providing seed money to presidential aspirants.

Beyond the role in campaign finance, organized interests can provide electoral assistance in other ways as well. It is difficult for a presidential candidate, especially a Democrat, to win election if he does not forge a strong coalition of groups. In the course of a campaign, a candidate makes countless appeals to sundry groups within the public: women, Hispanics, blacks, farmers, veterans, old people, young people, manufacturers, and so on. Such appeals are often mediated by the organizations that represent these groups of citizens. For example, in 1976 Jimmy Carter won the vigorous support of the powerful National Education Association by promising the NEA that if elected he would press hard for the establishment of a federal Department of Education. After his victory, Carter repaid his political debt, weathering several bruising battles with Congress before obtaining the passage of a bill creating the Department of Education.

This same sort of maneuvering continues after a successful presidential candidate takes office. If a president cares about reelection for himself or a successor from his party, he must try to please organized interests that can help secure that next victory. Thus, the months before a presidential election are likely to find the incumbent engaging in all sorts of courting behavior and using the levers of his office to increase the flow of benefits to important constituencies. In fact, some observers of contemporary presidential politics have argued that incumbent presidents have begun to mimic members of Congress in the constancy of their concern over reelection. Just as members of Congress are said to be always campaigning, presidents are said to have institutionalized their electoral machines to such an extent that White House staff operations have taken on the character of a "permanent campaign."[4]

For a contemporary president, the ability to get elected is by no means a guarantee of the power to get things done once in office.[5] Presidents need political allies. If they are to be successful in realizing a policy program, they need political support from organized interests in dealing with Congress. Therefore, recent presidents have gone to great lengths both to make potential beneficiaries aware of presidential policy proposals so as to generate support for them and to cultivate goodwill among potential opponents. They have found that organized interests have ongoing alliances with powerful congressional policymakers. Thus, presidents sometimes use their contacts among organized interests to facilitate access to key legislators. Also, the cooperation of interest organizations is often vital both in developing new policy initiatives and in implementing programs. What organizations are most frequently in a

[4]See Sidney Blumenthal, *The Permanent Campaign* (New York: Simon & Schuster, 1982).
[5]On the theme of the limitations of presidential power and the president's need to persuade, see Richard E. Neustadt, *Presidential Power* (New York: Wiley, 1980).

position to provide at the stage of policy formulation is information about the costs, feasibility, and consequences of proposed governmental action. In addition, the president often needs the cooperation of affected interests in carrying out policy. For example, when President Nixon imposed wage and price controls in 1971, he included representatives from both business and labor on administrative councils in order to minimize the opposition of these critically positioned interests. As a consequence of these mutual political needs of presidents and organized interests, the pathways of group influence in the White House are greater in number and variety than one might expect.

Institutionalizing Group Liaison

Recognizing these needs, all presidents from Franklin Roosevelt on have had staff assistance in maintaining liaison with organized interests in society.[6] In the 1970s President Ford institutionalized what had been an informal function by establishing the White House Office of Public Liaison, a staff agency designed to reach out to organized interests and provide them with special contacts within the White House. This office and its counterparts in successive administrations have served two functions: to act as advocates for the interests of various groups in the making of policy decisions, and to act as advocates for the interests of the administration in selling these decisions to affected groups.[7]

By the end of the Carter administration, this liaison operation had developed into a sophisticated system for communicating with outside interests, with at least seven assistants to deal with special constituencies. For example, a former president of the National Council of Senior Citizens served as the White House liaison to the aged. Other assistants dealt specifically with blacks, Jews, women, Hispanics, consumers, and the business community. Another group of staff members in the liaison office served as program managers in charge of liaison oversight for specific issues. This organizational structure permitted the White House to maintain contacts with some constituencies on a continuing basis and also to work with the special coalitions that crop up on an issue-by-issue basis.[8] This organization of the liaison office, of course, reflected the peculiar nature of the Democratic electoral coalition. Under Reagan the function of group liaison has continued, but has focused on different groups. In addition to links with business, Reagan's White House liaison operation has cultivated the blue-collar Catholic and evangelical Protestant groups whose electoral support was deemed critical.[9]

---

[6]On the early origins of public liaison staffing in the Roosevelt and Truman presidencies, see Joseph Pika, "White House Public Liaison: The Early Years," paper delivered at the Annual Meeting of the Midwest Political Science Association, Chicago, April 1984.

[7]See Pika, "The President and Interest Groups," p. 72.

[8]Information on Carter's liaison operation is drawn from Dom Bonafede, "To Anne Wexler, All the World Is a Potential Lobbyist," *National Journal,* September 8, 1979, pp. 1476–1479.

[9]See Dick Kirschten, "The Switch from Dole to Whittlesey Means the Election is Getting Closer," *National Journal,* April 30, 1983, pp. 884–885.

Direct Contacts with the White House

While the president's office of public liaison assumes the central responsibility for orchestrating relationships with groups, the president and his aides engage in frequent direct contacts with organized interests. These interactions differ from legislator-lobbyist contacts insofar as the president has too many demands on his time to allow direct access to a large number of groups. Even organizations that may be privileged because of their help in securing the president's election are not allowed access to the president at will.

For the most part, direct contacts are initiated by the president.[10] This shifts the balance in lobbying somewhat. Although all lobbying involves reciprocity, in legislative lobbying, it is more common for organizations to line up legislators in support of favored measures. With respect to the White House, it is the president's purposes rather than the organizations' that take precedence and his efforts to line up groups that merit primary emphasis. Often such meetings are called because the president is displeased with a private organization's policies (such as when the steel industry increases prices to the extent that the president fears a worsening of inflation) or because the president is eager to win the support of key groups for part of his legislative program.

However, the president's need to persuade others puts him in the position of being pressured in return. And some powerful organizations (especially those from which the president has derived crucial support in the past) can press their claims effectively in direct meetings with the president. But given the limits on the president's time, most direct contacts between organized interests and the White House involve presidential aides. Since modern presidents rely increasingly upon a large staff for information and advice, contacts with staff may be easier to come by—and no less productive—for an organization than direct contacts with the president.

Task Forces and Presidential Commissions

Another avenue of contact between the White House and organized interests is presidential advisory commissions and task forces. Essentially these are panels whose members are appointed by the president for the purpose of advising him or making recommendations to him on such problems as the sorry state of the postal system in the 1960s, the need for reform of social security financing mechanisms, or the best means of increasing employment for the handicapped.

These presidential advisory commissions provide benefits both to the organizations represented on them and to the White House. From the perspective of the participating interests, membership on such a panel may offer an unusual opportunity to define the issues and help shape the boundaries of public debate on an issue of concern to them. From the president's perspective, the presence of such a committee is also beneficial. If he chooses to propose legislation to

[10]Carol S. Greenwald, *Group Power* (New York: Praeger, 1977), p. 215.

Congress, the panel's favorable policy recommendations may furnish the pro-posal with enough political support for it to prevail in Congress. Moreover, these panels can also be a fertile source of bold, new policy ideas.[11]

It is not altogether clear how much influence such panels actually have on the determination of public policy. It is sometimes argued that their functions are only symbolic; public pressure is defused and the heat is taken off the president while a sticky issue is handed over to experts for study.[12] However, there is evidence that positive governmental action in response to the recom-mendations of these panels is more frequent than is widely believed.[13]

Influencing Appointments

Earlier chapters have discussed indirect forms of organized influence, among them electoral activity. Through the electoral process, organizations can have an impact on decisions in Washington by influencing the selection of the deci-sion makers. There is a second route to shaping policy outcomes indirectly by influencing the choice of government personnel, one which leads directly to the president. The Constitution empowers the president to make various executive and judicial appointments "with the Advice and Consent of the Senate." As the federal government has grown so, too, has the number of major appointive positions until it stands today at roughly four thousand.[14] Many organized interests try to influence these appointments, since they understand that their ability to protect or advance their interests may well be directly affected by the president's personnel selections.[15] A bare majority of the respondents in our Washington representatives survey, 53 percent, indicated that they use this technique, making it twenty-first on the list of 27 techniques of influence. Just under half of the corporations, trade associations, and citizens' groups and 80 percent of the unions indicated that they attempt to influence appointments.

Naturally, an organization's ability to influence appointments varies with its size, resources, and relations with both the president's party and the White House. Some organizations are actually guaranteed a role in the appointment process by statutory direction. For example, the law creating the Railroad Retirement Board specifies that "one member shall be appointed from recom-

[11]The derivation of substantive policy proposals is certainly not the only strategic purpose for which presidents use advisory commissions. For interesting suggestions as to some of their other uses, see Elizabeth Drew, "On Giving Oneself a Hotfoot: Government by Commission," *Atlantic Monthly,* May 1968, pp. 45–49.

[12]See Murray Edelman, *The Symbolic Uses of Politics* (Urbana: University of Illinois Press, 1964), Chapter 2.

[13]See Thomas Wolanin, *Presidential Advisory Commissions* (Madison: University of Wisconsin Press, 1975).

[14]See data in John W. Macy et al., eds., *America's Unelected Government: Appointing the President's Team* (Cambridge, MA: Ballinger, 1983), p. 6.

[15]The most thorough treatment of this subject is in G. Calvin Mackenzie, *The Politics of Presidential Appointments* (New York: Free Press, 1981). Our discussion relies heavily on Chapter 11 of Mackenzie's book.

mendations made by the representatives of the employees and one member shall be appointed from recommendations made by representatives of the carriers."[16]

Other groups have an unusually strong influence on appointments by virtue of tradition rather than statutory instruction. Usually such influence relates to the professional expertise required for the position under consideration. For example, ever since 1945 the American Bar Association has played an important role in the appointment of federal judges. Although the ABA is not usually directly involved in the selection of judicial candidates, the lawyers' association does screen candidates for adherence to some minimum standard of acceptability.[17] The ABA's evaluations are taken seriously by both the Justice Department (which makes recommendations to the president) and the Senate Judiciary Committee (which must confirm all nominees for seats on the federal bench). Similarly, the American Medical Association enjoys an unofficial role in the appointment of the Surgeon General, and the National Society of Professional Engineers expresses its view on the fitness of candidates to head the Geological Survey.[18] Most organized interests, however, do not enjoy even such a semiformal role in the appointment process.

In general, organized interests have a better chance of influencing an appointment if they apply pressure early in the appointment process—prior to the formal nomination stage. This is especially true when the group's goal is to prevent the appointment of an unpalatable candidate. If the group transmits an intense, negative reaction to the White House early enough, it may succeed in blocking the candidate before the president has committed himself through a formal nomination announcement, thus sparing both the White House and the candidate any severe embarrassment. If an organization is unsuccessful at the White House, however, it may have a second chance at the Senate. Senate confirmation hearings are generally quite open, and many groups can rely for help on allies in the Senate.

Lobbying the White House: A Brief Assessment

As suggested by this survey of the multiple avenues for organizational influence in the White House, there may be reason to question the notion, outlined earlier, that the presidency is a majoritarian institution insulated from pressures by narrow publics. For recent presidents the need to fortify their own political positions has led them to place great emphasis on cultivating good relations with organized interests. These presidential attempts to structure relations with groups through such means as White House liaison operations have

[16]45 *U.S. Code* 228J.

[17]On the role of the ABA in the judicial appointment process, see Harold W. Chase, *Federal Judges: The Appointing Process* (Minneapolis: University of Minnesota Press, 1972), and Joel B. Grossman, *Lawyers and Judges: The Politics of Judicial Selection* (New York: Wiley, 1965).

[18]Mackenzie, *Politics of Presidential Appointments,* p. 208.

served to increase the strength of organized interests in the system. Outside organizations now have regular contact with White House officials, from whom they learn more about the executive decision-making process and about the identity of key decision makers. The information and contacts that groups obtain through these interactions enable them to "insinuate themselves in the policy process in a way they had not been able to in earlier days."[19]

ORGANIZED INTERESTS AND THE AGENCIES

As important as the White House is as a target of activity, for many organizations the administrative and regulatory agencies of the executive branch are even more important. Two-thirds of the respondents in our Washington representatives survey indicated that executive agencies are a very important focus of organizational activity; only 6 percent deemed it not too important. The attention paid by organizations to the bureaucracy is a function of the powerful role these agencies play in the policymaking process. Charged primarily with implementing policies enacted by Congress and approved by the president, the agencies enjoy considerable discretion in applying these policies. Over the years, Congress has delegated to these agencies the quasi-legislative power to write the rules and regulations that actually put the policies into effect. Moreover, many agencies such as the Federal Trade Commission and the National Labor Relations Board are vested with quasi-judicial powers, allowing them to apply existing laws or rules to particular situations through case-by-case adjudication.

Much of the discretionary authority that agencies enjoy stems from the fact that Congress often writes vague or general laws, leaving the definition of specifics to the executive agencies that have the expertise and time to fill in the gaps and give the policy programmatic content. For example, Congress has passed laws prohibiting age discrimination in employment, but the Equal Employment Opportunity Commission decides what practices will be deemed discriminatory and establishes procedures for detecting and penalizing violators.

Because of the formidable discretionary powers that agencies exercise, organizations serious about protecting and advancing their interests work hard to influence agency decisions. These lobbying relationships are, however, reciprocal. Organized interests are in a position to supply agencies with several kinds of assistance critical for their survival and success. Policymakers in the bureaucracy need the kinds of information—both technical data and political intelligence—that organized interests command. Furthermore, executive agencies receive both their mandates and their funding from Congress. Because they are prohibited by Congress from engaging in legislative lobbying, many agencies look to organized interests to provide legislative lobbying services for them. Agency officials are especially likely to rely on the political support of orga-

[19]Kumar and Grossman, "The Presidency and Interest Groups," p. 308.

nized interests within their clienteles when Congress is considering agency budgets or contemplating executive reorganizations. In addition, organized interests can serve bureaucratic agencies by engaging in public relations activities on their behalf and by cooperating in program development and implementation.

There are many different ways in which organized groups are able to protect and advance their interests by working through the agencies. Some of them—for example, contacting policymakers directly, testifying at hearings, presenting research results and technical information, and doing favors—are analogous to techniques used to influence Congress.[20] Others, such as serving on advisory committees, are unique to the executive branch.

Lobbying Agency Personnel

As in congressional lobbying, some of the most productive contacts between lobbyists and executive branch policymakers are informal. When the rules of administrative procedure do not prohibit it, organized interests commonly try to cultivate the favor of mid-level agency staff personnel. Building good working relationships with agency staff can be enormously useful for lobbyists. For example, a friendly staffer may be the source of early warnings about likely administrative actions, thus allowing lobbyists extra time to develop a response. Close contacts may also furnish an organized interest with opportunities to comment informally on policy changes that may be incubating in the bureaucracy.[21] In return, interest organizations are able to provide agency staff with policy ideas and useful technical information, including forecasts and policy analyses. Clearly, then, these informal contacts between groups and the agencies facilitate an easy two-way flow of information. As on Capitol Hill, the currencies of exchange are credibility and reliable technical information; hence, such contacts can lead over time to the development of mutual trust.

Organized interests do not confine their attention to staff; they may also approach the political leadership of an agency in an effort to plead a case. To be sure, organizations deluge agency administrators with letters, position papers, and analyses in an effort to persuade them to take favorable action. Once again, however, the important organizational resource is information that can be of use to political appointees—who are concerned with maintaining the

[20]When we asked our respondents about the use of techniques of influence such as direct contacts with policymakers, testifying at hearings, and the like, we did not ask them to specify the specific arenas to which they apply these techniques. Therefore, the discussion in Chapter 12 of the survey results with respect to the use of such techniques applies to this chapter as well. Rather than repeat those data, in this chapter we shall present only those survey results that bear on techniques used exclusively in dealing with the executive branch.

[21]Jeffrey Berry describes such contacts at work between administrators of the food stamp program and lobbyists for the Community Nutrition Institute and the Food Research and Action Center. See *Feeding Hungry People: Rulemaking in the Food Stamp Program* (New Brunswick, NJ: Rutgers University Press, 1984), p. 96.

agency's autonomy and resources—in their efforts to keep Congress and the president at bay.

Participation in Rule-Making Proceedings

Organized interests are also involved in agency activities in more formal ways. Among the most important—once again, just as in Congress—is participation in the official proceedings that agencies use to formulate new rules and regulations. Seventy-eight percent of the respondents in our survey—in roughly equal proportions across all categories of groups—indicated that their organizations help draft regulations. By and large, rule-making hearings owe their existence to the Administrative Procedure Act, which was passed by Congress in 1946 to make sure that binding rules not be developed in private meetings behind closed doors. Agencies must announce in the *Federal Register* any proposed changes in existing rules and regulations or proposals for new ones. In addition, most agencies give interested parties the right to appear at an agency hearing on the proposal or, at least, to submit detailed comments outlining their positions.

In spite of these commonalities, such hearings come in many different forms. Some closely resemble the proceedings of a courtroom. The entire hearing is very formal and bound by strict rules of evidence and procedure. Parties typically file briefs, make oral arguments, and offer witnesses of their own, subject to cross-examination by all other intervenors. More frequently, however, hearings are less formal, more closely approximating a congressional hearing, in which witnesses submit written testimony, state their positions orally, and answer questions posed by the hearing officers. Transcripts of the hearings are kept and used by the agency in reaching a decision.

The amount of organizational participation in rule-making proceedings, through written comments and oral testimony, naturally varies with the number of groups that care about the issue at hand and the intensity of their concern: the more numerous the attentive publics and the greater the impact on their vital interests, the more extensive the participation. For example, when the Postal Rate Commission considers a general rate change for all classes of mail, there may be as many as 60 intervenors, including all the main mailing-industry trade associations, such as the Magazine Publishers Association, the Direct Mail Marketing Association, the American Newspaper Publishers Association, and the American Bankers Association. The hearings in such a case can go on for weeks or months and produce a hearing record—including the various filings, testimony of experts, interrogatories and answers, exhibits, briefs and replies, and oral arguments—thousands of pages in length.[22] By contrast,

---

[22] See John T. Tierney, *Postal Reorganization: Managing the Public's Business* (Boston: Auburn House, 1981), pp. 110–111. In the Postal Rate Commission's first rate case in the early 1970s, the hearing record was 13,000 pages long.

when agencies promulgate minor rules having minimal effects on program constituents, the rule-making proceedings may elicit only a handful of written comments and no oral statements at all.

Interest organizations are not always equally advantaged in administrative hearings processes. For example, in proceedings aimed at regulating business markets or activities, the regulated industry usually has access to the best data (perhaps the *only* relevant data), and other interested parties (such as citizens' groups) are often left in the position of having to try to discredit industry statistics or trying to draw contrary inferences from the data.[23]

In spite of the hurdles they face, citizens' groups that participate in formal administrative decision-making processes often have substantial effects on the outcomes. Examples include the successful four-year campaign by Ralph Nader's Health Research Group to persuade the Food and Drug Administration to ban red dye no. 2; the Environmental Defense Fund's successful efforts to induce the Environmental Protection Agency to stop most uses of DDT; public interest activist John Banzhaf's virtually solitary struggle to force the FCC to apply the "fairness doctrine" to cigarette commercials; and food stamp lobbyists' successful intervention in shaping regulations governing the program's benefits and eligibility requirements.[24]

Service on Advisory Committees

An even more formally institutionalized vehicle for participation by organized interests in executive policymaking processes is service on federal advisory committees.[25] Typically, such committees are created by an agency to provide advice on a continuing basis for regulating particular activities or industries within the agency's jurisdiction. In 1982 there were over 875 advisory committees in the federal government. Examples include the Health Insurance Benefits Advisory Council, for the Department of Health and Human Services; the Advisory Committee on Hog Cholera Eradication, for the Department of Agriculture; and the Space and Missile Systems Organization Advisory Group, for the Department of Defense. The members of such committees are usually involved in the particular activity or industry and are drawn from the agency's dominant clientele groups.

In our survey, three-quarters of the respondents—95 percent of those from unions, 74 percent each of those from corporations and trade associations, and 67 percent of those from citizens' groups—reported that their or-

---

[23] Peter H. Schuck, "Public Interest Groups and the Policy Process," *Public Administration Review* 37 (1977): 137.

[24] Ibid., p. 138. See also, Berry, *Feeding Hungry People,* pp. 90–100.

[25] This discussion of advisory committees relies heavily on Mark P. Petracca, "The National Executive and Private Interests—Federal Advisory Committees: The 'Steel Bridge' to Corporatism," paper delivered at the Annual Meeting of the American Political Science Association, Chicago, September 1983.

ganizations serve on advisory commissions and boards. While these figures suggest especially heavy union involvement in this activity, government data indicate that corporations are much more likely to serve on multiple committees. In 1976, each of 29 corporations had 20 or more seats on such panels: only 5 unions had so many seats.[26] Hence, although the proportion of unions reporting service on advisory committees is higher than for other kinds of organizations, the total volume of corporate participation is even larger.

Like so many other pathways of organized interest influence on government, this one is paved by mutual needs and interests. From an agency's viewpoint, advisory committees are valuable not only because they provide access to information when and where it is needed but also because they provide a means of channeling pressures from organized interests. An agency may find it preferable to give interest organizations representation on an advisory committee rather than to have them on the outside raising a fuss. Thus incorporated into the decision-making machinery, interest organizations add legitimacy to the policies they have helped to recommend.[27] Obviously, service on advisory committees also works to the advantage of organized groups. This form of participation provides them with valuable information about where the government stands on issues, what it intends to do, what programs it plans to institute, how internal agency procedures work, and so on. The advisory panels also serve as a vehicle through which industrial competitors may meet regularly, with the government's approval (and with de facto exemption from antitrust laws), to advise the government on matters of mutual interest.[28] But surely the most important benefit that advisory committees provide to organized interests is direct access for influencing and educating executive branch policymakers.[29]

In fact, many observers insist that advisory committees have much more than a consultative role—that they play an important role in policy initiation and determination.[30] Studies of specific committees provide substantial anecdotal evidence in support of the argument. An analysis of the implementation of the Medicare program concluded that the Health Insurance Benefits Advisory Council (with a membership representing beneficiaries, health care institutions and professionals, public health officials, and taxpayers) played a sub-

[26] See Lee Metcalf, "New Index Shows Personal and Corporate Influence on Federal Advisory Committees," *Congressional Record,* October 20, 1977, p. S–34626; tables reprinted in Petracca, "The National Executive and Private Interests," Tables 7 and 8.

[27] See Petracca, "The National Executive and Private Interests," for a more complete discussion of the many ways in which advisory committees are of value to government.

[28] Edward S. Herman, *Corporate Control, Corporate Power* (New York: Cambridge University Press, 1981), p. 216.

[29] See Henry H. Perritt, Jr., and James A. Wilkinson, "Open Advisory Committees and the Political Process: The Federal Advisory Committees Act After Two Years," *Georgetown University Law Review* 63 (1975): 728.

[30] See Avery Leiserson, *Administrative Regulation: A Study in Representation of Interests* (Chicago: University of Chicago Press, 1942), p. 11; William Boyer, *Bureaucracy on Trial* (Indianapolis, IN: Bobbs-Merrill, 1964), p. 27; and Don K. Price, *Government and Science* (New York: New York University Press, 1954), p. 200.

stantial role in shaping initial policy outcomes as well as the policy process. Officials of the Social Security Administration adapted their policies to reflect the council's consensus.[31]

It is clear that these committees institutionalize, on a sustained basis, the representation of organized interests in the policy process.[32] Several arguments are used to justify these arrangements. These committees, it is said, provide a mechanism whereby the solution of public problems can proceed through voluntary cooperation between the government and those most affected by policy decisions. In essence, then, such arrangements conform to the highest norms of participatory democracy.

However, such arrangements have their critics. To some, they constitute private government—the parceling out of public authority to private interests.[33] The critics argue that the institutionalized sharing of public power poses problems for accountability. How to make unelected bureaucrats accountable without forcing them to act as political operatives in a narrow partisan sense has long been a conundrum for democratic governance. The puzzle of bureaucratic accountability becomes even more complex when authority is being exercised, not by agency officials alone, but jointly with private organizations. Problems of accountability have traditionally been exacerbated by the fact that these committees tended to protect their operations from scrutiny—by failing to give public notice of scheduled meetings, closing them to the public, and giving only sketchy reports of the proceedings.[34] It is further argued that such arrangements pose problems for political equality. When public power is shared with private organizations in advisory committees, then those not represented on the committee are at a disadvantage. Traditionally, advisory committees have tended to include few representatives of the interests of broad publics and the disadvantaged. Thus, according to this view, such arrangements compromise the norm of one-person–one-vote.

[31] See Judith Feder, "Medicare Implementation and the Policy Process," *Journal of Health Politics, Policy and Law* 2 (1977): 175.

[32] As such, advisory committees stand as an American analogue to corporatist arrangements in Western European democracies whereby private associations are brought into government and given a regularized consultative role in formulating policy. Such arrangements of shared public-private power traditionally involve peak associations and focus on issues of broad scope. In the American context, the sharing of authority is more fragmented and less centralized, involving hundreds of committees in dozens of agencies and individual trade associations, corporations, unions, and other organized units rather than peak associations. Furthermore, the issues at stake are far narrower.

Corporatist arrangements in advanced capitalist systems have received considerable attention recently. See, for example, the essays contained in Philippe C. Schmitter and Gerhard Lehmbruch, eds., *Trends toward Corporatist Intermediation* (Beverly Hills, CA: Sage, 1979); Suzanne Berger, ed., *Organizing Interests in Western Europe* (Cambridge: Cambridge University Press, 1981); and Gerhard Lehmbruch and Philippe C. Schmitter, eds., *Patterns of Corporatist Policy-Making* (Beverly Hills, CA: Sage, 1982).

[33] For statements of this theme, see McConnell, *Private Power and American Democracy*, especially Chapters 8, 10; and Lowi, *The End of Liberalism*, especially Chapter 3.

[34] On this theme, see Mark V. Nadel, *Corporations and Political Accountability* (Lexington, MA: Heath, 1976), pp. 56-57.

Influencing Agencies Indirectly

In addition to attempts at direct influence, organized interests employ two strategies in order to shape policy outcomes in the executive branch indirectly: influencing staffing decisions and influencing the organizational structure of the executive branch. Just as organizations try to influence presidential appointments to see that those appointed to government posts are congenial to their interests and points of view, they seek to affect the countless agency staffing decisions that are not White House appointments. When an organization deals with an agency staffed by persons sympathetic to its interests—or, better yet, persons drawn from its own ranks—the organization is more likely to see its goals realized.

This is a common pattern—the so-called revolving door, discussed in Chapter 11. The expertise and experience of professionals representing organized interests make them logical candidates for agency appointments, and organizations are often successful in gaining executive branch positions for their staff and activists. Perhaps most conspicuous in this regard are the defense contractors whose former employees go to work for the Department of Defense. But the practice extends far beyond the Pentagon, touching a wide array of domestic social and regulatory agencies. Under the Carter administration, for example, many citizens' groups succeeded in placing their lobbyists on the inside of bureaus such as the Food and Nutrition Service, the agency that administers the food stamp program.[35] The Reagan administration hired at least 25 people from the U.S. Chamber of Commerce, appointing them to such positions as the president's speech writer on economic issues, White House deputy press secretary, and special assistant to the assistant secretary of the treasury for tax policy.[36]

For citizens sharing a common problem or concern, having strong advocates on the staff of an agency can make a substantial difference. An instructive case is that of the Architectural and Transportation Barriers Compliance Board (ATBCB), an agency in the Department of Health and Human Services. Created by the Rehabilitation Act of 1973, the board was mandated to establish minimum requirements so that buildings constructed or leased by certain federal agencies would be accessible to handicapped persons. Eleven positions on the board were reserved for members of the public; nine of them were filled with handicapped persons. The board's staff also included many persons with handicaps. Thus, the board and staff encompassed substantial representation of the handicapped and much more limited representation of those who might argue on behalf of containing costs. Not surprisingly, from roughly 1979 through 1981 the ATBCB became a militant advocate for the handicapped and

---

[35] See Berry, *Feeding Hungry People,* p. 94. Also see Juan Cameron, "Nader's Invaders Are Inside the Gates," *Fortune,* October 1977, pp. 252–262.

[36] Ann Crittenden, "A Stubborn Chamber of Commerce," *New York Times,* June 27, 1982, p. F4.

proposed sweeping and costly guidelines covering everything from parking spaces to handrails to water coolers to telephones. Although the rules were modified in the aftermath of acrimonious public debate about their costs, the handicapped members of the board had an undeniable policy impact.[37]

As usual, the ability of organized interests to influence agency appointments varies with a variety of factors—among them the groups' size, command of technical information and expertise, and relations with the president's party and the agency in question. Furthermore, the structure of an agency's constituency can have an impact on the ability of a particular organization to influence personnel decisions. If an agency has several clientele groups attentive to its activities, each of those groups is likely to have less influence over appointment decisions than if it were the agency's only client. For example, organized labor typically enjoys a great deal of influence on executive appointments in the Department of Labor, where it is the primary client. At the National Labor Relations Board, however, unions compete for influence over appointments with business groups having equally compelling interests. Not surprisingly, labor's preferences carry less weight at the NLRB than at the Department of Labor. Most groups are not the sole client of an agency and are, thus, forced into a competitive situation in trying to shape decisions on appointments.

Executive Reorganization   This steers us toward a more general point about the relationship between executive branch structure and organized interest influence. Politically active organizations have an interest in seeing that the executive branch is structured so as to maximize their influence. Thus, it is common for organized interests to become embroiled in battles over proposed executive reorganizations, often as the ally of an agency that is attempting to ward off an attack on its autonomy or administrative status. Frequently the goal is to protect either a situation in which the group is the sole client of an agency or one in which the group deals only with a single agency.[38]

Clientele groups fear that they will have to compete for resources and attention if consolidated into a larger organization with a more diverse clientele and responsibilities or that they will have to deal with multiple agencies instead of a single one. To see these protective instincts at work, consider the way organized interests got into the act in 1978 when Jimmy Carter officially proposed the creation of a cabinet-level Department of Education. A wide array of groups of differing resources and status promptly emerged to lead the battle to prevent agencies with which they had special ties from being swallowed by the new department. The Children's Defense Fund, a citizens' group working to protect the interests of children, argued that a relocation of the Head Start

---

[37]Felicity Barringer, "Truce Reached on Handicapped Access," *Washington Post,* December 2, 1981, p. A25.

[38]For an instructive primer on the political conflicts to which executive reorganizations give rise, see Patricia Rachal, *Federal Narcotics Enforcement: Reorganization and Reform* (Boston: Auburn House, 1982), especially Chapters 1–4, from which many of the following examples are culled.

program might well have negative effects, leading to a transformation of the experimental education program into just another "narrow classroom program" lost in the "rigidities" of a formal education establishment. The politically more powerful and well-financed veterans' lobby pressured for the exclusion of the Veterans Administration's educational programs from the Education Department as well. The veterans' groups feared the potential loss of "one-stop shopping" at the VA and the potential de-emphasis of educational programs for veterans in general if such programs were consolidated into a large department with interests ranging far afield of the needs of veterans.[39] In protesting these reorganization schemes, such groups not only are serving their own interests but are also doing a favor for an agency with which they deal on an ongoing basis. Thus, in yet another way, organized interests are able to provide assistance at the same time that they attempt to shape policy.

Using Other Political Actors as Leverage

When all efforts to apply direct and indirect pressure to an agency fail to bring about the desired policy results, organized interests have a final strategy at their disposal: they can seek assistance elsewhere in the government. Implicit within this discussion has been the vulnerability of the agencies to the president, the courts, and especially Congress. Hence, one way to influence what happens in an agency is by seeking the support and intervention of those in a position to control it. Sometimes this strategy leads to the president, who has the authority to appoint agency officials and, in some cases, to fire or overrule them as well. Sometimes this strategy leads to the courts. In this increasingly litigious society, it has become commonplace for organized interests aggrieved by federal regulatory actions to go to federal court to try to halt or change an agency's application of the law.

For the most part, however, it is to Congress that organized interests go for outside help in affecting the actions of agencies. Virtually every agency is subject to congressional intervention on behalf of organized interests. For example, the policy decisions and managerial initiatives of the U.S. Postal Service incur close congressional scrutiny and, often, reversal. When the Postal Service has tried to replace small, uneconomical post offices with cheaper, alternate forms of service, the National League of Postmasters has prevailed on members of Congress to restrict postal management's freedom to close offices. Whenever the Postal Service has tried to eliminate Saturday mail deliveries, the postal employee unions and some organizations representing weekly newspapers have successfully beseeched Congress to prevent the Postal Service from taking such a step.[40]

[39] Joel Havemann, "Carter Reorganization Plans—Scrambling for Turf," *National Journal,* May 20, 1978, p. 790.
[40] See Tierney, *Postal Reorganization,* Chapter 3.

Another example of congressional intervention on behalf of an organized interest occurred in 1982 when Congress vetoed a Federal Trade Commission rule requiring used car dealers to disclose information about major known defects in the automobiles they sell. Consumer advocates regarded the rule as a modest consumer protection measure, but the used car dealers contended that the rule would require expensive inspections to protect them from possible litigation, thereby adding to the cost of the cars on their lots. Since the Federal Trade Commission's 1980 authorization permitted Congress to veto the agency's rules if both chambers adopted a disapproval resolution, the used car dealers mounted an intense campaign of direct lobbying (including almost $1 million in contributions to the reelection coffers of members of Congress) in an effort to persuade legislators to veto the rule. Ultimately, both houses voted to kill the regulation.[41]

When an organization takes such a case to Congress, all the principles developed in Chapter 12 apply. Both direct and indirect techniques of influence may be mobilized. Success is most common when opposing interests are inattentive or widely diffused and when the organization has resources that command legislators' attention—such as a large, geographically distributed membership (like the postal employees' union) or a sizable political action committee (like the used car dealers').

ORGANIZATIONAL CAPTURE OF EXECUTIVE AGENCIES

The preceding discussion has made clear that agencies and private organizations often have close relationships and mutually reinforcing interests. So warm are these relationships and so compatible are these interests that so-called capture theorists among academic observers have charged that agencies in the executive branch act as the servants of their organized constituents rather than as the servants of the citizenry. In some cases, of course, agencies are set up overtly to organize and nurture a special public and to act as its advocate in the halls of government. Such agencies as the now-defunct Office for Economic Opportunity (established to administer the poverty program during the 1960s), the Department of Labor, and the Department of Agriculture—often called "clientele agencies"—fit this pattern. Other agencies are supposedly set up to sustain a more adversarial relationship with organized interests. In this regard, what usually comes to mind are regulatory agencies—governmental organizations ostensibly established to use public authority to ameliorate undesirable

---

[41]See Judy Sarasohn, "FTC's Car Rule Falls Victim to First Congressional Veto," *National Journal,* May 29, 1983, p. 1259. See also Kirk Brown, "Campaign Contributions and Congressional Voting," paper presented at the Annual Meeting of the American Political Science Association, Chicago, September 1983; and Patricia Theiler, "Wheelers and Dealers," *Common Cause,* October 1981, pp. 15–21.

consequences of unfettered market activity. Capture theorists note that even agencies designed to protect the public rather than a narrow constituency are highly responsive to the very interests they are set up to regulate.

Although it is commonplace to refer to "capture theory," there is neither a single theory nor any single mechanism by which groups are thought to capture agencies. Perhaps the classic variant of capture theory specifies that agencies pass through a series of phases that constitute a "life cycle."[42] According to this view, agencies begin their lives full of youthful enthusiasm to do battle on behalf of the public. As they mature, however, this élan gives way to realism until in old age these agencies become, at best, the protectors of the status quo and at worst the captives of the industries they are supposed to regulate.

The agency whose life history is frequently cited as conforming to this pattern is the first of the regulatory commissions, the Interstate Commerce Commission (ICC), created in 1887. Over the course of its long history, the commission has compiled an almost spotless record of guarding and promoting the interests of the dominant companies and unions in its jurisdiction. After a brief period of aggressive regulation, the ICC entered a premature old-age stage about the time of World War I. The poor performance of the railroads during wartime created a crisis, in response to which the federal government ceased to be a regulator and became instead a promoter. But as the economic and political vitality of the rails declined, the ICC became increasingly captured by a newly dominant constituency, the truckers. To protect the truckers, the ICC kept trucking rates high by restricting entry into the trucking business and by sanctifying the high rates set by the industry's own rate bureaus (which operated under antitrust immunity). The agency encouraged inefficiency in the industry by certifying only certain carriers to haul specific items under specific conditions (in some cases, requiring that trucks make return trips empty because they were not certified to carry goods on the back haul). Moreover, the ICC barely enforced its own truck safety code and household movers' code.[43]

In contrast to the view that agencies are captured over time as they age is the perspective that their capture is inevitable because it was never meant to be otherwise. In this view, "regulation is acquired by the industry and is designed and operated primarily for its benefit."[44] The Civil Aeronautics Board might be used to illustrate this perspective. Until 1974 the CAB was the very model of a

[42]This view of agency capture is supported by a collection of sociologists, legal scholars, and political scientists whose observations were summarized and articulated by Marver Bernstein, *Regulating Business by Independent Commission* (Princeton: Princeton University Press, 1955), pp. 74–95.

[43]See Fred A. Kramer, *Dynamics of Public Bureaucracy,* 2nd ed. (Cambridge, MA: Winthrop Publishers, 1981), pp. 44–45, and Stephen Chapman, "The ICC and the Truckers," *Washington Monthly,* December 1977, pp. 33–39.

[44]George J. Stigler, "The Theory of Economic Regulation," *Bell Journal of Economics and Management Science* 2 (1971): 3. Stigler is a conservative economist. For much the same argument

captured agency, apportioning routes and setting fares in such a way as to restrict competition and protect the airline industry. This state of affairs should not be considered surprising, however, since from its very inception the CAB was meant to nurture the fledgling airline industry.[45]

The Mechanisms of Capture

Just as there is no single theory of the origins of regulatory capture, there is no single explanation of how capture is perpetuated. Several factors—none of them mutually exclusive—are cited by scholars as mechanisms by which agency capture is maintained. To understand these various mechanisms, it is helpful to note some of the many reasons why there is a natural affinity between bureaucratic agencies and organized interests. Executive agencies and private organizations are the policy specialists in Washington politics. They have a kind of sustained involvement with the details of particular policies that distinguishes them from officials in Congress, the White House, and the courts, who deal with numerous policy issues and confront any one of them only sporadically. Consequently, mutual concerns and shared expertise underpin the familiarity that emanates from regular interaction. In view of these joint substantive policy concerns and the long-term, frequent contacts that bring together agency and organized interest, it is not surprising that common perspectives develop.

These common perspectives may be reinforced in still another way. Executive agencies are dependent on outside organizations for information. Frequently, the only pertinent and detailed information comes from an agency's client, either because the data are generated by, for example, a regulated industry that is the only repository of such information or because other organizations lack the resources necessary to generate policy-relevant data. When persons who might hold competing views lack organized expression or when opposing organizations lack the technical expertise to challenge the accuracy or assumptions of the prevailing information base, outcomes are affected. Earlier chapters have shown that a policy controversy looks very different to a policymaker depending on whether there is factual input from more than one source. In the absence of information from a rival perspective, the policymaker is more likely to be swayed by the information provided by a single organized interest.

Another commonly noted mechanism for perpetuating agency capture involves influence over agency staffing decisions. It is said that because of explicit or implicit pressure from organized interests, the agencies selectively

from a radical historian, see Gabriel Kolko, *Railroads and Regulation, 1877–1916* (Princeton: Princeton University Press, 1966), and Kolko, *Triumph of Conservatism* (New York: Free Press, 1963).

[45]On the history of the CAB, see Bradley Behrman, "Civil Aeronautics Board," in James Q. Wilson, ed., *The Politics of Regulation* (New York: Basic Books, 1980), pp. 75–120.

recruit personnel with attitudes favorable to agency clients.[46] What is more, agency officials are often recruited through the "revolving door"; that is, organized interests are often successful not only in guaranteeing that officials will be congenial, but also in placing their own members and staff in key agency positions. Agency officials who have been drawn from the ranks of organized interests are, of course, likely to be predisposed to be sympathetic to the needs and interests of those agency clients. In addition, these officials are subsequently lobbied by their former workmates. Hence the expected bonds of a common point of view are reinforced by links of friendship.

Of course, the revolving door operates in the other direction as well. Agency officials mindful that their days as public servants will not last forever, keep their eyes set on what they will do once they leave office. The one sure place where they can cash in on their expertise and personal contacts is with organized agency constituents. In the view of some capture theorists, agency officials eager to guarantee their future employability fashion policies favorable to the agency's special publics. In short, officials take care of clients so that the clients will take care of them.[47] That agency officials, especially commissioners and staff of independent regulatory agencies, often find employment with former agency clients has been well documented.[48] Conflict-of-interest laws place some limitations on the ability of former executive branch officials to take jobs in the private sector and to argue cases before their former agencies. However, just as when agency personnel are drawn from the regulated interest, when executive branch officials go through the revolving door to find employment with agency clients, former workmates end up lobbying one another and judging each others' cases.

Finally, to the extent that agencies depend upon the political support of their organized constituencies, they are also subject to capture. Organized interests may lend their patron agencies support not only in fending off unwanted reorganizations but also in securing an adequate budget.[49] We know, for example, that agencies with enthusiastic clientele support (such as the Social Security Administration) have an easier time getting what they want from Congress than do agencies that lack well-organized and active clientele groups (such as the Census Bureau, the Bureau of Labor Statistics, and the Weather Bureau).[50] For an agency the price of such assistance in maintaining bureaucratic auton-

[46]On this theme, see the discussion and bibliographical references in Paul J. Quirk, *Industry Influence in Federal Regulatory Agencies* (Princeton: Princeton University Press, 1981), Chapter 3.
[47]See George W. Hilton, "The Basic Behavior of Regulatory Commissions," *American Economic Review Papers and Proceedings* 62 (1962): 47–54, and Milton Russell and Robert B. Shelton, "A Model of Regulatory Agency Behavior," *Public Choice* 20 (1974): 47–62.
[48]See Common Cause, *Serving Two Masters: A Common Cause Study of Conflicts of Interest in the Executive Branch* (Common Cause, 1976); Louis Kohlmeier, *The Regulators* (New York: Harper & Row, 1969), p. 77; and Roger G. Noll et al., *Economic Aspects of Television Regulation* (Washington, DC: The Brookings Institution, 1973), pp. 123–124.
[49]See Quirk, *Industry Influence in Federal Regulatory Agencies,* Chapter 4.
[50]See Richard Fenno, *The Power of the Purse: Appropriations Politics in Congress* (Boston: Little, Brown, 1966), especially Chapter 8.

omy vis-à-vis Congress is the sacrifice of autonomy vis-à-vis the client.[51] Capture theorists are fond of citing the Bureau of Land Management (BLM) as an example of this form of capture. The BLM and its organizational predecessor, the Grazing Service, both exceptionally dependent on the livestock industry that spoke up for them in Congress, had difficulty reforming public range management in the face of resistance from the stockmen.[52]

Although the various strains of capture theory differ substantially in content, they all posit a situation in which organized interests acquire sufficient influence over administrative agencies as to permit them to advance their narrow interests at the expense of the general public. When this happens, the agency "becomes simply the governmental outpost of an enclave of private power—only able to exercise its public authority at the sufferance of private groups,"[53] and "conflict of interest is made a principle of government."[54]

Capture Theories Reconsidered

Although capture theories of one sort or another have long enjoyed widespread currency among scholars and journalists alike, recently they have come in for question and scrutiny. After all, if agencies are captured and if they govern so as to protect their clienteles, then why do those clients clamor so loudly for deregulation? Regulated industries complain continually of the oppressive regulations imposed on them by a meddlesome government. If captured agencies were directing their efforts toward protecting the regulated, then we would not expect to hear such pleas for relief. This line of reasoning leads us to suspect that capture theories are too simplistic.

Indeed, recent research on the behavior of executive agencies indicates that capture is not inevitable. For example, one recent study of the relations between organized interests and agencies in the energy policy area concludes:

> Bureaucratic agencies need not be pawns of the interest organizations that confront them. Besides being able to affect the incentives and disincentives for group participation, agencies may selectively cooperate or resist cooperating with groups, as best suit their administrative and political needs.[55]

Another recent study of four executive agencies (the Federal Trade Commission, the Civil Aeronautics Board, the Food and Drug Administration, and

---

[51] Francis E. Rourke, *Bureaucracy, Politics, and Public Policy*, 3d ed. (Boston: Little, Brown, 1984), pp. 57–59, 61.

[52] See McConnell, *Private Power and American Democracy*, pp. 200–211, and Phillip Foss, *Politics and Grass* (Seattle: University of Washington Press, 1960).

[53] Rourke, *Bureaucracy, Politics, and Public Policy*, pp. 63–64.

[54] Lowi, *The End of Liberalism*, p. 59.

[55] John Chubb, *Interest Groups and the Bureaucracy* (Stanford: Stanford University Press, 1983), pp. 260–261.

the National Highway Traffic Safety Administration) tested capture theories, not by examining whether the organized constituents of these agencies in fact exercise influence over policy outcomes, but by investigating whether the mechanisms alleged to sustain agency capture actually operate as they are said to. In particular, the following postulates of capture theory were examined for the four agencies: that agencies selectively recruit personnel with proindustry attitudes; that in order to enhance the agency's budget, officials must court their organized clients; and that because they hope to get private sector jobs with agency clients after retiring from government service, agency officials seek not to offend them and thus do not regulate vigorously. While the study found some confirmation for the last of these hypotheses, little support for the first two was uncovered.[56]

Finally, a set of studies of eight federal agencies shows a diversity of patterns of relationships between regulator and regulated—ranging from regulatory failure and receptivity to the wishes of the carriers at the Federal Maritime Commission, to hostility toward business among the occupational safety and health professionals at the Occupational Safety and Health Administration.[57] Taken together, the studies make clear that there is no single pattern of regulatory politics. Capture is not by any means the norm, and where capture occurs, it does not always last. Various case studies of agencies in action also demonstrate that an agency's politics and policies are determined by multiple factors in addition to the demands made by its special public—including, for example, the structure of its clientele, the professional credentials of agency officials, the precision of the instructions given by Congress, the demands of the president, the preferences of current agency leadership, and the intensity of public opinion.

An agency having several organized groups within its constituency is less likely to be responsive to the demands of a particular group—and thus less likely to be captured—than one having an undifferentiated clientele.[58] When there are competing groups within an agency's constituency, officials will have more than one place to turn for political support, future employment, and the like; hence, they are unlikely to get too deeply in debt to any single client. For example, in the early years of its existence, women's groups found that they could not count on the Equal Employment Opportunity Commission to take up the cudgel against gender-based employment discrimination, in spite of a backlog of complaints on the subject. The EEOC's failure to help women surely reflects (among other things) the fact that it has traditionally been a disorganized and underfunded agency with a weak statutory mandate. In addition, women's groups were forced to compete for limited attention and resources

[56]Quirk, *Industry Influence in Federal Regulatory Agencies.*
[57]Wilson, ed., *The Politics of Regulation.*
[58]There are many exceptions to this tendency, including two agencies already mentioned, the Interstate Commerce Commission and the Federal Maritime Commission.

with the EEOC's other client groups, including blacks and Hispanics, to whose needs the EEOC had accorded higher priority.[59]

It also seems that, when agency officials have norms of professional excellence by which their performance can be evaluated, capture is less likely. One study of the Federal Trade Commission makes the point that economists on the agency's staff see their audience as academia, not the commission itself or the business community. Consequently, they would neither make recommendations nor furnish analyses that would threaten their professional integrity. The lawyers on the FTC's staff are equally impervious to capture. Many of them wish to use their government service as an opportunity to learn a transportable set of legal skills and perceive that their future opportunities in the private bar will be enhanced to the extent that they can demonstrate their toughness and legal expertise.[60]

Case studies of agency politics make clear not only that there is tremendous variation across agencies in terms of relations with organized constituencies but also that relations between any particular agency and its clients are not static. Many factors can have an impact upon the zeal with which agencies carry out their responsibilities. For example, with the arrival in Washington of a new administration, new presidential directives and new agency appointees can produce a transformation of agency policy and, consequently, substantial alteration in the fortunes of the organized interests within its clientele. The Environmental Protection Agency (EPA) provides an especially interesting illustration. At the time it was created in 1970, the EPA was given a very detailed congressional mandate on the theory that precise statutory standards would allow the new agency to avoid capture by industry. The inflexible goals and timetables set by Congress did protect the EPA from capture, but Reagan's original appointees to the EPA changed the agency's policy dramatically, making it very responsive to the demands of industry.[61] This about-face was not, however, an example of capture as the result of either organizational imperatives or agency decline in middle age; rather, it reflected the Reagan adminis-

---

[59]On the early years of the EEOC and its unresponsiveness to women, see Jo Freeman, *The Politics of Women's Liberation* (New York: McKay, 1975), pp. 184–185.

[60]Robert A. Katzmann, *Regulatory Bureaucracy: The Federal Trade Commission and Antitrust Policy* (Cambridge: MIT Press, 1980), pp. 39–40, 76–85, 94. Suzanne Weaver has found a similar situation in the Antitrust Division of the Justice Department, where the staff attorneys' expectations of future employment in the private sector leads to vigorous enforcement of the law. See "Antitrust Division of the Department of Justice," in Wilson, ed., *The Politics of Regulation,* p. 135.

[61]On the history of the EPA throughout the 1970s, see Alfred Marcus, "Environmental Protection Agency," in Wilson, ed., *The Politics of Regulation,* pp. 267–303. On Reagan administration officials' efforts to emasculate the EPA (and on later charges of conflict of interest on the part of some of these officials), see Joanne Omang, "Internal Rifts, Huge Staff Cut Hint EPA Retreat on Programs, *Washington Post,* September 30, 1981, p. 1; Charles A. Radin, "Ex-aide to Gorsuch Target of Probe," *Boston Globe,* February 21, 1983, p. 11; and Mary Thornton, "Firm Under Cloud Got EPA Contract," *Washington Post,* February 22, 1983, p. 1.

tration's ideological commitment to free markets. In short, the EPA was not so much captured by industry as donated to it by the Reagan administration.

Finally, agencies change with the times. The vigor of agency activity often responds to the overall political climate, as periods of public ferment and pressure for governmental initiatives alternate with periods of public quiescence and political consolidation. During the 1960s, of course, politics was characterized by public agitation on behalf of, among other things, consumer protection and environmental preservation. These popular movements left an organizational residue of citizens' groups of various kinds that monitor the activities of the executive branch. Their influence on the agencies is often enhanced by their ability to enlist the aid of the media in drawing public attention to alleged misuses of administrative power. Such groups have had an impact on even such notoriously captured agencies as the Bureau of Land Management. The constituencies of most local administrators in the BLM now include not just the livestock and forest products industries but conservationists and recreationists as well. This expansion in the BLM's clientele has had a significant impact on its politics. The resulting pattern of group influence is therefore quite different from that once posited by the adherents of the capture thesis.[62]

In short, capture theories are simplistic as a description of the relations between organized interests and the agencies to which they are attentive. They do, however, have the virtue of sensitizing us to the possibility that private groups may occasionally acquire positions of great influence in agency decision-making processes, thus posing a perplexing puzzle for democracy. The problem is, of course, to insure that the processes of executive decision making are equally accessible to all and accountable to the public and their elected representatives, while simultaneously promoting efficiency and deference to expertise.

PROCEDURAL CHANGES IN ADMINISTRATIVE POLICYMAKING

Recognizing this fundamental problem, several steps have been taken in recent years to democratize policymaking in the executive branch. These changes are aimed at rendering the administrative process more accountable and more democratic in several ways: exposing the process to greater scrutiny by opening agency proceedings to the public and by making administrative information more readily available; limiting undue influence over policy by agency clients, especially in regulatory agencies; and correcting imbalances in representation by facilitating the participation of representatives of broad publics. These changes merit consideration, not only because of the importance of their substantive content and consequences, but also because they demonstrate the extent to which the structures and processes of government affect the behavior of organized interests.

[62] Paul Culhane, *Public Lands Politics: Interest Group Influence on the Forest Service and the Bureau of Land Management* (Baltimore: Johns Hopkins University Press, published for Resources for the Future, 1981), p. 334.

Opening Up the Process

In recent years there have been several important changes intended to open up regulatory and administrative processes to greater public scrutiny and access. Among the most significant is the Freedom of Information Act (FOIA). Originally passed in 1966, the Act requires federal agencies to provide citizens with access to public records upon request. The law provides exemptions for certain kinds of national defense materials, confidential personnel information and financial data, and some law enforcement files. Early experience under the Act showed that too much of the information in government files was classified as confidential, that government agencies were using exemption provisions "as a broad charter for the preservation and even the expansion of secrecy," and that requests for material often were met with bureaucratic delay and excessive charges.[63] As a consequence, in 1974 Congress amended the act to make it easier for the public to find out what the government is doing and to get information from it.

While the 1974 amendments have added to the administrative headaches of most federal agencies, the revised law has, by and large, made life easier for organized interests. Table 13.1 shows that 43 percent of the respondents in our Washington representatives survey indicated that the FOIA had made it easier for them to operate effectively; only 9 percent indicated that it had made things harder. The impact of the FOIA has not been uniform across various kinds of groups, however. Respondents from unions (93 percent) and citizens' groups (82 percent) were overwhelmingly likely to report the FOIA as having had benign effects. On the other hand, the act seems to have had less effect on corporations: two-thirds of those affiliated with corporations indicated that it has made no difference in their ability to operate effectively; 19 percent reported that it had made things easier.

By invoking the FOIA, organizations are able to garner substantive data and information that may otherwise be unavailable to them. Moreover, organized interests know that the information they acquire through a FOIA request may provide them with tactical advantages. For example, in January 1980 the Federal Insurance Administration (FIA) awarded the National Training and Information Center of Chicago (NTIC) a study contract to propose solutions to the problem of urban redlining. Concerned over the FIA's selection of a "militant, anti-insurance public interest group" to do the study, the Independent Insurance Agents of America (IIAA) filed a freedom of information request to learn more about the criteria used to choose NTIC, hoping that this information "could offer an opportunity to fault the selection of the study contractor, and undermine the credibility of a potentially unfairly damaging report."[64]

[63] See Francis E. Rourke, "Executive Secrecy: Change and Continuity," in Francis E. Rourke, ed., *Bureaucratic Power in National Politics,* 3d ed. (Boston: Little, Brown, 1978), p. 370.
[64] Independent Insurance Agents of America, "Window on Washington," *Independent Agent,* January 1981, p. 17.

**Table 13.1   THE IMPACT OF CHANGES IN THE EXECUTIVE BRANCH ON
ORGANIZATIONAL ABILITY TO OPERATE EFFECTIVELY**

How has change affected organization's ability to operate effectively—made it easier,
harder, or made relatively little difference?

	Easier	Little difference	Harder	
1. Freedom of Information Act	43%	48	9	= 100%
2. Sunshine laws	36%	53	12	= 101%
3. Conflict-of-interest laws governing employment in the private sector after government service	6%	83	11	= 100%
4. Restrictions on communications with government officials when cases are pending (ex parte rules)	3%	74	22	= 99%
5. Government financing of public interest representation at regulatory proceedings (intervenor financing)	14%	53	32	= 99%
6. Increasing authority of the Office Management and Budget to review agency rules	24%	35	41	= 100%

Percentage of respondents from different kinds of organizations saying that change has
made it easier to operate effectively

	Corporations	Trade associations	Unions	Citizens' groups
1. Freedom of Information Act	19%	38%	93%	82%
2. Sunshine laws	23	31	50	48
3. Conflict-of-interest laws	6	3	0	14
4. Ex parte rules	0	7	0	11
5. Intervenor financing	2	0	38	52
6. Increasing authority of OMB	38	40	6	5

Source: Washington Representatives Survey.

Shortly after the filing of the IIAA's request, the agency canceled the study
contract, stating that an internal office had already performed the task, rendering the outside contract unnecessary.

Another significant measure is the Sunshine Act of 1976, a piece of legislation containing many provisions designed to open up the administrative process and to alter patterns of influence within agencies. It requires some agencies
to open their proceedings to the public, and meetings of collegial bodies that
head federal agencies—with a few exceptions—must not be closed. The idea is,

of course, that such access gives anyone who shares a stake in the decision an opportunity to present a point of view. If all interested groups have access, final judgments have a better chance of being based on all relevant information, not on evidence garnered from a single source or on data illustrating a single perspective. However, it seems that there is tremendous variation in the extent to which agencies observe the requirement.[65]

Another effort aimed at opening up administrative proceedings focuses on federal advisory committees. In recognition of the threat to accountability posed by governing arrangements such as advisory committees, where policymaking has traditionally been carried on behind closed doors, Congress passed the Federal Advisory Committee Act of 1972. The FACA stipulates that all advisory committee meetings be open to public view and requires public notice of meetings in the *Federal Register* 15 days in advance. Assessments of the experience of the past decade indicate that compliance with the FACA has not been uniform, and the announcement of meetings and publication of records has been uneven.[66] Moreover, advisory committees still employ various techniques to prevent or at least forestall widespread public participation: proclaiming that space is limited; locating the meetings in buildings where access is restricted; and manipulating the meeting's agenda to close parts of it to the public.[67]

The congressional counterparts of these sunshine measures make it possible for lobbyists to scrutinize policymaking and to make sure that promises made previously are not broken if the going gets tough. However uneven the compliance with various executive branch sunshine provisions, they seem, on balance, to expand the number of opportunities for influence there as well. As shown in Table 13.1, a bare majority of the respondents in our survey indicated that sunshine laws make no difference in their organizations' ability to operate effectively. The remainder divided three to one: 36 percent indicated that it made life easier, and only 12 percent that it made life harder. Representatives of citizens' groups and of unions were especially likely to report that sunshine laws make life easier for them; however, even among corporate respondents, only 12 percent indicated that sunshine laws make it harder to operate effectively.

Limiting Undue Influence

A second set of measures is designed to limit the influence of agency clients. As Chapter 11 indicated, the Ethics in Government Act of 1978 aimed at diminish-

---

[65] Douglas B. Feaver, "Sunshine Act: Not an Open and Shut Case," *Washington Post,* September 29, 1981, p. A17.

[66] Petracca, "The National Executive and Private Interests," pp. 21–22.

[67] Barbara W. Turkheimer, "Veto By Neglect: The Federal Advisory Committee Act," *American University Law Review* 25 (1975): 68–71; noted in Petracca, "The National Executive and Private Interests," p. 22.

ing the incentive for officials to show favoritism to agency clients in the hope of securing future private sector employment. This act expanded statutory restrictions on the subsequent employment of high-ranking executive branch officials. The restrictions in the act are actually rather narrow: they prohibit former officials only from exploiting their government contacts and expertise as representatives of private interests seeking to influence their former agencies. The rules do not actually limit postgovernment employment, nor do they prevent individuals from assuming governmental posts that confer on them substantial responsibility over programs they tried to influence from the outside. The respondents in our Washington representatives survey confirmed that this measure has had only a limited impact. The overwhelming majority reported that it had made no difference in their ability to operate effectively, 11 percent said that it had made life harder, and 6 percent that it had made life easier. This view was shared across various kinds of organizations.

Also aimed at the limitation of undue influence are the *ex parte* rules contained in the Sunshine Act of 1976. Ex parte rules restrict communications with agency officials when cases are pending. The act prohibits outside interests from engaging in informal conversations with the intention of informing or influencing agency officials regarding either substantive or procedural matters before the agency. Agencies have some discretion over exactly what types of outside contacts are illegal and at what point during formal proceedings they become illegal.[68] Naturally, then, the effectiveness of these rules varies from agency to agency. But a study of the Nuclear Regulatory Commission, an agency long considered to be captured by the industry it regulates, found that the agency chose a strict definition of ex parte communications and based its policies largely on the formal record. As a consequence, none of the environmental groups in the agency's constituency felt disadvantaged by informal relationships between the agency and the industry once licensing and generic rulemaking proceedings began.[69] As shown in Table 13.1, three-fourths of our respondents reported that ex parte rules have made no difference in their ability to operate effectively; of the remainder, a mere 3 percent indicated that the rules had made things easier, and 22 percent that they had made things harder. Trade associations seem to be most inconvenienced by ex parte rules: 40 percent of their representatives indicated that ex parte rules have made life more difficult.

Balancing Representation

Perhaps the most radical of the recent reforms are those aimed at guaranteeing representation in executive branch proceedings to the kinds of interests that

[68]On ex parte communications, see Lawrence J. White, *Reforming Regulation: Process and Problems* (Englewood Cliffs, NJ: Prentice-Hall, 1981), Chapter 2.
[69]Chubb, *Interest Groups and the Bureaucracy,* p. 106. On the notion that the NRC is captured by the nuclear power industry, see Bernard Weinraub, "Nuclear Agency Called Too Close to Industry to Regulate it Properly," *New York Times,* October 16, 1983, pp. 1, 28.

have traditionally been excluded. Congress included in the Federal Advisory Committee Act of 1972 a stipulation that committee membership be "fairly balanced in terms of the points of view represented and the functions to be performed by the advisory committee."[70] Furthermore, in order to eliminate government by private interests, the FACA required that advisory committees were not to operate independently of the supervision of agency officials.

Once again, subsequent assessments indicate that compliance has not been uniform. The mandate for balance in committee membership has achieved mixed results. While some agencies have incorporated representatives of newly organized groups, others have resisted such expansion or have isolated representatives of emergent interests on newly formed committees, leaving the composition of older committees unchanged. The difficulties in achieving greater public participation stem not only from pressure generated by the organized interests that have traditionally dominated the committees and do not wish to see their influence diluted, but also from the needs of the agencies. Widened public participation conflicts with such traditional bureaucratic norms as expertise and efficiency; requirements for openness contradict the inevitable bureaucratic impulse to secrecy and institutional maintenance.[71] Hence, the transformation of the conduct of federal advisory committees is easier to legislate than to implement.

An even more direct and controversial step taken toward balancing representation in administrative proceedings is *intervenor financing*—governmental funding of participation by citizens' groups. Not surprisingly, this procedural innovation was enthusiastically supported by citizens' groups as a way to bridge what they deemed the "advocacy gap" that resulted from the monopoly of access enjoyed by narrowly focused and well-financed organizations. In brief, they argued that agency neglect of broad public interests in administrative proceedings emanated from the ability of large companies and trade associations to afford the surveys, statistics, lawyers, and consultants needed to participate effectively in complicated rule-making proceedings, which citizens' groups and smaller businesses could not. Therefore, they argued that the government should facilitate balanced representation in agency proceedings by helping citizens' groups to defray the costs of obtaining legal counsel, expert witnesses, adequate documentation, and the other requirements of effective participation.

Intervenor financing won congressional endorsement for several agencies in the mid-1970s. For example, Congress authorized the Federal Trade Commission to provide compensation for reasonable attorneys' fees, expert witnesses' fees, and other costs to small businesses and citizens' groups for partici-

---

[70] Public Law 92–463 as amended by PL 94–409; quoted in Joseph A. Pika, "Interest Groups and the Executive: Presidential Intervention," in Allan J. Cigler and Burdett A. Loomis, eds., *Interest Group Politics* (Washington, DC: CQ Press, 1983), p. 309. Our discussion of the FACA and its consequences draws heavily from Pika's more extended treatment.

[71] This issue is raised by Robert W. Kweit and Mary Grisez Kweit, "Bureaucratic Decision-Making: Impediments to Citizen Participation," *Polity* 12 (1980): 650.

pating in rule-making proceedings. With this congressional mandate and the enthusiastic support of the chairman at the time, the FTC implemented what came to be the government's most fully developed intervenor financing program. During 1979–1980 the FTC paid $351,049 to 54 witnesses for testimony about regulations on children's television programming, used cars, funeral homes, over-the-counter drugs, children's hearing aids, mobile homes, and home insulation.[72]

The concept of intervenor financing is controversial. Proponents of the practice say it reduces the imbalance in participation by industry and citizens' groups in executive branch proceedings and therefore makes them more equitable. The broader participation that results from intervenor financing may curb whatever pro-client tendencies that agencies may have by presenting decision makers with new ideas and information, reducing their dependence on data supplied by dominant clientele organizations, compelling them to seek accommodations with new groups, and aiding in the development of a more comprehensive record.[73]

Opponents of intervenor funding claim that the practice may simply encourage irresponsible participation in administrative proceedings and prolong proceedings that are already long and unwieldy. They argue that intervenor funding is duplicative and wasteful since top administrators and staff of public agencies are responsible for representing the public interest and already possess the kinds of expertise and resources needed to perform that function adequately.[74] Opponents also believe that funded intervenors may be coopted by the funding agencies over the long run, since agencies would tend to show favoritism toward persons or groups they know, who had testified effectively before the agency in the past and might be counted upon to make the kinds of arguments the agency wants to hear. Consequently, the independence of the participating groups would be compromised, the quality of the testimony would be tarnished, and the purpose of the intervention would be undermined.[75]

In view of the controversy, it is not surprising that there is more division of opinion over the effects of intervenor financing than over most of the other procedural changes considered. Table 13.1 shows that a bare majority of the respondents in our survey indicated that intervenor financing makes no difference in their organization's ability to operate effectively. Of the remainder, 14

[72]See Jeffrey M. Berry, "Maximum Feasible Dismantlement," *Citizen Participation,* November/December 1981, p. 5, and Pete Earley, "Rule-Makers No Longer Foster Public Input," *Washington Post,* April 7, 1982, p. A23.

[73]Joan B. Aron, "Citizen Participation at Government Expense," *Public Administration Review* 39 (1979): 480. See also R. D. Comfort, "Agency Assistance to Impecunious Intervenors," *Harvard Law Review* 88 (1975): 1816.

[74]See D. Stephen Cupps, "Emerging Problems of Citizen Participation," *Public Administration Review* 37 (1977): 480, 482.

[75]Aron, "Citizen Participation," p. 481. See also "Funding Public Participation in Regulatory Proceedings," *Regulation,* March/April 1978, p. 10.

percent reported that it makes things easier, and 32 percent that it makes things harder. However, there are real disparities across the various categories of organizations: 38 percent of the respondents from unions and 52 percent of the respondents from citizens' groups, but only 2 percent of those from corporations and none of those from trade associations, said that intervenor financing makes it easier to be effective. Furthermore, nearly two-thirds of the respondents from corporations and 41 percent of the respondents from trade associations, but only 10 percent of those from citizens' groups and none of those from unions, said that intervenor financing makes it harder to be effective.

In the months since we conducted our interviews, opponents of intervenor financing have attacked the practice successfully and have rendered the matter moot for the time being. Various actions by the courts, Congress, and Reagan-appointed officials effectively gutted intervenor financing with the result that nearly all the intervenor financing programs that existed when President Reagan took office have since been shut down.[76]

Increasing the Power of the OMB

A final procedural change in the executive branch—the substantial increase in the power of the Office of Management and Budget (OMB) over agency rule making—has even greater implications for organized interests. Less than a month after President Reagan assumed office in 1981, he issued Executive Order 12291 establishing new principles and procedures that alter and centralize the rule-making processes of all executive branch agencies. Under the terms of the presidential order, an agency cannot propose a major new rule—one that would have an economic impact of $100 million or more—unless it first prepares a "regulatory impact statement" of the costs and benefits of the proposed rule. The proposed rule and accompanying cost-benefit analysis must be submitted to OMB for its approval, thus making OMB the gatekeeper and central clearance point for federal regulations.[77]

The OMB has exercised its new responsibilities with zeal. Scores of proposed rules have been rejected or delayed and scores of existing rules have been reviewed without any explanation. For example, less than three months after the Reagan administration took office, OMB announced its plans to change the

---

[76]See Earley, "Rule-Makers No Longer Foster Public Input," *Washington Post,* April 7, 1982, p. A23; and Berry, "Maximum Feasible Dismantlement," p. 5.

[77]The powers granted to OMB by the order are substantial. For example, among the agency's powers are the ability to decide which rules or sets of rules are "major"; to waive requirements for any rules or class of rules in order to expedite rule making; to prescribe the procedures agencies are to follow in their regulatory impact analyses; and to extend the date of review beyond 30 days for final rules and regulatory impact analyses. See Executive Order 12291, 46 Fed. Reg. 13, 193 (February 17, 1981). For analysis of the order's procedural impact, see Robert S. Gilmour, "Controlling Regulation in the Reagan Administration: The Emergence of Central Clearance," paper delivered at the Annual Meeting of the New England Political Science Association, Newport, RI, April 1984.

tough environmental regulations scheduled to be imposed on diesel vehicles in the fall of 1984. The OMB move undid the work of the Environmental Protection Agency and was a victory for the automobile industry, which wanted to increase its production of diesel-powered cars and light trucks.[78]

This tremendous increase in OMB's power has important consequences for the behavior and influence of organized interests. Since this power shift gives the president greater control over rules and regulations adopted during his administration, it means that the OMB and the White House will become more important targets of lobbying activities. Organized interests that have lost their case in agency proceedings may use the OMB as a court of last resort, lobbying the president's management team in an effort to overturn the setback.

When asked about what effect these changes in regulatory procedure have had on the ability of their organizations to operate effectively, our respondents had widely varying answers. Almost two-thirds of them reported that these changes had made a difference to them, and 41 percent reported that it had made things more difficult. The replies are distributed quite unevenly across organizations. By and large, business organizations have fared rather better under this system than unions and citizens' groups: 38 percent of the respondents from corporations and 40 percent of the respondents from trade associations, but only 6 percent of those from unions and 5 percent of those from citizens' groups, said that the new authority of the OMB to review agency rules has made life easier; 75 percent of the respondents from unions and 62 percent of the respondents from citizens' groups, but only 18 percent of those from corporations and 37 percent of those from trade associations, said that it has made life harder.

Like some of the others, this change is controversial. OMB reviewers have an injudicious practice of engaging in informal, off-the-record dealings with affected interests, mostly from the business community. As the president and his staff aides engage in ex parte communications with external parties, there are concerns that not all concerned parties will have a chance to present their points of view and that regulatory decisions will be made on the basis of discussions and deals cloaked in executive privilege and unavailable for public review or judicial scrutiny.[79]

[78]Caroline Mayer, "OMB Usurping Rule Making, Group Charges," *Washington Post,* October 21, 1981, p. A25. According to one study, environmental regulations have been subjected to unusually close scrutiny by OMB. The Environmental Protection Agency and environmentally relevant units of the Department of Transportation account for more than 50 percent of the regulations returned by OMB for agency reconsideration. See Robert A. Shanley, "The Politics of Regulatory Oversight: The Reagan Administration's Executive Order 12291 and Environmental Policy," paper delivered at the Annual Meeting of the New England Political Science Association, Newport, RI, April 1984, p. 8.

[79]Gilmour, "Controlling Regulation in the Reagan Administration," pp. 20, 27. Also see Kenneth Culp Davis, *1982 Supplement to Administrative Law Treatise* (San Diego, CA: K.C. Davis Publishing Co., 1982), pp. 153–154, and Dick Kirschten, "The 20 Years War," *National Journal,* June 11, 1983, p. 1238.

The Impact of Procedural Changes on Organized Interests

The discussion so far has focused on the differential consequences for various kinds of groups of these individual executive branch changes; however, it is also important to assess the overall effects of the changes as a package. As we did when we considered the impact on organized interests of recent changes in Congress, we constructed a scale to indicate the net effects of all changes taken together. Once again, for each respondent we subtracted the number of changes that the respondent considered to make life harder from the number deemed to make life easier, and placed the respondents' organizations along the five categories of the scale. Table 13.2 presents the results of this operation. The figures for all organizations taken together (shown in the right-hand column) show the distribution of replies: 19 percent of our respondents indicated that these changes only make it easier to operate effectively, and 24 percent indicated that they only make it harder; in the middle, 28 percent of our respondents indicated that these reforms make no difference. Just as the changes in Congress did not affect all kinds of organizations in the same way, these executive branch changes have had a differential impact on various kinds of organizations. Although there are differences from one change to another, citizens' groups find them most congenial overall, followed in order by unions, trade associations, and corporations.[80]

A NOTE ON DEREGULATION

In understanding the explosion of organized interest involvement over the past couple of decades, we have been sensitive to the way in which expanded government activity generates activity from private interests. More recently, however, the government has withdrawn long-standing regulations in such key economic sectors as trucking, civil aviation, and telecommunications. It might be expected that as the government reduces its regulation of business, political activity by corporations and trade associations might constrict. Although it is not possible for us to put these expectations to any conclusive tests, we can consider what we learned in our interviews with Washington representatives from four corporations in a recently deregulated industry, the airlines.

Although the respondents from all four airlines indicated that deregulation makes life easier for their companies, they all remain very active politically, utilizing an average of 20 out of the 27 basic lobbying techniques outlined in Chapter 7. (For all corporations in the survey the average was 18.) Not only

[80] If the one Reagan era reform (the enhanced authority of the OMB to review regulations) is omitted from the scale, these relationships become even more pronounced: 71 percent of the respondents from citizens' groups and 62 percent of the respondents from unions, but only 12 percent of those from trade associations and 6 percent of those from corporations, fall into the "easier only" category.

Table 13.2 NET IMPACT OF CHANGES IN EXECUTIVE BRANCH[a]

Impact on organizational ability to operate effectively	Corporations	Trade associations	Unions	Citizens' groups	All organizations
Only easier	12%	19%	19%	24%	19%
Easier on balance	4	9	44	38	15
No change	35	25	19	24	28
Harder on balance	16	22	6	10	14
Only harder	33	25	12	5	24
	100%	100%	100%	101%	100%

[a]The figure for the net impact was calculated by subtracting the number of changes that were deemed to make it harder from the number deemed to make it easier.
Source: Washington Representatives Survey.

are they highly active, but all four of these companies report that they are *more* politically active now than they were before deregulation. On average, they have increased their use of 16 of the 27 techniques. (Across the whole sample, the corporate average was 13.) This is not to say, however, that nothing has changed. The issues have changed—from routes and fares to airports and airways. The principal target has changed—from the Civil Aeronautics Board to the Federal Aviation Administration. Our discussions with airline executives make clear that their corporations remain highly active politically. Thus, if the experience of one industry is any indication, substantial deregulation may not result in a wholesale contraction in corporate attempts to influence government—at least not in the short run.

SUMMARY

This chapter shows that the executive branch is a highly heterogeneous and permeable set of institutions affording organized interests many different points of access in their attempts to shape public policy. While the president is more insulated from direct pressure than are most other elected officials, there are many ways that organized interests can try to make presidential power work for them. The effectiveness that many groups enjoy in this regard stems in part from the increasing extent to which modern presidents rely on interest organizations both for electoral success and for help in pulling together political support for presidential initiatives.

This same kind of political calculus is the source of organized interest influence with the executive agencies. Interests and agencies rely on each other for political support, as well as for information and expertise. This dependence of most agencies on their attentive constituencies provides the outside groups with multiple means of influencing agency actions. Organizations participate formally in bureaucratic decision making through service on advisory committees and involvement in rule-making proceedings, and they participate informally by cultivating personal relationships with agency officials and staff.

Organized interests enjoy influence in bureaucratic decision making not because agencies are captive to organized groups but because agencies need their support and know that the most important weapon in the arsenal of organized interests is the ability to make trouble for bureaucrats. Indeed, what makes interest organizations so strong vis-à-vis administrative and regulatory agencies is that agencies recognize how vulnerable their own autonomy is. They know that organized interests have many other political actors and institutions to which they may effectively turn in an effort to overturn unfavorable agency decisions. Organizations may appeal successfully to the president and his aides, to the department heads and other political appointees, to the OMB, and especially to Congress and the public. In other words, there are many kinds of courts of appeal to which organized interests may go in an effort to shape or affect agency behavior. As the next chapter will demonstrate, not the least of these is the federal judiciary itself.

14

Going to Court

Although the popular image of interest representation places lobbyists at the doors of legislative and executive officials, the courts are also a political forum in which organized interests are active. The courts are crucial policymaking institutions in the American system, empowered to make authoritative decisions that not only settle particular disputes but make sweeping policies. Moreover, although the courts are sensitive to different kinds of political crosswinds from those that visit Congress and the executive branch, the judiciary is highly attuned to the articulation of political interests. Thus, just as organized interests work to influence the course of legislative and executive decisions, many organizations also try to influence judicial outcomes. Often organized interests resort to the courts either when they have lost in legislative or executive battles or when they are so certain of losing in those arenas that they figure it is not worth trying. Thus, the courts provide an alternative institutional forum in which they may succeed in forcing a change in policy or preventing some uncongenial policy from being implemented. In addition, interest organizations may go to court either to create legitimacy or precedent for some future change in policy or to focus the attention of Congress, the executive, and the public on some widely ignored problem or grievance.

This chapter has four principal purposes. First, it identifies briefly a few characteristics that distinguish the courts from other institutional arenas of organized interest activity. Second, it examines the various tactics and strategies organizations use in pursuing their goals through the courts. Third, it considers the profound effects of changes over the past fifteen years in the rules governing what kinds of matters may be brought to court for decision (and by whom) upon the activity of organized interests in the courts. Finally, it explores the question of what kinds of interests seem to benefit most from going to court.

THE COURTS AS AN ARENA FOR ORGANIZATIONAL ACTIVITY

To understand organized interests' use of the federal courts, it is important first to chart the institutional terrain. The Constitution requires only one federal court, the U.S. Supreme Court. All other federal courts and their jurisdictions have been established by Congress over the years. For the handling of cases that need not be decided by the Supreme Court, Congress has created two kinds of lower federal courts: "legislative" courts (special-purpose courts such as the territorial courts, the Court of Military Appeals, and the United States Claims Court) and "constitutional" courts (that exercise the judicial powers found in Article III of the Constitution).[1] The concern in this chapter is with the U.S. Supreme Court and the most important of the constitutional courts— the 12 United States (Circuit) Courts of Appeals and the 94 United States District Courts only.[2]

Just as it makes little sense to speak of "the Congress" or "the executive branch" as if these were monolithic institutions, it is risky to make blanket assertions about the federal courts or about the hundreds of judges who sit at their benches. Still, the established procedures and practices that govern the behavior of the federal courts promote sufficient consistency within the judiciary for us to make some general points about the courts as an arena for organized interest activity.

Many of the points made in previous chapters about legislative and administrative lobbying pertain either not at all or only in peculiar ways to the judiciary. For example, the courts differ from Congress and the executive as a forum for organizational activity with respect to the importance and character of access. In legislative and administrative lobbying, access to appropriate policymakers is critical for lobbying success. In the judicial arena, organization representatives have only indirect access to judges and only in formal courtroom settings governed by the strictest rules of procedure. Moreover, the kinds of inducements that help create access to legislative and administrative officials and facilitate dialogue with them—PAC contributions, honoraria, lunches at posh restaurants, the implied promise of future employment, and so on—play no role in the judicial setting.

There is no opportunity for "buttonholing" a judge in the corridors or

[1] See Henry J. Abraham, *The Judiciary: The Supreme Court in the Governmental Process*, 6th ed. (Boston: Allyn & Bacon, 1983), pp. 6–19.

[2] Consistent with our emphasis throughout on national politics, we are also excluding from our purview the separate court systems of the 50 states.

taking him out to lunch to discuss the merits of a case. Any kind of direct access to federal judges is considered inappropriate. For example, a lobbyist cannot make an appointment with a judge to urge him to decide a pending case in a way that would benefit his organization; the lobbyist would be shown the door. An incident described in a recent book detailing the inner workings of the Supreme Court illustrates the point. Thomas G. Corcoran, a former member of President Franklin Roosevelt's "brain trust" and a prominent Washington lawyer-lobbyist, once directly lobbied Justices Hugo Black and William J. Brennan for a rehearing of an antitrust case involving the El Paso Natural Gas Company, a Corcoran client; the Justices shooed Corcoran out as soon as the purpose of his visit became apparent. The book makes clear that this behavior was seen as so inappropriate as to be embarrassing.[3]

The judicial arena also differs from the legislative and the executive in the relative inability of the courts to act as self-starting policy initiators. Judges cannot seek out cases or issue decisions on whatever matters strike their fancy. Whereas policy entrepreneurs in Congress or the executive often identify and define problems, formulate solutions, and work for their adoption, courts cannot take that particular kind of initiative.[4] Consequently, organizations pursuing their goals through the courts may face a long, slow process requiring both patience and persistence. The slowness of the judicial process is magnified by the fact that decisions of the courts often have quite narrow application. Whereas Congress, for example, can formulate policies using broad standards that will apply generally to persons in similar situations, the courts must make policy on the basis of a case that presents a particular set of facts and a specific plea for relief. The court's task is to rule in a way that will resolve the immediate problem. Depending on how idiosyncratic the facts are, the judgment may or may not pertain to many other persons or groups; thus, an organization may have to go to court repeatedly to broaden the application of the judicial relief.

INFLUENCING THE COURTS WITHOUT FILING SUIT

The tactics used by organized interests in an effort to gain favorable policy outcomes from the courts are relatively limited in number—at least in comparison with the relatively wide array of tactics they have available to them in approaching Congress and the executive. Sometimes organizations pursue their interests through the courts without going into the courtroom. In times past it

[3]See Bob Woodward and Scott Armstrong, *The Brethren: Inside the Supreme Court* (New York: Simon & Schuster, 1979), pp. 88–96.

[4]However, as indicated later in this chapter, activist judges can play an important rule as agenda setters and entrepreneurial policymakers. Moreover, although the courts cannot solicit cases to serve as vehicles of judicial policymaking, the courts do have discretion in determining their own agendas through such gatekeeping mechanisms as the issuance of writs of certiorari and the application of rules governing "standing." Judges can pick and choose those issues they wish to address from among the thousands that come up in any particular year. On this last point, see Richard Neely, *How Courts Govern America* (New Haven: Yale University Press, 1981), pp. 49–50.

was not uncommon for politically active organizations to try to influence judicial decision making by picketing federal courthouses or by staging mass demonstrations. In 1949 huge demonstrations around the federal courthouse in New York where Communist party leaders were on trial led to the adoption of a federal law (reportedly drafted by the Supreme Court justices themselves) prohibiting any groups or individuals from parading or picketing outside courthouses in an effort to influence judges, jurors, witnesses, or officers of the court.[5]

Another tactic once used by organized interests in an effort to influence judges was the orchestration of the kinds of massive telegram and letter-writing campaigns discussed in Chapter 8. The application of this kind of pressure on the courts has been effectively checked ever since the early 1950s when Justice Hugo Black, in response to a barrage of letters and telegrams telling the members of the Court how to decide a case involving a stay of execution for a black prisoner sentenced to die in Mississippi, publicly denounced "the growing practice of sending telegrams to judges in order to have cases decided by pressure," insisting that he would not read them. He put organized interests on notice that "the courts of the United States are not the kind of instruments that can be influenced by such pressures."[6]

Although organized interests no longer try to bring direct pressure on judges, many do try to shape judicial outcomes through various external maneuvers, such as attempting to influence the selection of judges and attempting to shape opinion in the legal community about a particular issue or set of issues. Let us briefly examine these techniques of influencing judicial policymaking.

Influencing Judicial Appointments

Earlier chapters explored many indirect forms of concerted influence, including attempts by organizations to influence the selection of decision makers through both the electoral process and the appointment process. At the federal level, organized interests can influence judicial policymaking indirectly by attempting to influence the selection of persons to occupy judicial positions. All federal judges are appointed by the president, with the advice and consent of the Senate. Usually these nominations proceed fairly smoothly and the president's choice wins confirmation. However, sometimes it becomes clear that the candidate will have a rough time in the Senate and the president eventually withdraws the nomination. This happened in 1968 when strong criticism in the Senate led President Lyndon Johnson to withdraw two nominations to the Supreme Court. The president had wanted to elevate sitting Justice Abe Fortas

[5]Clement E. Vose, "Litigation as a Form of Pressure Group Activity," *Annals of the American Academy of Political and Social Sciences* 319 (September 1958): 28–29.
[6]Ibid.

to chief justice in the wake of Earl Warren's retirement, and to appoint Homer Thornberry, a federal district court judge from Texas, to replace Fortas as an associate justice. Republicans in the Senate argued that a "lame duck" president should not be permitted to make two appointments of such importance and that the decisions should be reserved to the incoming president.[7]

Sometimes a nomination is so offensive to organized interests that they expend substantial political capital in an effort to block the candidate's confirmation by the Senate. Convincing the Senate to refuse a president his choice on a court appointment is no small feat: only three Supreme Court nominees have been formally rejected by the Senate in the twentieth century. In each case— the nomination of John Parker by President Herbert Hoover, and President Nixon's nominations of Clement Haynsworth and G. Harold Carswell—labor organizations and civil rights groups led the successful attempts to block confirmation. Parker and Haynsworth were considered too conservative, particularly on policies concerning labor unions and desegregation. Carswell was attacked sharply on the grounds that his service as a federal district judge had been mediocre, and that he had been hostile in his handling of civil rights cases and had behaved rudely to black lawyers and black defendants.[8]

Supreme Court nominees are not alone among candidates for the federal bench in being subjected to the scrutiny of organized interests; other federal judicial nominees also must survive the litmus tests of attentive groups. For example, although his nomination was finally approved in the summer of 1984 after many months, Harvey Wilkinson, 3d, President Reagan's choice to fill a federal appellate court vacancy in Virginia, attracted intense criticism and organized opposition from groups such as the National Association for the Advancement of Colored People (NAACP) Legal Defense and Education Fund Inc., the Mexican-American Legal Defense and Education Fund, and the National Women's Political Caucus—all of which were critical of Wilkinson for what they regarded as his limited legal experience (especially in comparison to that of several minority and women candidates), his insensitivity to minority concerns, and his parochialism.[9]

Shaping Opinion in the Legal Community

Another indirect way in which organized interests may try to influence the decisions of the courts is through efforts to educate judges, lawyers, and other

---

[7]Abe Fortas served on the Court only a few more months. Revelations that he had accepted large amounts of cash from a wealthy industrialist under investigation by the Securities and Exchange Commission, forced him to resign during Richard Nixon's first year in office.

[8]On the controversies and group activities surrounding these nominations, see Richard Harris, *Decision* (New York: Dutton, 1971); Joel B. Grossman and Stephen L. Wasby, "Haynsworth and Parker: History Does Live Again," *South Carolina Law Review* 23 (1971): 345–359; and Grossman and Wasby, "The Senate and Supreme Court Nominations: Some Reflections," *Duke Law Journal* (1972): 557–591.

[9]David Margolick, "Critics Question Experience of Reagan's Choice for Judgeship," *New York Times,* April 1, 1984, p. 22.

members of the legal community on a particular issue or set of issues and to demonstrate to judges around the nation that there is growing support for a particular viewpoint. The principal form such efforts take is "law review lobbying"—publishing articles in law reviews and other legal journals or periodicals. The scholarly articles and "notes" that comprise law reviews typically advocate certain types of court decisions and legal reasoning or present scholarly analyses of constitutional issues or of legal remedies.

Normally, of course, the articles in law journals merely present the opinions of particular legal scholars. However, organized interests have found it useful to encourage sympathetic legal experts to write articles supporting a particular viewpoint. This can be especially useful where the existing body of legal precedents runs counter to the organization's aims. Judges read the legal periodicals and use them to provide themselves with the legal reasoning to move in a new direction and to bolster their position on a case.[10] As a consequence, if the organization can get some favorable scholarly articles published, its positions will enjoy greater legitimacy and support. The NAACP is an organization that has used this technique with great success. Mindful of the potential impact of law review articles in helping to overturn negative precedent, the NAACP has at various times worked hard to generate a large number of favorable law review articles before the presentation of one of its issues in the Court. As part of its drive to have judicial enforcement of restrictive covenants declared unconstitutional, the NAACP helped orchestrate the appearance, between 1946 and 1948, of more than thirty books and law review articles urging the Supreme Court to reverse itself on restrictive covenants.[11] In 1948 the Supreme Court did in fact outlaw restrictive covenants in *Shelley* v. *Kraemer,* a decision that according to one scholar "was an outgrowth of the complex group activity which preceded it."[12]

An organization that has followed the lead of the NAACP in making law review lobbying an instrumental part of its overall strategy is the Women's Rights Project (WRP), an organization established in 1971 by the American Civil Liberties Union to fight gender discrimination through litigation. The WRP sought to reach lawyers and judges—the persons on whom the organization's success would depend—by educating them as to the nature and importance of sex discrimination, the validity of the WRP's legal rationale against such discrimination, and the desirability of suggested remedies. As part of the strategy, the WRP's first director, Ruth Bader Ginsburg, spoke at gatherings of law students, professors, and practitioners. She coauthored a major text on sex

[10]See Chester A. Newland, "The Supreme Court and Legal Writing: Learned Journals as Vehicles of an Anti-Trust Lobby Today," *Georgetown Law Journal* 48 (1959): 105–143.
[11]See Clement E. Vose, *Constitutional Change* (Lexington, MA: Lexington Books, D.C. Heath, 1972), p. 227; Jack W. Peltason, *Federal Courts in the Political Process* (New York: Random House, 1955), p. 52; and Karen O'Connor, *Women's Organizations' Use of the Courts* (Lexington, MA: Heath, 1980), p. 26.
[12]Clement E. Vose, *Caucasians Only* (Berkeley: University of California Press, 1959), p. 252.

discrimination and wrote at least a half dozen scholarly articles that helped to build a body of legal opinion supportive of arguments that the WRP would later raise in court. Her hope, as she expressed it, "was that the judges might look and realize that this is a very large and important matter; so that we would guard against the tendency some might have who don't know and haven't thought about it, to see these cases almost as a joke."[13]

Of course, there is no way of measuring how frequently law journal articles are written by persons active on behalf of specific organizations or at the urging of organized interests. Nor is there any clear way of ascertaining the extent to which legal periodicals are decisive in the judgments of the courts. What is clear, however, is that the law journals provide a legitimate and respectable outlet for organized interests seeking to nurture within the legal community a favorable climate of opinion for their policy goals.

Important as these indirect attempts may be for some organizations, most of the activity of organized interests in the judicial arena consists of sponsoring (initiating, financing, and conducting) lawsuits or submitting briefs as *amici curiae* (friends of the court). Almost three-fourths (72 percent) of the respondents in our Washington representatives survey indicated that their organizations engage in some form of litigation, making it eighteenth on the list of 27 techniques of exercising influence. Ninety-five percent of the union respondents included this among the techniques their organizations use, followed by 83 percent of the trade associations, 79 percent of the citizens' groups, and 72 percent of the corporations. The following discussion examines in greater detail what form this activity takes. Later sections of this chapter explore the question of what kinds of organizations tend to be advantaged in the legal process. At this point, however, it is important to understand how widespread such activity is among organized interests.

SPONSORING LITIGATION

The most direct way in which organized interests use the judiciary in an effort to further their goals is through sponsorship of cases—providing the funds and legal expertise to take cases to court. Sponsoring litigation is not a step that all organizations are eager to take. Although the benefits may be substantial in the event of a legal victory, the planning and execution of litigation can be extraordinarily difficult, expensive, and time-consuming. Moreover, the consequences of an unfavorable court decision may be great, since it represents an immediate setback for the organization and also helps set a precedent that may serve to frustrate the organization's policy aspirations for years to come.[14]

[13]Quoted in Ruth B. Cowan, "Women's Rights Through Litigation: An Examination of the American Civil Liberties Union Women's Rights Project, 1971–1976," *Columbia Human Rights Law Review* 8 (1976): 389.

[14]Joseph F. Kobylka, "Organizational Response to a Changing Litigation Environment: The Effect of *Miller* v. *California* (1978) on the Litigation Patterns of Libertarian Organizations,"

Not surprisingly, organizations vary widely in their inclination to litigate. Many organizations rarely, if ever, engage in litigation, limiting their political efforts to other institutional arenas of government. Sometimes, organizations that normally avoid political activity go to court to protect some specific right or correct some particular wrong. For example, the Jehovah's Witnesses, a generally apolitical religious organization, brought a number of important cases to the Supreme Court during the 1940s and 1950s, some aimed at preventing local authorities from interfering with the group's aggressive proseletyzing practices, others aimed at striking down state laws requiring that all public school children must salute the flag—a practice, the Witnesses objected, that compelled them to "behold a graven image."[15]

There are, however, many organizations for which going to court is a principal activity. Many of these are public interest law firms which have emerged for the explicit—and usually exclusive—purpose of litigating. Most of these organizations work to protect the environment, the civil rights of minorities, or the interests of consumers or of the disadvantaged. Among them are organizations such as the Mexican-American Legal Defense and Education Fund, the Natural Resources Defense Council, the Center for Law and Social Policy, the Citizen's Communications Center, and the National Prison Project. However, as noted in Chapter 3, there is a new brand of conservative public interest law firms—such as the Pacific Legal Foundation and Americans for Effective Law Enforcement—active in the federal courts. Most organized interests, however, see litigation neither as their raison d'etre nor as something to be eschewed, but as an instrument to be used when it appears to be the best (or only) way of protecting or furthering organizational goals.

The substantive goals that organizations pursue through court action vary widely, from organizational maintenance (showing the members that the organization is working in their interests) to securing strategic leverage (relying on the publicity associated with the filing of a suit to force action by other political actors).[16] Perhaps the weightiest goals include establishing principles of constitutional right and challenging the constitutionality or legitimacy of legislative and executive actions, thus using the courts to provide the legitimacy for a wholesale change in a particular area of public policy.

Just as there are differences in the substantive goals that bring an organi-

---

paper delivered at the Annual Meeting of the Midwest Political Science Association, Chicago, April 1983, p. 3.

[15]On the major role of the Jehovah's Witnesses in bringing flag-salute cases to court, see David R. Manwaring, *Render unto Caesar: The Flag Salute Controversy* (Chicago: University of Chicago Press, 1962).

[16]For example, in 1981 the Environmental Defense Fund, criticizing the Interior Department for its slow pace in placing threatened species on the endangered species list, initiated a suit against James G. Watt, then Secretary of the Interior, in order to make him extend endangered species status to 44 eligible species. The Fish and Wildlife Service, responding to the publicity stirred up by the suit, announced that it would soon place the 44 species on the list. See Philip Shabecoff, "Environmental Unit Plans to Sue Watt to Speed Species Protection," *New York Times,* July 23, 1981, p. A20.

zation into the courtroom, there are differences in the political or strategic circumstances that impel them. Sometimes organizations go to court because they have no expectation of achieving their goals via other political avenues and regard the judiciary as the institution most likely to produce a victory. For example, black Americans in the 1940s and early 1950s had little prospect of securing civil rights by pursuing their goals in Congress or the state legislatures, where white allies were few in number and where the advancement of black interests had been stymied for generations. Consequently, the NAACP chose to shift the struggle for civil rights into a potentially more congenial institutional forum, waging a prolonged, carefully planned legal battle in the courts.[17]

Sometimes organized interests go to court because they have lost in earlier administrative or legislative battles and the courts are their only immediate hope of forestalling some undesired action. For example, throughout most of the 1970s a lobbying battle raged in Washington, both in Congress and before administrative agencies, over the desirability of a regulation requiring that cars be equipped with so-called passive restraints—airbags or seat belts that engage automatically when the car doors are closed. The insurance industry and consumers' groups supported the rule, seeing it as a way of overcoming the public's persistent failure to make regular use of conventional seat belts. The automobile industry, complaining about the costs of complying with the rule, continually lobbied against it.

After a protracted seesaw battle, the Reagan administration finally rescinded the rule in October 1981, saying the benefits were questionable. The insurance industry (represented by the National Association of Independent Insurers and State Farm Mutual Automobile Insurance Company), joined by consumer groups, challenged the action in court, claiming that the National Highway Traffic Safety Administration's rescission of the passive restraint standard was an abuse of administrative discretion. The U.S. Circuit Court of Appeals for the District of Columbia agreed, terming the Reagan Administration's action "arbitrary and capricious," and invalidated it. The automobile industry (represented by the Motor Vehicle Manufacturers Association) and the Reagan administration then appealed the case to the Supreme Court on the grounds that the appellate judges had overstepped the grounds of judicial review and had substituted their own policy preferences for those of the administration. In June 1983 the Supreme Court upheld the Circuit Court's decision, and required the administration to reconsider.[18]

---

[17]The NAACP is an organization whose court successes over the years (in the areas of restrictive covenants, capital punishment, employment discrimination, and, most conspicuously, school desegregation) have made it a model for many other organizations to imitate. On the various successes of the NAACP, see Richard Kluger, *Simple Justice* (New York: Random House, Vintage Books, 1977); Loren Miller, *The Petitioners: The Story of the U.S. Supreme Court and the Negro* (New York: Pantheon Books, 1966); Clement E. Vose, "NAACP Strategy in the Restrictive Covenant Cases," *Western Reserve Law Review* 6 (1955): 101–145; and Michael Meltsner, *Cruel and Unusual Punishment* (New York: Random House, 1973).

[18]The Reagan administration finally issued its new rule on July 11, 1984. The rule requires lawmakers to phase in the crash protection unless states representing two-thirds of the U.S. popu-

The Administrative Procedure Act encourages this kind of litigation by providing for redress when parties can show that agency actions are arbitrary and capricious or that there has been an abuse of executive discretion not in accordance with the law; that an agency is being deliberately dilatory or is acting outside its scope of authority; or that an agency's action will result in some irreparable harm.[19] Not surprisingly, virtually every regulation issued by such agencies as the Environmental Protection Agency and the Occupational Safety and Health Administration is challenged in court either by environmental and consumer groups or by industry.[20]

Test Cases

Often when an organization wants to get the courts to assess the constitutionality or application of a legislative or executive act, it files a lawsuit known as a test case. Since federal courts do not issue advisory opinions, an organization wishing a ruling on the act must somehow institute a suit that explicitly raises the issue of concern—that is, a case that contains an unambiguous presentation of the specific issue on which the group wants the courts to rule. The difficulty here is that courts will only decide those constitutional questions that are actually raised in the litigation and only if there are no other ways the judges can resolve the legal dispute.[21] Thus, in order to reduce as much as possible the chance that the courts will decide the case on some tangential issue, the test case has to be carefully devised. This sometimes leads organizations to violate the act intentionally as a way of inviting prosecution or to give it an opportunity to file a suit seeking to restrain enforcement.

Another way in which organizational litigants structure an appropriate test case is by scouring the country in search of someone whose circumstances make him or her a desirable plaintiff or defendant in the test case. But this process of searching for a case is complicated, and many factors must be considered in the selection of the vehicle for the test. Consider, for example, the difficulties faced by NAACP attorneys in the 1940s and 1950s as they patiently brought a series of test cases in their fight against segregation in the schools. They had to search nationwide for appropriate plaintiffs in whose names suits could be filed. In addition, the NAACP attorneys had to find persons who

lation pass laws by April 1, 1989, making seat-belt use mandatory, in which case the new regulation would not apply. This loophole is likely to have the immediate effect of shifting the battle over automobile crash protection from Washington (where it has been waged in various institutions since 1969) to the state legislatures. See Stephen Gettinger, "DOT Rule May Shift Air-Bag Battle to States," *Congressional Quarterly Weekly Report,* July 14, 1984, p. 1708.

[19]Carol Greenwald, *Group Power: Lobbying and Public Policy* (New York: Praeger, 1977), p. 278.

[20]See Steven Kelman, "Occupational Safety and Health Administration," in James Q. Wilson, ed., *The Politics of Regulation* (New York: Basic Books, 1980), p. 259, and Paul J. Culhane, "Natural Resources Policy: Procedural Change and Substantive Environmentalism," in Theodore J. Lowi and Alan Stone, eds., *Nationalizing Government: Public Policies in America* (Beverly Hills, CA: Sage, 1978), pp. 131–162.

[21]Walter E. Murphy and C. Herman Pritchett, *Courts, Judges, and Politics: An Introduction to the Judicial Process,* 3rd ed. (New York: Random House, 1979), pp. 536–537.

would still be in school by the time the cases reached the Supreme Court so that the cases would not be declared moot. Moreover, they had to find plaintiffs whose families were firmly settled in particular locales since a move to another city or state might also render a case moot.[22]

Class Actions

One of the ways that organized interests minimize such problems—as well as other difficulties such as the time and expense involved in bringing many similar cases—is by filing "class action" suits, which are lawsuits brought on behalf of the named plaintiff and all other persons similarly situated (for example, all children in segregated schools or all persons overcharged by a bank assessing illegal interest rates). Since the judicial decisions in these cases are typically far more sweeping in their application than is usually true (applying not just to the plaintiff but to a whole "class" of persons), they not only establish the principle of law (as a test case does) but have immediate application to many persons. Thus, not every person overcharged by the bank has to file a suit; if the plaintiff is victorious, the judicial remedy applies also to those for whom the plaintiff stands.

Class action suits also have the advantage of minimizing the possibility that the plaintiff will settle a case by compromise; usually the named plaintiff cannot take such a step in a class action without the court's permission. Class actions also have the advantage—from the sponsoring organization's perspective—of reducing the chance that the case will be dismissed as moot because the plaintiff has died, moved out of the area, or in some other way lost standing. Should any of these circumstances occur, the organization sponsoring the litigation merely needs to substitute as the plaintiff some other person similarly situated—another member of the "class."[23]

Because of the potential advantages of class action suits, many organizations have made them a standard part of their litigating strategies. One such organization is the Food Research and Action Center (FRAC), a liberal public interest law firm that focuses on improving the availability and quality of benefits through federal food programs for the poor and disadvantaged. When FRAC began its work in 1970, food law was a largely uncharted area, and the organization successfully worked through the courts to provide class action relief on behalf of the poor. For example, in 1973 FRAC won a class action suit that provided food stamp relief to thousands of persons who had been deprived of aid by administrative errors.[24]

Class action suits became quite common in the 1960s and 1970s, as organized interests used them in issues ranging from malapportionment of legisla-

[22]See Herbert Jacob, *Justice in America: Courts, Lawyers, and the Judicial Process,* 4th ed. (Boston: Little, Brown, 1984), pp. 39–40.
[23]Murphy and Pritchett, *Courts, Judges, and Politics,* p. 265.
[24]*Bermudez* v. *Butz,* U.S. Circuit Court of Appeals for D.C., 1973.

tures to the rights of prisoners, from antitrust suits against corporations to women's occupational rights.[25] In part this increase reflected an understanding by organized interests that a class action suit could call governmental attention to problems that were not being addressed by Congress or were being improperly handled by administrative agencies. The increase in class actions also reflected a 1966 liberalization of federal rules that provided financial incentives for lawyers to bring such cases to court. The change allowed that the attorneys' fees could come out of the total pool of financial damages awarded for all members of the class and not just for the lawyers' personal clients.[26]

By the mid-1970s, however, the large number of class action suits and their exceptional complexities (the difficulties of deciding who are legitimate members of a class and how settlements should be distributed) had become so much of a burden on the courts' work load that the Supreme Court moved to tighten the rules governing these suits.[27] In a class action suit initiated against stock brokerage houses for alleged overcharges of more than two million people, the court ruled that the persons bringing the suit would have to notify, at their own expense, all other persons in the class, or at least those identifiable through reasonable effort.[28] Needless to say, such notification is prohibitively expensive for most potential litigants, so the number of such cases has declined. Still, many of the barriers to class actions erected by the courts in the 1970s do not apply to civil rights cases, and organizations such as the Mexican-American Legal Defense and Education Fund continue to bring class action suits in matters involving employment discrimination, school desegregation, and immigration and naturalization.

Not every organization has both the means and the will necessary for the effective sponsorship of litigation. Selecting a case and seeing it through the initial adjudication may cost hundreds of thousands of dollars—and perhaps many times that to take a case all the way to the Supreme Court. For many organizations, such costs close off litigation as an avenue for the pursuit of group goals. For others, the costs present problems later on. For example, in 1977, after a lengthy and costly trial, the Women's Equity Action League had to abandon an important suit at the appeals stage because the group could not come up with the $40,000 it would cost merely to provide copies of the trial transcript from the initial adjudication.[29]

But resources are only one factor critical to successful litigation by an organized interest. Other factors that seem important are longevity (the ability

[25]Class action suits in federal courts nearly doubled during the 1970s. See Abraham, *The Judiciary,* p. 176n.

[26]See Jethro K. Lieberman, *The Litigious Society* (New York: Basic Books, 1981), p. 17.

[27]See *Zahn* v. *International Paper Co.,* 414 U.S. 211 (1973).

[28]*Eisen* v. *Carlisle & Jacquelin,* 417 U.S. 156 (1974). See also the limitations in *Oppenheimer Fund* v. *Sanders,* 437 U.S. 340 (1978). Stephen L. Wasby discusses both the *Zahn* and the *Eisen* cases in *The Supreme Court in the Federal Judicial System* (New York: Holt, Rinehart and Winston, 1978), pp. 116–117.

[29]O'Connor, *Women's Organizations' Use of the Courts,* p. 118.

to litigate over many years, slowly whittling away at negative precedents); staffing (highly skilled legal talent as well as competent clerical and administrative assistants); and a sharp issue focus (pursuing litigation in one issue area at a time, thus increasing the distinctive competence of the attorneys).[30] Even if these and other critical elements come together in an organization, the opportunities for error are many, and mistakes anywhere along the line—selecting a less than perfect test case, selecting an unfavorable jurisdiction in which to bring the case, misjudging the appropriate timing for the case—may sink the case. In view of the complexities of the process, it is little wonder that many organizations systematically avoid sponsoring litigation, preferring instead to participate through the filing of amicus curiae briefs.

AMICUS BRIEFS

Even if an organization is not directly involved as a sponsor of a suit, it may still play a role in the case by participating as a "friend of the court," or *amicus curiae,* providing the court with written briefs and on rare occasions with oral arguments that present the group's views on the issue before the court. Organizational participation through amicus briefs has several advantages. First, it is a relatively informal mode of participation, requiring only that the group first obtain the consent of all parties to the suit or, failing that, get special permission from the court.[31] More importantly, participation as an amicus provides an organization with an opportunity to have an input into the judicial policymaking process at only a fraction of the cost it would incur as a direct sponsor of the case. This role requires only the preparation, printing, and filing of a brief—a document usually no longer than twenty-five printed pages. Except for getting permission to file, there is not much more to it.[32] For organizations without access to considerable financing, submitting amicus briefs may be the only feasible mode of participation.

Organized interests use amicus briefs to provide the court with information or legal arguments that are not being presented by the actual parties to the suit or to introduce new arguments that allow the court to settle a case on grounds other than those presented in the parties' briefs. For example, in the landmark case of *Mapp* v. *Ohio* (1961), in which the Supreme Court held that illegally seized evidence could not be used in state criminal trials, the parties

---

[30] These are only some of the factors explored in O'Connor, *Women's Organizations' Use of the Courts.* See pp. 16–28 for others. For factors deemed important for success in constitutional litigation, see Frank J. Sorauf, *The Wall of Separation: The Constitutional Politics of Church and State* (Princeton: Princeton University Press, 1976), p. 73.

[31] This rule was adopted by the Supreme Court in 1949 in response to the justices' growing frustration with the increasing number of amicus briefs that were "propagandistic" in character and of little utility. See Karen O'Connor and Lee Epstein, "Court Rules and Workload: A Case Study of Rules Governing Amicus Curiae Participation," *Justice System Journal* 8 (1983): 35–45.

[32] Clement E. Vose, "Interest Groups and Litigation," paper prepared for delivery at the Annual Meeting of the American Political Science Association, New York, September 1981, p. 11.

argued the case on the issue of convicting someone for "mere possession" of obscene material—that is, without intent to sell. It was the American Civil Liberties Union, participating as an amicus, that raised the constitutional issue about the admissability of illegally seized evidence. And it was on this issue that the Court decided the case, not even reaching the issue raised by the litigants.[33]

The filing of an amicus brief is a technique strikingly similar to the principal techniques used by lobbyists in attempting to influence legislators and administrative officials. All are efforts to furnish decision makers with information that will influence them to make a decision favorable to the organization's interests. For example, when organizations such as Planned Parenthood, the National Organization for Women, and the American College of Obstetricians and Gynecologists filed amicus briefs in support of the pro-choice position in what was to become the landmark abortion case of *Roe* v. *Wade* (1973), they provided the Court with information and arguments asserting, among other things, that antiabortion statutes unduly interfered in the doctor-patient relationship. Amicus briefs filed on the other side by organizations such as Americans United for Life and the National Right to Life Committee focused on establishing that "from conception the child is a complex, dynamic rapidly growing organism," not a mere "blob of protoplasm."[34]

Participation as amici is also useful for organized interests as a way of making the court aware that others are attentive to the issue at hand and care intensely about it.[35] Surely this was one of the factors that led to the extensive participation by organized interests as amici curiae in the landmark affirmative action case, *Regents of the University of California* v. *Bakke* (1978). In this case, Allan Bakke complained that his denial of admission to the University of California's medical school at Davis because of racial quotas favoring minority applicants constituted "reverse discrimination." Fifty-eight amicus briefs were filed in this case by more than 100 organizations: 42 of the briefs backed the University of California's admissions policy; 16 supported Bakke, who won his case in a complex decision having ambiguous implications for affirmative action programs in admissions.[36]

As these examples suggest, the purpose of the amicus brief has undergone a transformation of sorts. Originally intended to provide the court with information that it might not otherwise have, the amicus brief has developed into an

[33]See Wasby, *The Supreme Court in the Federal Judicial System,* p. 131.

[34]See Austin Sarat, "Abortion and the Courts: Uncertain Boundaries of Law and Politics," in Allan P. Sindler, ed., *American Politics and Public Policy: Six Case Studies* (Washington, DC: CQ Press, 1982), pp. 134–135.

[35]Leo Pfeffer, "Amici in Church-State Litigation," *Law and Contemporary Problems* 44 (1981): 104–110.

[36]Murphy and Pritchett, *Courts, Judges, and Politics,* p. 267. For a listing of the organizations filing amicus briefs in the *Bakke* case, see Dennis S. Ippolito and Thomas G. Walker, *Political Parties, Interest Groups, and Public Policy: Group Influence in American Politics* (Englewood Cliffs, NJ: Prentice-Hall, 1980), pp. 405–406.

advocacy document used by interested parties to influence the court's decision. As one observer has put it: "The institution of the amicus curial brief has moved from neutrality to partisanship, from friendship to Advocacy."[37] But advocacy is not the only function amicus participation provides. Amicus participation is also a way for an organization to publicize its position on an issue, to educate its own members on the substantive points of an issue of shared concern, or to impress the members with the vitality of the Washington staff.

Whatever the reasons for organizations' participation through the filing of amicus briefs, this form of organizational activity, like most others, has been increasing in recent years. Whereas organized interests only rarely participated as amici curiae prior to World War II, this form of activity rose significantly after the war. One study found that organizations appeared as amici curiae in 23.8 percent of noncommercial cases decided by the Supreme Court between 1953 and 1966.[38] In the 1970s, organized interests' participation as amici increased dramatically, occurring in 53.4 percent of the 841 noncommercial, full-opinion Supreme Court cases decided between 1970 and 1980.[39] The increases in amicus participation are particularly conspicuous in certain issue areas. For example, there have been extraordinary increases in amicus participation in cases involving labor unions, free press issues, racial discrimination, and church-state relations.[40]

For the most part, groups that eschew amicus participation in favor of filing test cases do so because they want to have control over the development of cases—something that comes only with direct sponsorship of litigation. For example, the NAACP Legal Defense and Education Fund generally tries to sponsor employment discrimination cases, since sponsorship affords the or-

[37]Samuel Krislov, "The Amicus Curiae Brief: From Friendship to Advocacy," *Yale Law Journal* 72 (1963): 704.

[38]Nathan Hakman, "The Supreme Court's Political Environment: The Processing of Noncommercial Litigation," in Joel Grossman and Joseph Tanenhaus, eds., *Frontiers of Judicial Research* (New York: Wiley, 1969), pp. 209–210.

[39]Karen O'Connor and Lee Epstein, "Amicus Curiae Participation in U.S. Supreme Court Litigation: An Appraisal of Hakman's 'Folklore,'" *Law and Society Review* 16 (1981–1982): 311–320. When O'Connor and Epstein eliminated the criminal cases, which are significantly less likely to attract amicus support, they found the rate of amicus participation to be 63.8 percent. Other researchers have also found substantial increases in amicus participation in the period from 1955 to 1980. See Robert C. Bradley and Paul Gardner, Jr., "The Supreme Court and Amicus Briefs: A Study of Interest Group Access," paper presented at the Annual Meeting of the Midwest Political Science Association, Chicago, April 1983, p. 11.

We should note that although amicus participation is clearly an important avenue of interest expression in the judicial process, its relative importance as a technique used by organized interests may have been blown out of proportion by scholars who dwell on this form of group activity, in part because it is comparatively easy to acquire information about it simply by examining reported cases. By contrast it is much more difficult to identify when organized interests are the sponsors of the case since only the names of counsel are listed in reports, not their affiliations. See Vose, "Interest Groups and Litigation," p. 11.

[40]O'Connor and Epstein, "Amicus Curiae Participation in U.S. Supreme Court Litigation," p. 317.

ganization greater control over the development of the case, particularly at the trial court level where the handling of complicated issues such as the validity of job tests may strongly affect the outcome of the case.[41]

THE COURTS' ACCESSIBILITY TO ORGANIZED INTERESTS

A recurring theme throughout this book has been that procedural and institutional changes in government often have profound consequences for organized interest activity. In the judicial arena as well, an important change has taken place, affecting the courtroom activities of organized interests. In recent years the courts have made it easier for plaintiffs to pursue their goals in the courtroom and substantially altered the range of matters over which organizations may go to court.

Standing to Sue

In order to take a case into federal court, an organization must have "standing"—that is, there must be a real dispute between the plaintiff and the defendant, and it must be clear that the federal court can provide the plaintiff with some kind of relief through the issuance of a judicial order. The plaintiff must also have exhausted all available remedies before going to court. This means, for example, that persons aggrieved by administrative decisions must have used all the procedures available for correcting the action administratively before they can have standing to be heard in court. In addition, the timing must be right. If the case is brought too late, it may be considered moot; if it is brought too early, it may be dismissed as hypothetical. In the language of the judiciary, the case must be "ripe" for adjudication.[42]

Moreover, traditional criteria for "standing" required that the plaintiff show direct economic injury or direct personal impairment of his own constitutional or statutory rights. In other words, to have standing, litigants were required to have a personal interest at stake beyond that of other parties or of the general public. This meant that in situations where all citizens suffered equally, their concerns or grievances, if they were to be represented in court at all, had to be represented by the attorney general or another public official. It also meant, for example, that taxpayer suits (aimed at preventing the expenditure of public funds for a given purpose), permissible in most states, could not be brought in the federal courts. The Supreme Court had held in 1923 that such

[41]See Karen O'Connor and Lee Epstein, "The Importance of Interest Group Involvement in Employment Discrimination Litigation," *Black Law Journal* 7 (1982): 417–418. The proper handling of factual issues at the trial court level is especially important since it is too late to raise such matters when a case is on appeal.

[42]See Murphy and Pritchett, *Courts, Judges, and Politics,* p. 220.

suits were impermissible in federal courts because no taxpayer has a sufficient personal interest in the vast expenditure of federal funds to warrant standing.[43]

In the 1960s, the federal courts began to relax the rules of standing, thus permitting the litigation of disputes on a much broader range of issues than previously. The liberalization of the rules of standing took several different forms. One step was to make it easier for plaintiffs to bring cases involving some broad and diffuse public interests. In the case of *Flast* v. *Cohen* (1968), the Court opened the way for taxpayers to take cases to court challenging congressional expenditures (in this case, federal grants to parochial schools.)[44]

Five years later the court opened the door still further to broad public interests in the case of *U.S.* v. *Students Challenging Regulatory Action Procedure (SCRAP)* (1973). The plaintiffs, a group of George Washington University Law School students, had opposed the Interstate Commerce Commission's (ICC) approval of a temporary railroad freight rate increase where no environmental impact statement had been filed. The plaintiffs claimed that the rate increase would decrease the use of recycled goods, thereby producing more litter and other harmful effects on the parks in the Washington area that the students frequently visited for recreation. The ICC argued that the plaintiffs' allegation (that the harm extended to anyone who made use of the country's scenic resources and all who breathed the air) was too vague and unsubstantiated for them to be granted standing. The Supreme Court, however, upheld the plaintiffs' right to sue, stating: "To deny standing to persons who are in fact injured simply because many others are also injured would mean that the most injurious and widespread government actions could be questioned by nobody."[45] The decision in the *SCRAP* case was far-reaching in its effect. As one observer of environmental policy has put it: "After the Court granted SCRAP standing, it would be fair to say that environmentalist individuals or organizations who are part of a 'public' with even a broad and diffuse public interest can obtain standing and act essentially as 'private attorneys general.' "[46]

A second way in which the courts liberalized the rules on standing was by holding in a number of cases that injuries other than economic harm could be sufficient grounds for standing. One important case involved the Federal Power Commission's (FPC) approval in the early 1960s of the planned construction of a reservoir and pumping station on the Hudson River in New York. A coalition of conservation groups, concerned about the effect the project would have on the scenic value of the area, sought standing on aesthetic grounds for judicial review of the FPC's decision. The circuit court granted standing to the environ-

[43] *Frothingham* v. *Mellon,* 262 U.S. 447 (1923). Taxpayer suits at the state level are generally permissible on the theory that each taxpayer has an interest in how public money is spent, regardless of the amount he has contributed through taxes.

[44] *Flast* v. *Cohen,* 392 U.S. 83 (1968).

[45] 412 U.S. 669 (1973), 689.

[46] Culhane, "Natural Resources Policy: Procedural Change and Substantive Environmentalism," p. 206.

mentalists, holding that economic interest need not be the only basis for being an "aggrieved" party.[47] The court's recognition in this case of noneconomic interests as a basis for spending opened the gates for a flood of suits brought by organized interests against administrative decisions considered potentially harmful. For example, in a 1966 case the court granted standing to a church group that challenged the renewal of a television license for a station in Jackson, Mississippi, whose programming and hiring policies the church group deemed racist. The court again held that standing could not be restricted only to those with an economic interest in the matter.[48]

Yet another way in which the courts liberalized the rules on standing was by freeing potential plaintiffs of the burden of having to show that some specific constitutional or statutory boundary had been overstepped in causing injury. This change came as a result of a suit brought by the Association of Data Processing Service Organizations, a trade association representing data processors, challenging the authority of the Comptroller of the Currency to allow banks to provide data processing services. The data processors argued that the competition from the banks had caused them injury. Under the old rules of standing, the data processors would not have been able to get a court ruling because injury from competition alone was insufficient grounds for standing if there was no specific statutory language authorizing "adversely affected or aggrieved persons" to bring suit. In its decision in this case, the Supreme Court turned away from that kind of narrow, legalistic view of standing and decided that plaintiffs could have standing if they could show injury in fact and if the claim fell within a judicially inferred "zone of interest."[49] In other words, even in the absence of specific statutory language granting standing to parties aggrieved by particular administrative actions, the courts could grant standing if they inferred some protection to that interest in relevant statutes or in the Constitution.

In spite of the general relaxation in the rules on standing, the courts still exercise their power to limit access to the judiciary. For example, in the 1974 case of *U.S.* v. *Richardson,* the Supreme Court refused to grant standing to a taxpayer who was trying to compel the secretary of the treasury to publish an accounting of the receipts and expenditures of the Central Intelligence Agency, holding that a taxpayer's "generalized grievances about the conduct of the government" are an insufficient basis for standing.[50] More recently, the Supreme Court refused to grant standing to a group that wanted to stop the government from giving a surplus military hospital to the Valley Forge Chris-

[47] *Scenic Hudson Preservation Conference* v. *FPC,* 354 F.2d 608 (2d Cir. 1965).
[48] *Office of Communications of the United Church of Christ* v. *FCC,* 359 F.2d 94 (D.C. Cir., 1966).
[49] *Association of Data Processing Service Organizations* v. *Camp,* 397 U.S. 150 (1970). For a complete discussion of the implications of this and other cases in which the courts relaxed the rules on standing, see Karen Orren, "Standing to Sue: Interest Group Conflict in the Federal Courts," *American Political Science Review* 70 (1976): 723–741.
[50] *United States* v. *Richardson,* 418 U.S. 166 (1974).

tian College. The Court held that the group, Americans United for Separation of Church and State, had no right to block the property transfer in court because they suffered no personal injury other than their displeasure with the government's action. The case also did not fit the *Flast* loophole since the government was giving the church property instead of money.[51]

Nevertheless, the relaxation of the rules on standing in the 1960s and early 1970s vastly extended the possibilities of the lawsuit as a strategy for organized interests, allowing many kinds of plaintiffs to take the government to court for redress of grievances: pregnant women seeking abortions, citizens' groups opposed to the expenditure of public funds to support religious schools, residents displaced by urban renewal, and so on. Moreover, the changes in standing have affected not only the propensity of organized interests to go to court to challenge the government, but have also permitted organizations representing the interests of diffuse publics to use the courts to challenge the activities of other private organizations, thus changing, in particular, the relationship of business with the public. As one careful student of the subject has put it:

> [T]he liberalized approach [to standing] has enabled numerous environmental, consumer, historic-preservational, and other associations, as well as a wide variety of *ad hoc* citizens' groups to come before the courts to do battle with such diverse parties as land developers, lumber companies, and passenger railroads.[52]

PERSPECTIVES ON INTEREST GROUPS AND THE COURTS

One of the continuing concerns of this book has been to achieve some comprehension of who is represented in the politics of organized interests and how those patterns of interest representation contribute to who wins and loses in American politics. This interest implies a concern with resources as well—how they enhance effectiveness in politics and how these resources are distributed. The last two chapters have paid attention to the particular resources that have special relevance for political activity in the legislature and executive. The same questions must now be posed with respect to the courts, in order to understand whether there are certain kinds of organizations that are likely to find legal strategies especially productive.

As usual, an organization enjoys some advantage if it is well established and well funded. As the preceding discussion made clear, litigating is expensive. For some organizations, the costs of going to court are prohibitive. Furthermore, affluent organizations go to court from a position of strength. Among other things, they have the means to avail themselves of top attorneys. For

[51] *Valley Forge Christian College* v. *Americans United for Separation of Church and State,* 454 U.S. 464 (1982).
[52] Orren, "Standing to Sue," p. 735.

example, when the National Cable Television Association and the National Association of Broadcasters battle one another in court over regulatory issues, they can rely not only on their own cadre of attorneys but also on the expert litigators that they retain from Washington's best law firms.

Furthermore, organizations that command sufficient financial resources can combine a legal strategy with efforts to influence policy outcomes in other spheres. Policy accomplishments are rarely the result of the use of a single technique or concentration on a single institutional arena. Going to court, like other activities, is likely to produce the greatest leverage when it is used in strategic combination with other efforts.[53] Here again, wealthy and established organizations are at an advantage since they are more likely than poorer organizations to have organizational slack that permits them to conduct a variety of political activities simultaneously.

Moreover, well-endowed organizations are likely to be able to use their activities in court to tactical as well as strategic advantage. Consider in the following example how Sears Roebuck & Co. used a lawsuit not only to achieve its broad, strategic objective of getting the government off its back but also to achieve the more narrow, tactical purpose of mobilizing other corporations to challenge the government's conflicting affirmative action programs. In January 1979, Sears, the world's largest retailer, expecting to be sued by the federal Equal Employment Opportunity Commission over alleged job discrimination against women, blacks, and Mexican-Americans, filed its own lawsuit against the government, charging that the federal government's affirmative action programs had subjected Sears to conflicting requirements—that, for example, policies raising the mandatory retirement age and others designed to encourage employers to hire veterans and the handicapped had actually made it more difficult to hire minorities.

Hoping to mobilize other corporations similarly frustrated by government pressures, Sears introduced its lawsuit with a remarkable publicity blitz. On the day it filed suit, Sears held a press conference at its corporate headquarters in Chicago featuring its chairman of the board, Edward R. Telling, and Charles Morgan, Jr., a well-known civil rights lawyer who had prepared the suit for Sears. Then a phalanx of top Sears executives flew to Washington, where thanks to the efforts of Hill & Knowlton, a top Washington public relations firm hired by Sears to help publicize the suit, they met the next morning at breakfast with representatives of eight major publications. The team of Sears executives and lobbyists distributed a press kit containing a press release, the company's 57-page complaint against the government, and documents providing details on Sears's various efforts to hire and promote minorities and women.[54] Only better-off organizations have the kind of resources necessary to

---

[53]This point is made by Marc Galanter, "Why the 'Haves' Come Out Ahead: Speculations on the Limits of Legal Change," *Law and Society Review* 95 (1974): 151.

[54]James W. Singer, "Affirmative Action for Jobs—Is the Sears Suit on Target?" *National Journal,* March 10, 1979, pp. 384–388.

accompany their initiation of a lawsuit with this kind of carefully orchestrated public relations campaign.

There is some controversy regarding what kinds of interests are advantaged in the judicial process. Some scholars have suggested that the Supreme Court, like other institutions of government, is primarily interested in maintaining the political system. The argument here is that since the government looks to high-status groups for support, the Court is more responsive to their demands.[55] This argument has considerable merit: surely the judicial arena presents yet another point of access for politically powerful and advantaged groups; surely such groups have frequently advanced their interests through skillful use of the courts.

Over the past several decades, however, broad publics and underdog groups—the poor and the disadvantaged; racial, ethnic, and religious minorities; and all sorts of other political and economic have-nots—have won important victories in the judicial arena. Although the disadvantaged and broad publics have fared well in the courts over the past half century, one need only examine the conservative posture of the Court from the 1870s through the 1930s—and the ascendance of the conservative bloc on the Court in the 1983–1984 term—to see that there is nothing institutionally inevitable about this. That is, there is nothing in particular about the structure of the courts or of the legal process that inclines the judiciary to be the friend of the disadvantaged; it is the set of incumbents—the particular set of judges on the bench at any time—that matters. Over the course of American history, the courts have befriended various interests. In the early part of this century, the federal bench was quite sympathetic to business interests and declared unconstitutional numerous regulatory measures including a federal law to forbid the passage in interstate commerce of products made by companies employing children. Hence, the current status of the courts as an arena for successful activity by representatives of broad publics and the disadvantaged need not be permanent. Indeed, the Supreme Court's 1983–1984 term may signal that a shift has already taken place.

The Courts as Allies of Underdogs

Numerous factors help explain why the disadvantaged and broad publics have scored some notable successes in the courts in recent decades. First, the number of organizations representing such interests has increased substantially in

---

[55]This is the argument of S. Sidney Ulmer, cited in Robert C. Bradley and Paul Gardner, Jr., "The Supreme Court and Amicus Briefs: A Study of Interest Group Access," paper prepared for the Annual Meeting of the Midwest Political Science Association, Chicago, April 1983, p. 8. Others who argue that the Court is more sympathetic to "upperdog" or high-status interests include Robert Dahl, "Decision-Making in a Democracy: The Supreme Court as a National Policy-Maker," *Journal of Public Law* 6 (1957): 279–295; and William M. Landes and Richard A. Posner, "The Independent Judiciary in an Interest-Group Perspective," *Journal of Law and Economics* 18 (1975): 875–905.

recent years. Our data indicate that more than half of the civil rights groups and more than three-quarters of the citizens' groups, social welfare, and poor people's organizations with offices in Washington were founded since 1960. Many of these new organizations—such as the National Center for a Barrier Free Environment, the Environmental Defense Fund, the Lawyer's Committee for Civil Rights under Law, and the Migrant Legal Action Project, to name but a few—work almost exclusively through the courts to achieve their goals. They initiate their own cases aimed at achieving organizational objectives and also provide legal counsel for other groups that are too poor to hire their own attorneys.[56]

Furthermore, the government has adopted policies in recent years that make it profitable for traditionally disadvantaged groups to try to redress their grievances through legal action. Congressional activity during the 1960s and early 1970s left a body of law—civil rights and voting rights acts, consumer and environmental legislation—that such interests use as the basis of legal action. Congress has not only armed such interests with legal tools, but has actually helped them to go to court. A law passed by Congress in 1976 permits public interest law firms to collect their fees from defendants (including federal and state governments) when the firms have successfully litigated certain kinds of cases (usually having to do with civil rights, poverty, environmental protection, and consumer rights). This process, known as fee-shifting, has made it easier for resource-poor organizations to go to court, especially for the purpose of challenging the actions of the government.[57] In addition, as already indicated, the courts' liberalization of the rules on standing has given particular leverage to various citizens' groups in their battles with powerful industries and with the government.

The interests of political and economic have-nots have also been fur-

---

[56] A recent study indicates that liberal interest groups go to court—both as direct sponsors of cases and as amicus curiae—to a greater extent than do conservative interest groups. However, there has been an increase since 1969 in conservative interest group use of the courts. See Karen O'Connor and Lee Epstein, "The Rise of Conservative Interest Group Litigation," *Journal of Politics* 45 (1983): 479–489.

[57] The Reagan Administration has proposed sharp cutbacks on the authority of the courts to award fees to lawyers victorious over the federal government and has proposed putting caps on some of the fees. See Stuart Taylor, Jr., "Reagan Stalks Public Interest Lawyers' Fees," *New York Times,* February 19, 1982, p. A14. The Reagan administration's position on the awarding of fees to attorneys in public interest law firms was rebuffed by the Supreme Court in 1984 in the case of *Blum* v. *Stenson.* The administration, participating as an amicus in the case, had argued that fee awards to nonprofit firms should not be based on market rates but on the actual costs incurred in representation of the client. In other words, the Administration objected that the courts were ordering reimbursement of public interest attorneys at the same rates charged by attorneys in private practice; the administration felt this amounted to a windfall or subsidy for public interest law firms. The court found that the legislative history of the Civil Rights Attorneys' Fee Awards Act of 1976 "flatly contradicted" the administration's cost-based argument, and the court thus upheld the award of $79,000 in fees to the Legal Aid Society of New York, which had successfully represented a class of Medicaid recipients suing New York over an eligibility issue. See Elder Witt, "Court Widens Libel Reach, Rejects Reagan Antitrust Plea," *Congressional Quarterly Weekly Report,* March 24, 1984, p. 690.

thered in recent years by a decided trend toward judicial activism on the part of many federal judges who endorse the view that governmental intervention in economic and social affairs is appropriate and desirable. Activist judges see the federal government as having a positive obligation to regulate the economy, to safeguard constitutional rights, to protect citizens against discrimination, and even to compensate for past discrimination. Organized interests—for example, racial minorities, prisoners, and conservationists—that lack clout in the legislative and executive branches have taken advantage of this judicial activism, going to court in an effort to get judges to interpret constitutional rights broadly and to take over important government functions when elected and appointed officials neglect their duties. The following are but a few examples of the decisions of activist federal courts. They have decided that Mexican-American children have a constitutional right to bilingual education; eliminated a high school diploma as a requirement for a firefighter's job; ordered the equalization of school expenditures on teachers' salaries; closed some prisons and for others promulgated elaborate standards on such matters as food handling, recreation facilities, inmate employment and education, sanitation, lighting, and renovation; established equally comprehensive programs of care and treatment for the mentally ill confined in hospitals; and enjoined the construction of roads and bridges on environmental grounds.[58]

Of course, as in many other facets of political life, there is a dynamic at work here, a synergistic relationship between activist judges and activist litigants. Although judges can exercise substantial powers, they are limited in the kinds of matters they can take up. They can only make policy on cases brought to them, and organizational litigants serve that function. Moreover, until litigants get the court to interpret or apply a law, its benefits for them may remain latent. One observer of the courts has suggested that the implicit cooperation at work here has given rise to a new kind of "iron triangle" consisting of the courts, executive agencies, and organized interests. The idea is that Congress initiates the triple alliance by creating a statutory right and then withdrawing. The statutory right might be, for example, an adequate education for handicapped children. Then, if the regulations promulgated by the Department of Education to achieve this objective are unsatisfactory, or if the special education programs established by a locality are inadequate, the affected parties can bring suit in court. In an era of active judicial "administration" of statutes, with judges getting involved in the details of institutional operation, organized interests are emboldened to make demands on agencies—and go to court—to secure their rights.[59]

[58] We draw the examples from Donald Horowitz, *The Courts and Social Policy* (Washington, DC: The Brookings Institution, 1977), pp. 3–4.
[59] Martin Shapiro, "The Courts v. the President," *Journal of Contemporary Studies 4* (1981), p. 5. Shapiro's argument and the example illustrating it are cited in Roger H. Davidson and Walter J. Oleszek, *Congress and its Members* (Washington, DC: CQ Press, 1981), p. 350.

In addition, to the extent that the courts are structurally and procedurally insulated from the narrow application of political pressure by organized interests, they can be responsive to the supplications of the politically and economically weak if they so desire. This is not to say that the desires of the public at large have no influence on judicial policymaking; the courts are by no means freed from the need to be responsive to majority opinion and preferences, and judges cannot stray too far from the prevailing mood of the country without jeopardizing the legitimacy of the courts.[60] However, narrower interests have difficulty bringing their resources to bear directly on judges. As was indicated at the beginning of the chapter, many of the most expensive techniques of influence used by organized interests—orchestrated campaigns of grass roots pressure, campaign contributions, the offer of assorted inducements—are irrelevant, inappropriate, or statutorily proscribed in the judicial setting. Thus, while the courts cannot long ignore the preferences of the majority of citizens on issues about which they care deeply, they are insulated from the importunes of narrower organized interests.

Still, resources clearly matter. An impecunious organization cannot even contemplate sponsoring litigation. In addition, there are many ways in which resources can increase the effectiveness of a group's judicial strategy. But the advantage of well-off groups is reduced by their inability to apply their principal resources directly on the decision makers, and groups lacking in conventional political resources enjoy a more nearly equal footing in the courts. As one student of the courts puts it:

Court proceedings are judicial. They involve adversary proceedings between two parties viewed as equal individuals. Marginal groups can expect a much more favorable hearing from courts than from bodies which look beyond the individual to the strength he can bring into the arena.[61]

Data about the filing of amicus briefs by organizations allow us to investigate these considerations in a more systematic way.[62] We enumerated all the amicus briefs filed with the Supreme Court in two periods: the four terms beginning in October 1958 and the four terms beginning in October 1978. (We should note that we included only those briefs urging affirmance or reversal

[60]On this theme see Robert G. McCloskey, *The American Supreme Court* (Chicago: University of Chicago Press, 1960), p. 225 and passim.

[61]Martin Shapiro, "The Supreme Court and Freedom of Speech," in David F. Forte, ed., *The Supreme Court in American Politics: Judicial Activism* v. *Judicial Restraint* (Lexington, MA: Heath, 1972), p. 37.

[62]Because test cases are named for the individuals involved in the particular dispute rather than for the organization sponsoring the cases, it is difficult to use the Supreme Court cases themselves to examine systematically judicial activity by organized interests. For this reason, we (like other researchers) turned to amicus briefs as a source of systematic information.

and only those cases in which the lower court decision was either affirmed or reversed by the Court.) Following our usual procedure, we categorized the organization filing the brief. In addition, we noted whether the position urged in the brief was in fact adopted by the Court. Our first finding confirms a change upon which others have remarked—that there has been a tremendous expansion in amicus activity over the past couple of decades. A total of 216 briefs were filed in the earlier period, while 679 were filed in the later one. However, not all these amicus briefs were filed by private organizations. Many (33 percent in the earlier period and 24 percent in the later period) originated with governments—the Department of Justice or other agencies of the federal government, states and localities and their agencies, and other organizations from the intergovernmental lobby. Furthermore, a certain number of amicus briefs (9 percent of the total from 1958 through 1961 and 4 percent of the total from 1978 through 1981) were filed by individuals.

Table 14.1 summarizes the data for the amicus briefs filed by organized interests. (Because we have eliminated briefs originating with individuals or governments, the total numbers of briefs considered are lower than the figures given above.) The two left-hand columns allow us to compare the kinds of organizations that filed briefs in the two periods. What is clear is the remarkable expansion of amicus activity by organizations representing the interests of the disadvantaged and broad publics—interests that are underrepresented in other forms of pressure politics. There were no briefs filed by any civil rights or social welfare organizations or by groups representing women, the elderly, or the handicapped in the four terms beginning in October of 1958. However, 18 percent of all amicus briefs filed by organized interests in the four terms beginning in October 1978 originated with such groups. Thus, organizations representing the disadvantaged carry a much larger share of the weight of amicus activity than they do of other kinds of organized interest activity—for example, PAC giving.

Organizations representing broad publics also increased their share of amicus activity somewhat. At the same time, there was a transformation in the kinds of diffuse public interests that achieved organized advocacy in amicus briefs. In the earlier period, all but one of the 19 briefs originating with citizens' groups were filed by the American Civil Liberties Union (ACLU). While the ACLU is still an important source of amicus briefs—accounting for 30 percent of the 93 briefs filed in the later period—several other kinds of citizens' groups now engage in this activity as well. Of the briefs filed by citizens' groups in the later period, consumer groups were responsible for 9 percent, and environmental groups were responsible for 8 percent. What is more, in a significant shift, 38 percent of the amicus briefs filed by citizens' groups originated with conservative organizations.[63]

[63]Our findings confirm evidence presented in O'Connor and Epstein, "The Rise of Conservative Interest Group Litigation."

Table 14.1   FILING OF AMICUS BRIEFS BY ORGANIZATIONS

	Distribution of organizations filing briefs		Percentage of briefs in which Court took suggested action	
	1958–1961	1978–1981	1958–1961	1978–1981
Corporations	16%	8%	65%	65%
Trade and other business associations	25	21	23	45
Professional associations	16	10	40	62
Unions	15	10	83	57
Citizens' groups	15	19	39	53
Civil rights groups	—	9	—	61
Social welfare groups	—	4	—	45
Women/Elderly/ Handicapped	—	5	—	36
Other	13	14	50	58
	100%	100%		
	(N = 125)	(N = 493)		

Sources: The tally of amicus briefs for the 1958–1961 and 1978–1980 terms is based on information taken from the "Annotations and Briefs" section in *The United States Supreme Court Reports* (Lawyers' Edition, Second Series; Rochester, NY: The Lawyers' Co-operative Publishing Co.). Information for the 1981 term was taken from *United States Reports* (Washington, DC: Government Printing Office, 1984), vol. 454 and preliminary prints of vols. 455–458.

The two right-hand columns of Table 14.1, which show the percentage of briefs filed by a particular kind of organization in which the Court took the action suggested, give us some sense of the kinds of interests to which the Court responded. Comparing the two periods, trade and other business associations, professional associations, and citizens' groups were more likely—and unions less likely—to have been on the winning side in the later period. What is striking about the 1978–1981 period is how little difference there was among various kinds of organizations in terms of the likelihood of the Court's adopting the position urged in their briefs. Corporations, professional associations, and civil rights groups were somewhat more likely than trade and other business associations, social welfare groups, and especially groups representing women, the elderly, and the handicapped to have argued on behalf of the side that eventually won the case.[64] However, the differences are not substantial. Furthermore, this array does not show the Court as differentially responsive to

[64]To disaggregate the last figures: 56 percent of the amicus briefs filed by women's organizations were on the winning side; the analogous figures for groups representing the elderly and the handicapped were 20 and 29 percent, respectively.

arguments made by advocates of the interests of broad publics and the disadvantaged.

In short, these data suggest that what has changed most substantially is the distribution of amicus activity among various kinds of organizations, not the Court's favorability to different kinds of interests. The arguments made by business organizations were no more likely to face rejection by the Supreme Court than those made by advocates of the disadvantaged and broad publics. However, the interests of the latter groups were simply more likely to have been represented in recent years. This adds confirmation to one of the themes underlying this inquiry: that while representation of interests is not equivalent to political influence, it is a critical first step in the achievement of political influence.

SUMMARY

This chapter has examined the various ways in which organized interests use the federal courts to further their objectives. Although the informal and direct forms of lobbying common in the other branches are taboo in the judicial process, organized interests have several avenues open to them in trying to shape the outcomes of judicial decisions. Some of these are indirect. For example, organized interests may try to affect the appointment of persons to the federal bench or to educate judges and the rest of the legal community through the strategic publication of articles in prestigious law reviews and other legal periodicals.

Organized interests also get involved in the judicial process more directly. Most important, they file suits aimed at testing the constitutionality of some governmental action or raising questions about how a particular law or administrative regulation should be interpreted. Organized interests have achieved significant results through their litigation strategies, wringing from the courts policy decisions that they could not get Congress or the executive branch to make. In addition, many organizations file briefs as friends of the court, providing judicial decision makers with information and arguments in much the same way they do when testifying before a congressional or administrative hearing or furnishing the White House with a position paper on an issue.

Just as there is a dynamic relationship in other arenas between institutional structure and procedure, on the one hand, and organized interest activity, on the other, the procedural rules developed by the courts have an important impact on the courtroom activities of organized interests. The old rules on standing made it difficult for many groups to go to court, limiting access only to plaintiffs who met relatively narrow criteria. But the courts' liberalization of rules on standing in the 1960s and early 1970s paved the way for tidal waves of new group-sponsored litigation as organized interests took to the courts to challenge the actions of the government as well as of other private interests.

Finally, for a variety of reasons, some of the interests that are underrepresented within the Washington pressure community—the less advantaged and broad publics—have in recent years achieved some notable successes in the courts. This situation, however, is unlikely to be permanent and may change as there are changes in the ranks of judges. But judicial activity by organized interests has lent an important counterweight to the thrust of organized interest activity elsewhere in national politics.

15

Organized Interests and American Democracy

Our inquiry has led us down the side streets and through the back alleys of pressure politics. We have encountered scores of organizations along the way. For example, we have evaluated the claims of Preservation Action that it is a public interest group; enumerated the selective benefits provided to members of the Food Marketing Institute; examined the nature of organizational democracy inside the American Federation of Teachers; recounted the efforts of the Calorie Control Council in mobilizing the public against a proposed ban on the use of saccharin; analyzed the comprehensive electoral program fielded by the National Association of Home Builders; observed the intricate grass roots lobbying network established by the U.S. Chamber of Commerce; and described the legal strategy of the National Association for the Advancement of Colored People in filing test cases. These explorations have led to organizations like the National Education Association that have thousands of members and others like R. J. Reynolds Industries that are not even membership groups; organizations like the AFL-CIO tackling many issues and others like the National Rifle Association concentrating on a few; well-heeled organizations like the American Medical Association and straitened ones like the Low Income Housing Coalition; recent arrivals like the Environmental Defense Fund and old-timers like the American Bankers Association.

Having gotten down to cases in the preceding chapters, it is now appropriate to draw back from the welter of fascinating detail surrounding particular examples of organized interests in action and to reconsider some of the larger themes originally raised in the introduction. This concluding chapter reconsiders the following: the issue of how much the Washington pressure scene has changed since political scientists last took a serious look two decades ago; the validity of a linear model in which social disturbances produce collective interests and, in turn, interest organizations and, finally, collective efforts to influence public policy; the knotty question of whether organized interests, in fact, have much influence in American politics; and what this all means for democracy from the point of view of both the time-honored question of who governs and the question of whether anyone can govern at all. The discussion will draw wherever possible on the systematic data already presented. However, in order to address some of the issues most fundamental to an understanding of the role of organized pressure activity in American democracy, it will be necessary to go beyond the evidence assembled here and engage in some informed speculation.

THE CHANGING PRESSURE SCENE: MORE OF THE SAME

One of the continuing efforts throughout this inquiry has been to measure the extent of the changes that have taken place in Washington pressure politics since political scientists last gathered systematic information some two decades ago. Perhaps the most striking change in the activity of organized interests in the capital is how much it has expanded. As shown in Chapter 4, there are many more organizations on the scene than in the past. Many new organizations have been born in recent years. Fully 40 percent of the organizations about which we gathered data were founded since the beginning of the 1960s; even more remarkably, one in every four has appeared on the scene just since 1970. In addition, over the same period there has been a massive mobilization for politics of existing but hitherto apolitical organizations. In particular, large numbers of organizations have regularized their presence in politics by establishing offices in Washington to manage their government relations operations. Hence, not only are there many *new* organizations, but there are many more organizations *in politics*.

Although the vast increase in the *number* of organized interests involved in Washington politics constitutes a substantial change, there is considerably more continuity when it comes to the *kinds* of interests represented. Describing the Washington pressure community of the 1950s, E. E. Schattschneider observed not only that some interests are excluded altogether but also that some kinds of interests—those of the less advantaged and diffuse publics—are systematically less likely to achieve vigorous representation.[1] In spite of the emergence of many new organizations—ranging from Common Cause and the Friends of the Earth to the Food Research and Action Center and the Mexican-American Legal Defense and Education Fund—representing precisely such interests, the contours of the contemporary Washington pressure community hew closely to the outlines depicted by Schattschneider.

[1] See the discussion of Schattschneider's observations in Chapter 4.

As a matter of fact, the data presented in Chapter 4 make clear that, if anything, the distribution of organizations within the Washington pressure community is even more heavily weighted in favor of business organizations than it used to be. If all organizations having representation in Washington are considered, the proportion representing the interests of business has risen from 57 percent to 72 percent since 1960. The proportion of citizens' groups decreased from 9 percent to 5 percent of all organizations, and the proportion representing labor fell from 11 percent to 2 percent. Thus, while the single most appropriate word to describe the changing number of organizations involved in Washington is "more," in an important sense what we have found is "more of the same."

It is not simply that there are more organizations on the scene, but that these organizations are more active as well. Even considering that our sample was designed to include large and active organizations, when the multiple techniques that organizations use to influence political outcomes were probed, what was striking was just how much organizations do. However, they are not only doing a lot, but according to their own reports they are doing much more. Once again, however, the situation might be characterized as more of the same, for this remarkable increase in the volume of organized interest activity has brought very little change in substance. In short, the various techniques that fill the arsenal of the contemporary pressure organization are the same that have been used for decades. In examining the methods of interest representation, it seemed over and over again that techniques considered unique to our era have ample historical precedent. For example, while we ordinarily think of the use of carefully targeted direct mail as a peculiarly modern way to generate grass roots support, we saw that long before the age of the microchip the Anti-Saloon League amassed mailing lists of hundreds of thousands of names.

This degree of continuity might seem unremarkable were it not for the many significant alterations in the larger political environment over the same period. For example, in view of recent developments in mass-communication and data-processing technologies, we expected to find conspicuous increases in the use of computer- and media-based techniques of influence. Similarly, in light of the strengthening of the ties between congressional legislators and their districts, organized interests might now place special emphasis on certain approaches: to devote more energy to explaining the effects of bills on individual legislators' districts, bringing influential constituents to Washington to lobby their representatives, and the like. However, as shown in Chapter 7, there have been no selective increases in either the electronically related or the constituency-based modes of organized interest activity. Organizational use of these forms of interest representation has, of course, increased dramatically, but so too has the use of classic lobbying methods such as direct contact and consultation. In summary, then, while there has been an explosion in both the number of organizations active in Washington politics and the volume of their activity, in terms of both the kinds of interests represented and the kinds of techniques of influence mobilized, what we have found is more of the same.

ORGANIZED INTEREST POLITICS: AN INTERACTIVE APPROACH

At one time, group theorists of politics—who placed the politics of organized interests at the center of the American political process—construed pressure politics as a kind of political chain reaction. According to this perspective, disturbances to the equilibrium in the political environment would give rise to alterations in collectively perceived interests. If these jointly interested individuals had not already done so, they would form an organization that would in turn actively represent their interests before the government until a new, and more favorable, equilibrium could be established.[2]

This formulation is too simplistic. The question of where organizations come from, for example, is a complicated one. Organizational formation is not necessarily the spontaneous result of social disturbances and consequent redefinitions of joint politically relevant interests. Sometimes such dislocations in the political environment do not result in new organizations. Chapter 4 considered the aggregate set of interests represented by the Washington pressure community and concluded that there is nothing automatic about the emergence of interest organizations. A number of groups—ranging from public housing tenants to homemakers—whose members might be expected to have joint interests in government policy have no organized representation in Washington politics. Chapter 6 elaborated this empirical observation by reference to the formal theory of Mancur Olson, whose logic of collective action posits that there is nothing inevitable about the formation of organizations to do political battle on behalf of the jointly interested and that those who wish to start an organization or keep one going must be able to supply supporters with sufficient tangible or intangible benefits.

Furthermore, there are other patterns of organizational formation besides the spontaneous association of individuals sharing interests. A number of factors can serve as catalysts of organizational formation—including, not infrequently, the government itself. As shown in Chapters 5 and 6, not only do federal government funds (usually derived from contracts to carry out specific purposes) contribute substantially to the budgets of some organizations, but the government often takes the initiative in organizing unorganized constituencies. Over the course of this century, federal government activity has provided the impetus for the founding of organizations representing diverse groups, ranging from business to farmers to the poor.

[2]Such a model of politics emerges most clearly from the work of David Truman, *The Governmental Process* (New York: Knopf, 1951). However, a number of academic analysts of politics of the 1950s subscribed to it—at least implicitly.

Finally, the definition of joint interests need not precede organization; rather, the definition of interests involves a process of mutual influence between organization and members. Ongoing organizations often play a role in shaping the ways in which those with common interests understand their shared political concerns. Because the members of an organization's government relations staff are on the scene day in and day out, they have a knowledge of the potential effects of proposed policy changes that most organization members do not have. As shown in Chapter 6, one of the most important functions of a Washington office is to act as a kind of early warning system, informing members when their interests are threatened. In this process, interests are interpreted and, sometimes, created where none had existed before.

The Impact of the Political System on Organized Interests

It is not only the first part of the group theorist formulation—that which specifies the more or less automatic emergence of interest organizations in response to social changes and accompanying redefinitions of politically relevant interests—that requires revision. The second part of the formulation—that which posits unidirectional pressure placed on the political system by organized interests—also demands reassessment, for the relationship between the political system and organized interests is reciprocal. Interest organizations are not autonomous units; rather, they reflect the constitutional, institutional, legal, and electoral systems in which they are embedded. Over and over in the course of our inquiry, the multiple ways in which these aspects of the political environment impinge on pressure politics—in terms of how many and what kind of interest organizations emerge, the techniques they use, the strategies they adopt, and the extent of their influence—have become clear.

First of all, constitutional arrangements, federalism and separation of powers, create a receptive environment for organized interests; the existence of multiple institutional arenas implies that there are numerous points at which influence might be exerted. This situation has the effect not only of fostering pressure activity but also of encouraging certain kinds of strategies—in particular, attempts to locate policy controversies in the arenas most likely to yield a favorable outcome. In addition, it is possible to list numerous examples of laws and regulations that affect the choice of techniques of influence. For example, we saw in Chapter 5 that tax laws place restrictions on the lobbying activities of organizations enjoying 501(c)(3) tax status; in Chapter 10 that the Federal Electoral Campaign Act and subsequent Federal Election Commission rulings (in particular, the *Sun Oil* decision) have had the effect of encouraging the growth of political action committees (PACs); and in Chapter 14 that legal precedents defining when a plaintiff has standing have consequences for organizations' ability to go to court.

Furthermore, institutional arrangements have an impact. Chapter 12 described how changes in Congress have contributed to the recent explosion in organized interest activity. Chapter 13 showed how the structure of the executive branch—both the number of agencies with which an organization has dealings and the number of other clients with which it must compete for an agency's attention—can affect the amount of influence enjoyed by organized interests. Finally, even electoral outcomes make a difference. One of the themes of Chapter 9 was that although there is little consultation between party and organized interest leadership, election results—especially, as in 1980, when they change the dominant ideological complexion of the government—can alter the fortunes of organized interests.

There is another respect in which the unidirectional model of organized interest influence on government is inadequate as well. Organized interests are not battering rams attempting to bludgeon policymakers into making concessions; rather, they are engaged in complex relationships of mutual assistance and interdependence with public officials. This is hardly a novel observation with respect to the executive branch. The symbiotic nature of the relationships between client and agency was long ago described by the capture theorists. However, even in agencies that are not captured—and, as shown in Chapter 13, they frequently are not—policymakers depend in numerous ways on their organized constituents, particularly for information, but also for political support and sometimes for future employment. Furthermore, what is less frequently noted is the extent to which the relationships between organized interests and Congress are characterized by similar reciprocity. Once again, as shown in Chapter 12, Washington representatives are in a position to supply congressional policymakers with much that is valuable—not only information and political support, but also PAC contributions, speaking fees, various forms of entertainment, and so on. In yet another way, then, the paths connecting organized interests to other parts of society and the polity bear two-way traffic.

DO ORGANIZED INTERESTS HAVE INFLUENCE?

Throughout the preceding chapters, one of our ongoing preoccupations has been the question of representation—in particular, the question of what kind of interests achieve vigorous advocacy in organized interest politics. Representation is not, however, equivalent to influence. Political outcomes are decided by a multiplicity of factors, only one of which is organized interest activity, and political scientists of an earlier era erred in attributing to organized interests a virtually exclusive role in policy determination.[3] In concluding, it seems appropriate to address somewhat more directly the fundamental question of whether organized interests make a difference for policy.

The systematic evidence presented here—the sample survey of Washington representatives and the inventories of PACs and organizations having a

---

[3]For a discussion of the group theorists' perspective on the determination of policy, see Chapter 1.

presence in the capital—illuminates many important questions about organized interests, what they do, and whom they represent; it is not particularly appropriate, however, for tackling the issue of the policy impact of organized interest activity. Our data draw from the universe of Washington-based private organizations. In order to investigate in a systematic way the impact of organized interest activity on policy, it would be necessary somehow to sample from the universe of political controversies, construct detailed case studies, and then draw inferences about the extent of organized interest influence.[4] In so doing, the appropriate standard for assessing policy impact would not be whether the organization sustained a victory or a defeat, but whether the resolution of a particular political conflict reflects the efforts of organized interests. Sometimes organized interests are able to ameliorate the extent of a defeat; the apparent loss thus masks the degree to which things would have been worse had the organization not gotten involved. Similarly, victories may be false evidence of organizational effectiveness, for the outcome might have been determined by other factors (such as the support of key policymakers) rather than by organized interest activity. In short, in making inferences from cases about organized interest influence, what matters is not simply who won or lost, but whether the score would have been different had interest organizations not been active.

Our inquiry, of course, is studded with particular cases. However, there is good reason to believe that the cases presented are skewed systematically in the direction of demonstrating organized interest success. Inept or indifferent attempts at influence rarely make vivid illustrations of organized interests in action. Hence, in choosing cases as examples of particular techniques of influence, we have surely presented a disproportionate number in which the attempt at influence was effective.

The Weakness of Organized Interests

Although the cases included in the text might lead to the conclusion that organized interests enjoy great success in American politics, there are two bodies of evidence suggesting that, on the contrary, organized interests are in fact rather weak in their impact. One source of evidence is derived from comparisons of organized interest politics in the United States with that of other advanced industrial democracies. Although Americans have traditionally had a reputation for being a nation of joiners, and although associational life in the United States has a richness and variety that is probably unsurpassed, Americans are less likely than citizens of several other democracies to be members of organizations. In particular, Americans are somewhat less likely to be members of unions and professional or other occupationally related organizations; hence,

---

[4]For a more extended discussion of the points made in this paragraph and the one that follows, see Chapter 7.

such associations achieve a much higher density of membership in many European countries than they do in the United States.[5] Furthermore, there is more competition between organizations within broadly defined economic sectors here than elsewhere. The situation is especially notable in the field of agriculture, where two peak associations having markedly different ideological leanings, the National Farmers Union and the American Farm Bureau Federation, compete with one another. However, the same observation applies to organized labor, where three of the nation's largest unions (the National Education Association, the Teamsters, and the United Mine Workers) are not affiliated with the peak labor union, the AFL-CIO.[6]

In addition, in several European nations—among them the democracies of Scandinavia, Austria, and the Netherlands—organized interests have an official role in policymaking. Under such political arrangements, which are sometimes called *neocorporatist,* mechanisms providing for the equal representation of individuals on a geographic basis are supplemented by mechanisms providing for functional representation of organized interests—ordinarily by a relatively limited number of peak associations representing, for example, workers, employers, and farmers.[7] Such organizations are recognized and licensed by the state and attain a regularized role in policymaking through their integration into its administrative apparatus—through delegations of administrative power or participation on public councils or committees. Important government decisions are made only after consultation with major economic interests. For example, in many such systems, there is a national wage bargain, which is the outcome of negotiations among the national government, unions, and employer associations.

Analysts of European politics sometimes point out that this process of ongoing consultation gives organized interests an institutionalized role in governing that they lack in the United States. There are, however, many examples of private government on a narrower scale in American politics.[8] For example, certain organizations are accorded quasi-public status. Blue Cross plans and other "fiscal intermediaries" under the Medicare program bear much of the

[5]See the discussion and attendant references in Chapter 4.

[6]Graham K. Wilson discusses these examples in "Why Is There No Corporatism in the United States?" in Gerhard Lehmbruch and Philippe C. Schmitter, eds., *Patterns of Corporatist Policy-Making* (Beverly Hills, CA: Sage, 1982), pp. 221–222.

[7]For neocorporatist interpretations of interest representation in advanced industrial systems, see the essays contained in Philippe C. Schmitter and Gerhard Lehmbruch, eds., *Trends Toward Corporatist Intermediation* (Beverly Hills, CA: Sage, 1979); Suzanne Berger, ed., *Organizing Interests in Western Europe* (Cambridge: Cambridge University Press, 1981); and Lehmbruch and Schmitter, eds., *Patterns of Corporatist Policy-Making.* For explicit statements on the relevance of this perspective for the American case, see Robert H. Salisbury, "Why No Corporatism in America?," in Schmitter and Lehmbruch, eds., *Trends Toward Corporatist Intermediation,* pp. 213–230, and Wilson, "Why Is There No Corporatism in the United States?," pp. 219–236.

[8]See, in particular, Grant McConnell, *Private Power and American Democracy* (New York: Knopf, 1966). The self-regulatory policies described by Michael T. Hayes, ["The Semi-Sovereign Pressure Groups: A Critique of Theory and an Alternative Typology," *Journal of Politics* 40 (1978): 145, 154–155] involve delegation of government power to private interests.

administrative burden and share in much of the decision making for the massive health care financing program. Furthermore, in advisory committees within the executive branch, governmental authority is shared with private interests. However, as shown in Chapter 13, the members of these committees lack the official certification as representatives of particular constituencies that is conferred on them in other polities. Moreover, compared with the negotiations surrounding national wage agreements abroad, American advisory committees deal with narrower sets of issues and are less likely to be able to make binding policy decisions than their counterparts in neocorporatist systems.

There is, however, a price for the badge of official recognition. In order to make a credible case that they speak for their constituencies, organizations so certified must guarantee membership compliance with the results of the deliberations in which they have participated. In the process, rank-and-file members lose independence; union members, for example, are more constrained in rejecting negotiated settlements, a right they exercise regularly in the United States. Moreover, the organizations themselves lose autonomy and become, in a sense, creatures of the state. In addition, interests not enjoying the legitimating badge of state certification are frozen out of the process and enjoy no influence at all. Still, a very real case can be made that organized interests wield greater influence in certain capitals across the Atlantic than they do in Washington.

A second body of evidence suggesting that organized interests command only limited policy influence derives from studies of pressure politics in the United States conducted in the late 1950s and early 1960s. The group theorist orthodoxy positing pressure group determination of policy was soon supplanted by a counter-orthodoxy stressing the weakness of group influence.[9] According to the revisionist perspective, organized interests—far from deciding the broad outlines of policy—can merely hope to have an impact on the details of measures. This contention rests on several related assertions: that organized interests are too resource poor to mount much of a fight; that they have few inducements to offer policymakers; that they only approach their allies among public officials and, hence, waste effort preaching to the converted; that policymakers pay attention only to what they want to hear; and that organized pressure on one side of a policy controversy is invariably met by pressure on the opposite side.

These contentions were discussed at length in Chapter 12; many of the points made there with respect to Congress have relevance for the political system as a whole. Our arguments hinged in part on a somewhat different understanding of what constitutes nontrivial influence. We pointed out, for example, that while the broad outlines of policy are rarely dictated by organized interest preferences alone, the power to influence details—whether of congressional legislation, agency regulations, or judicial findings—is not a neg-

[9]See the discussion and attendant footnotes in Chapter 12.

ligible form of influence, for it is the particulars that govern the nature and extent of the impact, if any at all, a given policy will have. In addition, we argued that conspiring with allies can enhance policy effectiveness. Converting opponents is one route to political influence; collaborating with friends to design effective strategy is another.

The discussion also indicated that some of the empirical assertions adduced to demonstrate organized interest influence no longer hold, if they ever did. For example, if the stereotype of the overworked and underpaid lobbyist was ever accurate, it is no longer. Surely, the organizations we encountered vary substantially in the amount and adequacy of their resources; surely, some of them are forced to get by on relatively slender budgets; and surely, the Washington representatives whom we interviewed seem uniformly hardworking. Still, in general, their surroundings are hardly threadbare and their expense accounts hardly lean. By and large, it is simply inappropriate to characterize the contemporary world of Washington interest representation as resource starved.

Similarly, the contention that organized interests have no inducements to offer to policymakers does not hold up, if it ever did. The array of such inducements is impressive indeed—ranging from information, political support, and future jobs to, in the case of legislators, PAC contributions and fact-finding junkets. As a matter of fact, one of the themes throughout our inquiry has been to demonstrate the reciprocity of needs that links organized interests to policymakers.

Finally, organized pressure on one side of an issue is not always met with organized pressure on the other. Of course, organized interests frequently confront opposition from other organized interests. Still, various theories lead us to predict—and empirical evidence substantiates—that head-on conflicts between organized interests are not the norm. In short, while competition between organized interests sometimes vitiates organized interest influence, such rivalry is not inevitable.

When Do Organized Interests Wield Influence?

In light of the fragility of several of the pillars supporting the original argument about organized interest weakness, it becomes important to inquire into the circumstances under which they are especially likely to be influential. This question was discussed at some length in Chapter 12. Not surprisingly, many of the generalizations made there with respect to Congress have broader applicability. First, political influence varies with the nature of the demand. The point is often made that success is more likely when the objective is to kill a proposed measure than when the goal is to see one become policy. The fragmented nature of the American political process implies that there are so many opportunities for the exertion of political pressure, and thus so many opportunities for throwing up roadblocks to unwanted action, that it has a built-in bias in favor of the policy status quo. Hence, an organization seeking to stymie a threatening measure is in a much better position to prevail than one seeking positive policy action.

In addition, the probability of success appears to vary inversely with the scope of the demand. Organizations whose political ends are narrow and technical are more likely to be influential than those whose goals are more encompassing. In general, it is easier to affect the details of a policy than its broad outlines; and, as we have seen, this is not a negligible form of influence. This is a point having implications for our earlier discussion of the relative strength of organized interests in neocorporatist systems. Where such arrangements prevail, organized interests are able to have an impact on broad issues such as wage-price policy having societywide import. While organized interests in the American context lack this kind of impact, they frequently wield impressive influence on narrower issues.

Organized interest influence is also likely to increase with the availability of resources. One point made repeatedly is that money is only one of a number of political resources. Other resources—a large and active membership, an appealing cause, a dedicated staff, well-placed allies—can help compensate for an inadequate budget. However, as shown in Chapter 5, financial resources are very unevenly distributed among organizations, and some organizations—especially citizens' groups—indicate that lack of financial resources inhibits their policy effectiveness.

The probability of organized interest influence will also vary with the structure of the political conflict. The greater the number of helpful allies, the more effective organized interests are likely to be; the more extensive the competing pressures, the more limited the impact of organized interests. These allies and antagonists, whose support or opposition can do so much to alter the chances of organized interest success, come from various quarters. One potential source of support is the public. The public can be a natural ally—and increasingly in this electronic age, a created ally. The correlative of this point is, of course, that an organization facing actual or potential public hostility ordinarily adopts a strategy of keeping the issue at stake as narrowly confined and nearly invisible as possible so as not to mobilize opposition.

In addition to the public at large are the special publics whose assistance or opposition can be so critical. On one hand, it is clear that organized interests are increasingly likely to find it useful to act in coalition. When allied with other organized interests, they can create a rational division of labor, compound their resources, and multiply the number of contacts within the government. On the other hand, among the most formidable adversaries that organized interests confront are other organized interests. Organized pressure is much less likely to yield policy influence if it is met—as it often is—by opposing pressure. However, such countervailing activity by an opposing interest is hardly inevitable.

Contrary to the orthodox group theorists who attributed to government mere referee status in overseeing the group struggle, public officials inevitably throw their weight to one side of a controversy or another and thus constitute among the most important allies that organized interests can cultivate. We have seen that organized interests sometimes find natural allies within the government. An organization that has the good fortune to deal with a single agency within the executive branch and to be its sole client ordinarily finds itself with a valuable advocate in policy matters. Similarly, an organization whose cause is adopted by a policy entrepreneur may be able to overcome serious resource deficiencies and wield political influence. With respect to Congress, as shown in Chapter 12, legislators are subject to multiple and competing pressures. Therefore, organized interest influence in Congress is likely to be greatest on the kind of low-visibility issues that do not command public or media attention and do not engage strong ideological, partisan, or constituency pressures. Furthermore, as shown in Chapter 14, many activist judges in the federal courts have proved to be the patrons of interests that otherwise lack natural allies within the government.

These observations about the significance of public authorities as allies, in conjunction with our earlier observations about the fragmentation of American politics by federalism and separation of powers and the consequent proliferation of arenas in which policy is made, lead to one final generalization about the circumstances under which organized pressure is likely to have an impact on policy. Organized interests are more likely to be influential if they can locate a public controversy in the arena most likely to yield a favorable outcome. Our inquiry contains numerous examples of the successful use of this strategy. For example, during the 1950s civil rights groups—certain to make no headway against Jim Crow laws either in lily-white Southern legislatures or in a Congress dominated by Southern committee chairmen—made progress by taking test cases to court. It was only after the 1964 presidential election yielded an overwhelmingly Democratic Congress that legislative strategies became productive for civil rights groups. Similarly, soft drink companies threatened with FDA action on saccharin and auto dealers threatened with FTC action on used cars were able to transfer the locus of policy conflict from an executive agency to Congress. In this more congenial environment, the organized interests were able to forestall the proposed policy changes.

It is now possible to draw together the various strands of our argument about organized interest influence on policy matters. Early in the 1960s political scientists maintained that organized interests are weak in American politics. It seems both that they tended to discount too readily certain kinds of organized influence and that several of the empirical assertions underlying their analysis no longer hold. In particular, private organizations in Washington are, by and large, not starving for resources; they have significant inducements to offer public officials in exchange for cooperation; and organized activity on one side of a policy controversy is not always met by counterpressure from an opposing organization. Furthermore, although we do not have the kind of systematic sampling of policy controversies that would permit valid generalizations about the extent of policy impact enjoyed by organized interests, it seems reasonable to suggest that the involvement of organized interests is most likely to have consequences for political outcomes under the following circumstances: when the objective is to block proposed action rather than to nurture a new policy to fruition; when the issue at stake is narrow and technical and when it has low public and media visibility; when an organization has sufficient resources to pursue its goals vigorously; and when there is no opposition—and, preferably, active support—from the public, other organized interests, and public officials.

In short, we have encountered many cases in which organized interests clearly exercised significant influence and a number of instances in which an organization's best efforts came to naught. It seems appropriate to pose one final question: Do efforts to affect political outcomes ever backfire? In our files of case material, there are examples of victories that were Pyrrhic or defeats that were costly in terms of organizational maintenance—instances, for example, in which fighting a particular battle was so expensive that the organization was handicapped in fighting subsequent ones or in which the cost of position taking by leaders and staff was to alienate the rank and file. From the perspective of organizational maintenance, then, the organization would probably have been better off not to have gotten involved in the first place. Of the multitudes of examples reviewed, however, there is only one in which an organization was worse off in terms of the policy outcome than it was at the outset.[10] That is, our files contain just one case in which efforts at organized influence were not only unproductive but counterproductive with respect to policy. Thus, political activity by organized interests frequently results in the accomplishment of policy objectives; it sometimes nets no policy gains, but it almost never results in policy loss.

ORGANIZED INTERESTS AND PUBLIC LIFE IN AMERICA

It is impossible to conclude an inquiry of this sort without thinking once again about the "mischiefs of faction" and aiming some speculative remarks at the question of the implications for public life in America of the kind of vigorous organized interest process that we have described. In particular, two questions demand attention: how the existence of pressure politics as a vehicle for the

[10]The single case that we located in which an organization was worse off than it would have been had it never gotten involved is the Supreme Court decision in *Valley Forge Christian College v. Americans United for Separation of Church and State,* 454 U.S. 464 (1982), discussed in Chapter 14. The latter organization sued to stop the government from giving a surplus army hospital to a small Christian college. The Court ruled that Americans United did not have standing to sue because the members of the group did not suffer "injury in fact" and thus did not have the right to fight the property transfer in court. In this case, then, organized interest activity seems to have been actually counterproductive. Not only did Americans United sustain a total loss in this particular battle, but a policy emerged that rendered them unable to fight similar battles in the future.

expression of citizen concerns and preferences affects political outcomes in America; and whether, as some have suggested, the explosion in organized interest activity over the past two decades has so fragmented and factionalized our politics that it has become impossible for anyone to govern at all.

Organized Interests and American Politics: Who Governs?

It is widely accepted that procedure and substance cannot be divorced in the understanding of political life. Political arrangements have implications for political outcomes; particular sets of such arrangements tend to facilitate the expression of particular kinds of interests and provide likely arenas for the playing out of particular kinds of public controversies and, thus, to have implications for who wins and who loses in politics.[11] This inquiry has dwelled, of course, on a narrow slice of the arrangements that prevail in American politics. It now seems appropriate to consider how organized interest politics relates to the more general political process of which it is a part. Thus, we are led to inquire what sorts of biases are built into American politics by the fact that a relatively weak party system is supplemented by a relatively strong pressure system in linking citizens to politics.

The realm of pressure politics in America is one in which the range of politically relevant interests represented is not only remarkably broad but also more nearly comprehensive than in the past. It is also a realm in which power is not held by a narrow elite but is widely dispersed. It is, however, an arena that accommodates the conversion of private or market resources into political ones. Thus, interest politics is characterized by tremendous inequalities in representation and influence. In the course of our inquiry we have reviewed many changes having implications for the perpetuation of these inequalities. Some of them ameliorate inequalities among organized interests: both the emergence of new groups representing the poor, the ideologically committed, consumers, taxpayers, and environmentalists and the changes in congressional and administrative procedure that make it easier for such new groups to function have this effect. Others incline in the opposite direction. The mobilization of previously apolitical business interests, the rapid growth in the sums funneled to electoral campaigns through political action committees, and the development of expensive new techniques of public persuasion tend to exacerbate existing inequalities. In summary, then, it seems accurate to describe pressure politics as characterized by "dispersed inequalities" and to conclude that these inequalities are likely to persist for the foreseeable future.[12]

[11] E. E. Schattschneider points out that "all forms of political organization have a bias in favor of the exploitation of some kinds of conflict and the suppression of others. . . . Some issues are organized into politics while others are organized out." *The Semisovereign People* (New York: Holt, Rinehart and Winston, 1960), p. 71.

[12] The term "dispersed inequalities" is taken from Robert A. Dahl, *Who Governs?* (New Haven: Yale University Press, 1961), Chapter 7.

The overall thrust of organized interest politics is quite different from that envisioned by Madison. He feared tyranny of the majority as the pernicious consequence of factional politics, arguing that the ordinary operations of democratic procedure would prevent any minority faction from prevailing. On the contrary, it seems that the politics of organized pressure builds into the American system a minoritarian tendency to counterbalance the more majoritarian proclivities of other parts of the political process. In general, organized interest politics tends to facilitate the articulation of demands by the narrowly interested and well organized. By and large, the collectivities thus benefited are well heeled; business, in particular, finds pressure politics a useful mechanism for pursuing political goals. Larger aggregates, especially the less advantaged and those seeking nondivisible public goods, such as clean air and lower taxes, fare rather less well through the agency of organized interest politics than they do elsewhere in the American political process.[13]

This gross generalization—namely, that the central tendency of organized pressure politics is to offset the majoritarian propensities of other kinds of democratic politics by benefiting narrow publics, especially affluent ones, at the expense of broader aggregates—should immediately be qualified in several ways. First, it is clear that not all the narrow publics that have found organized interest politics an avenue to influence are privileged. It is possible to list a number of nonaffluent minorities—the elderly, the handicapped, prisoners, and blacks come to mind—that have used pressure politics to realize significant policy gains especially, but not exclusively, through the courts.

In addition, just because organized business interests fare well in pressure politics does not mean that the political interests of business are uniform.[14] There are various patterns of conflict and cooperation among organized business interests. Sometimes business interests are in direct conflict with one another: individual firms, for example, vie with each other in defense procurement; truckers and railroads compete at the Interstate Commerce Commission. On some issues, such as drug safety regulation, part of the business community—often a single industry—is involved, while the remainder is indifferent. On a few issues—for example, labor law reform or the establishment of a consumer agency (both of which were defeated during the late 1970s)—the business community as a whole is united. In spite of the diversity of patterns, however, systematic data indicate that, cooperation within the business com-

[13]To clarify what is meant here, it might be helpful to indicate the relationship between our discussion and the argument made by Charles E. Lindblom in *Politics and Markets* (New York: Basic Books, 1977). Lindblom's analysis parallels ours in its emphasis upon the political importance of the financial resources commanded by business (pp. 194–196) and its focus upon the way in which a pluralistic politics places those without such resources at a disadvantage (p. 141). Lindblom, however, takes the logic one step further by arguing (Chapter 13) that business has a "privileged position" with respect to the government and that business, therefore, enjoys differential success in politics. The evidence presented here, while in no way contradicting this contention, can be used neither to confirm nor to deny the state's enhanced responsiveness to business in market-oriented societies.

[14]See the discussions of this issue in Chapters 4 and 11.

munity is far more commonplace than conflict. When asked to name any consistent allies or antagonists, fully 88 percent of the business organizations (corporations and trade and other business associations) in our sample mentioned another member of the business community as an ally. (Of these, 23 percent named antagonists as well as allies from among the other members of the business community.) Only 4 percent named antagonists but no allies from the business community. In short, while business interests may be involved in head-on collisions with one another, such a pattern of business opposition is hardly the norm.

Advocating the Interests of the Underrepresented   Moreover, the relative inhospitality of pressure politics to the interests of the less advantaged and broad publics does not imply that such interests are completely ignored in American politics. Although the organizations representing such groups are neither the most numerous nor the most affluent in the Washington pressure community, and although the relative distribution of kinds of organizations has not been altered in their favor over the past few decades, the emergence of many new organizations representing broad public interests and those with few resources has given to such interests a more substantial ongoing presence than they had a generation ago. In addition, as we have seen, procedural changes in all three branches of government have made it easier for these organizations to be effective.

Moreover, broad publics and the disadvantaged sometimes achieve vicarious representation in our political system, benefiting from the efforts of narrower interests working on their own behalf in the political process. For example, welfare recipients have few, if any, organizations to represent their interests in Washington. However, the social service personnel employed by welfare agencies often act as advocates for these programs, thus promoting the interests of beneficiaries at the same time they protect their own jobs. Diffuse public interests sometimes benefit from such secondary advocacy as well. In particular, the interests that broad publics share in economic growth and in lower prices or taxes are often championed by narrower interests seeking their own political goals—frequently industries seeking to avoid costly regulations. Sometimes consumer and environmental interests benefit from such advocacy, as when insurance companies advanced the cause of consumer safety by supporting regulations requiring passive restraints in automobiles. However, narrow interests are less likely to take up the cudgel on behalf of the diffuse public interests in consumer protection or environmental preservation than on behalf of stimulating economic growth or keeping taxes and prices down.

In short, those who are less well represented sometimes benefit from the organized interest activity of the kinds of interests that predominate in pressure politics. However, such secondary advocacy is usually an imperfect substitute for direct participation in politics. There may be no interested organization to act as a patron. Furthermore, such organizations usually have their own political goals that may not coincide perfectly with the interests of those not directly represented. Thus, while the self-interested efforts of organizations acting on their own behalf can ameliorate inequalities in representation, they do not overcome such inequalities.

The interests of the less advantaged and broad publics achieve representation through other avenues of citizen politics—namely, electoral politics and protest activity. Observers of American politics have argued both that the interests of the less advantaged fare better in electoral politics than in pressure politics and that such interests are better served when there is vigorous competition between political parties.[15] Since the New Deal, the Democratic Party has served as an advocate of the interests of the less privileged, and both of the major periods of expansion of the American welfare state—the 1930s and the 1960s—occurred in the aftermath of landslide victories by the Democrats.

Because the barriers to entry into the Washington pressure community are sufficiently high as to force many new groups to operate outside of mainstream interest politics until they can establish a foothold as insiders, emergent demands of various kinds have frequently found expression in social movements and protest activity.[16] The citizen concerns that have initially been articulated through the medium of social protest—ranging from women's suffrage and temperance to nuclear disarmament and school prayer—are diverse indeed. They include many examples of efforts by the less advantaged (for example, the early labor and civil rights movements) and broad publics (for example, taxpayer revolts and the wildlife conservation movement as well as the various ideological publics concerned about such single issues as handgun control and the content of school textbooks). Of course, social movements often encompass an organized interest component. In some cases—the women's movement comes to mind—the organized interest sector and the protest sector coexist for a considerable period. Ordinarily, however, the protest wing of the movement atrophies with the establishment and growth of a mainstream organized interest wing.

The final reason that interests poorly represented in the Washington pressure community still receive attention in the policy process has to do with the nature of government. The orthodox group theorists erred in ignoring the independent leadership and influence exercised by public officials.[17] Contrary to what the group theorists would have us believe, the government is not some kind of anemometer measuring the force of the prevailing organized interest breezes. At various times and under various circumstances, various governmental institutions and actors have adopted the causes of the less advantaged and

[15] Both of these points are made by Schattschneider, *The Semisovereign People,* Chapter 5. Perhaps the most eloquent statement of the latter point can be found in V. O. Key, Jr., *Southern Politics* (New York: Knopf, 1949), Chapter 14.

[16] On this point see, for example, Theodore J. Lowi, *The Politics of Disorder* (New York: Basic Books, 1971), Chapters 1 and 2.

[17] This point is made by Robert A. Dahl in *Who Governs?,* p. 6.

broad publics. Sometimes, especially in periods of social ferment and unusual party polarization, Congress takes on this role. Sometimes it is the President who carries the banner. In the recent past, activist federal judges as well as policy entrepreneurs in both the legislative and executive branches have acted as advocates of such interests. There is, of course, nothing permanent about the responsiveness of particular institutions to the interests of the less advantaged and broad publics. One of the legacies of the appointments made by the Reagan administration (in conjunction with those made by other recent Republican administrations) may be to alter the nature of the kinds of publics with which the courts and policy entrepreneurs elsewhere in the federal government are most concerned.

Let us recapitulate our understanding of the contribution of organized pressure politics to the overall distribution of influence in American politics. The activities of organized interests build into the American political system a minoritarian counterweight to some of its more majoritarian tendencies. The minorities thus benefited—while not unanimous in their interests—are disproportionately but not uniformly affluent ones. Those who generally fare less well through pressure politics—in particular, the less advantaged and broad publics—are nevertheless heeded in the making of policy. There are several reasons for this: they have continuing representation within the Washington pressure community; they sometimes benefit from the efforts of narrower publics whose interests coincide with theirs; electoral and social movement politics are more hospitable to their interests; and those in government sometimes take up the cudgel on their behalf.

Handling New Demands in Democratic Polities   Once again, some brief comparisons with the nature of interest representation in other advanced capitalist democracies can illuminate our discussion. Substantial evidence from other democracies confirms the inference that, as opposed to pressure politics, party politics is a more effective vehicle for the interests of the broad majority of ordinary citizens, especially the less advantaged among them. Electoral politics in the United States, of course, is exceptional on two dimensions that are critical for our discussion: parties are weaker here than in most developed democracies, and there is no socialist or labor party alternative. Analysts comparing public outcomes across democratic polities have demonstrated strong correlations between the degree to which such parties of the left share in governing and a number of measures of public efforts on behalf of the ordinary citizen—the ability of the government to tax, the level of unemployment, various measures of inequality of wealth and income, various measures of the extensiveness and level of welfare state benefits.[18] These findings lend credence

[18]See, for example, Christopher Hewitt, "The Effect of Political Democracy and Social Democracy on Equality in Industrial Societies: A Cross-National Comparison," *American Sociological Review* 42 (1977): 450–464; Douglas A. Hibbs, "Political Parties and Macroeconomic Policy," *American Political Science Review* 71 (1977): 1467–1487; David R. Cameron, "The Expansion

to our conclusions about the characteristics of parties—as opposed to interest organizations—as representative mechanisms.

If advanced capitalist democracies with strong parties and social democratic or labor parties that share political power tend to be more hospitable to the class-based interests of broad aggregates, how do other interests fare in such systems? That is, how receptive are such polities to demands made by groups—women, environmentalists, regional and linguistic groups, and so on—that cut across the axes of party conflict?[19] Unfortunately, there are no systematic studies covering a large number of advanced capitalist democracies that seek to draw general conclusions about the circumstances under which such interests gain a receptive response. On the basis of case studies—a few of which make comparisons among nations—it is clear that in other democracies there has been no shortage of citizens' movements analogous to those we found active in the United States during the 1960s and 1970s.[20]

There is, however, a great deal of variation from country to country—even from movement to movement within the same country—in their success, in the degree to which they have desired and been able to penetrate mainstream politics, and in the strategies they have adopted for so doing. In some cases, citizens' movements—for example, the environmentalist, antinuclear movement in West Germany that became the basis for the Green party—attempt to enter electoral politics on their own. In others, the concerns of a citizens' movement—for example, the feminist movement in Sweden—have been addressed by at least one of the established parties, obviating the need for the formation of a new party. In still others, the citizens' movement—for example, the environmentalists in Italy—either by choice or by necessity remains entirely outside the realm of electoral politics. Interestingly, one cannot predict the electoral strategies movements will choose simply by knowing the electoral arrangements of the countries in which they are active. For example, in the Netherlands, where a system of proportional representation would seem to invite the establishment of new parties, environmentalists found their concerns addressed by the Radical party; in France, where a strong presidency and a single-mem-

---

of the Public Economy: A Comparative Analysis," *American Political Science Review* 72 (1978): 1243–1261; and Francis G. Castles, "The Impact of Parties on Public Expenditure," and J. Corina M. van Arnhem and Geurt J. Schotsman, "Do Parties Affect the Distribution of Incomes? The Case of Advanced Capitalist Democracies," both in Francis G. Castles, ed., *The Impact of Parties* (London: Sage, 1982), pp. 21–96, 283–284.

[19]Such questions take on particular meaning in political systems in which neocorporatist arrangements prevail in the organized interest sphere because such representative arrangements ordinarily involve state certification of more limited numbers of organizations as official emissaries of designated interests.

[20]See the following and the references they contain: Thomas R. Rochon, "Political Change in Ordered Societies: The Rise of Citizens' Movements," *Comparative Politics* 15 (1983): 351–373; Herbert Kitschelt, "New Social Movements in West Germany and the United States" (South Bend, IN: University of Notre Dame, September 1983); Steven Kelman, "Party Strength and System Governability in the Face of New Demands: The Case of Feminism" (Cambridge: John F. Kennedy School of Government, Harvard University, March 1984); David Vogel, "Cooperative Regulation: Environmental Protection in Great Britain," *Public Interest* 72 (1983): 88–106.

ber district system of representation would seem less hospitable to new parties, they formed the Ecologist party.[21]

In the United States a citizens' movement that seeks to supplement mass action with mainstream participation in politics ordinarily travels the route of pressure politics rather than the route of electoral politics. For example, while feminists in Sweden have been incorporated into the Social Democratic party, the American women's movement has spawned a number of mainstream pressure groups. This strategy seems much less common in other advanced capitalist democracies. It seems that it is easier in the United States than elsewhere for a citizens' movement to make the transition from protest politics to organized interest politics by institutionalizing an ongoing presence. Thus, it may be that American politics is more permeable than the politics of many other democracies to emergent interests that do not hew to the fault lines of party competition.[22]

This observation casts one of the themes of our inquiry in a somewhat different light. In responding to the group theorist orthodoxy (most frequently associated with David Truman) that politically relevant interests achieve organizational representation in pressure politics more or less automatically, we have stressed the barriers to entry into the arena of organized interest competition. It does not repudiate this emphasis to point out that, viewed from the perspective of other democratic systems, the filters restricting access to pressure politics are relatively porous. In short, while it is more difficult to establish an ongoing institutionalized presence in pressure politics than it is sometimes assumed to be, it is rather easier to do so in the American context than in many advanced capitalist democracies.

Too Much of a Good Thing?

Visitors to the floor of Yosemite Valley in earlier years were invariably awed by the majesty of the scene. As the years went by, the number of visitors and the number of automobiles, recreational vehicles, and motorcycles multiplied exponentially until the park bore witness to the kind of traffic and environmental degradation that, supposedly, only city dwellers are forced to endure. Thus, in an important way Yosemite has become a different place from what it once was. So it is with the politics of organized interests. Earlier in the chapter, in summarizing our findings with respect to changes in pressure politics, we characterized the situation as "more of the same." We now wish to return to this

[21] See Rochon, "Political Change in Ordered Societies," p. 361. With the exception of the example of Swedish feminists, which is taken from Kelman, "Party Strength and System Governability," all other examples are taken from Rochon.

[22] Philippe Schmitter argues that polities characterized by strong party systems and corporatist forms of interest representation are less hospitable than those with pluralist systems of interest representation to newly emergent interests. See "Interest Intermediation and Regime Governability in Contemporary Western Europe and North America," in *Organizing Interests in Western Europe,* ed. by Berger, pp. 319–324.

theme by making clear that, in politics as in national parks, more of the same is not simply the same.

The very ease with which new interests can gain access to the political system by setting up organizational shop in Washington has led a number of critics—who come from quite divergent points on the political spectrum—to argue that what we have now is too much of a good thing. Some of those who ascribe unfortunate consequences to the democratization of pressure politics focus on its meaning for economic performance. They argue that when interests are well organized and politically involved, narrow interests prevail over broad ones in policymaking. The consequences of this are far from benign, they argue, because such organizations will be able to extract concessions from the government—such as agricultural price supports or tax breaks for particular kinds of income—that benefit their narrowly based constituencies but produce widely shared costs. Moreover, the argument goes, the narrow interests will be able to stymie policies designed to confront problems having societywide implications—such as efforts to achieve hospital cost containment or independence from foreign energy sources—when those policies would impose disproportionate costs on their narrowly based constituencies. The upshot of such policy dominance by narrow interests is the erection of political barriers to effective economic performance and, consequently, slow economic growth coupled with inflation.[23]

Others of these critics worry about the effects of the massive mobilization of organized interests on the political process. One argument is that what has been called the "democratic surge" of the past couple of decades has rendered our politics shrill and unruly.[24] The contention that the incorporation of new interests into organized pressure politics has left our politics less temperate runs contrary to the view, once dominant among political scientists, that a democracy in which political demands are mediated by vigorously contending organized interests is *less* likely to be characterized by turbulence, disorder, and extremism.

[23]See Lester C. Thurow, *The Zero-Sum Society* (New York: Basic Books, 1980), Chapter 1, and Mancur Olson, *The Rise and Decline of Nations* (New Haven: Yale University Press, 1982), especially Chapter 3. With respect to the influence of pluralistic systems of interest representation on economic performance, Schmitter in "Interest Intermediation and Regime Governability" makes a similar argument to Olson's. However, Olson would probably not accept Schmitter's conclusions about the benign effects of corporatist consultation between organized interests and government on economic performance.

There are interesting affinities between Olson's conclusions about the effects of organized narrow interests upon policy and James Q. Wilson's fourfold categorization of types of policies (discussed in Chapter 4). In *The Rise and Decline of Nations,* however, Olson emphasizes the disincentives to narrow groups to act in a public-spirited manner. Wilson emphasizes the greater likelihood that narrow publics will be represented in the political process, a theme that echoes Olson's argument in *The Logic of Collective Action.*

[24]See Michel Crozier, Samuel P. Huntington, and Joji Watanuki, *The Crisis of Democracy: Report on the Governability of Democracies to the Trilateral Commission* (New York: New York University Press, 1975), especially Chapter 3; Samuel P. Huntington, "The Democratic Distemper," *The Public Interest* 41 (Fall 1975): 9–38; and Schmitter, "Interest Intermediation and Regime Governability." The phrase "democratic surge" is Huntington's.

According to this latter perspective, a spirited group process promotes stability and effective governance for two reasons. First, citizen demands are rendered more moderate when they are transmitted indirectly by organizations rather than directly by citizens acting on their own. In addition, the group process mobilizes into politics members of the "political stratum," who are more likely to be committed to the norms of procedural democracy than are ordinary citizens. Furthermore, according to this interpretation, when a plurality of organized interests is involved in politics, the probability of political polarization is reduced by the existence of crosscutting cleavages. That is, when there are multiple axes of political conflict in a society, groups that are antagonists on one issue are not likely to be antagonists on all others; hence, political animosities are not cumulative, and resultant political conflict is less intense.[25]

Those who worry about the consequences for governmental performance of the increase in organized interest activity have another concern as well. They argue not only that the intensification of organized interest involvement has made our politics strident and unruly but also that it undermines governmental effectiveness. According to this logic, two developments—the decline of the parties as aggregative institutions and the increasing responsiveness of legislators to the particularistic needs of their districts and the importunes and inducements of organized interests, rather than to the claims of programmatic effectiveness—further fragment a political system in which authority is already dispersed by separation of powers, federalism, and decentralization of authority within individual institutions. These tendencies, combined with the declining authority of government and the democratization of citizen inputs, produce a situation of policymaking paralysis and political overload. Confronted with a surfeit of citizen demands and an insufficiency of citizen patience, government cannot govern effectively.[26]

Our inquiry is only partially helpful in evaluating this line of reasoning. Certainly, it is unambiguous that there has been over the past twenty years an explosion in pressure activity—more organizations doing more to influence politics in Washington. Although at present the process has lost the shrillness

[25]See, for example, William Kornhauser, *The Politics of Mass Society* (New York: Free Press, 1959), especially pp. 76–90, and Robert A. Dahl, *Pluralist Democracy in the United States* (Chicago: Rand McNally, 1967), pp. 22–24, Chapters 13 and 14. (Dahl does not emphasize the importance of organized interests per se so much as the importance of multiple, noncumulative cleavages.) See, also, the discussions of this perspective in Michael Paul Rogin, *The Intellectuals and McCarthy* (Cambridge: MIT Press, 1967), pp. 15, 23–26, and Peter Bachrach, *The Theory of Democratic Elitism* (Boston: Little, Brown, 1967), Chapters 3 and 4.

[26]On this theme, see Crozier et al., *The Crisis of Democracy;* Huntington, "The Democratic Distemper"; Schmitter, "Interest Intermediation and Regime Governability" and the discussion of Crozier and others in Mark Kesselman, "The Conflictual Evolution of American Political Science," in J. David Greenstone, ed., *Public Values and Private Power in American Politics* (Chicago: University of Chicago Press, 1982), pp. 51–55.

The theme of the ungovernability of contemporary democracies is also treated in the essays contained in Richard Rose, ed., *Challenge to Governance: Studies in Overloaded Polities* (Beverly Hills, CA: Sage, 1980). In these essays, however, the emphasis is on the notion that modern welfare states undertake to do too much, rather than that they are subjected to too many demands.

and turbulence that characterized the 1960s, it remains far more contentious than it was when political scientists last examined it seriously. The ante has been raised substantially: the number of contending interests and the number of positions receiving vigorous advocacy have expanded greatly; moreover, the amount of activity and level of resources required to mount a credible political effort have increased significantly. This is the sense in which "more of the same" is not merely "the same". Furthermore, there is no indication that there is anything cyclical about this development. While it is clear that the intensity of political conflict varies over time with the nature of the issues at stake and the degree of public concern over political matters, there is no evidence that there will be a deflation in the arena of pressure politics. Given the imperatives of organizational maintenance, organized interest efforts, like prices, are probably sticky.

Our analysis sheds less light on the specific contention that the polity is ungovernable. The data cannot really be used to measure whether the capacity of the state to govern effectively has been overtaxed by the excess of demands generated by an expanded and more robust Washington pressure community. However, our observations do not lead to the conclusion that the federal government is about to collapse under the weight of the demands made by organized interests. Still, the organized interest explosion does seem to have introduced a potentially dysfunctional particularism into national politics. If those who make policy are forced to find an appropriate balance between deference to the exigencies of the short run and consideration of consequences for the long run, between acquiescence to the clearly expressed wishes of narrow groups that care intensely and respect for the frequently unexpressed needs of larger publics, the balance may have shifted too far in the direction of the near-term and the narrow.

The burden for maintaining this balance does not, however, fall to the organized interests. The right to petition government collectively is so fundamental and so constitutionally protected that it cannot be restrained. In an era when an expanded Washington pressure community speaks so loudly and so cacophonously, those who govern bear a special responsibility. This is not to suggest that public officials, especially elected ones, rely solely on their own judgment and ignore public preferences in making policy. Rather, their responses to the public should be informed by an understanding that the expressions of opinion transmitted by organized interests are selective; such communications clearly overrepresent the views of narrow, intense publics at the expense of broad, diffuse ones and the views of the affluent at the expense of the less advantaged. Similarly, their policy deliberations should reflect their awareness that the information, inducements, and services on which they rely emanate more readily from some interests than from others. There is a saying, sometimes attributed to Bismarck, that "a statesman is a politician who thinks about his grandchildren." At a time when the enlarged and more contentious nature of organized interest activity renders their presence especially vital, there may not be a sufficient supply of statesmen in the capital.

Curing the Mischiefs of Faction

Surely the federal government defended so vigorously by Madison in *The Federalist,* No. 10 has not cured the mischiefs of faction. Some observers have suggested a more frontal assault on the problem. According to one such observer: "Some of the problems of governance in the United States today stem from an 'excess of democracy'. . . . There are potentially desirable limits to the extension of political democracy. . . . What is needed is a greater degree of moderation in democracy."[27] Apart from the dilemma of knowing *how* to curb the "excess of democracy" and restore the balance needed for effective governance, any such palliative for the ills purportedly introduced by the explosion in organized interest activity has serious implications. First, to hush the voices clamoring for the attention of policymakers in Washington is to jeopardize the informational function of organized interest activity. As our inquiry has made abundantly clear, organized interests play an important role in supplying to public officials the information critical to the formulation of sound policy. To the extent that attempts to inform are inseparable from attempts to persuade, it would presumably be unwise to do anything that would check the flow of information to those who govern.

Furthermore, there are consequences for equality of any effort to quiet the din in Washington. It is sometimes suggested that a certain amount of public apathy in a democracy is useful in facilitating effective government.[28] But hushing the organized interests that operate on the political margins has implications for political equality as well as for governability. It would reinforce the existing distortion in the contours of the Washington pressure community and freeze out those who have not previously had the wherewithal to become involved in organized interest politics. Even to suggest that all organized interests exercise greater self-restraint overlooks the fact that many of the noisiest organizations on the Washington scene are those newcomers that in order to generate sympathy for their points of view are forced by their scanty resources to substitute attention-grabbing tactics for the quieter efforts that long-established groups with insider status can mount.

Finally, to urge that organized interests forebear in the name of civic virtue is to suggest that they yield one of the most fundamental rights of citizens in a democracy—the right to act collectively to achieve joint public purposes. Besides, Mancur Olson's logic of collective action offers little reason to expect voluntary discipline on the part of the many contending organizations

[27] Huntington, "The Democratic Distemper," pp. 26, 37, 38.
[28] Ibid., p. 30. A similar argument is made with respect to electoral politics in Bernard R. Berelson, Paul F. Lazarsfeld, and William N. McPhee, *Voting* (Chicago: University of Chicago Press, 1954), pp. 314–315.

so busily engaged in promoting political causes. To impose restraints on this activity from without is surely a remedy far more pernicious than the disease. This point brings us full circle, for it was Madison in *The Federalist,* No. 10, who dismissed in a sentence the folly of curing the mischiefs of faction by curtailing the liberty that sustains it. The contentiousness of pressure politics in our age may contribute to a circumstance in which we think more about ourselves than our grandchildren: it may place an untenable responsibility upon those who would presume to govern; but it may be a price we pay for the rights we enjoy as citizens.

The Washington Representatives Survey

Our sampling procedure bears elaboration. As we mentioned in the Preface, we wished to devise a technique that would somehow sample randomly from Washington interest group *activity,* rather than from Washington lobbyists or even the universe of organizations represented. Therefore, we wished to contrive a procedure whereby organizations with large, active, and affluent offices in Washington would have a higher probability of being selected than organizations fielding smaller, less active, and less well-financed operations.

We were able to locate a surrogate measure of a group's Washington activity by using the *National Journal*'s Index to Organizations. Until very recently the *National Journal* published a twice-yearly index listing the private organizations mentioned in its articles during the preceding six months. In any one index to organizations, the AFL-CIO might occupy several inches of column space, while the American Hotel and Motel Association might merit only a single entry. We assembled indexes over a four-year period (1977-1980) and sampled randomly from them by line, thus giving the more frequently mentioned groups a greater probability of being selected.

Not all the organizations listed in the *National Journal*'s Index have their own offices in Washington. We included in our sample only those organizations listed in *Washington Representatives—1981* as having their own Washington offices.[1] We eliminated those having only Washington-based legal counsel or consultants. Practical considerations dictated this decision. We deemed full-time organizational employees more likely to be intimately involved in many aspects of the organization's affairs and also, as

[1] Arthur C. Close ed., *Washington Representatives—1981* (Washington, DC: Columbia Books, 1981).

411

salaried employees, more likely than those who bill clients by the hour to share their time with us. Furthermore, focusing exclusively on organizational employees allowed us to obviate problems of professional-client confidentiality.

We also eliminated from the sample foreign governments and foreign corporations (because they are legally barred from lobbying Congress directly), research organizations like the Gallup Poll, and representatives of American subnational governments, such as the City of Provo, Utah, or the State of New Jersey. The issue of how to treat organizations of government workers is somewhat complicated. We decided to exclude those who lobby on behalf of *governments,* such as the Council of Chief State School Officers, but to retain those who lobby on behalf of their own private interests as public employees, such as the National Treasury Employees Union. What this meant in fact is that we eliminated organizations which governmental units (states, regional authorities, cities, and the like) join, but included those which individuals join.

The resulting sample contained 200 organizations—corporations, trade associations, unions, professional associations, civil rights groups, citizens' groups, and so on. We ultimately conducted interviews in 175 of these organizations.

In selecting the person within the organization to interview, we searched the personnel listing in the *Washington Representatives* directory for the one person whose job title indicated that he or she would have the broadest understanding of that organizations's involvement in politics. If, after an introductory letter and follow-up phone calls, that person was unable or unwilling to be interviewed, we asked to be put in touch with someone else in the organization having extensive experience in the organization and a comprehensive knowledge of its Washington activity. These interviews lasted approximately two hours each.

In order to ascertain what kinds of bias we had introduced by using our somewhat unusual sampling procedure, we conducted some further checks. Our concerns were dual. With respect to the various categories of Washington organizations, we wished to assess the effects, first, of having established as our sampling frame only those organizations mentioned in the *National Journal* rather than all those listed in the *Washington Representatives* directory; and, second, of having increased the probability that more frequently mentioned organizations would be chosen. To do so, we used the results of our enumeration of the nearly 3000 organizations meeting our criteria that were listed in the directory as having Washington offices. We also chose an unweighted random sample of 200 organizations from the *National Journal.* Table A.1 allows us to compare the distributions thus obtained with the weighted sample that we originally drew from the *National Journal.*

Our weighted sample of 200 organizations—and the 175 we actually interviewed—do not differ appreciably from the random sample of *National Journal* organizations in terms of the distribution of organizations into rough categories. There are some differences between the various *National Journal* samples and the distribution of the universe of organizations having Washington offices; however, the differences are exactly the opposite of what we had expected. When we drew our weighted sample, we were dismayed that 54 percent of the organizations represented business and assumed that the *National Journal*'s thorough coverage of economic affairs was responsible. In fact, although we oversampled corporations and undersampled trade associations somewhat, the overall total for business organizations was right on target. Contrary to our initial concern that our sample did not capture sufficient numbers of the antagonists of business—unions and citizens' groups—we actually oversampled those two categories

Table A.1 THE SAMPLES COMPARED

	All organizations having DC office	*National Journal* random sample	*National Journal* weighted sample	Actually interviewed
Corporations	22%	32%	30%	30%
Trade and other business associations	32	28	24	26
Professional associations	15	5	8	7
Unions	4	8	12	11
Citizens' groups	9	13	15	13
Civil rights/Social welfare	3	4	4	5
Other/Unknown	16	10	8	7
	101%	100%	101%	99%
	(N = 2694)	(N = 200)	(N = 200)	(N = 175)

substantially. We surmise that this is a consequence of the journalistic ethic of giving each side of the story more or less equal coverage, regardless of whether there is equal pressure activity on both sides. This supposition is lent credence by findings presented by Robert Salisbury.[2] He shows that *New York Times* references to organizations active on agricultural policy overrepresent citizens' groups and underrepresent corporations and trade associations. We should note that our sample is deficient in professional associations and in groups that defied classification. In the aggregate, however, our sample is quite representative of the categories of groups having offices in Washington.

[2]"Interest Groups: The Dominance of Institutions" (Mimeograph, Washington University, Saint Louis, 1983), p. 26.

appendix B

The Questionnaire

I'd like to ask you a series of questions about the Washington scene in general and about your organization in particular. Although nothing that I'll ask will be sensitive, I can assure you that your answers will remain anonymous. There are quite a few questions, but most of them can be answered rather quickly so this need not take too long. By the way, the answers to some of these questions may seem so obvious that you may wonder why I even bother to ask them. However, I will be talking to people in many different kinds of organizations, and those answers may be less obvious in other cases. I hope you will bear with me.

1. When was _____ established? _____

2. Is this the national headquarters of _____ or is your national headquarters located elsewhere?
    1. National headquarters
    2. Located elsewhere
    9. Don't know/No answer

3. When did your organization first establish an office in Washington? _____

4.a. How long have you been with this organization? _____
  b. How long have you been in government relations? _____

5.a. Have you ever worked for the federal government?
    1. Yes
    2. No (*Skip to Q. 6.*)
    9. Don't know/No answer
  b. Can you tell me what you did? (*Skip to Q. 7.*)

6.a. Has anybody else in this organization ever worked for the federal government?
    1. Yes

    2. No (*Skip to Q. 7.*)

    9. Don't know/No answer/Not relevant

  b. Can you tell me what they did?

7.*a.* Does your organization have a political action committee?

    1. Yes

    2. No (*Skip to Q. 8*)

    9. Don't know/No answer

  b. What is your PAC called?

8. (*If organization is fewer than 5 years old, skip to Q. 10.*) I'd like to ask you about how things are changing in Washington. From what you know about this organization, what changes have there been over the past decade in the way that it goes about trying to influence what goes on in Washington?

9. (*If not already answered in Q. 8.*) Over the last decade, has your organization become more active in Washington politics, less active in Washington politics, or has its level of activity stayed pretty much the same?

    1. More active

    2. Stayed the same

    3. Less active

    9. Don't know/No answer/New organization

10. As you know, organizations in Washington use many different techniques to try to influence either directly or indirectly what goes on in government.

  a. I am going to read you a long list of such techniques. After I read each one of them, please tell me whether your organization—or its associated PAC—uses that technique. (*If such techniques have been discussed in Q. 8*) By the way, you have already discussed some of them, but I'd like to go through the whole list with you.

  b. (*If the organization is fewer than 5 years old, skip.*) (*If organization does not use technique, skip.*) Is your organization doing that more frequently, less frequently, or about as frequently as it did ten years ago?

  c. (*Show card A.*) Now please read down this list and tell me which *three* of these activities consume the most in terms of time and resources for your organization. (*If respondent names only one or two*) Is there another one which also consumes a lot of time and resources?

  d. Are there any other techniques that your organization uses frequently that are not included on the list? (*Probe*) Which ones?

	Uses technique		Over last 10 years		
	Yes	No	More	About same	Less
1. Shaping the government's agenda by raising new issues and calling attention to previously ignored problems	1	2 9	1	2	3 9

	Uses technique			Over last 10 years		
	Yes	No		More	About same	Less	
2. Talking with people from the press and the media	1	2	9	1	2	3	9
3. Running advertisements in the media about your position on issues	1	2	9	1	2	3	9
*4. Sending letters to members of your organization to inform them about your activities	1	2	9	1	2	3	9
*5. Engaging in direct-mail fund raising for your organization	1	2	9	1	2	3	9
6. Inspiring letter-writing or telegram campaigns	1	2	9	1	2	3	9
7. Mounting grass roots lobbying efforts	1	2	9	1	2	3	9
8. Engaging in protests or demonstrations	1	2	9	1	2	3	9
9. Making financial contributions to electoral campaigns	1	2	9	1	2	3	9
10. Contributing work or personnel to electoral campaigns	1	2	9	1	2	3	9
11. Making public endorsements of candidates for office	1	2	9	1	2	3	9
12. Publicizing candidates' voting records	1	2	9	1	2	3	9
13. Testifying at hearings	1	2	9	1	2	3	9
14. Helping to draft legislation	1	2	9	1	2	3	9
15. Consulting with government officials to plan legislative strategy	1	2	9	1	2	3	9
16. Alerting Congressmen to the effects of a bill on their districts	1	2	9	1	2	3	9
17. Presenting research results or technical information	1	2	9	1	2	3	9
18. Having influential constituents contact their Congressmen's office	1	2	9	1	2	3	9
19. Contacting government officials directly to present your point of view	1	2	9	1	2	3	9
20. Doing favors for officials who need assistance	1	2	9	1	2	3	9
21. Entering into coalitions with other organizations	1	2	9	1	2	3	9

* Omit for corporations and nonmembership organizations.

	Uses technique			Over last 10 years			
	Yes	**No**		**More**	**About same**	**Less**	
22. Attempting to influence appointments to public office	1	2	9	1	2	3	9
23. Engaging in informal contacts with officials—at conventions, lunch, etc.	1	2	9	1	2	3	9
24. Serving on advisory commissions and boards	1	2	9	1	2	3	9
25. Helping to draft regulations, rules, or guidelines	1	2	9	1	2	3	9
26. Attempting to shape the implementation of policies	1	2	9	1	2	3	9
27. Filing suit or otherwise engaging in litigation	1	2	9	1	2	3	9

	Consumes time and resources		
	Mention	**No Mention**	
1. Shaping the government's agenda by raising new issues and calling attention to previously ignored problems	1	2	9
2. Talking with people from the press and the media	1	2	9
3. Running advertisements in the media about your position on issues	1	2	9
*4. Sending letters to members of your organization to inform them about your activities	1	2	9
*5. Engaging in direct-mail fund raising for your organization	1	2	9
6. Inspiring letter-writing or telegram campaigns	1	2	9
7. Mounting grass roots lobbying efforts	1	2	9
8. Engaging in protests or demonstrations	1	2	9
9. Making financial contributions to electoral campaigns	1	2	9
10. Contributing work or personnel to electoral campaigns	1	2	9
11. Making public endorsements of candidates for office	1	2	9
12. Publicizing candidates' voting records	1	2	9
13. Testifying at hearings	1	2	9
14. Helping to draft legislation	1	2	9
15. Consulting with government officials to plan legislative strategy	1	2	9
16. Alerting Congressmen to the effects of a bill on their districts	1	2	9
17. Presenting research results or technical information	1	2	9

* Code as 9 for corporations and nonmembership organizations.

	Consumes time and resources		
	Mention	**No Mention**	
18. Having influential constituents contact their Congressmen's office	1	2	9
19. Contacting government officials directly to present your point of view	1	2	9
20. Doing favors for officials who need assistance	1	2	9
21. Entering into coalitions with other organizations	1	2	9
22. Attempting to influence appointments to public office	1	2	9
23. Engaging in informal contacts with officials—at conventions, lunch, etc.	1	2	9
24. Serving on advisory commissions and boards	1	2	9
25. Helping to draft regulations, rules, or guidelines	1	2	9
26. Attempting to shape the implementation of policies	1	2	9
27. Filing suit or otherwise engaging in litigation	1	2	9

11.a. (*If respondent indicated in Q. 10 that organization inspires letter-writing campaigns or mounts grass roots lobbying efforts*)

It is sometimes said that Congressmen are skeptical of letter-writing campaigns or grassroots lobbying efforts that appear to lack spontaneity or to have been engineered. In your experience, is this a problem?

    1. Yes

    2. No (*Skip to Q. 12.*)

    9. Don't know/No answer/Not relevant

  b. How do you deal with it?

12. In 1980 many Americans were shocked by the implication of the Abscam scandals that members of Congress would engage in illegal activity by accepting bribes. From your experience around Washington, how common is that kind of illegal activity? Would you say that it goes on all the time, much of the time, some of the time, or only infrequently?

    1. All the time

    2. Much of the time

    3. Some of the time

    4. Only infrequently

    9. Don't know/No answer

13. As you know there are many points of contact for Washington activity—Congress, the White House, executive agencies, and the courts.

  a. Recognizing that the focus of your activity may change from issue to issue or even over the life span of a single issue, in general, how important is _____ as a focus of your organization's activity—very important, somewhat important, or not too important?

b. (*Skip if organization is fewer than 5 years old.*) Over the past decade has _____ become more important, less important, or stayed about the same as a focus for your organization's activity?

	Importance today				Over past 10 years		
	Very	**Some-what**	**Not**		**More**	**About same**	**Less**
1. Congress	1	2	3	9	1	2	3
2. The White House	1	2	3	9	1	2	3
3. Executive Agencies	1	2	3	9	1	2	3
4. The Courts	1	2	3	9	1	2	3

14. (*If Congress is not an important focus of activity in Q. 13, skip to Q. 15.*) Apart from other private organizations, which *two* of the political forces listed on this card do you consider to be your principal competition in influencing the decisions of members of Congress? (Show card B.)

	Mentioned	**Not mentioned**	
1. The White House	1	2	9
2. Members' constituencies	1	2	9
3. The political parties	1	2	9
4. Congressional staff members	1	2	9
5. Executive branch agencies	1	2	9
6. Public opinion	1	2	9
7. The media	1	2	9
8. Other members of Congress	1	2	9

15. There are many resources which make an organization effective in Washington. Some of them are listed on this card. (*Show card C.*)
   a. Please look over the list and tell me *in general* which two of them are most important for effectiveness in Washington politics.
   b. Which two of them are most important *to your organization?*
   c. Least important *in general?*
   d. Least important *to your organization?*
   e. If you could enhance your organization's stock of any of these, which two would you like to have more of?
      1. A large membership
      2. A large budget
      3. Control over technical information or expertise
      4. Well-known and respected leaders
      5. A reputation for being credible and trustworthy
      6. A wide circle of contacts
      7. Strategically placed allies
      8. An appealing cause

	In general				To your organization				Want more		
	Most	No mention	Least		Most	No mention	Least		Mention	No mention	
1. Membership	1	2	3	9	1	2	3	9	1	2	9
2. Budget	1	2	3	9	1	2	3	9	1	2	9
3. Information	1	2	3	9	1	2	3	9	1	2	9
4. Leaders	1	2	3	9	1	2	3	9	1	2	9
5. Reputation	1	2	3	9	1	2	3	9	1	2	9
6. Contacts	1	2	3	9	1	2	3	9	1	2	9
7. Allies	1	2	3	9	1	2	3	9	1	2	9
8. Cause	1	2	3	9	1	2	3	9	1	2	9

16. As you well know, government relations has become an increasingly technical enterprise in recent years, involving people with various kinds of special skills. I am going
to ask you about some of them.
   a. (*If Washington office is national headquarters*)
      Does your organization have _____ on its staff?
      (*If national headquarters is elsewhere*)
      Are _____ available to you—either as part of your Washington staff
      or from the national headquarters?
   b. (If yes) Do you also hire _____ from the outside?
      (If no) Do you hire _____ from the outside?

	On staff			From outside		
	Yes	No		Yes	No	
1. Lawyers	1	2	9	1	2	9
2. Public relations consultants	1	2	9	1	2	9
3. Pollsters	1	2	9	1	2	9
4. Specialists in direct-mail fund raising	1	2	9	1	2	9

17. Thinking about some policy issues on which your organization has been most effective in recent years, to what would you attribute your effectiveness? (*Probe, if necessary*) Incidentally, what was the issue?
18. Thinking about some policy issues on which organization has been least effective in
recent years, to what would you attribute these outcomes? (*Probe, if necessary*)
Incidentally, what was the issue?
19. Are there any organizations you consider to be your allies on most issues? (*Probe*)
Which ones?
20. Are there any organizations you consider to be your opponents on most issues?
(*Probe*) Which ones?
21. How would you compare the strength of your organization with that of its antagonists—would you say that your organization is stronger, about as strong, or weaker
than its opponents?
   1. Stronger
   2. About as strong
   3. Weaker
   9. Don't know/No answer
22. When you plan your political strategy on policy matters, how likely are you to
consult and cooperate with the following political actors—almost certainly, somewhat likely, or not too likely? (*Show card C1.*)

	Almost certainly	Somewhat likely	Not too likely	
1. Members of Congress	1	2	3	9
2. Party leaders in Congress	1	2	3	9

	Almost certainly	Somewhat likely	Not too likely	
3. Congressional committee staff members	1	2	3	9
4. Congressmen's personal staff members	1	2	3	9
5. Mid-level bureaucrats	1	2	3	9
6. Cabinet officers or their deputies	1	2	3	9
7. White House staff	1	2	3	9
8. Party leaders at the national committees	1	2	3	9
9. Friends in other private organizations	1	2	3	9
10. Influential grass roots contacts	1	2	3	9

23. Most groups are anxious not only to convey information to government officials, but to obtain information about what the government is doing. To keep yourself posted as to what the government is up to, how important is each of the following possible channels of information—very important, somewhat important, or not too important? (*Show card C2.*)

	Very	Somewhat	Not too	
1. Members of Congress	1	2	3	9
2. Party leaders in Congress	1	2	3	9
3. Congressional committee staff members	1	2	3	9
4. Congressmen's personal staff members	1	2	3	9
5. Mid-level bureaucrats	1	2	3	9
6. Cabinet officers or their deputies	1	2	3	9
7. White House staff	1	2	3	9
8. Party leaders at the national committees	1	2	3	9
9. Journalists	1	2	3	9
10. Friends in other private organizations	1	2	3	9
11. *The Federal Register* or other government publications	1	2	3	9
12. The trade press	1	2	3	9
13. Newspapers like the *Post* and the *Times*	1	2	3	9

24.a. How often do government officials or their staffs take the initiative—that is, *come to you* on a matter—frequently, from time to time, or rarely?
    1. Frequently
    2. From time to time
    3. Rarely (*Skip to Q. 25.*)
    9. Don't know/No answer
b. What do they ask for?

25.a. We have been discussing the communications between your organization and government officials. But many organizations spend a great deal of time and effort on communications with their own members or with corporate headquarters in order to let them know what the government is up to and how government policies will affect them. How much of the time and resources of your office here in Washington are devoted to these kinds of internal communications—a great deal, some, relatively little, almost none?

    1. A great deal
    2. Some
    3. Relatively little (*Skip to Q. 26.*)
    4. Almost none (*Skip to Q. 26.*)
    9. Don't know/No answer

  b. (*Membership organizations*)
In general, which is the more important component of the work of your organization—communications with government officials, on the one hand, or communications with your own members on the other?
(*Corporations*)
In general, which is the more important component of the work of your organization—communications with government officials, on the one hand, or communications with corporate headquarters, on the other?

    1. Government officials
    2. Equally important
    3. Own members

    (*If respondent indicated that the organization does not make financial contributions to electoral campaigns in Q. 10, skip to Q. 33.*)

Now I would like to change the subject and talk to you about the way in which your organization gets involved in the electoral process.

26. You mentioned before that your organizations—or its associated PAC—makes contributions to electoral campaigns. What are the criteria you use in selecting candidates to support?

27. There are many criteria an organization might use in selecting candidates to support. Some of them are listed on this card. (*Show card D.*) Of course, your organization probably takes many things into consideration in making these decisions, but would you select the *two* which are generally most important?

	Mention	No mention	
1. The candidate's party	1	2	9
2. The location of the candidate's district	1	2	9
3. The candidate's general ideology	1	2	9
4. The candidate's position on a few issues of special concern to your organization	1	2	9
5. The candidate's committee assignments	1	2	9
6. How close the race is	1	2	9
7. The candidate's position as a party leader or committee chairman	1	2	9
8. The size of the candidate's war chest relative to his opponent's	1	2	9

28.a. (*If not already answered*) Generally speaking, do you support Republicans, Democrats, or candidates of both parties equally?
>   1. Republicans
>   2. Both parties
>   3. Democrats
>   9. Don't know/No answer/No contributions

 b. (*If not already answered*) Generally speaking, do you support incumbents, challengers, or both equally?
>   1. Incumbents
>   2. Both equally
>   3. Challengers
>   9. Don't know/No answer/No contributions

29. Who in your organization is responsible for making decisions about which candidates to support?
(*If not answered*) How often do you/they meet?
(*If not answered*) How do you/they get the information on which to base these decisions?

30.a. We have been talking about how you select the candidates you support. What about when candidates themselves take the initiative—that is, come to you to seek support—how do they make the approach?
(*If not answered*) What do they ask for?
(*If candidates never approach group, skip to Q. 31.*)

 b. How often do you feel free to refuse these requests—most of the time, some of the time, or rarely?
>   1. Most of the time
>   2. Some of the time
>   3. Rarely
>   9. Don't know/No answer/Not relevant

 c. What might be the consequences for your organization if you were to refuse such a request? (*Probe, if necessary*) Do you ever feel that your interests would be damaged if you don't provide support for a candidate who asks for it? How so?

31.a. Do you ever have occasion to give to more than one candidate in a race for a single office?
>   1. Yes
>   2. No (*Skip to Q. 32.*)
>   9. Don't know/No answer/No contributions

 b. Under what circumstances might that happen?

32.a. Have you ever had to withdraw support from a candidate whom you had supported in a previous election?
>   1. Yes
>   2. No (*Skip to Q. 33.*)
>   9. Don't know/No answer/No contributions

 b. Under what circumstances might that happen?

33. As you well know, over the last decade there have been many changes in the way things work in Washington. I am going to read you a list of some of these changes. After I read each one, please tell me whether it has made it easier or harder for your organization to operate effectively—or has it made relatively little difference?

		No		
	Easier	**difference**	**Harder**	
1. The growth in Congressional staff	1	2	3	9
2. The increasing number of subcommittees in Congress	1	2	3	9
3. The increasing ability of Congress to generate its own information through service agencies like the Congressional Budget Office	1	2	3	9
4. Sunshine laws	1	2	3	9
5. Freedom of Information Act	1	2	3	9
6. Restrictions on communications with government officials when cases are pending—sometimes called ex parte rules	1	2	3	9
7. Conflict of interest rules governing employment in the private sector after government service	1	2	3	9
8. Government financing of public interest representation at regulatory proceedings—sometimes called intervenor financing	1	2	3	9
9. Changes in the congressional budgetary process	1	2	3	9
10. The increasing authority of OMB to review agency rules	1	2	3	9
11. The movement toward deregulation	1	2	3	9
12. The growing role of PACs in financing elections	1	2	3	9
13. Rules governing public disclosure of campaign contributions	1	2	3	9
14. The rise of environmental and consumer groups	1	2	3	9

34a. We have been discussing the changes which have taken place in Washington in the past ten years. More recently—that is, in the last eight or ten months—there have been many important changes in Washington since the 1980 election. Has the change to Republican control of the Senate and White House made any difference to your organization?

    1. Yes

    2. No (*Skip to Q. 35.*)

    9. Don't know/No answer

  b. In what way?

  c. (*If not already answered*) Has the outcome of the 1980 election affected the way you go about trying to influence policy? (*If necessary*) In what way? Has it changed your strategies? Has it changed your sets of governmental contacts?

  d. (*If not already answered*) Would you say that the influence enjoyed by your organization has increased, decreased, or pretty much stayed the same since the 1980 election?

1. Increased
2. Stayed the same
3. Decreased
9. Don't know/No answer

35. Of the many organizations that are active in Washington today, which two or three specific organizations do you consider to be the strongest and most powerful? (*Probe, if respondent names a category of organization such as unions, or corporations, rather than name specific organizations or industries.*) Any ones in particular?

36. What about ten years ago?

37. In the past decade are there any kinds of groups that have become more powerful in Washington? (*Probe*) Which ones?

38. Any kinds of groups whose power has declined? (*Probe*) Which ones?

Now, in concluding, let me ask you a few additional background questions about your organization. (*For corporations and nonmembership organizations, skip to Q. 44.*)

39. What is the approximate current membership of your organization?

40.a. Over and above representing their interests on political matters, does your organization perform any additional services or provide any special benefits for its members that are denied to nonmembers—things like educational programs, publications or newsletters, access to special facilities, research results, travel, or insurance benefits?

(*Probe*) Can you be more specific? Can you give any other examples?

b. (*If organization puts out publications or newsletters*) How often do you send out such publications or newsletters?

41. Organizations vary in terms of the degree to which members are involved and active—attend meetings and other functions, care about and express opinions on matters of concern to the organization. Overall, how would you describe the level of involvement of the members of your organization—would you say that most of them are quite involved, somewhat involved, or not too involved?

1. Quite involved
2. Somewhat involved
3. Not too involved
9. Don't know/No answer/Not relevant

42.a. Are the officers of this organization chosen in elections?

1. Yes
2. No (*Skip to Q. 44.*)
9. Don't know/No answer/Not relevant

b. Are there usually opposing candidates in these elections?

1. Yes
2. No (*Skip to Q. 44.*)
9. Don't know/No answer/Not relevant

c. Are there groups or factions from which these opposing candidates usually come?

1. Yes
2. No (*Skip to Q. 43.*)
9. Don't know/No answer/Not relevant

d. Can you explain a little about these groups?

43. Can you think of any matters which were at issue in recent elections in your organization?

44. Generally, speaking, how would you describe your organization—as liberal, middle of the road, or conservative?

    1. Liberal
    2. Middle of the road
    3. Conservative
    9. Don't know/No answer

45. Overall, is your organization closer to the Democratic party, to the Republican party, or to neither party?

    1. Democratic party
    2. Republican party
    3. Neither party
    9. Don't know/No answer

46.a. (*If respondent indicated in Q. 7 that organization has a PAC*)

    (*Noncorporate*)   Excluding its political action committee, what is the approximate annual budget of _____?

    (*Corporate*)   Excluding its political action committee, approximately how much does _____ budget annually for its government affairs operation? (*Skip to Q. 47.*)

    (*If no PAC*)   What is the approximate annual budget of _____?

    (*Noncorporate*)   Approximately how much does _____ budget annually for its government affairs operation? (*Skip to Q. 47.*)

    (*Corporate*)

  b. Washington organizations are financed in many different ways. Some possible sources of financial support are listed on this card. (*Show card E.*) Which of them are significant sources of funding for your organization—that is, account for 10 percent or more or your budget?

	Mention	No mention	
1. Dues of individual members	1	2	9
2. Dues of member organizations	1	2	9
3. Foundation grants	1	2	9
4. Corporate gifts and donations	1	2	9
5. Individual gifts and donations	1	2	9
6. Grants or contracts from the federal government	1	2	9
7. Income from investments or endowment	1	2	9
8. Staff generated revenue (e.g., sales of materials, staff lectures)	1	2	9

47. One last question, in your experience what are the greatest sources of frustration in being a Washington representative?

48. And what are the greatest sources of gratification in being a Washington representative?

appendix C

The Catalogue of Organizations

The catalogue of organizations includes all organizations, with the exception of the duplications explained below, listed in the *Washington Representatives—1981* directory as having an ongoing presence in Washington.[1] For organizations that maintain an office in Washington, the directory lists the address of the office and the names of important government affairs personnel; for those that do not, the directory lists the names of those hired as counsel or consultants to represent them. While it is surely the most nearly complete listing of private organizations having a sustained Washington presence, it is probably not an exhaustive inventory. Also, by taking the organizations listed in the directory as our universe, we neglect an important component of the pressure system: the hundreds of local organizations that are occasionally active in Washington politics.

In most cases it was clear how to classify an organization either from its name alone or from the brief description contained in the directory. If not, *The Encyclopedia of Associations* usually gave fuller information.[2] We also used this source, as well as various manuals put out by Moody's Investors Service, to ascertain the dates of founding of the organizations having their own offices in Washington.

In separating the organizations into 31 different categories, many subjective judgments were made. Certainly, others attempting such a catalogue would not arrive at precisely the figures presented here. However, the broad outlines of the distribution are so unmistakable that they would clearly have been unaffected had some subjective

---

[1]Arthur C. Close, ed., *Washington Representatives—1981* (Washington, DC: Columbia Books, 1981).
[2]Denise S. Akey, ed., *The Encyclopedia of Associations,* 13th and 17th eds. (Detroit: Gale Research Company, 1979 and 1983).

428

decisions been made differently. Given the expectation that the well heeled would be overrepresented in the pressure system, the decision was taken to make any subjective judgments in such a way as to reduce the number of groups representing business and professionals and to enhance the number representing diffuse publics and the disadvantaged. For example, associations of minority professionals or minority-owned businesses were classified not as professionals or trade associations but as minority organizations. Conservative citizens' groups devoted to the cause of promoting free enterprise were classified as citizens' groups even when it seemed that most of their support derived from business. In this way the final tally, which indicates a very substantial business and professional presence in Washington, does not overstate that presence.

The same end was achieved in another way. The directory includes many organizations that are subsidiaries or affiliates of other organizations listed. Whenever possible, these were cross-referenced, and duplicates were eliminated from the tally. Because so many of these affiliated organizations were businesses, this procedure, too, had the effect of depressing the number of business organizations in the total.

We also took a census of the nearly 3,000 political action committees included in the *PAC Directory*.[3] In categorizing PACs we used these same classificatory criteria.

[3]Marvin Weinberger and David U. Greevy, compilers, *The PAC Directory* (Cambridge, MA: Ballinger, 1982).

appendix **D**

Additional Tables

Table D.1 PERCENTAGE OF ORGANIZATIONS IN EACH CATEGORY USING
TECHNIQUES OF EXERCISING INFLUENCE

	Corporations	Trade associations	Unions	Citizens' groups
1. Testifying at hearings	98%	100%	100%	100%
2. Contacting officials directly	100	97	100	100
3. Informal contacts	98	97	95	96
4. Presenting research results	94	89	90	92
5. Sending letters to members	85	97	95	86
6. Entering into coalitions	96	91	100	92
7. Shaping implementation	90	91	85	92
8. Talking with press and media	67	89	95	96
9. Planning legislative strategy	90	89	85	83
10. Helping to draft legislation	86	94	85	74
11. Inspiring letter-writing campaigns	83	89	100	83
12. Shaping the government's agenda	79	77	85	100
13. Mounting grass roots lobbying	81	80	100	71
14. Having constituents contact	77	94	85	58
15. Drafting regulations	85	83	75	75
16. Serving on advisory commissions	74	74	95	67
17. Alerting members of Congress to effects	92	74	85	58
18. Filing suit	72	83	95	79
19. Contributing to campaigns	86	66	90	29
20. Doing favors for officials	62	56	68	54
21. Influencing appointments	48	49	80	46
22. Publicizing voting records	28	37	90	75
23. Direct-mail fund raising	19	37	65	75
24. Running ads in the media	31	31	55	33
25. Contributing work or personnel to campaigns	14	23	70	33
26. Endorsing candidates	8	9	95	29
27. Engaging in protests	0	3	90	25
Average number of techniques	18 (N = 52)	19 (N = 35)	24 (N = 20)	19 (N = 24)

Source: Washington Representatives Survey.

Table D.2 PERCENTAGE OF ORGANIZATIONS IN EACH CATEGORY INDICATING TECHNIQUE CONSUMES TIME AND RESOURCES

	Corporations	Trade associations	Unions	Citizens' groups
1. Contacting officials directly	44%	33%	13%	39%
2. Testifying at hearings	13	30	53	27
3. Presenting research or technical information	35	6	0	35
4. Mounting grass roots lobbying efforts	22	18	53	44
5. Shaping the government's agenda	11	24	33	27
6. Entering into coalitions with other organizations	30	24	7	17
7. Consulting to plan legislative strategy	20	30	7	14
8. Shaping the implementation of policies	18	33	0	17
9. Alerting members of Congress to the effects of bills	17	15	33	0
10. Sending letters to organization members	6	18	13	9
11. Helping to draft legislation	17	9	7	4
12. Engaging in informal contacts with officials	11	18	13	0
13. Inspiring letter-writing campaigns	2	12	20	9
14. Talking with the press and media	4	9	0	26
15. Contributing to campaigns	4	6	40	9
16. Helping to draft regulations	9	12	0	0
17. Having constituents contact their Reps.	0	12	13	4
18. Engaging in direct-mail fund raising	0	0	0	17
19. Serving on advisory commissions and boards	2	6	7	4
20. Filing suit	0	3	7	13
21. Running advertisements in the media	4	0	0	0
22. Publicizing candidates' voting records	0	0	0	9
23. Contributing work or personnel to campaigns	0	0	0	13
24. Doing favors for officials	2	0	0	0
25. Engaging in protests or demonstrations	0	0	7	0
26. Influencing appointments to public office	0	0	0	0
27. Endorsing candidates for office	0	0	0	0

Source: Washington Representatives Survey.

433

Table D.3 NETWORKS OF INFORMATION AND CONSULTATION

Importance of channels of information—Percent "very important"

	Corporations	Trade associations	Unions	Citizens' groups
1. Congressional committee staff members	92%	83%	90%	79%
2. Friends in other private organizations	62	70	58	83
3. Congressmen's personal staff members	70	60	74	79
4. Members of Congress	72	63	63	58
5. Newspapers like the *Post* and the *Times*	59	37	53	58
6. *The Federal Register* or other government publications	51	62	26	42
7. The trade press	42	60	39	65
8. Mid-level bureaucrats	47	42	10	17
9. Party leaders in Congress	37	43	47	25
10. White House staff	36	47	16	13
11. Journalists	19	45	5	50
12. Cabinet officers or their deputies	33	47	10	9
13. Party leaders at the national committees	2	14	21	12

Likelihood of consultation and cooperation—Percent "almost certainly"

	Corporations	Trade associations	Unions	Citizens' groups
1. Congressional committee staff members	85%	97%	74%	87%
2. Members of Congress	81	79	79	78
3. Friends in other private organizations	64	63	58	78
4. Congressmen's personal staff members	64	50	37	83
5. Influential grass roots contacts	29	74	58	82
6. Party leaders in Congress	42	45	63	22
7. Mid-level bureaucrats	26	38	0	4
8. White House staff	26	41	16	14
9. Cabinet officers or their deputies	26	34	10	14
10. Party leaders at the national committees	2	10	16	9

Source: Washington Representatives Survey.

Index

ABA. *See* American Bankers Association; American Bar Association

Abraham, Henry J., 359n, 369n

Abscam scandals, 264

ACA. *See* Americans for Constitutional Action

Academy for Implants and Transplants, 1

Access
  directly to policymakers, 292–295, 323, 327, 330–335, 359
  importance of, 100
  to information, 347, 349. *See also* Freedom of Information Act
  relationship to political influence, 164–165, 169, 253, 255, 267, 294

ACLU. *See* American Civil Liberties Union

Action on Smoking and Health, 39

ACU. *See* American Conservative Union

ADA. *See* Americans for Democratic Action

Adamany, David, 201n, 225n

Adams, Gordon, 267n, 270n, 271n, 276n

Administrative policymaking. *See* Executive agencies; Participation in rulemaking proceedings

Administrative Procedure Act, 332, 367

Advertising, 172–178
  advocacy, 175–176, 188
  image, 175–176

Advisory Committee on Hog Cholera Eradication, 333

Advisory committees, 333–335, 394

Advocacy groups, 45–47

Aerospace Industries Association of America, 72

AFBF. *See* American Farm Bureau Federation

AFL-CIO. *See* American Federation of Labor-Congress of Industrial Organizations

AFSCME. *See* American Federation of State, County and Municipal Employees

AFT. *See* American Federation of Teachers

Agricultural Extension Service (AES), 122

Agriculture, U.S. Department of, 333, 339

AHA. *See* American Hospital Association

Air Conditioning and Refrigeration Institute, 72

Air Line Pilots Association, 98

Alcohol, Tobacco, and Firearms, U.S. Bureau of (ATF), 192–193

Alexander, Herbert E., 223n, 229n, 230n, 247n, 252n

Almond, Gabriel A., 61n

AMA. *See* American Medical Association

Amalgamated Clothing and Textile Workers Union, 1, 164–167

American Academy of Physicians' Assistants, 121

American Agriculture Movement, 184

American Arts Alliance, 1

American Academy of Sports Physicians, 44

American Association of Retired Persons, 97

American Association of Sex Educators and Counselors, x

American Automobile Association, 128
American Bankers Association (ABA), xii, 144, 190, 332, 386
American Bar Association (ABA), 45, 329
American Business Network (Biznet), 187–188
American Civil Liberties Union (ACLU), 39, 45, 50, 135, 142, 321, 363, 371, 382
American Coalition of Citizens with Disabilities, 125
American College of Nurse Midwives, 1
American College of Obstetricians and Gynecologists, 371
American Committee on East-West Accord, 46
American Conservative Union (ACU), 48, 212, 214, 281
American Council on Education, 92
American Dental Association (ADA), 39
American Farm Bureau Federation (AFBF), 10, 43, 122, 393
American Federation of Labor-Congress of Industrial Organizations (AFL-CIO), 39, 40n, 42, 43, 72, 73, 98, 138, 142, 183, 186, 201, 208, 212, 282, 321, 386, 411
American Federation of State, County and Municipal Employees (AFSCME), 42, 56–57, 176
American Federation of Teachers (AFT), 29, 42, 138, 139, 176, 209, 386
American Foreign Service Association, 57
American Frozen Food Institute, 141
American Hospital Association (AHA), 40, 96–97, 135
American Hotel and Motel Association, 411
American Institute of Architects, 44, 137
American Institute of Certified Public Accountants, 294n
American Iron and Steel Institute, 41
American League of Lobbyists, 262
American Legion, 10, 24, 60, 168
American Medical Association (AMA), xii, 39, 45, 60, 92, 97, 98, 137, 163, 174, 201, 222, 254, 303, 329, 386
American Medical PAC (AMPAC), 222
American Nazi Party, 74, 135
American Newspaper Publishers Association, 332
American Nurses Association, 10, 44
American Petroleum Institute, 98, 163, 205
American Political Science Association (APSA), 140
American Public Transit Association, 92
American Retail Federation, 52
Americans for Constitutional Action (ACA), 53, 212, 214, 223
Americans for Democratic Action (ADA), 53, 201, 212, 214, 233

Americans for Effective Law Enforcement, 365
American Society for Personnel Administration, 44
American Society of Mechanical Engineers, 44, 145
American Soybean Association, 44
American Student Association, 69, 168
Americans United for Life, 371
Americans United for Separation of Church and State, 376n, 398n
American Telephone and Telegraph Company (AT&T), 172, 186, 192
American Textile Manufacturers Institute, 164
American Trial Lawyers Association, 97
Ames, Ruth E., 128n
Amicus curiae briefs, 364, 370–373, 381–382
distribution of, 382
growing number of, 372, 382
Aminoil, USA, 52
Anderson, James E., 44n
Anti-Saloon League, 197, 388
Appointments, 328–329, 336–337, 341–342, 361–362
Architectural and Transportation Barriers Compliance Board (ATBCB), 163, 336
Arms Control Association, 46
Armstrong, Scott, 360n
Aron, Joan B., 352n
Asher, Herbert, 177n
Asphalt Roofing Manufacturers Association, xii
Association of County Aging Programs, 56
Association of Data Processing Service Organizations v. *Camp,* 375
Association of Dress ·gs and Sauces, 141
Association of Form. r Members of Congress, 57
Association of Home Appliance Manufacturers, 72
Association of Public Welfare Attorneys, 44
AT&T. *See* American Telephone and Telegraph Company
ATBCB. *See* Architectural and Transportation Barriers Compliance Board
Atomic Industrial Forum (AIF), 72, 73, 298
Aviation Consumer Action Project, 111

Bachrach, Peter, 162n, 407n
Baer, Michael, 202n, 290n, 310n
Bailis, Lawrence Neil, 63n, 131n, 184n
Baker, Ross K., 316n
Bakke, Allan, 371
Balbus, Isaac D., 16n, 17n
Baldwin, Deborah, 191n
Bannon, Brad, 216n, 217n
Banzhaf, John, 333
Baratz, Morton S., 162n

Barone, Michael, 231n
Barringer, Felicity, 337n
Barry, Brian M., 16n, 26n, 27n, 28n, 128n, 130n, 131n
Bauer, Raymond A., x, 8n, 18n, 89n, 290n, 310n
Bayh, Birch, 216
Beer, Samuel H., 56n
Behrman, Bradley, 341n
Benditt, Theodore M., 26n
Benn, S. I., 16n, 17n, 26n
Bennetts, Leslie, 183n
Bentley, Arthur, ix, x(n), 16n, 17n, 27n
Berelson, Bernard R., 409n
Berg, Larry L., 248n
Berger, Suzanne, 335n, 393n
Bermudez v. *Butz,* 368n
Bernstein, Marver, 340n
Berry, Jeffrey M., xi, 29n, 33n, 74n, 92n, 121n, 131n, 201n, 202n, 331n, 333n, 336n, 352n, 353n
Bethlehem Steel Co., 97
BIPAC. *See* Business-Industry Political Action Committee
Bisky, G., 294n
Biznet. *See* American Business Network
Black, Hugo L., 360–361
BLM. *See* Land Management, U.S. Bureau of
Blue Cross, 96, 393
Blumenthal, Sidney, 325n
Blum v. *Stenson,* 379n
Bodenheimer, Edgar, 27n
Boeckel, Richard, 197n
Boffey, Phillip M., 174n
Bok, Derek C., 138n, 142n
Bonafede, Dom, 75n, 326n
Bone, Hugh, 201n
Boone and Crocket Club, 102
Bow Tie Manufacturers Association, 41
Boyer, William, 334n
Boyte, Harry C., 75n
Bradley, Robert C., 328n
Brennen, William J., 360
Bribery, 263–265, 268
Brick Institute of America, 126n
Broder, David S., 183n
Brotherhood of Railway and Airline Clerks, 222
Brown, Kirk F., 256n, 339n
Brown, Lawrence D., 283n
Brown, Warren, 183n
Browne, William P., 130n, 146n, 312n, 314n
Buchsbaum, Andrew, 294n
Buckley v. *Valeo,* 224–225, 257, 259
Budde, Bernadette, 253n
Burlington Northern Railroad, 91
Burnham, Walter Dean, 201n
Business-Industry Political Action Committee (BIPAC), 215, 245, 247

Business interests. *See also* Corporations; Trade associations
  conflicts with other interests, 285–287, 400
  multiple representation of, 71–73
Business Roundtable, 40–41, 72, 102, 293
Byssinosis controversy, 164–167

CAB. *See* Civil Aeronautics Board
Califano, Joseph A., 190
California League of Conservation Voters, 234n
Californians for Bilingual Education, 251n
Calorie Control Council (CCC), 163, 188–190, 386
Cameron, David R., 403n
Cameron, Juan, 336n
Campaign Contributions. *See* PAC Contributions; Political action committees
Campaign finance laws, 223–226
Campbell Soup Co., 1
Capture theories, 339–346, 391
Carswell, G. Harold, 362
Carter, Jimmy, 190, 215, 269, 325–326, 337
Carter administration, 305, 336
Casket Manufacturers Association of America, 1
Castles, Francis G., 404n
Cater, Douglass, 276n
Caterpillar Tractor, 40
Cause groups, 46–47, 51
CCC. *See* Calorie Control Council
CDF. *See* Children's Defense Fund
Census, U.S. Bureau of, 342
Center for Law and Social Policy, 10, 50, 365
Center for the Study of Petroleum Understanding and Research (SPUR), 109
Central Intelligence Agency (CIA), 31, 375
Chamber of Commerce, U.S., 40, 60, 72, 97, 122, 187, 205, 212, 293–294, 336, 386
Chappell, Henry W., 256n
Chase, Harold W., 329n
Chase Manhattan Bank, 144n
Chemical Manufacturers Association, 175
Children's Defense Fund (CDF), 46, 93, 181, 337
Child Welfare Adoption Assistance Act of 1980, 305
Child Welfare League of America, xii, 46
Chubb, John, xi(n), 343n, 350n
Church, Frank, 216
Citibank, 28
Citizens' Committee for the Right to Keep and Bear Arms, 234n
Citizens' Communications Center, 111, 365
Citizens for Highway Safety, 209
Citizens' groups, 28–35, 45–47, 81
  benefits provided by, 128

conservative, 29–30, 51, 203n, 382
ideological leanings of, 203n
level of resources, 33–34, 98, 100, 115–116, 178
sources of financial support, 50
Civil Aeronautics Board (CAB), 340, 343, 357
Civil rights and social welfare organizations, 24, 47, 81
Clamshell Alliance, 47
Clark, Timothy, 209n
Clark, Peter B., xi(n)
Class action suits, 368–370
Clausen, Aage R., 252n
Clean Air Act Working Group, 48
Clothespin Manufacturers of America, 79
Clowns of America, 44
Clymer, Adam, 217n
Coalition for a New Foreign and Military Policy, 295
Coalition for Peace through Strength, 46
Coalitions, 48–49, 108, 109n, 278–287, 306–307, 313, 396
changing patterns of conflict, 283–287
in distributive politics, 280
increasing importance of, 279
in redistributive politics, 281–282
in regulatory politics, 281
Cochrane, Clarke E., 26n, 27n
Coelho, Tony, 253
Cohen, Julius, 297n
Cohen, Richard E., 80n
Cohen, William S., 194
Coleman, James, 138n
Colgate, Craig, Jr., 40n
Collective good, 124
Collins, Laurence, 246n
Comford, R. D., 352n
Committee for Collective Security, 80
Committee for Humane Legislation, 251n
Committee for the Return of Confiscated German and Japanese Property, 78
Committee for the Survival of a Free Congress, 251
Committee of Railroad Shippers, 48
Committee on Political Education (COPE), 212
Committee on the Present Danger, 46
Committee to Re-Elect the President (CREEP), 223–224
Common Cause, xii, 28, 33n, 45, 48, 74, 94–95, 98, 112, 130n, 153, 186, 321, 342n, 387
Communications with organizational members, 142–146
functions of, 144–146
importance of, 143
Communications Workers of America, 186
Community Nutrition Institute, 331n

Comprehensive Employment and Training Act, 283n
Comptroller of the Currency, 375
Computer and Business Equipment Manufacturers' Association (CBEMA), 52
Conable, Barber, 314n
Conflict of interest laws, 271, 342, 349
Congress. See also Favors; Lobbying; Provision of information to officials; Sunshine laws; Testifying at hearings
growing number of subcommittees, 302–303, 308
impact of recent changes in, 301–310
increasing role of staff, 303–304, 308–309
Joint Committee on Atomic Energy, 303
Joint Committee on the Organization of Congress, 318
links between legislator and district, 156–157, 259, 292
need for information, 297
special interest caucuses, 316
as a target of pressure activity, 272
turnover in membership, 305–306
vulnerability to lobbying influence, 310–317
Congressional Budget Office (CBO), 308
Congress Watch, 48, 321
Conlan, Richard, 196
Conlan, Timothy J., 56n
Connolly, William E., 16n, 17n
Conservative Caucus, 94–95
Constantini, Edmond, 248n, 250n
Consumer Bankers Association, 243
Consumer Federation of America, 34, 45, 82, 111n
Consumers Union, 29, 39, 50, 85, 111
Cooper, Martha R., 122n
Corcoran, Thomas G., 360
Corporations, 49–50, 82
increasing involvement in politics, 287
nature of constituency, 69–71
Cosmetic, Toiletry and Fragrance Association, 1
Costain, Anne N., 307n, 311n
Costain, Douglas W., 307n, 311n
Council for Exceptional Children, 158
Council of Chief State School Officers, 412
Council of Economic Advisors, 324
Council of State Governments, 55
Council of State Planning Agencies, 56
Courts. See also Amicus curiae briefs; Appointments; Class action suits; Law review lobbying; Standing to sue; Test cases
as arena of organized interest activity, 359–360
costs of litigating, 369, 376, 381
impact of recent procedural changes on, 373–376

Courts (*Continued*)
  insulation from political pressure, 381
  responsiveness to broad publics and
    disadvantaged, 378–384
  sponsorship of litigation, 364–370
  structure of federal judiciary, 359
  as a target of pressure activity, 272
Covington and Burling, 99
Cowan, Ruth B., 364n
Crawford, Kate, 108–109
Crenson, Matthew A., 103n, 162n
Crittendon, Ann, 336n
Cronin, Thomas, 324n
Crozier, Michel, 406n, 407n
Culhane, Paul J., 346n, 367n, 374n
Culver, John, 253n
Cupps, D. Stephen, 352n

Dahl, Robert, ix, x(n), 2n, 9n, 35n, 59n, 64n,
  107n, 123n, 378n, 399n, 402n, 407n
Davidson, Roger H., 302n, 303n, 319n, 320n,
  380n
Davis, Kenneth Culp, 354n
Defenders of Wildlife, 45
Defense contractors, 270, 284, 336
Defense, U.S. Department of, 93, 269–270,
  295, 333
Del-Monte Corporation, 52
Demkovich, Linda, 188n
Democracy in organizations. *See*
  Organizational democracy
Democratic Congressional Campaign
  Committee, 253
Democratic party, nature of organized
  interest constituency, 326
Democratic Study Group, 196, 204n
Demonstrations, 149, 151, 182–184, 361
Deregulation, 355–357
Dexter, Lewis Anthony, x, 18n, 58n, 89n,
  144n, 145n, 290n, 311n, 313n, 314n
Diamond, Martin, 2n
Dickson, Douglas N., 230n
Direct mail, 191–193
Direct-mail fund raising, 93–95, 150–151,
  156–157
Direct Mail Marketing Association, 332
Disability Rights Center, 65
Distilled Spirits Council of the United
  States, 267
Dolan, Terry, 217
Dolbeare, Cushing, 108–109
Dole, Robert, 251
Door and Hardware Institute, 72n
Downey, Thomas, 253n
Drew, Elizabeth, 223n, 243n, 250n, 252n,
  253n, 328n
Dunlop, John T., 138n, 142n
duPont de Nemours and Co., E. I., 90
Duverger, Maurice, 133n

Eagleton, Thomas, 216
Earley, Peter, 352n, 353n
Easterbrook, Gregg, 262n
Eastland, Larry L., 248n
Eastman, Hope, 318n
Eckstein, Harry, 160n
Economic interests in politics, 23–24, 26
Edelman, Marion Wright, 181
Edelman, Murray, 328n
Edison Electric Institute, 72, 243
Education, U.S. Department of, 163, 325,
  337–338, 380
Education for All Handicapped Children
  Act, 158
EEOC. *See* Equal Employment Opportunity
  Commission, U.S.
Eisenhower, Dwight D., 55
Eisen v. *Carlisle & Jacquelin,* 369n
Eismeier, Theodore J., 226n, 239n, 253n
Election results, impact on organized
  interests, 204–206, 391
Electoral politics, organized interest
  involvement in, 7, 151, 206–219, 325.
  See also Endorsements; Party
  conventions; Political action
  committees; Scorecards; Targeting;
  Voter registration drives
Electronics Industries Association, 72
Elks, 60
El Paso Natural Gas Company, 360
Endorsements, 151, 217
Engstrom, Richard L., 55n
Entman, Robert M., 180n
Environmental Action, 216
Environmental Defense Fund, 74, 333, 365n,
  386
Environmental Policy Center, 90
Environmental Protection Agency (EPA),
  333, 345–346, 354, 367
EPA. *See* Environmental Protection Agency
Epstein, Edwin M., 229n
Epstein, Lee, 370n, 372n, 373n, 379n, 382n
Equal Employment Opportunity
  Commission, U.S. (EEOC), 330, 344,
  345, 377
Ethics in Government Act, 271, 349
Executive agencies. *See also* Advisory
  committees; Appointments; Conflict of
  interest laws; Deregulation; Executive
  reorganization; Freedom of Information
  Act; Intervenor financing; Lobbying;
  Participation in rulemaking
  proceedings; Sunshine laws
  capture theories, 339–346, 391
  impact of recent changes in, 346–357
  indirect influence by organized interests,
    336–337
  structure of clientele, 337–338, 342, 344,
    391, 397

as a target of organized interest activity, 272, 330
 vulnerability to Congress, 330, 338, 342
Executive Office of the President, 323
Executive Order 12291, 353
Executive reorganization, 337–338
Ex parte rules, 267, 350
Exxon, 10, 39, 50, 91

FACA. *See* Federal Advisory Committee Act
Fact-finding trips, 267–268. *See also* Inducements
Fair Budget Action Campaign (FBAC), 218
Fallows, Susan E., 298n
Farm groups, 43–44
Favors, performance of, 265–268, 300–301, 313
FCC. *See* Federal Communications Commission
FDA. *See* Food and Drug Administration
Feaver, Douglas B., 349n
FEC. *See* Federal Election Commission
FECA. *See* Federal Election Campaign Act
Feder, Judith, 335n
Federal Advisory Committee Act of 1972 (FACA), 349, 351
Federal Aviation Administration (FAA), 357
Federal Communications Commission (FCC), 86, 333
Federal Election Campaign Act (FECA) of 1971, 223, 390
 1974 amendments to, 223–225, 324–325
Federal Election Commission (FEC), 222–225, 230–234, 248–250, 390
Federal Insurance Administration (FIA), 347
Federalist, No. 10, 2–3, 198, 409–410
Federal Maritime Commission, 344
Federal Power Commission (FPC), 318, 374
Federal Register, 332
Federal Regulation of Lobbying Act of 1946, 75n, 318–321
Federal Trade Commission (FTC), 87, 109, 158, 163, 330, 339, 343, 345, 351, 397
Federation of American Hospitals, 96, 243
Fee shifting. *See* Class action suits
Fenno, Richard F., 156n, 259n, 293n, 342n
Ferejohn, John A., 156n
Financial Executives Institute, 44
Fiorina, Morris, 156n, 259n, 293n, 313n
Firestone Tire and Rubber Co., 50
First Amendment rights, 25, 159, 224–226, 257, 317
Fish and Wildlife Service, U.S., 365
Fisk, Winston Mills, 2n
501(c)(3) tax status, 91–92, 161, 186, 210, 218n, 390
Flast v. *Cohen,* 374, 376
Flathman, Richard, 26n
FMC Corporation, 186, 187n

FOIA. *See* Freedom of Information Act
Food and Drug Administration (FDA), 163, 180–181, 188–190, 270, 333, 343, 397
Food and Nutrition Service, 336
Food Marketing Institute, 127, 386
Food Research and Action Center (FRAC), 51n, 163, 315n, 331n, 368, 387
Footwear Distributors PAC, 234n
Ford, Gerald, 326
Ford Motor Company, 90
Foreign Agents Registration Act of 1938, 54n, 318
Foristel, James, 303n
Fortas, Abe, 361, 362n
Foss, Phillip, 343n
Foundation of the Wall and Ceiling Industry, 72n
Fowler, Linda L., 212n, 214n
FPC. *See* Federal Power Commission
FRAC. *See* Food Research and Action Center
Frank, Alan Dodds, 54n
Frank, Barney, 191
Franklin, Grace A., 276n, 280n, 283n
Freedom of Information Act, 347–348
Freeman, J. Leiper, 276n
Freeman, Jo, 345n
Free rider problem, 102, 124–125
Frendreis, John P., 256n
Friends of the Earth, 10, 34, 45, 80, 85, 387
Friedrich, Carl J., 26n
Fritschler, A. Lee, 174n, 276n, 311n
Frolich, Norman, 126n
Froman, Lewis A., 315n
Frothingham v. *Mellon,* 374n
FTC. *See* Federal Trade Commission
Full Employment Action Council, 47
Full Employment Act of 1946, 282
Full Employment and Balanced Growth Act of 1978, 282
Fund for a Democratic Majority, 251
Fund raisers, 243, 301
Futures Industry Good Government PAC, 234n

Gable, Richard W., 263n
Gais, Thomas L., xi(n), 152n, 277n
Galanter, Marc, 377n
Galli, Anthony, 172n
Gamson, William, 21n
Gardner, Paul, 190n, 378n
Garfinkel, Herbert, 2n
Garson, G. David, x(n)
General Dynamics Corporation, 222
General Dynamics Voluntary Political Contribution Plan, 222
General Electric Co., xii, 50, 72–73, 295n
General Motors Corp. (GM), 10, 50, 293
General Telephone and Electronics (GTE), 40

Geological Survey, U.S., 329
Gerlach, Luther P., 133n
Gerrard, Michael, 176n
Gettinger, Stephen, 367n
Gilmour, Robert S., 353n, 354n
Ginsburg, Ruth Bader, 363
Glass, Andrew J., 41n
Glickman, Dan, 253n
Godwin, R. Kenneth, 158n, 161n
Goel, M. L., 61n
Goldberg, Nicholas, 230n
Golembiewski, Robert T., x(n)
Gopoian, David J., 237n, 239n
Gordon, Michael R., 98n, 181n
Gouldner, Alvin, 133n
Grass roots lobbying, 7, 145, 156, 184–197, 361
  effectiveness of, 194–196
Grazing Service, U.S., 343
Green, Mark, 98n, 253n, 266n, 294n
Greenpeace, 181
Greenstone, J. David, 16n, 21n, 142n
Greenwald, Carol S., 327n, 367n
Gregg, Sandra R., 183n
Grossman, Joel B., 329n, 362n
Grossman, Michael Baruch, 324n, 330n
Group theories of politics, ix–xii, 7, 391, 396, 402, 407
  criticisms of, x–xi, 7–8
Gun Control Act of 1968, 192
Gun Owners of America, 192
Gup, Ted, 267n
Gusfield, Joseph R., 25n
Guzzardi, Walter, Jr., 281n

Hadley, Charles D., 201n
Haider, Donald H., 55n
Haggerty, Brian A., 223n, 247n
Hakman, Nathan, 372n
Hammond, Susan Webb, 316n
Handgun control, 94
Handgun Control, Inc., 233n
Handler, Edward, 229n, 230n, 231n, 239n, 241n
Handlin, Mary, 4n
Handlin, Oscar, 4n
Hanna, Marcus A., 221, 223
Hardin, Russell, 128n, 131n
Harris, Richard, 362n
Hart, Gary, 153
Hatch, Orrin, 243
Havemann, Joel, 338n
Hawaiian Golfers for Good Government, 222
Haydon, William, 266n
Hayes, Michael T., xi(n), 74n, 140n, 282n, 290n, 311n, 312n, 393n
Haynsworth, Clement, 362
Head Start Program, 337–338

Health, Education, and Welfare, U.S.
  Department of, 190
Health and Human Services, U.S.
  Department of, 333, 336
Health Care Financing Administration, U.S., 96
Health Industries Manufacturers
  Association, 72
Health Insurance Benefits Advisory Council
  (HIBAC), 333–334
Health Research Group, 333
Heclo, Hugh, 276n
Held, Virginia, 26n
Herbers, John, 74n
Herman, Edward S., 334n
Herring, Pendleton, 181n, 197n
Hershey, Robert D., 98n
Hershey Foods, 50
Hess, Stephen, 324n
Hetzner, Candace, 26n
Hewitt, Christopher, 403n
Hibbs, Douglas A., 403n
Hill and Knowlton, 377
Hilton, George W., 342n
Hired professionals in government relations, 98–100
Hirschmann, Albert O., 15n, 134–135
Holcomb, John, 223n, 240n
Holt, Cooper T., 213n
Honoraria, 266–268. *See also* Inducements
Hoover, Herbert, 362
Hornblower, Margaret, 51n
Horowitz, Donald, 380n
House of Representatives, U.S. *See also*
  Congress
  Appropriations Committee, 295
  Rules Committee, 301
  Ways and Means Committee, 96, 267
Huckshorn, Robert J., 200n, 209n
Hughes Helicopters Inc., 295
Humphrey-Hawkins bill. *See* Full
  Employment and Balanced Growth Act
Hunt, Albert R., 98n, 242n
Hunt, Margaret A., 310n
Huntington, Samuel P., 305n, 406n, 407n, 409n

IBM. *See* International Business Machines, Inc.
ICC. *See* Interstate Commerce Commission
ILGWU. *See* International Ladies Garment
  Workers Union
Image advertising. *See* Advertising
Independent Insurance Agents of America
  (IIAA), 347
Independent Petroleum Association, 206n, 213
Inducements, 265–268, 294–295, 300, 312, 323, 359, 391, 395

Information, provision of, 265, 297–300, 330, 331, 341, 391, 395, 409
Institutional advertising. *See* Advertising
Interest groups. *See* Interest organizations; Organized interests
Interest organizations. *See also* Organized interests
  categories of, 39–51
  distribution of, 66–71, 75–82
  emergence of, 121–131
  growing number of, 75, 153, 378, 387
  variation in agenda size, 51–54, 111
Interests in politics. *See also* Political preferences
  nature of, 14–37
  objective approach to, 17, 19–23
  relationship to preferences, 16–23
  subjective approach to, 17–19
Intergovernmental Lobby, 10n, 55–57, 93n, 122–123
Interior, U.S. Department of, 365n
International Association of Machinists, 230n
International Brotherhood of Electrical Workers, 42
International Brotherhood of Teamsters, 42, 98, 215, 392
International Business Machines, Inc. (IBM), 40, 50
International City Management Association, 55
International Ladies Garment Workers Union (ILGWU), 42, 43
International Longshoremen's Association (ILA), 43
International Longshoremen's and Warehousemen's Union, 214
International Paper Company, 222
International Typographers' Union, 138
International Union of Bricklayers, 42
Interstate Commerce Commission, U.S. (ICC), 340, 344n, 374, 400
Intervenor financing, 351–353
Ippolito, Dennis S., 371
Ireland, Andy, 243
Iron law of oligarchy, 133
Iron triangles, 276–278. *See also* Subgovernments
Isaacson, Walter, 253n
Issue networks, 267–278, 300
Italian American Forum, 73

Jackson, Brooks, 223n, 254n, 266n
Jacob, Herbert, 368n
Jacobs, Andrew, 253n
Jacobson, Gary C., 250n, 258n
Japanese American Citizens League, 73
Javits, Jacob, 269
Jeffe, Sherry Bebitch, 248n
Jehovah's Witnesses, 365

Jennings, M. Kent, 61n
Jessup, David, 250n
Johnson, Lyndon B., 361
Johnson, Samuel, 15
Jones, Charles O., 30n
Jones, Ruth S., 247n
Justice, U.S. Department of, 329, 382

Kansas City Board of Public Utilities, 56
Katzmann, Robert A., 345n
Keefe, William J., 296n
Keller, Bill, 48n, 180n, 187n, 190n, 192n, 194n, 195n, 196n, 212n, 213n, 216n, 293n, 296n
Kelley, Stanley, Jr., 98n, 174n
Kelman, Steven, 367n, 404n, 405n
Kentucky Gasoline Dealers Association PAC, 234n
Kesselman, Mark, 407n
Key, V. O., Jr., 139n, 174n, 178n, 402n
King, Anthony, 159n
King, Joel, 248n, 250n
Kingdon, John W., 158n, 159n, 253n, 313n
Kirkland, Lane, 183
Kirkwood, Ronn, 190n
Kirschten, Dick, 326n, 354n
Kissinger, Henry, 127
Kitschelt, Herbert, 404n
Kluger, Richard, 366n
Kobylka, Joseph F., 364n
Kohlmeier, Louis, 342n
Kolko, Gabriel, 341n
Kornhauser, William, 9n, 407n
Kraft Foods, 50
Kramer, Fred A., 340n
Krislov, Samuel, 16n, 372n
Ku Klux Klan, 74
Kumar, Martha Joynt, 324n, 330n
Kweit, Mary Grisez, 351n
Kweit, Robert W., 351n

Labor, U.S. Department of, 276, 278, 337, 339
Labor Statistics, U.S. Bureau of, 342
Labor unions, 42–43, 81, 127
  differences of interest among members, 136
  electoral involvement of, 210
  level of resources, 115–116
  locals, 43
  operating unions, 42–43
  organizational democracy in, 137–140
Ladd, Everett Carll, 201n
Landes, William, 378n
Land Management, U.S. Bureau of (BLM), 343, 346
Langley, Monica, 230n
Latham, Earl L., ix, x(n), 7n
Latus, Margaret Ann, 217n
Law review lobbying, 363–364

Lawyer-lobbyists, 99. *See also* Hired
  government relations professionals
Lawyer's Committee for Civil Rights under
  Law, 74, 379
Lazarsfeld, Paul F., 409n
Leach, James, 253n
Leadership Conference on Civil Rights
  (LCCR), 49
League of Conservation Voters (LCV), 212,
  234n
League of the United Latin American
  Citizens, 249
League of Women Voters, 11, 134, 321
Lear, Norman, 193
Legal Aid Society of New York, 379n
Legislative liaison officers. *See* Lobbying, by
  the federal executive branch
Legislative Reorganization Act of 1946, 318
Lehmbruch, Gerhard, 335n, 393n
Leiserson, Avery, 334n
Lesher, Stephan, 262n
Levine, L. Erwin, 158n
Levitan, Sar A., 122n
Lewis, Karen De W., 90n
Liberty Lobby, xii, 10
Liberman, Jethro K., 369
Lijphart, Arendt, 36n
Lindblom, Charles E., 64n, 400n
Lippmann, Walter, 264n
Lipsen, Charles B., 262n
Lipset, Seymour Martin, 137n, 138n
Lipsky, Michael, 182n
Litigation. *See* Courts
Litton Industries, 295n
Lobbying, 10n, 149, 152, 261, 289–295, 322.
  See also Bribery; Coalitions; Congress;
  Executive agencies; Favors;
  Inducements; President; Provision of
  information; Testifying at hearings
  by-product theory of, 132
  effects of changes in Congress on,
    301–310, 390
  executive branch, 331–332
  factors determining success of, 314–317,
    395–397
  by the federal executive branch, 55
  by foreign governments, 54
  impact on policy, 310–317
  increasing professionalism of, 261–263,
    268
  institutional targets of, 271–274, 292, 313,
    395
  judicial, 359–360
  networks of information and consultation,
    274–276
  presidential, 323–324, 327, 329
  purposes of, 290, 292
  social lobbying, 294–295

Lobbyists
  recruitment of, 268–271, 342
  regulation of, 317–321
Lockheed Corp., 243, 300
Log Homes Council, 72n
Londgren, Richard, 176n
Loomis, Burdett A., 187n
Lowi, Theodore, x, 36n, 279–283, 287, 312,
  324n, 343n

Maass, Arthur, 27n
McCarthy, Frank, 253n
McCleary, Richard, 256n
McCloskey, Robert G., 381n
McConnell, Grant, x, 36n, 71n, 122n, 136n,
  324n, 335n, 343n, 393n
McFarland, Andrew S., 30n, 32n, 33n, 74n,
  130n, 131n
McGraw, Dickinson, 256n
Machiavelli, Niccolo, 15–16
MacKenzie, G. Calvin, 328n, 329n
McKinley, William, 221, 223
McPhee, William N., 409n
McQuaid, Kim, 40n
McRae, Kenneth, 36n
Macy, John W., 328n
Madison, James, 2, 3, 15, 26, 35, 124n, 198,
  400, 409–410
Magazine Publishers Association, 332
Malbin, Michael J., 208n, 227n, 250n, 254n,
  259n, 304n
Maine Retail Grocers Association, 194
Mansbridge, Jane J., 64n
Manwaring, David R., 365n
Mapp v. *Ohio*, 370
March, David, 130n
Marcus, Alfred, 345n
Marmor, Theodore R., 18n, 282n
Marsh, David, 130n
Martin Marietta Corp., 295n
Marwell, Gerald, 128n
Massachusetts Welfare Rights Organization
  (MWRO), 63, 130, 184
Massie, Robert K., 187n
Matasar, Ann B., 230n
Mayer, Caroline E., 33n, 354n
Mayhew, David, 156n, 259n, 293n, 313n
Media. *See* Organized interests, relations
  with the media
Media Access Project, 50
Media distribution services, 180
Medicare, 18, 20, 42, 96, 282, 334, 393
Meier, Kenneth J., 297n
Meltsner, Michael, 366n
Membership organizations, 39–49, 100–103,
  120–147
Membership in organizations, 59–63, 392
  barriers to, 61–63, 130
  incentives for, 125–130

rationality of, 124–126, 130–131
socioeconomic skew, 60–63
Merchant Marine Act of 1936, 318
Metcalf, Lee, 334n
Mexican-American Legal Defense and
 Education Fund, 68n, 362, 365, 369, 387
Michels, Robert, 133–134, 137, 141n, 146n
Migrant Legal Action Project, 74, 379
Milbrath, Lester W., x, 8n, 49n, 61n, 123n,
 144n, 146n, 264n, 310n, 314n
Miller, Loren, 366n
Miller, Warren E., 247n, 252n, 313n
Miller, William H., 187n
Mills, Wilbur, 269
Mintz, Morton, 230n
Mitnick, Barry M., 26n, 27n
Mobile Homes Dealers National
 Association, 79
Mobil Oil Corp., 28, 176, 230
Mobil PAC, 230
Moe, Terry M., xi(n), 128
Momboissee, Raymond M., 29n
Mondale, Walter, 208, 216
Moped Association of America, xii
Moral Majority, 53, 193, 201
Morehouse, Sarah McCally, 202n
Morgan, Charles, Jr., 377
Margolick, David, 362n
Morris, Gerald, 138n
Motor Vehicle Manufacturers' Association,
 366
Mouzelis, Nicos P., 137n
Moynihan, Daniel Patrick, 153, 305
Mueller, Carl G., 144n
Mulhollan, Daniel P., 316n, 320n
Mulkern, John R., 229n, 230n, 231n, 241n
Multi-issue groups, 52–53
Murphy, Walter E., 367n, 368n, 371n, 373n
MWRO. See Massachusetts Welfare Rights
 Organization

NAACP. See National Association for the
 Advancement of Colored People
Nader, Ralph, 28, 48, 74, 111, 281, 321,
 332–333
Nadel, Mark V., 335n
NAHB. See National Association of Home
 Builders
NAM. See National Association of
 Manufacturers
NARAL. See National Abortion Rights
 Action League
National Abortion Rights Action League
 (NARAL), 39, 46, 94
National Alliance of Business, 93
National Association for the Advancement
 of Colored People (NAACP), 10, 39, 50,
 68n, 74, 93, 362, 363, 366n, 367, 386,
 372

National Association of Beer Wholesalers,
 222
National Association of Black Women
 Attorneys, 66
National Association of Broadcasters, xii,
 72, 98, 377
National Association of Business PACs, 230
National Association of Counties, 55
National Association of County Park and
 Recreation Officials, 56
National Association of Federal
 Veterinarians, 44
National Association of Home Builders
 (NAHB), 1, 52, 72, 146, 219, 386
National Association of Independent
 Colleges and Universities, 209
National Association of Independent
 Insurers, 366
National Association of Insured Persons,
 111
National Association of Letter Carriers, 39,
 146, 180, 228, 245, 300
National Association of Manufacturers
 (NAM), 11, 40, 48, 72–73, 90, 281, 282
National Association of Railroad Passengers,
 111
National Association of Realtors, 10, 254
National Association for Retarded Children,
 158
National Association of Social Workers, 209
National Association of State Aviation
 Officials, 56
National Association of the Deaf, 46
National Association of Truck Stop
 Operators, 269
National Association of Wheat Growers, 44
National Audubon Society, 39, 128
National Automobile Dealers Association,
 158, 243
National Beauty Culturists League, 66
National Cable Television Association, 73,
 121, 377
National Cattlemen's Association's
 Cattlemen's Action Legislative Fund
 (CALF), 222
National Center for a Barrier Free
 Environment, 74, 379
National Citizens Committee for Nursing
 Home Reform, 164
National Coal Association, 73
National Coalition for Bankruptcy Reform,
 48
National Coalition to Ban Handguns, 163
National Committee for an Effective
 Congress, 53, 221
National Computer Graphics Association,
 121
National Committee to Liberalize the Tariff
 Laws on Art, 78

National Conference of Catholic Charities, 47
National Conservative Political Action Committee (NCPAC), 53, 216, 217, 225, 252
National Cotton Council, 44
National Council of Churches, 1, 142
National Council of Senior Citizens, 210, 326
National Education Association (NEA), xii, 98, 124, 163, 194, 208, 227, 325, 386, 392
National Electrical Manufacturers Association, 73
National Farmers Union (NFU), 43, 393
National Federation of Fishermen, 125
National Federation of Independent Business (NFIB), 40, 213
National Food Processors Association, 141
National Governors Association, 57, 93n
National Governors Conference, 55, 56
National Grange, 43
National Highway Traffic Safety Administration, U.S., 344, 366
National Labor Relations Board, U.S. (NLRB), 71, 330, 337
National League of Cities, 55
National League of Postmasters, 338
National Low Income Housing Coalition, 107, 108, 386
National Military Wives Association, 66
National Milk Producers Association, 44
National Organization for Women (NOW), 11, 40n, 47, 66, 98, 103, 208, 216, 371
National Pretzel Bakers Institute, 141
National Prison Project, 50, 365
National Pro-life Political Action Committee, 221
National Rifle Association, 36, 94–95, 386
National Rifle Association Political Victory Fund, 234n
National Right to Life Committee, 46, 94–95, 371
National Right to Work Committee, 94–95
National Rural Housing Coalition, 47
National Savings and Loan League, 93
National Security Council, 324
National Society of Professional Engineers, 329
National Tax Limitation Committee, 34, 45
National Taxpayers Union (NTU), 29, 45
National Training and Information Center (NTIC), 347
National Treasury Employees Union, 412
National Urban Coalition, 74, 93
National Urban League, 47, 74, 93
National Women's Political Caucus, 362
National Women's Political Caucus Campaign Support Committee, 233n
Natural Resources Defense Council, 365

NCPAC. *See* National Conservative Political Action Committee
NEA. *See* National Education Association
Neely, Richard, 360n
Nelson, Gaylord, 269
Neocorporatism, 335n, 392–394
Nerkin, Ira, 109, 110, 131
Neustadt, Richard E., 325
Newland, Chester A., 363n
New York State Board of Education, 56
NFIB. *See* National Federation of Independent Business
NFU. *See* National Farmers Union
Nie, Norman H., 61n, 201n
Niemi, Richard G., 61n
Nixon, Richard M., 223, 326, 362n
NLRB. *See* National Labor Relations Board
Noll, Roger G., 342n
Noneconomic interests in politics, 24–26
Nonmembership organizations, 49–51
NOW. *See* National Organization for Women
NTU. *See* National Taxpayers Union

Occupational Safety and Health Administration, U.S., 344, 367
O'Connor, Karen, 363n, 369n, 370n, 372n, 373n, 379n, 382n
Odegard, Peter, 197n
Office for Economic Opportunity, 339
Office of Communications of the United Church of Christ v. *Federal Communications Commission,* 375n
Office of Management and Budget (OMB), 323, 353–354, 355n
Ogul, Morris S., 296n
Oleszek, Walter J., 319n, 320n, 380n
Olson, Mancur, x, 35n, 68n, 102, 123–131, 132n, 312, 389, 406n, 409
Omang, Joanne, 345n
OMB. *See* Office of Management and Budget
Oppenheim, Felix E., 26n
Oppenheim, Joe A., 126n
Oppenheimer Fund v. *Saunders,* 369n
Organizational democracy, 132–143
Organizational entrepreneurs, 131
Organizational maintenance, xi, 112, 142
Organizational resources, 88–118
  allies in government as, 315, 397
  appealing cause as, 171
  comparability of, 110–112
  distribution of, 113–116, 117–118, 396
  expertise and skills as, 97
  government as a source of, 92–93, 122–123, 389
  information as, 95–97, 144
  level of, x, 7, 89–90, 311, 395
  membership as, 100–103
  money as, 89–90, 171, 396

organization itself as, 109–110, 165–168
relationship to policy influence, 316, 396
relative importance of, 103–107
reputation and credibility as, 103, 298
sources of, 90–94
Organizational staff, 97–98
responsiveness to membership, 141–142
Organized interests. *See also* Interest
  organizations; Lobbying
choice of political strategies and tactics,
  157–162
definition of, 9–11
emergence of, 65, 389–405
and governability, 9, 407–409
increasing activity of, ix, 1, 5, 75, 80–81,
  152–156, 277, 302, 307, 378, 388
inevitability of organized opposition,
  84–85, 312–313, 315, 395
influence in politics, x–xi, 7–9, 162–168,
  310–317, 391–398
patterns of conflict and cooperation
  among, 279–287
processes of mutual influence, 6–7,
  287–290, 330, 334, 389–391, 395
relations with the media, 178–182
role in American democracy, 3–4, 9,
  398–410
techniques of influence, 5, 149–152,
  156–157, 162, 388–389
Ornstein, Norman J., 305n
Orren, Karen, 375n, 376n
Oulette, Roland, 262
Outdoor Advertisers Association of America,
  267

PAC contributions, 265, 268, 300, 312, 323,
  391. *See also* Campaign finance laws;
  Political action committees
criteria used in giving, 238–239
influence on policy, 252–256
recipients of, 231–233
role in guaranteeing access, 245–246, 253
split giving, 241–242
Pacific Legal Foundation (PLF), 29–30,
  50–51, 365
PACs. *See* Political action committees
Page, Benjamin I., 324n
Paisley, William J., 177n
Paletz, David L., 180n
Panetta, Leon, 253n
Parker, John, 362
Parker Pen Co., 50
Participation in rulemaking proceedings,
  332–333
Party conventions, 204, 208–209
Peak, G. Wayne, 174n, 177n, 178n
Peak business associations, 40–41
Pear, Robert, 164n
Peirce, Neal R., 136n
Peltason, Jack W., 363n

Penn Central Corp., 91
People for the American Way, 193
Pepsico, 189
Perlez, Jane, 216n
Perritt, Henry H., 334n
Perry, James M., 229n
Peterson, Mark A., xi(n), 277n
Petracca, Mark P., 324n, 333n, 334n, 349n
Petrocik, John, 201n
Pfeffer, Leo, 321n
Pharmaceutical Manufacturers Association
  (PMA), 124
Pianin, Eric, 183n
Pickle Packers International, 141
Pika, Joseph, 324n, 351n
Pincus, Walter, 295n
Pious, Richard M., 55n
Pitkin, Hanna Fenichel, 16n, 17n, 132n
Plamenatz, John, 16n
Planned Parenthood Federation of America,
  93, 371
PLF. *See* Pacific Legal Foundation
Policy entrepreneurs, 84, 315, 397
Political action committees, 221–260, 301,
  359. *See also* Campaign finance laws;
    Fund raisers; PAC contributions
distribution of, 248–252
donations of technical services, 217
freedom in rejecting candidates' requests,
  243–246
imbalance in representation of interests,
  247–252, 255
implications for democracy, 256–260
increasing activity of, 222
independent expenditures by, 225, 259
internal management of, 226–229
methods of solicitation by, 229–231
nonconnected, 222
regulation of, 223–226
requests from candidates, 242–246
role in increasing participation, 247
strategies of giving, 231–241
Political parties
organized interests as constituencies of,
  202, 209
relationship to organized interests,
  200–206
Political preferences
determination of, 20, 23, 390
intensity of, 35–36
relationship to political activity, 20–21, 36
role of taste in, 22–23
Pollock, Phillip H., 226n, 239n, 253n
Polsby, Nelson, 16n, 17n
Pool, Ithiel de Sola, x, 8n, 18n, 89n, 290n
Posner, Richard A., 378n
Postal Rate Commission, U.S., 332
Postal Service, U.S., 338
Post Card Manufacturers Association, 41

Potato Chip/Snack Food Association, 127, 222
Pound, Edward F., 266n
Preservation Action, 31–32, 386
President, U.S. *See also* Appointments; Lobbying; Presidential advisory commissions; Task forces
  cultivation of organized interests, 325–326
  organized interest liaison operations of, 326
  as a target of pressure activities, 272, 324
Presidential advisory commissions, 327–328
Press conferences, 181
Pressure groups. *See* Interest organizations; Organized interests
Price, Don K., 334n
Pritchett, Herman, 367n, 368n, 371n, 373n
Professional associations, 44–45, 82
  benefits provided by, 44, 127
Protest movements, incorporation into organized interest politics, 401, 405
Protests. *See* Demonstrations
Provision of information to officials, 265, 297–300
Proxy lobbying, 193–194
PTA (Parent Teachers Association), 60
Public and private interests in politics, nature of, 26–35
Public Citizen, 48, 74, 80, 111
Public interest groups. *See* Citizens' groups
Public interest law firms, 50–51, 365
Public interests in politics, definition of, 26–32
Public relations firms, 99, 171, 175, 377. *See also* Hired professionals in government relations
Public Utilities Holding Company Act of 1935, 318

Quirk, Paul J., 270n, 342n, 344n

Rachal, Patricia, 193n, 337n
Radin, Charles A., 345n
Railroad Retirement Board, U.S., 328
Railway Labor Executives Association, 140
Railway Progress Institute, 73
Ranney, Austin, 201n
RCA (Radio Corporation of America), 112
Realtor's Political Action Committee (RPAC), 229
Reagan, Ronald W., 146, 168, 183, 205, 217, 218, 276, 325, 345, 355n, 362
Reagan administration, 164, 168, 176, 181, 205, 273, 278, 336, 345–346, 366n, 379n, 403n
Recreational Vehicle Industry Association (RVIA), 1, 127
Rees, W. J., 16n, 26n
Reeve, Andrew, 16n
Rehabilitation Act of 1973, 336

Regents of the University of California v. *Bakke,* 371
Republican Congressional Campaign Committee, 204n
Republican party, nature of organized interest constituency, 326
Representation of interests by organizations, 5–6, 63–87, 165, 389, 401–402. *See also* Access; Interest organizations; Washington pressure community
  implications for political influence, 85–86, 165–168, 384, 391
  problems of political equality, 63–65, 385, 399
Resilient Floor Covering Institute, 72n
Resources. *See* Organizational resources
Responsible Citizens Political League, 222
Revolving door. *See* Lobbyists, recruitment of
Rice, Ronald E., 177n
Ripley, Randall B., 276n, 280n, 283n, 315n
R. J. Reynolds Industries, 52, 386
R. J. Reynolds Tobacco Company, 175n
Roberts, Steven V., 136n, 156n, 184n, 314n
Robinson, Walter V., 208n
Rochon, Thomas R., 404n, 405n
Rockwell International, 295n
Roe v. *Wade,* 371
Rogin, Michael P., 407n
Romano, Lois, 243n
Roosevelt, Franklin D., 326, 360
Roosevelt, Theodore, 102
Rose, Richard, 407n
Rosellini, Lynn, 243n, 305n
Rosenstone, Steven J., 61n
Ross, Robert L., 312n
Rostenkowski, Daniel, 267
Rothenberg, Stuart, 225n, 259n
Rothman, Stanley, x(n)
Rourke, Francis E., 343n, 347n
Russell, Milton, 342n
RVIA. *See* Recreational Vehicle Industry Association

Sabato, Larry, 94n, 192n, 193n, 227n, 248n
Saccharin controversy, 185–190
Salisbury, Robert H., xi, 49n, 63n, 121n, 122n, 131n, 132n, 413
Samuelson, Robert J., 252n
Sarasohn, Judy, 339n
Sarat, Austin, 371n
Sayre, William, 281n
Scenic Hudson Preservation Conference v. *Federal Power Commission,* 375n
Schattschneider, E. E., 35n, 36n, 59n, 74–75, 87, 123n, 201n, 312, 387, 399, 402
Schlozman, Daniel A., 94–95
Schlozman, Kay Lehman, 18n, 59n, 86n, 157n, 282n, 283n, 302n

Schmitter, Phillippe C., 20n, 335n, 393n, 405n, 406n, 407n
Schneider, William, 215n
Schotsman, Geurt J., 404n
Schriftgiesser, Karl, 89n, 294n, 318n, 319n
Schubert, Glendon, 26n
Schuck, Peter H., 333n
Scorecards, 210–214, 217
Scott, Andrew, 310n
Sea-Land Service, 52
Sears Roebuck and Company, 377
Secretary of the Treasury, U.S., 375
Securities and Exchange Commission, U.S., 318, 362
Selective benefits, 126–128
Senate, U.S. *See also* Congress
  confirmation of presidential appointees, 328–329, 361–362
  Finance Committee, 305
  Judiciary Committee, 329
  Labor and Human Resources Committee, 243
Senior PAC, 249
Serrin, William, 138
Sethi, Prakash S., 175n, 179n
Shabecoff, Philip, 80n, 365n
Shakespeare, William, 106
Shanley, Robert A., 354n
Shannon, James, 253n
Shapiro, Martin, 380n, 381n
Shell Oil Co., 40
Shelley v. *Kraemer,* 363
Shelton, Robert B., 342n
Shields, Mark, 216n
Shribman, David, 153n, 305n, 314n
Sierra Club, 32, 45, 50, 91, 94–95, 128, 191, 321
Singer, James W., 50n, 51n, 377n
Single issue groups, 51–52
Six PAC, 222
Smith, Richard A., 297n
Snack-PAC, 222
Social Security, 42, 53
Social Security Administration (SSA), 335, 342
Society of Mechanical Engineers, 145
Society of the Plastics Industry, 73
Solar Lobby, 82
Sorauf, Frank J., 26n, 27n, 230n, 252n, 370n
Space and Missile Systems Organization Advisory Group, 333
SPUR. *See* Center for Strategic Petroleum Understanding and Research
Standard Oil, xii
Standing to sue, 373–376, 390
Stanfield, Rochelle L., 93n, 107n, 109n
State Department, U.S., 93
State Farm Mutual Automobile Insurance Co., 366
Stevens, Arthur G., 316n

Stigler, George J., 340n
Stokes, Donald E., 313n, 252n
Students in politics, 19
Subgovernments, 276–278
Sun Oil Co., 224, 390
Sun Oil decision, 223–225, 390
Sunshine Act of 1976, 348, 350
Sunshine laws, 304–305, 308–309, 348–349
Surgeon General, U.S., 329

Taft-Hartley Act, 42
Targeting, 216–217
Task forces, 327–328
Taylor, Elizabeth, 243
Taylor, Paul, 163n
Taylor, Stuart, 271n, 379
Teamster union. *See* International Brotherhood of Teamsters
Teledyne Ryan Aeronautical, 295n
Telling, Edward R., 377
Test cases, 50, 367–368, 372
Testifying at hearings, 149, 152, 295–297
Theiler, Patricia, 339n
Thornberry, Homer, 362
Thornton, Mary, 345n
Thurow, Lester C., 406n
Tierney, John T., 157n, 193n, 302n, 332n, 338n
Tillman Act of 1907, 223
Time, Inc., 91
Tobacco Institute, 174, 194
Tocqueville, Alexis de, 59
Tolchin, Martin, 266n
Trade associations, benefits provided by, 41, 126–127
Transportation, U.S. Department of, 354n
Treasury, U.S. Department of, 264
Trow, Martin, 138n
Truman, David B., ix, x(n), 16n, 17n, 27n, 121–123, 296n, 314n, 326n, 389n
Truman, Harry S, 174
Turkheimer, Barbara W., 349n
Turner, Henry A., 264n

UAW. *See* United Auto Workers
Ujifusa, Grant, 231n
Ukrainian National Information Service, 73
Ulmer, S. Sidney, 378n
Union of Journeymen Horseshoers, 42
United Auto Workers, 90, 159, 254
United Brotherhood of Carpenters and Joiners, 42
United Hatters, Cap and Millinery Workers, 42
United Mine Workers, 10, 138–139, 393
U.S. Circuit Court of Appeals for the District of Columbia, 366
U.S. Conference of Mayors, 55, 93n
U.S. Hang Gliding Association, 121
U.S. League of Savings Institutions, 190

U.S. v. *Harriss,* 320
U.S. v. *Richardson,* 375
U.S. v. *Slaughter,* 320n
U.S. v. *Students Challenging Regulatory
    Action Procedure (SCRAP),* 374
U.S. Wheat Associates, 51
United Steelworkers of America, 42, 138,
    222, 248
United Steelworkers of America Political
    Action Fund, 222
University of California, 10, 371

VFW. *See* Veterans of Foreign Wars
Valley Forge Christian College, 378–379
Valley Forge Christian College v. *Americans
    United for Separation of Church and
    State,* 376n, 398n
Van Louizen, J. R., 297n
Verba, Sidney, 18n, 59n, 61n, 86n, 201n,
    282n, 283n
Veterans Administration, U.S. (VA), 338
Veterans of Foreign Wars (VFW), 24, 168,
    212
Vogel, David, 32n, 74n, 80n, 286n, 404n
Vogler, David, 280n, 282n
Voluntary Contributors for Better
    Government, 222
Vose, Clement E., 361n, 363n, 366n, 370n
Voter registration drives, 218
Voters for Choice, 222

Wagner Act, 126n
Waldman, Michael, 266n
Walker, Charls, 262, 269
Walker, Jack L., xi(n), 74n, 75n, 80n, 92n,
    122n, 123n, 131n, 152n, 277n, 312n
Walker, Thomas G., 55n, 371n
Ward, Samuel, 89, 294
Ware, Alan, 16n
Warner, John, 243
Warren, Earl, 362
Wasby, Stephen L., 362n, 369n, 371n
Washington pressure community
    barriers to entry, 109–110, 401
    definition of, 58
    imbalance in representation, xi, 5–6, 26,
        33, 58–59, 65–82, 86, 110, 116–117, 123,
        130, 387–388, 399, 409
    inclusiveness, 123, 387
    recent changes in, 74–82
Washington representatives, definition of,
    11–12. *See also* Lobbyists

Washington Representatives Survey, xii,
    411–427
Watanuki, Joji, 406n
Waterman, Richard W., 256n
Water Quality Improvement Act of 1970, 85
Watt, James G., 365n
Weather Bureau, U.S., 342
Weaver, Suzanne, 345n
Weinraub, Bernard, 350n
Weisbrod, Burton A., 33n
Weissberg, Robert, 36n
Welch, W. P., 256n
Welding Institute, 73
Western Airlines, 50
Wexler, Anne, 269, 326n
Wexler, Elizabeth, 158n
Weyerhaeuser Company, 175
Whitaker and Baxter, 174
White, Lawrence J., 350n
White House Office of Public Liaison, 326
Wiggins, Charles W., 312n, 314n
Wilderness Society, 269
Wilkinson, Harvey, 362
Wilkinson, James A., 334n
Wills, Gary, 2n
Wilson, Graham K., 80n, 393n
Wilson, James Q., xi, 35n, 49n, 59n, 83–85,
    122n, 128–129, 131n, 134n, 142n, 183n,
    184n, 280n, 283, 312, 344n, 406n
Wirth, Timothy E., 254n
Witt, Elder, 379
Wolanin, Thomas, 328n
Wolfe, Tom, 25
Wolfinger, Raymond E., 61n
Women's Equity Action League (WEAL),
    47, 369
Women's Rights Project, 363–364
Woodward, Bob, 360n
WRP. *See* Women's Rights Project

Yiannakis, Diana, 256n
Young, James S., 316n
Young, Oran R., 126n
Young Americans for Freedom, 39
Young Americans for Freedom PAC, 249n

Zahn v. *International Paper Co.,* 369n
Zeigler, Harmon L., 174n, 177n, 178n, 194n,
    202n, 290n, 310n
Zero Population Growth, 1
Ziegler, Ron, 269
Zisk, Betty H., 177n